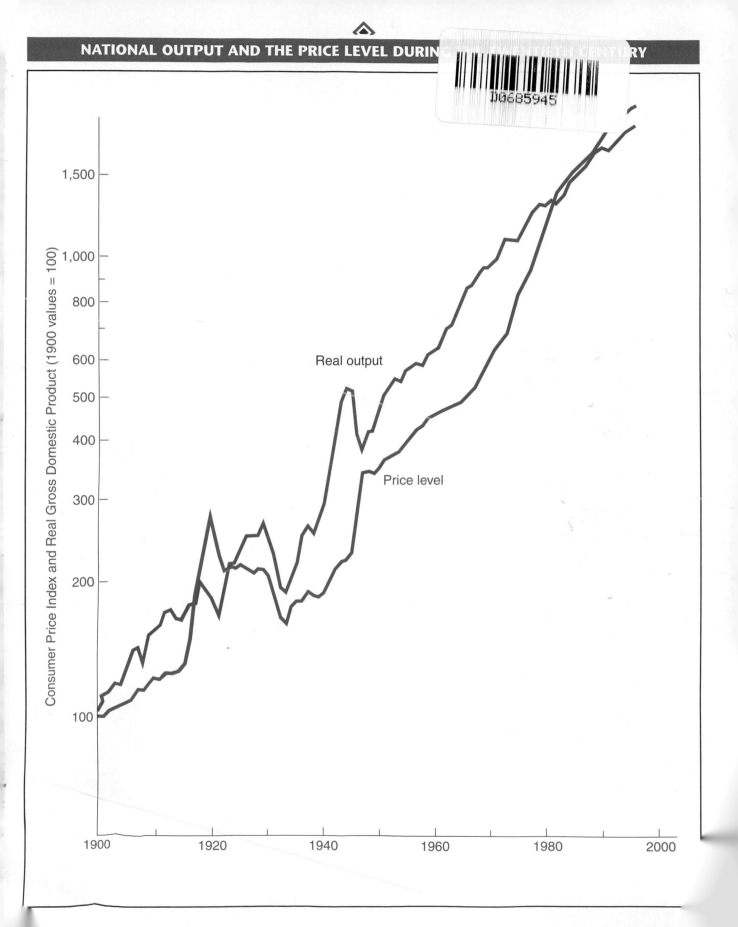

MICROECONOMICS

MICROECONOMICS

SIXTEENTH EDITION

PAUL A. SAMUELSON
Institute Professor Emeritus
Massachusetts Institute of Technology

WILLIAM D. NORDHAUS
A. Whitney Griswold Professor of Economics
Yale University

Irwin
McGraw-Hill

Boston   Burr Ridge, IL   Dubuque, IA   Madison, WI   New York   San Francisco   St. Louis
Bangkok   Bogotá   Caracas   Lisbon   London   Madrid
Mexico City   Milan   New Delhi   Seoul   Singapore   Sydney   Taipei   Toronto

Irwin/McGraw-Hill

A Division of The **McGraw·Hill** Companies

MICROECONOMICS

This book is printed on acid-free paper.

domestic   2 3 4 5 6 7 8 9 0   VNH VNH   9 0 0 9 8

ISBN 0-07-057953-9

VP/Editorial Director: Michael Junior
Publisher: Gary Burke
Sponsoring editor: Lucille Sutton
Developmental editor: Kezia Pearlman
Marketing manager: Nelson Black
Project manager: Terri Edwards
Production supervisor: Tanya Nigh
Cover and interior designer: Suzanne Montazer
Compositor: York Graphic Services, Inc.
Typeface: New Baskerville
Printer: Von Hoffmann Press, Inc.

Library of Congress Cataloging-in-Publication Data
Samuelson, Paul Anthony, 1915–
      Microeconomics / Paul A. Samuelson, William D. Nordhaus. —
      16th ed.
          p.   cm.
      Portions of this text have been taken from Economics, sixteenth
      edition.
      Includes index.
      ISBN 0-07-057953-9 (acid-free paper)
      1. Microeconomics.   I. Nordhaus, William D.   II. Samuelson, Paul
Anthony, 1915– Economics.   III. Title.
      HB172.S155   1998
      338.5—dc21   97-38898
                                                                      CIP

http://www.mhhe.com

ABOUT THE AUTHORS

PAUL A. SAMUELSON, founder of the renowned MIT graduate department of economics, was trained at the University of Chicago and Harvard. His many scientific writings brought him world fame at a young age, and in 1970 he was the first American to receive a Nobel Prize in economics. One of those rare scientists who can communicate with the lay public, Professor Samuelson wrote an economics column for *Newsweek* for many years and was economic adviser to President John F. Kennedy. He testifies often before Congress and serves as academic consultant to the Federal Reserve, the U.S. Treasury, and various private, nonprofit organizations. Professor Samuelson, between researches at MIT and tennis games, is a visiting professor at New York University. His six children (including three triplet boys) have contributed 15 grandchildren.

WILLIAM D. NORDHAUS is one of America's eminent economists. Born in Albuquerque, New Mexico, he was an undergraduate at Yale, received his Ph.D. in economics at MIT, and is now the A. Whitney Griswold Professor of Economics at Yale University and on the staff of the Cowles Foundation for Research in Economics. His economic research has spanned a wide variety of topics—including the environment, price measurement, energy, technological change, economic growth, and trends in profits and productivity. In addition, Professor Nordhaus takes a keen interest in economic policy. He served as a member of President Carter's Council of Economic Advisers from 1977 to 1979, was Provost of Yale University from 1986 to 1988, and writes occasionally for the *New York Times* and other periodicals. He regularly teaches the Principles of Economics course at Yale. Professor Nordhaus and his family live the urban life in New Haven, Connecticut, and share an enthusiasm for music, hiking, and skiing.

To

Our

Children

and

Students

CONTENTS IN BRIEF

CONTENTS

A NOTE FROM THE PUBLISHER

This is the fiftieth year that it has been our privilege and our pleasure at McGraw-Hill to publish Paul Samuelson's and, later, Samuelson and William Nordhaus's *Economics*. In that time, Professor Samuelson defined the field of economics in this remarkable book. Millions of students have been taught how economics can unravel the mysteries and problems of modern societies, problems that go to the heart of how, and how well, we live.

As William Nordhaus joined Professor Samuelson at the helm, this book continued to introduce later generations to the power of economic science. And as the ideas of monetarism, rational expectations, and supply-side economics captured the headlines, this book calmly included them in its presentation without crowding out the basic truths of the Keynesian and classical models. Today's students learn that economics can also shine a bright light on environmental problems, on dilemmas of health care, and on how to reckon the opportunity cost of a college education.

Keynes wryly observed, "In the long run, we are all dead." Now, sixteen editions later, I'm not so sure. We seem to have quite a pulse rate.

Gary Burke
Publisher

A GOLDEN BIRTHDAY

At its fiftieth birthday, this *Economics* has witnessed an exciting half-century of progress in economics. Our subject has come a long way. But there is so much farther to go before this, or any social science, can make pretense to be anywhere near an exact science. Economics will always be as much an art as a science, but still there's a world of difference between informed economics and just plain bad economics.

Today the number of jobs for economists has exploded. Statistical databases—inside government, in private industry, and within academia—are many times more comprehensive than they were in the late 1940s. Now information gets reported sooner, and computers give us access to statistical facts and knowledge with the speed of light. No branch of production has benefited more from the advance of computer hardware and technology than research in political economy itself. And that includes economic theory and applied economics.

And yet the fundamentals remain broadly intact. History—at least economic history—has taught the world certain basic economic principles that have been learned and tested the hard way. Repeated recessions and inflationary booms have been the economists' substitute for the chemists' controlled laboratory experiments. The tragic comedies of Russian and Chinese communistic organization of production and distribution have robbed three generations of the potential fruits of rising standards of material life. At the same time, the completely free market mechanism has not been able to bring all of humankind measurable near-equality of opportunity and outcome.

Because of "the poor we have always with us," the modern democratic state has evolved everywhere into a "mixed economy"—neither pure laissez-faire market mechanism nor Robin Hood utopia. Alas, only by their study of the rudiments of economics can the citizenry understand and decide about where should lie the *golden mean* between the selfishness of individual initiative and the regulatory, stabilizing, and redistributive functions of government. The mixed economy must, perforce, be the "limited mixed economy."

A Time to Look Back

A fiftieth birthday is a good time to look back. What is the story that emerges from this history of a trend-setting bestseller? How did this textbook come to be? Gaze back to 1945. Germany and Japan were defeated and American colleges were nearly overflowing with people returning from World War II. At the same time, the science of economics was entering a golden age. The Great Depression of 1929–1935 had finally been licked by forceful programs that threw out the window the old orthodoxies of do-nothing monetary and fiscal policies. Britain and America had later mobilized their economies for war in a way that Hitler, Mussolini, and Hirohito had never dreamed of. And, though we could not know it in 1945, the Marshall Plan and American occupation of Japan were about to set the stage for miraculous decades of postwar economic growth.

College students deserved to understand all this. But, as teachers of my generation knew to our sorrow, the best-selling economics textbooks were seriously out-of-date. No wonder beginners were bored. My students at Harvard and MIT often had that glassy-eyed look.

In 1948, when *Economics* was first published, the word "macroeconomics"—the study of what determines a society's unemployment, its price level and inflation rate, and its rate of overall real GNP growth—was not even in the dictionary! But had *Economics* not brought guns-and-butter choices into elementary microeconomics, someone, somewhere, would soon have done so. The time was ripe for a revolutionary approach to introductory economics. The real question is: Why me?

I was back from the MIT Radiation Laboratory, where I had worked at the mathematical job of designing automatic servomechanisms to ward off enemy bombers, and I "thirsted" for a return to economic research and teaching. And I was 30 years old, a good age to write a text or innovate a treatise. By chance, my advanced work, *Foundations of Economic Analysis,* which was to win me a Nobel Prize in economics 25 years later, was already in press.

However, in those days, a promising scholar was not supposed to write textbooks—certainly not basic texts for freshmen and sophomores. Only hacks were supposed to do that. But because I had already published so many research articles, it seemed that my reputation and prospects for lifetime tenure could allow me the elbowroom to respond positively to the request for a new textbook by my department head at MIT. Being cocky, even brash, in those good old days, I had only myself to please. And I agreed it was high time that we got some of the leaders in economic research back in the trenches of general education.

The Long Grind of Creation

Starting a project is easy. Bringing it to full term involves enormous labor and great travail. As soon as each chapter was written, the mimeograph machine ground it out for testing on our MIT students. I found it demanding but pleasant work. But what I naively thought might be a year's job turned into three years of writing and rewriting. And my tennis suffered, as weekends and summer vacation had to be devoted to the task of reducing to plain and understandable prose the fundamental complexities of economic science. Even the traditional diagrams of economics, I discovered, needed redesigning if the "dismal science of economics" was to become the exciting subject it really is.

The Moment of Truth

In the autumn of 1948 the first edition of *Economics* rolled off the presses. No matter how hard the advance work or how optimistic the dreams, one can of course never be sure how the future will turn out. Fortunately, from the word go, this novel approach to economics seemed to have hit a responsive chord. Colleges big and small opted for the new book, and as each fresh printing was sold out, *Economics* was back again for new press runs.

When a Guggenheim fellowship took me to Europe, I checked each main bookstore in major cities for the availability of translations into French, German, Italian, Spanish, and Swedish. And in addition to experiencing the natural vanity of an author, I was pleased as an educator to see that the citizenry, who would be deciding global policies, was being exposed to the pros and cons of up-to-date mainstream economics.

Reviews of the book speeded up the bandwagon. The first came from the pen of John Kenneth Galbraith, then an editor of the conservative business magazine *Fortune.* He predicted that the next generation would learn its economics from Samuelson's *Economics.* And although praise is sweet to an author's ears, I confess that the durability of the book's dominance did surprise me. Galbraith turned out to be more prescient than I, and *Economics* did set a new and lasting pattern. Most of its successful rivals have been written in its general evolving mode, and it is heartwarming that much of the competition has come from the pens of personal friends.

Rough Pebbles along the Way

Not always has it been fun and games. In the reactionary days of Senator Joseph McCarthy, when accusations of radicalism were being launched from the pulpit and in the classroom, my book got its share of condemnation. A conservative alumnus of MIT warned university president Karl Compton that Paul Samuelson would jeopardize his scholarly reputation if he were allowed to publish his apologetics for the "mixed economy." Dr. Compton replied that the day his faculty was subjected to censorship would be the day of his resignation from office. It all seems slightly comical four decades later, but it was no joke to be a teacher at a public university when many of the fashionable textbooks of the time were being denounced as subversive. (One excellent text, which came out a year before mine, was killed in its infancy by vicious charges of Marxism that were false from the beginning.) Actually, when your cheek is smacked from the Right, the pain may be assuaged in part by a slap from the Left. *Anti-Samuelson,* a two-volume critique authored in the 1960s when student activism was boiling over on campuses here and abroad, portrayed me as an apologist for the laissez-faire world of markets where dog eats dog, a veritable running jackal of capitalism.

Each cold wind imparts a useful lesson, and I learned to write with special care wherever controversial matters were concerned. It was certainly not that I was perfect in all things. Rather, it was that I could only gain by leaning over backward to state fairly the arguments against the positions popular in mainstream economics.

And by dealing carefully and fully with the contending schools within the mainstream, the work kept its representative status as a reference source book. Even Soviet Russia had felt a translation was mandatory, and within a month the entire supply of translated copies had been exhausted. (Experts tell me that in Stalin's day my book was kept on the special reserve shelf in the library, along with books on sex, forbidden to all but the specially licensed readers.) In the post–Cold War era, new translations have been authorized in Hungary, the Czech Republic, Croatia, Bosnia, Serbia, Romania, and other Eastern European countries as well as in China, Japan, Vietnam, and two-score other countries.

The Ever-Young Child

Just as a child takes on an individual identity distinct from a parent's, so it was with the *Economics*. At first I was in command of it; later it took over in its own right and came to be in charge of me. As the years passed, my hair turned from blond to brown and then to gray. But like the portrait of Dorian Gray, which never grew old, *Economics* remained forever 21. Its cover turned from green to blue and from brown to black; and now it turns to gold. Aided by hundreds of letters and suggestions to the author from students and teachers, the economics inside the covers evolved and developed. A historian of mainstream economic doctrines, like a paleontologist who studies the bones and fossils in different layers of the earth, could date the ebb and flow of ideas by analyzing how Edition 1 was revised to Edition 2 and, eventually, to Edition 16.

And so it went. Hard, hard work—but ever so rewarding. Finally came the day when the call of tennis was too strong to be denied. To McGraw-Hill I said: "I've paid my dues. Let others carry on as I enjoy the good life of an emeritus professor, cultivating the researches that interest me most." McGraw-Hill had a ready answer: "Let us find you a coauthor. We'll make a list of congenial economists whose competence and views you admire." And so the search for the perfect William Nordhaus began.

Yale is only 150 miles from MIT, and it was there that the real Nordhaus was to be found. It only helped that Bill had earned his Ph.D. at MIT. And in the days since then he has won his spurs serving on the President's Council of Economic Advisers and doing tours of duty in Cambridge (England), Delhi, and Vienna. Like Gilbert and Sullivan or Rogers and Hart, we turned out to be a most congenial team.

And so, as in the classic tales, we have lived happily ever after. What matters is that the book stays young, pointing to where the mainstream of economics will be flowing.

Science or Art?

Why has economics become in most colleges one of the largest elective courses? The reasons are many. Economics deals with the real life around us. On the job. At the store. When inflation comes, it hits us all. When recession strikes, the tide goes out for all the boats. And the early bird that seeks the worm needs to know about supply and demand. The same goes for the senior citizen constrained to live on a limited pension and for the young idealist determined to improve and reform society.

Good sense economics is not all obvious. The common sense you bring with you from home to college will not let you understand why a rich country and a poor country can both gain great benefit from free international trade at the same time. (And your senator won't understand the point either without taking a good course in *comparative advantage*.) On the other hand, *after* you have mastered instruction in so-called microeconomics and macroeconomics, there will remain no mysteries. If it doesn't make good sense, it isn't good economics.

A first course in economics will not make you a master of all its intricate and esoteric topics. But this I can tell you, based upon students' experience everywhere: your best course in economics will be your introductory course. After you have stepped into this new strange garden of ideas, the world will never be quite the same. And when, years from now, you look back on the experience, even what you didn't quite understand at the time will have perceptibly ripened.

Enjoy!

Paul A. Samuelson
Massachusetts Institute of Technology
Cambridge, Massachusetts
1998

PREFACE

1998 marks the fiftieth anniversary of this textbook. Over the last half-century, the economic world has changed enormously. In 1948, most people were living in piles of rubble from World War II, international financial markets were in a state of shock, and much of Eurasia was entering the long despotic night of socialist central planning.

Fifty Years of Economics

Economics at midcentury also lived in a different world. It was contending with the increasing virulence of business cycles, trying to explain depressions and hyperinflations and stock-market crashes, and debating the superiority of socialism and market capitalism.

At century's end, the economic world, and the world of economics, have evolved tremendously. America's total output has quadrupled in the last five decades, and the average real income has doubled during this period. Outside the United States, the changes are even more dramatic. Dozens of countries have rejected the socialist experiment and adopted market systems, and strong economic growth has been experienced in countries as diverse as Ireland, Botswana, and the Philippines. At no time in recorded history have so many enjoyed such a sustained period of economic growth as they have during the Great Peace of 1948–1998.

You might think that prosperity would lead to a declining interest in economic affairs. Paradoxically, an understanding of the enduring truths of economics has become even more vital in the affairs of people and nations. The United States has grappled with slow growth in living standards and large government budget deficits, even as structural changes in American industries have shaken managers, workers, and entire communities. The world has become increasingly interconnected as computers and communications create an ever-more-competitive global marketplace. Countries like Russia or Poland, which are making the transition from central planning, need a firm understanding of the institutions of a market economy if they are to make a successful transition. At the same time, there is growing concern about international environmental problems and the need to forge agreements to preserve our precious natural heritage. All these fascinating changes are part of the modern drama that we call economics.

Fifty Years of *Economics*

For half a century, this book has served as the standard-bearer for the teaching of elementary economics in classrooms in America and throughout the world. Each new edition has distilled the best thinking of economists about how markets function and about what society can do to improve people's living standards.

But economics has changed profoundly since the first edition of this text appeared in 1948. Economics is above all a living and evolving organism. The need to keep *Economics* at the frontier in the rapidly evolving world economy affords the authors an exciting opportunity to present the latest thinking of modern economists and to show how the subject can contribute to a more prosperous world.

Our task in these pages is straightforward: to present a clear, accurate, and interesting introduction to the principles of modern economics and to the institutions of the American and world economy. Our primary goal is to survey economics. In doing this we emphasize the basic economic principle that will endure beyond today's headlines.

THE SIXTEENTH EDITION

Economics is a dynamic science—changing to reflect the shifting trends in economic affairs, in the environment, in the world economy, and in society at large. As economics and the world around it evolve, so does this book. Ten features differentiate this edition from earlier ones:

1. *The Core Truths of Economics.* Often, economics appears to be an endless procession of new puzzles, problems, and difficult dilemmas. But as experienced teachers have learned, there are a few basic concepts that underpin all of economics. Once these basic concepts have been mastered, learning is much quicker and more enjoyable. We have therefore chosen to focus on the central core of economics—on those enduring truths which will be just as important in the twenty-first century as they were in the twentieth. Microeconomic concepts such as scarcity, efficiency, the gains from trade, and the principle of comparative advantage will never lose their central role in economics as long as scarcity itself exists. The use of marginal analysis revolutionizes decision making. Students of macroeconomics must receive a firm grounding in the concepts of aggregate supply and demand and must understand the role of national and international monies. Students will learn the widely accepted theory of economic growth, but they should also understand controversial theories of the business cycle.

2. *Innovation in the Economy.* One of the striking features of the modern economy is the rapidity of innovations in virtually every sector. We are accustomed to the dizzying speed of invention in computers, where new products and software appear monthly. Nowhere in recorded history do we find such a raid rate of improvement as has been seen for computers over the last three decades. But other sectors are also witnessing rapid innovation. The pulse of change is rapid virtually everywhere in the modern economy—we run in athletic equipment made of miraculous new materials and relax while listening to crystal-clear audio equipment. Our understanding of economic trends and policies must reflect this rapid change in our societies.

Economics is increasingly attentive to rapid innovation. In macroeconomics, new economic growth theories emphasize the importance of technology, invention, and human capital in the growth process. In microeconomics, we have included a new section on the economics of information, showing how externalities in the production of information and new technologies lead to market failures. A case study of the economics of the Internet explores the dilemmas of pricing information.

3. *Innovation in Economics.* In addition, we emphasize innovations in economics itself. Economists are innovators, and economic ideas can produce tidal waves when they are applied to real-world problems. Among the important innovations studied here is the application of economics to our environmental problems through "emissions trading" plans. Other important economic innovations discussed are improved regulatory mechanisms and radical ideas such as European monetary unification. One of the most influential economic innovations of the last few years involves the measurement of consumer prices. Economists have persuasively argued that better techniques for measuring prices show much more rapid improvement in the quality of goods and services; the striking implication of these analyses is that we may have dramatically underestimated the growth in living standards in recent years.

4. *Small Is Beautiful.* Economics has increased its scope greatly over the last half-century. The flag of economics flies over its traditional territory of the marketplace but also covers the environment, legal studies, statistical and historical methods, art, gender and racial discrimination, and even family life. But at its core, economics is the science of choice. And this means that we, as the authors, have to choose the most important and enduring issues for this text. In a survey as in a meal, small is beautiful because it is digestible.

Choosing the subjects for this text required many hard choices. To select these topics, we surveyed teachers and leading scholars to determine which ones were most crucial for an informed citizenry and a new generation of economists. We drew up a list of key ideas and said sad farewell to many appendices and sections. At every stage, we asked whether the material was, as best as we could predict, necessary for a student's understanding of the economics of the twenty-first century. Only when a subject passed this test was it included. The result of this campaign is a book that has lost more than one-quarter of its weight in the last two editions. Farming, labor unions, and Marxian economics have been trimmed to make room for environmental economics, information economics, and real business cycles.

5. Policy Issues at Century's End. Each generation of economists finds new challenges to contend with in the attempt to understand the evolving economic policy problems. Three areas that have been at the forefront of economics in the last decade have received expanded treatment in the sixteenth edition. As human societies grow, they begin to overwhelm the environment and ecosystems of the natural world around us. *Environmental economics,* presented in Chapter 18, helps students understand the externalities associated with economic activity and analyzes different approaches to making human economies compatible with natural systems. A second area of growing importance has been *health-care economics.* As humans become more affluent, they naturally pay more attention to their own health and longevity, and the result is a rapidly growing share of national output devoted to health care. But health care poses fundamental economic dilemmas as the principles of equality and universal coverage collide with the fact of scarcity. Chapter 19 analyzes these questions and presents some innovative ideas about how to resolve these dilemmas. A third growing area is international economics.

6. The Incredible Shrinking Globe. A century ago, the leading military strategist of the age, Captain A. T. Mahan, declared in his important book

The Influence of Sea Power on History: "Whether they will or no, Americans must now begin to look outward." President Bill Clinton echoed these words when he wrote about economic affairs, "There is simply no way to close our borders and return to the insular days. To try to do so would be an exercise in futility, doomed not only to fail but to lower living standards in the process." Americans are learning that no nation is an island. Immigration and international trade have profound effects on the goods that are available, the prices we pay, and the wages we earn. Labor economists have found that the surge of uneducated immigrants over the last two decades has been an important contributor to the declining real wages of unskilled workers. Development economists have found striking results regarding the impact of economic openness on economic growth. No complete understanding of modern economics is possible without a thorough grounding in the world economy. The sixteenth edition continues to increase the material devoted to international economics and the interaction between international trade and domestic economic events.

7. Triumph of the Market. One leitmotif in this edition is what we call "rediscovery of the market." All around the world, nations are discovering the power of the market as a tool for allocating resources. The most dramatic examples were the fall of communism in the former Soviet Union and Eastern Europe and the breakdown of Chairman Mao's one-party bureaucracy in China. Nation after nation rejected the command economy and began to move to the market. In 1990, Poland embarked on a grand experiment of undergoing "shock therapy" by introducing markets into much of its economy. Russia started down the road by liberalizing prices in 1991 but seemed to take one step backwards for every two steps forward. Nowhere was the transition painless. Virtually every country found that the road to the market was filled with obstacles such as raging inflation, high unemployment, and sharp declines in real wages and output. But by 1997, signs of recovery were found in those transition economies that had moved decisively.

The market was rediscovered in market economies as well. Many countries deregulated industries or privatized industries that had been in the public sectors. The results were generally favorable as productivity rose and prices fell in those sectors. Countries were applying market principles to novel areas, for example, by allowing pollution permits to be bought and sold or auctioning off the radio spectrum. These topics are part of the sixteenth edition's analysis of how market economies promote efficiency but also of the need for limited public controls.

8. *Emphasis on History and Policy.* Students study economics to understand the rapidly changing world around them. For this reason, economics is at its core an empirical science. It first aims to explain the world around us and then helps us devise economic policies, based on sound economic principles, that can enhance the living standards of people at home and abroad.

Drawing upon history, economic chronicles, and the experience of the authors, the sixteenth edition continues to emphasize the use of case studies and empirical evidence to illustrate economic theories. The rediscovery of the market is made vivid when we examine how central planning failed or the way the East Asian economies have grown so rapidly. The dilemmas involved in combating poverty become real when we understand the 1996 welfare reforms or the problems of the current health-care system. Our appreciation of macroeconomic analysis increases when we see how government deficits in the 1980s lowered national saving and slowed capital accumulation in the United States or when we examine the promises and pitfalls of the European Monetary Union.

The microeconomic chapters draw upon case studies, economic history, business decisions, and real-world experience to illustrate the fundamental principles. Examples such as the economics of addictive substances, the health-care crisis, the threat of greenhouse warming, the minimum-wage debate, performance regulation, trading pollution permits, and the history of stock markets help bring the theorems of microeconomics to life. Game theory becomes serious—and has striking implications—when applied to pollution or winner-take-all games. Established ideas such as the negative income tax can be used in innovative ways to resolve seemingly impossible policy dilemmas such as providing universal and affordable health care.

This "hands-on" approach to economics allows students to understand better the relevance of economic analysis to real-world problems. The abstract notion of scarcity becomes concrete when we see its implications for whether we have a good job, a healthy environment, adequate health care, and a secure nest egg for our retirement.

9 *Clarity.* Although there are many new features in the sixteenth edition, the pole star for our pilgrimage in preparing this edition has been to present economics in a clear and student-friendly way. Students enter the classroom with a wide range of backgrounds and with many preconceptions about the way the world works. Our role is not to change their values. Rather, we want students first to understand the enduring economic principles and then to be able to apply them to make the world a better place for them, their families, and their communities. Nothing aids understanding better than a clear and simple exposition. We have labored over every page to improve this survey of introductory economics. We have received thousands of comments and suggestions from teachers and students and have incorporated their counsel in the sixteenth edition.

Optional Matter

Economics courses range from one-quarter surveys to year-long intensive honors courses. This textbook has been carefully designed to meet all situations. The more advanced materials have been put in separate appendices or specially designated sections. These will appeal to curious students and to students in demanding courses that survey the entire discipline thoroughly. We have included advanced questions for discussion to test the mettle of the most dedicated student.

If yours is a fast-paced course, you will appreciate the careful layering of the more advanced material. Hard-pressed courses can skip the advanced sections, covering the core of economic analysis without losing the thread of the economic reasoning. This book will challenge the most advanced young scholar. Indeed, many of today's leading economists have written to say they've relied upon *Economics* all along their pilgrimage to the Ph.D.

Format

The sixteenth edition employs a set of in-text logos and material to help illustrate the central topics. You will find three distinctive logos: warnings for the fledgling economist, examples of economics in action, and biographical material on the great economists of the past and present. But these central topics are not sitting off by themselves in unattached boxes. Rather, they are integrated right into the chapter so that students can read them without breaking their train of thought. Keep these logos in mind as you read through the text:

 is a warning that students should pause to ensure that they understand a difficult or subtle point.

 is an interesting example or application of the analysis, and often it represents one of the major innovations of modern economics.

 presents biographies of important economic figures. Sometimes these are famous economists like Adam Smith, while at other times they are people who introduced economics into public policy.

New features in this edition include fresh end-of-chapter questions, with a special accent upon short problems that reinforce the major concepts surveyed in the chapter. Terms printed in bold type in the text mark the first occurrence and definition of the most important words that constitute the language of economics.

But these many changes have not altered one bit the central stylistic beacon that has guided *Economics* since the first edition: to use simple sentences, clear explanations, and concise tables and graphs.

Auxiliary Teaching and Study Aids

Students of this edition will benefit greatly from the *Study Guide*. This carefully designed aid has been prepared by Laurence Miners and Kathryn Nantz of Fairfield University who worked in close collaboration with us in our revision. Both when used alongside classroom discussions and when employed independently for self-study, the *Study Guide* has proved to be an impressive success. There is a full-text *Study Guide,* as well as micro and macro versions.

In addition, instructors will find the *Instructor's Resource Manual and Test Bank* useful for planning their courses and preparing multiple sets of test questions in both print and computerized formats. Moreover, Irwin/McGraw-Hill has designed a beautiful set of two-color overhead transparencies for presenting the tabular and graphical material in the classroom. The graphs and figures in this edition can also be viewed electronically as Powerpoint slides. The slides can be downloaded from our website (http://www.mhhe.com). These items can all be obtained by contacting your local Irwin/McGraw-Hill sales representative.

Economics in the Computer Age

The electronic age has revolutionized the way that scholars and students can access information. In economics, the information revolution allows us quick access to economic statistics and research. One of the new features of the sixteenth edition is the section "Economics and the Internet," which appears just before Chapter 1. This little section provides a road map for the state of economics on the Information Superhighway.

Two new interactive tutorials are available with this edition: *The Microeconomics and Macroeconomics Interactive CD-ROM* and *WinEcon*.

Developed by Charles Link and Jeffrey Miller at the University of Delaware, *The Microeconomics and Macroeconomics Interactive CD-ROM* offers students a rich, easy-to-use menu covering the six core topics in introductory economics. Both tutorials have a real-world focus: newspaper and magazine articles highlight economic concepts and interactive videos allow students to "interview" business leaders.

WinEcon is an interactive software package offering over 75 hours of tutorial material. It includes self-assessment questions and exams, economic databases, and an economic glossary and references to leading economic texts. It is the first computer-based learning package to cover the entire first-year economics syllabus. *WinEcon* combines two products in one: teaching software and student tools, and

WinEcon Lecturer with tests, exam, course manage-ment, and customization program. *WinEcon* was developed at the University of Bristol with the help of the Teaching and Learning Technology Pro-gramme Economics Consortium (TLTP), a group of eight UK university economics departments.

Students can also purchase *The Power of Macroeco-nomics* and *The Power of Microeconomics,* which contain lessons directly tied to this text. *The Power of Macro-economics* and *The Power of Microeconomics* are lively combinations of Powerpoint and audio designed to reinforce economics concepts. *The Power of Macroeco-nomics* and *The Power of Microeconomics* were devel-oped by Peter Navarro at the University of California at Irvine, Graduate School of Management.

Acknowledgments

This book has two authors but a multitude of col-laborators. We are profoundly grateful to colleagues, reviewers, students, and McGraw-Hill's staff for con-tributing to the timely completion of the sixteenth edition of *Economics.*

Colleagues at MIT, Yale, and elsewhere who gra-ciously contributed their comments and suggestions include William C. Brainard, William Buiter, E. Cary Brown, John Geanakoplos, Robert J. Gordon, Lyle Gramely, Paul Joskow, Alfred Kahn, Richard Levin, Robert Litan, Barry Nalebuff, Merton J. Peck, Gustav Ranis, Paul Craig Roberts, Herbert Scarf, Robert M. Solow, James Tobin, Janet Yellen, and Gary Yohe.

In addition, we have benefited from the tireless devotion of those whose experience in teaching ele-mentary economics is embodied in this edition. We are particularly grateful to the reviewers of the six-teenth edition. They include

Nik Mustapha Raja Abdullah, *University of Pertan-ian—Malaysia*

Marion Beaumont, *California State University—Long Beach*

Tom Beveridge, *The University of North Carolina—Greenville*

Erwin A. Blackstone, *Temple University*

Parantop Busu, *Fordham University*

Kevin Carey, *University of Miami*

Anthony Chen, *Woodbury University*

Jen-Chi Cheng, *Wichita State University*

Evangelos Djimopoulos, *Fairleigh Dickinson University*

George Euskirchen, *Thomas Moore College*

Gary Galles, *Pepperdine University*

Erwin Kelly, *California State University—Sacramento*

James F. McCarley, *Albion College*

Myra Moore, *Texas Christian University*

Ibrahim M. Oweiss, *Georgetown University*

Walter Park, *American University*

J. Hanns Pichler, *Economic Theory Institute*

Thomas Shea, *Springfield College*

Bo Shippen, *Macon University*

David Sisk, *San Francisco State University*

Sebastian Thomas, *St. Francis College*

Lawrence Weiser, *University of Wisconsin—Stevens Point*

George Zestos, *Christopher Newport University*

Students at MIT, Yale, and other colleges and universities have served as an "invisible college." They constantly challenge and test us, helping to make this edition less imperfect than its predecessor. Although they are too numerous to enumerate, their influence is woven through every chapter. The statis-tical and historical material was prepared and double-checked by Joseph Boyer and Andrew Pearl-man. Nancy King and Glena Ames provided help in word processing. Marnie Wiss coordinated the edito-rial process at the authors' end.

This project would have been impossible without the skilled team from McGraw-Hill who nurtured the book at every stage. We particularly would like to thank, in chronological order to their appearance on the scene, Economics Editor Lucille Sutton, Developmental Editor Kezia Pearlman, Project Man-agers Sharla Volkersz and Terri Edwards, Production Manager Tanya Nigh, and Marketing Manager Nel-son Black. This group of skilled professionals turned a pile of diskettes and a mountain of paper into a finely polished work of art.

A WORD TO THE SOVEREIGN STUDENT

You have read in the history books of waves of revo-lutions that shake civilizations to their roots—reli-gious conflicts, wars for political liberation, struggles against colonialism and imperialism. Over the last decade, economic revolutions in Eastern Europe, in the former Soviet Union, in China, and elsewhere have wrenched those societies. Young people battered down walls, overthrew established authority, and agitated for democracy and a market economy because of discontent with their centralized socialist governments. Students like yourselves are marching, and even going to jail, to win the right to study radical ideas and learn from Western textbooks like this one in hopes that they may enjoy the freedom and economic prosperity of democratic market economies.

The Intellectual Marketplace

Just what is the market that Russian and Chinese students are agitating for? In the pages that follow, you will learn about the markets for stocks and bonds, French francs and Russian rubles, unskilled labor and highly trained neurosurgeons. You have probably read in the newspaper about the gross domestic product, the consumer price index, the stock market, and the unemployment rate. After you have completed a thorough study of the chapters in this textbook, you will know precisely what these words mean. Even more important, you will also understand the economic forces that influence and determine them.

There is also a marketplace of ideas, where contending schools of economists fashion their theories and try to persuade their scientific peers. You will find in the chapters that follow a fair and impartial review of the thinking of the intellectual giants of our profession—from the early economists like Adam Smith, David Ricardo, and Karl Marx to modern-day titans like John Maynard Keynes, Milton Friedman, and Robert Solow.

Skoal!

As you begin your journey into the land of markets, it would be understandable if you are somewhat anxious. But take heart. The fact is that we envy you, the beginning student, as you set out to explore the exciting world of economics for the first time. This is a thrill that, alas, you can experience only once in a lifetime. So, as you embark, we wish you bon voyage!

Paul A. Samuelson
William D. Nordhaus

ECONOMICS AND THE INTERNET

The electronic age has revolutionized our lives in many ways. The impact on scholars and students has been particularly profound because it allows inexpensive and rapid access to vast quantities of information. The Internet—which is a huge and growing public network of linked computers and information—is changing the way we shop, do business, share our culture, and communicate with our friends and family.

In economics, the information revolution allows us quick access to economic statistics and research. With just a few clicks of a mouse, we can find out about the most recent unemployment rate, track down information on poverty and incomes, or delve into the intricacies of our banking system. A few years ago, it might take weeks to dig out the data necessary to analyze an economic problem. Today, with a computer and a little practice, that same task can be done in a few minutes.

This book is not a manual for driving on the Information Superhighway. That skill can be learned in classes on the subject or from informal tutorials. Rather, we want to provide a road map which shows the locations of economic data and research. With this map and rudimentary skills at navigating the Web, you can explore the various sites and find a rich array of data, information, studies, and chat rooms.

Data and Institutions. The Internet is an indispensable source of useful data and other information. Since most economic data are provided by governments, the first place to look is the Web pages of government agencies and international organizations. A neat starting point for the government's economic statistics is *The White House Briefing Room* found on the Web at ***http://www.whitehouse.government/fsbr/esbr.html.*** This site will take you to the major statistical agencies of the federal government. Another place to find general data is the Department of Commerce, which encompasses the Bureau of Economic Analysis (BEA) (***http://www.bea.doc.gov***) and Census Bureau (***http://www.census.gov***). The BEA site includes all data and articles published in the *Survey of Current Business,* including the national income and product accounts, international trade and investment flows, output by industry, economic growth, personal income and labor series, and regional data.

The Census site goes well beyond a nose count of the population. It also includes the economic census as well as information on housing, income and poverty, government finance, agriculture, foreign trade, construction, manufacturing, transportation, and retail and wholesale trade. In addition to making Census publications available, the Census site allows users to create custom extracts of popular microdata sources including the Survey of Income and Program Participation, Consumer Expenditure Survey, Current Population Survey, American Housing Survey, and, of course, the most recent census.

The Bureau of Labor Statistics (*http://stats.bls.gov*) allows easy access to commonly requested labor data, including employment and unemployment, prices and living conditions, compensation, productivity, and technology. Also available are labor-force data from the Current Population Survey and payroll statistics from the Current Employment Statistics Survey.

A useful source for financial data is Federal Reserve Economic Data (*http://www.stls.frb.org/fred*). This site, hosted by the St. Louis branch of the Fed, provides historical U.S. economic and financial data, including daily interest rates, monetary and business indicators, exchange rates, balance-of-payments data, and price indices. In addition, the Office of Management and Budget (*http://www.access.gpo.gov/su_docs/budget/index.html*) makes available the federal budget and related documents.

Two other sites are useful entry points for U.S. government statistics. FedStats (*http://www.fedstats.gov*) provides links to over 70 government agencies that produce statistical information. Sources are organized by subject or by agency, and the contents are fully searchable. The Commerce Department operates a huge database at *http://www.stat-usa.gov*, but use of parts of this database requires a subscription (which may be available at your college or university).

International statistics are often harder to find. The World Bank (*http://www.worldbank.org*) has information on its programs and publications at its site, as does the International Monetary Fund, or IMF (*http://www.imf.org*). The United Nations website has links to most international institutions and their databases (*http://www.unsystem.org*). For many international comparisons, the Penn-World Tables are available at the National Bureau of Economic Research (*http://www.nber.org/pwt56.html*) as well as many other sites. Another good source of information about high-income countries is the Organisation for Economic Cooperation and Development, or OECD (*http://www.oecd.org*). The OECD's website contains an array of data on economics, education, health, science and technology, agriculture, energy, public management, and other topics. Additionally, the CIA world factbook (*www.odci.gov/cia/publications/nsolo/wfb-all.html*) has a wide range of unspooky economic and other information about any country in the world.

Economic Research and Journalism. The Internet is rapidly becoming the world's library.

Newspapers, magazines, and scholarly publications are increasingly posting their writing in electronic form. Most of these present what is already available in the paper publications. Some interesting sources can be found at the *Economist* (*http://economist.com*), the *Wall Street Journal* (*http://www.wsj.com*), and the on-line-only *Slate* magazine (*http://www.slate.com*). Current policy issues are discussed at *http://www.policy.com*, and you can play budget games with the "National Budget Simulator" at (*http://socrates.berkeley.edu:3333/budget/budget.html*).

For scholarly writings, many journals are making their contents available on-line. WebEc (*http://netec.wustl.edu/%7eadnetec/WebEc/journals.html*) offers a comprehensive list of links to economics journals. For working papers, the National Bureau of Economic Research (NBER) website (*http://www.nber.org*) contains current economic research. The NBER site also contains general resources, including links to data sources and the official U.S. business-cycle dates. More generally, Washington University maintains an archive of working papers from myriad sources, usefully organized by topic.

Two excellent general purpose websites for economics are Bill Goffe's *Resources for Economists on the Internet* (*http://econwpa.wustl.edu/EconFAQ/EconFAQ.html*) and WebEc (*http://netec.wustl.edu*).

Did someone tell you that economics is the dismal science? You can chuckle over economist jokes (mostly at the expense of economists) at *http://netec.wustl.edu/JokEc.html*.

A Word of Warning. Note that, because of rapid technological change, this list will soon be out of date. New sites with valuable information and data are appearing every day . . . and others are disappearing almost as rapidly.

Before you set off into the wonderful world of the Web, we would pass on to you some wisdom from experts. Remember the old adage, you only get what you pay for:

Warning: Be careful to determine that your sources and data are reliable. The Internet and other electronic media are notorious: easy to use and equally easy to abuse.

The Web costs you nothing, and that price may sometimes overstate its value. But there are many diamonds buried in the mountains of bits.

PART ONE
BASIC CONCEPTS

CHAPTER 1
THE FUNDAMENTALS OF ECONOMICS

It is not from the benevolence of the butcher, the brewer, or the baker that we expect our dinner, but from their regard to their own interest.

Adam Smith, The Wealth of Nations *(1776)*

A. INTRODUCTION

Pause for a moment to consider the paradoxical words above, penned in 1776 by Adam Smith, the founder of modern economics. That same year was also marked by the American Declaration of Independence. It is no coincidence that both ideas appeared at the same time. Just as the American revolutionaries were proclaiming freedom from tyranny, Adam Smith was preaching a revolutionary doctrine emancipating trade and industry from the shackles of a feudal aristocracy.

In the last two centuries, most of the world has experienced an era of unimagined prosperity. In the United States and other high-income countries, most people today can afford to buy far more than the bare necessities of food, clothing, and shelter. Superfast personal computers, high-tech home entertainment centers, and fast air transportation to any part of the globe are examples of an astonishing range of goods and services that have become part of everyday life. Developing countries have also seen their standards of living rise rapidly in recent years.

But widespread prosperity has not brought economic security. In an average year, 10 million Americans lose their jobs and almost 100,000 businesses go bankrupt. About 14 percent of households are

designated as poor, and the number is almost 50 percent among households headed by black females. Many families worry about the catastrophic financial consequence of illness because they have no health insurance. The affluent society is an anxious society.

For most of human history, people who experienced economic misfortunes lived on the mercy of their families or friends. Starting about a century ago, governments introduced the "welfare state," which provided social insurance and income support to needy people. Gradually, poor people in rich countries got access to minimal levels of income, food, and health care. But rising taxes and growing government spending on health care and public pensions have produced a revolt of the middle class, which is the taxed class. In 1996, the United States removed its guarantee of income support for poor families. Everywhere, countries are rethinking the boundaries between state and market, trying to balance the growing need for providing public services with the increasing clamor for cutting taxes and shrinking government.

This is the age of the global marketplace. Today, money, goods, and information cross national borders more readily than ever before. In earlier times,

3

we did business with people down the street or in the next town, and we bought mainly local goods. Today, we ride in the "world car." Look at this world car or at a fast computer. It incorporates materials, labor, capital, and innovations from around the world. The rise of the global marketplace raises new challenges. Who can best adapt to increased foreign competition? Who can quickly adapt to the information age? The stakes are high. To the winners go the profits, while the losers lag behind.

For Whom the Bell Tolls

As you begin your studies, you are probably wondering, Why study economics? Understanding the role of government and the challenges of the global marketplace are only two reasons why people study economics today.

Some people study economics because they hope to make money. Others worry that they will be illiterate if they cannot understand the laws of supply and demand. Many people are interested in learning about how we can improve our environment or why inequality in the distribution of income in the United States has risen so sharply in recent years.

All these reasons, and many more, make good sense. Still, we have come to realize, there is one overriding reason for learning the basic lessons of economics: All your life—from cradle to grave and beyond—you will run up against the brutal truths of economics. As a voter, you will make decisions on issues—on the government deficit, on taxes, on free trade, on inflation and unemployment—that cannot be understood until you have mastered the rudiments of this subject.

Choosing your life's occupation is the most important economic decision you will make. Your future depends not only on your own abilities but also on how economic forces beyond your control affect your wages. Also, economics may help you invest the nest egg you save from your earnings. Of course, studying economics cannot make you a genius. But without economics the dice of life are loaded against you.

There is no need to belabor the point. We hope you will find that, in addition to being useful, economics is a fascinating field in its own right. Generations of students, often to their surprise, have discovered how stimulating economics can be.

SCARCITY AND EFFICIENCY: THE TWIN THEMES OF ECONOMICS

What, then, is economics? Over the last 30 years the study of economics has expanded to include a vast range of topics. What are the major definitions of this growing subject? The important ones are that economics[1]

- studies how the prices of labor, capital, and land are set in the economy, and how these prices are used to allocate resources.
- explores the behavior of the financial markets, and analyzes how they allocate capital to the rest of the economy.
- examines the distribution of income, and suggests ways that the poor can be helped without harming the performance of the economy.
- looks at the impact of government spending, taxes, and budget deficits on growth.
- studies the swings in unemployment and production that make up the business cycle, and develops government policies for improving economic growth.
- examines the patterns of trade among nations, and analyzes the impact of trade barriers.
- looks at growth in developing countries, and proposes ways to encourage the efficient use of resources.

This list is a good one, yet you could extend it many times over. But if we boil down all these definitions, we find one common theme:

Economics is the study of how societies use scarce resources to produce valuable commodities and distribute them among different people.

Behind this definition are two key ideas in economics: that goods are scarce and that society must use its resources efficiently. Indeed, economics is an important subject because of the fact of scarcity and the desire for efficiency.

Take **scarcity** first. If infinite quantities of every good could be produced or if human desires were

---

[1] This list contains several specialized terms from economics, and to master the subject, you will need to understand its vocabulary. If you are not familiar with a particular word or phrase, you should consult the Glossary at the back of this book. The Glossary contains most of the major technical economic terms used in this book. All terms printed in boldface are defined in the Glossary.

fully satisfied, what would be the consequences? People would not worry about stretching out their limited incomes, because they could have everything they wanted; businesses would not need to fret over the cost of labor or health care; governments would not need to struggle over taxes or spending, because nobody would care. Moreover, since all of us could have as much as we pleased, no one would be concerned about the distribution of incomes among different people or classes.

In such an Eden of affluence, there would be no **economic goods,** that is, goods that are scarce or limited in supply. All goods would be free, like sand in the desert or seawater at the beach. Prices and markets would be irrelevant. Indeed, economics would no longer be a useful subject.

But no society has reached a utopia of limitless possibilities. Goods are limited, while wants seem limitless. Even after two centuries of rapid economic growth, production in the United States is simply not high enough to meet everyone's desires. If you add up all the wants, you quickly find that there are simply not enough goods and services to satisfy even a small fraction of everyone's consumption desires. Our national output would have to be many times larger before the average American could live at the level of the average doctor or lawyer. And outside the United States, particularly in Africa and Asia, hundreds of millions of people suffer from hunger and material deprivation.

Given unlimited wants, it is important that an economy make the best use of its limited resources. That brings us to the critical notion of **efficiency**. Efficiency denotes the most effective use of a society's resources in satisfying people's wants and needs.

More specifically, the economy is producing efficiently when it cannot increase the economic welfare of anyone without making someone else worse off.

The essence of economics is to acknowledge the reality of scarcity and then figure out how to organize society in a way which produces the most efficient use of resources. That is where economics makes its unique contribution.

Microeconomics and Macroeconomics

Adam Smith is usually considered the founder of the field of **microeconomics,** the branch of economics which today is concerned with the behavior of individual entities such as markets, firms, and households. In *The Wealth of Nations*, Smith considered how individual prices are set, studied the determination of prices of land, labor, and capital, and inquired into the strengths and weaknesses of the market mechanism. Most important, he identified the remarkable efficiency properties of markets and saw that economic benefit comes from the self-interested actions of individuals. All these are still important issues today, and while the study of microeconomics has surely advanced greatly since Smith's day, he is still cited by politicians and economists alike.

The other major branch of our subject is **macroeconomics,** which is concerned with the overall performance of the economy. Macroeconomics did not even exist in its modern form until 1935, when John Maynard Keynes published his revolutionary *General Theory of Employment, Interest and Money*. At the time, England and the United States were still stuck in the Great Depression of the 1930s, and over one-quarter of the American labor force was unemployed. In his new theory Keynes developed an analysis of what causes unemployment and economic downturns, how investment and consumption are determined, how central banks manage money and interest rates, and why some nations thrive while others stagnate. Keynes also argued that governments had an important role in smoothing out the ups and downs of business cycles. Although macroeconomics has progressed far since his first insights, the issues addressed by Keynes still define the study of macroeconomics today.

The two branches—microeconomics and macroeconomics—converge to form modern economics. At one time the boundary between the two areas was quite distinct; more recently, the two subdisciplines have merged as economists have applied the tools of microeconomics to such topics as unemployment and inflation.

THE LOGIC OF ECONOMICS

Economic life is an enormously complicated hive of activity, with people buying, selling, bargaining, investing, persuading, and threatening. The ultimate purpose of economic science and of this text is to understand this complex undertaking. How do economists go about their task?

Economists use the *scientific approach* to understand economic life. This involves observing economic affairs and drawing upon statistics and the historical record. For complex phenomena like the impacts of budget deficits or the causes of inflation, historical research has provided a rich mine of insights. Often, economics relies upon analyses and theories. Theoretical approaches allow economists to make broad generalizations, such as those concerning the advantages of international trade and specialization or the disadvantages of tariffs and quotas.

A final approach is the use of statistical analyses. Economists have developed a specialized technique known as **econometrics,** which applies the tools of statistics to economic problems. Using econometrics, economists can sift through mountains of data to extract simple relationships. For example, in recent years people have argued about the impact of a higher minimum wage on employment. From dozens of studies, economists have concluded that it is *likely* that raising the minimum wage will reduce employment of low-wage workers. This knowledge is essential to policymakers who are struggling with the question of how high to set the minimum wage.

Budding economists must also be alert to common fallacies in economic reasoning. Because economic relationships are often complex, involving many different variables, it is easy to become confused about the exact reason behind events or the impact of policies on the economy. The following are some of the common fallacies encountered in economic reasoning:

- *The post hoc fallacy.* The first fallacy involves the inference of causality. *The post hoc fallacy occurs when we assume that, because one event occurred before another event, the first event caused the second event.*[2] An example of this syndrome occurred in the Great Depression of the 1930s in the United States. Some people had observed that periods of business expansions were preceded or accompanied by rising prices. From this, they concluded that the appropriate remedy for depres-

sion was to raise wages and prices. This idea led to a host of legislation and regulations to prop up wages and prices in an inefficient manner. Did these measures promote economic recovery? Almost surely not. Indeed, they probably slowed recovery, which did not occur until total spending began to rise as the government increased military spending in preparation for World War II.

- *Failure to hold other things constant.* A second pitfall is failure to hold other things constant when thinking about an issue. For example, we might want to know whether raising tax rates will raise or lower tax revenues. Some people have put forth the seductive argument that we can eat our cake and have it too. They argue that cutting tax rates will at the same time raise government revenues and lower the budget deficit. They point to the Kennedy-Johnson tax cuts of 1964, which lowered tax rates sharply and were followed by an increase in government revenues in 1965. Ergo, they argue, lower tax rates produce higher revenues.

  What is wrong with this reasoning? This argument overlooks the fact that the economy grew from 1964 to 1965. Because people's incomes grew during that period, government revenues also grew, even though tax rates were lower. Careful studies indicate that revenues would have been even higher in 1965 had tax rates not been lowered in 1964. Hence, this analysis fails to hold other things (namely, total incomes) constant.

  Remember to hold other things constant when you are analyzing the impact of a variable on the economic system.

- *The fallacy of composition.* Sometimes we assume that what holds true for part of a system also holds true for the whole. In economics, however, we often find that the whole is different from the sum of the parts. *When you assume that what is true for the part is also true for the whole, you are committing the fallacy of composition.*

  Here are some true statements that might surprise you if you ignore the fallacy of composition: (1) If one farmer has a bumper crop, she has a higher income; if all farmers produce a record crop, farm incomes will fall. (2) If one

---

[2] Post hoc is shorthand for *post hoc, ergo propter hoc.* Translated from the Latin, the full expression means "after this, therefore necessarily because of this."

person receives a great deal more money, that person will be better off; if everyone receives a great deal more money, the society is likely to be worse off. (3) If a high tariff is put on the product of a particular industry, the producers in that industry are likely to profit; if high tariffs are put on all industries, most producers and consumers will be worse off. (4) When teachers grade on a curve, grades are a "zero-sum game": if one student performs well, he will raise his grade; if all students perform well, the average grade is unchanged.

These examples contain no tricks or magic. Rather, they are the results of systems of interacting individuals. When individuals interact, often the behavior of the aggregate looks very different from the behavior of individual people.

We mention these fallacies only briefly in this introduction. Later, as we introduce the tools of economics, we will reinforce this discussion and provide examples of how inattention to the logic of economics can lead you to false and sometimes costly errors. When you reach the end of this book, you can look back to see why each of these paradoxical examples is true.

COOL HEADS AT THE SERVICE OF WARM HEARTS

Since the time of Adam Smith, economics has grown from a tiny acorn into a mighty oak. Under its spreading branches we find explanations of the gains from international trade, advice on how to reduce unemployment and inflation, formulas for investing your retirement funds, and even proposals for selling the rights to pollute. Throughout the world, economists are laboring to collect data and improve our understanding of economic trends.

You might well ask, What is the purpose of this army of economists measuring, analyzing, and calculating? The ultimate goal of economic science is to improve the living conditions of people in their everyday lives. Increasing the gross domestic product is not just a numbers game. Higher incomes mean good food, warm houses, and hot water. They mean safe drinking water and inoculations against the perennial plagues of humanity.

They mean even more. Higher incomes allow governments to build schools so that young people can learn to read and develop the skills necessary to operate complex technologies. As incomes rise further, nations can afford deep scientific inquiries into biology and discover yet other vaccines against yet other diseases. With the resources freed up by economic growth, talented artists have the opportunity to write poetry and compose music, while others have the leisure time to read, to listen, and to perform. Although there is no single pattern of economic development, and the evolution of culture will differ around the world, freedom from hunger, disease, and the elements is a universal human aspiration.

But centuries of human history also show that warm hearts alone will not feed the hungry or heal the sick. Determining the best route to economic progress requires cool heads, ones that objectively weigh the costs and benefits of different approaches, trying as hard as humanly possible to keep the analysis free from the taint of wishful thinking. Sometimes, economic progress will require shutting down an outmoded factory. Sometimes, as when the formerly socialist countries adopted market principles, things get worse before they get better. Choices are particularly difficult in the field of health care, where limited resources literally involve life and death.

You may have heard the saying, "From each according to his ability, to each according to his need." Governments have learned that no society can long operate solely on this utopian principle. To maintain a healthy economy, governments must preserve incentives for people to work and to save. Societies can shelter for a while those who become unemployed, but if social insurance becomes too generous, people come to depend upon the government. If they begin to believe that the government owes them a living, this may dull the sharp edge of enterprise. Just because government programs derive from lofty purposes does not mean that they should be pursued without care and efficiency.

Society must find the right balance between the discipline of the market and the generosity of the welfare state. By using cool heads to inform our warm hearts, economic science can do its part in ensuring a prosperous and just society.

B. THE THREE PROBLEMS OF ECONOMIC ORGANIZATION

Every human society—whether it is an advanced industrial nation, a centrally planned economy, or an isolated tribal nation—must confront and resolve three fundamental economic problems. Every society must have a way of determining *what* commodities are produced, *how* these goods are made, and *for whom* they are produced.

Indeed, these three fundamental questions of economic organization—*what, how,* and *for whom*—are as crucial today as they were at the dawn of human civilization. Let's look more closely at them:

- *What* commodities are produced and in what quantities? A society must determine how much of each of the many possible goods and services it will make, and when they will be produced. Will we produce pizzas or shirts today? A few high-quality shirts or many cheap shirts? Will we use scarce resources to produce many consumption goods (like pizzas)? Or will we produce fewer consumption goods and more investment goods (like pizza-making machines), which will boost production and consumption tomorrow.

- *How* are goods produced? A society must determine who will do the production, with what resources, and what production techniques they will use. Who farms and who teaches? Is electricity generated from oil, from coal, or from the sun? With much air pollution or with little?

- *For whom* are goods produced? Who gets to eat the fruit of economic activity? Or, to put it formally, how is the national product divided among different households? Are many people poor and a few rich? Do high incomes go to managers or athletes or workers or landlords? Will society provide minimal consumption to the poor, or must they work if they are to survive?

 Warning: In thinking about economic questions, we must distinguish questions of fact from questions of fairness. Positive economics describes the facts of an economy, while normative economics involves value judgments.

Positive economics deals with questions such as: Why do doctors earn more than janitors? Does free trade raise or lower wages for most Americans? What is the economic impact of raising taxes? Although these are difficult questions to answer, they can all be resolved by reference to analysis and empirical evidence. That puts them in the realm of positive economics.

Normative economics involves ethical precepts and norms of fairness. Should poor people be required to work if they are to get government assistance? Should unemployment be raised to ensure that price inflation does not become too rapid? Should the United States penalize China because it is pirating U. S. books and CDs? There are no right or wrong answers to these questions because they involve ethics and values rather than facts. They can be resolved only by political debate and decisions, not by economic analysis alone.

MARKET, COMMAND, AND MIXED ECONOMIES

What are the different ways that a society can answer the questions of *what, how,* and *for whom?* Different societies are organized through *alternative economic systems,* and economics studies the various mechanisms that a society can use to allocate its scarce resources.

We generally distinguish two fundamentally different ways of organizing an economy. At one extreme, government makes most economic decisions, with those on top of the hierarchy giving economic commands to those further down the ladder. At the other extreme, decisions are made in markets, where individuals or enterprises voluntarily agree to exchange goods and services, usually through payments of money. Let's briefly examine each of these two forms of economic organization.

In the United States and most democratic countries, most economic questions are solved by the market. Hence their economic systems are called market economies. A **market economy** is one in which individuals and private firms make the major decisions about production and consumption. A system of prices, of markets, of profits and losses, of incentives and rewards determines *what, how,* and *for whom.* Firms produce the commodities that yield the highest profits (the *what*) by the techniques of production that are least costly (the *how*). Consumption is determined by individuals' decisions about how to spend the wages and property incomes generated by their labor and property ownership (the *for whom*). The extreme case of a market economy, in which the government keeps its hands off economic decisions, is called a **laissez-faire** economy.

By contrast, a **command economy** is one in which the government makes all important decisions about production and distribution. In a command economy, such as the one which operated in the Soviet Union during most of this century, the government owns most of the means of production (land and capital); it also owns and directs the operations of enterprises in most industries; it is the employer of most workers and tells them how to do their jobs; and it decides how the output of the society is to be divided among different goods and services. In short, in a command economy, the government answers the major economic questions through its ownership of resources and its power to enforce decisions.

No contemporary society falls completely into either of these polar categories. Rather, all societies are **mixed economies,** with elements of market and command. There has never been a 100 percent market economy (although nineteenth-century England came close).

Today most decisions in the United States are made in the marketplace. But the government plays an important role in overseeing the functioning of the market; governments pass laws that regulate economic life, produce educational and police services, and control pollution. Most societies today operate mixed economies.

C. SOCIETY'S TECHNOLOGICAL POSSIBILITIES

Every gun that is made, every warship launched, every rocket fired signifies, in the final sense, a theft from those who hunger and are not fed.

President Dwight D. Eisenhower

Each economy has a stock of limited resources—labor, technical knowledge, factories and tools, land, energy. In deciding *what* and *how* things should be produced, the economy is in reality deciding how to allocate its resources among the thousands of different possible commodities and services. How much land will go into growing wheat? Or into housing the population? How many factories will produce computers? How many will make pizzas? How many children will grow up to play professional sports or to be professional economists or to program computers?

Faced with the undeniable fact that goods are scarce relative to wants, an economy must decide how to cope with limited resources. It must choose among different potential bundles of goods (the *what*), select from different techniques of production (the *how*), and decide in the end who will consume the goods (the *for whom*).

INPUTS AND OUTPUTS

To answer these three questions, every society must make choices about the economy's inputs and outputs. **Inputs** are commodities or services that are used to produce goods and services. An economy uses its existing *technology* to combine inputs to produce outputs. **Outputs** are the various useful goods or services that result from the production process and are either consumed or employed in further production. Consider the "production" of pizza. We say that the eggs, flour, heat, pizza oven, and chef's skilled labor are the inputs. The tasty pizza is the output. In education, the inputs are the time of the faculty, the laboratories and classrooms, the textbooks, and so on, while the outputs are educated and informed citizens.

Another term for inputs is **factors of production.** These can be classified into three broad categories: land, labor, and capital.

- *Land*—or, more generally, natural resources—represents the gift of nature to our productive processes. It consists of the land used for farming or for underpinning houses, factories, and roads; the energy resources that fuel our cars and heat our homes; and the nonenergy resources like copper and iron ore and sand. In today's congested world, we must broaden the scope of natural resources to include our environmental resources, such as clean air and drinkable water.
- *Labor* consists of the human time spent in production—working in automobile factories, tilling the land, teaching school, or baking pizzas. Thousands of occupations and tasks, at all skill levels, are performed by labor. It is at once the most familiar and the most crucial input for an advanced industrial economy.
- *Capital* resources form the durable goods of an economy, produced in order to produce yet other goods. Capital goods include machines, roads, computers, hammers, trucks, steel mills, automobiles, washing machines, and buildings. As we will later see, the accumulation of specialized capital goods is essential to the task of economic development.

Restating the three economic problems in terms of inputs and outputs, a society must decide (1) *what* outputs to produce, and in what quantity; (2) *how* to produce them—that is, by what techniques inputs should be combined to produce the desired outputs; and (3) *for whom* the outputs should be produced and distributed.

THE PRODUCTION-POSSIBILITY FRONTIER

Societies cannot have everything they want. They are limited by the resources and the technology available to them. Take defense spending as an example.

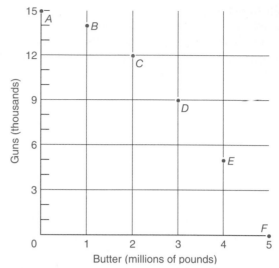

FIGURE 1-1. The Production Possibilities in a Graph

This figure displays the alternative combinations of production pairs from Table 1-1.

Alternative Production Possibilities		
Possibilities	Butter (millions of pounds)	Guns (thousands)
A	0	15
B	1	14
C	2	12
D	3	9
E	4	5
F	5	0

TABLE 1-1. Limitation of Scarce Resources Implies the Guns-Butter Tradeoff

Scarce inputs and technology imply that the production of guns and butter is limited. As we go from A to B . . . to F, we are transferring labor, machines, and land from the gun industry to butter and can thereby increase butter production.

Countries are always being forced to decide how much of their limited resources goes to their military and how much goes into other activities (such as new factories or education). Some countries, like Japan, allocate about 1 percent of their national output to their military. The United States spends 5 percent of its national output on defense, while a fortress economy like North Korea spends up to 20 percent of its national output on the military. The more output that goes for defense, the less there is available for consumption and investment.

Let us dramatize this choice by considering an economy which produces only two economic goods, guns and butter. The guns, of course, represent military spending, and the butter stands for civilian spending. Suppose that our economy decides to throw all its energy into producing the civilian good, butter. There is a maximum amount of butter that can be produced per year. The maximal amount of butter depends on the quantity and quality of the economy's resources and the productive efficiency with which they are used. Suppose 5 million pounds of butter is the maximum amount that can be produced with the existing technology and resources.

At the other extreme, imagine that all resources are instead devoted to the production of guns. Again, because of resource limitations, the economy can produce only a limited quantity of guns. For this example, assume that the economy can produce 15,000 guns of a certain kind if no butter is produced.

These are two extreme possibilities. In between are many others. If we are willing to give up some butter, we can have some guns. If we are willing to give up still more butter, we can have still more guns.

A schedule of possibilities is given in Table 1-1. Combination F shows the extreme where all butter and no guns are produced, while A depicts the opposite extreme where all resources go into guns. In between—at E, D, C, and B—increasing amounts of butter are given up in return for more guns.

How, you might well ask, can a nation turn butter into guns? Butter is transformed into guns not physically but by the alchemy of diverting the economy's resources from one use to the other.

We can represent our economy's production possibilities more vividly in the diagram shown in Figure 1-1. This diagram measures butter along the horizontal axis and guns along the vertical one. (If you are unsure about the different kinds of graphs or about how to turn a table into a graph, consult the appendix to this chapter.) We plot point F in Figure 1-1 from the data in Table 1-1 by counting over 5 butter units to the right on the horizontal axis and going up 0 gun units on the vertical axis; similarly, E is obtained by going 4 butter units to the right and going up 5 gun units; and finally, we get A by going over 0 butter units and up 15 gun units.

If we fill in all intermediate positions with new rust-colored points representing all the different combinations of guns and butter, we have the con-

tinuous rust curve shown as the *production-possibility frontier,* or *PPF,* in Figure 1-2.

The **production-possibility frontier** (or *PPF*) shows the maximum amounts of production that can be obtained by an economy, given its technological knowledge and quantity of inputs available. The *PPF* represents the menu of goods and services available to society.

Putting the *PPF* to Work

The *PPF* in Figure 1-2 was drawn for guns and butter, but the same analysis applies to any choice of goods. Thus the more resources the government uses to build public goods like highways, the less will be left to produce private goods like houses; the more we choose to consume of food, the less we can consume of clothing; the more society decides to consume today, the less can be its production of capital goods to turn out more consumption goods in the future.

FIGURE 1-2. A Smooth Curve Connects the Plotted Points of the Numerical Production Possibilities

This frontier shows the schedule along which society can choose to substitute guns for butter. It assumes a given state of technology and a given quantity of inputs. Points outside the frontier (such as point *I*) are infeasible or unattainable. Any point inside the curve, such as *U,* indicates that the economy has not attained productive efficiency, as occurs when unemployment is high during severe business cycles.

The Production-Possibility Frontier

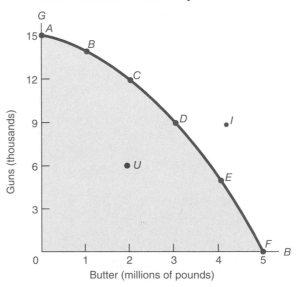

The graphs of Figures 1-3 to 1-5 present some important applications of *PPF*s. Figure 1-3 shows the effect of economic growth on a country's production possibilities. An increase in inputs, or improved technological knowledge, enables a country to produce more of all goods and services, thus shifting out the *PPF*. The figure also illustrates that poor countries must devote most of their resources to food production while rich countries can afford more luxuries as productive potential increases.

Figure 1-4 depicts the electorate's choice between private goods (bought at a price) and public goods (paid for by taxes). Poor countries can afford little of public goods like public health and scientific research. But with economic growth, public goods as well as environmental quality take a larger share of output.

Figure 1-5 portrays an economy's choice between (*a*) current-consumption goods and (*b*) investment or capital goods (machines, factories, etc.). By sacrificing current consumption and producing more capital goods, a nation's economy can grow more rapidly, making possible more of *both* goods (consumption and capital) in the future.

The production-possibility frontier can also show the crucial economic notion of tradeoffs. To take one important case, time is scarce. People have limited time available to pursue different activities. For example, as a student, you might have 10 hours to study for upcoming tests in economics and history. If you study only history, you will get a high grade there and do poorly in economics, and vice versa. Treating the grades on the two tests as the "output" of your studying, sketch out the *PPF* for grades, given your limited time resources. Alternatively, if the two student commodities are "grades" and "fun," how would you draw this *PPF*? Where are you on this frontier? Where are your lazy friends?

Opportunity Costs

Life is full of choices. Because resources are scarce, we must always consider how to spend our limited incomes or time. When you decide whether

---

FIGURE 1-3. Economic Growth Shifts the *PPF* Outward

(a) Before development, the nation is poor. It must devote almost all its resources to food and enjoys few comforts. **(b)** Growth of inputs and technological change shift out the *PPF*. With economic growth, a nation moves from *A* to *B*, expanding its food consumption little compared with its increased consumption of luxuries. It can increase its consumption of both goods if it desires.

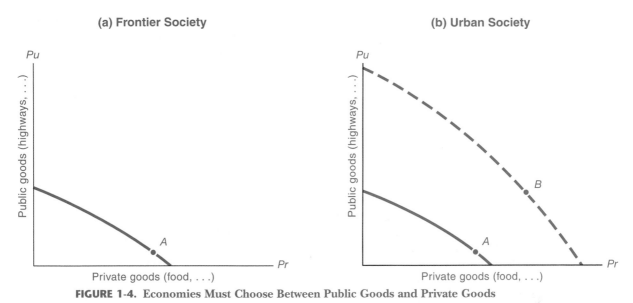

FIGURE 1-4. Economies Must Choose Between Public Goods and Private Goods

(**a**) A poor frontier society lives from hand to mouth, with little left over for public goods like superhighways or public health. (**b**) A modern urbanized economy is more prosperous and chooses to spend more of its higher income on public goods and government services (roads, environmental protection, and education).

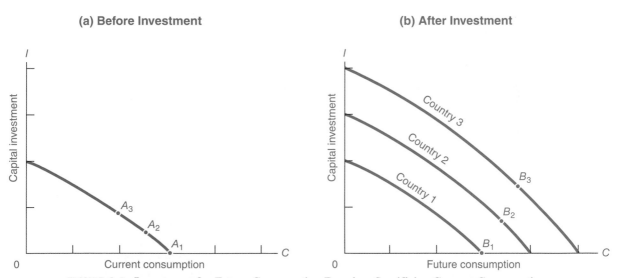

FIGURE 1-5. Investment for Future Consumption Requires Sacrificing Current Consumption

A nation can produce either current-consumption goods (pizzas and concerts) or investment goods (pizza ovens and concert halls). (**a**) Three countries start out even. They have the same *PPF*, shown in the panel on the left, but they have different investment rates. Country 1 does no investment for the future and remains at A_1 (merely replacing machines). Country 2 abstains modestly from consumption and invests at A_2. Country 3 sacrifices a great deal of current consumption and invests heavily. (**b**) In the following years, countries that invest more heavily forge ahead. Thus thrifty Country 3 has shifted its *PPF* far out, while Country 1's *PPF* has not moved at all. Countries that invest heavily have higher investment *and* consumption in the future.

to study economics, buy a car, or go to college, in each case you must consider how much the decision will cost in terms of forgone opportunities. The cost of the forgone alternative is the *opportunity cost* of the decision.

The concept of opportunity cost can be illustrated using the *PPF*. Examine the frontier in Figure 1-2, which shows the tradeoff between guns and butter. Suppose the country decides to increase its gun purchases from 9000 guns at *D* to 12,000 units at *C*. What is the opportunity cost of this decision? You might calculate the cost in dollar terms. But in economics we always need to "pierce the veil" of money to examine the *real* impacts of alternative decisions. On the most fundamental level, the opportunity cost of moving from *D* to *C* is the butter that must be given up to produce the extra guns. In this example, the opportunity cost of the 3000 extra guns is 1 million pounds of butter forgone.

Or consider the real-world example of the cost of opening a gold mine near Yellowstone National Park. The developer argues that the mine will have but a small cost because the fees for Yellowstone will hardly be affected. But an economist would answer that the dollar receipts are too narrow a measure of cost. We should ask whether the unique and precious qualities of Yellowstone might be degraded if a gold mine were to operate, with the accompanying noise, water and air pollution, and degradation of amenity value for visitors. While the dollar cost might be small, the opportunity cost in lost wilderness values might be large indeed.

In a world of scarcity, choosing one thing means giving up something else. The **opportunity cost** of a decision is the value of the good or service forgone.

Efficiency

All of our explanations up to now have implicitly assumed that the economy is producing efficiently—that is, it is on, rather than inside, the production-possibility frontier. Remember that efficiency means that the economy's resources are being used as effectively as possible to satisfy people's needs and desires. One important aspect of overall economic efficiency is *productive efficiency*. Productive efficiency occurs when an economy cannot produce more of one good without producing less of another good; this implies that the economy is on its production-possibility frontier.

Let's see why productive efficiency requires being on the *PPF*. Start in the situation shown by point *D* in Figure 1-2. Say the market calls for another million pounds of butter. If we ignored the constraint shown by the *PPF*, we might think it possible to produce more butter without reducing gun production, say, by moving to point *I*, to the right of point *D*. But point *I* is outside the frontier, in the "infeasible" region. Starting from *D*, we cannot get more butter without giving up some guns. Hence point *D* displays productive efficiency, while point *I* is infeasible.

Productive efficiency occurs when society cannot increase the output of one good without cutting back on another good. Productive efficiency means that an economy is on its production-possibility frontier.

One further point about productive efficiency can be illustrated using the *PPF*: Being on the *PPF* means that producing more of one good inevitably requires sacrificing other goods. When we produce more guns, we are substituting guns for butter. Substitution is the law of life in a full-employment economy, and the production-possibility frontier depicts the menu of society's choices.

Unemployed Resources and Inefficiency.
Even casual observers of modern life know that society has unemployed resources in the form of idle workers, idle factories, and idled land. When there are unemployed resources, the economy is not on its production-possibility frontier at all but, rather, somewhere *inside* it. In Figure 1-2, point *U* represents a point inside the *PPF*; at *U*, society is producing only 2 units of butter and 6 units of guns. Some resources are unemployed, and by putting them to work, we can increase our output of all goods; the economy can move from *U* to *D*, producing more butter and more guns and improving the economy's efficiency. We can have our guns and eat more butter too.

One source of inefficiency occurs during business cycles. From 1929 to 1933, in the Great Depression, the total output produced in the United States declined by almost 25 percent. This occurred not because the *PPF* shifted in but because various shocks reduced spending and pushed the economy inside its *PPF*. Then the buildup for World War II expanded demand, and output grew rapidly as the economy pushed back to the *PPF*. Similar forces were at work in much of the industrial world between 1990 and 1996 as macroeconomic factors pushed Europe and Japan inside their *PPFs*.

Business-cycle depressions are not the only reason why an economy might be inside its *PPF*. An economy might suffer from inefficiency or dislocations because of strikes, political changes, or revolution. Such a case occurred during the early 1990s in countries that threw off their socialist planning systems and adopted free markets. Because of the disruptive changes, output fell and unemployment rose as firms responded to changing markets and the new rules of capitalism. No period of history saw such sustained declines in output as the economies in transition experienced after 1990.

However, economists expect that this "real business cycle" will be but a temporary setback. Already, those economies that have made the most thorough reforms—such as Poland or the Czech Republic—have turned the corner and are beginning to recover. Their *PPF*s are once again shifting outward, and their incomes are likely to surpass the incomes of countries like Ukraine or Belarus, which have been reluctant reformers.

As we close this introductory chapter, let us return briefly to our opening theme, Why study economics? Perhaps the best answer to the question is a famous one given by Keynes in the final lines of *The General Theory of Employment, Interest and Money*:

> The ideas of economists and political philosophers, both when they are right and when they are wrong, are more powerful than is commonly understood. Indeed the world is ruled by little else. Practical men, who believe themselves to be quite exempt from any intellectual influences, are usually the slaves of some defunct economist. Madmen in authority, who hear voices in the air, are distilling their frenzy from some academic scribbler of a few years back. I am sure that the power of vested interests is vastly exaggerated compared with the gradual encroachment of ideas. Not, indeed, immediately, but after a certain interval; for in the field of economic and political philosophy there are not many who are influenced by new theories after they are twenty-five or thirty years of age, so that the ideas which civil servants and politicians and even agitators apply to current events are not likely to be the newest. But, soon or late, it is ideas, not vested interests, which are dangerous for good or evil.

To understand how the powerful ideas of economics apply to the central issues of human societies—ultimately, this is why we study economics.

SUMMARY

A. Introduction

1. What is economics? Economics is the study of how societies choose to use scarce productive resources that have alternative uses, to produce commodities of various kinds, and to distribute them among different groups. We study economics to understand not only the world we live in but also the many potential worlds that reformers are constantly proposing to us.

2. Goods are scarce because people desire much more than the economy can produce. Economic goods are scarce, not free, and society must choose among the limited goods that can be produced with its available resources.

3. Microeconomics is concerned with the behavior of individual entities such as markets, firms, and households. Macroeconomics views the performance of the economy as a whole. Through all economics, beware of the fallacy of composition and the post hoc fallacy, and remember to keep other things constant.

B. The Three Problems of Economic Organization

4. Every society must answer three fundamental questions: *what, how,* and *for whom? What* kinds and quantities are produced among the wide range of all possible goods and services? *How* are resources used in producing these goods? And *for whom* are the goods produced (that is, what is the distribution of income and consumption among different individuals and classes)?

5. Societies answer these questions in different ways. The most important forms of economic organization today are *command* and *market*. The command economy is directed by centralized government control; a market economy is guided by an informal system of prices and profits in which most decisions are made by private individuals and firms. All societies have different combinations of command and market; all societies are mixed economies.

C. Society's Technological Possibilities

6. With given resources and technology, the production choices between two goods such as butter and guns can be summarized in the *production-possibility frontier* (*PPF*). The *PPF* shows how the production of one good (such as guns) is traded off against the production of another good (such as butter). In a world of scarcity, choosing one thing means giving up something else. The value of the good or service forgone is its opportunity cost.

7. Productive efficiency occurs when production of one good cannot be increased without curtailing production of another good. This is illustrated by the *PPF.* When an economy is on its *PPF,* it can produce more of one good only by producing less of another good.

8. Production-possibility frontiers illustrate many basic economic processes: how economic growth pushes out the frontier, how a nation chooses relatively less food and other necessities as it develops, how a country chooses between private goods and public goods, and how societies choose between consumption goods and capital goods that enhance future consumption.

9. Societies are sometimes inside their production-possibility frontier. When unemployment is high or when revolution or inefficient government regulations hamper economic activity, the economy is inefficient and operates inside its *PPF.*

CONCEPTS FOR REVIEW

Fundamental Concepts

scarcity and efficiency
free goods vs. economic goods
macroeconomics and microeconomics
normative vs. positive economics
fallacy of composition, post hoc fallacy
"keep other things constant"
cool heads, warm hearts

Key Problems of Economic Organization

what, how, and *for whom*
alternative economic systems:
    command vs. market
laissez-faire
mixed economies

Choice Among Production Possibilities

inputs and outputs
production-possibility frontier (*PPF*)
productive efficiency and inefficiency
opportunity cost

QUESTIONS FOR DISCUSSION

1. The great English economist Alfred Marshall (1842–1924) invented many of the tools of modern economics, but he was most concerned with the application of these tools to the problems of society. In his inaugural lecture, Marshall wrote:

   It will be my most cherished ambition to increase the numbers who Cambridge University sends out into the world with cool heads but warm hearts, willing to give some of their best powers to grappling with the social suffering around them; resolved not to rest content till they have opened up to all the material means of a refined and noble life. (*Memorials of Alfred Marshall*, A. C. Pigou, ed. (MacMillan and Co., London, 1925), p. 174 with minor edits.)

   Explain how the cool head might provide the essential positive economic analysis to implement the normative value judgments of the warm heart. Do you agree with Marshall's view of the role of the teacher? Do you accept his challenge?

2. The late George Stigler, an eminent conservative Chicago economist, wrote as follows:

   No thoroughly egalitarian society has ever been able to construct or maintain an efficient and progressive economic system. It has been universal experience that some system of differential rewards is necessary to stimulate workers. [*The Theory of Price*, 3d ed. (Macmillan, New York, 1966), p. 19.]

   Are these statements positive or normative economics? Discuss Stigler's view in light of Alfred Marshall's quote in Question 1. Is there a conflict?

3. Define each of the following terms carefully and give examples: *PPF*, scarcity, productive efficiency, inputs, outputs.

4. In deciding how to use your scarce time and income, determine what the opportunity cost would be for you of going to a movie before your economics exam. What is the opportunity cost of buying a car?

5. Assume that Econoland produces haircuts and shirts with inputs of labor. Econoland has 1000 hours of labor available. A haircut requires ½ hour of labor, while a shirt requires 5 hours of labor. Construct Econoland's production-possibility frontier.

6. Assume that scientific inventions have doubled the productivity of society's resources in butter production without altering the productivity of gun manufacture. Redraw society's production-possibility frontier in Figure 1-2 to illustrate the new trade-off.

7. Many scientists believe that we are rapidly depleting our natural resources. Assume that there are only two inputs (labor and natural resources) producing two goods (concerts and gasoline) with no improvement in society's technology over time. Show what would happen to the *PPF* over time as natural resources are exhausted. How would invention and technological improvement modify your answer? On the basis of this example, explain why it is said that "economic growth is a race between depletion and invention."

8. Say that Diligent has 10 hours to study for upcoming tests in economics and history. Draw a *PPF* for grades, given Diligent's limited time resources. If Diligent studies inefficiently by listening to loud music and chatting with friends, where will Diligent's grade "output" be relative to the *PPF*? What will happen to the grade *PPF* if Diligent increases study inputs from 10 hours to 15 hours?

APPENDIX 1
HOW TO READ GRAPHS

A picture is worth a thousand words.

Chinese Proverb

Before you can master economics, you must have a working knowledge of graphs. They are as indispensable to the economist as a hammer is to a carpenter. So if you are not familiar with the use of diagrams, invest some time in learning how to read them—it will be time well spent.

What is a *graph*? It is a diagram showing how two or more sets of data or variables are related to one another. Graphs are essential in economics because, among other reasons, they allow us to analyze economic concepts and examine historical trends.

You will encounter many different kinds of graphs in this book. Some graphs show how variables change over time (see, for example, the inside of the front cover); other graphs show the relationship between different variables (such as the example we will turn to in a moment). Each graph in the book will help you understand an important economic law or trend.

THE PRODUCTION-POSSIBILITY FRONTIER

The first graph that you encountered in this text was the production-possibility frontier. As we showed in the body of this chapter, the production-possibility frontier, or *PPF*, represents the maximum amounts of a pair of goods or services that can both be produced with an economy's given resources assuming that all resources are fully employed.

Let's follow up an important application, that of choosing between food and machines. The essential data for the *PPF* are shown in Table 1A-1, which is very much like the example in Table 1-1. Recall that each of the possibilities gives one level of food production and one level of machine production. As the quantity of food produced increases, the production of machines falls. Thus, if the economy produced 10 units of food, it could produce a maximum of 140 machines, but when the output of food is 20 units, only 120 machines can be manufactured.

Production-Possibility Graph

The data shown in Table 1A-1 can also be presented as a graph. To construct the graph, we represent each of the table's pairs of data by a single point on a two-dimensional plane. Figure 1A-1 displays in a graph the relationship between the food and machines outputs shown in Table 1A-1. Each pair of numbers is represented by a single point in the graph. Thus the row labeled "A" in Table 1A-1 is graphed as point *A* in Figure 1A-1, and similarly for points *B*, *C*, and so on.

In Figure 1A-1, the vertical line at left and the horizontal line at bottom correspond to the two variables—food and machines. A **variable** is an item of interest that can be defined and measured and that takes on different values at different times or places. Important variables studied in economics are prices,

Alternative Production Possibilities		
Possibilities	Food	Machines
A	0	150
B	10	140
C	20	120
D	30	90
E	40	50
F	50	0

TABLE 1A-1. The Pairs of Possible Outputs of Food and Machines

The table shows six potential pairs of outputs that can be produced with the given resources of a country. The country can choose one of the six possible combinations.

quantities, hours of work, acres of land, dollars of income, and so forth.

The horizontal line on a graph is referred to as the *horizontal axis,* or sometimes the *X axis.* In Figure 1A-1, food output is measured on the black horizontal axis. The vertical line is known as the *vertical axis,* or *Y axis.* In Figure 1A-1, it measures the number of machines produced. Point *A* on the vertical axis stands for 150 machines. The lower left-hand corner where the two axes meet is called the *origin.* It signifies 0 food and 0 machines in Figure 1A-1.

FIGURE 1A-1. Six Possible Pairs of Food-Machines Production Levels

This figure shows the data of Table 1A-1 in graphical form. The data are exactly the same, but the visual display presents the data more vividly.

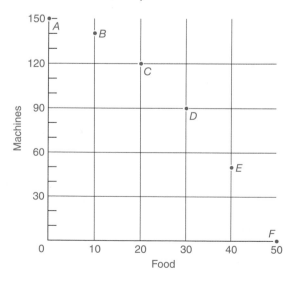

A Smooth Curve. In most economic relationships, variables can change by small amounts as well as by the large increments shown in Figure 1A-1. We therefore generally draw economic relationships as continuous curves. Figure 1A-2 shows the *PPF* as a smooth curve in which the points from *A* to *F* have been connected.

By comparing Table 1A-1 and Figure 1A-2, we can see why graphs are so often used in economics. The smooth *PPF* reflects the menu of choice for the economy. It is a visual device for showing what types of goods are available in what quantities. Your eye can see at a glance the relationship between machine and food production.

Slopes and Lines

Figure 1A-2 depicts the relationship between maximum food and machine production. One important way to describe the relationship between two variables is by the slope of the graph line.

The **slope** of a line represents the change in one variable that occurs when another variable changes. More precisely, it is the change in the variable *Y* on the vertical axis per unit change in the variable *X* on the horizontal axis. For example, in Figure 1A-2,

FIGURE 1A-2.

A smooth curve fills in between the plotted pairs of points, creating the production-possibility frontier.

The Production-Possibility Frontier

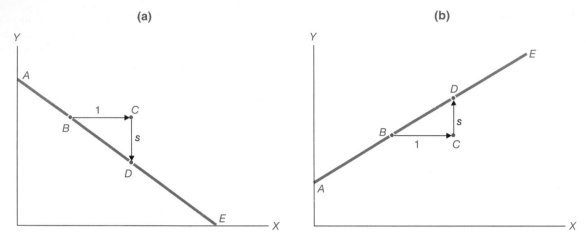

FIGURE 1A-3. Calculation of Slope for Straight Lines

It is easy to calculate slopes for straight lines as "rise over run." Thus in both (**a**) and (**b**), the numerical value of the slope is rise/run = $CD/BC = s/1 = s$. Note that in (**a**), CD is negative, indicating a negative slope, or an inverse relationship between X and Y.

say that food production rose from 25 to 26 units. The slope of the curve in Figure 1A-2 tells us the precise change in machinery production that would take place. *Slope is an exact numerical measure of the relationship between the change in* Y *and the change in* X.

We can use Figure 1A-3 to show how to measure the slope of a straight line, say, the slope of the line between points B and D. Think of the movement from B to D as occurring in two stages. First comes a horizontal movement from B to C indicating a 1-unit increase in the X value (with no change in Y). Second comes a compensating vertical movement up or down, shown as s in Figure 1A-3. (The movement of 1 horizontal unit is purely for convenience. The formula holds for movements of any size.) The two-step movement brings us from one point to another on the straight line.

Because the BC movement is a 1-unit increase in X, the length of CD (shown as s in Figure 1A-3) indicates the change in Y per unit change in X. On a graph, this change is called the *slope* of the line $ABDE$.

Often slope is defined as "the rise over the run." The *rise* is the vertical distance; in Figure 1A-3, the rise is the distance from C to D. The *run* is the horizontal distance; it is BC in Figure 1A-3. The rise over the run in this instance would be CD over BC. Thus the slope of BD is CD/BC.

The key points to understand about slopes are the following:
1. The slope can be expressed as a number. It measures the change in Y per unit change in X, or "the rise over the run."
2. If the line is straight, its slope is constant everywhere.
3. The slope of the line indicates whether the relationship between X and Y is direct or inverse. *Direct relationships* occur when variables move in the same direction (that is, they increase or decrease together); *inverse relationships* occur when the variables move in opposite directions (that is, one increases as the other decreases).

Thus a negative slope indicates the X-Y relation is inverse, as it is in Figure 1A-3(a). Why? Because an increase in X calls for a decrease in Y.

People sometimes confuse slope with the appearance of steepness. This conclusion is often valid— but not always. The steepness depends on the scale of the graph. Panels (a) and (b) in Figure 1A-4 both portray exactly the same relationship. But in (b), the horizontal scale has been stretched out compared with (a). If you calculate carefully, you will see that the slopes are exactly the same (and are equal to ½).

FIGURE 1A-4. Steepness **Is Not the Same as Slope** Note that even though (**a**) looks steeper than (**b**), they display the same relationship. Both have slope of ½, but the *X* axis has been stretched out in (**b**).

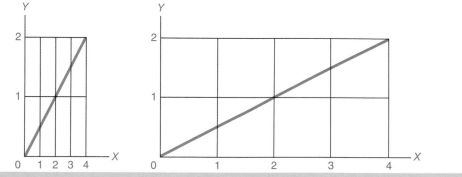

Slope of a Curved Line. A curved or non-linear line is one whose slope changes. Sometimes we want to know the slope *at a given point*, such as point *B* in Figure 1A-5. We see that the slope at point *B* is positive, but it is not obvious exactly how to calculate the slope.

To find the slope of a smooth curved line at a point, we calculate the slope of the straight line that just touches, but does not cross, the curved line at the point in question. Such a straight line is called a *tangent* to the curved line. Put differently, the slope of a curved line at a point is given by the slope of the straight line that is tangent to the curve at the given point. Once we draw the tangent line, we find the slope of the tangent line with the usual right-angle measuring technique discussed earlier.

To find the slope at point *B* in Figure 1A-5, we simply construct straight line *FBJ* as a tangent to the curved line at point *B*. We then calculate the slope of the tangent as *NJ/MN*. Similarly, the tangent line *GH* gives the slope of the curved line at point *D*.

Another example of the slope of a nonlinear line is shown in Figure 1A-6. This shows a typical micro-economics curve, which is dome shaped and has a

FIGURE 1A-5. Tangent as Slope of Curved Line
By constructing a tangent line, we can calculate the slope of a curved line at a given point. Thus the line *FBMJ* is tangent to smooth curve *ABDE* at point *B*. The slope at *B* is calculated as the slope of the tangent line, i.e., as *NJ/MN*.

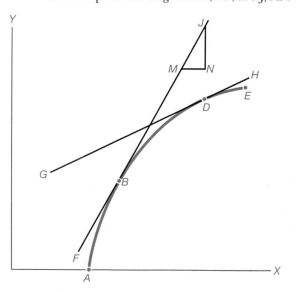

FIGURE 1A-6. Different Slopes of Nonlinear Curves
Many curves in economics first rise, then reach a maximum, then fall. In the rising region from *A* to *C* the slope is positive (see point *B*). In the falling region from *C* to *E* the slope is negative (see point *D*). At the curve's maximum, point *C*, the slope is zero. (What about a U-shaped curve? What is the slope at its minimum?)

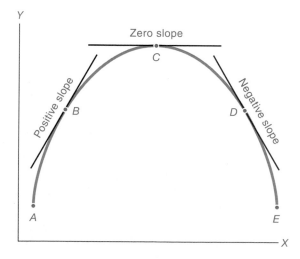

maximum at point *C.* We can use our method of slopes-as-tangents to see that the slope of the curve is always positive in the region where the curve is rising and negative in the falling region. At the peak or maximum of the curve, the slope is exactly zero. A zero slope signifies that a tiny movement in the *X* variable around the maximum has no effect on the value of the *Y* variable.[1]

Shifts of and Movement Along Curves

An important distinction in economics is that between shifts of curves and movement along curves. We can examine this distinction in Figure 1A-7. The inner production-possibility frontier reproduces the *PPF* in Figure 1A-2. At point *D* society chooses to produce 30 units of food and 90 units of machines. If society decides to consume more food with a given *PPF,* then it can *move along* the *PPF* to point *E.* This movement along the curve represents choosing more food and fewer machines.

Suppose that the inner *PPF* represents society's production possibilities for 1990. If we return to the same country in 2000, we see that the *PPF* has *shifted* from the inner 1990 curve to the outer 2000 curve. (This shift would occur because of technological change or because of an increase in labor or capital available.) In the later year, society might choose to be at point *G,* with more food and machines than at either *D* or *E.*

The point of this example is that in the first case (moving from *D* to *E*) we see movement along the curve, while in the second case (from *D* to *G*) we see a shift of the curve.

Some Special Graphs

The *PPF* is one of the most important graphs of economics, one depicting the relationship between two economic variables (such as food and machines or guns and butter). You will encounter other types of graphs in the pages that follow.

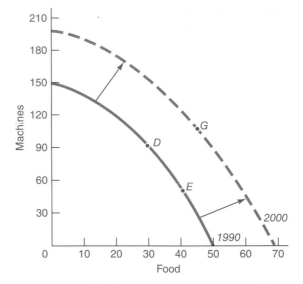

FIGURE 1A-7. Shift of Curves Versus Movement Along Curves

In using graphs, it is essential to distinguish *movement along* a curve (such as from high-investment *D* to low-investment *E*) from a *shift of* a curve (as from *D* in an early year to *G* in a later year).

Time Series. Some graphs show how a particular variable has changed over time. Look, for example, at the graphs on the inside front cover of this text. The left-hand graph shows a time series, since the American Revolution, of a significant macroeconomic variable, the ratio of the federal government debt to total gross domestic product, or *GDP*—this ratio is the *debt-GDP ratio.* Time-series graphs have time on the horizontal axis and variables of interest (in this case, the debt-GDP ratio) on the vertical axis. This graph shows that the debt-GDP ratio has risen sharply during every major war.

Scatter Diagrams. Sometimes individual pairs of points will be plotted, as in Figure 1A-1. Often, combinations of variables for different years will be plotted. An important example of a scatter diagram from macroeconomics is the *consumption function,* shown in Figure 1A-8. This scatter diagram shows the nation's total disposable income on the horizontal axis and total consumption (spending by households on goods like food, clothing, and housing) on the vertical axis. Note that consumption is very closely linked to income, a vital clue for understanding changes in national income and output.

---

[1] For those who enjoy algebra, the slope of a line can be remembered as follows: A straight line (or linear relationship) is written as $Y = a + bX$. For this line, the slope of the curve is b, which measures the change in Y per unit change in X.

A curved line or nonlinear relationship is one involving terms other than constants and the X term. An example of a nonlinear relationship is the quadratic equation $Y = (X - 2)^2$. You can easily verify that the slope of this equation is negative for $X < 2$ and positive for $X > 2$. What is its slope for $X = 2$?

FIGURE 1A-8. Scatter Diagram of Consumption Function Shows Important Macroeconomic Law Observed points of consumption spending fall near the *CC* line, which displays average behavior over time. Thus, the rust-colored point for 1990 is so near the *CC* line that it could have been quite accurately predicted from that line even before the year was over. Scatter diagrams allow us to see how close the relationship is between two variables.

Consumption Relates to Income

Diagrams with More Than One Curve. Often it is useful to put two curves in the same graph, thus obtaining a "multicurve diagram." The most important example is the *supply-and-demand diagram*, shown in Chapter 3 (see page 52). Such graphs can show two different relationships simultaneously, such as how consumer purchases respond to price (demand) and how business production responds to price (supply). By graphing the two relationships together, we can determine the price and quantity that will hold in a market.

This concludes our brief excursion into graphs. Once you have mastered these basic principles, the graphs in this book, and in other areas, can be both fun and instructive.

SUMMARY TO APPENDIX

1. Graphs are an essential tool of modern economics. They provide a convenient presentation of data or of the relationships among variables.
2. The important points to understand about a graph are: What is on each of two axes (horizontal and vertical)? What are the units on each axis? What kind of relationship is depicted in the curve or curves shown in the graph?
3. The relationship between the two variables in a curve is given by its slope. The slope is defined as "the rise over the run," or the increase in *Y* per unit increase in

X. If it is upward- (or positively) sloping, the two variables are directly related; they move upward or downward together. If the curve has a downward (or negative) slope, the two variables are inversely related.
4. In addition, we sometimes see special types of graphs: time series, which show how a particular variable moves over time; scatter diagrams, which show observations on a pair of variables; and multicurve diagrams, which show two or more relationships in a single graph.

CONCEPTS FOR REVIEW

Elements of Graphs

horizontal, or X, axis
vertical, or Y, axis

slope as "rise over run"
slope (negative, positive, zero)
tangent as slope of curved line

Examples of Graphs

time-series graphs
scatter diagrams
multicurve graphs

QUESTIONS FOR DISCUSSION

1. Consider the following problem: After your 8 hours a day of sleep, you have 16 hours a day to divide between leisure and study. Let leisure hours be the X variable and study hours be the Y variable. Plot the straight-line relationship between all combinations of X and Y on a blank piece of graph paper. Be careful to label the axes and mark the origin.

2. In question 1, what is the slope of the line showing the relationship between study and leisure hours? Is it a straight line?

3. Let us say that you absolutely need 6 hours of leisure per day, no more, no less. On the graph, mark the point that corresponds to 6 hours of leisure. Now consider a *movement along the curve*: Assume that you decide that you need only 4 hours of leisure a day. Plot the new point.

4. Next show a *shift of the curve*: You find that you need less sleep, so you have 18 hours a day to devote to leisure and study. Draw the new (shifted) curve.

5. Keep a record of your leisure and study for a week. Plot a time-series graph of the hours of leisure and study each day. Next plot a scatter diagram of hours of leisure and hours of study. Do you see any relationship between the two variables?

CHAPTER 2
THE SHIFTING BOUNDARY
BETWEEN MARKETS AND GOVERNMENT

The important thing for Government is not to do things which individuals are doing already, and to do them a little better or a little worse; but to do those things which at present are not done at all.

John Maynard Keynes, "The End of Laissez Faire" (1926)

One of the principal problems of political economy —emphasized by the opening quote from Keynes— is deciding on the appropriate boundary between state and market. We can better understand the issues if we examine how the boundaries evolved to their present point. In medieval times, the aristocracy and town guilds directed much of the economic activity in Europe and Asia. However, about two centuries ago, governments began to exercise less and less power over prices and production methods. Gradually, the restraints of feudalism were replaced by what we call the "market mechanism" or "competitive capitalism."

In most of Europe and North America, the nineteenth century became the age of **laissez-faire**. This doctrine, which translates as "leave us alone," holds that government should interfere as little as possible in economic affairs and leave economic decisions to the interplay of supply and demand in the marketplace. Many governments espoused this economic philosophy in the middle of the nineteenth century.

Nevertheless, by the end of the century, the unbridled excesses of capitalism led the United States and the industrialized countries of Western Europe to retreat from full laissez-faire. Governments assumed a steadily expanding economic role, regulating monopolies, collecting income taxes, and taking on such tasks as providing support for the elderly (social security). This new system, called the **welfare state**, is one in which markets direct the detailed activities of day-to-day economic life while governments regulate social conditions and provide pensions, health care, and other aspects of the social safety net.

Under the guiding hand of government, the market economies of Western Europe and North America flourished in the three decades after World War II. Those years witnessed an unprecedented period of sustained economic growth and prosperity. Then, around 1980, the tides shifted again, as conservative governments in many countries began to reduce taxes and deregulate government's control over the economy. Particularly influential was the "Reagan revolution," which changed public attitudes about taxes and government and reversed the trends in U.S. federal spending on civilian programs.

The most dramatic turn toward the market came in Russia and the socialist countries of Eastern Europe. After decades of extolling the advantages of central planning and a government-run command economy, these countries started to make the difficult transition to a decentralized, market economy. China, while still run by the dictatorship of the Communist party, has enjoyed an economic boom in the late 1980s and early 1990s by allowing markets to operate within its borders. Developing countries like Taiwan, Thailand, and Chile have enjoyed rapid income growth by embracing capitalism and reducing the role of government in their economies.

This capsule history of the shifting balance between state and market will naturally raise many questions. What exactly is a market economy, and what makes it so powerful? What is the "capital" in "capitalism"? What government controls are needed to help markets? The time has come to understand the principles that lie behind the market economy and to review government's role in economic life.

A. WHAT IS A MARKET?

Not Chaos, but Economic Order

We usually take for granted the smooth running of the economy. When you go to the supermarket, the items you want—bread, cereal, and bananas—are usually on the shelf. You pay your bill, pop the food in your mouth, and have a juicy meal. What could be simpler?

If you pause for a moment and look more closely, you may begin to appreciate the complexity of the economic system that provides your daily bread. The food may have passed through five or ten links before getting to you, traveling for days or months from every state and every corner of the globe as it moved along the chain of farmers, food processors, packagers, truckers, wholesalers, and retailers. It seems almost a miracle that food is produced in suitable amounts, gets transported to the right place, and arrives in a palatable form at the dinner table.

But the true miracle is that this entire system works without coercion or centralized direction by anybody. Literally millions of businesses and consumers engage in voluntary trade, and their actions and purposes are invisibly coordinated by a system of prices and markets. Nobody decides how many chickens will be produced, where the trucks will drive, and when the supermarkets will open. Still, in the end, the food is in the store when you want it.

Markets perform similar miracles around us all the time, as can easily be seen if only we observe our economy carefully. Thousands of commodities are produced by millions of people, willingly, without central direction or master plan. Indeed, with a few important exceptions (like the military, police, and schools) most of our economic life proceeds without government intervention, and that's the true wonder of the social world.

The Market Mechanism

A market economy is an elaborate mechanism for coordinating people, activities, and businesses through a system of prices and markets. It is a communication device for pooling the knowledge and actions of billions of diverse individuals. Without central intelligence or computation, it solves problems of production and distribution involving billions of unknown variables and relations, problems that are far beyond the reach of even today's fastest supercomputer. Nobody designed the market, yet it functions remarkably well. *In a market economy, no single individual or organization is responsible for production, consumption, distribution, and pricing.*

How do markets determine prices, wages, and outputs? Originally, a market was an actual place where buyers and sellers could engage in face-to-face bargaining. The *marketplace*—filled with slabs of butter, pyramids of cheese, layers of wet fish, and heaps of vegetables—used to be a familiar sight in many villages and towns, where farmers brought their goods to sell. In the United States today there are still important markets where many traders gather together to do business. For example, wheat and corn are traded at the Chicago Board of Trade, oil and platinum are traded at the New York Mercantile Exchange, and gems are traded at the Diamond District in New York City.

More generally, a market should be thought of as a mechanism by which buyers and sellers can determine prices and exchange goods and services. There are markets for almost everything, from art to pollution. A market may be centralized, like the stock market. It may be decentralized, as in the case of houses or labor. Or it may exist only electronically, as in the case of many financial assets and services, which are traded by computer. The crucial characteristic of a market is that it brings buyers and sellers together to set prices and quantities.

A **market** is a mechanism by which buyers and sellers interact to determine the price and quantity of a good or service.

In a market system, everything has a **price**, which is the value of the good in terms of money (the role of money will be discussed in Section B of this chapter). Prices represent the terms on which people and firms voluntarily exchange different commodities. When I agree to buy a used Ford from a dealer for $4050, this agreement indicates that the Ford is worth more than $4050 to me and that the $4050 is worth more than the Ford to the dealer. The used-car market has determined the price of a used Ford and, through voluntary trading, has allocated this good to the person for whom it has the highest value.

In addition, prices serve as *signals* to producers and consumers. If consumers want more of any good, the price will rise, sending a signal to producers that more supply is needed. For example, every summer, as families set out on their vacations, the demand for gasoline rises, and so does the price. The higher price encourages oil companies to increase gasoline production and, at the same time, discourages travelers from lengthening their trips.

On the other hand, if a commodity such as cars becomes overstocked, dealers and automobile companies will lower their prices in order to reduce their inventory. At the lower price, more consumers will want cars, and producers will want to make fewer cars. As a result, a balance, or equilibrium, between buyers and sellers will be restored.

What is true of the markets for consumer goods is also true of markets for factors of production, such as land or labor. If computer programmers rather than textile workers are needed, job opportunities will be more favorable in the computing field. The price of computer programmers (their hourly wage) will tend to rise, and that of textile workers will tend to fall, as they did during the 1980s. The shift in relative wages will attract workers into the growing occupation.

The nursing crisis of the 1980s shows the labor market at work. During that decade the growth in the health-care sector led to an enormous expansion of nursing jobs with far too few trained nurses to fill them. Hospitals offered all sorts of fringe benefits to attract nurses, including subsidized apartments, low-cost on-site child care, and signing bonuses as high as $10,000. One hospital even ran a lottery for nurses, with the prize being a gift certificate at a nearby department store. But what really attracted people into the nursing profession was rising wages. Between 1983 and 1992, the pay for registered nurses rose almost 70 percent, so they were making about as much money as the average accountant or architect. The rising pay drew so many people into nursing that by 1992 the nursing shortage had disappeared in most parts of the country.

Prices coordinate the decisions of producers and consumers in a market. Higher prices tend to reduce consumer purchases and encourage production. Lower prices encourage consumption and discourage production. Prices are the balance wheel of the market mechanism.

Market Equilibrium. At every moment, some people are buying while others are selling; firms are inventing new products while governments are passing laws to regulate old ones; foreign companies are opening plants in America while American firms are selling their products abroad. Yet in the midst of all this turmoil, markets are constantly solving the *what, how,* and *for whom.* As they balance all the forces operating on the economy, markets are finding a **market equilibrium of supply and demand.**

A market equilibrium represents a balance among all the different buyers and sellers. Depending upon the price, households and firms all want to buy or sell different quantities. The market finds the equilibrium price that simultaneously meets the desires of buyers and sellers. Too high a price would mean a glut of goods with too much output; too low a price would produce long lines in stores and a deficiency of goods. Those prices for which buyers desire to buy exactly the quantity that sellers desire to sell yield an equilibrium of supply and demand.

How Markets Solve the Three Economic Problems

We have just described how prices help balance consumption and production (or demand and supply) in an individual market. What happens when we put all the different markets together—gasoline, cars, land, labor, capital, and everything else? These markets work simultaneously to determine a *general equilibrium* of prices and production.

By matching sellers and buyers (supply and demand) in each market, a market economy simultaneously solves the three problems of *what, how,* and *for whom.* Here is an outline of a market equilibrium:

1. *What* goods and services will be produced is determined by the dollar votes of consumers—not every 2 or 4 years at the polls, but in their daily purchase decisions. The money that they pay into businesses' cash registers ultimately provides the payrolls, rents, and dividends that consumers, as employees, receive as income.

    Firms, in turn, are motivated by the desire to maximize profits. **Profits** are net revenues, or the difference between total sales and total costs. Firms abandon areas where they are losing profits; by the same token, firms are lured by high profits into production of goods in high demand. A familiar example is Hollywood. If one film makes huge profits—say, a film about a cute dinosaur and an evil scientist—other studios will rush to produce imitations.

2. *How* things are produced is determined by the competition among different producers. The best way for producers to meet price competition and maximize profits is to keep costs at a minimum by adopting the most efficient methods of production. Sometimes change is incremental and consists of little more than tinkering with the machinery or adjusting the input mix to gain a cost advantage, which can be very important in a competitive market. At other times there are drastic shifts in technology, as with steam engines displacing horses because steam was cheaper per unit of useful work, or airplanes replacing railroads as the most efficient mode for long-distance travel. Right now we are in the midst of just such a transition to a radically different technology, with computers replacing typewriters, paper, and many white-collar workers.

3. *For whom* things are produced—who is consuming, and how much—depends, in large part, on the supply and demand in the markets for factors of production. Factor markets (i.e., markets for factors of production) determine wage rates, land rents, interest rates, and profits. Such prices are called *factor prices.* The same person may receive wages from a job, dividends from stocks, interest from a certificate of deposit, and rent from a piece of property. By adding up all the revenues from factors, we can calculate the person's market income. The distribution of income among the population is thus determined by the amounts of factors (person-hours, acres, etc.) owned and the prices of the factors (wage rates, land rents, etc.).

Be warned, however, that incomes reflect much more than the rewards for sweaty labor or abstemious saving. High incomes come also from large inheritances, good luck, favorable location, and skills highly prized in the marketplace. Those with low incomes are often pictured as lazy, but the truth is that low incomes are generally the result of poor education, discrimination, or living where jobs are few and wages are low. When we see someone on the unemployment line, we might say, "There, but for the grace of supply and demand, go I."

Monarchs of the Marketplace

Who rules a market economy? Do giant companies like General Electric and AT&T call the tune? Or perhaps Congress and the President? Or the advertising moguls from Madison Avenue? If we examine the structure of a market economy carefully, we see a dual monarchy shared by *consumers and technology.* Consumers direct by their innate and acquired tastes—as expressed by their dollar votes—the ultimate uses to which society's resources are channeled. They pick the point on the production-possibility frontier (*PPF*).

But consumers alone cannot dictate *what* goods will be produced. The available resources and technology place a fundamental constraint on their choices. The economy cannot go outside its *PPF.* You can fly to Hong Kong, but there are no flights to Mars. An economy's resources, along with the available science and technology, limit the candidates for the dollar votes of consumers. Consumer demand has to dovetail with business supply of goods. So business cost and supply decisions, along with consumer demand, help determine what is produced.

Not every technology, however, will find a use. From the Stanley Steamer—a car that ran on steam—to the Premiere smokeless cigarette, which was smokeless but also tasteless, history is full of products that found no markets. How do useless products die off? Is there a government agency that pronounces upon the value of new products? No such agency is necessary. Rather, it is profits which serve as the rewards and penalties for businesses and guide the market mechanism.

Like a farmer using a carrot and a stick to coax a donkey forward, the market system deals out profits and losses to induce firms to produce desired goods efficiently.

A Picture of Prices and Markets

We can picture the circular flow of economic life in Figure 2-1 on page 30. The diagram provides an overview of how consumers and producers interact to determine prices and quantities for both inputs and outputs. Note the two different kinds of markets in the circular flow. At the top are the product markets, or the flow of outputs like pizza and shoes; at the bottom are the markets for inputs or factors of production like land and labor. Further, see how decisions are made by two different entities, households and businesses.

Households buy goods and sell factors of production; businesses sell goods and buy factors of production. Households use their income from sale of labor and other inputs to buy goods from businesses; businesses base their prices of goods on the costs of labor and property. Prices in goods markets are set to balance consumer demand with business supply; prices in factor markets are set to balance household supply with business demand.

All this sounds complicated. But it is simply the total picture of the intricate web of interdependent supplies and demands, interconnected through a market mechanism to solve the economic problems of *what, how,* and *for whom.* Look at Figure 2-1 carefully. A few minutes spent studying it will surely help you understand the workings of a market economy.

The Invisible Hand and "Perfect Competition"

The orderliness of the market system was first recognized by Adam Smith, whose classic work *The Wealth of Nations* (1776) is still read today. Smith proclaimed the principle of the **"invisible hand."** This principle holds that, in selfishly pursuing only his or her personal good, every individual is led, as if by an

invisible hand, to achieve the best good for all. Smith held that in this best of all possible worlds, government interference with market competition is almost certain to be injurious. In one of the most famous passages in all of economics, Smith saw harmony between private interest and public interest:

> Every individual endeavors to employ his capital so that its produce may be of greatest value. He generally neither intends to promote the public interest, nor knows how much he is promoting it. He intends only his own security, only his own gain. And he is in this led by an invisible hand to promote an end which was no part of his intention. By pursuing his own interest he frequently promotes that of society more effectually than when he really intends to promote it.[1]

Smith's insight about the functioning of the market mechanism has inspired modern economists—both the admirers and the critics of capitalism. Economic theorists have proved that under restrictive conditions a perfectly competitive economy is efficient (remember that an economy is producing efficiently when it cannot increase the economic welfare of anyone without making someone else worse off).

After two centuries of experience and thought, however, we recognize the scope and realistic limitations of this doctrine. We know that there are "market failures" and that markets do not always lead to the most efficient outcome. One set of market failures concerns monopolies and other forms of imperfect competition. A second failure of the invisible hand comes when there are spillovers or externalities outside the marketplace—positive externalities such as scientific discoveries and negative spillovers such as pollution. A final reservation comes when the income distribution is politically or ethically unacceptable. When any of these elements occur, Adam Smith's invisible-hand doctrine breaks down and government may want to step in to mend the flawed invisible hand.

In summary:

Adam Smith discovered a remarkable property of a competitive market economy. Under perfect competition and with no market failures, markets will squeeze as many useful goods and services out of the available resources as is possible. But where monopolies or pollution or similar market failures become pervasive, the remarkable efficiency properties of the invisible hand may be destroyed.

---

[1] Adam Smith, *The Wealth of Nations,* 1776.

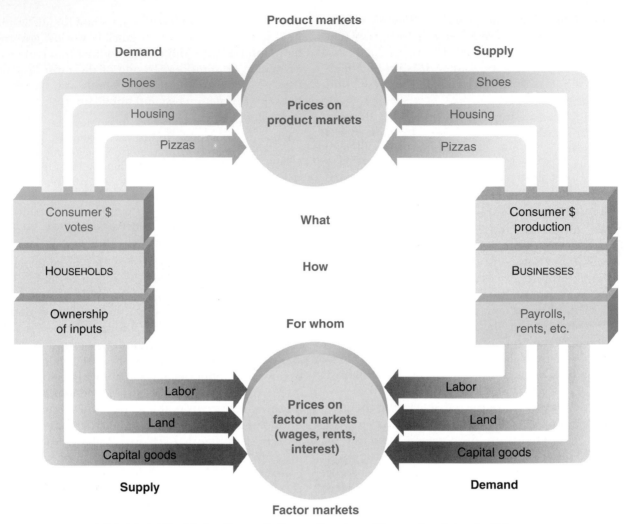

FIGURE 2-1. The Market System Relies on Supply and Demand to Solve the Trio
of Economic Problems

We see here the circular flow of a market economy. Dollar votes of households interact with
business supply in the product markets at top, helping to determine *what* is produced. Further, business demand for inputs meets the public's supply of labor and other inputs in the
factor markets below to help determine wage, rent, and interest payments; incomes thus
influence *for whom* goods are delivered. Business competition to buy factor inputs and sell
goods most cheaply determines *how* goods are produced.

 **Adam Smith: Founding father of eco-
nomics.** "For what purpose is all the toil and
bustle of this world? What is the end of avarice and ambition, of the pursuit of wealth, of power, and pre-
eminence?" Thus wrote Adam Smith (1723–1790), of Scot-
land, who glimpsed for the social world of economics

what Isaac Newton recognized for the physical world of
the heavens. Smith answered his questions in *The Wealth
of Nations* (1776), where he explained the self-regulating
natural order by which the oil of self-interest lubricates
the economic machinery in an almost miraculous fashion.
Smith believed that the toil and bustle had the effect of

improving the lot of the common man and woman. "Consumption is the sole end and purpose of all production."

Smith was the first apostle of economic growth. At the dawn of the Industrial Revolution, he pointed to the great strides in productivity brought about by specialization and the division of labor. In a famous example, he described the specialized manufacturing of a pin factory in which "one man draws out the wire, another straightens it, a third cuts it," and so it goes. This operation allowed 10 people to make 48,000 pins in a day, whereas if "all wrought separately, they could not each of them make twenty, perhaps not one pin a day." Smith saw the result of this division of labor as "universal opulence which extends itself to the lowest ranks of the people." Imagine what he would think if he returned today to see what two more centuries of economic growth have produced!

Smith wrote hundreds of pages railing against countless cases of government folly and interference. Consider the seventeenth-century guild master who was attempt-ing to improve his weaving. The town guild decided, "If a cloth weaver intends to process a piece according to his own invention, he should obtain permission from the judges of the town to employ the number and length of threads that he desires after the question has been considered by four of the oldest merchants and four of the oldest weavers of the guild." Smith argued that such restrictions—whether imposed by government or by monopolies, whether on production or on foreign trade—limit the proper workings of the market system and ultimately hurt both workers and consumers.

None of this should suggest that Smith was an apologist for the establishment. He had a distrust of all entrenched power, private monopolies as much as public monarchies. He was for the common people. But, like many of the great economists, he had learned from his research that the road to waste is paved with good intentions.

Above all, it is Adam Smith's vision of the self-regulating "invisible hand" that is his enduring contribution to modern economics.[2]

B. TRADE, MONEY, AND CAPITAL

Since the time of Adam Smith, market economies have evolved enormously. Advanced capitalist economies, such as the United States, Western Europe, and Japan, have three distinguishing features: trade and specialization, money, and capital.

- An advanced economy is characterized by an elaborate network of *trade,* among individuals and countries, that depends on great *specialization* and an intricate division of labor.
- The economy today makes extensive use of *money,* or the means of payment. The flow of money is the lifeblood of our system. Money provides the yardstick for measuring the economic value of things and for financing trade.
- Modern industrial technologies rest on the use of vast amounts of *capital:* precision machinery,

large-scale factories, and stocks of inventories. Capital goods leverage human labor power into a much more efficient factor of production and allow productivity many times greater than that possible in an earlier age.

TRADE, SPECIALIZATION, AND DIVISION OF LABOR

Compared to the economies of the 1700s, today's economies depend on the specialization of individuals and firms, connected by an extensive network

---

[2] An eloquent introduction to the lives of the great economists can be found in Robert L. Heilbroner, *The Worldly Philosophers* (Simon and Schuster, New York, 1980).

of trade. Western economies have enjoyed rapid economic growth as increasing specialization has allowed workers to become highly productive in particular occupations and to trade their output for the commodities they need.

Specialization occurs when people and countries concentrate their efforts on a particular set of tasks—it permits each person and country to use to best advantage its specific skills and resources. One of the facts of economic life is that, rather than have everyone do everything in a mediocre way, it is better to establish a *division of labor*—dividing production into a number of small specialized steps or tasks. A division of labor permits tall people to become basketball players, numerate people to teach, and persuasive people to sell cars.

In our economic system, it sometimes takes many years to receive the training for particular careers—it takes 14 years to become a certified neurosurgeon. Capital and land are also highly specialized. Land can be specialized, as in the vineyard lands of California and France, which it has taken decades to cultivate. The computer program that went along with the labor to write this textbook took over a decade to be developed, but it is useless at managing an oil refinery or solving large numerical problems. One of the most impressive examples of specialization is the computer chip that manages automobiles and increases their efficiency.

The enormous efficiency of specialization allows the intricate network of trade among people and nations that we see today. Very few of us produce a single finished good; we make but the tiniest fraction of what we consume. We might teach a small part of one college's curriculum, or empty coins from parking meters, or separate the genetic material of fruit flies. In exchange for this specialized labor, we will receive an income adequate to buy goods from all over the world.

The idea of *gains from trade* forms one of the central insights of economics. Different people or countries tend to specialize in certain areas and then to engage in the voluntary exchange of what they produce for what they need. Japan has grown enormously productive by specializing in manufacturing goods such as automobiles and consumer electronics; it exports much of its manufacturing output to pay for imports of raw materials. By contrast, countries which have tried the strategy of becoming self-sufficient, attempting to produce most of what they consume, have discovered that this is the road to stagnation. Trade can enrich all nations and increase *everyone's* living standards.

To summarize:

Advanced economies engage in specialization and division of labor, which increase the productivity of their resources. Individuals and countries then voluntarily trade goods in which they specialize for others' products, vastly increasing the range and quantity of consumption and having the potential to raise everyone's living standards.

MONEY: THE LUBRICANT OF EXCHANGE

If specialization permits people to concentrate on particular tasks, money then allows people to trade their specialized outputs for the vast array of goods and services produced by others. What is money? **Money** is the means of payment or exchange—that is, the currency and checks that we use when we buy things. But more than that, money is a lubricant that facilitates exchange. When everyone trusts and accepts money as payment for goods and debts, trade is facilitated. Just imagine how complicated economic life would be if you had to barter goods for goods every time you wanted to buy a pizza or go to a concert. What services could you offer Sal's Pizza? And what about your education—what could you barter with your college for tuition that it needs? Because everyone accepts money as the medium of exchange, the need to match supplies and demands is enormously simplified.

Governments control the money supply through their central banks. But like other lubricants, money can get gummed up. It can grow out of control and cause a hyperinflation, in which prices increase very sharply. When that happens, people concentrate on spending their money quickly, before it loses its value, rather than investing it for the future. That's what happened to several Latin American countries in the 1980s, and many former socialist economies in the 1990s, when they had inflation rates exceeding 1000 percent or even 10,000 percent per year. Imagine getting your paycheck and having it lose 20 percent of its value by the end of the week!

Proper management of the money supply is one of the major issues for government macroeconomic policy in all countries.

CAPITAL

An advanced industrial economy like the United States uses an enormous amount of buildings, machinery, computers, and so on. These are the factors of production called **capital**, a produced factor of production, a durable input which is itself an output of the economy.

Most of us do not realize how much our daily activities rely, directly or indirectly, on capital, including our houses, the highways we drive on, and the wires that bring electricity and cable TV to our homes. The total net amount of capital stock in the economy is almost $18.5 trillion—including government-owned, business, and residential capital. On average, this is more than $70,000 per person.

As we have seen, capital is one of the three major factors of production. The other two, land and labor, are often called *primary factors of production.* That means their supply is mostly determined by non-economic factors, such as the fertility rate and the country's geography. Capital, by contrast, has to be produced before you can use it. For example, some companies build textile machinery, which is then used to make shirts; some companies build farm tractors, which are then used to help produce corn.

Note that capital inherently involves time-consuming, roundabout methods of production. In fact, people learned long ago that indirect and roundabout production techniques often are more efficient than direct methods of production. For example, the most direct method of catching fish is to wade into a stream and grab fish with your hands, but this yields more frustration than fish. By using a fishing rod (which is capital equipment), fishing time becomes more productive in terms of fish caught per day. By using even more capital, in the form of nets and fishing boats, fishing becomes productive enough to feed many people and provide a good living to those who operate the specialized nets and equipment.

Growth from the Sacrifice of Current Consumption. If people are willing to save—to abstain from present consumption and wait for future consumption—society can devote resources to new capital goods. A larger stock of capital helps the economy grow faster by pushing out the *PPF.* Look back at Figure 1-5 to see how forgoing current

consumption in favor of investment adds to future production possibilities. High rates of saving and investment help explain how Japan, Korea, and other Asian countries have grown so fast. By comparison, many economists believe that the U.S. economy is lagging behind other countries in the growth race because it saves and invests too little.

Is there no limit to the amount of useful capital? Should we continue to boost productivity by adding more capital, by replacing all direct processes with more productive, roundabout ones and all roundabout processes with still more roundabout processes. While this seems sensible, it has a high cost because too much roundabout investment would cause too great a reduction in today's consumption. Investing resources to give every worker an advanced degree, to remove 99.9 percent of pollution, and to build a dense subway system under every city would certainly increase productivity. But the payoff would not be worth the enormous cost in consumption.

We summarize as follows:

Much of economic activity involves forgoing current consumption to increase our capital. Every time we invest—building a new factory or road, increasing the years or quality of education, or increasing the stock of useful technical knowledge—we are enhancing the future productivity of our economy and increasing future consumption.

Capital and Private Property

In a market economy, capital typically is privately owned, and the income from capital goes to individuals. Every patch of land has a deed, or title of ownership; almost every machine and building belongs to an individual or corporation. *Property rights* bestow on their owners the ability to use, exchange, paint, dig, drill, or exploit their capital goods. These capital goods also have market values, and people can buy and sell the capital goods for whatever price the goods will fetch. *The ability of individuals to own and profit from capital is what gives capitalism its name.*

However, while our society is one built on private property, property rights are limited. Society determines how much of "your" property you may bequeath to your heirs and how much must go in inheritance and estate taxes to the government. Society determines how much your factory can pollute and where you can park your car. Even your home is not your castle: you must obey zoning laws and, if necessary, make way for a road.

Interestingly enough, the most valuable economic resource, labor, cannot be turned into a commodity that is bought and sold as private property. Since the abolition of slavery, it has been against the law to treat human earning power like other capital assets. You are not free to sell yourself; you must rent yourself at a wage.

 Property rights for capital and pollution: Property rights define the ability of individuals or firms to own, buy, sell, and use the capital goods and other property in a market economy. These rights are enforced through the legal framework, which constitutes the set of laws within which an economy operates. An efficient and acceptable legal framework for a market economy includes the definition of property rights, the laws of contract, and a system for adjudicating disputes. As the ex-communist countries are discovering, it is very difficult to have a market economy when there are no laws enforcing contracts or guaranteeing that a company can keep its own profits. And when the legal framework breaks down, as in the former Yugoslavia or sometimes even in impoverished urban areas of America, people begin to fear for their lives and have little time or inclination to make long-term investments for the future. Production falls and the quality of life deteriorates. Indeed, many of the most horrifying African famines were caused by civil war and the breakdown in the legal order, not by bad weather.

The environment is another example where poorly designed property rights harm the economy. Water and air are generally common property, meaning that no one owns and controls them. As the saying goes, everyone's business is nobody's business. As a result, people do not weigh all the costs of their actions. Someone might throw trash into the water or emit smoke into the air because the costs of dirty water or foul air are borne by other people. By contrast, people are less likely to throw trash on their own lawn or burn coal in their own living room because they themselves will bear the costs. In recent years, economists have proposed extending property rights to environmental commodities by selling or auctioning permits to pollute and allowing them to be traded on markets. Preliminary evidence suggests that this extension of property rights has given much more powerful incentives to reduce pollution efficiently.

Specialization, trade, money, and capital form the key to the productiveness of an advanced economy. But note as well that they are closely interrelated. Specialization creates enormous efficiencies, while increased production makes trade possible. Use of money allows trade to take place quickly and efficiently. Without the facility for trade and exchange that money provides, an elaborate division of labor would not be possible. Money and capital are related because the funds for buying capital goods are funneled through financial markets, where people's savings can be transformed into other people's capital.

C. THE ECONOMIC ROLE OF GOVERNMENT

An ideal market economy is one in which all goods and services are voluntarily exchanged for money at market prices. Such a system squeezes the maximum benefits out of a society's available resources without government intervention. In the real world, however, no economy actually conforms totally to the idealized world of the smoothly functioning invisible hand. Rather, every market economy suffers from imperfections which lead to such ills as excessive pollution, unemployment, and extremes of wealth and poverty.

For that reason, no government anywhere in the world, no matter how conservative, keeps its hands off the economy. In modern economies governments take on many tasks in response to the flaws in the market mechanism. The military, the police, the national weather service, and highway construction are all typical areas of government activity. Socially useful ventures such as space exploration and scientific research benefit from government funding. Governments may regulate some businesses (such as banking and garbage collection) while subsidizing others (such as education and health care). And governments tax their citizens and redistribute some of the proceeds to the elderly and needy.

But for all the wide range of possible activities, governments have three main economic functions in a market economy. These functions are increasing efficiency, promoting equity, and fostering macroeconomic stability and growth.

1. Governments increase *efficiency* by promoting competition, curbing externalities like pollution, and providing public goods.
2. Governments promote *equity* by using tax and expenditure programs to redistribute income toward particular groups.
3. Governments foster *macroeconomic stability and growth*—reducing unemployment and inflation while encouraging economic growth—through fiscal policy and monetary regulation.

We will examine briefly each function.

EFFICIENCY

Adam Smith recognized that the virtues of the market mechanism are fully realized only when the checks and balances of perfect competition are present. What is meant by **perfect competition**? It means that all goods and services have a price and are traded on markets. It also means that no firm or consumer is large enough to affect the market price. For example, the wheat market is perfectly competitive because the largest wheat farm, producing only a minuscule fraction of the world's wheat, can have no appreciable effect upon the price of wheat.

The invisible-hand doctrine applies to economies in which all the markets are perfectly competitive. In such a circumstance, markets will produce an efficient allocation of resources, so the economy is on its production-possibility frontier. When all industries are subject to the checks and balances of perfect competition, as we will see later in this book, markets will produce the efficient bundle of outputs using the most efficient techniques and the minimum amount of inputs.

Alas, there are many ways that markets can fall short of perfect competition. The three most important involve imperfect competition, such as monopolies; externalities, such as pollution; and public goods, such as national defense and highways. In each case, market failure leads to inefficient production or consumption, and government can play a useful role in curing the disease.

Imperfect Competition

One serious deviation from an efficient market comes from *imperfect competition* or *monopoly* elements. Whereas under perfect competition no firm or consumer can affect prices, **imperfect competition** occurs when a buyer or seller can affect a good's price. For example, if the telephone company or a labor union is large enough to influence the price of phone service or labor, respectively, some degree of imperfect competition has set in. When imperfect competition arises, society may move inside its *PPF*. This would occur, for example, if a single seller (a monopolist) raised the price of a good sky-high to earn extra profits. The output of that good would be reduced below the most efficient level, and the efficiency of the economy would thereby suffer. In such a situation, the invisible-hand property of markets may be violated.

What is the effect of imperfect competition, which is the ability of a large firm to affect the price in a given market? Imperfect competition leads to prices that rise above cost and to consumer purchases that are reduced below efficient levels. The pattern of too high price and too low output is the hallmark of the inefficiencies associated with imperfect competition.

In reality, almost all industries possess some measure of imperfect competition. Airlines, for example, may have no competition on some of their routes but face several rivals on others. The extreme case of imperfect competition is the *monopolist*—a single supplier who alone determines the price of a particular good or service.

Over the last century, most governments have taken steps to curb the most extreme forms of imperfect competition. Governments sometimes regulate the prices and profits of monopolies such as local water, telephone, and electric utilities. In addition, government antitrust laws prohibit actions such as price fixing or agreeing to divide up markets. The most important check to imperfect competition, however, is the opening of markets to competitors, whether they be domestic or foreign. Few monopolies can long withstand the attack of competitors unless governments protect them through tariffs or regulations.

Externalities

A second type of inefficiency arises when there are spillovers or externalities, which involve involuntary imposition of costs or benefits. Market transactions involve voluntary exchange in which people exchange goods or services for money. When a firm buys a chicken to make frozen drumsticks, it buys the chicken from its owner in the chicken market, and the seller receives the full value of the hen. When you buy a haircut, the barber receives the full value for time, skills, and rent.

But many interactions take place outside markets. While airports produce a lot of noise, they generally do not compensate the people living around the airport for disturbing their peace. On the other hand, some companies which spend heavily on research and development have positive spillover effects for the rest of society. For example, researchers at AT&T invented the transistor and launched the electronic revolution, but AT&T's profits increased by only a small fraction of the global social gains. In each case, an activity has helped or hurt people outside the market transaction; that is, there was an economic transaction without an economic payment.

Externalities (or spillover effects) occur when firms or people impose costs or benefits on others outside the marketplace.

Governments are today often more concerned with negative externalities than positive ones. As our society has become more densely populated and as the production of energy, chemicals, and other materials increases, negative externalities or spillover effects have grown from little nuisances into major threats. This is where governments come in. Government *regulations* are designed to control externalities like air and water pollution, damage from strip mining, hazardous wastes, unsafe drugs and foods, and radioactive materials.

In many ways, governments are like parents, always saying no: Thou shalt not expose thy workers to dangerous conditions. Thou shalt not pour out poisonous smoke from thy factory chimney. Thou shalt not sell dangerous drugs. Thou shalt not drive without wearing thy seat belt. And so forth. Finding the exactly correct regulations is a difficult task, requiring complex science and economics, and subject to heavy political pressure, but few today would argue for returning to the unregulated economic jungle where firms can dump plutonium wherever they want.

Public Goods

While negative externalities like pollution or global warming command most of the headlines, positive externalities may well be economically more significant. Important examples of positive externalities are construction of a highway network, operation of a national weather service, support of basic science, and provision of measures to enhance public health. These are not goods which can be bought and sold in markets. Adequate private production of these public goods will not occur because the benefits are so widely dispersed across the population that no single firm or consumer has an economic incentive to provide the service and capture the returns.

The extreme example of a positive externality is a public good. **Public goods** are commodities for which the cost of extending the service to an additional person is zero and which it is impossible to exclude individuals from enjoying.[3] The best example of a public good is national defense. When a nation protects its freedoms and way of life, it does so for all its inhabitants, whether they want the protection or not and whether they pay for it or not.

Because private provision of public goods is generally insufficient, government must step in to encourage the production of public goods. In buying public goods like national defense or lighthouses, government is behaving exactly like any other large spender. By casting sufficient dollar votes in certain directions, it causes resources to flow there. Once

---

[3] Lighthouses are an interesting example of a public good provided by government. They save lives and cargos. Lighthouse signals are a "public good" because it costs no more to warn 100 ships than to warn a single ship of the rocks and shoals. In an earlier age, lighthouses were sometimes privately owned, and lighthouse owners attempted to collect fees from ships in port. But private provision encounters a "free-rider" problem that can lead to underprovision and underfinancing of such socially desirable goods. We have here a positive externality, a divergence between private and social benefit, which is efficiently provided free of charge.

the dollar votes are cast, the market mechanism then takes over and channels resources to firms so that the lighthouses or tanks get produced.

Taxes. Government must find the revenues to pay for its public goods and for income-redistribution programs. Such revenues come from taxes levied on personal and corporate incomes, on wages, on sales of consumer goods, and on other items. All levels of government—city, state, and federal—collect taxes to pay for their spending.

Taxes sound like another "price"—in this case the price we pay for public goods. But taxes differ from prices in one crucial respect: taxes are not voluntary. Everyone is subject to the tax laws; we are all obligated to pay for our share of the cost of public goods. Of course, through our democratic process, we as citizens choose both the public goods and the taxes to pay for them. However, the close connection between spending and consumption that we see for private goods does not hold for taxes and public goods. I pay for a hamburger only if I want one, but I must pay my share of the taxes used to finance defense and public education even if I don't care a bit for these activities.

EQUITY

Our discussion of market failures like monopoly or externalities focused on defects in the allocative role of markets—imperfections that can be corrected by judicious intervention. But assume for the moment that the economy functioned with complete efficiency—always on the production-possibility frontier and never inside it, always choosing the right amount of public versus private goods, and so forth. Even if the market system worked perfectly, it might still lead to a flawed outcome.

Markets do not necessarily produce a fair distribution of income. A market economy may produce unacceptably high levels of inequality of income and consumption.

Why might the market mechanism produce an unacceptable solution to the question of *for whom*? The reason is that incomes are determined by a wide variety of factors, including effort, education, inheritance, factor prices, and luck. The resulting income distribution may not correspond to a fair outcome. Moreover, recall that goods follow dollar votes and not the greatest need. A rich man's cat may drink the

milk that a poor boy needs to remain healthy. Does this happen because the market is failing? Not at all, for the market mechanism is doing its job—putting goods in the hands of those who have the dollar votes. If a country spends more fertilizing its lawns than feeding poor children, that is a defect of income distribution, not of the market. Even the most efficient market system may generate great inequality.

Often the income distribution in a market system is the result of accidents of birth. Every year *Forbes* magazine lists the 400 richest Americans, and it's impressive how many of them either received their wealth by inheritance or used inherited wealth as a springboard to even greater wealth. Would everyone regard that as necessarily right or ideal? Probably not. Should someone be allowed to become a billionaire simply by inheriting 5000 square miles of rangeland or the family's holding of oil wells? That is the way the cookie crumbles under laissez-faire capitalism.

For most of American history, economic growth was a rising tide that lifted all boats, raising the incomes of the poor as well as those of the rich. But over the last two decades, changes in family structure and declining wages of the less skilled and less educated have reversed the trend. With a return to greater emphasis on the market has come greater homelessness, more children living in poverty, and deterioration of many of America's central cities.

Income inequalities may be politically or ethically unacceptable. A nation does not need to accept the outcome of competitive markets as predetermined and immutable; people may examine the distribution of income and decide it is unfair. If a democratic society does not like the distribution of dollar votes under a laissez-faire market system, it can take steps to change the distribution of income.

Let's say that voters decide to reduce income inequality. What tools could the government use? First, it can engage in *progressive taxation*, taxing large incomes at a higher rate than small incomes. It might impose heavy taxes on wealth or on large inheritances to break the chain of privilege. The federal income and inheritance taxes are examples of such redistributive progressive taxation.

Second, because low tax rates cannot help those who have no income at all, governments can make *transfer payments*, which are money payments to people. Such transfers today include aid for the elderly, blind, and disabled and for those with dependent children, as well as unemployment insurance for the jobless. This system of transfer payments provides a "safety net" to protect the unfortunate from privation. And, finally, governments sometimes subsidize consumption of low-income groups by providing food stamps, subsidized medical care, and low-cost housing—though in the United States, such spending comprises a relatively small share of total spending.

These programs have become increasingly unpopular in the last two decades. As the real wages of the middle class have stagnated, people naturally ask why they should support the homeless or able-bodied people who do not work. What can economics contribute to debates about equality? Economics as a science cannot answer such normative questions as how much of our market incomes—if any—should be transferred to poor families. This is a political question that can be answered only at the ballot box.

Economics can analyze the costs or benefits of different redistributive systems. Economists have devoted much time to analyzing whether different income-redistribution devices (such as taxes and food stamps) lead to social waste (e.g., people work less or buy drugs rather than food). They have also studied whether giving poor people cash rather than goods is likely to be a more efficient way of reducing poverty. Economics cannot answer questions of how much poverty is acceptable and fair, but it can help design more effective programs to increase the incomes of the poor.

MACROECONOMIC GROWTH AND STABILITY

Since its origins, capitalism has been plagued by periodic bouts of inflation (rising prices) and recession (high unemployment). Since World War II, for example, there have been nine recessions in the United States, some putting millions of people out of work.

Today, thanks to the intellectual contribution of John Maynard Keynes and his followers, we know how to control the worst excesses of the business cycle. By careful use of fiscal and monetary policies, governments can affect output, employment, and inflation. The *fiscal policies* of government are the power to tax and the power to spend. *Monetary policy* involves determining the supply of money and interest rates; these affect investment in capital goods and other interest-rate-sensitive spending. Using these two fundamental tools of macroeconomic policy, governments can influence the level of total spending, the rate of growth and level of output, the levels of employment and unemployment, and the price level and rate of inflation in an economy.

Governments in advanced industrial countries successfully applied the lessons of the Keynesian revolution over the last half-century. Spurred on by active monetary and fiscal policies, the market economies witnessed a period of unprecedented economic growth in the three decades after World War II.

In the 1980s, governments became more concerned with also designing macroeconomic policies to promote long-term objectives, such as economic growth and productivity. (*Economic growth* denotes the growth in a nation's total output, while *productivity* represents the output per unit input or the efficiency with which resources are used.) For example, tax rates were lowered in most industrial countries in order to improve incentives for saving and production. Many economists emphasized the importance of public saving through smaller budget deficits as a way to increase national saving and investment.

Macroeconomic policies for stabilization and economic growth include fiscal policies (of taxing and spending) along with monetary policies (which affect interest rates and credit conditions). Since the development of macroeconomics in the 1930s, governments have succeeded in curbing the worst excesses of inflation and unemployment.

Table 2-1 summarizes the economic role played by government today. It shows the important governmental functions of promoting efficiency, achieving a fairer distribution of income, and pursuing the macroeconomic objectives of economic growth and stability. In all advanced industrial societies we find a mixed economy in which the market determines output and prices in most individual sectors while government steers the overall economy with programs of taxation, spending, and monetary regulation.

TWILIGHT OF THE WELFARE STATE?

In 1942, the great Austrian-born Harvard economist Joseph Schumpeter argued that the United States

Failure of market economy	Government intervention	Current examples of government policy
Inefficiency:		
Monopoly	Encourage competition	Antitrust laws, deregulation
Externalities	Intervene in markets	Antipollution laws, antismoking ordinances
Public goods	Encourage beneficial activities	Build lighthouses, subsidize scientific research
Inequality:		
Unacceptable inequalities of income and wealth	Redistribute income	Progressive taxation of income and wealth
		Income-support programs (e.g., food stamps)
Macroeconomic problems:		
Business cycles (high inflation and unemployment)	Stabilize through macroeconomic policies	Monetary policies (e.g., changes in money supply and interest rates)
		Fiscal policies (e.g., taxes and spending programs)
Slow economic growth	Stimulate growth	Invest in education
		Raise national savings rate by reducing budget deficit

TABLE 2-1. Government Can Remedy the Shortcomings of the Market

was "capitalism living in an oxygen tent" on its march to socialism. Capitalism's success would breed alienation and self-doubt, sapping its efficiency and innovation. The next quarter-century saw sustained growth in government's involvement in the economies of North America and Western Europe *along with the most impressive economic performance ever recorded.*

The return to more-normal growth rates in the last two decades has been accompanied by increased skepticism about government's role. Critics of government say that the state is overly intrusive; governments create monopoly; government failures are just as pervasive as market failures; high taxes distort the allocation of resources; social security reduces saving; environmental regulation dulls the spirit of enterprise; government attempts to stabilize the economy must fail at best and increase inflation at

worst; and inflation chokes off investment. In short, for some, government is the problem rather than the solution.[4]

These views remind us how easy it is to take the achievements of the last century for granted. They remind us of the tendency to credit ourselves for successes while blaming others—particularly the government—for failures. In economics as in life, success has many parents, while failure is an orphan. Diatribes against government forget the many successes of collective action over the last century. We have reduced malnutrition and conquered many terrible diseases like smallpox. Government programs have increased literacy and life expectancy. Macro-

---

[4] For an eloquent account of economic controversies over the last three decades, see Paul Krugman, *Peddling Prosperity* (Norton, New York, 1994).

economic successes have reduced the sting of inflation and unemployment, while government transfer programs have brought health care to the poor and improved the quality of life for the aged. State-supported science has penetrated the atom, discovered the DNA molecule, and explored outer space.

Of course, these successes did not belong to governments alone. Governments harnessed private ingenuity through the market mechanism to help achieve these social aims. And, in some cases, governments were like orators who didn't know when enough was enough. Government's successes and failures remind us that drawing the right boundary between market and government is an enduring problem. The tools of economics are indispensable to help societies find the *golden mean* between *laissez faire* market mechanisms and democratic rules of the road: the good Mixed Economy is, perforce, the Limited Mixed Economy. But those who would reduce government to the constable plus a few lighthouses are living in the last century. An efficient and humane society requires both halves of the mixed system— market and government. Operating a modern economy without both is like trying to clap with one hand.

SUMMARY

A. What Is a Market?

1. In an economy like the United States, most economic decisions are made in markets, which serve as mechanisms by which buyers and sellers meet to trade and to determine prices and quantities for commodities. Adam Smith proclaimed that the *invisible hand* of markets would lead to the optimal economic outcome as individuals pursue their own self-interest. And while markets are far from perfect, they have proved remarkably effective at solving the problems of *how*, *what*, and *for whom*.

2. The market mechanism works as follows to determine the what and the how: The dollar votes of people affect prices of goods; these prices serve as guides for the amounts of the different goods to be produced. When people demand more of a good, businesses can profit by expanding production of that good. Under perfect competition, a business must find the cheapest method of production, efficiently using labor, land, and other factors; otherwise, it will incur losses and be eliminated from the market.

3. At the same time that the *what* and *how* problems are being resolved by prices, so is the problem of *for whom*. The distribution of income is determined by the ownership of factors of production (land, labor, and capital) and by factor prices. People possessing fertile land or the ability to hit home runs will earn many dollar votes to buy consumer goods. Those without property and with skills, color, or sex that the market does not value will receive low incomes.

B. Trade, Money, and Capital

4. As economies develop, they become more specialized. Division of labor allows a task to be broken into a number of smaller chores that can each be mastered and performed more quickly by a single worker. Specialization arises from the increasing tendency to use roundabout methods of production that require many specialized skills. As individuals and countries become increasingly specialized, they tend to concentrate on particular commodities and trade their surplus output for goods produced by others. Voluntary trade, based on specialization, benefits all.

5. Trade in specialized goods and services today relies on money to lubricate the wheels of trade. Money is the universally acceptable medium of exchange—currency and checks. It is used to pay for everything from apple tarts to zebra skins. By accepting money, people and nations can specialize in producing a few goods and trade them for others; without money, we would waste much time constantly bartering one good for another.

6. Capital goods—produced inputs such as machinery, structures, and inventories of goods in process—permit roundabout methods of production that add much to a nation's output. These roundabout methods take time and resources to get started and therefore require a temporary sacrifice of present consumption in order to increase future consumption. The rules that define how capital and other assets can be bought, sold, and used are the system of property rights. In no economic system are private-property rights unlimited.

C. The Economic Role of Government

7. Although the market mechanism is an admirable way of producing and allocating goods, sometimes market failures lead to deficiencies in the economic outcomes. Government may step in to correct these failures. Government's role in a modern economy is to ensure efficiency, to correct an unfair distribution of income, and to promote economic growth and stability.

8. Markets fail to provide an efficient allocation of resources in the presence of imperfect competition or externalities. Imperfect competition, such as monopoly, produces high prices and low levels of output. To combat these conditions, governments regulate businesses or put legal antitrust constraints on business behavior. Externalities arise when activities impose costs or bestow benefits that are not paid for in the marketplace. Governments may decide to step in and regulate these spillovers (as it does with air pollution) or provide for *public goods* (as in the case of public health).

9. Markets do not necessarily produce a fair distribution of income; they may spin off unacceptably high inequality of income and consumption. In response, governments can alter the pattern of incomes (the *for whom*) generated by market wages, rents, interest, and dividends. Modern governments use taxation to raise revenues for transfers or income-support programs that place a financial safety net under the needy.

10. Since the development of macroeconomics in the 1930s, government has undertaken a third role: using fiscal powers (of taxing and spending) and monetary policy (affecting credit and interest rates) to promote long-run economic growth and productivity and to tame the business cycle's excesses of inflation and unemployment. Since 1980, the blend of the mixed economy called the welfare state has been on the defensive in the enduring struggle over the boundary between state and market.

CONCEPTS FOR REVIEW

The Market Mechanism

market, market mechanism
markets for goods and for factors of
    production
prices as signals
market equilibrium
perfect and imperfect competition
Adam Smith's invisible-hand doctrine

Features of a Modern Economy

specialization and division of labor
money
factors of production (land, labor,
    capital)
capital, private property, and property
    rights

Government's Economic Role

efficiency, equity, stability
inefficiencies: monopoly and exter-
    nalities
inequity of incomes under markets
macroeconomic policies:
    fiscal and monetary policies
    stabilization and growth

QUESTIONS FOR DISCUSSION

1. What determines the composition of national output? In some cases, we say that there is "consumer sovereignty," meaning that consumers decide how to spend their incomes on the basis of their tastes and market prices. In other cases, decisions are made by political choices of legislatures. Consider the following examples: transportation, education, police, energy efficiency of appliances, health-care coverage, television advertising. For each, describe whether the allocation is by consumer sovereignty or by political decision. Would you change the method of allocation for any of these goods?

2. Consider the following cases of government intervention in the economy: regulations to limit air pollution, research on an AIDS vaccine, income supplements to the elderly, price regulation of a local water monopoly, a monetary-policy step to curb inflation. What role of government is being pursued in each case?

3. When a good is limited, some means must be found to ration the scarce commodity. Some examples of rationing devices are auctions, ration coupons, and first-come, first-served systems. What are the strengths and weaknesses of each? Explain carefully in what sense a market mechanism "rations" scarce goods and services.

4. The circular flow of goods and inputs illustrated in Figure 2-1 has a corresponding flow of dollar incomes and spending. Draw a circular-flow diagram for the dollar flows in the economy, and compare it with the circular flow of goods and inputs. What is the role of money in the dollar circular flow?

5. This chapter discusses many "market failures," areas in which the invisible hand guides the economy poorly, and describes the role of government. Is it possible that there are, as well, "government failures," government attempts to curb market failures that are worse

than the original market failures? Think of some examples of government failures. Give some examples in which government failures are so bad that it is better to live with the market failures than to try to correct them.

6. Give three examples of specialization and division of labor. In what areas are you and your friends thinking of specializing? What might be the perils of *over* specialization?

7. "Lincoln freed the slaves. With one pen stroke he destroyed much of the capital the South had accumulated over the years." Comment.

8. The table to the right shows some of the major expenditures of the federal government. Explain how each one relates to the economic role of government.

Major Expenditure Categories for Federal Government	
Budget category	Federal spending, 1998 ($, billion)
Social security	384
National defense	259
Income security	247
Interest on public debt	250
Natural resources and environment	22
Administration of justice	24
Science and technology	16

Source: Office of Management and Budget, *Budget of the United States Government,* Fiscal Year 1998.

CHAPTER 3
BASIC ELEMENTS OF SUPPLY AND DEMAND

> The level of the sea is not more surely kept, than is the equilibrium of value in society, by the demand and supply: the artifice or legislation punishes itself, by reactions, gluts, and bankruptcies.
>
> *Ralph Waldo Emerson (1860)*

VOLATILE MARKETS

Markets are akin to the weather. They are always changing, dynamic, unpredictable, subject to frequent periods of storm and calm, complex, and fascinating. As with the weather, careful study of markets also shows certain forces and patterns underneath the daily and apparently random movements. The essential tool for understanding the movement of prices and outputs in individual markets is called the analysis of supply and demand.

Take the example of gasoline prices, illustrated in Figure 3-1 on the next page. (This shows the "real gasoline price," or the price corrected for movements in the general price level.) Demand for gasoline and other oil products rose sharply after World War II as people fell in love with the automobile and moved increasingly to the suburbs. Next, in the 1970s, supply restrictions, wars among producers, and revolutions reduced production, with the consequent price spikes seen after 1973 and 1979. Then, as a result of energy conservation, smaller cars, and price wars, the real price of gasoline fell sharply, from about $2.50 per gallon in 1980 to around $1.40 in 1996.

What lay behind these dramatic shifts? Econom-

ics has a very powerful tool for explaining these and many other changes in the economic environment. It is called the *theory of supply and demand*. This theory shows how consumer preferences determine consumer demand for commodities, while business costs are the foundation of the supply of commodities. The increases in the price of gasoline occurred either because the demand for gasoline had gone up or because the supply of oil had decreased. The same is true for every market, from computers to diamonds to land: changes in supply and demand drive changes in output and prices. If you understand how supply and demand work, you have gone a long way toward understanding a market economy.

This chapter introduces the notions of supply and demand, and it shows how they operate in competitive markets for *individual commodities*. We begin with demand curves and then discuss supply curves. Using these basic tools, we will see how the market price is determined (or reaches its competitive equilibrium) where these two curves intersect—where the forces of demand and supply are just in balance. It is the movement of prices, the price mechanism, which brings supply and demand into balance or equilibrium. This chapter closes with some examples of how supply-and-demand analysis can be applied.

43

FIGURE 3-1. The Volatile Price of Gasoline

Gasoline prices have fluctuated widely over the last three decades. The little wiggle at the end —the price run-up before the 1996 U.S. presidential election—led to widespread charges of profiteering and a call for a reduction of the federal gasoline tax. You can easily understand the social unrest provoked by the enormous price increases in the 1970s. Supply and demand are crucial for understanding these trends. (Source: U.S. Departments of Energy and Labor. The price of gasoline has been converted into 1996 prices using the consumer price index.)

A. THE DEMAND SCHEDULE

Both common sense and careful scientific observation show that the amount of a commodity people buy depends on its price. The higher the price of an article, other things being constant,[1] the fewer units

consumers are willing to buy. The lower its market price, the more units of it are bought.

There exists a definite relationship between the market price of a good and the quantity demanded of that good, other things held constant. This relationship between price and quantity bought is called the **demand schedule,** or the **demand curve.**

Let's look at a simple example. Table 3-1 presents a hypothetical demand schedule for cornflakes. At

---

[1] Later in this chapter we discuss the other factors that influence demand, including income and tastes. The term "other things held constant" simply means we are varying the price without changing any of these other determinants of demand.

Demand Schedule for Cornflakes		
	(1)	(2)
	Price ($ per box) P	Quantity demanded (millions of boxes per year) Q
A	5	9
B	4	10
C	3	12
D	2	15
E	1	20

TABLE 3-1. The Demand Schedule Relates Quantity Demanded to Price

At each market price, consumers will want to buy a certain quantity of cornflakes. As the price of cornflakes falls, the quantity of cornflakes demanded will rise.

each price, we can determine the quantity of cornflakes that consumers purchase. For example, at $5 per box, consumers will buy 9 million boxes per year.

At a lower price, more cornflakes are bought. Thus, at a cornflakes price of $4, the quantity bought is 10 million boxes. At yet a lower price (P) equal to $3, the quantity demanded (Q) is still greater, at 12 million. And so forth. We can determine the quantity demanded at each listed price in Table 3-1.

THE DEMAND CURVE

The graphical representation of the demand schedule is the *demand curve.* We show the demand curve in Figure 3-2, which graphs the quantity of cornflakes demanded on the horizontal axis and the price of cornflakes on the vertical axis. Note that quantity and price are inversely related, Q going up when P goes down. The curve slopes downward, going from northwest to southeast. This important property is called the *law of downward-sloping demand.* It is based on common sense as well as economic theory and has been empirically tested and verified for practically all commodities—cornflakes, gasoline, college education, and illegal drugs being a few examples.

Law of downward-sloping demand: When the price of a commodity is raised (and other things are held constant), buyers tend to buy less of the commodity. Similarly, when the price is lowered, other things being constant, quantity demanded increases.

Why does quantity demanded tend to fall as price rises? For two reasons. First is the **substitution effect.** When the price of a good rises, I will substitute other similar goods for it (as the price of beef rises, I eat more chicken). A second reason for the depressing effect of price increases on purchases is the **income effect.** This comes into play because when a price goes up, I find myself somewhat poorer than I was before. If gasoline prices double, I have in effect less real income, so I will naturally curb my consumption of gasoline and other goods.

Market Demand

Our discussion of demand has so far referred to "the" demand curve. But whose demand is it? Mine? Yours? Everybody's? The fundamental building block for demand is individual tastes and needs. However, in this chapter we will always focus on the *market demand,* which represents the sum total of all

FIGURE 3-2. A Downward-Sloping Demand Curve Relates Quantity Demanded to Price

In the demand curve for cornflakes, prices (P) are measured on the vertical axis while quantity demanded (Q) is measured on the horizontal axis. Each pair of (P,Q) numbers from Table 3-1 is plotted as a point and then a smooth curve is passed through the points to give us a demand curve, *DD.* The negative slope of the demand curve illustrates the law of downward-sloping demand.

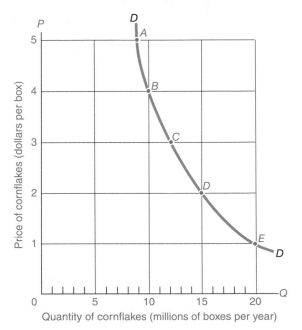

individual demands. The market demand curve is found by adding together the quantities demanded by all individuals at each price. The market demand is what is observable in the real world.

Does the market demand curve obey the law of downward-sloping demand? It certainly does. If prices drop, for example, the lower prices attract new customers, through the substitution effect. In addition, a price reduction will induce extra purchases of goods by existing consumers, through both the income and substitution effects. Conversely, a rise in the price of a good will cause some of us to buy less.

We can illustrate the law of downward-sloping demand for the case of personal computers (PCs). In the early 1980s, the price of PCs was astronomical, and they were found in few businesses and even fewer homes. People used typewriters or pens to write papers and did calculations by hand.

But the prices of PCs fell sharply in the last decade, and the lower prices enticed new buyers. As more and more people could afford them, PCs came to be widely used for work, for school, and for fun. Even today, the computer revolution is unfinished. As prices for personal computers drop further, even more people will find it worthwhile to buy their first PC or to buy an extra one.

Behind the Demand Curve

What determines the market demand curve for cornflakes or gasoline or computers? A whole array of factors influences how much will be demanded at a given price: average levels of income, the size of the population, the prices and availability of related goods, individual and social tastes, and special influences.

- The *average income* of consumers is a key determinant of demand. As people's incomes rise, individuals tend to buy more of almost everything, even if prices don't change. Automobile purchases tend to rise sharply with higher levels of income.
- The *size of the market*—measured, say, by the population—clearly affects the market demand curve. California's 32 million people tend to buy 32 times more apples and cars than do Rhode Island's 1 million people.

- The prices and availability of *related goods* influence the demand for a commodity. A particularly important connection exists among substitute goods—ones that tend to perform the same function, such as cornflakes and oatmeal, pens and pencils, small cars and large cars, or oil and natural gas. Demand for good A tends to be low if the price of substitute product B is low. (For example, if the price of beef rises, will that increase or decrease the demand for chicken?)
- In addition to these objective elements, there is a set of subjective elements called *tastes* or *preferences*. Tastes represent a variety of cultural and historical influences. They may reflect genuine psychological or physiological needs (for liquids, love, or excitement). And they may include artificially contrived cravings (for cigarettes, drugs, or fancy sports cars). They may contain a large element of tradition or religion (eating beef is popular in America but taboo in India, while curried jellyfish is a delicacy in Japan but would make many Americans gag).
- Finally, *special influences* will affect the demand for particular goods. The demand for umbrellas is high in rainy Seattle but low in sunny Phoenix; the demand for air conditioners will rise in hot weather; the demand for automobiles will be low in New York, where public transport is plentiful and parking is a nightmare. In addition, expectations about future economic conditions, particularly prices, may have an important impact on demand.

The determinants of demand are summarized in Table 3-2, which uses automobiles as an example.

A Change in Demand

As economic life evolves, demand changes incessantly. Demand curves sit still only in textbooks.

Why does the demand curve shift? Because the influences other than the good's price change. For example, there are many possible reasons why the American demand for cars grew sharply from 1950 to 1997: the average real income of Americans almost doubled; the adult population rose by more than half; and there was a decline in the availability of alternative forms of local transportation (bus,

Factors affecting the demand curve	Example for automobiles
1. **Average income**	As incomes rise, people increase car purchases.
2. **Population**	A growth in population increases car purchases.
3. **Prices of related goods**	Lower gasoline prices raise the demand for cars.
4. **Tastes**	Having a new car becomes a status symbol.
5. **Special influences**	Special influences include availability of alternative forms of transportation, safety of automobiles, expectations of future price increases, etc.

TABLE 3-2. Many Factors Affect the Demand Curve

trolley, and rail). The result of all these changes was a rightward shift in the demand curve for cars.

The net effect of the changes in underlying influences is what we call an *increase in demand*. An increase in the demand for automobiles is illustrated in Figure 3-3 as a rightward shift in the demand curve. Note that the shift means that more cars will be bought at every price.

You can test yourself by answering the following questions: Will a warm winter shift the demand curve for heating oil leftward or rightward? Why? What will happen to the demand for baseball tickets if young people lose interest in baseball and watch basketball instead? What will a sharp fall in the price of personal computers do to the demand for typewriters? What happens to the demand for a college education if wages are falling for blue-collar jobs which don't require a college degree?

FIGURE 3-3. Increase in Demand for Automobiles
As elements underlying demand change, the demand for automobiles is affected. Here we see the effect of rising average income, increased population, and lower gasoline prices on the demand for automobiles. We call this shift in the demand curve an increase in demand.

 Do not confuse movement along curves with shift of curves. Great care must be taken not to confuse a change in demand (which denotes a shift of the demand curve) with a change in the quantity demanded (which means moving to a different point on the same demand curve after a price change).

A change in demand occurs when one of the elements underlying the demand curve shifts. Take the case of pizzas. As incomes increase, consumers will want to buy more pizzas even if pizza prices do not change. In other words, higher incomes will increase demand and shift the demand curve for pizzas out and to the right. This is a shift in the demand for pizzas.

Distinguish this from a change in quantity demanded that occurs because consumers tend to buy more pizzas as pizza prices fall, all other things remaining constant. Here, the increased purchases result not from an increase in demand but from the price decrease. This change represents *a movement along* the demand curve, not a *shift of* the demand curve. A movement along the demand curve means that other things were held constant when price changed.

B. THE SUPPLY SCHEDULE

Let us now turn from demand to supply. The supply side of a market typically involves the terms on which businesses produce and sell their products. The supply of tomatoes tells us the quantity of tomatoes that will be sold at each tomato price. More precisely, the supply schedule relates the quantity supplied of a good to its market price, other things constant. In considering supply, the other things that are held constant include costs of production, prices of related goods, and government policies.

The **supply schedule** (or **supply curve**) for a commodity shows the relationship between its market price and the amount of that commodity that producers are willing to produce and sell, other things held constant.

THE SUPPLY CURVE

Table 3-3 shows a hypothetical supply schedule for cornflakes, and Figure 3-4 plots the data from the table in the form of a supply curve. These data show that at a cornflakes price of $1 per box, no cornflakes at all will be produced. At such a low price, breakfast cereal manufacturers might want to devote their factories to producing other types of cereal, like bran flakes, that earn them more profit than

cornflakes. As the price of cornflakes increases, ever more cornflakes will be produced. At ever-higher cornflakes prices, cereal makers will find it profitable to add more workers and to buy more automated cornflakes-stuffing machines and even more cornflakes factories. All these will increase the output of cornflakes at the higher market prices.

Figure 3-4 shows the typical case of an upward-sloping supply curve for an individual commodity. One important reason for the upward slope is "the law of diminishing returns" (a concept we will learn more about later). Wine will illustrate this important law. If society wants more wine, then additional labor will have to be added to the limited land sites suitable for producing wine grapes. Each new worker will be adding less and less extra product. The price needed to coax out additional wine output is there-

Supply Schedule for Cornflakes		
	(1) Price ($ per box) P	(2) Quantity supplied (millions of boxes per year) Q
A	5	18
B	4	16
C	3	12
D	2	7
E	1	0

TABLE 3-3. Supply Schedule Relates Quantity Supplied to Price
The table shows, for each price, the quantity of cornflakes that cornflakes makers want to produce and sell. Note the positive relation between price and quantity supplied.

FIGURE 3-4. Supply Curve Relates Quantity Supplied to Price
The supply curve plots the price and quantity pairs from Table 3-3. A smooth curve is passed through these points to give the upward-sloping supply curve, *SS*.

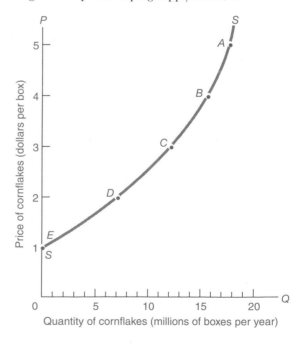

fore higher. By raising the price of wine, society can persuade wine producers to produce and sell more wine; the supply curve for wine is therefore upward-sloping. Similar reasoning applies to many other goods as well.

Behind the Supply Curve

In examining the forces determining the supply curve, the fundamental point to grasp is that producers supply commodities for profit and not for fun or charity. For example, a cereal maker will supply more cornflakes at higher prices because it is profitable to do so; conversely, when the price of cornflakes falls below the cost of production, cereal makers will switch to other lines of business.

One major element underlying the supply curve is the *cost of production*. When production costs for a good are low relative to the market price, it is profitable for producers to supply a great deal. When production costs are high relative to price, firms produce little, switch to the production of other products, or may simply go out of business.

Production costs are primarily determined by the *prices of inputs* and *technological advances*. The prices of inputs such as labor, energy, or machinery obviously have a very important influence on the cost of producing a given level of output. For example, when oil prices rose sharply in the 1970s, the increase raised the price of energy for manufacturers, increased their production costs, and lowered their supply. As computer prices fell over the last three decades, businesses increasingly substituted computerized for manual technologies, as in payroll or accounting operations.

An equally important determinant of production costs is *technological advances*, which consist of changes that lower the amount of inputs needed to produce the same quantity of output. Such advances include everything from actual scientific breakthroughs to better application of existing technology or simply reorganization of the flow of work. For example, manufacturers have become much more efficient over the last decade or so. It takes far fewer hours of labor to produce an automobile today than it did just 10 years ago. This advance enables car makers to produce more automobiles at the same cost. Or, to give another example, if a computer program allows a new customer to open a checking account with a few quick entries

on a computer screen, that, too, lowers the cost of production.

But production costs are not the only ingredient that goes into the supply curve. Firms are always alert to alternative opportunities to use their productive assets. So supply is also influenced by the *prices of related goods,* particularly goods that can be readily substituted for one another as outputs of the production process. If the price of one production substitute rises, the supply of another substitute will decrease. For example, auto companies typically make several different car models in the same factory. If there's more demand for one model, and its price rises, they will switch more of their assembly lines to making that model, and the supply of the other models will fall. Or if the demand and price for trucks rise, the entire factory can be converted to making trucks, and the supply of cars will fall.

Government policy also has an important impact on the supply curve. Environmental and health considerations determine what technologies can be used, while taxes and minimum-wage laws can significantly raise input prices. In the local electricity market, government regulations influence both the number of firms that can compete and the prices they charge. And government trade policies have a major impact upon supply. For instance, when a free-trade agreement opens up the U.S. market to Mexican goods, the supply of Mexican goods increases.

Finally, *special influences* affect the supply curve. The weather exerts an important influence on farming and on the ski industry. The computer industry has been marked by a keen spirit of innovation, which has led to a continuous flow of new products. Market structure will affect supply, and expectations about future prices often have an important impact upon supply decisions.

Table 3-4 on page 50 highlights the important determinants of supply, using automobiles as an example.

Shifts in Supply

Businesses are constantly changing the mix of products and services they provide. What lies behind these changes in supply behavior?

Supply changes when any influences other than the commodity's own price change. In terms of a supply curve, we say that supply increases (or decreases) when the amount supplied increases (or decreases) at each market price.

Factors affecting the supply curve	Example for automobiles
1. **Technology**	Computerized manufacturing lowers production costs and increases supply.
2. **Input prices**	A reduction in the wage paid to autoworkers lowers production costs and increases supply.
3. **Prices of related goods**	If truck prices fall, supply of cars rises.
4. **Government policy**	Removing quotas and tariffs on imported automobiles increases automobile supply.
5. **Special influences**	If the government lowers standards on pollution-control equipment, supply of cars may increase.

TABLE 3-4. Supply Is Affected by Production Costs and Other Factors

When automobile prices change, producers change their production and quantity supplied, but the supply and the supply curve do not shift. By contrast, when other influences affecting supply change, supply changes and the supply curve shifts.

We can illustrate a shift in supply for the automobile market. Supply would increase if the introduction of cost-saving computerized design and

manufacturing reduced the labor required to produce cars, if autoworkers took a pay cut, if Japanese automakers were allowed to export more cars to the United States, or if the government removed some of the regulatory requirements on the industry. Any of these elements would increase the supply of automobiles in the United States at each price. Figure 3-5 illustrates an increase in supply of automobiles.

To test your understanding of supply shifts, think about the following: What would happen to the world supply curve for oil if a revolution in Saudi Arabia led to declining oil production? What would happen to the supply curve for tomatoes in the United States if quotas on Mexican tomatoes were imposed to pander to Florida tomato growers in an election year? What happens to the supply curve for computers if Intel introduces a new Sextium chip that dramatically increases computing speeds?

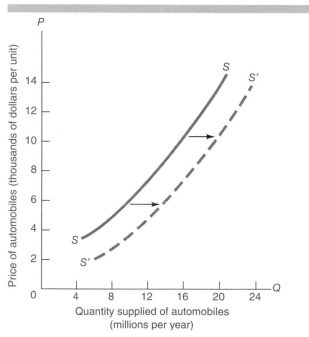

FIGURE 3-5. Increased Supply of Automobiles
As production costs fall or Japanese competition increases, the supply of automobiles increases. At each price, domestic and foreign producers will supply more automobiles, and the supply curve therefore shifts to the right. (What would happen to the supply curve if Congress put a restrictive quota on automobile imports?)

 Reminder on shifts of curves vs. movements along curves: As you answer the questions above, make sure to keep in mind the difference between moving along a curve and a shift of the curve. Look back at the gasoline-price curve in Figure 3-1 on page 44. When the price of oil rose and the production of oil declined because of political disturbances in the 1970s, these changes resulted from an inward shift in the supply curve. When sales of gasoline declined in response to the higher price, that was a movement along the demand curve. How would you describe a rise in chicken production that was induced by a rise in chicken prices? What about the case of a rise in chicken production because of a fall in the price of chicken feed?

C. EQUILIBRIUM OF SUPPLY AND DEMAND

Up to this point we have been considering demand and supply in isolation. We know the amounts that are willingly bought and sold at each price. We have seen that consumers demand different amounts of cornflakes, cars, and computers as a function of these goods' prices. Similarly, producers willingly supply different amounts of these and other goods depending on their prices. But how can we put both sides of the market together?

The answer is that supply and demand interact to produce an equilibrium price and quantity, or a market equilibrium. The **market equilibrium** comes at that price and quantity where the forces of supply and demand are in balance. At the equilibrium price, the amount that buyers want to buy is just equal to the amount that sellers want to sell. The reason we call this an equilibrium is that, when the forces of supply and demand are in balance, there is no reason for price to rise or fall, as long as other things remain unchanged.

Let us work through the cornflakes example in Table 3-5 to see how supply and demand determine a market equilibrium; the numbers in this table come from Tables 3-1 and 3-3. To find the market price and quantity, we find a price at which the amounts desired to be bought and sold just match. If we try a price of $5 per box, will it prevail for long? Clearly not. As row A in Table 3-5 shows, at $5 pro-

ducers would like to sell 18 million boxes per year while demanders want to buy only 9. The amount supplied at $5 exceeds the amount demanded, and stocks of cornflakes pile up in supermarkets. Because too few consumers are chasing too many cornflakes, the price of cornflakes will tend to fall, as shown in column (5) of Table 3-5.

Say we try $2. Does that price clear the market? A quick look at row D shows that at $2 consumption exceeds production. Cornflakes begin to disappear from the stores at that price. As people scramble around to find their desired cornflakes, they will tend to bid up the price of cornflakes, as shown in column (5) of Table 3-5.

We could try other prices, but we can easily see that the equilibrium price is $3, or row C in Table 3-5. At $3, consumers' desired demand exactly equals producers' desired production, each of which is 12 units. Only at $3 will consumers and suppliers both be making consistent decisions.

A market equilibrium comes at the price at which quantity demanded equals quantity supplied. At that equilibrium, there is no tendency for the price to rise or fall. The equilibrium price is also called the *market-clearing price*. This denotes that all supply and demand orders are filled, the books are "cleared" of orders, and demanders and suppliers are satisfied.

TABLE 3-5. Equilibrium Price Comes Where Quantity Demanded Equals Quantity Supplied
The table shows the quantities supplied and demanded at different prices. Only at the equilibrium price of $3 per box does amount supplied equal amount demanded. At too low a price there is a shortage and price tends to rise. Too high a price produces a surplus, which will depress price.

	Combining Demand and Supply for Cornflakes				
	(1)	(2)	(3)	(4)	(5)
	Possible price ($ per box)	Quantity demanded (millions of boxes per year)	Quantity supplied (millions of boxes per year)	State of market	Pressure on price
A	5	9	18	Surplus	↓Downward
B	4	10	16	Surplus	↓Downward
C	3	12	12	Equilibrium	Neutral
D	2	15	7	Shortage	↑Upward
E	1	20	0	Shortage	↑Upward

EQUILIBRIUM WITH SUPPLY AND DEMAND CURVES

We often show the market equilibrium through a supply-and-demand diagram like the one in Figure 3-6; this figure combines the supply curve from Figure 3-4 with the demand curve from Figure 3-2. Combining the two graphs is possible because they are drawn with exactly the same units on each axis.

We find the market equilibrium by looking for the price at which quantity demanded equals quantity supplied. *The equilibrium price comes at the intersection of the supply and demand curves, at point* C.

How do we know that the intersection of the supply and demand curves is the market equilibrium? Let us repeat our earlier experiment. Start with the initial high price of $5 per box, shown at the top of the price axis in Figure 3-6. At that price, suppliers want to sell more than demanders want to buy. The result is a *surplus,* or excess of quantity supplied over quantity demanded, shown in the figure by the black line labeled "Surplus." The arrows along the curves show the direction that price tends to move when a market is in surplus.

At a low price of $2 per box, the market shows a *shortage,* or excess of quantity demanded over quantity supplied, here shown by the black line labeled "Shortage." Under conditions of shortage, the competition among buyers for limited goods causes the price to rise, as shown in the figure by the arrows pointing upward.

We now see that the balance or equilibrium of supply and demand comes at point *C, where the supply and demand curves intersect.* At point *C,* where the price is $3 per box and the quantity is 12 units, the quantities demanded and supplied are equal: there are no shortages or surpluses; there is no tendency for price to rise or fall. At point *C* and only at point *C,* the forces of supply and demand are in balance and the price has settled at a sustainable level.

The equilibrium price and quantity come at that level where the amount willingly supplied equals the amount willingly demanded. In a competitive market, this equilibrium is found at the intersection of the supply and demand curves. There are no shortages or surpluses at the equilibrium price.

Effect of a Shift in Supply or Demand

The analysis of the supply-and-demand apparatus can do much more than tell us about the equi-

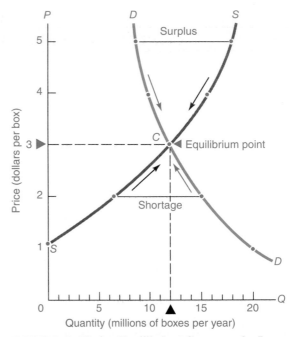

FIGURE 3-6. Market Equilibrium Comes at the Intersection of Supply and Demand Curves
The market equilibrium price and quantity come at the intersection of the supply and demand curves. At a price of $3, at point *C,* firms willingly supply what consumers willingly demand. When price is too low (say, at $2), quantity demanded exceeds quantity supplied, shortages occur, and the price is driven up to equilibrium. What occurs at a price of $4?

librium price and quantity. It can also be used to predict the impact of changes in economic conditions on prices and quantities. Let's change our example to the staff of life, bread. Suppose that a spell of bad weather raises the price of wheat, a key ingredient of bread. That shifts the supply curve for bread to the left. This is illustrated in Figure 3-7(*a*), where the bread supply curve has shifted from *SS* to *S'S'.* In contrast, the demand curve has not shifted; people have the same desire for their daily sandwich whether the harvest is good or bad.

What happens in the bread market? The bad harvest causes bakers to produce less bread at the old price, so quantity demanded exceeds quantity supplied. The price of bread therefore rises, encouraging

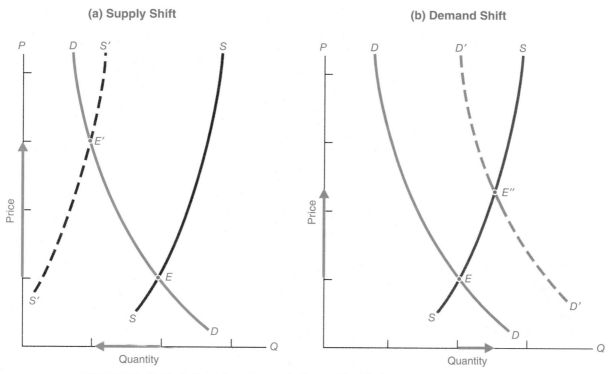

FIGURE 3-7. Shifts in Supply or Demand Change Equilibrium Price and Quantity

(**a**) If supply shifts leftward, a shortage will develop at the original price. Price will be bid up until quantities willingly bought and sold are equal, at new equilibrium E'. (**b**) A shift in the demand curve leads to excess demand. Price will be bid up as equilibrium price and quantity move upward to E''.

production and thereby raising quantity supplied, while simultaneously discouraging consumption and lowering quantity demanded. The price continues to rise until, at the new equilibrium price, the amounts demanded and supplied are once again equal.

As Figure 3-7(a) shows, the new equilibrium is found at E', the intersection of the new supply curve $S'S'$ and the original demand curve. Thus a bad harvest (or any leftward shift of the supply curve) raises prices and, by the law of downward-sloping demand, lowers quantity demanded.

Suppose that new baking technologies lower costs and therefore increase supply. That means the supply curve shifts down and to the right. Draw in a new $S'S''$ curve, along with the new equilibrium E'''. Why is the equilibrium price lower? Why is the equilibrium quantity higher?

We can also use our supply-and-demand apparatus to examine how changes in demand affect the market equilibrium. Suppose that there is a sharp increase in family incomes, so everyone wants to eat more bread. This is represented in Figure 3-7(b) as a "demand shift" in which, at every price, consumers demand a higher quantity of bread. The demand curve thus shifts *rightward* from DD to $D'D'$.

The demand shift produces a shortage of bread at the old price. A scramble for bread ensues, with long lines in the bakeries. Prices are bid upward until supply and demand come back into balance at a higher price. Graphically, the increase in demand has changed the market equilibrium from E to E'' in Figure 3-7(b).

For both examples of shifts—a shift in supply and a shift in demand—a variable underlying the

	Demand and supply shifts	Effect on price and quantity
If demand rises . . .	The demand curve shifts to the right, and . . .	Price ↑ Quantity ↑
If demand falls . . .	The demand curve shifts to the left, and . . .	Price ↓ Quantity ↓
If supply rises . . .	The supply curve shifts to the right, and . . .	Price ↓ Quantity ↑
If supply falls . . .	The supply curve shifts to the left, and . . .	Price ↑ Quantity ↓

TABLE 3-6. The Effect on Price and Quantity of Different Demand and Supply Shifts

demand or supply curve has changed. In the case of supply, there might have been a change in technology or input prices. For the demand shift, one of the influences affecting consumer demand—incomes, population, the prices of related goods, or tastes—changed and thereby shifted the demand schedule (see Table 3-6).

When the elements underlying demand or supply change, this leads to shifts in demand or supply and to changes in the market equilibrium of price and quantity.

Interpreting Changes in Price and Quantity

Let's go back to our bread example. Suppose that you go to the store and see that the price of bread has doubled. Does the increase in price mean that the demand for bread has risen, or does it mean that bread has become more expensive to produce? The correct answer is that without more information, you don't know—it could be either one, or even both. Let's look at another example. If fewer airline tickets are sold, is the cause that airline fares have gone up or that demand for air travel has gone down? Airlines will be most interested in the answer to this question.

Economists deal with these sorts of questions all the time: When prices or quantities change in a market, does the situation reflect a change on the supply side or the demand side? Sometimes, in simple situations, looking at price and quantity simultaneously gives you a clue about whether it's the supply curve that's shifted or the demand curve. For example, a

rise in the price of bread accompanied by a *decrease* in quantity suggests that the supply curve has shifted to the left (a decrease in supply). A rise in price accompanied by an *increase* in quantity indicates that the demand curve for bread has probably shifted to the right (an increase in demand).

This point is illustrated in Figure 3-8. In both panel (*a*) and panel (*b*), quantity goes up. But in (*a*) the price rises, and in (*b*) the price falls. Figure 3-8(*a*) shows the case of an increase in demand, or a shift in the demand curve. As a result of the shift, the equilibrium quantity demanded increases from 10 to 15 units. The case of a movement along the demand curve is shown in Figure 3-8(*b*). In this case, a supply shift changes the market equilibrium from point *E* to point *E''*. As a result, the quantity demanded changes from 10 to 15 units. But demand does not change in this case; rather, quantity demanded increases as consumers move along their demand curve from *E* to *E''* in response to a price change.

 The elusive concept of equilibrium: The notion of equilibrium is one of the most elusive concepts of economics. We are familiar with equilibrium in our everyday lives from seeing, for example, an orange resting at the bottom of a bowl or a pendulum at rest. In economics, equilibrium means that the different forces operating on a market are in balance, so the resulting price and quantity align the desires of purchasers and suppliers. Too low a price means that the forces are *not* in balance—that the forces attracting demand are greater than the forces attracting supply, so there is excess

FIGURE 3-8. Shifts of and Movements along Curves
Start out with initial equilibrium at E and a quantity of 10 units. In (**a**), an increase in demand (i.e., a shift of the demand curve) produces a new equilibrium of 15 units at E'. In (**b**), a shift in supply results in a movement along the demand curve from E to E''.

demand or a shortage. We also know that a competitive market is a mechanism for producing equilibrium. If price is too low, demanders will bid up the price to the equilibrium level.

The notion of equilibrium is tricky, however, as is seen by the statement of a leading pundit: "Don't lecture me about supply and demand equilibrium. The supply of oil is always equal to the demand for oil. You simply can't tell the difference." The pundit is right in an accounting sense. Clearly the oil sales recorded by the oil producers should be exactly equal to the oil purchases recorded by the oil consumers. But this bit of arithmetic cannot repeal the laws of supply and demand. More important, if we fail to understand the nature of economic equilibrium, we cannot hope to understand the way that different forces affect the marketplace.

In economics, we are interested in knowing the quantity of sales that will clear the market, that is, the equilibrium quantity. We also want to know the price at which

consumers willingly buy what producers willingly sell. Only at this price will both buyers and sellers be satisfied with their decisions. Only at this price and quantity will there be no tendency for price and quantity to change. Only by looking at the equilibrium of supply and demand can we hope to understand such paradoxes as the fact that immigration may not lower wages in the affected cities, that land taxes do not raise rents, and that bad harvests raise (yes, raise!) the incomes of farmers.

Supply, Demand, and Immigration

A fascinating and important example of supply and demand, full of complexities, is the role of immigration in determining wages. If you ask people, they are likely to tell you that immigration into California or Florida surely lowers the wages of people in those regions. It's just supply and demand. They might point to Figure 3-9(*a*), which shows a

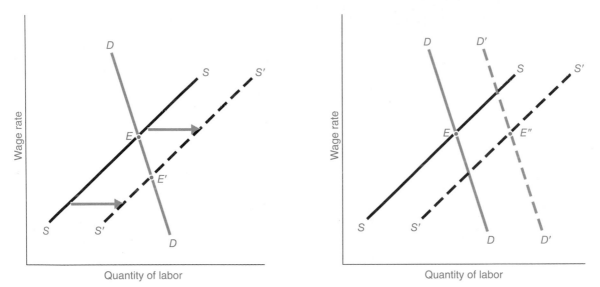

FIGURE 3-9. Analysis of Supply and Demand Must Hold All Other Things Constant
In (**a**), new immigrants cause the supply curve for labor to shift from SS to $S'S'$, lowering
equilibrium wages. What if immigrants go only to cities with growing labor markets? Then,
as shown in (**b**), the wage may not fall if demand shifts right to $D'D'$ at the same time as supply shifts.

supply-and-demand analysis of immigration. According to this analysis, immigration into a region shifts
the supply curve for labor to the right and pushes
down wages.

Careful economic studies cast doubt on this simple proposition, however. A recent survey of the evidence concludes:

> [The] effect of immigration on the labor market out-
> comes of natives is small. There is no evidence of eco-
> nomically significant reductions in native employ-
> ment. Most empirical analysis ... finds that a 10
> percent increase in the fraction of immigrants in the
> population reduces native wages by at most 1 percent.[2]

How can we explain the small impact of immigration on wages? The main mistake is to forget how
mobile the American population is and that the

impact of immigration will quickly spread around
the entire country. For example, immigrants may
move to cities where they can get jobs—that is, people move to those cities where the demand for labor
is already rising because of a strong local economy.

This possibility is illustrated in Figure 3-9(*b*),
where a shift in labor supply to S' is associated with a
higher demand curve, D'. The new equilibrium wage
at E'' is the same as the original wage at E. Another
possibility is that native-born residents move out (or
do not move in) when immigrants move in, so total
supply of labor is unchanged. This would leave the
supply curve for labor in its original position and
leave the wage unchanged.

How do economists sort out the possible reasons
for the puzzling finding that immigration is not associated with depressed city wages? The key step in iso-
lating the impact of a single variable is to hold other
things constant. This means that all other variables
must be held constant while the variable under consideration is changed. If we want to measure the

[2] Rachel M. Friedberg and Jennifer Hunt, "The Impact of
Immigrants on Host Country Wages, Employment, and
Growth," *Journal of Economic Perspectives* (Spring 1995),
pp. 23–44.

impact of immigration on wages, we must examine the effect of new immigrants when the strength of the local economy and the number of native-born residents in a city are unchanged—that is, when these "other things" are held constant. Unless you exclude the effects of other changing variables, you cannot accurately gauge the impact of immigration.

The same principle holds in doing a supply-and-demand analysis of any market. As much as possible, when you are examining the impact of a supply or demand shift, you must try to keep all other things constant.

RATIONING BY PRICES

Let us now take stock of what the market mechanism accomplishes. By determining the equilibrium prices and quantities of all inputs and outputs, the market allocates or rations out the scarce goods of the society among the possible uses. Who does the rationing? A planning board? Congress or the President? No. The marketplace, through the interaction of supply and demand, does the rationing. This is *rationing by the purse.*

What goods are produced? This is answered by the signals of the market prices. High oil prices stim-ulate oil production, whereas low food prices drive resources out of agriculture. Those who have the most dollar votes have the greatest influence on what goods are produced.

For whom are goods produced? The power of the purse dictates the distribution of income and consumption. Those with higher incomes end up with larger houses, more clothing, and longer vacations. When backed up by cash, the most urgently felt needs get fulfilled through the demand curve.

Even the *how* question is decided by supply and demand. When corn prices are low, it is not profitable for farmers to use expensive tractors and irrigation systems, and only the best land is cultivated. When oil prices are high, oil companies drill in deep offshore waters and employ novel seismic techniques to find oil.

With this introduction to supply and demand, we begin to see how desires for goods, as expressed through demands, interact with costs of goods, as reflected in supplies. Further study will deepen our understanding of these concepts and will show how this tool can be applied to other important areas. But even this first survey will serve as an indispensable tool for interpreting the economic world in which we live.

SUMMARY

1. The analysis of supply and demand shows how a market mechanism solves the three problems of *what, how,* and *for whom.* It shows how dollar votes decide the prices and quantities of different goods and services. A market blends together demands, coming from consumers who are spreading their incomes among available goods and services, with supplies, such as those provided by businesses interested in maximizing their profits.

A. The Demand Schedule

2. A demand schedule shows the relationship between the quantity demanded and the price of a commodity, other things held constant. Such a demand schedule, depicted graphically by a demand curve, holds constant other things like family incomes, tastes, and the prices of other goods. Almost all commodities obey the *law of downward-sloping demand,* which holds that quantity demanded falls as a good's price rises. This law is represented by a downward-sloping demand curve.

3. Many influences lie behind the demand schedule for the market as a whole: average family incomes, population, the prices of related goods, tastes, and special influences. When these influences change, the demand curve will shift.

B. The Supply Schedule

4. The supply schedule (or supply curve) gives the relationship between the quantity of a good that producers desire to sell—other things constant—and that good's price. Quantity supplied generally responds positively to price, so the supply curve rises upward and to the right.

5. Elements other than the good's price affect its supply. The most important influence is the commodity's production cost, determined by the state of technology and by input prices. Other elements in supply include the prices of related goods, government policies, and special influences.

C. Equilibrium of Supply and Demand

6. The equilibrium of supply and demand in a competitive market is attained at a price at which the forces of supply and demand are in balance. The equilibrium price is the price at which the quantity demanded just equals the quantity supplied. Graphically, we find the equilibrium as the intersection of the supply and demand curves. At a price above the equilibrium, producers want to supply more than consumers want to buy, which results in a surplus of goods and exerts downward pressure on price. Similarly, too low a price generates a shortage, and buyers will therefore tend to bid price upward to the equilibrium.

7. Shifts in the supply and demand curves change the equilibrium price and quantity. An increase in demand, which shifts the demand curve to the right, will increase both equilibrium price and quantity. An increase in supply, which shifts the supply curve to the right, will decrease price and increase quantity demanded.

8. To use supply-and-demand analysis correctly, we must (*a*) distinguish a change in demand or supply (which produces a shift in a curve) from a change in the quantity demanded or supplied (which represents a movement along a curve); (*b*) hold other things constant, which requires distinguishing the impact of a change in a commodity's price from the impact of changes in other influences; and (*c*) look always for the supply-and-demand equilibrium, which comes at the point where forces acting on price and quantity are in balance.

9. Competitively determined prices ration the limited supply of goods among those with the demands.

CONCEPTS FOR REVIEW

supply-and-demand analysis
demand schedule or curve, *DD*
law of downward-sloping demand
influences affecting demand curve

supply schedule or curve, *SS*
influences affecting supply curve
equilibrium price and quantity

shifts in supply and demand curves
all other things held constant
rationing by prices

QUESTIONS FOR DISCUSSION

1. **a.** Define carefully what is meant by a demand schedule or curve. State the law of downward-sloping demand. Illustrate the law of downward-sloping demand with two cases from your own experience.
   b. Define the concept of a supply schedule or curve. Show that an increase in supply means a rightward and downward shift of the supply curve. Contrast this with the rightward and upward shift in the demand curve implied by an increase in demand.

2. What might increase the demand for hamburgers? What would increase the supply? What would inexpensive frozen pizzas do to the market equilibrium for hamburgers? To the wages of teenagers who work at McDonald's?

3. Explain why the price in competitive markets settles down at the equilibrium intersection of supply and demand. Explain what happens if the market price starts out too high or too low.

4. Explain why each of the following is *false*:
   a. A freeze in Brazil's coffee-growing region will lower the price of coffee.
   b. "Protecting" American tomato producers from Mexican tomato imports will lower tomato prices in the United States.

   c. The rapid increase in college tuitions will lower the demand for college.
   d. The war against drugs, with increased interdiction of imported cocaine, will lower the price of domestically produced marijuana.

5. The four laws of supply and demand are the following:
   a. An increase in demand generally raises price and raises quantity demanded.
   b. A decrease in demand generally _____ price and _____ quantity demanded.
   c. An increase in supply generally lowers price and raises quantity demanded.
   d. A decrease in supply generally _____ price and _____ quantity demanded.
   Fill in the blanks. Demonstrate each law with a supply-and-demand diagram.

6. For each of the following, explain whether quantity demanded changes because of a demand shift or a price change, and draw a diagram to illustrate your answer:
   a. As a result of decreased military spending, the price of Army boots falls.
   b. Fish prices fall after the pope allows Catholics to eat meat on Friday.

c. An increase in gasoline taxes lowers the consumption of gasoline.

d. After the Black Death struck Europe in the fourteenth century, wages rose.

7. Examine the graph for the price of gasoline in Figure 3-1, page 44. Then, using a supply-and-demand diagram, illustrate the impact of each of the following on price and quantity demanded:

a. Improvements in transportation lower the costs of importing oil into the United States in the 1960s.

b. After the 1973 war, oil producers cut oil production sharply.

c. After 1980, smaller automobiles get more miles per gallon.

d. A record-breaking cold winter in 1995–1996 unexpectedly raises the demand for heating oil.

8. From the following data, plot the supply and demand curves and determine the equilibrium price and quantity:

Supply and Demand for Pizzas		
Price ($ per pizza)	Quantity demanded (pizzas per semester)	Quantity supplied (pizzas per semester)
10	0	40
8	10	30
6	20	20
4	30	10
2	40	0
0	125	0

What would happen if the demand for pizzas tripled at each price? What would occur if the price were initially set at $4 per pizza?

PART TWO

MICROECONOMICS: SUPPLY, DEMAND, AND PRODUCT MARKETS

CHAPTER 4
APPLICATIONS OF SUPPLY AND DEMAND

The Age of Chivalry is gone; that of sophisters, economists, and calculators has succeeded.

Edmund Burke

Having completed our introductory survey, we begin our study of microeconomics, which is concerned with the behavior of the individual markets that make up the economy. Individual markets contain most of the grand sweep and drama of economic history and the controversies of economic policy. Within the confines of microeconomics we will study the reasons for the vast disparities in earnings between neurosurgeons and textile workers. Microeconomics is crucial to understanding why computer prices have fallen so dramatically and why the use of computers has expanded exponentially. We cannot hope to understand the bitter debates about health care or the minimum wage without applying the tools of supply and demand to these sectors. Even topics such as illegal drugs or crime and punishment are usefully illuminated by considering the way the demand for addictive substances differs from that for other commodities.

Our survey of microeconomics will proceed in three parts. In this part, we focus on the behavior of *product markets,* the markets for all the goods and services that firms produce. We will examine where consumer demand comes from, how businesses make decisions, and how prices and profits efficiently coordinate the allocation of scarce economic resources

in a perfectly competitive market. We will also examine the market failures that arise when monopolies or other forms of imperfect competitors dominate industry.

Then in Part Three we turn to the study of *factor markets,* which are the markets for factors of production such as labor, capital, and land. These critical markets affect us all, because the prices of these factors—wages, interest, and rent—help determine what income workers, investors, and landowners will receive. We will see how prices in these markets are set and how they affect the distribution of income in a market economy.

Looking further down the road, in Part Four we examine the critical role of government in the modern market economy. We will see how the government must balance *efficiency* and *fairness* in its taxation and spending policies. We will also study how government regulation can both help and hurt the workings of the economy and how government policies can help alleviate the poverty and hardship resulting from the market distribution of income. Finally, we will turn our attention to environmental economics, which proposes ways to halt environmental degradation without harming economic growth.

A. ELASTICITY OF DEMAND AND SUPPLY

Here we start our study of product markets. We have already seen in Chapter 3 how supply and demand can be combined to produce market equilibrium. The theory of supply and demand can be used to answer a wide range of important and interesting questions. For example, when a new tax is put on gasoline, do drivers bear the burden of the tax or does it fall on the oil companies? Does raising the minimum wage help workers or hurt them? Should the airlines raise ticket prices to increase their profits, or will lower ticket prices increase the number of passengers so much that profits actually rise?

In order to turn supply and demand curves into truly useful tools, we need to know *how much* supply and demand respond to changes in price. Some purchases, like those for vacation travel, are very sensitive to price changes. Others, like food or electricity, are necessities for which consumer purchases respond very little to price changes. These issues are analyzed using the crucial concept of elasticity, which is a way of quantifying how responsive quantities supplied and demanded are to changes in prices. The payoff will come in the second half of the chapter, when we use this new tool to examine the microeconomic impacts of taxes and other types of government intervention.

PRICE ELASTICITY OF DEMAND

Let's look first at the response of consumer demand to price changes:

The **price elasticity of demand** (sometimes simply called **price elasticity**) measures how much the quantity demanded of a good changes when its price changes. The precise definition of price elasticity is the percentage change in quantity demanded divided by the percentage change in price.

Goods vary enormously in their price elasticity, or sensitivity to price changes. When the price elasticity of a good is high, we say that the good has "elastic" demand, which means that its quantity demanded responds greatly to price changes. When the price elasticity of a good is low, it is "inelastic" and its quantity demanded responds little to price changes.

For necessities like food, fuel, shoes, and prescription drugs demand tends to be inelastic. Such items are the staff of life and cannot easily be forgone when their prices rise. By contrast, you can substitute other goods when luxuries like European holidays, 17-year-old Scotch whiskey, and Italian designer clothing rise in price.

In addition, goods that have ready substitutes tend to have more elastic demand than those that have no substitutes. If all food or footwear prices were to rise 20 percent tomorrow, you would hardly expect people to stop eating or to go around barefoot, so food and footwear demands are price-inelastic. On the other hand, if mad-cow disease drives up the price of British beef, people can turn to beef from other countries or to lamb or poultry for their meat needs. Therefore, British beef shows a high price elasticity.

The length of time that people have to respond to price changes also plays a role. A good example is that of gasoline. Suppose you are driving across the country when the price of gasoline suddenly increases. Is it likely that you will sell your car and abandon your vacation? Not really. So in the short run, the demand for gasoline may be very inelastic.

In the long run, however, you can adjust your behavior to the higher price of gasoline. You can buy a smaller and more fuel-efficient car, ride a bicycle, take the train, move closer to work, or carpool with other people. For many goods, the ability to adjust consumption patterns implies that demand elasticities are higher in the long run than in the short run.

Economic factors determine the size of price elasticities for individual goods: elasticities tend to be higher when the goods are luxuries, when substitutes are available, and when consumers have more time to adjust their behavior.

Calculating Elasticities

If we can observe how much quantity demanded changes when price changes, we can calculate the elasticity. The precise definition of price elasticity, E_D, is the percentage change in quantity demanded divided by the percentage change in price.

We can calculate the coefficient of price elasticity numerically according to the following formula:

Price elasticity of demand = E_D

$$= \frac{\text{percentage change in quantity demanded}}{\text{percentage change in price}}$$

Now we can be more precise about the different categories of price elasticity:

- When a 1 percent change in price calls forth more than a 1 percent change in quantity demanded, the good has **price-elastic demand.** For example, if a 1 percent increase in price yields a 5 percent decrease in quantity demanded, the commodity has a highly price-elastic demand.
- When a 1 percent change in price evokes less than a 1 percent change in quantity demanded, the good has **price-inelastic demand.** This case occurs, for instance, when a 1 percent increase in price yields only a 0.2 percent decrease in demand.
- One important special case is **unit-elastic demand,** which occurs when the percentage change in quantity is exactly the same as the percentage change in price. In this case, a 1 percent increase in price yields a 1 percent decrease in demand. We will see later that this condition implies that total expenditures on the commodity (which equal $P \times Q$) stay the same even when the price changes.

To illustrate the calculation of elasticities, let us examine the simple case of the response to a price increase which is shown in Figure 4-1. In the original situation, price was 90 and quantity demanded was 240 units. A price increase to 110 led consumers to reduce their purchases to 160 units. In Figure 4-1, consumers were originally at point A but moved along their demand schedule to point B when the price rose.

Table 4-1 shows how we calculate price elasticity. The price increase is 20 percent, with the resulting

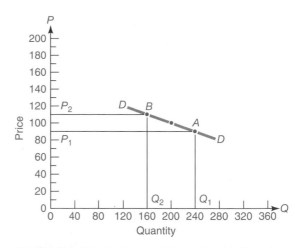

FIGURE 4-1. Elastic Demand Shows Large-Quantity Response to Price Change

Market equilibrium is originally at point A. In response to a 20 percent price increase, quantity demanded declines 40 percent, to point B. Price elasticity is $E_D = 40/20 = 2$. Demand is therefore elastic in the region from A to B.

quantity decrease being 40 percent. The price elasticity of demand is evidently $E_D = 40/20 = 2$. The price elasticity is greater than 1, and this good therefore displays price-elastic demand in the region from A to B.

In practice, calculating elasticities is somewhat tricky, and we emphasize three key steps where you have to be especially careful. First, note that we drop the minus signs from the numbers by treating all percentage changes as positive. That means all elasticities are positive, even though prices and quantities

TABLE 4-1. Example of Good with Elastic Demand

Consider the situation where price is raised from 90 to 110. According to the demand curve, quantity demanded falls from 240 to 160. Price elasticity is the ratio of percentage change in quantity divided by percentage change in price. We drop the minus sign from the numbers so that all elasticities are positive.

Case A: Price = 90 and quantity = 240

Case B: Price = 110 and quantity = 160

Percentage price change = $\Delta P/P = 20/100 = 20\%$

Percentage quantity change = $\Delta Q/Q = {}^-80/200 = {}^-40\%$

Price elasticity = $E_D = 40/20 = 2$

demanded move in opposite directions because of the law of downward-sloping demand.

Second, note that the definition of elasticity uses percentage changes in price and demand rather than actual changes. That means that a change in the units of measurement does not affect the elasticity. So whether we measure price in pennies or dollars, the price elasticity stays the same.

A third point concerns the exact procedure for calculating percentage changes in price and quantity. The formula for a percentage change is $\Delta P/P$. The value of ΔP in Table 4-1 is clearly $20 = 110 - 90$. But it's not immediately clear what value we should use for P in the denominator. Is it the original value of 90, the final value of 110, or something in between?

For very small percentage changes, such as from 100 to 99, it doesn't much matter whether we use 99 or 100 as the denominator. But for larger changes, the difference is significant. To avoid ambiguity, we always take the average price to be the base price for calculating price changes. In Table 4-1, we used the average of the two prices $[P = (90 + 110)/2 = 100]$ as the base or denominator in the elasticity formula. Similarly, we used the average quantity $[Q = (160 + 240)/2 = 200]$ as the base for measuring the percentage change in quantity. The exact formula for calculating elasticity is therefore

$$E_D = \frac{\Delta Q}{(Q_1 + Q_2)/2} \div \frac{\Delta P}{(P_1 + P_2)/2}$$

where P_1 and Q_1 represent the original price and quantity and P_2 and Q_2 stand for the new price and quantity.

Price Elasticity in Diagrams

It's possible to determine price elasticities in diagrams as well. Figure 4-2 illustrates the three cases of elasticities. In each case, price is cut in half and consumers change their quantity demanded from A to B.

In Figure 4-2(a), a halving of price has tripled quantity demanded. Like the example in Figure 4-1, this case shows price-elastic demand. In Figure 4-2(c), cutting price in half led to only a 50 percent increase in quantity demanded, so this is the case of price-inelastic demand. The borderline case of unit-elastic demand is shown in Figure 4-2(b); in this example, the doubling of quantity demanded exactly matches the halving of price.

Figure 4-3 displays the important polar extremes where the price elasticities are infinite and zero, or completely elastic and completely inelastic. Completely inelastic demands, or ones with zero elasticity, are ones where the quantity demanded responds not at all to price changes; such demand is seen to be a vertical demand curve. By contrast, when demand is infinitely elastic, a tiny change in price will lead to an indefinitely large change in quantity demanded, as in the horizontal demand curve in Figure 4-3.

FIGURE 4-2. Price Elasticity of Demand Falls into Three Categories

Numerical Calculation of Elasticity Coefficient						
Q	ΔQ	P	ΔP	$\dfrac{Q_1 + Q_2}{2}$	$\dfrac{P_1 + P_2}{2}$	$E_D = \dfrac{\Delta Q}{(Q_1 + Q_2)/2} \div \dfrac{\Delta P}{(P_1 + P_2)/2}$
0		6				
	10		2	5	5	$\dfrac{10}{5} \div \dfrac{2}{5} = 5 > 1$
10		4				
	10		2	15	3	$\dfrac{10}{15} \div \dfrac{2}{3} = 1$
20		2				
	10		2	25	1	$\dfrac{10}{25} \div \dfrac{2}{1} = 0.2 < 1$
30		0				

TABLE 4-2. Calculation of Price Elasticity along a Linear Demand Curve
ΔP denotes the change in price, i.e., $\Delta P = P_2 - P_1$, while $\Delta Q = Q_2 - Q_1$. To calculate numerical elasticity, percentage change of price equals price change ΔP divided by average price; the percentage change in output is calculated as $\Delta Q/Q$, where Q is given by the average Q. Treating all figures as positive numbers, the resulting ratio gives numerical price elasticity of demand, E_D. Note that for a straight line, elasticity is high at the top, low at the bottom, and exactly 1 in the middle.

FIGURE 4-3. Perfectly Elastic and Inelastic Demands
Polar extremes of demand are vertical demand curves, which represent perfectly inelastic demand ($E_D = 0$), and horizontal demand curves, which show perfectly elastic demand ($E_{D'} = \infty$).

 Warning: Elasticity is not the same as slope.
We must always remember not to confuse the elasticity of a curve with its slope. This distinction is easily seen when we examine the straight-line demand curves

that are often found in illustrative examples. We often depict demand curves as linear or straight lines because they are easy to draw. So it's only natural to ask, What is the price elasticity of a straight-line demand curve?

That question turns out to have a surprising answer. Along a straight-line demand curve, the price elasticity varies from zero to infinity! Table 4-2 gives a detailed set of elasticity calculations using the same technique as that in Table 4-1. This table shows that linear demand curves start out with high price elasticity, where price is high and quantity is low, and end up with low elasticity, where price is low and quantity high.

This illustrates an important point. When you see a demand curve in a diagram, it is in general not true that a steep slope for the demand curve means inelastic demand and a flat slope signifies elastic demand. The slope is not the same as the elasticity because the demand curve's slope depends upon the changes in P and Q, whereas the elasticity depends upon the percentage changes in P and Q. The only exceptions are the polar cases of completely elastic and inelastic demands.

One way to see this point is to examine Figure 4-2(b). This demand curve is clearly not a straight line with constant slope. Yet it has a constant demand elasticity of $E_D = 1$ because the percentage change in price is everywhere equal to the percentage change in quantity. So remember: Elasticity is definitely different from slope.

Figure 4-4 illustrates the pitfall of confusing slope and elasticity. This figure plots a linear or straight-line demand curve. Because it is linear, it has the same slope everywhere. But the top of the line, near *A*, has a very small percentage price change and a very large percentage quantity change, and elasticity is extremely large. Therefore, price elasticity is relatively large when we are high on the linear *DD* curve. Conversely, when we are in the bottom part of the linear demand curve, the price elasticity is less than unity. Near the horizontal axis, price elasticity is close to zero.

More generally, above the midpoint *M* of any straight line, demand is elastic, with $E_D > 1$. At the midpoint, demand is unit-elastic, with $E_D = 1$. Below the midpoint, demand is inelastic, with $E_D < 1$.

In summary, while the extreme cases of completely elastic and completely inelastic demand can be determined from the slopes of the demand curves alone, for the in-between cases, which correspond to virtually all goods, elasticities cannot be inferred by slope alone (see Figure 4-5 for one way to calculate elasticity from a diagram).[1]

---

[1] A simple trick will allow you to calculate the price elasticity of a demand curve: *The elasticity of a straight line at a point is given by the ratio of the length of the line segment below the point to the length of the line segment above the point.*

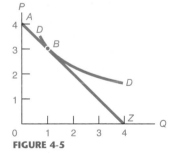

FIGURE 4-5

To see this, first examine Fig. 4-4. Note that at the midpoint *M* the length of the segment above (*AM*) and that of the segment below (*MZ*) are exactly equal; hence the elasticity is *MZ/AM* = 1. At point *B*, this formula yields $E_D = BZ/AB$ = 3/1 = 3; at *R*, $E_D = 1/3$.

Knowing how to calculate E_D for a straight line enables you to calculate it for any point along a curved demand curve, as shown in Fig. 4-5. (1) Draw the straight line tangent to the curve at your point (e.g., at *B* in Fig. 4-5), and then (2) calculate E_D for the straight line at that point (e.g., E_D at *B* = 3). The result will be the correct elasticity for the curve at point *B*.

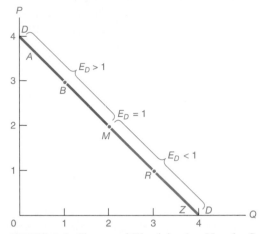

FIGURE 4-4. Slope and Elasticity Are Not the Same Thing All points on the straight-line demand curve have the same slope. But above the midpoint, demand is elastic; below it, demand is inelastic; at the midpoint, demand is unit-elastic. Only in the case of vertical or horizontal curves, shown in Fig. 4-3, can you infer the price elasticity from slope alone.

ELASTICITY AND REVENUE

One important application of elasticity is to help clarify whether a price increase will raise or lower revenue. This is a key question for many businesses, ranging from airlines to restaurants to magazines, which must decide whether it is worthwhile to raise prices and whether the higher prices make up for lower demand. Let's look at the relationship between price elasticity and total revenue.

Total revenue is by definition equal to price times quantity (or $P \times Q$). If consumers buy 5 units at $3 each, total revenue is $15. If you know the price elasticity of demand, you know what will happen to total revenue when price changes:

1. When demand is price-inelastic, a price decrease reduces total revenue.
2. When demand is price-elastic, a price decrease increases total revenue.
3. In the borderline case of unit-elastic demand, a price decrease leads to no change in total revenue.

For example, business travelers have an inelastic demand for air travel, so an increase in business fares tends to raise revenue. By contrast, leisure travelers have a much more elastic demand for air travel, because they have a far greater choice about where and when they are traveling. As a result, raising leisure fares tends to decrease revenue.

 Fly the financial skies of "Elasticity Air." Understanding the demand elasticities of their passengers' travel is worth billions of dollars each year to U.S. airlines. Ideally, airlines would like to charge the highest price they can to business travelers, while charging leisure passengers a low-enough price to fill up all their empty seats. That is how they would raise revenues and maximize profits.

But if they charge low-elasticity business travelers one price and high-elasticity leisure passengers a lower price, the airlines have a big problem—keeping the two classes of passengers separate. How can they stop the low-elasticity business travelers from buying up the cheap tickets meant for the leisure travelers and not let high-elasticity leisure flyers take up seats that business passengers would have been willing to buy? The airlines have solved their problem by engaging in "price discrimination" among their different customers in a way that exploits different price elasticities. (*Price discrimination* is the practice of charging different prices for the same service to different customers.) Airlines offer discount fares for travelers who plan ahead and who tend to choose times when prices are low. At the same time, airlines might require a stay over Saturday night to get the discount fare, a rule that discourages business travelers who would like to get home for the weekend. Also, discounts are often unavailable at the last minute because many business trips are unplanned expeditions to handle an unforeseen crisis—another case of price-inelastic demand. Airlines have devised extremely sophisticated computer programs to manage their seat availability as a way of ensuring that their low-elasticity passengers cannot benefit from discount fares. As a result, their profits have continued to be healthy while they fill their planes with budget travelers.

The Paradox of the Bumper Harvest

We can use elasticities to illustrate one of the most famous paradoxes of all economics: the paradox of the bumper harvest. Imagine that in a particular year nature smiles on farming. A cold winter kills off the pests; spring comes early for planting; there are no killing frosts; rains nurture the growing shoots; and a sunny October allows a record crop to come to market. At the end of the year, family Jones happily settles down to calculate its income for the year. The Joneses are in for a major surprise: *The good weather and bumper crop have lowered their and other farmers' incomes.*

How can this be? The answer lies in the elasticity of demand for foodstuffs. The demands for basic food products such as wheat and corn tend to be inelastic; for these necessities, consumption changes very little in response to price. But this means farmers as a whole receive less total revenue when the harvest is good than when it is bad. The increase in supply arising from an abundant harvest tends to lower the price. But the lower price doesn't increase quantity demanded very much. The implication is that a low price elasticity of food means that large harvests (high Q) tend to be associated with low revenue (low $P \times Q$).

These ideas can be illustrated by referring back to Figure 4-2. We begin by showing how to measure revenue in the diagram itself. Total revenue is the product of price times quantity, $P \times Q$. Further, the area of a rectangle is always equal to the product of its base times its height. Therefore, total revenue at any point on a demand curve can be found by examining the area of the rectangle determined by the P and Q at that point.

Next, we can check the relationship between elasticity and revenue for the unit-elastic case in Figure 4-2(*b*). Note that the shaded revenue region ($P \times Q$) is $1000 million for both points A and B. The shaded areas representing total revenue are the same because of offsetting changes in the Q base and the P height. This is what we would expect for the borderline case of unit-elastic demand.

We can also see that Figure 4-2(*a*) corresponds to elastic demand. In this figure, the revenue rectangle expands from $1000 million to $1500 million when price is halved. Since total revenue goes up when price is cut, demand is elastic.

In Figure 4-2(*c*) the revenue rectangle falls from $40 million to $30 million when price is halved, so demand is inelastic.

Which diagram illustrates the case of agriculture, where a bumper harvest means lower total revenues for farmers? Clearly it is Figure 4-2(*c*).

Value of demand elasticity	Description	Definition	Impact on revenues
Greater than one ($E_D > 1$)	Elastic demand	Percentage change in quantity demanded *greater* than percentage change in price	Revenues *increase* when price decreases
Equal to one ($E_D = 1$)	Unit-elastic demand	Percentage change in quantity demanded *equal* to percentage change in price	Revenues *unchanged* when price decreases
Less than one ($E_D < 1$)	Inelastic demand	Percentage change in quantity demanded *less* than percentage change in price	Revenues *decrease* when price decreases

TABLE 4-3. Elasticities: Summary of Crucial Concepts

Which represents the case of vacation travel, where a lower price could mean higher revenues? Surely Figure 4-2(*a*).

Table 4-3 shows the major points to remember about price elasticities.

PRICE ELASTICITY OF SUPPLY

Of course, consumption is not the only thing that changes when prices go up or down. Businesses also respond to price in their decisions about how much to produce. Economists define the price elasticity of supply as the responsiveness of the quantity supplied of a good to its market price.

More precisely, the **price elasticity of supply** is the percentage change in quantity supplied divided by the percentage change in price.

Suppose the amount supplied is completely fixed, as in the case of perishable fish brought to market to be sold at whatever price they will fetch. This is the limiting case of zero elasticity, or completely inelastic supply, which is a vertical supply curve.

At the other extreme, say that a tiny cut in price will cause the amount supplied to fall to zero, while the slightest rise in price will coax out an indefinitely large supply. Here, the ratio of the percentage change in quantity supplied to percentage change in price is extremely large and gives rise to a horizontal supply curve. This is the polar case of infinitely elastic supply.

Between these extremes, we call supply elastic or inelastic depending upon whether the percentage change in quantity is larger or smaller than the percentage change in price. In the borderline unit-elastic case, where price elasticity of supply equals 1, the percentage increase of quantity supplied is exactly equal to the percentage increase in price.

You can readily see that the definitions of price elasticities of supply are exactly the same as those for price elasticities of demand. The only difference is that for supply the quantity response to price is positive, while for demand the response is negative.

The exact definition of the price elasticity of supply, E_S, is as follows:

$$E_S = \frac{\text{percentage change in quantity supplied}}{\text{percentage change in price}}$$

Figure 4-6 displays three important cases of supply elasticity: (a), the vertical supply curve, showing completely inelastic supply; (c), the horizontal supply curve, displaying completely elastic supply; and (b), an intermediate case of a straight line, going through the origin, illustrating the borderline case of unit elasticity.[2]

What factors determine supply elasticity? The major factor influencing supply elasticity is the ease with which production in the industry can be increased. If all inputs can be readily found at going market prices, as is the case for the textile industry,

---

[2] You can determine the elasticity of a supply curve that is not a straight line in the fashion described for the demand curve in footnote 1 on page 68 by drawing the straight line that lies tangent to the curve at a point and measuring the elasticity of the tangential straight line.

then output can be greatly increased with little increase in price. This would indicate that supply elasticity is relatively large. On the other hand, if production capacity is severely limited, as is the case for the mining of South African gold, then even sharp increases in the price of gold will call forth but a small response in production of South African gold; this would be inelastic supply.

Another important factor in supply elasticities is the time period under consideration. A given change in price tends to have a larger effect on amount supplied as the time for suppliers to respond increases. For very brief periods after a price increase, firms may be unable to increase their inputs of labor, materials, and capital, so supply may be very price-inelastic. However, as time passes and businesses can hire more labor, build new factories, and expand capacity, supply elasticities will become larger.

We can use Figure 4-6 to illustrate how supply may change over time for the fishing case. Supply curve (a) might hold for fish on the day it is brought to market, where it is simply auctioned off for whatever it will bring. Curve (b) might hold for the intermediate run of a year or so, with the given stock of fishing boats and before new labor is attracted to the industry. Over the very long run, as new fishing boats are built, new labor is attracted, and new fish farms

are constructed, the supply of fish might be very price-elastic, as in case (c) in Figure 4-6.

Supply Elasticities

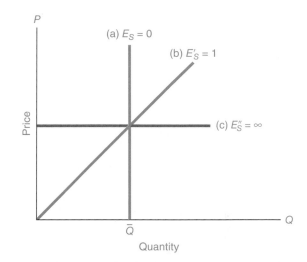

FIGURE 4-6. Supply Elasticity Depends upon Producer Response to Price

When supply is fixed, supply elasticity is zero, as in curve (a). Curve (c) displays an indefinitely large quantity response to price changes. Intermediate case (b) arises when the percentage quantity and price changes are equal.

B. APPLICATIONS TO CURRENT ECONOMIC ISSUES

Having laid the groundwork with our study of elasticities, we show how the tools can assist our understanding of many of the basic economic trends and policy issues. We begin with one of the major transformations since the Industrial Revolution, the decline of agriculture. Next, we examine the implications of taxes on an industry, using the example of a gasoline tax. We then analyze the consequences of various types of government intervention in markets.

THE ECONOMICS OF AGRICULTURE

Our first application of supply-and-demand analysis comes from agriculture. The first part of this section

lays out some of the economic fundamentals of the farm sector. Then we will use the theory of supply and demand to study the effects of government intervention in agricultural markets.

Long-Run Relative Decline of Farming

Farming was once our largest single industry. A hundred years ago, half the American population lived and worked on farms, but that number has declined to less than 3 percent of the work force today. At the same time, prices for farm products have fallen relative to incomes and other prices in the economy. As Table 4-4 shows, over the last half-century, median family income has more than doubled. By contrast, farm incomes have stagnated. Farm-state senators fret about the decline of the family farm.

A single diagram can explain the cause of the sagging trend in farm prices better than libraries of books and editorials. Figure 4-7 shows an initial equilibrium with high prices at point *E*. Observe what happens to agriculture as the years go by. Demand for food increased slowly because most foods are necessities; the demand shift is consequently modest in comparison to growing average incomes.

What about supply? Although many people mistakenly think that farming is a backward business, statistical studies show that productivity (output per unit of input) has grown more rapidly in agriculture than in most other industries. Important advances include mechanization through tractors, combines, and cotton pickers; fertilization and irrigation; selective breeding; and development of new seeds. All these innovations have vastly increased the productivity of agricultural inputs. Rapid productivity growth has increased supply greatly, as shown by the supply curve's shift from *SS* to *S'S'* in Figure 4-7.

What must happen at the new competitive equilibrium? Sharp increases in supply outpaced modest increases in demand, producing a downward trend in farm prices relative to other prices in the economy. And this is precisely what has happened in recent decades, as is seen in Table 4-4.

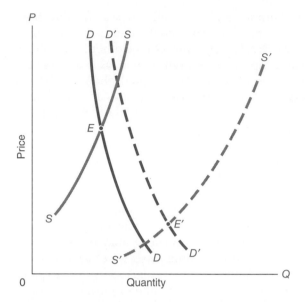

FIGURE 4-7. Agricultural Distress Results from Expanding Supply and Price-Inelastic Demand

Equilibrium at *E* represents conditions in the farm sector decades ago. Demand for farm products tends to grow more slowly than the impressive increase in supply generated by technological progress. Hence competitive farm prices tend to fall. Moreover, with price-inelastic demand, farm incomes decline with increases in supply.

TABLE 4-4. Farm Prices Have Declined and Farm Incomes Have Lagged

Since World War II, productivity in farming has increased sharply, resulting in a dramatic drop in the relative prices of farm products. Farm prices today are but 34 percent of their 1947 level. The stagnation of farm incomes is explained by a correct supply-and-demand analysis. (Source: U.S. Bureau of the Census and U.S. Department of Labor.)

Item	1994 level* (1947 = 100)
Real median family income	210
Real farm incomes	95
Real farm prices	34

*"Real" levels are the dollar values corrected by the change in the general price level as measured by the consumer price index.

Crop Restrictions. In response to falling incomes, farmers have often lobbied the federal government for economic assistance. Over the years, governments at home and abroad have taken many steps to help farmers. They have raised prices through price supports; they have curbed imports through tariffs and quotas; and they sometimes simply sent checks to farmers who agreed *not* to produce on their land.

The paradox of the bumper harvest has an interesting application here. *Many governments attempt to help farmers by reducing their production.* How could this be in the interests of farmers? Figure 4-8 shows the economics of this policy. If the Department of Agriculture requires every farmer to reduce the amount of production, the effect is a shifting of the supply curve up and to the left. Because food demands are inelastic, crop restrictions not only raise the price of crops but also tend to raise farmers' total revenues

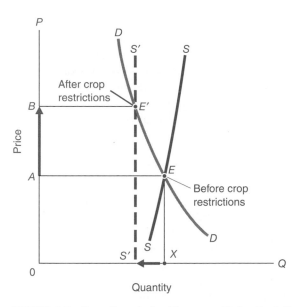

FIGURE 4-8. Crop-Restriction Programs Raise Both Price and Farm Income

Before the crop restriction, the competitive market produces an equilibrium with low price at *E*. When government restricts production, the supply curve is shifted leftward to *S'S'*, moving the equilibrium to *E'* and raising price to *B*. With inelastic demand, confirm that new revenue rectangle 0*BE'S'* is larger than original revenue rectangle 0*AEX*.

and earnings. Just as bumper harvests hurt farmers, crop restrictions tend to raise farm incomes. Of course, consumers are hurt by the crop restrictions and higher prices—just as they would be if a flood or drought created a scarcity of food.

Production restrictions are typical of government market interferences that raise the incomes of one group at the expense of others. We will see in later chapters that this kind of policy is inefficient: The gain to farmers is actually less than the harm to consumers.

IMPACT OF A TAX ON PRICE AND QUANTITY

Governments levy taxes on a wide variety of commodities—on cigarettes and alcohol, on payrolls and profits. Supply-and-demand analysis can help us predict who will bear the true burden of a tax and how a tax will affect output.

As an example, we will look at the case of a gasoline tax to illustrate the way that taxes affect market output and price. Although American politicians periodically make a fuss about them, gasoline taxes are far lower in the United States than in most European countries, where gas taxes are $2 to $5 per gallon—as compared to around 50 cents on average in the United States. Many economists and environmentalists advocate much higher gasoline taxes for the United States. They point out that higher taxes would curb consumption, and thereby reduce pollution and our dependence on insecure foreign sources of oil.

For concreteness, say that the government decided to raise the tax by $1 per gallon. Prudent legislators would of course be reluctant to raise gas taxes so sharply without a firm understanding of the consequences of such a move. They would want to know the incidence of the tax. *By incidence we mean the ultimate economic impact or burden of a tax.* Just because businesses write a check for the taxes does not mean that the taxes in fact reduce their profits. By using supply and demand, we can analyze who actually bears the burden, or what the incidence is, of the tax.

It could be that the burden of the tax is shifted forward to the consumers, if the retail price of gasoline goes up by the full $1 of the tax. Or perhaps consumers cut back so sharply on gasoline purchases that the burden of the tax is shifted back completely onto the oil companies. Where the actual impact lies between these extremes can be determined only from supply-and-demand analysis.

Figure 4-9 on page 74 provides the answer. It shows the original pretax equilibrium at *E*, the intersection of the original *SS* and *DD* curves, at a gasoline price of $1 a gallon and total consumption of 100 billion gallons per year. We portray the imposition of a $1 tax in the retail market for gasoline as an upward shift of the supply curve, with the demand curve remaining unchanged. The demand curve does not shift because the quantity demanded at each retail price is unchanged after the gasoline-tax increase. Note that the demand curve for gasoline is relatively inelastic.

By contrast, the supply curve definitely does shift upward by $1. The reason is that producers are willing to sell a given quantity (say, 100 billion gallons) only if they receive the same *net* price as before. That

FIGURE 4-9. Gasoline Tax Falls on Both Consumer and Producer

What is the incidence of a tax? A $1 tax on gasoline shifts the supply curve up $1 everywhere, giving a new supply curve, S'S', parallel to the original supply curve, SS. This new supply curve intersects DD in the new equilibrium at E', where price to consumers has risen 90 cents and producers' price has fallen 10 cents. The rust arrows show changes in P and Q.

is, at each quantity supplied, the market price must rise by exactly the amount of the tax. If producers had originally been willing to sell 80 billion gallons at $0.90 per gallon, they would still be willing to sell the same amount at a retail price of $1.90 (which, after subtracting the tax, yields the producers the same $0.90 per gallon).

What will be the new equilibrium price? The answer is found at the intersection of the new supply and demand curves, or at E', where S'S' and DD meet. Because of the supply shift, the price is higher. Also, the quantity supplied and demanded is reduced. If we read the graph carefully, we find that the new equilibrium price has risen from $1 to about $1.90. The new equilibrium output, at which supply and demand are in equilibrium, has fallen from 100 billion to about 80 billion gallons.

Who ultimately pays the tax? What is its incidence? Clearly the oil industry pays a small fraction, for it receives only 90 cents ($1.90 less the $1 tax) rather than $1. But the consumer bears most of the burden, with the retail price rising 90 cents, because supply is relatively price-elastic whereas demand is relatively price-inelastic.

Subsidies. If taxes are used to discourage consumption of a commodity, subsidies are used to encourage production. One pervasive example of subsidies comes in agriculture. You can examine the impact of a subsidy in a market by shifting *down* the supply curve. The general rules for subsidies are exactly parallel to those for taxes.

General Rules on Tax Shifting. Gasoline is just a single example of how to analyze tax shifting. Using this apparatus we can understand how cigarette taxes affect both the prices and consumption of cigarettes; how taxes or tariffs on imports affect foreign trade; and how property taxes, social security taxes, and corporate-profit taxes affect land prices, wages, and interest rates.

The key issue in determining the incidence of a tax is the relative elasticities of supply and demand. If demand is inelastic relative to supply, as in the case of gasoline, most of the cost is shifted to consumers. By contrast, if supply is inelastic relative to demand, as is the case for land, then most of the tax is shifted to supply. Here is the general rule for determining the incidence of a tax:

The incidence of a tax is determined by the effect on prices and quantities in supply-and-demand equilibrium. In general, the burden or incidence depends upon the relative elasticities of demand and supply. A tax is shifted forward to consumers if the demand is inelastic relative to supply; a tax is shifted backward to producers if supply is relatively more inelastic than demand.

MINIMUM FLOORS AND MAXIMUM CEILINGS

Sometimes, rather than taxing or subsidizing a commodity, the government legislates maximum or minimum prices. History is full of examples. From biblical days, governments have limited the interest rates that lenders can charge (so-called usury laws). In wartime, governments often impose wage and price controls to prevent spiraling inflation. During the energy crisis of the 1970s, there were controls on gasoline prices. Today, there are increasingly stringent limitations on the prices that doctors or hospitals can charge, and many large cities, including New

York, have rent controls on apartments. Proposals to increase the minimum wage are among the most controversial issues of economic policy.

These kinds of interferences with the laws of supply and demand are genuinely different from those in which the government imposes a tax and then lets the market act through supply and demand. Although political pressures always exist to keep prices down and wages up, experience has taught that sector-by-sector price and wage controls tend to create major economic distortions. Nevertheless, as Adam Smith well knew when he protested against mercantilist policies of an earlier age, most economic systems are plagued by inefficiencies stemming from well-meaning but inexpert interferences with the mechanisms of supply and demand. Setting maximum or minimum prices in a market tends to produce surprising and sometimes perverse economic effects. Let's see why.

Two important examples of government intervention are the minimum wage and price controls on gasoline. These will illustrate the surprising side effects that can arise when governments interfere with market determination of price and quantity.

The Minimum-Wage Controversy

The minimum wage sets a minimum on what employers are allowed to pay workers. In the United States, the federal minimum wage began in 1938 when the government required that covered workers in covered industries be paid at least 25 cents an hour. At that time, the minimum wage was about 40 percent of the average manufacturing wage. The minimum wage was raised occasionally, and by 1996 it had reached $4.25 per hour, which was only 33 percent of the average manufacturing wage rate. Because the minimum wage had declined relative to average earnings, President Clinton proposed and Congress passed a minimum-wage increase to $5.15 per hour in 1997.

This is an issue that divides even the most eminent economists. For example, Nobel laureate Gary Becker stated flatly, "Hike the minimum wage, and you put people out of work." Another group of Nobel Prize winners countered, "We believe that the federal minimum wage can be increased by a moderate amount without significantly jeopardizing employment opportunities." Yet another leading economist,

Alan Blinder of Princeton and former economic adviser to President Clinton, wrote as follows:

> The folks who earn the lowest wages have been suffering for years. They need all the help they can get, and they need it in a hurry. About 40 percent of all minimum-wage employees are the sole wage earner in their households, and about two-thirds of the teenagers earning the minimum wage live in households with below-average incomes. Frankly, I do not know whether a modest minimum-wage increase would decrease employment or not. If it does, the effect will likely be very small. (*New York Times*, May 23, 1996.)

How can nonspecialists sort through the issues when the experts are so divided? How can we resolve these apparently contradictory statements? To begin with, we should recognize that statements on the desirability of raising the minimum wage contain personal value judgments. Such statements might be informed by the best positive economics and still make different recommendations on important policy issues.

A cool-headed analysis indicates that the minimum-wage debate centers primarily on issues of interpretation rather than fundamental disagreements on empirical findings. Begin by looking at Figure 4-10 on page 76, which depicts the market for unskilled workers. The figure shows how a minimum wage rate sets a floor for most jobs. As the minimum wage rises above the market-clearing equilibrium at M, the total number of jobs moves up the demand curve to E, so employment falls. The gap between labor supplied and labor demanded is shown as U. This represents the amount of unemployment.

Using supply and demand, we see that there is likely to be a rise in unemployment and a decrease in employment of low-skilled workers. But how large will these magnitudes be? And what will be the impact on the wage income of low-income workers? On these questions, we can look at the empirical evidence.

Most studies indicate that a 10 percent increase in the minimum wage would reduce employment of teenagers by between 1 and 3 percent. The impact on adult employment is even smaller. Some recent studies put the employment effects very close to zero, and one set of studies suggests that employment might even increase. So a careful reading of the quotations from the eminent economists indicates that some economists consider small to be "insignificant" while others emphasize the existence of at least some

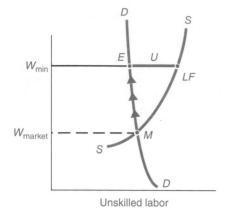

Unskilled labor

FIGURE 4-10. Effects of a Minimum Wage

Setting the minimum-wage floor at W_{min}, high above the free-market equilibrium rate at W_{market}, results in forced equilibrium at E. Employment is reduced, as the arrows show, from M to E. Additionally, unemployment is U, which is the difference between labor supplied at LF and employment at E. If the demand curve is inelastic, increasing the minimum wage will increase the income of low-wage workers. To see this, pencil in the rectangle of total wages before and after the minimum-wage increase.

job losses. Our example in Figure 4-10 shows a case where the *employment* decline is very small while the *unemployment* increase is quite large.

Another factor in the debate relates to the impact of the minimum wage on incomes. Virtually every study concludes that the demand for low-wage workers is price-inelastic. The results we just cited indicate that the price elasticity is between 0.1 and 0.3. This implies that raising the minimum wage would increase the incomes of low-income workers as a whole. Roughly speaking, a 10 percent increase in the minimum wage will increase the incomes of the affected groups by 7 to 9 percent.

The impact on incomes is yet another reason why people may disagree about the minimum wage. Those who are particularly concerned about the welfare of low-income groups may feel that modest inefficiencies are a small price to pay for higher incomes. Others—who worry more about the cumulative costs of market interferences or about the impact of higher costs upon prices, profits, and international competitiveness—may hold that the inefficiencies are too high a price. Yet another

group might believe that the minimum wage is an inefficient way to transfer buying power to low-income groups; this third group would prefer using direct income transfers or government wage subsidies rather than gumming up the wage system. How important are each of these three concerns to *you*? Depending upon your priorities, you might reach quite different conclusions on the advisability of increasing the minimum wage.

Energy Price Controls

Another example of government interference comes when the government legislates a maximum price ceiling. This occurred in the United States in the 1970s, and the results were sobering. We return to our analysis of the gasoline market to see how price ceilings function.

Let's set the scene. Suppose there is suddenly a crisis in the oil industry. This has happened time and again because of political disturbances in the Middle East due to war and revolution. We saw in Figure 3-1 the results of the 1973 and 1979 disturbances on the price of gasoline.

Politicians, seeing the sudden jump in prices, rise to denounce the situation. They claim that consumers are being "gouged" by profiteering oil companies. They worry that the rising prices threaten to ignite an inflationary spiral in the cost of living. They fret about the impact of rising prices on the poor and elderly. They call upon the government to "do something." In the face of rising prices, the U.S. government might be inclined to listen to these arguments and place a ceiling on oil prices, as it did from 1973 to 1981.

What are the effects of such a ceiling? Suppose the initial price of gasoline is $1 a gallon. Then, because of a drastic cut in oil supply, the market price of gasoline rises to $2 a gallon. Now consider the gasoline market after the supply shock. In Figure 4-11, the post-shock equilibrium is given at point E. Enter the government, which passes a law setting the maximum price for gasoline at the old level of $1 a gallon. We can picture this legal maximum price as the ceiling-price line CJK in Figure 4-11.

At the legal ceiling price, quantities supplied and demanded do not match. Consumers want more gasoline than producers are willing to supply at the controlled price. This is shown by the gap between *J* and *K*. This gap is so large that before long the pumps run dry. Somebody will have to go without the desired gasoline. If the free market were allowed to operate, the market would clear with a price of $2 or more; consumers would grumble but would willingly pay the higher price rather than go without fuel.

But the market cannot clear because it is against the law for producers to charge a higher price. There follows a period of frustration and shortage— a game of musical cars in which somebody is left without gasoline when the pump runs dry. The inadequate supply of gasoline must somehow be rationed. Initially, this may be done through a "first come, first served" approach, with or without limiting sales to each customer. Lines form, and much time has to be spent foraging for fuel.

Eventually, some kind of nonprice rationing mechanism evolves. For gasoline and other storable goods, the shortage is often managed by making people wait in line—rationing by the queue. Sometimes people who have privileged access to the good engage in black-market sales, which are illegal transactions above the regulated price. There is great waste as people spend valuable time trying to secure their needs. Sometimes, governments design a more efficient system of nonprice rationing based on formal allocation or coupon rationing.

Under coupon rationing, each customer must have a coupon as well as money to buy the goods— in effect, there are two kinds of money. When rationing is adopted and coupons are meted out according to "need," shortages disappear because demand is limited by the allocation of the coupons. Just how do ration coupons change the supply-and-demand picture? Clearly, the government must issue just enough of them to lower the demand curve to *D′D′* in Figure 4-11, where supply and the new demand balance at the ceiling price.

Price controls on goods like energy, with or without formal rationing, have fallen out of favor in most market economies. The only area where they are significant today is medical care. History has shown

FIGURE 4-11. Price Controls Produce Shortages
Without a legal price ceiling, price would rise to *E*. At the ceiling price of $1, supply and demand do not balance, and shortages break out. Some method of rationing, formal or informal, is needed to allocate the short supply and bring the actual demand down to *D′D′*.

that legal and illegal evasions of price controls grow over time, and the inefficiencies eventually overwhelm whatever favorable impacts the controls might have on consumers. Particularly when there is room for ample substitution (i.e., when elasticities of supply or demand are high), price controls are costly and difficult to administer.

But there is a deeper lesson here: Goods are always scarce. Society can never fulfill everyone's wishes. In normal times, price itself rations the scarce supplies. When governments step in to interfere with supply and demand, prices no longer fill the role of rationers. Waste, inefficiency, and aggravation are certain companions of such interferences.

This concludes our survey of supply-and-demand analysis. In the next few chapters we investigate the foundations of demand and supply in consumer choice and business costs. These chapters will help to explain patterns of pricing in competitive and monopolistic markets and to show why competitive markets lead to an efficient (although possibly inequitable) allocation of resources.

▲

SUMMARY

A. Elasticity of Demand and Supply

1. Price elasticity of demand measures the quantitative response of demand to a change in price. Price elasticity of demand (E_D) is defined as the percentage change in quantity demanded divided by the percentage change in price. That is,

   Price elasticity of demand $= E_D$

   $$= \frac{\text{percentage change in quantity demanded}}{\text{percentage change in price}}$$

   In this calculation, the sign is taken to be positive, and P and Q are averages of old and new values.

2. We divide price elasticities into three categories: (*a*) Demand is elastic when the percentage change in quantity demanded exceeds the percentage change in price; that is, $E_D > 1$. (*b*) Demand is inelastic when the percentage change in quantity demanded is less than the percentage change in price; here, $E_D < 1$. (*c*) When the percentage change in quantity demanded exactly equals the percentage change in price, we have the borderline case of unit-elastic demand, where $E_D = 1$.

3. Price elasticity is a pure number, involving percentages; it should not be confused with slope.

4. The demand elasticity tells us about the impact of a price change on total revenue. Demand is elastic if a price reduction increases total revenue; demand is inelastic if a price reduction decreases total revenue; in the unit-elastic case, a price change has no effect on total revenue.

5. Price elasticity of demand tends to be low for necessities like food and shelter and high for luxuries like snowmobiles and air travel. Other factors affecting price elasticity are the extent to which a good has ready substitutes, the length of time that consumers have to adjust to price changes, and the fraction of the consumer budget spent on the commodity.

6. Price elasticity of supply measures the percentage change of output supplied by producers when the market price changes by a given percentage.

B. Applications to Current Economic Issues

7. One of the most fruitful arenas for application of supply-and-demand analysis is agriculture. Improvements in agricultural technology mean that supply increases greatly, while demand for food rises less than proportionately with income. Hence free-market prices for foodstuffs tend to fall. No wonder governments have adopted a variety of programs, like crop restrictions, to prop up farm incomes.

8. A commodity tax shifts the supply-and-demand equilibrium. The tax's burden (or incidence) will fall more heavily on consumers than on producers to the degree that the demand is inelastic relative to supply.

9. Governments occasionally interfere with the workings of competitive markets by setting maximum ceilings or minimum floors on prices. In such situations, quantity supplied need no longer equal quantity demanded; ceilings lead to excess demand, while floors lead to excess supply. Sometimes, the interference may raise the incomes of a particular group, as in the case of farmers or low-skilled workers. Often, distortions and inefficiencies result.

CONCEPTS FOR REVIEW

Elasticity Concepts

price elasticity of demand, supply
elastic, inelastic, unit-elastic demand
$E_D = \%$ change in $Q / \%$ change in P
determinants of elasticity

total revenue $= P \times Q$
relationship of elasticity and revenue
   change

Applications of Supply and Demand

incidence of a tax
rationing by price
distortions from price controls
rationing by prices vs. coupons

QUESTIONS FOR DISCUSSION

1. "A good harvest will generally lower the income of farmers." Illustrate this proposition using a supply-and-demand diagram.

2. For each pair of commodities, state which you think is the more price-elastic and give your reasons: perfume and salt; penicillin and ice cream; automobiles and automobile tires; ice cream and chocolate ice cream.

3. "The price drops by 1 percent, causing the quantity demanded to rise by 2 percent. Demand is therefore elastic, with $E_D > 1$." If you change 2 to 1/2 in the first

sentence, what two other changes will be required in the quotation?

4. Consider a competitive market for apartments. What would be the effect on the equilibrium output and price after the following changes (other things held equal)? In each case, explain your answer using supply and demand.

   a. A rise in the income of consumers
   b. A $10-per-month tax on apartment rentals
   c. A government edict saying apartments could not rent for more than $200 per month
   d. A new construction technique allowing apartments to be built at half the cost
   e. A 20 percent increase in the wages of construction workers

5. Explain and show graphically how the 1990–1991 embargo of Iraqi oil exports affected oil supply and demand and thereby the equilibrium oil price and quantity.

6. A conservative critic of government programs has written, "Governments know how to do one thing well. They know how to create shortages and surpluses." Explain this quotation using examples like the minimum wage or interest-rate ceilings. Show graphically that if the demand for unskilled workers is price-elastic, a minimum wage will decrease the total earnings (wage times quantity demanded of labor) of unskilled workers.

7. Consider what would happen if a tariff of $2000 were imposed on imported automobiles. Show the impact of this tariff on the supply and the demand, and on the equilibrium price and quantity, of American automobiles. Explain why American auto companies and autoworkers often support import restraints on automobiles.

8. Elasticity problems:

   a. The world demand for crude oil is estimated to have a short-run price elasticity of 0.05. If the initial price of oil were $3 per barrel, what would be the effect on oil price and quantity of an embargo that curbed world oil supply by 5 percent? (For this problem, assume that the oil-supply curve is completely inelastic.)

   b. To show that elasticities are independent of units, refer to Table 3-1. Calculate the elasticities between each demand pair. Change the price units from dollars to pennies; change the quantity units from millions of boxes to tons, using the conversion of 10,000 boxes equals 1 ton. Then recalculate the elasticities in the first two rows. Explain why you get the same answer.

   c. Demand studies find that the price elasticity of demand for crack is 0.1. Suppose that half the crack users in New York City support their habit by criminal activities. Using supply-and-demand analysis, show the impact on crime in New York City of a tough law-enforcement program that decreases the supply of crack into the New York market by 50 percent. What would be the effect on criminal activities and on drug use of legalizing crack if this lowered the price of crack by 90 percent? Discuss the impact on price and addiction of a program that successfully rehabilitated half of the crack users.

   d. Can you explain why farmers during a depression might approve of a government program requiring that pigs be killed and buried under the ground?

CHAPTER 5
DEMAND AND CONSUMER BEHAVIOR

What is a cynic? A man who knows the price of everything and the value of nothing.

Oscar Wilde

Each day we make countless decisions about how to allocate our scarce money and time. Should we eat breakfast or sleep late? Spend our evenings reading or visit with friends? Buy a new car or fix our old one? Spend our income today or save for the future? As we balance competing demands and desires, we make the choices that define our lives.

The results of these individual choices are what underlie the demand curves and price elasticities that we saw in earlier chapters. In this chapter we extend our survey of demand by looking at the basic principles of consumer choice and behavior. We shall see how the process of individuals' pursuing their most preferred bundle of consumption goods explains observed patterns of market demand, and we will learn how to measure the benefits that each of us receives from participating in a market economy.

CHOICE AND UTILITY THEORY

In explaining consumer behavior, *economics relies on the fundamental premise that people tend to choose those goods and services they value most highly.* To describe the way consumers choose among different consumption possibilities, economists a century ago developed the notion of *utility.* From the notion of utility, they were able to derive the demand curve and explain its properties.

What do we mean by "utility"? In a word, **utility** denotes satisfaction. More precisely, it refers to how consumers rank different goods and services. If basket A has higher utility than basket B for Smith, this ranking indicates that Smith prefers A over B. Often, it is convenient to think of utility as the subjective pleasure or usefulness that a person derives from consuming a good or service. But you should definitely resist the idea that utility is a psychological function or feeling that can be observed or measured. Rather, utility is a scientific construct that economists use to understand how rational consumers divide their limited resources among the commodities that provide them with satisfaction. *In the theory of demand, we say that people maximize their utility, which means that they choose the bundle of consumption goods that they most prefer.*

Marginal Utility and the Law of Diminishing Marginal Utility

How does utility apply to the theory of demand? Say that consuming the first unit of ice cream gives you a certain level of satisfaction or utility. Now imagine consuming a second unit. Your total utility goes up because the second unit of the good gives you some additional utility. What about adding a third and fourth unit of the same good? Eventually, if you eat enough ice cream, instead of adding to your satisfaction or utility, it makes you sick!

80

This leads us to the fundamental economic concept of marginal utility. When you eat an additional unit of ice cream, you will get some additional satisfaction or utility. The increment to your utility is called **marginal utility.**

The expression "marginal" is a key term in economics and always means "extra." Marginal utility denotes the additional utility arising from consumption of an additional unit of a commodity.

A century ago, when economists thought about utility, they enunciated the **law of diminishing marginal utility.** This law states that the amount of extra or marginal utility declines as a person consumes more and more of a good.

What is the reason for this law? Utility tends to increase as you consume more of a good. However, according to the law of diminishing marginal utility, as you consume more and more, your total utility will grow at a slower and slower rate. Growth in total utility slows because your marginal utility (the extra utility added by the last unit consumed of a good) diminishes as more of the good is consumed. The diminishing marginal utility results from the fact that your enjoyment of the good drops off as more and more of it is consumed.

The law of diminishing marginal utility states that, as the amount of a good consumed increases, the marginal utility of that good tends to diminish.

A Numerical Example

We can illustrate utility numerically as in Table 5-1. The table shows in column (2) that total utility (U) enjoyed increases as consumption (Q) grows, but it increases at a decreasing rate. Column (3) measures marginal utility as the extra utility gained when 1 extra unit of the good is consumed. Thus as the individual consumes 2 units, the marginal utility is $7 - 4 = 3$ units of utility (call these units "utils").

Focus next on column (3). The fact that marginal utility declines with higher consumption illustrates the law of diminishing marginal utility.

Figure 5-1 on page 82 shows graphically the data on total utility and marginal utility from Table 5-1. In part (a), the gray blocks add up to the total utility at each level of consumption. In addition, the smooth gray curve shows the smoothed utility level for fractional units of consumption. It shows utility

(1) Quantity of a good consumed Q	(2) Total utility U	(3) Marginal utility MU
0	0	
		4
1	4	
		3
2	7	
		2
3	9	
		1
4	10	
		0
5	10	

TABLE 5-1. Utility Rises with Consumption
As we consume more of a good or service like pizza or concerts, total utility increases. The increment of utility from one unit to the next is the "marginal utility"—the extra utility added by the last extra unit consumed. By the law of diminishing marginal utility, the marginal utility falls with increasing levels of consumption.

increasing, but at a decreasing rate. Figure 5-1(b) depicts marginal utilities. Each of the gray blocks of marginal utility is the same size as the corresponding block of total utility in (a). The straight black line in (b) is the smoothed curve of marginal utility.

The law of diminishing marginal utility implies that the marginal utility (MU) curve in Figure 5-1(b) must slope downward. This is exactly equivalent to saying that the total utility curve in Figure 5-1(a) must look concave, like a dome.

Relationship of Total and Marginal Utility. Using Figure 5-1, we can easily see that the total utility of consuming a certain amount is equal to the sum of the marginal utilities up to that point. For example, assume that 3 units are consumed. Column (2) of Table 5-1 shows that the total utility is 9 units. In column (3) we see that the sum of the marginal utilities of the first 3 units is also $4 + 3 + 2 = 9$ units.

Examining Figure 5-1(b), we see that the total area under the marginal utility curve at a particular level of consumption—as measured either by blocks or by the area under the smooth MU curve—must equal the height of the total utility curve shown for the same number of units in Figure 5-1(a).

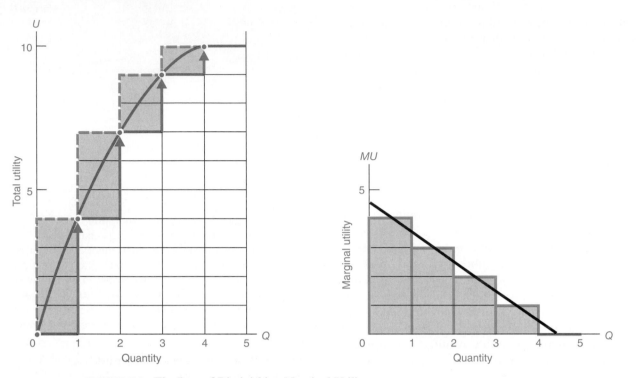

(a) Total Utility

(b) Marginal Utility

FIGURE 5-1. The Law of Diminishing Marginal Utility

Total utility in (**a**) rises with consumption, but it rises at a decreasing rate, showing diminishing marginal utility. This observation led early economists to formulate the law of downward-sloping demand.

The gray blocks show the extra utility added by each new unit. The fact that total utility increases at a decreasing rate is shown in (**b**) by the declining steps of marginal utility. If we make our units smaller, the steps in total utility are smoothed out and total utility becomes the smooth gray curve in (**a**). Moreover, smoothed marginal utility, shown in (**b**) by the black downward-sloping smooth curve, becomes indistinguishable from the slope of the smooth curve in (**a**).

Whether we examine this relationship using tables or graphs, we see that total utility is the sum of all the marginal utilities that were added from the beginning.

History of Utility Theory

Modern utility theory has its source in *utilitarianism,* which has been one of the major currents of Western intellectual thought for the last two centuries. The notion of utility arose soon after 1700, as the basic ideas of mathematical probability were being developed. Thus Daniel Bernoulli, a member of a brilliant Swiss family of mathematicians, observed in 1738 that people act as if the dollar they

stand to gain in a fair bet is worth less to them than the dollar they stand to lose. This means that they are averse to risk and that successive new dollars of wealth bring them smaller and smaller increments of true utility.[1]

An early introduction of the utility notion into the social sciences was accomplished by the English philosopher Jeremy Bentham (1748–1831). After studying legal theory, and under the influence of Adam Smith's doctrines, Bentham turned to the study of the principles necessary for drawing up

---

[1] The economics of risk, uncertainty, and gambling are examined in Chapter 11.

social legislation. He proposed that society should be organized on the "principle of utility," which he defined as the "property in any object . . . to produce pleasure, good or happiness or to prevent . . . pain, evil or unhappiness."[2] All legislation, according to Bentham, should be designed on utilitarian principles, to promote "the greatest happiness of the greatest number." Among his other legislative proposals were quite modern-sounding ideas about crime and punishment in which he suggested that raising the "pain" to the criminal by harsh punishments would deter crimes.

Bentham's views about utility seem elementary to many people today. But they were revolutionary 200 years ago because they emphasized that social and economic policies should be designed to achieve certain practical results, whereas earlier justifications were generally based upon tradition, the will of the monarch, or religious doctrines. Today, many political thinkers defend their legislative proposals with utilitarian notions of what will make the largest number of people best off.

The next step in the development of utility theory came when the neoclassical economists—such as William Stanley Jevons (1835–1882)—extended Bentham's utility concept to explain consumer behavior. Jevons thought economic theory was a "calculus of pleasure and pain," and he showed that rational people would base their consumption decisions on the extra or marginal utility of each good. Many utilitarians of the nineteenth century believed that utility was a psychic reality—directly and cardinally measurable, like length or temperature. They looked to their own sentiments for affirmation of the law of diminishing marginal utility.

Ordinal Utility. Economists today generally reject the notion of a cardinal, measurable utility that is attached to consumption of ordinary goods like shoes or pasta. Instead, we can easily derive demand curves without ever mentioning the notion of utility. What counts for modern demand theory is the principle of **ordinal utility.** Under this approach, we examine only the preference ranking of bundles of commodities. Ordinal utility asks, "Is A preferred to B?" Using such preference rankings,

we can establish firmly the general properties of market demand curves described in this chapter and in its appendix.[3]

EQUIMARGINAL PRINCIPLE: EQUAL MARGINAL UTILITIES PER DOLLAR FOR EVERY GOOD

We now want to use utility theory to explain consumer demand and to understand the nature of demand curves. For this purpose, we need to know the condition under which I, as a consumer, am most satisfied with my market basket of consumption goods. We say that a consumer attempts to maximize his or her utility, which means that the consumer chooses the most preferred bundle of goods from what is available.

Can we see what a rule for such an optimal decision would be? Certainly I would not expect that the last egg I am buying brings exactly the same marginal utility as the last pair of shoes I am buying, for shoes cost much more per unit than eggs. A more sensible rule would be: If good A costs twice as much as good B, then buy good A only when its marginal utility is at least twice as great as good B's marginal utility.

This leads to the *equimarginal principle* that I should arrange my consumption so that every single good is bringing me the same marginal utility per dollar of expenditure. In such a situation, I am attaining maximum satisfaction or utility from my purchases.

Equimarginal principle: The fundamental condition of maximum satisfaction or utility is the equimarginal principle. It states that a consumer having a fixed income and facing given market prices of goods

---

[2] *An Introduction to the Principles of Morals* (1789). Note that the term "utility" was used by Bentham in quite a different way from today's usage, in which utility is something that is useful.

[3] A statement such as "Situation A is preferred to situation B"—which does not require that we know how much A is preferred to B—is called *ordinal*, or dimensionless. Ordinal variables are ones that we can rank in order, but for which there is no measure of the quantitative difference between the situations. We might rank pictures in an exhibition by order of beauty without having a quantitative measure of beauty.

For certain special situations the concept of *cardinal*, or dimensional, utility is useful. An example of a cardinal measure comes when we say that a substance at 100 K (kelvin) is twice as hot as one at 50 K. People's behavior under conditions of uncertainty is today often analyzed using a cardinal concept of utility. This topic will be examined further in Chapter 11.

will achieve maximum satisfaction or utility when the marginal utility of the last dollar spent on each good is exactly the same as the marginal utility of the last dollar spent on any other good.

Why must this condition hold? If any one good gave more marginal utility per dollar, I would increase my utility by taking money away from other goods and spending more on that good—until the law of diminishing marginal utility drove its marginal utility per dollar down to equality with that of other goods. If any good gave less marginal utility per dollar than the common level, I would buy less of it until the marginal utility of the last dollar spent on it had risen back to the common level.[4] The common marginal utility per dollar of all commodities in consumer equilibrium is called the *marginal utility of income.* It measures the additional utility that would be gained if the consumer could enjoy an extra dollar's worth of consumption.

This fundamental condition of consumer equilibrium can be written in terms of the marginal utilities (*MU*s) and prices (*P*s) of the different goods in the following compact way:[5]

$$\frac{MU_{\text{good 1}}}{P_1} = \frac{MU_{\text{good 2}}}{P_2}$$

$$= \frac{MU_{\text{good 3}}}{P_3} = \cdots$$

$$= MU \text{ per \$ of income}$$

---

[4] At a few places in economics the indivisibility of units is important and cannot be glossed over. Thus, Cadillacs cannot be divided into arbitrarily small portions the way juice can. Suppose I buy one Cadillac, but definitely not two. Then the marginal utility of the first car is enough larger than the marginal utility of the same number of dollars spent elsewhere to induce me to buy this first unit. The marginal utility that the second Cadillac would bring is enough less to ensure I do not buy it. When indivisibility matters, our equality rule for equilibrium can be restated as an inequality rule.

[5] The discerning reader will wonder whether the following mathematical condition seems to imply cardinal, or dimensional, utility (see footnote 3). In fact it does not. An ordinal utility measure is one that we can stretch while always maintaining the same greater-than or less-than relationship (like measuring with a rubber band). If the utility scale is stretched (say, by doubling or multiplying times 3.1415), then you can see that all the numerators in the condition are changed by the same amount, so the consumer equilibrium condition still holds. This is shown in the appendix to this chapter by the use of indifference curves.

Why Demand Curves Slope Downward

Using the fundamental rule for consumer behavior, we can easily see why demand curves slope downward. For simplicity, hold the common marginal utility per dollar of income constant. Then increase the price of good 1. With no change in quantity consumed, the first ratio (i.e., $MU_{\text{good 1}}/P_1$) will be below the *MU* per dollar of all other goods. The consumer will therefore have to readjust the consumption of good 1. The consumer will do this by (*a*) lowering the consumption of good 1, (*b*) thereby raising the *MU* of good 1, until (*c*) at the new, reduced level of consumption of good 1, the new marginal utility per dollar spent on good 1 is again equal to the *MU* per dollar spent on other goods.

Therefore, a higher price for a good reduces the consumer's desired consumption of that commodity; this shows why demand curves slope downward.

Leisure and the Optimal Allocation of Time

A Spanish toast to a friend wishes "health, wealth, and the time to enjoy them." This saying aptly captures the idea that we must allocate our time budgets in much the same way as we do our dollar budgets. Indeed, our time budget is even more constrained than our dollar budget because we have only 24 hours a day whether we are rich or poor in dollars. Let's see how our earlier analysis of allocating scarce dollars applies to time.

Consider leisure, often defined as "time which one can spend as one pleases." Leisure brings out our personal eccentricities. The seventeenth-century philosopher Francis Bacon held that the purest of human pleasures was gardening. The modern British statesman Winston Churchill wrote of his holiday: "I have had a delightful month building a cottage and dictating a book: 200 bricks and 2000 words a day."

Whatever *your* tastes, the principles of utility theory can apply well. Suppose that, after satisfying all your obligations, you have 3 hours a day of free time and can devote it to gardening, laying bricks, or writing history. What is the best way to allocate your time? Let's ignore the possibility that time spent on some of these activities might be an investment that will enhance your earning power in the future. Rather, assume that these are all pure consumption or utility-yielding pursuits. The principles of consumer choice suggest that you will make the best use of your time when you equalize the marginal utilities of the last minute spent on each activity.

To take another example, suppose you want to maximize your knowledge in your courses but you have only a limited amount of time available. Should you study each subject for the same amount of time? Surely not. You may find that an equal study time for economics, history, and chemistry will not yield the same amount of knowledge in the last minute. If the last minute produces a greater marginal knowledge in chemistry than in history, you would raise your total knowledge by shifting additional minutes from history to chemistry, and so on, until the last minute yields the same incremental knowledge in each subject.

The same rule of maximum utility per hour can be applied to many different areas of life, including charitable activities, improving the environment, or losing weight. It is not merely a law of economics. It is a law of rational choice.

 Consumers as wizards? A word of caution is in order about how we view consumers. We do not expect consumers to be wizards. They may make most decisions in a routine and unthinking way. What is assumed is that consumers are fairly consistent in their tastes and actions—that they do not flail around in unpredictable ways, making themselves miserable by persistent errors of judgment or arithmetic. If enough people act consistently, avoiding erratic changes in buying behavior and generally choosing their most preferred commodities, our scientific theory will provide a reasonably good approximation to the facts.

AN ALTERNATIVE APPROACH: SUBSTITUTION EFFECT AND INCOME EFFECT

The concept of marginal utility has helped explain the fundamental law of downward-sloping demand. But over the last few decades, economists have developed an alternative approach to analysis of demand—one that makes no mention of marginal utility. This alternative approach uses "indifference curves," which are explained in the appendix to this chapter, to rigorously and consistently produce the major propositions about consumer behavior. This approach also helps explain the factors that tend to make the responsiveness of quantity demanded to price—the price elasticity of demand—large or small.

Indifference analysis asks about the substitution effect and the income effect of a change in price. By looking at these, we can see why the quantity demanded of a good declines as its price rises.

Substitution Effect

The first factor explaining downward-sloping demand curves—the substitution effect—is obvious. If the price of coffee goes up while other prices do not, then coffee has become relatively more expensive.

When coffee becomes a more expensive beverage, less coffee and more tea or cola will be bought. Similarly, because sending electronic mail is cheaper and quicker than sending letters through the regular mail, people are increasingly relying on electronic mail for correspondence. More generally, the **substitution effect** says that when the price of a good rises, consumers will tend to substitute other goods for the more expensive good in order to satisfy their desires more inexpensively.

Consumers, then, behave the way businesses do when the rise in price of an input causes firms to substitute low-priced inputs for high-priced inputs. By this process of substitution, businesses can produce a given amount of output at the least total cost. Similarly, when consumers substitute toward less expensive goods, they are buying a given amount of satisfaction at less cost.

Income Effect

In addition, when your money income is fixed, a price increase is just like a reduction in your "real income," which signifies the actual amount of goods and services that your money income can buy. When a price rises and money incomes are fixed, consumers' real incomes fall and they are likely to buy less of almost all goods (including the good whose price has risen). This produces the **income effect**, which denotes the impact of a price change on a good's quantity demanded that results from the effect of the price change on consumers' real incomes. Because a lower real income generally leads to lower consumption, the income effect will normally reinforce the substitution effect in making the demand curve downward-sloping.

To obtain a quantitative measure of the income effect, we examine a good's **income elasticity.** This term denotes the percentage change in quantity demanded divided by the percentage change in income, holding other things, such as prices, constant. High income elasticities, such as are found for airline travel or yachts, indicate that the demand for these goods rises rapidly as income increases. Low income elasticities, such as for food or cigarettes, denote a weak response of demand as income rises.

Income and substitution effects combine to determine the major characteristics of different commodities. Under some circumstances the resulting demand curve is very price-elastic, as where the consumer has been spending a good deal on the commodity and ready substitutes are available. In this case both the income and the substitution effects are strong and the quantity demanded responds strongly to a price increase.

But consider a commodity like salt, which requires only a small fraction of the consumer's budget. Salt is not easily replaceable by other items and is needed in small amounts to complement more important items. For salt, both income and substitution effects are small, and demand will tend to be price-inelastic.

FROM INDIVIDUAL TO MARKET DEMAND

Having analyzed the principles underlying a single individual's demand for coffee or electronic mail, we next examine how the entire market demand derives from the individual demand. *The demand curve for a good for the entire market is obtained by summing up the quantities demanded by all the consumers.* Each consumer has a demand curve along which the quantity demanded can be plotted against the price; it generally slopes downward and to the right. If all consumers were exactly alike in their demands and if there were 1 million consumers, we could think of the market demand curve as a million-fold enlargement of each consumer's demand curve.

But people are not all exactly alike. Some have high incomes, some low. Some greatly desire coffee; others prefer cola. To obtain the total market curve, all we have to do is calculate the sum total of what all the different consumers will consume at any given price. We then plot that total amount as a point on the market demand curve. Or, if we like, we might construct a numerical demand table by summing the quantities demanded for all individuals at each market price.[6]

The market demand curve is the sum of individual demands at each price. Figure 5-2 shows how to add individual *dd* demand curves horizontally to get the market *DD* demand curve.

Demand Shifts

We know that changes in the price of coffee affect the quantity of coffee demanded. We know this from budget studies, from historical experience, and from examining our own behavior. We discussed briefly in Chapter 3 some of the important nonprice determinants of demand. We now review the earlier discussion in light of our analysis of consumer behavior.

An increase in income tends to increase the amount we are willing to buy of most goods. Necessities tend to be less responsive than most goods to income changes, while luxuries tend to be more responsive to income. And there are a few anomalous goods, known as inferior goods, for which purchases may shrink as incomes increase because people can afford to replace them with other, more desirable goods. Soup bones, intercity bus travel, and used TVs are examples of inferior goods for many Americans today.

What does all this mean in terms of the demand curve? The demand curve shows how the quantity of a good demanded responds to a change in its own price. But the demand is also affected by the prices of other goods, by consumer incomes, and by special influences. The demand curve was drawn on the assumption that these other things were held constant. But what if these other things change? Then the whole demand curve will shift to the right or to the left.

Figure 5-3 illustrates changes in factors affecting demand. Given people's incomes and the prices for other goods, we can draw the demand curve for coffee as *DD.* Assume that price and quantity are at point *A.* Suppose that incomes rise while the prices of coffee and other goods are unchanged. Because coffee is a normal good with a positive income elasticity, people will increase their purchases of coffee. Hence the demand curve for coffee will shift to the

---

[6] Here and in other chapters, we label *individual* demand and supply curves with lowercase letters (*dd* and *ss*), while using uppercase letters (*DD* and *SS*) for the *market* demand and supply curves.

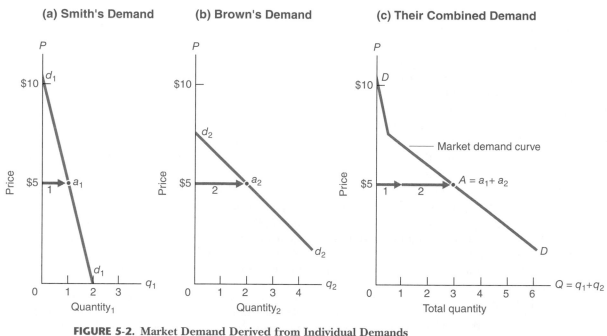

FIGURE 5-2. Market Demand Derived from Individual Demands

We add all individual consumers' demand curves to get the market demand curve. At each price, such as $5, we add quantities demanded by each person to get the market quantity demanded. The figure shows how, at a price of $5, we add horizontally Smith's 1 unit demanded to Brown's 2 units to get the market demand of 3 units.

right, say, to $D'D'$, with A' indicating the new quantity demanded of coffee. If incomes should fall, then we would expect a reduction in demand and in quantity bought. This downward shift we illustrate by $D''D''$ and by A''.

Substitutes and Complements

Everyone knows that raising the price of beef will decrease the amount of beef demanded. We have seen that it will also affect the demand for other commodities. For example, a higher price for beef will increase the demand for substitutes like chicken. A higher beef price may lower the demand for goods like hamburger buns and ketchup that are used along with beef hamburgers. It will probably have little effect on the demand for economics textbooks.

We say, therefore, that beef and chicken are substitute products. Goods A and B are **substitutes** if an increase in the price of good A will increase the demand for substitute good B. Hamburgers and hamburger buns, or cars and gasoline, on the other hand, are complementary products; they are called **complements** because an increase in the price of good A causes a decrease in the demand for its complementary good B. In between are **independent**

FIGURE 5-3. Demand Curve Shifts with Changes in Income or in Other Goods' Prices

As incomes increase, consumers generally want more of a good, thus increasing demand or shifting demand outward (explain why higher incomes shift DD to $D'D'$). Similarly, a rise in the price of a substitute good increases or shifts out the demand curve (e.g., from DD to $D'D'$). Explain why a decrease in income would generally shift demand to $D''D''$. Why would a decrease in chicken prices shift hamburger demand to $D''D''$?

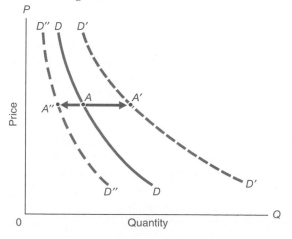

goods, such as beef and textbooks, for which a price change for one good has no effect on the demand for the other. Try classifying the pairs turkey and cranberry sauce, oil and coal, college and textbooks, shoes and shoelaces, salt and shoelaces.

Say Figure 5-3 represented the demand for beef. A fall in the price of chickens may well cause consumers to buy less beef; the beef demand curve would therefore shift to the left, say, to $D''D''$. But what if the price of hamburger buns were to fall? The resulting change on DD, if there is one, will be in the direction of increased beef purchases, a rightward shift of the demand curve. Why do we see this difference in response? Because chicken is a rival or substitute product for beef, while hamburger buns are complements to beef.

Review of key concepts:

- The substitution effect occurs when a higher price leads to substitution of other goods for the good whose price has risen.
- The income effect is the change in the quantity demanded of a good because the change in its price has the effect of changing a consumer's real income.
- Income elasticity is the percentage change in quantity demanded of a good divided by the percentage change in income.
- Goods are substitutes if an increase in the price of one increases the demand for the other.
- Goods are complements if an increase in the price of one decreases the demand for the other.
- Goods are independent if a price change for one has no effect on the demand for the other.

Empirical Estimates of Price and Income Elasticities

For many economic applications, it is essential to have numerical estimates of price elasticities. For example, an automobile manufacturer will want to know the impact on sales of the higher car prices that result from installation of costly pollution-control equipment; a college needs to know the impact of higher tuition rates on student applications; and a publisher will calculate the impact of higher textbook prices on its sales. All these applications require a numerical estimate of price elasticity.

Commodity	Price elasticity
Tomatoes	4.60
Green peas	2.80
Legal gambling	1.90
Taxi service	1.20
Furniture	1.00
Movies	0.87
Shoes	0.70
Legal services	0.61
Medical insurance	0.31
Bus travel	0.20
Residential electricity	0.13

TABLE 5-2. Selected Estimates of Price Elasticities of Demand

Estimates of price elasticities of demand show a wide range of variation. Elasticities are generally high for goods for which ready substitutes are available, like tomatoes or peas. Low price elasticities exist for those goods like electricity which are essential to daily life and which have no close substitutes. [Source: Heinz Kohler, *Intermediate Microeconomics: Theory and Applications,* 2d ed. (Scott Foresman, New York, 1986).]

Similar decisions depend on income elasticities. A government planning its road or rail network will estimate the impact of rising incomes on automobile travel; the federal government must calculate the effect of higher incomes on energy consumption in designing policies for air pollution or global warming; in determining the necessary investments for generating capacity, electrical utilities require income elasticities for estimating electricity consumption.

Economists have developed useful statistical techniques for estimating price and income elasticities. The quantitative estimates are derived from market data on quantities demanded, prices, incomes, and other variables. Tables 5-2 and 5-3 show selected estimates of elasticities.

THE ECONOMICS OF ADDICTION

In a free-market economy, government generally lets people decide what to buy with their money. If some individuals want to eat ice cream rather than pizza, we assume that they know what is best for them and that in the interests of personal freedom the government should respect their preferences. In some cases, but sparingly and with great hesitation, the government decides to overrule private adult decisions. These are cases of *merit goods,* whose consumption is thought intrinsically worthwhile (to be contrasted with *demerit goods,* whose consumption is deemed harmful). For these goods, we recognize that some consumption activities have such serious effects that overriding private decisions may be desirable. Today, most societies provide for free public education and emergency health care; on the other hand, society also penalizes or forbids consumption of such harmful substances as cigarettes, alcohol, and heroin.

One of the most controversial cases of demerit goods concerns addiction. An addictive substance is one for which the desire to consume depends significantly on past consumption. The hooked smoker, the addicted crack user, may regret bitterly the acquired habit; but, such is the nature of addiction, one cannot resist the habit after it has become established. A regular user of cigarettes or heroin is much more likely to desire these substances than is a nonuser. Moreover, for highly addictive goods, demand is likely to be quite price-inelastic. By contrast, for conventional goods, demands today are not likely to depend so directly on consumption patterns yesterday.

TABLE 5-3. Income Elasticities for Selected Products
Income elasticities are high for luxuries, whose consumption grows rapidly relative to income. Negative income elasticities are found for *inferior goods,* whose demand falls as income rises. Demand for many staple commodities, like clothing, grows proportionally with income. [Source: Heinz Kohler, *Intermediate Microeconomics: Theory and Applications,* 2d ed. (Scott Foresman, New York, 1986).]

Commodity	Income elasticity
Automobiles	2.50
Owner-occupied housing	1.50
Furniture	1.50
Books	1.40
Restaurant meals	1.00
Clothing	1.00
Physicians' services	0.75
Tobacco	0.64
Eggs	0.37
Margarine	−0.20
Pig products	−0.20
Flour	−0.36

The markets for addictive substances are big business. Annual cigarette expenditures today are around $50 billion, while those on alcohol are about $30 billion. Numbers for illegal drugs are obviously conjectural, but estimates of total spending range from $20 to $50 billion annually. Consumption of these substances raises major public policy issues because addictive substances may harm the users and often impose costs and harms on society. The harms to users include early mortality and a wide range of medical problems in the case of cigarettes; 10,000 highway fatalities a year attributed to alcohol; binges and psychosis in the use of crack cocaine; and failures in school, job, and family, along with high levels of AIDS, from intravenous heroin use. Harms to society include the predatory crime that addicts of high-priced drugs engage in, the costs of providing medical care to unhealthy drug users, and the rapid spread of communicable disease, especially AIDS and pneumonia.

One policy approach, often followed in the United States, is to prohibit the sale and use of addictive substances and to enforce prohibition with criminal sanctions. Economically, prohibition can be interpreted as a sharp upward shift in the supply curve. After the upward shift, the price of the addictive substance is much higher. During Prohibition (1920–1933), alcohol prices were approximately 3 times higher than before. Estimates are that cocaine currently sells for at least 20 times its free-market price.

But what has happened to quantity demanded, to the use, of addictive substances? And how does the prohibition affect the injuries to self and to society? To answer these questions, we need to consider the nature of the demand for addictive substances. The evidence indicates that casual consumers of illegal drugs have cheap substitutes like alcohol and tobacco and thus will have relatively high price elasticity of demand. By contrast, hard-core users are often addicted to particular substances and have price-inelastic demands.

One possible outcome is shown in Figure 5-4. This illustrates the impact of moving from legalized drugs to drug prohibition by tightening supply from *SS* to *S'S'* for the hard-core users of a highly addictive substance like heroin. In this case, demand is highly price-inelastic. As a result of the shift in supply and rise in price, total spending on drugs increases sharply. For such drugs, the outlays may be so great

FIGURE 5-4. Demand for Addictive Substances by Hard-Core Users

Demand for addictive substances is very price-inelastic for hard-core users of drugs like heroin. As a result, if the street price rises after prohibition shifts supply from SS to $S'S'$, total spending on drugs will rise from $0HCG$ to $0ABF$. For drugs that are highly price-inelastic, this implies that spending on drugs will rise sharply when supply is restrained. What will happen to criminal activity after prohibition if a substantial fraction of the income of addicts is obtained by theft and prostitution? Can you see why some people would argue for reduced drug enforcement or even legalization in this case?

that the user engages in predatory crime. The results, in the view of two economists who have studied the subject, are that "the market in illegal drugs promotes crime, destroys inner cities, spreads AIDS, corrupts law enforcement officials and politicians, produces and exacerbates poverty, and erodes the moral fabric of society."[7]

Others argue that drug use is highly price-sensitive, especially for casual users, as is shown in Figure 5-5. For example, a teenager might experiment with an addictive substance if it is affordable, while a high price (accompanied by low availability) would be unlikely to tempt that person down the road to addiction. In this case, supply restraints are likely to both lower use sharply and reduce spending on addictive substances.

---

[7] The quote is from Jeffrey A. Miron and Jeffrey Zwiebel, "The Economic Case against Drug Prohibition," *Journal of Economic Perspectives* (Fall 1995), pp. 175–192, which is an excellent nontechnical survey of the economics of drug prohibition.

One of the major difficulties with regulating addictive substances comes because of the patterns of substitution. Many drugs appear to be close substitutes. As a result, experts caution, raising the price of one substance mainly serves to drive users to other harmful substances. For example, states that have criminal penalties for marijuana use tend to have higher teenage consumption of alcohol and tobacco.

Clearly, social policy toward addictive substances raises extremely complex issues. But the economic theory of demand provides some important insights into the impacts of alternative approaches. First, it suggests that raising the prices of harmful addictive substances can reduce the number of casual users who will be attracted into the market. Second, it cautions us that many of the negative consequences of illegal drugs result from the prohibition of addictive substances rather than from their consumption. Many thoughtful observers conclude with the paradoxical observation that the overall costs of addictive substances—to users, to other people, and to the ravaged inner cities in which the drug trade thrives—would be lower if government prohibition were relaxed and the resources currently devoted to supply restrictions were instead put into treatment and counseling.

THE PARADOX OF VALUE

More than two centuries ago, in *The Wealth of Nations*, Adam Smith posed the paradox of value:

> Nothing is more useful than water; but it will scarce purchase anything. A diamond, on the contrary, has scarce any value in use; but a very great quantity of other goods may frequently be had in exchange for it.

In other words, how is it that water, which is essential to life, has little value, while diamonds, which are generally used for conspicuous consumption, command an exalted price?

Although it troubled Adam Smith 200 years ago, we can today resolve this paradox as follows: "The supply and demand curves for water intersect at a very low price, while supply and demand for diamonds are such that their equilibrium price is very high." Having said that, we would naturally go on to ask, "But why do supply and demand for water intersect at such a low price?" The answer is that diamonds are very scarce and the cost of getting extra

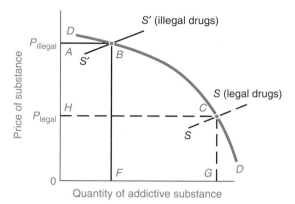

FIGURE 5-5. Demand for Addictive Substances by Casual Users

Demand may be quite elastic for casual users (those who are not addicted or for whom substitute products are readily available). In this case, restrictions or price increases will have significant impact on use. Moreover, because demand is price-elastic, total spending on drugs falls from 0*HCG* to 0*ABF* with restrictions. This depicts the argument of those who would severely limit the availability of addictive substances.

oncs is high, while water is relatively abundant and costs little in many areas of the world.

Yet this answer still does not reconcile the cost information with the equally valid fact that the world's water is vastly more critical than the world's supply of diamonds. We need to add a second truth: The total utility from water consumption does not determine its price or demand. Rather, water's price is determined by its marginal utility, by the usefulness of the last glass of water. Because there is so much water, the last glass sells for very little. Even though the first few drops are worth life itself, the last few are needed only for watering the lawn or washing the car. *We thus find that an immensely valuable commodity like water sells for next to nothing because its last drop is worth next to nothing.*

As one student put the matter: The theory of economic value is easy to understand if you just remember that in economics the tail wags the dog. It is the tail of marginal utility that wags the dog of prices and quantities.

We can resolve the paradox of value as follows: The more there is of a commodity, the less is the relative desirability of its last little unit. It is therefore clear why water has a low price and why an absolute necessity like air could become a free good. In both cases, it is the large quantities that pull the marginal utilities so far down and thus reduce the prices of these vital commodities.

CONSUMER SURPLUS

The paradox of value emphasizes that the recorded money value of a good (measured by price times quantity) may be very misleading as an indicator of the total economic value of that good. The measured economic value of the air we breathe is zero, yet air's contribution to welfare is immeasurably large.

The gap between the total utility of a good and its total market value is called **consumer surplus.** The surplus arises because we "receive more than we pay for" as a result of the law of diminishing marginal utility.

We have consumer surplus basically because we pay the same amount for each unit of a commodity that we buy, from the first to the last. We pay the same price for each egg or glass of water. Thus we pay for *each* unit what the *last* unit is worth. But by our fundamental law of diminishing marginal utility, the earlier units are worth more to us than the last. Thus, we enjoy a surplus of utility on each of these earlier units.

Figure 5-6 illustrates the concept of consumer surplus in the case where money provides a firm measuring rod for utility. Here, an individual consumes water, which has a price of $1 per gallon. This is shown by the horizontal rust line at $1 in Figure 5-6. The consumer considers how many gallon jugs to buy at that price. The first gallon is highly valuable, slaking extreme thirst, and the consumer is willing to pay $9 for it. But this first gallon costs only the market price of $1, so the consumer has gained a surplus of $8.

Consider the second gallon. This is worth $8 to the consumer, but again costs only $1, so the surplus is $7. And so on down to the ninth gallon, which is worth only 50 cents to the consumer, and so it is not bought. The consumer equilibrium comes at point *E*, where 8 gallons of water are bought at a price of $1 each.

But here we make an important discovery: Even though the consumer has paid only $8, the total value of the water is $44. This is obtained by adding up each of the marginal utility columns (= $9 + $8 + ··· + $2). Thus the consumer has gained a surplus of $36 over the amount paid.

Consumer Surplus for an Individual

FIGURE 5-6. Because of Diminishing Marginal Utility, Consumer's Satisfaction Exceeds What Is Paid

The downward-sloping demand for water reflects the diminishing marginal utility of water. Note how much excess or surplus satisfaction occurs from the earlier units. Adding up all the gray surpluses ($8 of surplus on unit 1 + $7 of surplus on unit 2 + · · · + $1 of surplus on unit 8), we obtain the total consumer surplus of $36 on water purchases.

In the simplified case seen here, the area between the demand curve and the price line is the total consumer surplus.

Figure 5-6 examines the case of a single consumer purchasing water. We can also apply the concept of consumer surplus to a market as a whole. The market demand curve in Figure 5-7 is the horizontal summation of the individual demand curves. The logic of the individual consumer surplus carries over to the market as a whole. The area of the market demand curve above the price line, shown as *NER* in Figure 5-7, represents the total consumer surplus.

Because consumers pay the price of the last unit for all units consumed, they enjoy a surplus of utility over cost. Consumer surplus measures the extra utility that consumers receive over what they pay for a commodity.

Applications of Consumer Surplus

The concept of consumer surplus is useful in helping evaluate many government decisions. For example, how can the government decide on the value of building a new highway or of preserving a recreation site? Suppose a new highway has been proposed. Being free to all, it will bring in no revenue. The value to users will be found in time saved or in safer trips and can be measured by the individual consumer surplus. To avoid difficult issues of interpersonal utility comparisons, we assume that there are 10,000 users, all identical in every respect.

By careful experimentation, we determine that each individual's consumer surplus is $350 for the highway. The highway will raise consumer economic welfare if its total cost is less than $3.5 million (10,000 × $350). Economists use consumer surplus when they are performing a *cost-benefit analysis*, which attempts to determine the costs and benefits of a

FIGURE 5-7. Total Consumer Surplus Is the Area under the Demand Curve and above the Price Line

The demand curve measures the amount consumers would pay for each unit consumed. Thus the total area under the demand curve (*0REM*) shows the total utility attached to the consumption of water. By subtracting the market cost of water to consumers (equal to *0NEM*), we obtain the consumer surplus from water consumption as the gray triangle *NER*. This device is useful for measuring the benefits of public goods and the losses from monopolies and import tariffs.

Consumer Surplus for a Market

government program. Generally, an economist would recommend that a free road should be built if its total consumer surplus exceeds its costs. Similar analyses have been used for environmental questions such as whether to preserve wilderness areas for recreation or whether to require new pollution-abatement equipment.

The concept of consumer surplus also points to the enormous privilege enjoyed by citizens of modern societies. Each of us enjoys a vast array of enormously valuable goods that can be bought at low prices. This is a humbling thought. If you know someone who is bragging about *his* economic productivity, or explaining how high *her* real wages are, suggest a moment of reflection. If they were transported with their specialized skills to an uninhabited desert island, how much would their wages buy? Indeed, without capital machinery, without the cooperation of others, and without the technological knowledge which each generation inherits from the past, how much could any of us produce? It is only too clear that all of us reap the benefits of an eco-

nomic world we never made. As the great British sociologist L. T. Hobhouse said:

> The organizer of industry who thinks that he has "made" himself and his business has found a whole social system ready to his hand in skilled workers, machinery, a market, peace and order—a vast apparatus and a pervasive atmosphere, the joint creation of millions of men and scores of generations. Take away the whole social factor and we [are] but . . . savages living on roots, berries, and vermin.

We have now completed our survey of how consumer preferences interact with prices and incomes to determine the demand for goods and services. But what of business? What of the production and supply of the goods that consumers demand? The next two chapters turn to this other partner in supply and demand. Once our survey of business decisions is complete, we will have a fuller understanding of the forces that lie behind the two curves that dance through the pages of textbooks and indeed through economic life itself.

SUMMARY

1. Market demands or demand curves are explained as stemming from the process of individuals' choosing their most preferred bundle of consumption goods and services.

2. Economists explain consumer demand by the concept of utility, which denotes the relative satisfaction that a consumer obtains from using different commodities. The additional satisfaction obtained from consuming an additional unit of a good is given the name *marginal utility*, where "marginal" means the extra or incremental utility. The law of diminishing marginal utility states that as the amount of a commodity consumed increases, the marginal utility of the last unit consumed tends to decrease.

3. Economists assume that consumers allocate their limited incomes so as to obtain the greatest satisfaction or utility. To maximize utility, a consumer must satisfy the *equimarginal principle* that the marginal utilities of the

last dollar spent on each and every good must be equal.

Only when the marginal utility per dollar is equal for apples, bacon, coffee, and everything else will the consumer attain the greatest satisfaction from a limited dollar income. But be careful to note that the marginal utility of a \$50-per-ounce bottle of perfume is not equal to the marginal utility of a 50-cent glass of cola. Rather, their marginal utilities divided by price per unit are all equal in the consumer's optimal allocation. That is, their marginal utilities per last dollar, *MU/P*, are equalized.

4. Equal marginal utility per unit of resource is a fundamental rule of choice that transcends demand theory and dollars. If you want to allocate any limited resource among competing uses, you can benefit by transferring from the low marginal advantage per unit of resource to the high marginal advantage until a final equilib-

rium is reached at which all marginal advantages per unit of resource have become equal. An important application of this rule is the use of time.

5. The market demand curve for all consumers is derived by adding horizontally the separate demand curves of each consumer. A demand curve can shift for many reasons. For example, a rise in income will normally shift *DD* rightward, thus increasing demand; a rise in the price of a substitute good (e.g., chicken for beef) will also create a similar upward shift in demand; a rise in the price of a complementary good (e.g., hamburger buns for beef) will in turn cause the *DD* curve to shift downward and leftward. Still other factors—changing tastes, population, or expectations—can affect demand.

6. We can gain added insight into the factors that cause downward-sloping demand by separating the effect of a price rise into substitution and income effects. (*a*) The substitution effect occurs when a higher price leads to substitution of other goods to meet satisfactions; (*b*) the income effect means that a price increase lowers real income and thereby reduces the desired consumption of most commodities. For most goods, substitution and income effects of a price increase reinforce one another and lead to the law of downward-sloping demand. We measure the quantitative responsiveness of demand to income by the income elasticity, which measures the percentage change in quantity demanded divided by the percentage change in income.

7. Remember that it is the tail of marginal utility that wags the market dog of prices and quantities. This point is emphasized by the concept of *consumer surplus*. We pay the same price for the last quart of milk as for the first. But, because of the law of diminishing marginal utility, marginal utilities of earlier units are greater than that of the last unit. This means that we would have been willing to pay more than the market price for each of the earlier units. The excess of total value over market value is called consumer surplus. Consumer surplus reflects the benefit we gain from being able to buy all units at the same low price. In simplified cases, we can measure consumer surplus as the area between the demand curve and the price line. It is a concept relevant for many public decisions—such as deciding when the community should incur the heavy expenses of a road or bridge or set aside land for a wilderness area.

CONCEPTS FOR REVIEW

utility, marginal utility
utilitarianism
law of diminishing marginal utility
demand shifts from income and
    other sources
ordinal utility

equimarginal principle of equal *MU*
    of last dollar spent on each good:
    $MU_1/P_1 = MU_2/P_2 = \cdots$
    $= MU$ per \$ of income
market demand vs. individual
    demand

income elasticity
substitutes, complements, independent goods
substitution effect and income effect
merit goods, demerit goods
paradox of value
consumer surplus

QUESTIONS FOR DISCUSSION

1. Explain the meaning of utility. What is the difference between total utility and marginal utility? Explain the law of diminishing marginal utility and give a numerical example.

2. Each week, Tom Wu buys two hamburgers at \$2 each, eight cokes at \$0.50 each, and eight slices of pizza at \$1 each, but he buys no hot dogs at \$1.50 each. What can you deduce about Tom's marginal utility for each of the four goods?

3. Which pairs of the following goods would you classify as complementary, substitute, or independent goods:

beef, ketchup, lamb, cigarettes, gum, pork, radio, television, air travel, bus travel, taxis, and paperbacks? Illustrate the resulting shift in the demand curve for one good when the price of another good goes up. How would a change in income affect the demand curve for air travel? The demand curve for bus travel?

4. Why is it wrong to say, "Utility is maximized when the marginal utilities of all goods are exactly equal"? Correct the statement and explain.

5. How much would you be willing to pay each year rather than give up *all* movies? How much do you

spend on movies? Estimate roughly your consumer surplus.

6. Consider the following table showing the utility of different numbers of days skied each year:

Number of days skied	Total utility ($)
0	0
1	30
2	55
3	73
4	88
5	98
6	98

Construct a table showing the marginal utility for each day of skiing. Assuming that there are 1 million people with preferences shown in the table, draw the market demand curve for ski days. If lift tickets cost $20 per day, what are the equilibrium price and quantity of days skied?

7. For each of the commodities in Table 5-2, calculate the impact of a doubling of price on quantity demanded. Similarly, for the goods in Table 5-3, what would be the impact of a 50 percent increase in consumer incomes?

8. As you add together the identical demand curves of more and more people (in a way similar to the procedure in Figure 5-2), the market demand curve becomes flatter and flatter on the same scale. Does this fact indicate that the elasticity of demand is becoming larger and larger? Explain your answer carefully.

9. An interesting application of supply and demand to addictive substances compares alternative techniques for supply restriction. For this problem, assume that the demand for addictive substances is inelastic.

   a. One approach (used today for heroin and cocaine and for alcohol during Prohibition) is to reduce supply at the nation's borders. Show how this raises price and increases the total income of the suppliers in the drug industry.

   b. An alternative approach (followed today for tobacco and alcohol) is to tax the goods heavily. Using the tax apparatus developed in Chapter 4, show how this reduces the total income of the suppliers in the drug industry.

   c. Comment on the difference between the two approaches.

10. Suppose you are very rich and very fat. Your doctor has advised you to limit your food intake to 2000 calories per day. What is your consumer equilibrium for food consumption?

APPENDIX 5
GEOMETRICAL ANALYSIS
OF CONSUMER EQUILIBRIUM

A century ago, the economist Vilfredo Pareto (1848–1923) discovered that all the important elements of demand theory could be analyzed without the utility concept. Pareto developed what are today called indifference curves. This appendix presents the modern theory of indifference analysis and then derives the major conclusions of consumer behavior with that new tool.

THE INDIFFERENCE CURVE

Start by assuming that you are a consumer who buys different combinations of two commodities, say, food and clothing, at a given set of prices. For each combination of the two goods, assume that you prefer one to the other or are indifferent between the pair. For example, when asked to choose between combination A of 1 unit of food and 6 units of clothing and combination B of 2 units of food and 3 of clothing, you might (1) prefer A to B, (2) prefer B to A, or (3) be indifferent between A and B.

Now suppose that A and B are equally good in your eyes—that you are indifferent as to which of them you receive. Let us consider some other combinations of goods about which you are likewise indifferent, as listed in the table for Figure 5A-1.

Figure 5A-1 shows these combinations diagrammatically. We measure units of clothing on one axis and units of food on the other. Each of our four combinations of goods is represented by its point, A,

B, C, D. But these four are by no means the only combinations among which you are indifferent. Another batch, such as 1½ units of food and 4 of clothing, might be ranked as equal to A, B, C, or D, and there are many others not shown. The curved contour of Figure 5A-1, linking up the four points, is an **indifference curve.** The points on the curve represent consumption bundles among which the consumer is indifferent; all are equally desirable.

Law of Substitution

Indifference curves are drawn as bowl-shaped, or convex to the origin. Hence, as you move downward and to the right along the curve—a movement that implies increasing the quantity of food and reducing the units of clothing—the curve becomes flatter. The curve is drawn in this way to illustrate a property that seems most often to hold true in reality and which we call the law of substitution:

The scarcer a good, the greater its relative substitution value; its marginal utility rises relative to the marginal utility of the good that has become plentiful.

Thus, in going from *A* to *B* in Figure 5A-1, you would swap 3 of your 6 clothing units for 1 extra food unit. But from *B* to C, you would sacrifice only 1 unit of your remaining clothing supply to obtain a third food unit—a 1-for-1 swap. For a fourth unit of food, you would sacrifice only ½ unit from your dwindling supply of clothing.

96

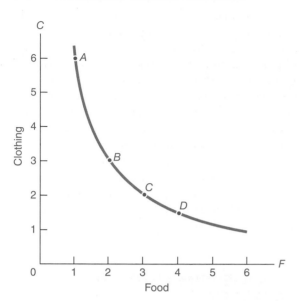

A Consumer's Indifference Curve

Indifference Combinations

	Food	Clothing
A	1	6
B	2	3
C	3	2
D	4	1½

FIGURE 5A-1. Indifference Curves for a Pair of Goods
Getting more of one good compensates for giving up some of the other. The consumer likes situation *A* exactly as much as *B*, *C*, or *D*. The food-clothing combinations that yield equal satisfaction are plotted as a smooth indifference curve. This is convex from below in accord with the law of substitution, which says that as you get more of a good, its substitution ratio, or the indifference-curve's slope, diminishes.

If we join the points *A* and *B* of Figure 5A-1, we find that the slope of the resulting line (neglecting its negative sign) has a value of 3. Join *B* and *C*, and the slope is 1; join *C* and *D*, and the slope is ½. These figures—3, 1, ½—are the *substitution ratios* (sometimes called the *marginal rates of substitution*) between the two goods. As the size of the movement along the curve becomes very small, the closer the substitution ratio comes to the actual slope of the indifference curve.

The slope of the indifference curve is the measure of the goods' relative marginal utilities, or of the substitution terms on which—for very small changes—the consumer would be willing to exchange a little less of one good in return for a little more of the other.

An indifference curve that is convex in the manner of Figure 5A-1 conforms to the law of substitution. As the amount of food you consume goes up—and the clothing goes down—food must become relatively cheaper and cheaper in order for you to be persuaded to take a little extra food in exchange for a little sacrifice of clothing. The precise shape and slope of an indifference curve will, of course, vary from one consumer to the next, but the typical shape will take the form shown in Figures 5A-1 and 5A-2.

The Indifference Map

The table in Figure 5A-1 is one of an infinite number of possible tables. We could start with a more preferred consumption situation and list some of the different combinations that would bring the consumer this higher level of satisfaction. One such table might have begun with 2 food units and 7 clothing units; another with 3 food units, 8 clothing units. Each table could be portrayed graphically; each has a corresponding indifference curve.

Figure 5A-2 shows four such curves; the curve from Figure 5A-1 is labeled U_3. This diagram is analogous to a geographical contour map. A person who walks along the path indicated by a particular height contour on such a map is neither climbing nor descending; similarly, the consumer who moves from one position to another along a single indifference curve enjoys neither increasing nor decreasing satisfaction from the change in consumption. Only a few

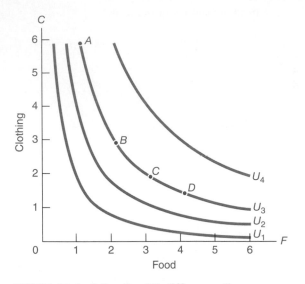

FIGURE 5A-2. A Family of Indifference Curves
The curves labeled U_1, U_2, U_3, and U_4 represent indifference curves. Which indifference curve is most preferred by the consumer?

of the possible indifference curves are shown in Figure 5A-2.

Note that as we increase both goods and thus move in a northeasterly direction across this map, we are crossing successive indifference curves; hence, we are reaching higher and higher levels of satisfaction (assuming that the consumer gets greater satisfaction from receiving increased quantities of both goods). Curve U_3 stands for a higher level of satisfaction than U_2; U_4, for a higher level of satisfaction than U_3; and so forth.

BUDGET LINE OR BUDGET CONSTRAINT

Now let us set a particular consumer's indifference map aside for a moment and give the consumer a fixed income. He has, say, $6 per day to spend, and he is confronted with fixed prices for each food and clothing unit—$1.50 for food, $1 for clothing. It is clear that he could spend his money on any one of a variety of alternative combinations of food and clothing. At one extreme, he could buy 4 food units and no clothing; at the other, 6 clothing units and no food. The table with Figure 5A-3 illustrates some of the possible ways in which he could allocate his $6.

Figure 5A-3 plots these five possibilities. Note that all the points lie on a straight line, labeled *NM*. Moreover, any other attainable point, such as $3\frac{1}{3}$ food units and 1 clothing unit, lies on *NM*. The straight budget line *NM* sums up all the possible combinations of the two goods that would just exhaust the consumer's income.[1] The slope of *NM* (neglecting its sign) is $\frac{3}{2}$, which is the ratio of the food price to the clothing price. The meaning of the slope is that, given these prices, every time our consumer gives up 3 clothing units (thereby dropping down 3 vertical units on the diagram), he can gain 2 units of food (i.e., move right 2 horizontal units).

We call *NM* the consumer's *budget line* or *budget constraint.*

THE EQUILIBRIUM POSITION OF TANGENCY

Now we are ready to put our two parts together. The axes of Figure 5A-3 are the same as those of Figures 5A-1 and 5A-2. We can superimpose the gray budget line *NM* upon this rust consumer indifference map, as shown in Figure 5A-4 on page 100. The consumer is free to move anywhere along *NM*. Positions to the right and above *NM* are not allowed because they require more than $6 of income; positions to the left and below *NM* are irrelevant because the consumer is assumed to spend the full $6.

Where will the consumer move? Obviously, to that point which yields the greatest satisfaction—that is, to the highest possible indifference curve—which in this case must be at the rust point *B*. At *B*, the budget line just touches, but does not cross, the indifference curve U_3. At this point of tangency, where the budget line just kisses but does not cross an indifference contour, is found the highest utility contour the consumer can reach.

Geometrically, the consumer is at equilibrium where the slope of the budget line (which is equal to

---

[1] This is so because, if we designate quantities of food and clothing bought as F and C, respectively, total expenditure on food must be 1.50F$ and total expenditure on clothing, 1C$. If daily income and expenditure are $6, the following equation must hold: $6 = \$1.50F + \$1C$. This is a linear equation, the equation of the budget line *NM*. Note:

Arithmetic slope of *NM* = $1.50 \div \$1$
= price of food $\div$ price of clothing

A Consumer's Budget Line

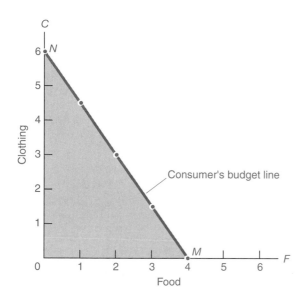

Alternative Consumption Possibilities

	Food	Clothing
M	4	0
	3	1½
	2	3
	1	4½
N	0	6

FIGURE 5A-3. Income Constrains Consumer Spending
The budget limit on expenditures can be seen in a numerical table. The total cost of each budget (reckoned as $1.50F + $1C$) adds up to exactly $6 of income. We can plot the budget constraint as a straight line whose absolute slope equals the P_F/P_C ratio. NM is the consumer's budget line. When income is $6, with food and clothing prices $1.50 and $1, the consumer can choose any point on this budget line. (Why is its slope $1.50/$1 = ³⁄₂?)

the ratio of food to clothing prices) is exactly equal to the slope of the indifference curve (which is equal to the ratio of the marginal utilities of the two goods).

Consumer equilibrium is attained at the point where the budget line is tangent to the highest indifference curve. At that point, the consumer's substitution ratio is just equal to the slope of the budget line.

Put differently, the substitution ratio, or the slope of the indifference curve, is the ratio of the marginal utility of food to the marginal utility of clothing. So our tangency condition is just another way of stating that the ratio of prices must be equal to the ratio of marginal utilities; in equilibrium, the consumer is getting the same marginal utility from the last penny spent on food as from the last penny spent on clothing. Therefore, we can derive the following equilibrium condition:

$$\frac{P_F}{P_C} = \text{substitution ratio} = \frac{MU_F}{MU_C}$$

This is exactly the same condition as we derived for utility theory in the main part of this chapter.

CHANGES IN INCOME AND PRICE

Two important applications of indifference curves are frequently used to consider the effects of (*a*) a change in money income and (*b*) a change in the price of one of the two goods.

Income Change

Assume, first, that the consumer's daily income is halved while the two prices remain unchanged. We could prepare another table, similar to the table for Figure 5A-3, showing the new consumption possibilities. Plotting these points on a diagram such as Figure 5A-5, we should find that the new budget line occupies the position $N'M'$ in Figure 5A-5. The line has made a parallel shift inward.[2] The consumer is

---

[2] The equation of the new $N'M'$ budget line is now $3 = $1.50F + $1C.$

Consumer's Equilibrium

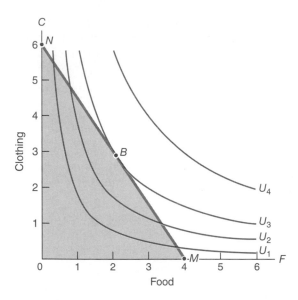

FIGURE 5A-4. Consumer's Most Preferred and Feasible Consumption Bundle Is Attained at B

We now combine the budget line and indifference contours on one diagram. The consumer reaches the highest indifference curve attainable with fixed income at point B, which is the tangency of the budget line with highest indifference curve. At tangency point B, substitution ratio equals price ratio P_F/P_C. This means that all goods' marginal utilities are proportional to their prices, with the marginal utility of the last dollar spent on every good being equalized.

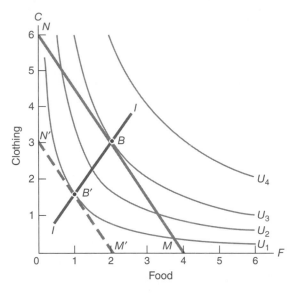

FIGURE 5A-5. Effect of Income Change on Equilibrium

An income change shifts the budget line in a parallel way. Thus, halving income to $3 shifts NM to N'M', moving equilibrium to B'. (Show what raising income to $8 would do to equilibrium. Estimate where the new tangency point would come.)

now free to move only along this new (and lower) budget line; to maximize satisfaction, he will move to the highest attainable indifference curve, or to point B'. A tangency condition for consumer equilibrium applies here as before.

Single Price Change

Now return our consumer to his previous daily income of $6, but assume that the price of food rises from $1.50 to $3 while the price of clothing is unchanged. Again we must examine the change in the budget line. This time we find that it has pivoted on point N and is now NM'', as illustrated in Figure 5A-6.[3]

The common sense of such a shift is clear. Since the price of clothing is unchanged, point N is just as

available as it was before. But since the price of food has risen, point M (which represents 4 food units) is no longer attainable. With food costing $3 per unit, only 2 units can now be bought with a daily income of $6. So the new budget line still passes through N, but it must pivot at N and pass through M'', which is to the left of M.

Equilibrium is now at B'', and we have a new tangency situation. Higher food price has definitely reduced food consumption, but clothing consumption may move in either direction. To clinch your understanding, work out the cases of an increase in income and a fall in the price of clothing or food.

DERIVING THE DEMAND CURVE

We are now in a position to derive the demand curve. Look carefully at Figure 5A-6. Note that as we increased the price of food from $1.50 per unit to $3 per unit, we kept other things constant. Tastes as represented by the indifference curves did not change, and money income and the price

---

[3] The budget equation of NM'' is now $6 = $3F + $1C.

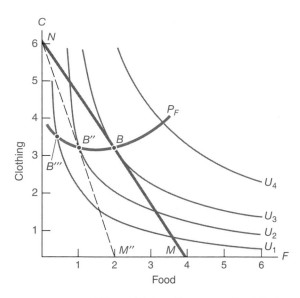

FIGURE 5A-6. Effect of Price Change on Equilibrium
A rise in the price of food makes the budget line pivot on *N*, rotating from *NM* to *NM″*. The new tangency equilibrium is at *B″*, with less food but either more or less clothing.

of clothing stayed constant. Therefore, we are in the ideal position to trace the demand curve for food. At a price of $1.50, the consumer buys 2 units of food, shown as equilibrium point *B*. When the price rises to $3 per unit, the food purchased is 1 unit, at equilibrium point *B″*. If you draw in the budget line corresponding to a price of $6 per unit of food, the equilibrium occurs at point *B‴*, and food purchases are 0.45 units.

Now plot the price of food against the purchases of food, again holding other things constant. You will have derived a neat downward-sloping demand curve from indifference curves. Note that we have done this without ever needing to mention the term "utility"—basing the derivation solely on measurable indifference curves.

SUMMARY TO APPENDIX

1. An indifference curve depicts the points of equally desirable consumption bundles. The indifference contour is usually drawn convex (or bowl-shaped) in accordance with the law of diminishing relative marginal utilities.

2. When a consumer has a fixed money income, all of which she spends, and is confronted with market prices of two goods, she is constrained to move along a straight line called the budget line or budget constraint. The line's slope will depend on the ratio of the two market prices; how far out it lies will depend on the size of her income.

3. The consumer will move along this budget line until reaching the highest attainable indifference curve. At this point, the budget line will touch, but not cross, an indifference curve. Hence, equilibrium is at the point of tangency, where the slope of the budget line (the ratio of the prices) exactly equals the slope of the indifference curve (the substitution ratio or the ratio of the marginal utilities of the two goods). This gives additional proof that, in equilibrium, marginal utilities are proportional to prices.

4. A fall in income will move the budget line inward in a parallel fashion, usually causing less of both goods to be bought. A change in the price of one good alone will, other things being constant, cause the budget line to pivot so as to change its slope. After a price or income change, the consumer will again attain a new tangency point of highest satisfaction. At every point of tangency, the marginal utility per dollar is equal in every use. By comparing the new and old equilibrium points, we trace the usual downward-sloping demand curve.

CONCEPTS FOR REVIEW

indifference curves
slope or substitution ratio
budget line or budget constraint

convexity of indifference curves and law of diminishing relative marginal utilities

optimal tangency condition: $P_F/P_C =$ substitution ratio $= MU_F/MU_C$

CHAPTER 6
PRODUCTION AND BUSINESS ORGANIZATION

The business of America is business.

Calvin Coolidge

Before we can eat our daily bread, someone must bake it. The productive capacity of a country—the number of loaves of bread, barrels of oil, kilowatt-hours of electricity, and so forth—is the measure of a country's economic potential. Productive capacity is determined by the size and quality of the labor force, by the quantity and quality of the capital stock, by the nation's technical knowledge along with the ability to use that knowledge, and by the nature of public and private institutions. Why are living standards high in North America? Low in tropical Africa? For answers, we should look to how well the machine of production is running.

Our goal is to understand how market forces determine the supply of goods and services. Over the next three chapters we will lay out the essential concepts of production, cost, and supply and show how they are linked. First we explore the fundamentals of production theory, showing how firms transform inputs into desirable outputs. Production theory also helps us understand why productivity and living standards have risen over time and how firms manage their internal activities.

Building on our knowledge of production, Chapter 7 then develops the essential concepts of business cost. Businesses decide what inputs to employ in production on the basis of the costs and productivities of various inputs. Finally, we use the theory of production and cost to show how businesses decide how much output to produce. This is the basis for the supply curve we first saw in our basic analysis of supply and demand.

A. THEORY OF PRODUCTION AND MARGINAL PRODUCTS

BASIC CONCEPTS

Productive activities are as diverse as life itself. A farm takes fertilizer, seed, land, and labor and turns them into wheat or corn. Modern factories take inputs such as energy, raw materials, computerized machinery, and labor and use them to produce tractors, TVs, or tubes of toothpaste. An airline takes airplanes, fuel, labor, and computerized reservation systems and provides passengers with the ability to travel quickly from one end of the country to the other. An accounting firm takes pencils, computers, paper, office space, and labor and produces audits or tax returns for its clients.

Our discussion assumes that the farm, factory, airline, and accounting firm always strive to produce efficiently, or at lowest cost. That is, they always attempt to produce the maximum level of output for a given dose of inputs, avoiding waste whenever possible. Later on, in deciding what goods or services to produce and sell, firms are assumed to maximize economic profits as well.

The Production Function

We have spoken of inputs like land and labor and outputs like wheat and toothpaste. But if you have a fixed amount of inputs, how much output can you get? In practice, the answer depends on the state of technology and engineering knowledge. On any day, given the available technical knowledge, land, machinery, and so on, only a certain quantity of tractors or toothpaste can be obtained from a given amount of labor. The relationship between the amount of input required and the amount of output that can be obtained is called the *production function.*

The **production function** specifies the maximum output that can be produced with a given quantity of inputs. It is defined for a given state of engineering and technical knowledge.

For example, we can imagine a book of technical specifications that shows the production function for generating electricity. On one page there are specifications for different-size gas turbines, showing their inputs (initial capital cost, fuel consumption, and the amount of labor needed to run the turbine) and their outputs (amount of electricity generated). The next page includes descriptions of several sizes of coalfired generating plants, showing inputs and outputs. Yet other pages describe nuclear power plants, solar power stations, and so forth. Together they constitute the production function for electricity generation.

Or consider the humble task of ditchdigging. Outside our windows in America, we see a large and expensive tractor, driven by one person with another to supervise. This team can easily dig a trench 5 feet deep and 50 feet long in 2 hours. When we visit China, we see 50 laborers armed only with picks. The same trench might take an entire day. These two techniques—one very capital-intensive and the other highly labor-intensive—represent the production function for ditchdigging.

There are literally millions of different production functions—one for each and every product or service. Most of them are not written down anywhere. In areas of the economy where technology is changing rapidly, like telecommunications and biotechnology, production functions may become obsolete soon after they are used. And some, like the blueprints of a medical laboratory or cliff house, are specially designed for a specific location and purpose and would be useless anywhere else. Nevertheless, economists have found that production functions are a useful way of describing the productive capabilities of a firm.

Total, Average, and Marginal Product

Starting with a firm's production function, we can calculate three important production concepts: total, average, and marginal product. We begin by computing the total physical product, or **total product**, which designates the total amount of output produced, in physical units such as bushels of wheat or number of telephone calls produced. Figure 6-1(*a*) and column (2) of Table 6-1 illustrate the concept of total product. For this example, they show how total product responds as the amount of labor applied is increased. The total product starts at zero for zero labor and then increases as additional units of labor are applied, reaching a maximum of 3900 units when 5 units of labor are used.[1]

Once we know the total product, it is easy to derive an equally important concept, the marginal product. Recall that the term "marginal" means "extra."

The **marginal product** of an input is the extra product or output added by 1 extra unit of that input while other inputs are held constant.

For example, assume that we are holding land, machinery, and all other inputs constant. Then labor's marginal product is the extra output obtained by adding 1 unit of labor. The third column of Table 6-1 calculates the marginal product. The marginal product of labor starts at 2000 for the first unit of labor and then falls to only 100 units for the

---

[1] In this chapter we talk of "units of labor" as being one input into the production process. How are units of labor measured? It is customary to measure labor in terms of hours of work (person-hours) to reflect the fact that people work different numbers of hours per week. For simplicity, however, we simply refer to numbers of workers and assume that each person works the same number of hours.

(1) Units of labor	(2) Total product	(3) Marginal product	(4) Average product
0	0		
		2,000	
1	2,000		2,000
		1,000	
2	3,000		1,500
		500	
3	3,500		1,167
		300	
4	3,800		950
		100	
5	3,900		780

TABLE 6-1. Total, Marginal, and Average Product

The table shows the total product that can be produced for different inputs of labor when other inputs (capital, land, etc.) and the state of technical knowledge are unchanged. From total product, we can derive important concepts of marginal and average products.

fifth unit. Marginal product calculations such as this are crucial for understanding how wages and other factor prices are determined.

The final concept is the **average product**, which equals total output divided by total units of input. The fourth column of Table 6-1 shows the average product of labor as 2000 units per worker with one worker, 1500 units per worker with two workers, and so forth. In this example, average product falls through the entire range of increasing labor input.

Figure 6-1 plots the total and marginal products from Table 6-1. Study this figure to make sure you understand that the blocks of marginal products in (*b*) are related to the changes in the total product curve in (*a*).

The Law of Diminishing Returns

Using production functions, we can understand one of the most famous laws in all economics, the law of diminishing returns:

The **law of diminishing returns** holds that we will get less and less extra output when we add additional doses of an input while holding other inputs fixed. In other words, the marginal product of each unit of input will decline as the amount of that input increases, holding all other inputs constant.

The law of diminishing returns expresses a very basic relationship. As more of an input such as labor

is added to a fixed amount of land, machinery, and other inputs, the labor has less and less of the other factors to work with. The land gets more crowded, the machinery is overworked, and the marginal product of labor declines.

The law of diminishing returns can be fleshed out by putting ourselves in the boots of a farmer performing an agricultural experiment illustrated by Table 6-1. Given a fixed amount of land and other inputs, assume that we use no labor inputs at all. With zero labor input there is no corn output. Hence, Table 6-1 records zero product when labor is zero.

Now add 1 unit of labor to the same fixed amount of land. We observe that 2000 bushels of corn are produced. In the next stage in our controlled experiment, we continue to hold other inputs fixed and go from 1 unit of labor to 2 units of labor. What is the impact of the added labor on production? The second unit of labor adds only 1000 bushels of additional output, which is less than what the first unit of labor added. The third unit of labor has an even lower marginal product than does the second, and the fourth unit adds yet a bit less. The hypothetical experiment reported in Table 6-1 thus illustrates the law of diminishing returns.

Figure 6-1 also illustrates the law of diminishing returns for labor, holding land and other inputs constant. Here we see that the marginal product curve declines as labor inputs increase, which is the precise meaning of diminishing returns. In Figure 6-1(*a*), diminishing returns are seen as a concave or dome-shaped total product curve.

What is true for labor is also true for land and any other input. We can interchange land and labor, now holding labor constant and varying land. Land's marginal product is the change in total output that results from 1 additional unit of land, with all other inputs held constant. We can calculate the marginal product of each input (labor, land, machinery, water, fertilizer, etc.), and the marginal product would apply to any output (wheat, corn, steel, soybeans, and so forth). We would find that other inputs also tend to show the law of diminishing returns.

 Economics at work: Diminishing returns. The law of diminishing returns makes good economic sense. In the case of farming, output will

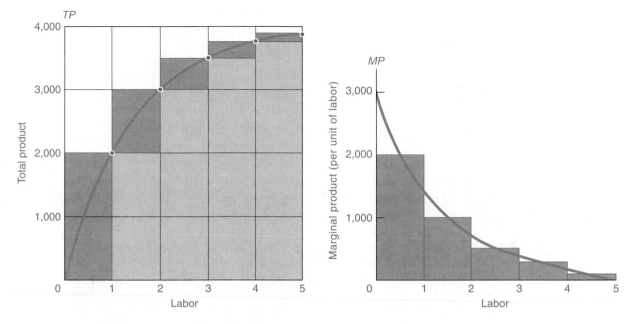

(a) Total Product

(b) Marginal Product

FIGURE 6-1. Marginal Product Is Derived from Total Product

Diagram (**a**) shows the total product curve rising as additional inputs of labor are added, holding other things constant. However, total product rises by smaller and smaller increments as additional units of labor are added (compare the increments of the first and the fifth worker). By smoothing between points, we get the rust-colored total product curve.

Diagram (**b**) shows the declining steps of marginal product. Make sure you understand why each dark rectangle in (**b**) is equal to the equivalent dark rectangle in (**a**). The area in (**b**) under the rust-colored marginal product curve (or the sum of the dark rectangles) adds up to the total product in (**a**).

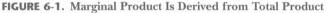

increase sharply as we add labor—the fields will be more thoroughly seeded and weeded, irrigation ditches will be neater, and scarecrows better oiled. At some point, however, the additional labor becomes less and less productive. The third hoeing of the day or the fourth oiling of the machinery adds little to output. Eventually, output grows very little as more people crowd onto the farm; too many tillers spoil the crop.

Diminishing returns are a key factor in explaining why many countries in Asia are so poor. Living standards in crowded China and India are low because there are so many workers per acre of land and not because farmers are ignorant or fail to respond to economic incentives.

We can also use the example of studying to illustrate the law of diminishing returns. You might find that the

first hour of studying economics on a given day was productive—you learned new laws and facts, insights and history. The second hour might find your attention wandering a bit, with less learned. The third hour might show that diminishing returns had set in with a vengeance—so that by the next day you could remember nothing of what you had read during the third hour. Does the law of diminishing returns suggest why the hours devoted to studying should be spread out rather than crammed into the day before exams?

The law of diminishing returns is a widely observed empirical regularity rather than a universal truth like the law of gravity. It has been found in numerous empirical studies, but exceptions have also been uncovered. Moreover, diminishing returns might not hold for all levels of production. The very first inputs of labor might actually show increasing marginal products, since a minimum amount of labor may be needed just to walk to the field and pick up a shovel. Notwithstanding these reservations, diminishing returns will prevail in most situations.

RETURNS TO SCALE

Diminishing returns and marginal products refer to the response of output to an increase of a *single* input when all other inputs are held constant. We saw that increasing labor while holding land constant would increase food output by ever-smaller increments.

But sometimes we are interested in the effect of increasing *all* inputs. For example, what would happen to wheat production if land, labor, water, and other inputs were increased by the same proportion? Or what would happen to production of tractors if the quantities of labor, computers, robots, steel, and factory space were all doubled? These questions refer to the *returns to scale*, or the effects of scale increases of inputs on the quantity produced. Put differently, the returns to scale reflect the responsiveness of total product when *all* the inputs are increased proportionately. Three important cases should be distinguished:

- **Constant returns to scale** denote a case where a change in all inputs leads to a proportional change in output. For example, if labor, land, capital, and other inputs are doubled, then under constant returns to scale output would also double. Many handicraft industries (such as haircutting in America or handloom operation in a developing country) show constant returns.
- **Increasing returns to scale** arise when an increase in all inputs leads to a more-than-proportional increase in the level of output. For example, an engineer planning a small-scale chemical plant would generally find that increasing the inputs of labor, capital, and materials by 10 percent will increase the total output by more than 10 percent. Engineering studies have determined that many manufacturing processes enjoy

modestly increasing returns to scale for plants up to the largest size used today.
- **Decreasing returns to scale** occur when a balanced increase of all inputs leads to a less-than-proportional increase in total output. In many processes, scaling up may eventually reach a point beyond which inefficiencies set in. These might arise because the costs of management or control become large. One case has occurred in electricity generation, where firms found that when plants grew too large, risks of plant failure grew too large. Many productive activities involving natural resources, such as growing wine grapes or providing clean drinking water to a city, show decreasing returns to scale.

Production shows increasing, decreasing, or constant returns to scale when a balanced increase in all inputs leads to a more-than-proportional, less-than-proportional, or just-proportional increase in output.

One of the common findings of engineers is that modern mass-production techniques require that factories be a certain minimum size. Chapter 2 showed that as output increases, firms may divide production into smaller steps, taking advantage of specialization and division of labor. In addition, large-scale production allows intensive use of specialized capital equipment, automation, and computerized design and manufacturing to perform simple and repetitive tasks quickly.

What kind of returns prevail in production today? Economists often think that most production activities should be able to attain constant returns to scale. They reason that if production can be adjusted by simply replicating existing plants over and over again, the producer would simply be multiplying both inputs and output by the same number. In such a case, you would observe constant returns to scale for any level of output.

Productivity. Economies of scale and mass production have fueled much of the economic growth of nations over the last century. Most production processes are many times larger than they were during the nineteenth century. A large ship in the mid-nineteenth century could carry 2000 tons of goods, while the largest supertankers today carry over 1 million tons of oil.

What would be the effect of a general increase in the scale of economic activity? If increasing returns prevailed, the larger scale of inputs and production would lead to greater productivity—where **productivity** is a concept measuring the ratio of total output to a weighted average of inputs. Suppose that the typical firm's inputs increased by 1 percent and that because of economies of scale output increased by 3 percent. We then calculate that productivity (output per unit of input) rose by 2 ($= 3 - 1$) percent. This example suggests that increases in a nation's per capita output and living standards may result in part from exploiting increasing returns to scale in production.

While increasing returns to scale are potentially large in many sectors, at some point decreasing returns to scale may take hold. As firms become larger and larger, the problems of management and coordination become increasingly difficult. In relentless pursuit of greater profits, a firm may find itself expanding into more geographic markets or product lines than it can effectively manage. A firm can have only one chief executive officer, one chief financial officer, one board of directors. With less time to study each market and spend on each decision, top managers may become insulated from day-to-day production and begin to make mistakes.

Like empires that have been stretched too thin, such firms find themselves exposed to invasion by smaller and more agile rivals. Those who study management report that the world's largest automobile manufacturer, General Motors, became increasingly isolated from the outside world and from competitive pressures. As a result, it was slow to respond to changes in the automobile market when oil prices rose in the 1970s, and it lost much market share to smaller and nimbler firms. Hence, while technology might ideally allow constant or increasing returns to scale, the need for management and supervision may eventually lead to decreasing returns to scale in giant firms.

SHORT RUN AND LONG RUN

Production requires not only labor and land but also time. Pipelines cannot be built overnight, and once built they last for decades. Farmers cannot change crops in midseason. It often takes a decade to plan, construct, test, and commission a large power plant. Moreover, once capital equipment has been put in the concrete form of a power plant on the Tennessee River or a giant petrochemical factory in Mexico, the capital cannot be economically dismantled and moved to another location or transferred to another use.

To account for the role of time in production and costs, we distinguish two different time periods. We define the **short run** as a period in which firms can adjust production by changing variable factors such as materials and labor but cannot change fixed factors such as capital. The **long run** is a period sufficiently long so that all factors including capital can be adjusted.

To understand these concepts more clearly, consider the way the production of steel might respond to changes in demand. Say that Nippon Steel is operating its furnaces at 70 percent of capacity when an unexpected increase in the demand for steel occurs because of the need to rebuild from an earthquake in Japan or California. To adjust to the higher demand for steel, the firm can increase production by increasing worker overtime, hiring more workers, and operating its plants and machinery more intensively. The factors which are increased in the short run are called *variable* factors. We define the short run as the period in which production can be changed by changing variable inputs.

Suppose that the increase in steel demand persisted for an extended period of time, say, several years. Nippon Steel would examine its capital needs and decide that it should increase its productive capacity. More generally, it might examine all its *fixed* factors, those that cannot be changed in the short run because of physical conditions or legal contracts. The period of time over which all inputs, fixed and variable, can be adjusted is called the long run. In the long run, Nippon might add new and more efficient production processes, install a rail link or new computerized control system, or build a plant in Mexico. When all factors can be adjusted, the total amount of steel will be higher and the level of efficiency can increase.

Efficient production requires time as well as conventional inputs like labor. We therefore distinguish two different time periods in production and cost analysis. The short run is the period of time in which only some inputs, the variable inputs, can be adjusted. In the short run, fixed factors, such as plant and equipment, cannot be fully modified or adjusted. The long run is the period in which all factors employed by the firm can be changed, including capital.

TECHNOLOGICAL CHANGE

Economic history records that total output in the United States has grown more than tenfold since the turn of the century. Part of that gain has come from increased inputs, such as labor and machinery. But much of the increase in output has come from technological change, which improves productivity and raises living standards.

Technological change refers to improvements in the processes for producing goods and services, changes in old products, or introduction of new products. Some examples of technological change are dramatic: wide-body jets that increased the number of passenger-miles per unit of input by almost 50 percent; fiber optics that have lowered cost and improved reliability in telecommunications; and improvements in computer technologies that have increased computational power by more than 1000 times in three decades. Other forms of technological change are more subtle, as is the case when a firm adjusts its production process to reduce waste and increase output.

We distinguish *process innovation*, which occurs when new engineering knowledge improves production techniques for existing products, from *product innovation*, whereby new or improved products are introduced in the marketplace. For example, a process innovation allows firms to produce more output with the same inputs or to produce the same output with fewer inputs. In other words, a process innovation is equivalent to a shift in the production function.

Figure 6-2 illustrates how technological change, in the form of a process innovation, would shift the total product curve. The lower line represents the feasible output, or production function, for a particular industry in the year 1995. Suppose that productivity, or output per unit of input, in this industry is rising at 4 percent per year. If we return to the same industry a decade later, we would likely see that changes in technical and engineering knowledge have led to an almost 50 percent improvement in output per unit of input $[(1.04)^{10} = 1.48]$.

Now let's consider technological change which leads to new products. Product innovations are

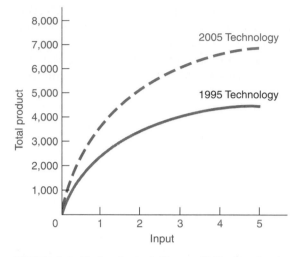

FIGURE 6-2. Technological Change Shifts Production Function Upward

The solid line represents maximum producible output for each level of inputs given the state of technical knowledge in 1995. As a result of improvements in technology and management practices, technological change shifts the production function upward, here allowing 50 percent greater output to be produced in 2005 for each level of input.

much harder to quantify than process innovations, but they are probably even more important in raising living standards over the long run. Today's array of goods and services is clearly far different from what prevailed just 50 years ago. In producing this textbook, the authors used computer software, microprocessors, color monitors, and Internet databases that were not available when the last edition was written. Medicine, communications, and entertainment are other areas where product innovations have been critical. The very notion of cellular telephones would have been unimaginable just 20 years ago. For fun, and to see this point, try to find any commodity or production process that has not changed since your grandparents were your age!

Figure 6-2 shows the happy case of a technological advance. Is the opposite case—technological regress—possible? For a well-functioning market economy, the answer is no. Indeed, that is one of the key advantages of a market economy over an economy ruled by government dictates or tradition. Inferior technologies tend to be discarded in a market economy, while superior technologies—ones with higher productivity—are introduced because they will increase the profits of the innovating firms. If, for example, someone invented a new type of photocopying machine that cost twice as much as existing varieties, no sensible profit-oriented firm would produce such a machine, and if a wrongheaded firm were to produce it, no sensible person would purchase it.

When there are market failures, however, technological regress might occur even in a market economy. An unregulated company might introduce a socially wasteful process, say, one dumping toxic wastes into a stream, because the wasteful process was cheaper to operate. But the economic advantage arises only because the social costs of pollution are not included in the firm's calculations of costs of production. If pollution costs were included in a firm's decisions, say, by strict liability rules or pollution taxes, the retrogressive process would no longer be profitable. In competitive markets, inferior products follow the Neanderthal man into extinction.

THE AGGREGATE PRODUCTION FUNCTION FOR THE UNITED STATES

Now that we have examined the principles of production theory, we can apply these theories to measure how well the whole U.S. economy has been performing. To do this, we need to look at what's happened to total output, to the quantity of inputs (like labor, capital, and land), and to total productivity. Because they involve serious problems of measurement, all such magnitudes must be calculated with great care. Yet they are useful in giving a broad description of an economy's overall behavior.

Empirical studies of the aggregate production function date back to the 1920s, when Paul Douglas (a professor at the University of Chicago and later a U.S. senator) analyzed data for manufacturing. Over the last 30 years some of the best minds of economics have examined this subject, including John Kendrick, Edward Denison, Robert Solow (a winner of the Nobel Prize in economics for his work in this area), and Dale Jorgenson. The goal of these studies was to understand how economic growth depends upon capital, labor, and productivity growth. Recall

from our earlier discussion that productivity measures the total quantity of output per unit of input. Productivity growth denotes the rate of growth of the level of productivity. For example, if output per worker is 100 units in 1996 and it grows to 102.5 units in 1997, we say that productivity growth was 2.5 percent per year.

In measuring productivity, we denote *labor productivity* as the amount of output per unit of labor; *capital productivity* as output per unit of capital; and *total factor productivity* as output per unit of total inputs of capital and labor.

Empirical Findings. What have economic studies found? Here are a few of the important results:

- Total factor productivity has been increasing throughout this century because of technological progress and higher levels of worker education and skill. The average rate of total productivity growth has been slightly under $1\frac{1}{2}$ percent per year during the twentieth century. Average real output per worker has grown slightly faster than the rate of growth of total factor productivity.
- The capital stock has been growing faster than the number of worker-hours. As a result, labor has a growing quantity of capital goods to work with; hence labor productivity and wages have tended to rise even faster than the $1\frac{1}{2}$ percent per year attributable to productivity growth alone.
- The rate of return on capital (the rate of profit) might have been expected to encounter diminishing returns because each capital unit now has less labor to cooperate with it. In fact, capital's rate of return has remained about the same.
- In the last two decades, all measures of productivity have shown a marked growth slowdown. From 1973 to 1996, total factor productivity grew only $\frac{3}{4}$ percent per year. Because of slow growth in productivity, real wages and living standards have grown slowly in the United States since the early 1970s.

A final encouraging word: Although measured productivity growth has been slow in the last few years, recent empirical studies suggest that we have seriously underestimated productivity growth. Studies of medical care, capital-goods pricing, computer software, and lighting indicate that our measuring rod for productivity may be badly flawed. One particularly important shortcoming is the failure to account for the economic value of new products. For example, when compact discs replace records, our measures of productivity do not include the improvement in durability and sound quality. One

study found that productivity in treatment of heart attacks was 5 percent per year more rapid than the conventional measure. If further studies confirm these tentative conclusions, we may find that productivity growth over the last quarter-century was significantly faster—maybe even double—the meager $\frac{3}{4}$ percent per year reported in the official statistics.

B. BUSINESS ORGANIZATIONS

THE NATURE OF THE FIRM

So far we have talked about production functions as if they were machines that could be operated by anyone: put a pig in one end and get sausage out the other. In reality, almost all production is done by specialized organizations—the small, medium, and large businesses that dominate the landscape of modern economies. Why does production generally take place in firms rather than in our basements?

Firms or business enterprises exist for many reasons, but the most important are to exploit economies of mass production, to raise funds, and to organize the production process. The most compelling factor leading to the organization of production in firms arises from *economies of mass production.* Efficient production requires specialized machinery and factories, assembly lines, and the division of labor into many small operations. Studies indicate that efficient production of automobiles requires production rates of at least 300,000 units per year.

We could hardly expect that workers would spontaneously gather to perform each task correctly and in the right sequence. Instead, we need firms to coordinate the production process, purchasing or renting land, capital, labor, and materials. If there were no need for specialization and division of labor, we could each produce our own electricity, digital watch, and compact disc in our own backyard. We obviously cannot perform such feats, so

efficiency generally requires large-scale production in businesses.

A related function of firms is *raising resources* for large-scale production. Developing a new commercial aircraft costs well over $1 billion; the research and development expenses for a new computer microprocessor, like Intel's Pentium chip, are just as high. Where are such funds to come from? In the nineteenth century, businesses could often be financed by wealthy risk-taking individuals. But the days of such fabulously wealthy captains of industry are past. Today, in a private-enterprise economy, most funds for production must come from company profits or from money borrowed in financial markets. Indeed, efficient production by private enterprise would be virtually unthinkable if corporations could not raise billions of dollars each year for new projects.

A third reason for the existence of firms is to *manage the production process.* The manager is the person who organizes production, introduces new ideas or products or processes, makes the business decisions, and is held accountable for success or failure. Production cannot, after all, organize itself. Someone has to supervise the construction of a new factory, negotiate with labor unions, and purchase materials and supplies.

If you were to purchase the franchise for an AA baseball team, you would have to rent a stadium, hire baseball players, negotiate with people for concessions, hire ushers, deal with unions, and sell tickets.

Once all these factors of production are engaged, someone has to monitor their daily activities to ensure that the job is being done effectively and honestly.

Production is organized in firms because efficiency generally requires large-scale production, the raising of significant financial resources, and careful management and monitoring of ongoing activities.

BIG, SMALL, AND INFINITESIMAL BUSINESSES

Production in a market economy takes place in a wide variety of business organizations—from the tiniest individual proprietorships to the giant corporations that dominate economic life in a capitalist economy. There are currently more than 18 million different businesses in America. The majority of these are tiny units owned by a single person—the individual proprietorship. Others are partnerships, owned by two or perhaps two hundred partners. The largest businesses tend to be corporations.

Tiny businesses predominate in numbers. But in sales and assets, in political and economic power, and in size of payroll and employment, the few hundred largest corporations dominate the economy.

The Individual Proprietorship

At one end of the spectrum are the individual proprietorships, the classic small businesses often called "mom-and-pop" stores. A small store might do a few hundred dollars of business per day and barely provide a minimum wage for the owners' efforts.

These businesses are large in number but small in total sales. For most small businesses, a tremendous amount of personal effort is required. The self-employed often work 50 or 60 hours per week and take no vacations, yet the average lifetime of a small business is only a year. Still, some people will always want to start out on their own. Theirs may be the successful venture that gets bought out for millions of dollars.

The Partnership

Often a business requires a combination of talents—say, lawyers or doctors specializing in different areas. Any two or more people can get together and form a partnership. Each agrees to provide some fraction of the work and capital, to share some percentage of the profits, and of course to share the losses or debts.

Today, partnerships account for only a small fraction of total economic activity. The reason is that partnerships pose certain disadvantages that make them impractical for large businesses. The major disadvantage is *unlimited liability*. General partners are liable without limit for all debts contracted by the partnership. If you own 1 percent of the partnership and the business fails, you will be called upon to pay 1 percent of the bills and the other partners will be assessed their 99 percent. But if your partners cannot pay, you may be called upon to pay all the debts even if you must sell off your prize possessions to do so.

The peril of unlimited liability and the difficulty of raising funds explain why partnerships tend to be confined to small, personal enterprises such as agriculture and retail trade. Partnerships are simply too risky for most situations.

The Corporation

The bulk of economic activity in an advanced market economy takes place in private corporations. Centuries ago, corporate charters were awarded by special acts of the monarch or legislature. The British East India Company was a privileged corporation and as such it practically ruled India for more than a century. In the nineteenth century, railroads often had to spend as much money on getting a charter through the legislature as on preparing their roadbeds. Over the past century, laws have been passed that allow almost anyone the privilege of forming a corporation for almost any purpose.

Today, a **corporation** is a form of business organization, chartered in one of the fifty states or abroad and owned by a number of individual stockholders. The corporation has a separate legal identity, and indeed is a legal "person" that may on its own behalf buy, sell, borrow money, produce goods and services, and enter into contracts. In addition, the corporation enjoys the right of *limited liability*, whereby each owner's investment in the corporation is strictly limited to a specified amount.

The central features of a modern corporation are the following:

- The ownership of a corporation is determined by the ownership of the company's common stock. If you own 10 percent of a corporation's shares, you have 10 percent of the ownership. Publicly owned corporations are valued on stock exchanges, like the New York Stock Exchange. It is in such stock markets that the titles to the largest corporations are traded and that much of the nation's risk capital is invested.
- In principle, the shareholders control the companies they own. They collect dividends in proportion to the fraction of the shares they own, and they elect directors and vote on many important issues. But don't think that the shareholders have a significant role in running giant corporations. In practice, shareholders of giant corporations exercise virtually no control because they are too dispersed to overrule the entrenched managers.
- The corporation's managers and directors have the legal power to make decisions for the corporation. They decide what to produce and how to produce it. They negotiate with labor unions and decide whether to sell the firm if another firm wishes to take it over. When the newspaper announces that a firm has laid off 20,000 workers, this decision was made by the managers. The shareholders own the corporation, but the managers run it.

Advantages and Disadvantages of Corporations. Why are corporations so predominant in a market economy? Simply because it is an extremely efficient way to engage in business. A corporation is a legal person that can conduct business. Also, the corporation may have perpetual succession or existence, regardless of how many times the shares of stock change hands. Corporations are hardly little democracies, so their managers can make decisions quickly, and often ruthlessly, which is in stark contrast to the way economic decisions are made by legislatures.

In addition, corporate stockholders enjoy limited liability, which protects them from incurring the debts or losses of the corporation beyond their initial contribution. If we buy $1000 of stock, we cannot lose more than our original investment.

Corporations face one major disadvantage: There is an extra tax on corporate profits. For an unincorporated business, any income after expenses is taxed as ordinary personal income. The corporation is treated differently in that corporate income is doubly taxed—first as corporate profits and then as individual income on dividends. The double taxation of corporations has been severely criticized by some economists in recent years, although most countries continue to find corporate income a convenient source of tax revenues.

Because efficient production often requires large-scale enterprises, with billions of dollars of capital, investors need a way to pool their funds. Corporations, with limited liability and a convenient management structure, can attract large supplies of private capital, produce a variety of related products, and pool risks.

THE ECONOMICS OF ORGANIZATIONS

This overview of the organizations of modern capitalism can provide only the barest hint of the richness of the *economics of organizations*. The last few years have seen a concerted effort by economists to understand why organizations take the particular form they do and why decisions are made in the controlled hierarchy of firms rather than by the arm's-length contracts of markets. Economists like Ronald Coase, Kenneth Arrow, Herbert Simon, and Oliver Williamson point to the importance of transaction costs in determining the boundaries between firm and market.

Those who study economic history point to the vital importance of organizational efficiency and innovation in increasing productivity. Railroads not only brought wheat from farm to market but also introduced time zones. Indeed the very notion of being "on time" first became crucial when being off schedule produced train wrecks. History shows how crucial organizations are for the achievement of human goals. As the sad story of centrally planned economies so clearly shows, without the organizational genius of the modern private-enterprise firm, all the land, labor, and capital would work for naught.

SUMMARY

A. Basic Concepts

1. The relationship between the quantity of output (such as wheat, steel, or automobiles) and the quantities of inputs (of labor, land, and capital) is called the production function. Total product is the total output produced. Average product equals total output divided by the total quantity of inputs. We can calculate the marginal product of a factor as the extra output added for each additional unit of input while holding all other inputs constant.

2. According to the law of diminishing returns, the marginal product of each input will generally decline as the amount of that input increases, when all other inputs are held constant.

3. The returns to scale reflect the impact on output of a balanced increase in all inputs. A technology in which doubling all inputs leads to an exact doubling of outputs displays constant returns to scale. When doubling inputs leads to less than double (more than double) the quantity of output, the situation is one of decreasing (increasing) returns to scale.

4. Because decisions take time to implement, and because capital and other factors are often very long-lived, the reaction of production may change over different time periods. The short run is a period in which variable factors, such as labor or material inputs, can be easily changed. In the long run, the capital stock (a firm's machinery and factories) can depreciate and be replaced. In the long run, all inputs, fixed and variable, can be adjusted.

5. Technological change refers to a change in the underlying techniques of production, as occurs when a new product or process of production is invented or an old product or process is improved. In such situations, the same output is produced with fewer inputs or more output is produced with the same inputs. Technological change shifts the production function upward.

6. Attempts to measure an aggregate production function for the American economy tend to corroborate theories of production and marginal products. In this century, technological change has increased the productivity of both labor and capital. Total factor productivity (measuring the ratio of total output to total inputs) has grown at around $1\frac{1}{2}$ percent per year over the twentieth century, although since 1970 the rate of productivity growth has slowed markedly and real wages have stopped growing. But underestimating the importance of new and improved products may lead to a significant underestimate of productivity growth.

B. Business Organizations

7. In a market economy, production is organized in firms—with some economic activity in tiny one-person proprietorships, some in partnerships, and the bulk in corporations.

8. Each kind of enterprise has advantages and disadvantages. Small businesses are flexible, can market new products, and can disappear quickly. But they suffer from the fundamental disadvantage of being unable to accumulate large amounts of capital from a dispersed group of investors. Today's large corporation, granted limited liability by the state, is able to amass billions of dollars of capital by borrowing from banks, bondholders, and stock markets.

9. In a modern economy, firms produce most goods and services because economies of mass production necessitate that output be produced at high volumes, the technology of production requires much more capital than a single individual would willingly put at risk, and efficient production requires careful management and coordination of the tasks by a centrally directed entity.

CONCEPTS FOR REVIEW

inputs, outputs, production function
total, average, and marginal product
diminishing marginal product and
    the law of diminishing returns
constant, increasing, and decreasing
    returns to scale

short run vs. long run
technological change: process innovation, product innovation
productivity
aggregate production function

reasons for firms: scale economies, financial needs, management
major business forms: individual proprietorship, partnership, corporation
unlimited and limited liability

QUESTIONS FOR DISCUSSION

1. Explain the concept of a production function. Describe the production function for hamburgers, concerts, haircuts, and a college education.
2. In the following table, which describes the actual production function for oil pipelines, fill in the missing values for marginal products and average products:

(1) Pumping horsepower	(2) Total product (barrels per day)	(3) 18-inch pipe Marginal product (barrels per day per hp)	(4) Average product (barrels per day per hp)
10,000	86,000		
20,000	114,000		
30,000	134,000		
40,000	150,000		
50,000	164,000		

3. Using the data in question 2, plot the production function of output against horsepower. On the same graph, plot the curves for average product and marginal product.
4. Suppose you are running the food concession at the athletic events for your college. You sell hot dogs, colas, and potato chips. What are your inputs of capital, labor, and materials? If the demand for the hot dogs declines, what steps could you take to reduce output in the short run? In the long run?
5. An important distinction in economics is between shifts in the production function and movements along the production function. For the food concession in question 4, give an example of both a shift of and a movement along the hot-dog production function. Illustrate each with a graph of the relation between hot-dog production and labor employed.
6. Substitution occurs when firms replace one input for another, as when a farmer uses tractors rather than labor when wages rise. Consider the following changes in a firm's behavior. Which represent substitution of one factor for another with an unchanged technology, and which represent technological change? Illustrate each with a graphical production function.
   a. When the price of oil increases, a firm replaces an oil-fired plant with a gas-fired plant.
   b. A chemical company decides to replace its old coal-fired electrical generation equipment with a newly invented gas turbine, reducing costs by 20 percent.
   c. Over the period 1970–1995, a typesetting firm decreases its employment of typesetters by 200 workers and increases its employment of computer operators by 100 workers.
   d. After a successful unionization drive for clerical workers, a college buys personal computers for its faculty and reduces its secretarial work force.
7. Consider a firm that produces wheat with land and labor inputs. Define and contrast diminishing returns and decreasing returns to scale. Explain why it is possible to have diminishing returns for one input and constant returns to scale for both inputs.
8. Show that if the marginal product is always decreasing, the average product is always above the marginal product.
9. List 5 products that are important to you today. For each, describe how product, process, or organizational inventions have affected the product over the last century.

CHAPTER 7

ANALYSIS OF COSTS

Costs merely register competing attractions.

Frank Knight, **Risk, Uncertainty, and Profit** (*1921*)

Everywhere that production goes, costs follow close behind like a shadow. In a world of scarcity, firms have to pay for their inputs: steel, screws, solvents, engineers, secretaries, computers, telephones, lights, and pencils. Profitable businesses are acutely aware of this simple fact as they set their production strategies, since every dollar of unnecessary costs reduces the firm's profits by that same dollar. Indeed, too much production can be as dangerous as too little; history shows that overexpansion can often drive a fast-growing company into bankruptcy, by pushing up costs far faster than revenues.

But the role of costs goes far beyond influencing the level of production. Smart businesses also pay close attention to their costs when they are making

their operating decisions. Is it cheaper to hire a new worker or to pay overtime? To open a new factory or expand an old one? To invest in new machinery at home or relocate production abroad? Businesses want to choose that method of production which is efficient, which produces the most at the lowest costs.

This chapter is devoted to a thorough analysis of cost. First we consider the full array of economic costs, including the all-important notion of marginal costs. Then we examine how business accountants measure cost in practice. Finally, we look at the notion of opportunity cost, a broad concept that can be applied to a wide range of decisions. This comprehensive study of cost will lay the foundation for understanding the supply decisions of business firms.

A. ECONOMIC ANALYSIS OF COSTS

TOTAL COST: FIXED AND VARIABLE

Consider a firm that produces a quantity of output (denoted by q) using inputs of capital, labor, and materials. The firm buys these inputs in the factor markets. A profit-minded firm will keep an eagle eye

on its costs to maintain profitability. The firm's accountants have the task of calculating the total dollar costs incurred at each level of q.

Table 7-1 on page 116 shows the total cost (TC) for each different level of output q. Looking at columns (1) and (4), we see that TC goes up as q

115

(1) Quantity *q*	(2) Fixed cost *FC* ($)	(3) Variable cost *VC* ($)	(4) Total cost *TC* ($)
0	55	0	55
1	55	30	85
2	55	55	110
3	55	75	130
4	55	105	160
5	55	155	210
6	55	225	280

TABLE 7-1. Fixed, Variable, and Total Costs

The major elements of a firm's costs are its fixed costs (which do not vary at all when output changes) and variable costs (which increase as output increases). Total costs are equal to fixed plus variable costs: $TC = FC + VC$.

goes up. This makes sense because it takes more labor and other inputs to produce more of a good; extra factors involve an extra money cost. It costs $110 in all to produce 2 units, $130 to produce 3 units, and so forth. In our discussion, we assume that the firm always produces output at the lowest possible cost.

Fixed Cost

Columns (2) and (3) of Table 7-1 break total cost into two components: total fixed cost (*FC*) and total variable cost (*VC*).

What are a firm's **fixed costs**? Sometimes called "overhead" or "sunk costs," they consist of items such as rent for factory or office space, contractual payments for equipment, interest payments on debts, salaries of tenured faculty, and so forth. These must be paid even if the firm produces no output, and they will not change if output changes. For example, a law firm might have an office lease which runs 10 years and remains an obligation even if the firm shrinks to half its previous size. Because *FC* is the amount that must be paid regardless of the level of output, it remains constant at $55 in column (2).

Variable Cost

Column (3) of Table 7-1 shows variable cost (*VC*). **Variable costs** are those which vary as output changes. Examples include materials required to produce output (such as steel to produce automobiles), production workers to staff the assembly lines, power to operate factories, and so on. In a super-

market, checkout clerks are a variable cost, since managers can easily adjust the clerks' hours worked to match the number of shoppers coming through the store.

By definition, *VC* begins at zero when *q* is zero. It is the part of *TC* that grows with output; indeed, the jump in *TC* between any two outputs is the same as the jump in *VC*. Why? Because *FC* stays constant at $55 throughout and cancels out in the comparison of costs between different output levels.

Let us summarize these cost concepts:

Total cost represents the lowest total dollar expense needed to produce each level of output *q*. *TC* rises as *q* rises.

Fixed cost represents the total dollar expense that is paid out even when no output is produced; fixed cost is unaffected by any variation in the quantity of output.

Variable cost represents expenses that vary with the level of output—such as raw materials, wages, and fuel—and includes all costs that are not fixed.

Always, by definition,

$$TC = FC + VC$$

 Minimum attainable costs. Anyone who has managed a business knows that when we write down a cost schedule like the one in Table 7-1, we make the firm's job look altogether too simple. Why so? Because much hard work lies behind Table 7-1. To attain the lowest level of costs, the firm's managers have to make sure that they are paying the least possible amount for necessary materials such as energy, that the lowest-cost engineering techniques are incorporated into the factory layout, that employees are being honest, and that countless other decisions are made in the most economical fashion. As a result of such managerial effort, the fixed and variable costs shown in Table 7-1 are the minimum costs necessary for the firm to produce that level of output.

DEFINITION OF MARGINAL COST

Marginal cost is one of the key concepts of economics. **Marginal cost** (*MC*) denotes the extra or additional cost of producing 1 extra unit of output. Say a firm is producing 1000 compact discs for a total cost of $10,000. If the total cost of producing 1001 discs is $10,006, the marginal cost of production is $6 for the 1001st disc.

Sometimes, the marginal cost of producing an extra unit of output can be quite low. For an airline flying planes with empty seats, the added cost of another passenger is simply the cost of the peanuts and snack; no additional capital (planes) or labor (pilots and flight attendants) is necessary. In other cases, the marginal cost of another unit of output can be quite high. Consider an electric utility. Under normal circumstances, it can generate enough power using only its lowest-cost, most efficient plants. But on a hot summer day, when everyone's air conditioners are running and electric demand is high, the utility may be forced to turn on its old, high-cost, inefficient generators. This added electric power comes at a high marginal cost to the utility.

Table 7-2 uses the data from Table 7-1 to illustrate how we calculate marginal costs. The rust-colored

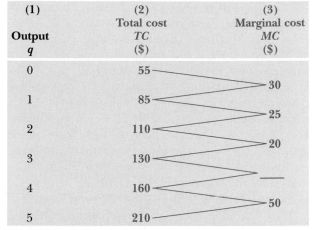

(1) Output q	(2) Total cost TC ($)	(3) Marginal cost MC ($)
0	55	
		30
1	85	
		25
2	110	
		20
3	130	
		___
4	160	
		50
5	210	

TABLE 7-2. Calculation of Marginal Cost

Once we know total cost, it is easy to calculate marginal cost. To calculate the MC of the fifth unit, we subtract the total cost of the four units from the total cost of the five units, i.e., $MC = \$210 - \$160 = \$50$. Fill in the blank for the marginal cost of the fourth unit.

FIGURE 7-1. The Relationship between Total Cost and Marginal Cost

This figure graphs the data from Table 7-2. Marginal cost in (**b**) is found by calculating the extra cost added in (**a**) for each unit increase in output. Thus to find the MC of producing the fifth unit, we subtract $160 from $210 to get MC of $50. A smooth black curve has been drawn through the points of TC in (**a**), and the smooth black MC curve in (**b**) links the discrete steps of MC.

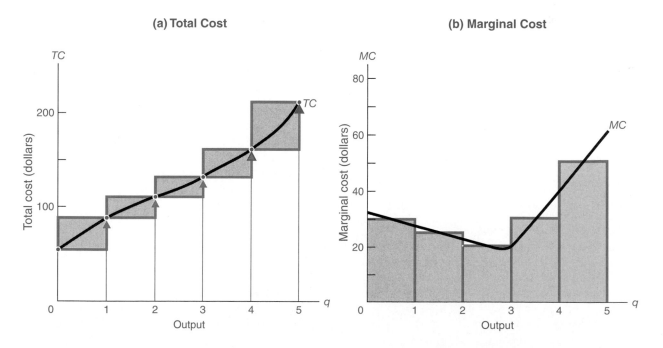

MC numbers in column (3) of Table 7-2 come from subtracting the *TC* in column (2) from the *TC* of the subsequent quantity. Thus the *MC* of the first unit is $30 (= $85 − $55). The marginal cost of the second unit is $25 (= $110 − $85). And so on.

Instead of getting *MC* from the *TC* column, we could get the *MC* figures by subtracting each *VC* number of column (3) of Table 7-1 from the *VC* in the row below it. Why? Because variable cost always grows exactly like total cost, the only difference being that *VC* must—by definition—start out from 0 rather than from the constant *FC* level. (Check that 30 − 0 = 85 − 55, and 55 − 30 = 110 − 85, and so on.)

The marginal cost of production is the additional cost incurred in producing 1 extra unit of output.

Marginal Cost in Diagrams. Figure 7-1 illustrates total cost and marginal cost. It shows that *TC* is related to *MC* in the same way that total product is related to marginal product or that total utility is related to marginal utility.

What kind of shape would we expect actual *MC* curves to have? Empirical studies have found that for most production activities in the short run (i.e., when the capital stock is fixed), marginal cost curves are U-shaped like the one shown in Figure 7-1(*b*). This U-shaped curve falls in the initial phase, reaches a minimum point, and finally begins to rise.

AVERAGE COST

We complete our catalog of the cost concepts important in economics and business with a discussion of different kinds of average or unit cost. Table 7-3 expands the data of Tables 7-1 and 7-2 to include three new measures: average cost, average fixed cost, and average variable cost.

TABLE 7-3. All Cost Concepts Derive from Total Cost Schedule

We can derive all the different cost concepts from the *TC* in column (4). Columns (5) and (6) are the important ones to concentrate on: incremental or marginal cost is calculated by subtraction of adjacent rows of *TC* and is shown in the rust color. The lighter numbers of smoothed *MC* come from Fig. 7-2(*b*). In column (6) note the point of minimum cost of $40 on the U-shaped *AC* curve in Fig. 7-2(*b*). (Can you see why the starred *MC* equals the starred *AC* at the minimum? Also, calculate and fill in all the missing numbers.)

(1)	(2)	(3)	(4)	(5)	(6)	(7)	(8)
	Fixed cost	Variable cost	Total cost	Marginal cost per unit	Average cost per unit	Average fixed cost per unit	Average variable cost per unit
Quantity	FC	VC	$TC = FC + VC$	MC	$AC = \dfrac{TC}{q}$	$AFC = \dfrac{FC}{q}$	$AVC = \dfrac{VC}{q}$
q	($)	($)	($)	($)	($)	($)	($)
0	55	0	55	33	Infinity	Infinity	Undefined
				30			
1	55	30	85	27	85	55	30
				25			
2	55	55	110	22	55	$27\frac{1}{2}$	$27\frac{1}{2}$
				20			
3	55	75	130	21	$43\frac{1}{3}$	$18\frac{1}{3}$	25
				30			
4*	55	105	160	40*	40*	$13\frac{3}{4}$	$26\frac{1}{4}$
				50			
5	55	155	210	60	42	11	____
				60			
6	55	225	280	80	$46\frac{2}{3}$	$9\frac{1}{6}$	$37\frac{1}{2}$
				90			
7	55	____	370	100	$52\frac{6}{7}$	$7\frac{6}{7}$	45
				110			
8	55	____	480	120	60	$6\frac{7}{8}$	$53\frac{1}{8}$

*Minimum level of average cost.

Average or Unit Cost

Like marginal cost, average cost (*AC*) is a concept widely used in business; by comparing average cost with price or average revenue, businesses can determine whether or not they are making a profit. **Average cost** is the total cost divided by the total number of units produced, as shown in column (6) of Table 7-3. That is,

$$\text{Average cost} = \frac{\text{total cost}}{\text{output}} = \frac{TC}{q} = AC$$

In column (6), when only 1 unit is produced, average cost has to be the same as total cost, or $85/1 = $85. But for $q = 2$, $AC = TC/2 = $110/2 = $55, as shown. Note that average cost, at first, falls lower and lower. (We shall see why in a moment.) *AC* reaches a minimum of $40 at $q = 4$, and then slowly rises.

Figure 7-2 plots the cost data shown in Table 7-3. Figure 7-2(*a*) depicts the total, fixed, and variable costs at different levels of output. Figure 7-2(*b*) shows the different average cost concepts, along with a smoothed marginal cost curve. Graph (*a*) shows how total cost moves with variable cost while fixed cost remains unchanged.

Now turn to graph (*b*). This plots the U-shaped *AC* curve and aligns *AC* right below the *TC* curve from which it is derived.

Finally, Figure 7-3 shows how marginal cost is related to the slope of the total cost curve.

Average Fixed and Variable Cost

Just as we separated total cost into fixed and variable cost, we can also break average cost into fixed and variable components. **Average fixed cost** (*AFC*) is defined as *FC/q*. Since total fixed cost is a constant, dividing it by an increasing output gives a steadily falling average fixed cost curve [see column (7) of Table 7-3]. In other words, as a firm sells more output, it can spread its overhead cost over more and more units. For example, a software firm may have a large staff of programmers to develop a new graphics program. The number of copies sold does not

---

FIGURE 7-2. All Cost Curves Can Be Derived from the Total Cost Curve

(**a**) Total cost is made up of fixed cost and variable cost. (**b**) The rust-colored curve of marginal cost falls and then rises, as indicated by the lighter *MC* figures given in column (5) of Table 7-3. The three average cost curves in (**b**) are calculated by dividing total, fixed, and variable cost by total output:

$$AC = TC/q \quad AVC = VC/q \quad AFC = FC/q$$

Also, $$AC = AVC + AFC$$

Note that *MC* intersects *AC* at its minimum.

(a) Total, Fixed, and Variable Cost

(b) Average Cost, Marginal Cost

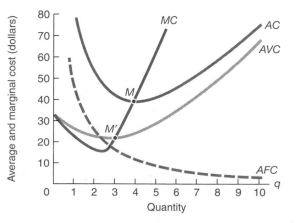

Relation between Slope and Marginal Cost

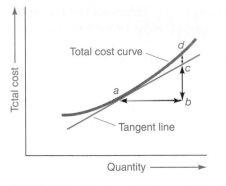

FIGURE 7-3. Relation of Slope and Marginal Cost

Focus a microscope on the total cost curve, examining the cost of going from an output of 3999 to 4000. The figure clarifies the distinction between (1) *MC* as incremental cost for a finite-step change in output and (2) *MC* as the cost for an infinitesimal change in output measured by the tangent. The distance from *a* to *b* represents 1 extra unit of output. The *b* to *d* distance represents the resulting increase in total cost. Hence *MC* = (*d* − *b*)/(*b* − *a*), which is the first and simplest definition of marginal cost.

The second definition of marginal cost is as the slope of the total cost curve. The slope of the curve at point *a* is given by the slope of the tangent at point *a*, which is given by the distance from *b* to *c* divided by the distance from *a* to *b*. In the limit for a smooth curve, as the size of the output increment becomes smaller and smaller and we recalculate the ratios in the new, smaller triangle, the discrepancy between the two definitions becomes negligible. That is, *bd/bc* approaches 1 as *b* approaches *a*.

directly affect how many programmers are necessary, making them a fixed cost. So if the program is a best-seller, the *AFC* of the programmers is low; if the program is a failure, their *AFC* is high.

The dashed gray *AFC* curve in Figure 7-2(*b*) is a hyperbola, approaching both axes: it drops lower and lower, approaching the horizontal axis as the constant *FC* gets spread over more and more units. If we allow fractional units of *q*, *AFC* starts infinitely high as finite *FC* is spread over ever-tinier *q*.

Average variable cost (*AVC*) equals variable cost divided by output, or *AVC* = *VC/q*. As you can see in both Table 7-3 and Figure 7-2(*b*), for this example *AVC* first falls and then rises.

Minimum Average Cost

Do not confuse average cost with marginal cost—it's an easy mistake to make. Indeed, average cost can be much higher or lower than marginal cost, as Figure 7-2(*b*) shows.

But Figure 7-2(*b*) also shows that there is an important link between *MC* and *AC:* When the *MC* of an added unit of output is below its *AC*, its *AC* is declining. And when *MC* is above *AC*, *AC* is increasing. At the point where *MC* equals *AC*, the *AC* curve is flat. For the typical U-shaped *AC* curve, the point where *MC* equals *AC* is also the point where *AC* hits its minimum level. Check this for yourself on the graph.

To summarize:

When marginal cost is below average cost, it is pulling average cost down; when *MC* just equals *AC*, *AC* is neither rising nor falling and is at its minimum; when *MC* is above *AC*, it is pulling *AC* up. Hence, at the bottom of a U-shaped *AC*, *MC* = *AC* = minimum *AC*.

This is a critical relationship. It means that a firm searching for the lowest average cost of production should look for the level of output at which marginal costs equal average costs.

Why is this so? If *MC* is below *AC*, the last unit produced costs less than the average cost of all the previous units produced. If the last unit costs less than the previous ones, the new *AC* (i.e., the *AC* including the last unit) must be less than the old *AC*, so *AC* must be falling. By contrast, if *MC* is above *AC*, the last unit costs more than the average cost of the previous units. Hence the new average cost (the *AC* including the last unit) must be higher than the old *AC*. Finally, when *MC* is just equal to *AC*, the last unit costs exactly the same as the average cost of all previous units. Hence the new *AC*, the one including the last unit, is equal to the old *AC;* the *AC* curve is flat when *AC* equals *MC*.

To better understand the relationship between *MC* and *AC*, study the curves in Figure 7-2(*b*) and the numbers in Table 7-3. Note that for the first 3 units, *MC* is below *AC*, and *AC* is therefore declining. At exactly 4 units, *AC* equals *MC*. Over 4 units, *MC* is above *AC* and pulling *AC* up steadily. Graphically, that means the rising *MC* curve will intersect the *AC* curve precisely at the point where it turns upward: *the* AC *curve is always pierced at its minimum point by the rising* MC *curve.* In terms of our cost curves, if the *MC* curve is below the *AC* curve, the *AC* curve must be falling.

 Marginals, averages, and grades: We can illustrate the *MC* and *AC* relationship using college grade averages. Let *AG* be your average grade (or cumulative grade average up to now) and *MG* be your grade average for this year, which we will call the "marginal grade average" because it is the last one. When *MG* is below *AG*, it will pull the new *AG* down. Thus, if your *AG* for the first 2 years is 3 and your *MG* for your junior year is 2, the new *AG* (at the end of your junior year) is $2\frac{2}{3}$. Similarly, if your *MG* in your third year is higher than your *AG* up till then, your new *AG* will be pulled up. Where *MG* equals *AG*, *AG* will be flat over time, or unchanged. The same relation holds for average cost and marginal cost.

THE LINK BETWEEN PRODUCTION AND COSTS

What determines a firm's cost curve? Clearly the prices of inputs like labor and land are important factors influencing costs. Higher rents and wages mean higher costs, as any business manager will tell you.

But the cost curve for a firm also depends very closely on the firm's production function. To see this, note that if technological improvements allow the firm to produce the same output with fewer inputs, the firm's costs will fall, and the cost curve will shift down.

Indeed, if you know factor prices and the production function, you can calculate the cost curve. Suppose a firm is aiming to produce a particular level of output. The production function (plus factor prices) will tell us what is the least costly combination of inputs the firm can select that can yield that output. Calculate the total cost of the least-cost bundle of inputs. When we do that for every possible level of output, we have the total cost shown in Tables 7-1 through 7-3.

We can see the derivation of cost from production data in the simple numerical example shown in Table 7-4. Suppose Farmer Smith rents 10 acres of land and can hire farm labor to produce wheat. Per period, land costs $5.5 per acre and labor costs $5 per worker. Using up-to-date farming methods, Smith can produce according to the production function shown in the first three columns of Table 7-4. In this example, land is a fixed cost (because Farmer Smith operates under a 10-year lease), while labor is a variable cost (because farmworkers, unlike faculty members, can easily be hired and fired).

TABLE 7-4. Costs Are Derived from Production Data and Input Costs

Farmer Smith rents 10 acres of wheatland and employs variable labor. According to the farming production function, careful use of labor and land allows the inputs and yields shown in columns (1) to (3) of the table. At input prices of $5.5 per acre and $5 per worker, we obtain Smith's cost of production shown in column (6). All other cost concepts (such as those shown in Table 7-3) can be calculated from the total cost data.

(1) Output (tons of wheat)	(2) Land inputs (acres)	(3) Labor inputs (workers)	(4) Land rent ($ per acre)	(5) Labor wage ($ per worker)	(6) Total cost ($)
0	10	0	5.5	5	55
1	10	6	5.5	5	85
2	10	11	5.5	5	110
3	10	15	5.5	5	130
4	10	21	5.5	5	160
5	10	31	5.5	5	210
6	10	45	5.5	5	280
7	10	63	5.5	5	370
8	10	85	5.5	5	480

Using the production data and the input-cost data, for each level of output we calculate the total cost of production shown in column (6) of Table 7-4. As an example, consider the total cost of production for 3 tons of wheat. Using the given production function, Smith can produce this quantity with 10 acres of land and 15 farmhands. The total cost of producing 3 tons of wheat is (10 acres × $5.5 per acre) + (15 workers × $5 per worker) = $130. Similar calculations will give all the other total cost figures in column (6) of Table 7-4.

Note that these total costs are identical to the ones shown in Tables 7-1 through 7-3, so the other cost concepts shown in the tables (i.e., *MC, FC, VC, AC, AFC,* and *AVC*) are also applicable to the production-cost example of Farmer Smith.

Diminishing Returns and U-Shaped Cost Curves

The relationship between cost and production helps us explain why average cost curves tend to be U-shaped. Recall that Chapter 6's analysis of production distinguished two different time periods, the short run and the long run. The same concepts can be applied to costs as well:

- The *short run* is the period of time that is long enough to adjust variable inputs, such as materials and production labor, but too short to allow all inputs to be changed. In the short run, fixed or overhead factors such as plant and equipment cannot be fully modified or adjusted. Therefore, in the short run, typically labor and materials costs are variable costs, while capital costs are fixed.
- In the *long run,* all inputs can be adjusted—including labor, materials, and capital. Hence, in the long run, all costs are variable and none are fixed.[1]

Note that whether a particular cost is fixed or variable depends on the length of time we are considering. In the short run, for example, the number of planes that an airline owns is a fixed cost. But over the longer run, the airline can clearly control the size of its fleet by buying or selling planes. Indeed, there is an active market in used planes, making it relatively easy to dispose of unwanted planes. Typi-

cally, in the short run, we will consider capital to be the fixed cost and labor to be the variable cost. That is not always true (think of your college's tenured faculty), but generally labor inputs can be adjusted more easily than can capital.

Why is the cost curve U-shaped? Consider the short run in which capital is fixed but labor is variable. In such a situation, there are diminishing returns to the variable factor (labor) because each additional unit of labor has less capital to work with. As a result, the marginal cost of output will rise because the extra output produced by each extra labor unit is going down. In other words, diminishing returns to the variable factor will imply an increasing short-run marginal cost. This shows why diminishing returns lead to rising marginal costs after some point.

Figure 7-4, which contains exactly the same data as Table 7-4, illustrates the point. It shows that the region of increasing marginal product corresponds to falling marginal costs, while the region of diminishing returns implies rising marginal costs.

We can summarize the relationship between the productivity laws and the cost curves as follows:

In the short run, when factors such as capital are fixed, variable factors tend to show an initial phase of increasing returns followed by diminishing returns. The corresponding cost curves show an initial phase of declining marginal costs followed by increasing *MC* after diminishing returns have set in.

CHOICE OF INPUTS BY THE FIRM

Marginal Products and the Least-Cost Rule

Every firm must decide *how* to produce its output. Should electricity be produced with oil or coal? Should cars be assembled in the United States or Mexico? Should classes be taught by faculty or graduate students? We now complete the link between production and cost by using the marginal product concept to illustrate how firms select the least-cost combinations of inputs.

In our analysis, we will rely on the fundamental assumption that *firms minimize their costs of production.* This cost-minimization assumption actually makes good sense not only for perfectly competitive firms but for monopolists or even nonprofit organizations like colleges or hospitals. It simply states that the

[1] For a more complete discussion of the long and short runs, see Chapter 6.

(a) Diminishing Returns . . .

(b) . . . Produce Upward-Sloping *MC*

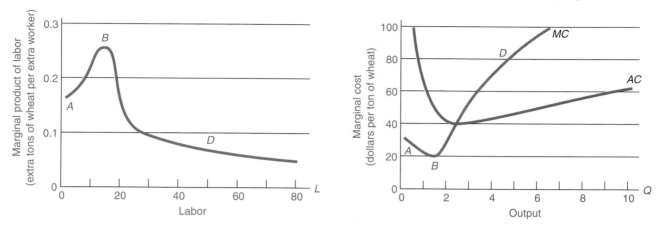

FIGURE 7-4. Diminishing Returns and U-Shaped Cost Curves

The U-shaped marginal cost curve in (**b**) arises from the shape of the marginal product curve in (**a**). With fixed land and variable labor, the marginal product of labor in (**a**) first rises to the left of *B*, peaks at *B*, and then falls at *D* as diminishing returns to labor set in.

The marginal cost curve derives from production data. In the region to the left of *B* in (**b**)—such as at point *A*—rising marginal product means that marginal cost is falling; at *B*, peak marginal product occurs at minimum marginal cost; in the region to the right of *B*, say, at *D*, as the marginal product of labor falls, the marginal cost of producing output increases.

Overall, increasing and then diminishing marginal product to the variable factor produces a U-shaped marginal cost curve.

firm should strive to produce its output at the lowest possible cost and thereby have the maximum amount of revenue left over for profits or for other objectives.

A simple example will illustrate how a firm might decide between different input combinations. Say a firm's engineers have calculated that the desired output level of 9 units could be produced with two possible options. In both cases, energy (*E*) costs $2 per unit while labor (*L*) costs $5 per hour. Under option 1, the input mix is *E* = 10 and *L* = 2. Option 2 has *E* = 4 and *L* = 5. Which is the preferred option? At the market prices for inputs, total production costs for option 1 are ($2 × 10) + ($5 × 2) = $30, while total costs for option 2 are ($2 × 4) + ($5 × 5) = $33. Therefore, option 1 would be the preferred least-cost combination of inputs.

More generally, there are usually many possible input combinations, not just two. But we don't have to calculate the cost of every different combination of inputs in order to find the one which costs the least. Here's a simple way to find the least-cost combination: Start by calculating the marginal product of each input, as we did in Chapter 6. Then divide the

marginal product of each input by its factor price. *This gives you the marginal product per dollar of input.* The cost-minimizing combination of inputs comes when the marginal product per dollar of input is equal for all inputs. That is, the marginal contribution to output of each dollar's worth of labor, of land, of oil, and so forth, must be just the same.

Following this reasoning, a firm will minimize its total cost of production when the marginal product per dollar of input is equalized for each factor of production. This is called the least-cost rule.

Least-cost rule: To produce a given level of output at least cost, a firm should buy inputs until it has equalized the marginal product per dollar spent on each input. This implies that

$$\frac{\text{Marginal product of } L}{\text{Price of } L}$$

$$= \frac{\text{marginal product of } A}{\text{price of } A} = \cdots$$

This rule for firms is exactly analogous to what consumers do when they maximize utilities, as we saw in Chapter 5. In analyzing consumer choice, we saw that to maximize utility, consumers should buy goods so that the marginal utility per dollar spent on each consumer good is equalized for all commodities.

What is the rationale for the least-cost rule? Let's say that land costs $800 an acre and labor costs $8 per hour. No one of sound mind would expect to achieve least cost if land and labor were chosen so that their marginal *physical* products were equal. If the marginal products of land and labor were both $100 worth of wheat, equal marginal products would mean that $800 of extra land would produce $100 of wheat while $8 of extra labor would also produce $100 of wheat. Clearly this is inefficient, and the firm would want to decrease inputs of land and increase inputs of labor. Examine the situation of $800 of extra land producing $1200 of wheat while $8 of extra labor produces $12 of extra wheat. This is clearly the efficient input mix because the marginal products per dollar of land and labor are equal, so the firm is minimizing its costs of production.

Another way of understanding the least-cost rule is the following: Break each factor into units worth $1 each. (In our earlier energy-labor example, $1 of labor would be one-fifth of an hour, while $1 of energy would be $\frac{1}{2}$ unit.) Then the least-cost rule states that the marginal product of each dollar-unit of input must be equalized.

A corollary of the least-cost rule is the substitution rule.

Substitution Rule: If the price of one factor falls while all other factor prices remain the same, firms will profit by substituting the now-cheaper factor for all the other factors.

Let's take the case of labor (L). A fall in the price of labor will raise the ratio MPL/P_L above the MP/P ratio for other inputs. Raising the employment of L lowers MP_L by the law of diminishing returns and therefore lowers MPL/P_L. Lower price and MP of labor then bring the marginal product per dollar for labor back into equality with that ratio for other factors.

B. ECONOMIC COSTS AND BUSINESS ACCOUNTING

From General Motors down to the corner deli, businesses use more or less elaborate systems to keep track of their costs. Many of the cost categories in business accounting look very similar to the concepts of economic cost we learned above. But there are some important differences between how businesses measure costs and how economists would do it. In this section we will lay out the rudiments of business accounting and point out the differences and similarity with economic costs.

THE INCOME STATEMENT, OR STATEMENT OF PROFIT AND LOSS

Let us start with a small company, called Hot Dog Ventures, Inc. As the name suggests, this company sells gourmet frankfurters in a small store. The operation consists of buying the materials (hot dogs, top-flight buns, expensive mustard, espresso coffee beans) and hiring people to prepare and sell the food. In addition, the company has taken out a loan of $100,000 for its cooking equipment and other restaurant furnishings, and it must pay rent on its store. The founders of Hot Dog Ventures have big aspirations, so they incorporated the business and issued common stock (see Chapter 6 on forms of business organization).

To determine whether Hot Dog Ventures is earning a profit, we must turn to the **income statement**, or—as many companies prefer to call it—the statement of profit and loss, shown in Table 7-5. This statement reports the following: (1) Hot Dog Venture's revenues from sales in 1997, (2) the expenses to be charged against those sales, and (3) the net income, or profits remaining after expenses have been deducted. This gives the fundamental identity of the income statement:

Net income (or profit) =

total revenue − total expenses

Income Statement of Hot Dog Ventures, Inc.
(July 1, 1997, to December 31, 1997)

(1)	Net sales (after all discounts and rebates)		$250,000
	Less cost of goods sold:		
(2)	Materials	$ 50,000	
(3)	Labor cost	90,000	
(4)	Miscellaneous operating costs (utilities, etc.)	10,000	
(5)	Less overhead costs:		
(6)	Selling and administrative costs	15,000	
(7)	Rent for building	5,000	
(8)	Depreciation	15,000	
(9)	Operating expenses	$185,000	185,000
(10)	Net operating income		$ 65,000
	Less:		
(11)	Interest charges on equipment loan		6,000
(12)	State and local taxes		4,000
(13)	Net income (or profit) before income taxes		$ 55,000
(14)	Less: Corporation income taxes		18,000
(15)	**Net income (or profit) after taxes**		**$ 37,000**
(16)	Less: Dividends paid on common stock		15,000
(17)	Addition to retained earnings		$ 22,000

TABLE 7-5. The Income Statement Shows Total Sales and Expenses for a Period of Time

This definition gives the famous "bottom line" of profits that firms want to maximize. And in many ways, business profits are close to an economist's definition of economic profits. Let's next examine the profit-and-loss statement in more detail, starting from the top. The first line gives the revenues, which were $250,000. Lines 2 through 9 represent the cost of different inputs into the production process. For example, the labor cost is the annual cost of employing labor, while rent is the annual cost of using the building. The selling and administrative costs include the cost of advertising the store and running the back office, while miscellaneous operating costs include the cost of electricity.

The first three cost categories—materials, labor cost, and miscellaneous operating costs—basically correspond to the variable cost of the firm, or its *cost of goods sold*. The next three categories, lines 6 through 8, correspond to the firm's fixed costs, since in the short run they cannot be changed.

Line 8 shows a term we haven't seen before, *depreciation*, which relates to the cost of capital goods.

Firms can either rent capital or own their capital goods. In the case of the building, which Hot Dog Ventures rented, we deducted the rent in item (7) of the income statement.

When the firm owns the capital good, the treatment is more complicated. Suppose the cooking equipment has an estimated useful lifetime of 10 years, at the end of which it is useless and worthless. In effect, some portion of the cooking equipment is "used up" in the productive process each year. We call the amount used up "depreciation," and calculate that amount as the cost of the capital input for that year. **Depreciation** measures the annual cost of a capital input that a company actually owns itself.

The same reasoning would apply to any capital goods that a company owns. Trucks wear out, computers become obsolete, and buildings eventually begin to fall apart. For each of these, the company would take a depreciation charge. There are a number of different formulas for calculating each year's depreciation, but each follows two major principles: (*a*) The total amount of depreciation over the asset's lifetime must equal the capital good's historical cost or purchase price; (*b*) the depreciation is taken in annual accounting charges over the asset's accounting lifetime, which is usually related to the actual economic lifetime of the asset.

We can now understand how depreciation would be charged for Hot Dog Ventures. The equipment is depreciated according to a 10-year lifetime, so the $150,000 of equipment has a depreciation charge of $15,000 per year (using the simplest "straight-line" method of depreciation). If Hot Dog Ventures owned its store, it would have to take a depreciation charge for the building as well.

Adding up all the costs so far gives us the operating expenses (line 9). The net operating income is net revenues minus operating expenses (line 1 minus line 9). Have we accounted for all the costs of production yet? Not quite. Line 11 includes the annual cost of interest on the $100,000 loan. This should be thought of as the cost of borrowing the financial capital. While this is a fixed cost, it is typically kept separate from the other fixed costs. State and local taxes, such as property taxes, are treated as another expense. Deducting lines 11 and 12 gives a total of $55,000 in profits before income taxes. How are these profits divided? Approximately $18,000 goes to the federal government in the form of corporate income taxes. That leaves a profit of $37,000 after taxes. Dividends of $15,000 on the common stock are paid, leaving $22,000 to be plowed back as retained earnings in the business. Again, note that profits are a residual of sales minus costs.

THE BALANCE SHEET

Business accounting is concerned with more than the profits and losses that are the economic driving force. Business accounts also include the **balance sheet**, which is a picture of financial conditions on a given date. This statement records what a firm, person, or nation is worth at a given point in time. On one side of the balance sheet are the **assets** (valuable properties or rights owned by the firm). On the other side are two items, the **liabilities** (money or obligations owed by the firm) and **net worth** (or net value, equal to total assets minus total liabilities).

One important distinction between the income statement and the balance sheet is that between stocks and flows. A **stock** represents the level of a variable, such as the amount of water in a lake or, in this case, the dollar value of a firm. A **flow** variable represents the change per unit of time, like the flow of water in a river or the flow of revenue and expenses into and out of a firm. *The income statement measures the flows into and out of the firm, while the balance sheet measures the stocks of assets and liabilities at the end of the accounting year.*

The fundamental identity or balancing relationship of the balance sheet is that total assets are balanced by total liabilities plus the net worth of the firm to its owners:

$$\text{Total assets} = \text{total liabilities} + \text{net worth}$$

We can rearrange this relationship to find

$$\text{Net worth} = \text{assets} - \text{liabilities}$$

Let us illustrate this by considering Table 7-6, which shows a simple balance sheet for Hot Dog Ventures, Inc. On the left are assets, and on the right are liabilities and net worth. A blank space has been deliberately left next to the net worth entry because the only correct entry compatible with our fundamental balance sheet identity is $200,000. *A balance sheet must always balance because net worth is a residual defined as assets minus liabilities.*

To illustrate how net worth always balances, suppose that hot dogs valued at $40,000 have spoiled. Your accountant reports to you: "Total assets are down $40,000; liabilities remain unchanged. This means total net worth has decreased by $40,000, and I have no choice but to write net worth down from the previous $200,000 to only $160,000." That's how accountants keep score.

Accounting Conventions

In examining the balance sheet in Table 7-6 you might well ask, How are the values of the different items measured? How do the accountants know that the buildings are worth $100,000?

The answer is that accountants use a set of agreed-upon rules or accounting conventions to answer most questions. The most important assumption used in a balance sheet is that the value placed on almost every item reflects its *historical costs*. This differs from the economist's concept of "value," as we will see in the next section. For example, the inventory of hot-dog buns is valued at the price that was paid for them. A newly purchased fixed asset—a piece of equipment or

Balance Sheet of Hot Dog Ventures, Inc.
(December 31, 1997)

Assets		Liabilities and net worth	
		Liabilities	
Current assets:		Current liabilities:	
Cash	$ 20,000	Accounts payable	$ 20,000
Inventory	80,000	Notes payable	30,000
Fixed assets:		Long-term liabilities:	
Equipment	150,000	Bonds payable	100,000
Buildings	100,000		
		Net worth	
		Stockholders' equity:	
		Common stock	....
Total	$350,000	Total	$350,000

TABLE 7-6. The Balance Sheet Records the Stock of Assets and Liabilities, plus Net Worth, of a Firm at a Given Point in Time

a building—is valued at its purchase price (this being the historical cost convention). Older capital is valued at its purchase price minus accumulated depreciation, thus measuring the gradual decline in usefulness of capital goods. Accountants use historical cost because it reflects an objective evaluation and is easily verified.

In Table 7-6 current assets are convertible into cash within a year, while fixed assets represent capital goods and land. Most of the specific items listed are self-explanatory. Cash consists of coins, currency, and money on deposit in the bank. Cash is the only asset whose value is exact rather than an estimate.

On the liabilities side, accounts payable and notes payable are sums owed to others for goods bought or for borrowed funds. Bonds payable are long-term loans floated in the market. The last item

on the balance sheet is net worth, or stockholders' equity. This is the net value of the firm's assets less liabilities, when valued at historical cost. The net worth must equal $200,000.

We summarize our analysis of accounting concepts as follows:

1. The income statement shows the flow of sales, cost, and revenue over the year or accounting period. It measures the flow of dollars into and out of the firm over a specified period of time.
2. The balance sheet indicates an instantaneous financial picture or snapshot. It is like a measure of the stock of water in a lake. The major items are assets, liabilities, and net worth.

C. OPPORTUNITY COSTS

In this section we look at costs from yet another angle. Remember that one of the cardinal tenets of economics is that resources are scarce. That means every time we choose to use a resource one way,

we've given up the opportunity to utilize it another way. That's easy to see in our own lives, where we must constantly decide what to do with our limited time and income. Should we go to a movie or study for next week's test? Should we travel in Mexico or buy a car? Should we get postgraduate or professional training or begin work right after college?

In each of these cases, making a choice in effect costs us the opportunity to do something else. The alternative forgone is called the opportunity cost, which we met briefly in Chapter 1 and develop more thoroughly here. The immediate dollar cost of going to a movie instead of studying is the price of a ticket, but the opportunity cost also includes the possibility of getting a higher grade on the exam. The opportunity costs of a decision include all its consequences, whether they reflect monetary transactions or not.

Decisions have opportunity costs because choosing one thing in a world of scarcity means giving up something else. The **opportunity cost** is the value of the good or service forgone.

One important example of opportunity cost is the cost of going to college. If you went to a public university, you might calculate the total costs of tuition, books, and travel to be approximately $14,000 in 1996. Does this mean that $14,000 is your opportunity cost of going to school? Definitely not! You must include as well the opportunity cost of the *time* spent studying and going to classes. A full-time job for a 19-year-old high school graduate would on average pay around $16,000 in 1996. If we add up both the actual expenses and the earnings forgone, we would find that the opportunity cost of college is $30,000 (equal to $14,000 + $16,000) rather than $14,000 per year.

Business decisions have opportunity costs, too. Do all opportunity costs show up on the profit-and-loss statement? Not necessarily. In general, business accounts include only transactions in which money actually changes hands. By contrast, the economist always tries to "pierce the veil of money" to uncover the real consequences that lie behind the dollar flows and to measure the true *resource costs* of an activity. Economists therefore include all costs—whether they reflect monetary transactions or not.

There are several important opportunity costs that do not show up on income statements. For example, in many small businesses, the family may put in many unpaid hours, which are not included as accounting costs. Nor do business accounts include a capital charge for the owner's financial contributions. Nor do they include the cost of the environ-

mental damage that occurs when a business dumps toxic wastes into a stream. But from an economic point of view, each of these is a genuine cost to the economy.

Let's illustrate the concept of opportunity cost by considering the owner of Hot Dog Ventures. The owner puts in 60 hours a week but earns no "wages." At the end of the year, as Table 7-5 showed, the firm earns a profit of $22,000—pretty good for a neophyte firm.

Or is it? The economist would insist that we should consider the value of a factor of production regardless of how the factor happens to be owned. We should count the owner's own labor as a cost even though the owner does not get paid directly but instead receives compensation in the form of profits. Because the owner has alternative opportunities for work, we must value the owner's labor in terms of the lost opportunities.

A careful examination might show that Hot Dog's owner could find a similar and equally interesting job working for someone else and earning $45,000. This represents the opportunity cost or earnings forgone because the owner decided to become the unpaid owner of a small business rather than the paid employee of another firm.

Therefore, the economist continues, let us calculate the true economic profits of the hot-dog firm. If we take the measured profits of $22,000 and subtract the $45,000 opportunity cost of the owner's labor, we find a net *loss* of $23,000. Hence, although the accountant might conclude that Hot Dog Ventures is economically viable, the economist would pronounce that the firm is an unprofitable loser.

OPPORTUNITY COST AND MARKETS

At this point, however, you might well say: "Now I'm totally confused. First I learned that price is a good measure of true social cost in the marketplace. Now you tell me that opportunity cost is the right concept. Can't you economists make up your minds?"

Actually, there is a simple explanation: *In well-functioning markets price equals opportunity cost.* Assume that a commodity like coal is bought and sold in a competitive market. If I bring my ton of coal to market, I will receive a number of bids from prospective buyers: $25.02, $24.98, $25.01. These represent the values of my coal to, say, three electric utilities. I pick the highest—$25.02. The opportunity cost of this sale is the value of the best available alternative— that is, the second-highest bid at $25.01—which is almost identical to the price that is accepted. As the market approaches perfect competition, the bids get closer and closer until in the limit the second-highest bid (which is our definition of opportunity cost) exactly equals the highest bid (which is the price). In competitive markets, numerous buyers compete for resources to the point where price is bid up to the best available alternative and is therefore equal to the opportunity cost.

Opportunity Costs outside Markets.

The concept of opportunity cost is particularly crucial when you are analyzing transactions that take place outside markets. How do you measure the value of a road or a park? Of a health or safety regulation? Even the allocation of student time can be explained using opportunity cost.

- The notion of opportunity cost explains why students watch more TV the week after exams than the week before exams. Watching TV right before an exam has a high opportunity cost, for the alternative use of time (studying) would have high value in improving grade performance. After exams, time has a lower opportunity cost.
- Say the federal government wants to drill for oil off the California coast. A storm of complaints is heard. A defender of the program states, "What's all the ruckus about? There's valuable oil out there, and there is plenty of seawater to go around. This is very low-cost oil for the nation." In fact, the opportunity cost might be very high. If drilling leads to oil spills that spoil the beaches, it might reduce the recreational value of the ocean. That opportunity cost might not be easily measured, but it's every bit as real as the value of oil under the waters.

The Road Not Traveled.

Opportunity cost, then, is a measure of what has been given up when we make a decision. Consider what Robert Frost had in mind when he wrote:

> Two roads diverged in a wood, and I—
> I took the one less traveled by,
> And that has made all the difference.

What other road did Frost have in mind? An urban life? An avocation where he would not be able to write of roads and walls and birches? Imagine the immeasurable opportunity cost to all of us if Robert Frost had taken the road more traveled by.

But let us return from the poetic to practical concepts of cost. The crucial point to grasp is this:

Economic costs include, in addition to explicit money outlays, those opportunity costs incurred because resources can be used in alternative ways.

SUMMARY

A. Economic Analysis of Costs

1. Total cost (*TC*) can be broken down into fixed cost (*FC*) and variable cost (*VC*). Fixed costs are unaffected by any production decisions, while variable costs are incurred on items like labor or materials which increase as production levels rise.

2. Marginal cost (*MC*) is the extra total cost resulting from 1 extra unit of output. Average total cost (*AC*) is the sum of ever-declining average fixed cost (*AFC*) and average variable cost (*AVC*). Short-run average cost is generally represented by a U-shaped curve that is always intersected at its minimum point by the rising *MC* curve.

3. Useful rules to remember are

$$TC = FC + VC \quad AC = \frac{TC}{q} \quad AC = AFC + AVC$$

At the bottom of U-shaped *AC*, *MC* = *AC* = minimum *AC*.

4. Costs and productivity are like mirror images. When the law of diminishing returns holds, the marginal product falls and the *MC* curve rises. When there is an initial stage of increasing returns, *MC* initially falls.

5. We can apply cost and production concepts to understand a firm's choice of the best combination of factors of production. Firms that desire to maximize profits will want to minimize the cost of producing a given level of output. In this case, the firm will follow the least-cost

rule: different factors will be chosen so that the marginal product per dollar of input is equalized for all inputs. This implies that $MP_L/P_L = MP_A/P_A = \cdots$.

B. Economic Costs and Business Accounting

6. To understand accounting, the most important relationships are:
   a. The character of the income statement (or profit-and-loss statement); the residual nature of profits; depreciation on fixed assets
   b. The fundamental balance sheet relationship between assets, liabilities, and net worth; the breakdown of each of these into financial and fixed assets; and the residual nature of net worth

C. Opportunity Costs

7. The economist's definition of costs is broader than the accountant's. Economic cost includes not only the obvious out-of-pocket purchases or monetary transactions but also more subtle opportunity costs, such as the return to labor supplied by the owner of a firm. These opportunity costs are tightly constrained by the bids and offers in competitive markets, so price is close to opportunity cost for marketed goods and services.

8. The most important application of opportunity cost arises for nonmarket goods—those like clean air or health or recreation—whose services may be highly valuable even though they are not bought and sold in markets.

CONCEPTS FOR REVIEW

Analysis of Costs

total costs: fixed and variable
marginal cost
least-cost rule:

$$\frac{MP_L}{P_L} = \frac{MP_A}{P_A} = \frac{MP_{\text{any factor}}}{P_{\text{any factor}}}$$

$TC = FC + VC$
$AC = TC/q = AFC + AVC$

Accounting Concepts

income statement: sales, cost, profits
fundamental balance sheet identity

assets, liabilities, and net worth
stocks vs. flows
opportunity cost
cost concepts in economics and
   accounting

QUESTIONS FOR DISCUSSION

1. Explain the difference between marginal cost and average cost. Why should AVC always look much like MC? Why is MC the same when computed from VC as from TC?

2. To the $55 of fixed cost in Table 7-3, add $90 of additional FC. Now calculate a whole new table, with the same VC as before but new $FC = \$145$. What happens to MC, AVC? To TC, AC, AFC? Can you verify that minimum AC is now at $q^* = 5$ with $AC = \$60 = MC$?

3. Explain why MC cuts AC and AVC at the bottom of their U's.

4. "Compulsory military service allows the government to fool itself and the people about the true cost of a big army." Compare the budget cost and the opportunity cost of a voluntary army (where army pay is high) and compulsory service (where pay is low). What does the concept of opportunity cost contribute to analyzing the quotation?

5. Consider the data in Table 7-7, which contains a situation similar to that in Table 7-4.
   a. Calculate the TC, VC, FC, AC, AVC, and MC. On a piece of graph paper, plot the AC and MC curves.
   b. Assume that the price of labor doubles. Calculate a new AC and MC. Plot the new curves and compare them with those in **a**.
   c. Now assume that total factor productivity doubles (i.e., that the level of output doubles for each input combination). Repeat the exercise in **b**. Can you see two major factors that tend to affect a firm's cost curves?

6. Explain the fallacies in each of the following:
   a. Average costs are minimized when marginal costs are at their lowest point.
   b. Because fixed costs never change, average fixed cost is a constant for each level of output.
   c. Average cost is rising whenever marginal cost is rising.
   d. The opportunity cost of drilling for oil in Yosemite Park is zero because no firm produces anything there.
   e. A firm minimizes costs when it spends the same amount on each input.

(1) Output (tons of wheat	(2) Land inputs (acres)	(3) Labor inputs (workers)	(4) Land rent ($ per acre)	(5) Labor wage ($ per worker)
0	15	0	12	5
1	15	6	12	5
2	15	11	12	5
3	15	15	12	5
4	15	21	12	5
5	15	31	12	5
6	15	45	12	5
7	15	63	12	5

TABLE 7-7.

7. In 1997 a company has $10 million of net sales and $9 million of costs of all kinds (including taxes, rentals, etc.) and rents its equipment and plant. Its inventory doesn't change in the year. It pays no dividends. Draw up its simplified 1997 income statement.

8. At the end of 1996, the company in question 7 owes no money, having been completely financed by common stock. Fill in the year-end balance sheet for 1996 using the data provided in Table 7-8. Then, using the data and income statement from question 7, complete the balance sheet for 1997 in Table 7-8.

TABLE 7-8.

	Assets (end of year)			Liabilities and net worth (end of year)	
	1996	1997		1996	1997
			Liabilities	0	0
			Net worth		
Total	$50 million	....	Total		

APPENDIX 7
PRODUCTION, COST THEORY, AND DECISIONS OF THE FIRM

The production theory described in Chapter 6 and the cost analysis of this chapter are among the fundamental building blocks of microeconomics. A thorough understanding of production and cost is necessary for an appreciation of how economic scarcity gets translated into prices in the marketplace. This appendix develops these concepts further and introduces the concept of an equal-product curve, or isoquant.

A NUMERICAL PRODUCTION FUNCTION

Production and cost analysis have their roots in the concept of a production function, which shows the maximum amount of output that can be produced with various combinations of inputs. Table 7A-1 starts with a numerical example of a constant-returns-to-scale production function, showing the amount of inputs along the axes and the amount of output at the grid points of the table.

Along the left-hand side are listed the varying amounts of land, going from 1 unit to 6 units. Along the bottom are listed amounts of labor, which also go from 1 to 6. Output corresponding to each land row and labor column is listed inside the table.

If we are interested in knowing exactly how much output there will be when 3 units of land and

2 units of labor are available, we count up 3 units of land and then go over 2 units of labor. The answer is seen to be 346 units of product. (Can you identify

TABLE 7A-1. A Tabular Picture of a Production Function Relating Amount of Output to Varying Combinations of Labor and Land Inputs

When you have 3 land units and 2 labor units available, the engineer tells you the maximum obtainable output is 346 units. Note the different ways to produce 346. Do the same for 490. (The production function shown in the table is a special case of the Cobb-Douglas production function, one given by the formula $Q = 100\sqrt{2LA}$.)

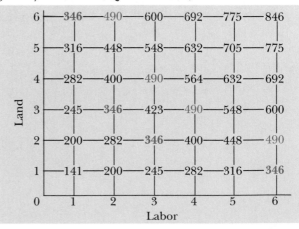

some other input combinations to produce $q = 346$?) Similarly, we find that 3 units of land and 6 of labor produce 600 units of q. Remember that the production function shows the maximum output available given engineering skills and technical knowledge available at a given time.

THE LAW OF DIMINISHING MARGINAL PRODUCT

Table 7A-1 can nicely illustrate the law of diminishing returns. First recall that the marginal product of labor is the extra production resulting from 1 additional unit of labor when land and other inputs are held constant. At any point in Table 7A-1, we can find the marginal product of labor by subtracting the output from the number on its right in the same row. Thus, when there are 2 units of land and 4 units of labor, the marginal product of an additional laborer would be 48, or 448 minus 400 in the second row.

By the "marginal product of land" we mean, of course, the extra product resulting from 1 additional unit of land when labor is held constant. It is calculated by comparing adjacent items in a given column. Thus, when there are 2 units of land and 4 units of labor, the marginal product of land is shown in the fourth column as $490 - 400$, or 90.

We can easily find the marginal product of each of our two factors by comparing adjacent entries in the vertical columns or horizontal rows of Table 7A-1.

Having defined the concept of marginal product of an input, we now can easily define the law of diminishing returns: The law of diminishing returns states that as we increase one input and hold other inputs constant, the marginal product of the varying input will, at least after some point, decline.

To illustrate this, hold land constant in Table 7A-1 by sticking to a given row—say, the row corresponding to land equal to 2 units. Now let labor increase from 1 to 2 units, from 2 to 3 units, and so forth. What happens to q at each step?

As labor goes from 1 to 2 units, the level of output increases from 200 to 282 units, or by 82 units. But the next dose of labor adds only 64 units, or $346 - 282$. Diminishing returns have set in. Still further additions of a single unit of labor give us, respectively, only 54 extra units of output, 48 units, and finally 42 units. You can easily verify that the law holds for other

rows and that the law holds when land is varied and labor held constant.

We can use this example to verify our intuitive justification of the law of diminishing returns—the assertion that the law holds because the fixed factor decreases relative to the variable factor. According to this explanation, each unit of the variable factor has less and less of the fixed factor to work with. So it is natural that extra product should drop off.

If this explanation is to hold water, output should increase proportionately when both factors are increased together. When labor increases from 1 to 2 and land simultaneously increases from 1 to 2, we should get the same increase in product as when both increase *simultaneously* from 2 to 3. This can be verified in Table 7A-1. In the first move we go from 141 to 282, and in the second move the product increases from 282 to 423, an equal jump of 141 units.

LEAST-COST FACTOR COMBINATION FOR A GIVEN OUTPUT

The numerical production function shows us the different ways to produce a given level of output. But

---

TABLE 7A-2. Inputs and Costs of Producing a Given Level of Output

Assume that the firm has chosen 346 units of output. Then it can use any of the four choices of input combinations shown as A, B, C, and D. As the firm moves down the list, production becomes more labor-intensive and less land-intensive. Fill in the missing numbers.

The firm's choice among the different techniques will depend on input prices. When $P_L = \$2$ and $P_A = \$3$, verify that the cost-minimizing combination is C. Show that lowering the price of land from \$3 to \$1 leads the firm to a more land-intensive combination at B.

	(1) Input Combinations		(3) Total cost when $P_L = \$2$ $P_A = \$3$ ($)	(4) Total cost when $P_L = \$2$ $P_A = \$1$ ($)
	Labor L	Land A		
A	1	6	20	___
B	2	3	13	7
C	3	2	12	___
D	6	1	15	___

which of the many possibilities should the firm use? If the desired level of output is $q = 346$, there are no less than four different combinations of land and labor, shown as A, B, C, and D in Table 7A-2.

As far as the engineer is concerned, each of these combinations is equally good at producing an output of 346 units. But the manager, interested in minimizing cost, wants to find the combination that costs least.

Let us suppose that the price of labor is $2 and the price of land $3. The total costs when input prices are at this level are shown in the third column of Table 7A-2. For combination A, the total labor and land cost will be $20, equal to $(1 \times \$2) + (6 \times \$3)$. Costs at B, C, and D will be, respectively, $13, $12, and $15. At the assumed input prices, C is the least costly way to produce the given output.

If either of the input prices changes, the equilibrium proportion of the inputs will also change so as to use less of the input that has gone up most in price. (This is just like the substitution effect of Chapter 5's discussion of consumer demand.) As soon as input prices are known, the least-cost method of production can be found by calculating the costs of different input combinations.

Equal-Product Curves

The commonsense numerical analysis of the way in which a firm will combine inputs to minimize costs can be made more vivid by the use of diagrams. We will take the diagrammatic approach by putting together two new curves, the equal-product curve and the equal-cost line.

Let's turn Table 7A-1 into a continuous curve by drawing a smooth curve through all the points that yield $q = 346$. This smooth curve, shown in Figure 7A-1, indicates all the different combinations of labor and land that yield an output of 346 units. This is called an **equal-product curve** or **isoquant** and is analogous to the consumer's indifference curve discussed in the appendix to Chapter 5. You should be able to draw on Figure 7A-1 the corresponding equal-product curve for output equal to 490 by getting the data from Table 7A-1. Indeed, an infinite number of such equal-product contour lines could be drawn in.

Equal-Cost Lines

Given the price of labor and land, the firm can evaluate the total cost for points *A, B, C,* and *D* or for

---

FIGURE 7A-1. Equal-Product Curve

All the points on the equal-product curve represent the different combinations of land and labor that can be used to produce the same 346 units of output.

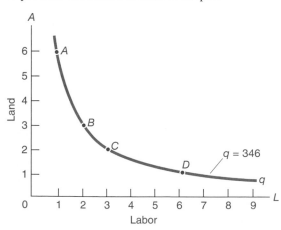

FIGURE 7A-2. Equal-Cost Lines

Every point on a given equal-cost line represents the same total cost. The lines are straight because factor prices are constant, and they all have a negative slope equal to the ratio of labor price to land price, $2/$3, and hence are parallel.

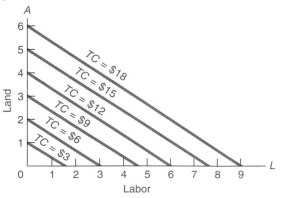

Substituting Inputs to Minimize Cost of Production

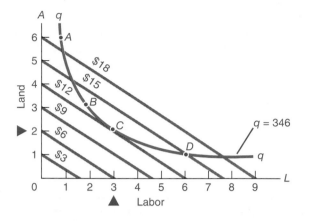

FIGURE 7A-3. Least-Cost Input Combination Comes at C

The firm desires to minimize its costs of producing a given output of 346. It thus seeks out the least expensive input combination along its rust-colored equal-product curve. It looks for the input combination that is on the lowest of the equal-cost lines. Where the equal-product curve touches (but does not cross) the lowest equal-cost line is the least-cost position. This tangency means that factor prices and marginal products are proportional, with equalized marginal products per dollar.

any other point on the equal-product curve. The firm will minimize its costs when it selects that point on its equal-product curve that has the lowest total cost.

An easy technique for finding the least-cost method of production is to construct **equal-cost lines**. This is done in Figure 7A-2, where the family of parallel straight lines represents a number of equal-cost curves when the price of labor is $2 and the price of land $3.

To find the total cost for any point, we simply read off the number appended to the equal-cost line going through that point. The lines are all straight and parallel because the firm is assumed to be able to buy all it wishes of either input at constant prices. The lines are somewhat flatter than 45° because the price of labor P_L is somewhat less than the price of land P_A. More precisely, we can always say that the arithmetic value of the slope of each equal-cost line must equal the ratio of the price of labor to that of land—in this case $P_L/P_A = \frac{2}{3}$.

Equal-Product and Equal-Cost Contours: Least-Cost Tangency

Combining the equal-product and equal-cost lines, we can determine the optimal, or cost-minimizing, position of the firm. Recall that the optimal input combination comes at that point where the given output of $q = 346$ can be produced at least cost. To find such a point, simply superimpose the single rust-colored equal-product curve upon the family of gray equal-cost lines, as shown in Figure 7A-3. The firm will always keep moving along the rust-colored convex curve of Figure 7A-3 as long as it is able to cross over to lower cost lines. Its equilibrium will therefore be at C, where the equal-product curve touches (but does not cross) the lowest equal-cost line. This is a point of tangency, where the slope of the equal-product curve just matches the slope of an equal-cost line and the curves are just kissing.

We already know that the slope of the equal-cost curves is P_L/P_A. But what is the slope of the equal-product curve? Recall from Chapter 1's appendix that the slope at a point of a curved line is the slope of the straight line tangent to the curve at the point in question. For the equal-product curve, this slope is a "substitution ratio" between the two factors. It depends upon the relative marginal products of the two factors of production, namely, MP_L/MP_A—just as the rate of substitution between two goods along a consumer's indifference curve was earlier shown to equal the ratio of the marginal utilities of the two goods (see the appendix to Chapter 5).

Least-Cost Conditions

Using our graphical apparatus, we have therefore derived the conditions under which a firm will minimize its costs of production:

1. The ratio of marginal products of any two inputs must equal the ratio of their factor prices:

Substitution ratio

$$= \frac{\text{marginal product of labor}}{\text{marginal product of land}}$$

$$= \begin{array}{c} \text{slope of} \\ \text{equal-product} \\ \text{curve} \end{array} = \frac{\text{price of labor}}{\text{price of land}}$$

2. We can also rewrite condition 1 in a different and illuminating way. From the last equation it follows that the marginal product per dollar received from the (last) dollar of expenditure must be the same for every productive factor:

$$\frac{\text{Marginal product of } L}{\text{Price of } L}$$

$$= \frac{\text{marginal product of } A}{\text{price of } A} = \cdots$$

But you should not be satisfied with abstract explanations. Always remember the commonsense economic explanation which shows how a firm will distribute its expenditure among inputs to equalize the marginal product per dollar of spending.

SUMMARY TO APPENDIX

1. A production-function table lists the output that can be produced for each labor column and each land row. Diminishing returns to one variable factor, when other factors are held fixed or constant, can be shown by calculating the decline of marginal products in any row or column.

2. An equal-product curve or isoquant depicts the alternative input combinations that produce the same level of output. The slope, or substitution ratio, along such an equal-product curve equals relative marginal products (e.g., MP_L/MP_A). Curves of equal total cost are parallel lines with slopes equal to factor-price ratios (P_L/P_A). Least-cost equilibrium comes at the tangency point, where an equal-product curve touches but does not cross the lowest TC curve. In least-cost equilibrium, marginal products are proportional to factor prices, with equalized marginal product per dollar spent on all factors (i.e., equalized MP_i/P_i).

CONCEPTS FOR REVIEW

equal-product curves
parallel lines of equal TC
substitution ratio = MP_L/MP_A

P_L/P_A as the slope of parallel equal-TC lines

least-cost tangency condition:
$MP_L/MP_A = P_L/P_A$ or MP_L/P_L
$= MP_A/P_A$

QUESTIONS FOR DISCUSSION

1. Show that raising labor's wage while holding land's rent constant will steepen the gray equal-cost lines and move tangency point C in Figure 7A-3 northwest toward B with the now-cheaper input substituted for the input which is now more expensive. If we substitute capital for labor, restate the result. Should union leaders recognize this relationship?

2. What is the least-cost combination of inputs if the production function is given by Table 7A-1 and input prices are as shown in Figure 7A-3, where $q = 346$? What would be the least-cost ratio for the same input prices if output doubled to $q = 692$? What has happened to the "factor intensity," or land-labor ratio? Can you see why this result would hold for any output change under constant returns to scale?

CHAPTER 8
THE BEHAVIOR OF PERFECTLY COMPETITIVE MARKETS

Cost of production would have no effect on competitive price if it could have none on supply.

John Stuart Mill

We now come to one of the most important topics in economics: how firms respond to the price signals that the market sends them. Common sense tells us that an astute business will increase production if the price of its product goes up. For example, if the price of oil rises, we would expect that oil companies will drill deeper and in more remote locations.

But armed with our knowledge of production and costs, we can achieve a much sharper understanding of the supply behavior of competitive firms and industries. In this chapter we will establish three key propositions. First, we see that the supply decisions of a firm depend upon its marginal cost of production. Second, we show that in the long run firms will enter or exit an industry until the profits in that industry are driven to zero. Finally, we show that a perfectly competitive industry will be efficient, meaning that there is no reorganization of production that can make everybody better off.

A. SUPPLY BEHAVIOR OF THE COMPETITIVE FIRM

Business enterprises are crucial to an efficient market economy. High-income nations are populated by businesses that produce efficiently and generate new products rapidly. But how exactly does a business enterprise behave? How much should a perfectly competitive firm produce?

BEHAVIOR OF A COMPETITIVE FIRM

How much wheat should Farmer Smith produce if wheat sells at $3 per bushel? How many pairs of shoes should tiny Fabiola's Fabulous Formfitters pro-

duce and sell if the market price of shoes is $40? These questions concern the supply behavior of perfectly competitive firms. In this chapter, we will assume that our competitive firm *maximizes profits*, which are equal to total revenues minus total costs. Profit maximization requires that the firm manage its internal operations efficiently (prevent waste, encourage worker morale, choose efficient production processes, and so forth) and make sound decisions in the marketplace (buy the correct quantity of inputs at least cost and choose the optimal level of output).

Why would a firm want to maximize profits? Profits are like the net earnings or take-home pay of a corporation. They represent the amount a firm can pay in dividends to the owners, reinvest in new plant and equipment, or employ to make financial investments. All these activities increase the value of the firm to its owners.

 Reminder on key terms: Because profits involve both costs and revenues, the firm must have a good grasp of its cost structure. Turn back to Table 7-2 in the last chapter to make sure you are clear on the important concepts of total cost, average cost, and marginal cost. Recall as well that the world of perfect competition is the world of price-takers. A perfectly competitive firm is so small relative to its market that it cannot affect the market price; it simply takes the price as given. When Farmer Smith sells a homogeneous product like wheat, she sells to a large pool of buyers who are willing to pay the market price of $3 per bushel. Just as most households must accept the prices that are charged by grocery stores or movie theaters, so must competitive firms accept the market prices of the wheat or oil or shoes that they produce.

We can depict a price-taking perfect competitor by examining the way the market looks to a competitive firm. Figure 8-1 shows the contrast between the industry demand curve (the *DD* curve) and the demand curve facing a single competitive firm (the *dd* curve). Because a competitive industry is populated by firms that are small relative to the market, the firm's segment of the demand curve is but a tiny segment of the industry's curve. Graphically, the competitive firm's portion of the demand curve is so small that, to the lilliputian eye of the perfect competitor, the firm's *dd* demand curve looks completely horizontal or infinitely elastic. Figure 8-1 illustrates how the elasticity of demand for a single competitor appears very much greater than that for the entire market.

Because competitive firms cannot affect the price, the price for each unit sold is the extra revenue that the firm will earn. For example, at a market price of $40 per unit, the competitive firm can sell all it wants at $40. If it decides to sell 101 units rather than 100 units, its revenue goes up by exactly $40.

Recall these key points:

1. Under perfect competition, there are many small firms, each producing an identical product and each too small to affect the market price.
2. The perfect competitor faces a completely horizontal demand (or *dd*) curve.
3. The extra revenue gained from each extra unit sold is therefore the market price.

Competitive Supply Where Marginal Cost Equals Price

Given its costs, demand, and desire to maximize profits, how does a competitive firm decide on the amount that it will supply? Clearly, the amount of output supplied will depend upon the costs of production. Take the supply of bicycles as an example. No sane firm would supply bicycles at a dollar a dozen, for that price would not even cover the cost of the seats. On the other hand, if bicycles were selling at $10 million apiece, everyone would rush in to open up new bicycle firms. Under normal circumstances, a firm's output decision is not so obvious and will involve the marginal cost of producing output. Let's see how.

Say *you* are managing Fabiola's Fabulous Formfitters and deciding on the profit-maximizing output. The data in Table 8-1 can help us understand the determinants of the supply decisions of a competitive

---

FIGURE 8-1. Demand Curve Looks Horizontal to a Perfect Competitor

The industry demand curve is on the left, showing inelastic demand at competitive equilibrium at *A*. However, the perfect competitor on the right has such a tiny part of the market that demand looks completely horizontal (i.e., perfectly elastic). The perfect competitor can sell all it wants at the market price.

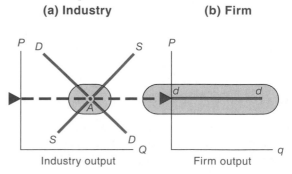

(a) Industry   **(b) Firm**

		Supply Decision of Competitive Firm				
(1)	(2)	(3) Marginal cost per unit MC ($)	(4)	(5)	(6)	(7)
Quantity q	Total cost TC ($)		Average cost AC ($)	Price P ($)	Total revenue TR ($)	Profit π ($)
0	55,000					
1,000	85,000	27	85	40	40,000	−45,000
2,000	110,000	22	55	40	80,000	−30,000
3,000	130,000	21	43.33	40	120,000	−10,000
3,999	159,960.01	38.98	40.000+	40	159,960	−0.01
		39.99				
4,000	160,000	40	40	40	160,000	0
		40.01				
4,001	160,040.01	40.02	40.000+	40	160,040	−0.01
5,000	210,000	60	42	40	200,000	−10,000

TABLE 8-1. Profit Is Maximized at Production Level Where Marginal Cost Equals Price
This table uses the same cost data as that analyzed in the previous chapter (see Table 7-3). We made a tiny adjustment in output to find the cost levels around the point of minimum average cost at 4000 units. The dark rust-colored marginal cost figures in column (3) are the numbers that are read off the smoothed *MC* curve. The light rust-colored *MC* numbers in column (3) between the rows are the exact *MC* calculated between output levels in column (1).

firm like Fabiola's. (Note that this table contains the same cost data in thousands as Table 7-3 in the previous chapter.) For this example, assume that the market price for shoes is $40 per unit. Say Fabiola's starts out by selling 3000 pairs. This yields total revenue of $40 × 3000 = $120,000 with total cost of $130,000, so the firm incurs a loss of $10,000.

Now you look at your operations and see that if you sell more shoes, the revenue from each unit is $40 while the marginal cost is only $21. Additional units bring in more than they cost. So you raise production to 4000 pairs. At this output, the firm has revenues of $40 × 4000 = $160,000 and costs of $160,000, so profits are zero.

Flush with your success, you decide to boost output some more, to 5000 pairs. At this output, the firm has revenues of $40 × 5000 = $200,000 and costs of $210,000. Now you're losing $10,000 again. What went wrong?

When you go back to your books, you see that at the output level of 5000, the marginal cost is $60, which is

more than the price of $40, so you are losing $20 (equal to price minus *MC*) on the last unit produced. Now you and your accountant see the light:

The maximum-profit output comes at that output where marginal cost equals price.

The reason underlying this proposition is that the competitive firm can always make additional profit as long as the price is greater than the marginal cost of the last unit. Total profit reaches its peak—is maximized—when there is no longer any extra profit to be earned by selling extra output. At the maximum-profit point, the last unit produced brings in an amount of revenue exactly equal to that unit's cost. What is that extra revenue? It is the price per unit. What is that extra cost? It is the marginal cost.

Let's test this rule by looking at Table 8-1. Starting at the maximum-profit output of 4000 units, if Fabiola's sells 1 more unit, that unit would bring a price of $40 while the marginal cost of that unit is $40.01. So the firm would lose money on the 4001st

FIGURE 8-2. Firm's Supply Curve Is Its Rising Marginal Cost Curve
For a profit-maximizing competitive firm, the upward-sloping marginal cost (*MC*) curve is
the firm's supply curve. For market price at *d′d′*, the firm will supply output at intersection
point at *A*. Explain why intersection points at *B* and *C* represent equilibria for prices at *d* and
d″ respectively.

unit. Similarly, the firm would lose $0.01 if it pro-
duced 1 less unit. This shows that the firm's maximum-profit output comes at exactly $q = 4000$, where
price equals marginal cost.

**Rule for a firm's supply under perfect competi-
tion:** A firm will maximize profits when it produces
at that level where marginal cost equals price:

$$\text{Marginal cost} = \text{price} \quad \text{or} \quad MC = P$$

Figure 8-2 illustrates a firm's supply decision
diagrammatically. When the market price of output is $40, the firm consults its cost data in Table 8-
1 and finds that the production level corresponding to a marginal cost of $40 is 4000 units. Hence,
at a market price of $40, the firm will wish to pro-
duce and sell 4000 units. We can find that profit-
maximizing amount in Figure 8-2 at the intersection of the price line at $40 and the *MC* curve at
point *B*.

In general, then, the firm's marginal cost curve
can be used to find its optimal production schedule:
the profit-maximizing output will come where the
price intersects the marginal cost curve.

We choose the example so that at the profit-maximizing output the firm has zero profits, with total
revenues equal to total costs. (Recall that these are
economic profits and include all opportunity costs,
including the owner's labor and capital.) Point *B* is
the **zero-profit point**, the production level at which
the firm makes zero profits; at the zero-profit point,
price equals average cost, so revenues just cover
costs.

What if the firm chooses the wrong output? If the
market price were $50, the firm should choose out-
put at intersection point *A* in Figure 8-2. We can calculate the loss of profit if the firm mistakenly produces at *B* when price is at $50 by the shaded gray
triangle in Figure 8-2. This depicts the surplus of
price over *MC* for production between *B* and *A*.
Draw in a similar shaded triangle above *A* to show
the loss from producing too much.

The general rule then is:

A profit-maximizing firm will set its output at that
level where marginal cost equals price. Diagrammatically, this means that a firm's marginal cost curve is
also its supply curve.

Total Cost and the Shutdown Condition

Our general rule for firm supply leaves open one possibility—that the price will be so low that the firm will want to shut down. Isn't it possible that at the $P = MC$ equilibrium, Fabiola's may be losing a truckful of money and want to shut down? In general, a firm will want to shut down in the short run when it can no longer cover its variable costs.

For example, suppose the firm were faced with a market price of $35, shown by the horizontal $d''d''$ line in Figure 8-2. At that price, MC equals price at point C, a point at which the price is actually less than the average cost of production. Would the firm want to keep producing even though it was incurring a loss?

Surprisingly, the correct answer is yes. The firm should *minimize its losses*, which is the same thing as maximizing profits. Because the firm's fixed costs are $55,000, producing at point C would result in a loss of only $20,000. Hence, continuing to operate would mean losing $20,000, whereas shutting down would involve losing $55,000. The firm should therefore continue to produce.

To understand this point, remember that a firm must still cover its contractual commitments even when it produces nothing. In the short run, the firm must pay fixed costs such as interest to the bank, rentals on the shoe factory, patent royalties to Fabiola, and directors' salaries. The balance of the firm's costs are variable costs, such as those for materials, production workers, and fuel. It will be advantageous to continue operations, with $P = MC$, as long as revenue minus variable costs covers some part of these fixed costs.

The critically low market price at which revenues just equal variable costs (or, equivalently, at which losses exactly equal fixed costs) is called the **shutdown point.** For prices above the shutdown point, the firm will produce along its marginal cost curve because, even though the firm might be losing money, it would lose more money by shutting down. For prices below the shutdown point, the firm will produce nothing at all because by shutting down the firm will lose only its fixed costs. This gives the shutdown rule:

Shutdown rule: The shutdown point comes where revenues just cover variable costs or where losses are equal to fixed costs. When the price falls below the level where revenues are equal to variable costs, the firm will minimize its losses by shutting down.

Zero-Profit and Shutdown Prices

FIGURE 8-3. Firm's Supply Curve Travels Down the *MC* Curve to the Shutdown Point

The firm's supply curve corresponds to its *MC* curve as long as revenues exceed variable costs. Once price falls below P_S, the shutdown point, losses are greater than fixed costs, and the firm shuts down. Hence the solid rust-colored curve is the firm's supply curve.

Explain why the firm has positive, zero, and negative profits for price above, at, and below the price of the *dd* curve.

Figure 8-3 shows the shutdown and zero-profit points for a firm. The zero-profit point comes where price is equal to *AC*, while the shutdown level of output comes where price is equal to *AVC*. Therefore, the firm's supply curve is the solid rust line in Figure 8-3. It goes up the vertical axis to the price corresponding to the shutdown point; jumps to the shutdown point at M', where P equals the level of *AVC*; and then continues up the *MC* curve for prices above the shutdown price.

The analysis of shutdown conditions leads to the surprising conclusion that profit-maximizing firms may in the short run continue to operate even though they are losing money. This condition will hold particularly for firms that are heavily indebted and therefore have high fixed costs (the airlines being a good example). For these firms, as long as losses are less than fixed costs, profits are maximized and losses are minimized when they pay the fixed costs and still continue to operate.

Unemployment in the drilling industry: A striking example of the shutdown rule at work is seen in the oil industry. In 1985, when the price of crude oil was $27 a barrel, there were about 35,000 oil wells drilled in the United States. But by the next year, the number of wells being drilled had fallen to less than 19,000, a drop of almost half. Had the oil fields run dry?

Hardly. Rather, what happened was that the average price of oil fell dramatically, to only $14 a barrel. It was the profits, not the wells, that dried up. As a result, the companies just shut the drilling rigs down. This works in reverse, as well. During the Persian Gulf war in 1990, the price of oil skyrocketed and drilling activity increased as drilling became more profitable.

B. SUPPLY BEHAVIOR IN COMPETITIVE INDUSTRIES

Our discussion up to now has concerned only the individual firm. But a competitive market comprises many firms, and we are interested in the behavior of all firms together, not just a single firm. How can we move from the one to the many? From Fabiola's to the entire shoe industry?

SUMMING ALL FIRMS' SUPPLY CURVES TO GET MARKET SUPPLY

Suppose we are dealing with a competitive market for shoes. At a given price, firm A will bring so many shoes to market, firm B will bring another quantity, and so on for firms C, D, etc. In each case, the quantity supplied will be determined by each firm's marginal costs. The *total* quantity brought to market at a given price will be the *sum* of the individual quantities that firms supply at that price.[1]

This reasoning leads to the following relationship between individual and market supplies:

To get the market supply curve for a good, we must add horizontally the supply curves of all the individual producers of that good.

Figure 8-4 illustrates this for two firms. To get the industry's supply curve *SS*, add horizontally, at the same price, all firms' supply curves *ss*. At a price of $40, firm A will supply 4000 units while firm B will supply 11,000 units. Therefore, the industry supply

curve, shown in Figure 8-4(*c*), adds the two supplies together and finds total industry supply of 15,000 units at a price of $40. If there are 2 million rather than 2 firms, we would still derive industry output by adding all the 2 million individual-firm quantities at the going price. Horizontal addition of output at each price gives us the industry supply curve.

SHORT-RUN AND LONG-RUN EQUILIBRIUM

At the turn of the century, Cambridge University's great economist Alfred Marshall helped forge the supply-and-demand tools we use today. He noticed that in the short run, demand shifts produce greater price adjustments and smaller quantity adjustments than they do in the long run. We can understand this observation by distinguishing two time periods for market equilibrium that correspond to different cost categories: (1) *short-run* equilibrium, when any increase or decrease in output must use the same fixed amount of plant and equipment, and (2) *long-run* equilibrium, when all factors are variable, so firms can abandon old plants or build new ones and firms can enter or exit the industry.

Let's illustrate this distinction with an example. Consider the market for fresh fish, supplied by a local fishing fleet. Suppose the demand for fish increases; this case is shown in Figure 8-5(*a*) on page 144 as a shift from *DD* to *D'D'*. With higher prices, fishing captains will want to increase their catch. In the short run, they cannot build new boats, but they can hire extra

---

[1] Recall that the *DD* market demand curve is similarly obtained by horizontal summation of individual *dd* demand curves.

FIGURE 8-4. Add All Firms' Supply Curves to Derive Market Supply

The diagrams show how the market supply curve (*SS*) is composed of two individual supply curves (*ss*). We horizontally add quantities supplied by each firm at $40 to get total market supply at $40. This applies at each price and to any number of firms. If there are 1000 firms identical to firm A, the market supply curve would look like firm A's supply curve with a thousandfold change of horizontal scale.

crews and work longer hours. Increased inputs of variable factors will produce a greater quantity of fish along the *short-run supply curve $S_S S_S$*, shown in Figure 8-5(*a*). The short-run supply curve intersects the new demand curve at *E′*, the point of short-run equilibrium.

In the long run, the higher prices coax out more shipbuilding, attract more sailors into the industry, and induce new firms to enter the industry. This gives us the *long-run supply curve $S_L S_L$* in Figure 8-5(*b*) and the long-run equilibrium at *E″*. The intersection of the long-run supply curve with the new demand curve yields the long-run equilibrium attained when all economic conditions (including the number of ships, shipyards, and firms) have adjusted to the new level of demand.

The Long Run for a Competitive Industry

Our analysis of zero-profit conditions showed that firms might stay in business for a time even though they are unprofitable. This situation is possible particularly for firms with high fixed capital costs. With this analysis we can understand why in business

downturns many of America's largest companies, such as General Motors, stayed in business even though they were losing billions of dollars.

Such losses raise a troubling question: Is it possible that capitalism is heading toward "euthanasia of the capitalists," a situation where increased competition produces chronic losses? For this question, we need to analyze the long-run shutdown conditions. We showed that firms shut down when they can no longer cover their variable costs. But in the long run, *all* costs are variable. A firm that is losing money can pay off its bonds, release its managers, and let its leases expire. In the long run, all commitments are once again options. Hence, in the long run firms will produce only when price is at or above the zero-profit condition where price equals average cost.

There is, then, a critical zero-profit point below which long-run price cannot remain if firms are to stay in business. In other words, long-run price must cover out-of-pocket costs such as labor, materials, equipment, taxes, and other expenses, along with opportunity costs such as competitive return on the owner's invested capital. That means long-run price must be equal to or above total long-run average cost.

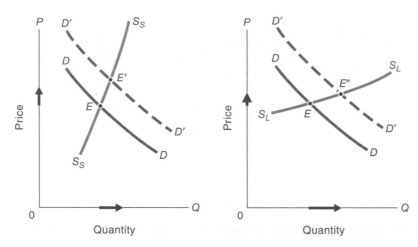

FIGURE 8-5. Effect of Increase in Demand on Price Varies in Different Time Periods
We distinguish between periods in which firms have time to make (**a**) adjustments of labor
and variable factors (short-run equilibrium) and (**b**) full adjustment of all factors, fixed as
well as varying (long-run equilibrium). The longer the time for adjustments, the greater the
elasticity of supply response and the less the rise in price.

What happens if the long-run price falls below
this critical zero-profit level? Firms, not making a
profit, will start leaving the industry. The market supply curve will shift to the left, and the price will rise
(draw the graph for yourself). Eventually, the price
will rise enough so that the industry is no longer
unprofitable.

But the process works in the other direction, as
well. Suppose that the long-run price is above total
long-run average cost, so firms are making positive
economic profits. Now suppose entry into the industry is absolutely free in the long run, so any number
of identical firms can come into the industry and
produce at exactly the same costs as those firms
already in the industry. In this situation, new firms
will be attracted by prospective profits, the supply
curve shifts to the right, and price falls. Eventually it
falls to the zero-profit level, so it is no longer profitable for other firms to enter the industry.

The conclusion is that in the long run, the price
in an industry will tend toward the critical point
where identical firms just cover their full competitive
costs. Below this critical long-run price, firms would
leave the industry until price returns to long-run
average cost. Above this long-run price, new firms
would enter the industry, thereby forcing market

price back down to the long-run equilibrium price
where all competitive costs are just covered.

Zero-profit long-run equilibrium: When an industry is supplied by competitive firms with identical
cost curves, and when firms can enter and leave the
industry freely, the long-run equilibrium condition is
that price equals marginal cost equals the minimum
long-run average cost for each identical firm:

$$P = MC = \text{minimum long-run } AC = \text{zero-profit price}$$

This is the long-run *zero-economic-profit* condition.

Long-Run Industry Supply. What is the
shape of the long-run supply curve for an industry?
Suppose that an industry has free entry of identical
firms. If the identical firms use general inputs, such
as unskilled labor, that can be attracted from the vast
ocean of other uses without affecting the prices of
those general inputs, we get the case of constant
costs shown by the horizontal $S_L S_L$ supply curve in
Figure 8-6.

By contrast, suppose some of the inputs used in
the industry are in relatively short supply—for example, fertile vineyard land for the wine industry or
scarce beachfront properties for summer vacations.
Then the supply curve for the wine or vacation

industry must be upward-sloping, as shown by $S_L S_L'$ in Figure 8-6.

Why must the long-run supply curve of industries using scarce factors be rising? We must invoke the law of diminishing returns. For the case of the rare vineyard land, when firms apply increasing inputs of labor to fixed land, they receive smaller and smaller increments of wine-grape output; but each dose of labor costs the same in wages, so the MC of wine rises. This long-run rising MC means that the long-run supply curve must be rising.

What can we conclude about the long-run profitability of competitive capitalism? We have found that the forces of competition tend to push firms and industries toward a zero-profit long-run state. Those industries that are profitable tend to attract entry of new firms, thereby driving down prices and reducing profits toward zero. By contrast, those industries that are suffering losses tend to drive firms out as they seek industries with better profit opportunities. Prices and profits then tend to rise. *The long-run equilibrium in a competitive industry is therefore one with no economic profits.*

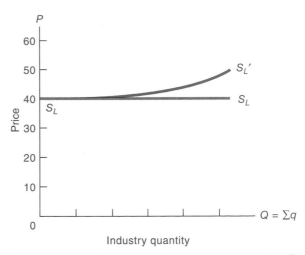

FIGURE 8-6. Long-Run Industry Supply Depends on Cost Conditions

With entry and exit free and any number of firms able to produce on identical, unchanged cost curves, the long-run $S_L S_L$ curve will be horizontal at each firm's minimum average cost or zero-profit price. If the industry uses a specific factor, such as scarce beachfront property, the long-run supply curve must slope upward like $S_L S_L'$ as higher production employs less well-suited inputs.

C. SPECIAL CASES OF COMPETITIVE MARKETS

We have now developed the basic apparatus of supply and demand. This section probes more deeply into supply-and-demand analysis. We first consider certain general propositions about competitive markets and then continue with some special cases.

GENERAL RULES

We analyzed above the impact of demand and supply shifts in competitive markets. These findings apply to virtually any competitive market, whether it is for codfish, brown coal, Douglas fir, Japanese yen, IBM stock, or petroleum. Are there any general rules? The propositions that follow investigate the impact of shifts in supply or demand upon the price and quantity bought and sold. Remember always that by a shift in demand or supply we mean a shift in the demand or supply curve or schedule, not a movement along the curve.

Demand rule: (*a*) Generally, an increase in demand for a commodity (the supply curve being unchanged) will raise the price of the commodity. (*b*) For most commodities, an increase in demand will also increase the quantity demanded. A decrease in demand will have the opposite effects.

Supply rule: An increase in supply of a commodity (the demand curve being constant) will generally lower the price and increase the quantity bought and sold. A decrease in supply has the opposite effect.

These two rules of supply and demand summarize the qualitative effects of shifts in supply and demand. But the quantitative effects on price and quantity depend upon the exact shapes of the supply and demand curves. In the cases that follow, we will see the response for a number of important cost and supply situations.

Constant Cost

Production of many manufacturing items, such as textiles, can be expanded by merely duplicating factories, machinery, and labor. Producing 200,000 shirts per day simply requires that we do the same thing as we did when we were manufacturing 100,000 per day, but on a doubled scale. In addition, assume that the textile industry uses land, labor, and other inputs in the same proportions as the rest of the economy.

In this case the long-run supply curve SS in Figure 8-7 is a horizontal line at the constant level of unit costs. A rise in demand from DD to D'D' will shift the new intersection point to E', raising Q but leaving P the same.

Increasing Costs and Diminishing Returns

We noted in the last section cases where a product uses an input in limited supply, such as wine grapes that require a certain kind of soil and climate. Such sites are limited in number. The annual output of wine can be increased to some extent by adding more labor and fertilizer to each acre of land. But as we saw in Chapter 6, the law of diminishing returns will eventually operate if variable factors of production, such as labor and fertilizer, are added to fixed amounts of a factor such as land.

As a result of diminishing returns, the marginal cost of producing wine increases as wine production rises. Figure 8-8 shows the rising supply curve SS. How will price be affected by an increase in demand? The figure shows that higher demand will increase the price of this good even in the long run with identical firms and free entry and exit.

Fixed Supply and Economic Rent

Some goods or productive factors are completely fixed in amount, regardless of price. There is only one *Mona Lisa* by da Vinci. Nature's original endowment of land can be taken as fixed in amount. Raising the price offered for land cannot create an additional corner at 57th Street and Fifth Avenue in New York City. Raising the pay of star athletes is unlikely to change their effort. When the quantity supplied is constant at every price, the payment for the use of such a factor of production is called **rent** or **pure economic rent**.

When supply is independent of price, the supply curve is vertical in the relevant region. Land will continue to contribute to production no matter what its price. Figure 8-9 shows the case of land, for which a higher price cannot coax out any increase in output.

An increase in the demand for a fixed factor will affect only the price. Quantity supplied is

FIGURE 8-7. Constant-Cost Case

FIGURE 8-8. Increasing-Cost Case

FIGURE 8-9. Factors with Fixed Supply Earn Rent

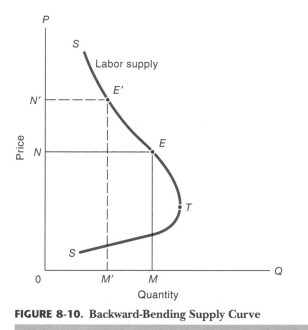

FIGURE 8-10. Backward-Bending Supply Curve

unchanged. And the rise in price exactly equals the upward shift in demand.

When a tax is placed upon the fixed commodity, the effect is that the price received by the supplier is reduced by exactly the amount of the tax. The tax is completely paid by (or "shifted" back to) the supplier (say, the landowner). The supplier absorbs the entire tax out of economic rent. The consumer buys exactly as much of the good or service as before and at no higher price.

Backward-Bending Supply Curve

Firms in poor countries noted that when they raised wages, the local workers often worked fewer hours. When the wage was doubled, instead of continuing to work 6 days a week, the workers might work 3 days and go fishing for the other 3 days. The same has been observed in high-income countries. As improved technology raises real wages, people feel that they want to take part of their higher earnings in the form of more leisure and early retirement. Chapter 5 described income and substitution effects, which explain why a supply curve might *bend backward*.

Figure 8-10 shows what a supply curve for labor might look like. At first the labor supplied rises as higher wages coax out more labor. But beyond point *T*, higher wages lead people to work fewer hours and to take more leisure. An increase in demand raises

the price of labor, as was stated in the demand rule at the beginning of this section. But note why we were cautious to add "for most commodities" to demand rule (*b*), for now the increase in demand decreases the quantity of labor supplied.

Verification of backward-bending supply can be found in many areas. One of the most interesting examples came when oil-rich countries curbed their production of oil after the price of oil quadrupled in the early 1970s.

Shifts in Supply

All the above discussions dealt with a shift in demand and no shift in supply. To analyze the supply rule, we must now shift supply, keeping demand constant. If the law of downward-sloping demand is valid, increased supply must decrease price and increase quantity demanded. You should draw your own supply and demand curves and verify the following quantitative corollaries of the supply rule:

(*c*) An increased supply will decrease *P* most when demand is inelastic.

(*d*) An increased supply will increase *Q* least when demand is inelastic.

What are commonsense reasons for these rules? Illustrate with cases of elastic demand for autos and of inelastic demand for electricity.

D. EFFICIENCY AND EQUITY OF COMPETITIVE MARKETS

EVALUATING THE MARKET MECHANISM

One of the remarkable features of the last decade has been the "rediscovery of the market." Many countries have abandoned the heavy-handed interventionism of government command and regulation for the subtle coordination of the invisible hand. Having reviewed the basic operation of competitive markets, let's ask how well they perform. Do they deserve high grades for satisfying people's economic needs? Is society getting many guns and much butter for a given amount of inputs? Or does the butter melt on the way to the store, while the guns have crooked barrels? We will give a preliminary answer to these questions at this point; a full answer must be postponed to Chapter 15, after we have analyzed factor markets.

The Concept of Efficiency

The answer to these questions lies in the concept of **allocative efficiency** (or **efficiency**, for short). An economy is efficient when it provides its consumers with the most desired set of goods and services, given the resources and technology of the economy.

Allocative efficiency (or **efficiency**) occurs when no possible reorganization of production can make anyone better off without making someone else worse off. Under conditions of allocative efficiency, one person's satisfaction or utility can be increased only by lowering someone else's utility.

We can think of the concept of efficiency intuitively in terms of the production-possibility frontier. An economy is clearly inefficient if it is inside the *PPF*. If we move out to the *PPF*, no one need suffer a decline in utility. At a minimum, an efficient economy is on its *PPF*. But efficiency goes further and requires not only that the right mix of goods be produced but also that these goods be allocated among consumers to maximize consumer satisfactions.

Efficiency of Competitive Equilibrium

One of the major results in all economics is that the allocation of resources by ideal competitive markets is efficient. This important result assumes that

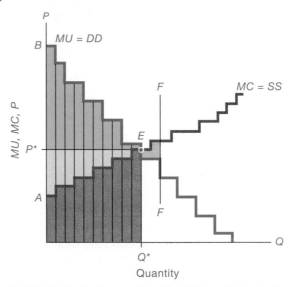

FIGURE 8-11. At Competitive Equilibrium Point *E*, the Marginal Costs and Utilities of Food Are Exactly Balanced Many identical farmer-consumers bring their food to market. The upward-stepping *MC* = *SS* curve adds together the marginal cost curves, while the downward-stepping *MU* = *DD* curve represents the consumer valuation of food. At competitive market equilibrium *E*, the marginal gain from the last unit of food is exactly equal to the marginal labor cost required to produce the last unit of food at *E*.

The cost of producing food (the disutility of sweaty labor) is shown by the dark gray slices. Vertical rust-color slices under *MU* and above *MC* are the net economic gain from the competitive equilibrium at *E*. Note that no reorganization of production can attain a larger net gain of the rust-color area as compared to a competitive market. For example, the light gray area to the right of *E* shows the economic loss from producing too much food at *FF*.

all markets are perfectly competitive and that there are no externalities like pollution. However, even if the economy is efficient, this says nothing about the fairness of the distribution of income in competitive markets. In this section, we use a simplified example to illustrate the general principles underlying the efficiency of competitive markets.

Consider an idealized situation where all individuals are identical. Further assume: (*a*) Each person works at growing food. As people increase their work, and leisure hours are therefore curtailed, each additional hour of work becomes increasingly tiresome. (*b*) Each extra unit of food consumed brings diminished marginal utility (*MU*). (*c*) Because food production takes place on fixed plots of land, by the law of diminishing returns, each extra minute of work brings less and less extra food.

Figure 8-11 shows supply and demand for our simplified competitive economy. When we sum horizontally the identical supply curves of our identical farmers, we get the upward-stepping *MC* curve. As we saw earlier in this chapter, the *MC* curve is also the industry's supply curve, so the figure shows *MC* = *SS*. Also, the demand curve is the horizontal summation of the identical individuals' marginal utility (or demand-for-food) curves; it is represented by the downward-stepping *MU* = *DD* curve for food in Figure 8-11.

The intersection of the *SS* and *DD* curves shows the competitive equilibrium for food. At point *E*, farmers supply exactly what consumers want to purchase at the equilibrium market price. Each person will be working up to the critical point where the declining marginal-utility-of-consuming-food curve intersects the rising marginal-cost-of-growing-food curve.

A careful analysis of this competitive equilibrium will show that it is efficient. At the competitive equilibrium at point *E* in Figure 8-11, the representative consumer will have higher utility than with any other feasible allocation of resources. This is so because at competitive equilibrium *E*, the marginal utility of the consumed good (*MU*) equals the price (*P*), which in turn equals the marginal cost of producing the good (*MC*). As the following three-step process shows, if *MU* = *P* = *MC*, then the allocation is efficient.

1. *P* = *MU*. Consumers choose food purchases up to the amount where *P* = *MU*. As a result, every person is gaining *P* utils of satisfaction from the last unit of food consumed.
2. *P* = *MC*. As producers, each person is supplying food up to the point where the price of food exactly equals the *MC* of the last unit of food supplied (the *MC* here being the cost in terms of the disutility of the sweaty labor needed to produce the last unit of food). The price then is the utils of satisfaction lost by working that last bit of time

needed to grow that last unit of food.
3. Putting these two equations together, we see that *MU* = *MC*. This means that the utils gained from the last unit of food consumed exactly equal the utils lost from the sweaty labor required to produce that last unit of food. *It is exactly this condition—that the marginal gain to society from the last unit consumed equals the marginal cost to society of that last unit produced—which guarantees that a competitive equilibrium is efficient.*

Equilibrium with Many Consumers and Markets

Let us now turn from our simple parable about identical farmer-consumers to an economy populated by millions of different firms, hundreds of millions of people, and countless commodities. Can a perfectly competitive economy still be efficient in this more complex world?

The answer is "yes," or better yet, "yes, if . . . " Efficiency requires some stringent conditions that are addressed in later chapters. These include having reasonably well-informed consumers, perfectly competitive producers, and no externalities like pollution or improved knowledge. For such economies, a system of perfectly competitive markets will earn the economist's gold star of allocational efficiency.

Figure 8-12 illustrates how a competitive system brings out a balance between utility and cost for a single commodity with nonidentical firms and consumers. On the left, we add horizontally the demand curves for all consumers to get the market curve *DD* in the middle. On the right, we add all the separate firms' *MC* curves to get the industry *SS* curve in the middle.

At the competitive equilibrium at point *E*, consumers on the left get the quantity they are willing to purchase of the good at the price reflecting efficient social *MC*. On the right, the equilibrium market price also allocates production efficiently among firms. The gray area under *SS* in the middle represents the minimized sum of gray cost areas on the right. Each firm is setting its output so that *MC* = *P*. Production efficiency is achieved because there is no reorganization of production that would allow the same level of industry output to be produced at lower cost.

Many Goods. Our economy produces not only food but also clothing, movies, vacations, and many other commodities. How does our analysis apply when consumers must choose among many products?

The principles are exactly the same, but now we recall one further condition: Utility-maximizing consumers spread their dollars among different goods until the marginal utility of the last dollar is equalized for each good consumed. In this case, as long as the ideal conditions are met, a competitive economy is efficient with a multitude of goods and factors of production.

In other words, a perfectly competitive economy is efficient when private and social costs and utilities coincide. Each industry must balance *MC* and *MU*. For example, if movies have 2 times the *MC* of hamburgers, the *P* and the *MU* of movies must also be twice those of hamburgers. Only then will the *MU*s, which are equal to the *P*s, be equal to the *MC*s. By equating price and marginal cost, competition guarantees that an economy can attain allocative efficiency.

The perfectly competitive market is a device for synthesizing (*a*) the willingness of people possessing dollar votes to pay for goods as represented by demand with (*b*) the marginal costs of those goods as represented by firms' supply. Under certain conditions, competition guarantees efficiency, in which no consumer's utility can be raised without lowering another consumer's utility. This is true even in a world of many factors and products.

The Central Role of Marginal-Cost Pricing

This chapter has stressed the importance of competition and marginal cost in attaining an efficient allocation of resources. But the importance of marginal cost extends far beyond perfect competition. Using marginal cost to achieve production efficiency holds for any society or organization trying to make the most effective use of its resources—whether that entity is a capitalist or socialist economy, a profit-maximizing or non-profit organization, a university or a church, or even a family.

FIGURE 8-12. Competitive Market Integrates Consumers' Demands and Producers' Costs
(**a**) Individual demands are shown on the left. We add the consumers' *dd* curves horizontally to obtain the market demand *DD* curve in the middle.
(**b**) The market brings together all consumer demands and firm supplies to reach market equilibrium at *E*. The horizontal price-of-food line shows where each consumer on the left and each producer on the right reach equilibrium. At *P**, see how each consumer's *MU* is equated to each firm's *MC*, leading to allocative efficiency.
(**c**) For each competitive firm, profits are maximized when the supply curve is given by the rising *MC* curve. The gray area depicts each firm's cost of producing the amount at *E*. At prices equal to marginal cost, the industry produces output at the least total cost.

(a) Consumers' Demands   (b) Industry Output   (c) Firms' Supplies

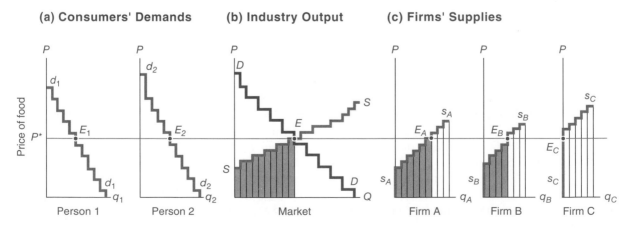

The essential role of marginal cost in a market economy is this: Only when prices are equal to marginal costs is the economy squeezing the maximum output and satisfaction from its scarce resources of land, labor, and capital.

Only when each firm has its own marginal cost equal to each other firm's *MC*—as will be the case when each *MC* has been set equal to a common price—will the industry be producing its total output at minimum total cost. Only when price is equal to marginal cost for all firms will society be on its production-possibility frontier.

The use of marginal cost as a benchmark for efficient resource allocation is applicable to all economic problems and not just to profit-maximizing firms. Say that you are convinced that "market socialism" should replace central planning in China. Your socialist firms will surely want to produce wheat efficiently. Efficiency requires that the marginal cost of wheat and all other goods be set by equating some kind of price with the marginal cost of production for each and every farm and firm.

Or suppose that you have been charged with solving a critical environmental problem, such as global warming or acid rain. You will soon find that marginal cost will be crucial to attaining your environmental objectives most efficiently. By ensuring that the marginal costs of reducing emissions or of cleaning the environment are equalized in every sector, you can guarantee that your environmental objectives are being reached at the lowest possible costs. Even noble goals should be efficiently attained in a world of scarcity.

Two Cheers for the Market, but Not Three

We have seen that markets have remarkable efficiency properties. But we cannot say that laissez-faire capitalism produces the greatest happiness of the greatest numbers. Nor does it necessarily result in the fairest possible use of resources. Why not? Because people are not equally endowed with purchasing power. Some are very poor through no fault of their own, while others are very rich through no virtue of their own. So the weighting of dollar votes, which lie behind the individual demand curves, may look unfair.

A system of prices and markets may be one in which a few people have most of the income and wealth. They may have inherited the society's scarce land or may own valuable patents and oil fields. The economy might be highly efficient, squeezing a great amount of guns and butter from its resources, but the rich few are eating the butter or feeding it to their poodles, while the guns are merely protecting the butter of the rich.

A society does not live on efficiency alone. Philosophers and the populace ask, Efficiency for what? And for whom? A society may choose to change a laissez-faire equilibrium to improve the equity or fairness of the distribution of income and wealth. The society may decide to sacrifice efficiency to improve equity. Is society satisfied with outcomes where the maximal amount of bread is produced? Or will modern democracies take loaves from the wealthy and pass them out to the poor?

There are no correct answers here. These are normative questions that are answered in the political arena by democratic voters or autocratic planners. Positive economics cannot say what steps governments should take to improve equity. But economics can offer some insights into the efficiency of different government policies that affect the distribution of income and consumption.

SUMMARY

A. Supply Behavior of the Competitive Firm

1. A perfectly competitive firm is one that can sell all the output it wants at the going market price. Competitive firms are assumed to maximize their profits. To maximize profits, the competitive firm will choose that output level at which price equals the marginal cost of production, i.e., $P = MC$. Diagrammatically, the competitive firm's equilibrium will come where the rising *MC* curve intersects its horizontal demand curve.

2. Variable costs must be taken into consideration in determining a firm's short-run shutdown point. Below the shutdown point, the firm loses more than its fixed

costs. It will therefore shut down and produce nothing when price falls below the shutdown price.

3. A competitive industry's long-run supply curve, S_LS_L, must take into account the entry of new firms and exodus of old ones. In the long run, all of a firm's commitments expire. It will stay in business only if price is at least as high as long-run average costs. These costs include out-of-pocket payments to labor, lenders, material suppliers, or landlords and opportunity costs, such as returns on the property assets owned by the firm.

B. Supply Behavior in Competitive Industries

4. Each firm's rising MC curve is its supply curve. To obtain the supply curve of a group of competitive firms, we add horizontally their separate supply curves. The supply curve of the industry hence represents the marginal cost curve for the competitive industry as a whole.

5. Because firms can adjust production over time, we distinguish two different time periods: (*a*) short-run equilibrium, when variable factors like labor change but fixed factors like capital and the number of firms do not change, and (*b*) long-run equilibrium, when the numbers of firms and plants, and all other conditions, adjust completely to the new demand conditions.

6. In the long run, when firms are free to enter and leave the industry, and where no one firm has any particular advantage of skill or location, competition will eliminate any excess profits earned by existing firms in the industry. So, just as free exit means price cannot fall below the zero-profit point, free entry means price cannot exceed long-run average cost in long-run equilibrium.

7. When an industry can expand by replication without pushing up the prices of its factors of production, the resulting long-run supply curve will be horizontal. When an industry uses factors specific to it, its long-run supply curve will slope upward.

C. Special Cases of Competitive Markets

8. Recall the general rules that apply to competitive supply and demand: Under the demand rule, an increase in the demand for a commodity (the supply curve being unchanged) will generally raise the price of the commodity and also increase the quantity demanded. A decrease in demand will have the opposite effects.

Under the supply rule, an increase in the supply of a commodity (the demand curve being constant) will generally lower the price and increase the quantity sold. A decrease in supply has the opposite effects.

9. Important special cases include constant and increasing costs, completely inelastic supply (which produces economic rents), and backward-bending supply. These special cases will explain many important phenomena found in markets.

D. Efficiency and Equity of Competitive Markets

10. The analysis of competitive markets sheds light on the efficient organization of a society. Allocative efficiency occurs when there is no way of reorganizing production and distribution such that everyone's satisfaction can be improved. Put differently, an economy is efficient when no individual can be made better off without making another individual worse off.

11. Under ideal conditions, a competitive economy attains allocative efficiency. Efficiency requires that all firms are perfect competitors and that there are no externalities like pollution or improved information. Efficiency comes because (*a*) when consumers maximize satisfaction, the marginal utility just equals the price; (*b*) when competitive producers supply goods, they choose output so that marginal cost just equals price; (*c*) Since $MU = P$ and $MC = P$, it follows that $MU = MC$. Thus the marginal social cost of producing a good under perfect competition just equals its marginal utility valuation.

12. The outcome of competitive markets, even when efficient, may not be socially desirable. Competitive markets by themselves will not necessarily ensure outcomes that correspond to the society's ideals about the fair distribution of income and consumption. Societies may modify the laissez-faire equilibrium to change the income distribution to correct for a perceived unfairness of dollar votes of demand.

CONCEPTS FOR REVIEW

Competitive Supply

$P = MC$ as maximum-profit condition
firm's *ss* supply curve and its MC
   curve
zero-profit condition, where
   $P = MC = AC$

shutdown point, where
   $P = MC = AVC$
summing individual *ss* curves to get
   industry SS
short-run and long-run equilibrium
long-run zero-profit condition

Efficiency and Equity

allocative efficiency
conditions for allocative efficiency:
   $MU = P = MC$
efficiency of competitive markets
efficiency vs. equity

QUESTIONS FOR DISCUSSION

1. Explain why each of the following statements about profit-maximizing competitive firms is incorrect. Restate each one correctly.
   a. A competitive firm will produce output up to the point where price equals average variable cost.
   b. A firm's shutdown point comes where price is less than minimum average cost.
   c. A firm's supply curve depends only on its marginal cost. Any other cost concept is irrelevant for supply decisions.
   d. The $P = MC$ rule for competitive industries holds for upward-sloping, horizontal, and downward-sloping MC curves.
   e. The competitive firm sets price equal to marginal cost.

2. Explain why a firm might supply goods at a loss.

3. One of the most important rules of economics, business, and life is the *sunk-cost principle*, "Let bygones be bygones." This means that sunk costs (which are bygone in the sense that they are unrecoverably lost) should be ignored when decisions are being made. Only future costs, involving marginal and variable costs, should count in making rational decisions.

   To see this, consider the following: We can calculate fixed costs in Table 8-1 as the cost level when output is 0. What are fixed costs? What is the profit-maximizing level of output for the firm in Table 8-1 if price is $40 while fixed costs are $0? $55,000? $100,000? $1,000,000,000? Minus $30,000? Explain the implication for a firm trying to decide whether to shut down.

4. Examine the cost data shown in Table 8-1. Calculate the supply decision of a profit-maximizing competitive firm when price is $21, $40, and $60. What would the level of total profit be for each of the three prices? What would happen to the exit or entry of identical firms in the long run at each of the three prices?

5. Using the cost data shown in Table 8-1, calculate the price elasticity of supply between $P = 40$ and $P = 40.02$ for the individual firm. Assume that there are 2000 identical firms, and construct a table showing the industry supply schedule. What is the industry price elasticity of supply between $P = 40$ and $P = 40.02$?

6. Examine Figure 8-12 to see that competitive firm C is not producing at all. Explain the reason why the profit-maximizing output level for firm C is at $q_C = 0$. What would happen to total industry cost of production if firm C produced 1 unit while firm B produced 1 less unit than the competitive output level?

   Say that firm C is a mom-and-pop grocery store. Why would chain grocery stores A and B drive C out of business? How do you feel about keeping C in business? What would be the economic impact of legislation that divided the market in three equal parts between the mom-and-pop store and chain stores A and B?

7. Often, consumer demand for a commodity will depend upon the use of durable goods, such as housing or transportation. In such a case, demand will show a time-varying pattern of response similar to that of supply. A good example is gasoline. In the short run the stock of automobiles is fixed, while in the long run consumers can buy new automobiles or bicycles.

   What is the relationship between the time period and the price elasticity of demand for gasoline? Sketch the short-run and long-run demand curves for gasoline. Show the impact of a decline in the supply of gasoline in both periods. Describe the impact of an oil shortage on the price of gasoline and the quantity demanded in both the long run and the short run. State two new rules of demand, (c) and (d), parallel to the rules of supply (c) and (d), that relate the impact of a shift in supply on price and quantity in the long run and the short run.

8. Interpret this dialogue:
   A: "How can competitive profits be zero in the long run? Who will work for nothing?"
   B: "It is only *excess* profits that are wiped out by competition. Managers get paid for their work; owners get a normal return on capital in competitive long-run equilibrium—no more, no less."

9. Consider three firms which are emitting sulfur into the California air. We will call supply the units of pollution control or reduction. Each firm has a cost-of-reduction schedule, and we will say that these schedules are given by the MC curves of firms A, B, and C in Figure 8-12.
   a. Interpret the "market" supply or MC schedule for reducing sulfur emissions, shown in the middle of Figure 8-12.
   b. Say that the pollution-control authority decides to seek 10 units of pollution control. What is the efficient allocation of pollution control across the three firms?
   c. Say that the pollution-control authority decides to have the first two firms produce 5 units each of pollution control. What is the additional cost?
   d. Say that the pollution authority decides upon a "pollution charge" to reduce pollution to 10 units. Can you identify what the appropriate charge would be using Figure 8-12? Can you say how each firm would respond? Would the pollution reduction be efficient?
   e. Explain the importance of marginal cost in the efficient reduction of pollution in this case.

CHAPTER 9
IMPERFECT COMPETITION AND ITS POLAR CASE OF MONOPOLY

The monopolists, by keeping the market constantly understocked, ... sell their commodities much above the natural price, and raise their emoluments, whether they consist in wages or profit.

Adam Smith, **The Wealth of Nations**

Perfectly competitive markets are the ideal in today's economy: much looked for, seldom found. When you buy your car from Ford or Toyota, your hamburgers from McDonald's or Wendy's, or your computer from IBM or Apple, you are dealing with firms large enough to affect the market price. Indeed, most markets in the economy are dominated by a handful of large firms, often only two or three. Welcome to the world you live in, the world of imperfect competition.

A. PATTERNS OF IMPERFECT COMPETITION

In this chapter and the next one we study the major kinds of imperfect competition—monopoly, oligopoly, and monopolistic competition. We shall see that for a given technology, prices are higher and outputs are lower under imperfect competition than under perfect competition. But imperfect competitors have virtues along with these vices, however. Large firms exploit economies of large-scale production and are responsible for much of the innovation that propels long-term economic growth. If you understand how imperfectly competitive markets work, you will have a much deeper understanding of modern industrial economies.

 Reminder on the meaning of perfect competition: Recall that a perfectly competitive market is one in which every firm is too small to affect the market price. That means no matter how much a firm produces, it can sell its entire production at the going market price. A perfect competitor therefore has no reason to undercut the market price. Moreover, it will not raise its price above the market price, because then the firm will sell nothing—consumers would rather buy from its lower-priced competitors.

By the strict definition, few markets in the U.S. economy are perfectly competitive. Think of the following: aircraft, aluminum, automobiles, batteries, breakfast cereals, chewing gum, cigarettes, electricity, refrigerators, and wheat. How many of these are sold in perfectly competitive markets? Certainly not aircraft, aluminum, or automobiles. Until World War II there was only one aluminum company, Alcoa. Even today, the four largest U.S. firms produce three-quarters of U.S. aluminum output. The world commercial aircraft market is dominated by only two firms, Boeing and Airbus. In the automotive industry, too, the top five automakers (including Toyota and Honda) have almost 80 percent of the U.S. car and light-truck market.

What about batteries, breakfast cereals, chewing gum, cigarettes, and refrigerators? These markets are dominated even more completely by a relatively small number of companies. Nor does the market in electricity meet the definition of perfect competition. In most towns, a single company generates and markets all the electricity used by the populace. Very few of us will find it economical to own our own generator or windmill!

Looking at the list above, you will find that only wheat falls within our strict definition of perfect competition. All the other goods, from autos to cigarettes, fail the competitive test for a simple reason: Some of the firms in the industry can affect the market price by changing the quantity they sell. To put it another way, they have some control over the price of their output.

Definition of Imperfect Competition

If a firm can appreciably affect the market price of its output, the firm is classified as an "imperfect competitor."

Imperfect competition prevails in an industry whenever individual sellers have some measure of control over the price of their output.

Imperfect competition does not imply that a firm has absolute control over the price of its product. Take the cola market, where Coca-Cola and Pepsi together have the major share of the market, and imperfect competition clearly prevails. If the average price of other producers' sodas in the market is 75 cents, Pepsi may be able to set the price of a can at 70 or 80 cents and still remain a viable firm. The firm could hardly set the price at $40 or 5 cents a can because at those prices it would go out of business. We see, then, that an imperfect competitor has some but not complete discretion over its prices.

Moreover, the amount of discretion over price will differ from industry to industry. In some imperfectly competitive industries, the degree of monopoly power is very small. In the retail computer business, for example, more than a few percent difference in price will usually have a significant effect upon a firm's sales. In the monopolistic electricity distribution business, on the other hand, changes of 10 percent or more in the price of electricity will have only a small effect on a firm's sales in the short run.

It is important to recognize that imperfect competition does not preclude intense rivalry in the marketplace. Imperfect competitors often struggle vigorously to increase their market shares. Still, intense rivalry should be distinguished from perfect competition. Rivalry encompasses a wide variety of behavior, from advertising that attempts to shift out the demand curve to improving product quality. Perfect competition says nothing about rivalry but simply denotes that no single firm in the industry can affect the market price.

Graphical Depiction. Figure 9-1 on page 156, shows graphically the difference between perfect and imperfect competition. Figure 9-1(*a*) reminds us that a perfect competitor faces a horizontal demand curve, indicating that it can sell all it wants at the going market price. An imperfect competitor, in contrast, faces a downward-sloping demand curve. Figure 9-1(*b*) shows that if an imperfectly competitive firm increases its sales, it will definitely depress the market price of its output as it moves down its *dd* demand curve.

We can also see the difference between perfect and imperfect competition in terms of price elasticity. *For a perfect competitor, demand is perfectly elastic; for an imperfect competitor, demand has a finite elasticity.* A careful measurement will show that the price elasticity is around 2 at point *B* in Figure 9-1(*b*).

VARIETIES OF IMPERFECT COMPETITORS

A modern industrial economy like the United States is a jungle populated with many species of imperfect

FIGURE 9-1. **Acid Test for Imperfect Competition Is Downward Tilt of Firm's Demand Curve**

(**a**) The perfectly competitive firm can sell all it wants along its horizontal *dd* curve without depressing the market price. (**b**) But the imperfect competitor will find that its demand curve slopes downward as higher price drives sales down. And unless it is a sheltered monopolist, a cut in its rivals' prices will appreciably shift its own demand curve leftward to *d'd'*.

competition. The dynamics of the personal computer industry, driven by rapid improvements in technology, are different from the patterns of competition in the not-so-lively funeral industry. Nevertheless, much can be learned about an industry by paying careful attention to its market structure, particularly the number and size of sellers and how much of the market the largest sellers control. Economists classify imperfectly competitive markets into three different market structures.

Monopoly

How imperfect can imperfect competition get? The most extreme case is **monopoly:** a single seller with complete control over an industry. (It is called a "monopolist," from the Greek words *mono* for "one" and *polist* for "seller.") It is the only firm producing in its industry, and there is no industry producing a close substitute.

True monopolies are rare today. Indeed, they typically exist only with some form of government protection. For example, a pharmaceutical company which discovers a new wonder drug will be granted a patent, which gives it monopoly control over that drug for a number of years. Another important

example of monopoly is a franchised local utility, such as a firm that provides your electricity or water. In such cases there is truly a single seller of a service with no close substitutes. But in today's highly competitive economy, even protected monopolists must reckon with competition. The pharmaceutical company will find that a rival will produce a similar drug; telephone companies that were monopolists a decade ago now must reckon with cellular telephones. *In the long run, no monopolist is completely secure from attack by competitors.*

Oligopoly

The term **oligopoly** means "few sellers." Few, in this context, can be a number as small as 2 or as large as 10 or 15 firms. The important feature of oligopoly is that each individual firm can affect the market price. In the airline industry, the decision of a single airline to lower fares can set off a price war which brings down the fares charged by all its competitors.

Oligopolistic industries are relatively common in the U.S. economy, especially in the manufacturing, transportation, and communications sectors. For example, there are only a few car makers, even though the automobile industry sells many different models. The same is true in the market for household appliances: stores are filled with many different models of refrigerators and dishwashers, all made by a handful of companies. You might be surprised to know that the breakfast cereal industry is an oligopoly dominated by a few firms even though there seem to be endless varieties of cereals.

Competition vs. rivalry: When studying oligopolies, it is important to remember that imperfect competition is not the same as no competition. In many oligopolistic industries, competition is very brisk. Indeed, some of the most vigorous rivalries in the economy are in markets where there are but a few rival firms. Just look at the cutthroat competition in the airline industry, where often only two or three airlines will fly a particular route, but they still engage in periodic fare wars.

Monopolistic Competition

The last category of imperfect competition is **monopolistic competition;** this occurs when a large number of sellers produce differentiated products. This market structure resembles perfect competition in that there are many sellers, none of whom have a large share of the market. It differs from perfect competition in that the products sold by different firms are not identical. **Differentiated products** are ones whose important characteristics vary; for example, for automobiles, important characteristics include size, performance, fuel economy, and safety. Because companies sell slightly different products, they can sell at slightly different prices.

The classic case of monopolistic competition is the retail gasoline market. You may go to the local Exxon station, even though it charges slightly more, because it is on your way to work. But if the price at Exxon rises more than a few pennies above the competition, you might switch to the Mobil station a short distance away.

Indeed, this example illustrates that one important source of product differentiation comes from location. It takes time to go to the bank or the grocery store, and the amount of time needed to reach different stores will affect our shopping choices. In economic language, the total opportunity cost of goods (including the cost of time) will depend upon how far we live from a store. Because the opportunity cost of local shops is lower, people generally tend to shop in nearby locations. This consideration also explains why large shopping complexes are so popular: they allow people to buy a wide variety of goods while economizing on shopping time. The product differentiation that comes from different locations is an important reason why these tend to be monopolistically competitive markets.

Product quality is an increasingly important part of product differentiation today. Goods differ in their characteristics as well as their prices. Most IBM-compatible personal computers these days can all run the same software, and there are many manufacturers. Yet the personal computer industry is a monopolistically competitive industry, because computers differ in speed, size, memory, repair services, and ancillaries like CD-ROMs, internal modems, and sound systems. Indeed, a whole batch of monopolistically competitive computer magazines is devoted to explaining the differences between the computers produced by the monopolistically competitive computer manufacturers!

Table 9-1 on page 158 gives a picture of the various possible categories of imperfect and perfect competition. This table is an important summary of the different kinds of market structure and warrants careful study.

Joan Robinson of Cambridge: Anyone who believes that economists are a dull lot never met Joan Robinson (1903–1983), who, along with Edward Chamberlin (1867–1967) of Harvard University, developed the theory of imperfect competition in the 1930s. Robinson, of Cambridge University, England, was justly renowned for taking controversial positions. She made her first mark in 1933 with the publication of *The Economics of Imperfect Competition.* This landmark book questioned the assumption of perfect competition that had dominated the economics profession and started economics down the road toward analysis of more realistic market structures.

Later, as one of the earliest and most visible proponents of Keynesian macroeconomics, Robinson engaged in heated disputes with several prominent American economists on the meaning of capital and the viability of capitalism. Toward the end of her career she increasingly worried about the instability of the capitalist system, the distribution of income, and the social value of capitalists. "Owning capital is not a productive activity," she wrote, adding: "It is clear enough that income from property is not the reward of waiting but the reward of employing a good stock broker." Did her iconoclastic views prevent her from being the first woman to win a Nobel Prize? Some believe so, but notwithstanding this slight she stands as one of the intellectual giants of twentieth-century economics.

SOURCES OF MARKET IMPERFECTIONS

Why do certain industries display near-perfect competition while others are dominated by a handful of large firms? Most cases of imperfect competition can be traced to two principal causes. First, industries tend to have fewer sellers when there are significant economies of large-scale production and decreasing costs. Under these conditions, large firms can simply produce more cheaply and then undersell small firms, which cannot survive.

Second, markets tend toward imperfect competition when there are "barriers to entry" that make it difficult for new competitors to enter an industry. In some cases, the barriers may arise from government laws or regulations which limit the number of competitors. In other cases, there may be reasons why it is simply too expensive for a new competitor to break into a market. We will examine both sources of imperfect competition.

Costs and Market Imperfection

The technology and cost structure of an industry help determine how many firms that industry can support and how big they will be. The key is whether there are economies of scale in an industry. If there are economies of scale, a firm can decrease its average costs by expanding its output, at least up to a point. That means bigger firms will have a cost advantage over smaller firms.

TABLE 9-1. Alternative Market Structures

Most industries are imperfectly competitive. Here are the major features of different market structures.

	Types of Market Structures			
Structure	Number of producers and degree of product differentiation	Part of economy where prevalent	Firm's degree of control over price	Methods of marketing
Perfect competition	Many producers; identical products	Financial markets and agricultural products	None	Market exchange or auction
Imperfect competition				
Monopolistic competition (many differentiated sellers)	Many producers; many real or perceived differences in product	Retail trade (pizzas, beer, . . .)		
Oligopoly	Few producers; little or no difference in product	Steel, chemicals, . . .	Some	Advertising and quality rivalry; administered prices
	Few producers; products are differentiated	Cars, cereals, . . .		
Monopoly	Single producer; product without close substitutes	Local electricity and water utilities ("natural monopolies")	Considerable, but usually regulated	Advertising and service promotion

Industry	(1) Share of U.S. output needed by a single firm to exploit economies of scale (%)	(2) Actual average market share of top three firms (%)	(3) Main reason for economies of large-scale operations
Beer brewing	10–14	13	Need to create a national brand image and to coordinate investment
Cigarettes	6–12	23	Advertising and image differentiation
Glass bottles	4–6	22	Need for central engineering and design staff
Cement	2	7	Need to spread risk and raise capital
Refrigerators	14–20	21	Marketing requirements and length of production runs
Petroleum	4–6	8	Spread risk on crude-oil ventures and coordinate investment

TABLE 9-2. Industrial Competition Is Based on Cost Conditions
A classic study examined different products to determine if cost conditions could lie behind existing concentration patterns. Column (1) shows the estimate of the point where the long-run average cost curve begins to turn up, as a share of industry output. Compare this with the average market share of each of the top three firms in column (2). [Source: F. M. Scherer, Alan Beckenstein, Erich Kaufer, and R. D. Murphy, *The Economics of Multi-Plant Operation: An International Comparisons Study* (Harvard University Press, Cambridge, Mass., 1975).]

What is the result? When economies of scale prevail, one or a few firms will expand their outputs to the point where they produce a significant part of the industry's total output. The industry then becomes imperfectly competitive. Perhaps a single monopolist will dominate the industry; a more likely outcome is that a few large sellers will control most of the industry's output; or there might be a large number of firms, each with slightly different products. Whatever the outcome, we must inevitably find some kind of imperfect competition instead of the atomistic perfect competition of price-taking firms.

Many industries enjoy increasing returns to scale. Numerous detailed econometric and engineering studies confirm that many nonagricultural industries show declining average long-run costs. For example, Table 9-2 shows the results of one study of six U.S. industries. It suggests that in many industries the point of minimum average cost occurs at a large fraction of industry output—10 or 20 or even 50 percent. These industries will tend to be oligopolistic, since they can support only a few large producers.

To understand further how costs may determine market structure, let's look at a case which is favorable for perfect competition. Figure 9-2(c) on page 160 shows an industry where the point of minimum average cost is reached at a relatively low level of output. Any firm which tries to expand its output beyond this point will find its costs rapidly rising. As a result, this industry can support the large number of efficiently operating firms that are needed for perfect competition. Figure 9-2(c) illustrates the cost curves in the perfectly competitive farm industry.

Now consider Figure 9-2(b), which shows an industry where firms enjoy increasing returns to scale up to a point, above which the scale economies are exhausted and average costs begin to increase. However, the *AC* curve does not turn up soon enough to avoid the breakdown of perfect competition: the industry total demand curve *DD* is only big enough to enable a relatively small number of firms to coexist at the point of minimum average cost. Such a cost structure will tend to lead to oligopoly. Most manufacturing industries in the United States—including steel, automobiles, cement, and oil—have a demand and cost structure similar to the one in Figure 9-2(b).

Finally, look at Figure 9-2(a), which illustrates the extreme case of *natural monopoly*. In Figure 9-2(a), the firm is shown to have average and marginal

FIGURE 9-2. Market Structure Depends on Relative Cost and Demand Factors
Cost and demand conditions affect market structures. In perfectly competitive (**c**), total industry demand *DD* is so vast relative to the efficient scale of a single seller that the market allows viable coexistence of numerous perfect competitors. In (**b**), costs turn up at a higher level of output relative to total industry demand *DD*. Coexistence of numerous perfect competitors is impossible, and oligopoly will emerge. When costs fall rapidly and indefinitely, as in the case of natural monopoly in (**a**), one firm can expand to monopolize the industry.

costs that fall forever. It displays perpetual increasing returns to scale. As output grows, the firm can charge lower and lower prices and still make a profit, since its average cost is falling. So peaceful competitive coexistence of thousands of perfect competitors will be quite impossible because one large firm is so much more efficient than small firms.

A few years ago, economists believed that many industries were natural monopolies. Utilities such as telephone, electricity, water, and natural gas were regarded as natural monopolies because they have high fixed costs and a relatively low cost of providing an additional phone call or an additional kilowatt-hour of electricity. Recent technological advances, however, weaken the argument that these industries are natural monopolies. Most of the U.S. population is now served by two cellular telephone networks, which use radio waves instead of wires. Similar trends in other industries are breaking down the impediment to entry in these industries.

Barriers to Entry

Although cost differences are the most important factor behind market structures, barriers to entry can also increase concentration. **Barriers to**

entry are factors that make it hard for new firms to enter an industry. When barriers are high, an industry may have few firms and limited pressure to compete. Economies of scale act as one common type of barrier to entry, but there are others, including legal restrictions, high cost of entry, advertising, and product differentiation.

Legal Restrictions. Governments sometimes restrict competition in certain industries. Important legal restrictions include patents, entry restrictions, and foreign-trade tariffs and quotas. A *patent* is granted to an inventor to allow temporary exclusive use (or monopoly) of the product or process that is patented. For example, pharmaceutical companies are often granted valuable patents on new drugs in which they have invested hundreds of millions of dollars. Governments grant patent monopolies to encourage inventive activity. Without the prospect of patent protection, a company or a sole inventor might be unwilling to devote time and resources to research and development.

Governments also impose *entry restrictions* on many industries. Typically, utilities, such as telephone, electricity, and water, are given *franchise monopolies* to serve an area. In these cases, the firm gets an exclusive right to provide a service, and in return the firm agrees to limit its profits and provide universal service in the area even when some customers might be unprofitable.

Finally, governments can impose *import restrictions*, which have the effect of keeping out foreign competitors. It could very well be that a single country's market for a product is only big enough to support two or three firms in an industry, while the world market is big enough to support a large number of firms. Then a protectionist policy might change the industry structure from Figure 9-2(*c*) to (*b*) or even to (*a*). When markets are broadened by abolishing tariffs in a large free-trade area, vigorous and effective competition is encouraged and monopolies tend to lose their power. One of the most dramatic examples of increased competition has come in the European Union, which has lowered tariffs among member countries steadily over the last three decades and has benefited from larger markets for firms and lower concentration of industry.

High Cost of Entry.
In addition to legally imposed barriers to entry, there are economic barriers as well. In some industries the price of entry simply may be very high. Take the commercial aircraft industry, for example. The high cost of designing and testing new airplanes serves to discourage potential entrants into the market. It is likely that only two companies—Boeing and Airbus—can afford the $10 to $15 billion that the next generation of aircraft will cost to develop.

In addition, companies build up intangible forms of investment, and such investments might be very expensive for any potential new entrant to match. Consider the software industry. Once a spreadsheet program (like Lotus 1-2-3) or a word-processing program (like Microsoft Word) has achieved wide acceptability, potential competitors find it difficult to make inroads into the market. Users, having learned one program, are reluctant to switch to another. Consequently, in order to get people to try a new program, any potential entrant will need to run a big promotional campaign, which is expensive and may still result in the failure to produce a profitable product.

Advertising and Product Differentiation.
Sometimes it is possible for companies to create barriers to entry for potential rivals by using advertising and product differentiation. Advertising can create product awareness and loyalty to well-known brands. For example, Pepsi and Coca-Cola spend together hundreds of millions of dollars per year advertising their brands, which makes it very expensive for any potential rivals to enter the cola market.

In addition, product differentiation can impose a barrier to entry and increase the market power of producers. In many industries—such as breakfast cereals, automobiles, household appliances, and cigarettes—it is common for a small number of manufacturers to produce a vast array of different brands, models, and products. In part, the variety appeals to the widest range of consumers. But the enormous number of differentiated products also serves to discourage potential competitors. The demands for each of the individual differentiated products will be so small that they will not be able to support a large number of firms operating at the bottom of their U-shaped cost curves. The result is that perfect competition's *DD* curve in Figure 9-2(*c*) contracts so far to the left that it becomes like the demand curves of monopoly and oligopoly shown in Figure 9-2(*a*) and (*b*). Hence, differentiation, like tariffs, produces greater concentration and more imperfect competition.

B. MARGINAL REVENUE AND MONOPOLY

In this section we will consider the most extreme form of imperfect competition, monopoly. Our analysis will illustrate the major drawbacks of imperfect competition, which are that it restricts output and raises prices. As an essential part of this analysis, we will define a new concept, marginal revenue,

	Total and Marginal Revenue		
(1) Quantity q	(2) Price $P = AR = TR/q$ ($)	(3) Total revenue $TR = P \times q$ ($)	(4) Marginal revenue MR ($)
0	200	0	
			+200
			+180
1	180	180	
			+160
			+140
2	160	320	
			+120
			+100
3	140	420	
			+80
4	120	480	
			+40
			+20
5	100	500	
			0
			−20
6	80	480	
			−40
			−60
7	60	___	
			−80
			−100
8	40	320	
			−140
9	___	180	
			−160
			−180
10	0	0	

TABLE 9-3. Marginal Revenue Is Derived from Demand Schedule
Total revenue (TR) in column (3) comes from multiplying P by q. To get marginal revenue (MR), we increase q by a unit and calculate the change in total revenue. MR is less than P because of the lost revenue from lowering the price on previous units to sell another unit of q. Note that MR is at first positive when demand is elastic. But after demand turns inelastic, MR becomes negative even though price is still positive.

which will turn out to have important applications for oligopolists and perfect competitors as well.

THE CONCEPT OF MARGINAL REVENUE

Price, Quantity, and Total Revenue

Suppose that a firm finds itself in possession of a complete monopoly in its industry. The firm might be the fortunate owner of a patent for a new anti-cancer drug, or it might have an exclusive franchise to sell electricity in a region. If the monopolist wishes to maximize its profits, what price should it charge and what output level should it produce?

To answer these questions, we need a new concept, marginal revenue (or MR). From the firm's demand curve, we know the relationship between price (P) and quantity sold (q). These are shown in columns (1) and (2) of Table 9-3 and as the black demand curve (dd) for the monopolist in Figure 9-3(a).

We next calculate the total revenue at each sales level by multiplying price times quantity. Column (3) of Table 9-3 shows how to calculate the **total revenue** (TR), which is simply P times q. Thus 0 units bring in TR of 0; 1 unit brings in $TR = \$180 \times 1 = \$180$; 2 units bring in $\$160 \times 2 = \$320$; and so forth.

In this example of a straight-line or linear demand curve, total revenue at first rises with output, since the reduction in P needed to sell the extra q is moderate in this upper, elastic range of the demand curve. But when we reach the midpoint of the straight-line demand curve, TR reaches its maximum. This comes at $q = 5$, $P = \$100$, with $TR = \$500$. Increasing q beyond this point brings the firm into the inelastic demand region. For inelastic demand, a 1 percent price cut produces less than a 1 percent sales increase, so total revenue falls as price is cut. Figure 9-3(b) shows TR to be dome-shaped, rising from zero at a very high price to a maximum of $500 and then falling to zero as price approaches zero.

How could you find the price at which revenues are maximized? You would see in Table 9-3 that TR is maximized when $q = 5$ and $P = 100$. This is the point where the demand elasticity is exactly 1.

Note that the price per unit can be called average revenue (AR) to distinguish it from total revenue. Hence, we get $P = AR$ by dividing TR by q (just as we earlier got AC by dividing TC by q). Verify that if column (3) had been written down before column (2), we could have filled in column (2) by division.

Marginal Revenue and Price

The final new concept is marginal revenue.

Marginal revenue (MR) is the change in revenue that is generated by an additional unit of sales. MR can be either positive or negative.

Table 9-3 shows marginal revenue in column (4). MR is calculated by subtracting the total revenues of adjacent outputs. When we subtract the TR we get by selling q units from the TR we get by selling $q + 1$ units, the difference is extra revenue or MR. Thus, from $q = 0$ to $q = 1$, we get $MR = \$180 - \$0$. From $q = 1$ to $q = 2$, MR is $\$320 - \$180 = \$140$.

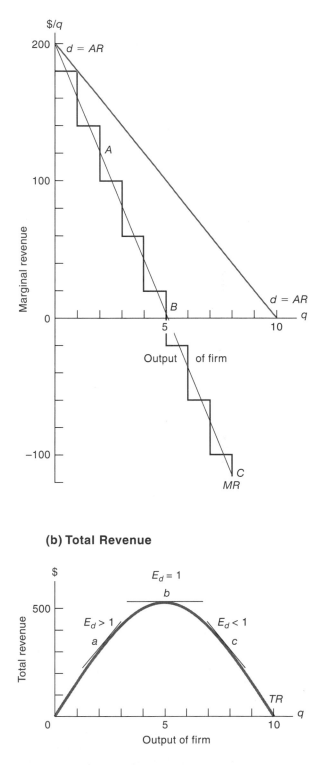

(a) Marginal Revenue

(b) Total Revenue

FIGURE 9-3. Marginal Revenue Curve Comes from Demand Curve

(**a**) The rust-colored steps show the increments of total revenue from each extra unit of output. MR falls below P from the beginning. MR becomes negative when dd turns inelastic. Smoothing the incremental steps of MR gives the smooth, thin rust-colored MR curve, which in the case of straight-line dd will always have twice as steep a slope as dd. (**b**) Total revenue is dome-shaped—rising from zero where $q = 0$, to a maximum (where dd has unitary elasticity) and then falling back to zero where $P = 0$. TR's slope gives smoothed MR just as jumps in TR give steps of incremental MR. (Source: Table 9-3.)

MR is positive until we arrive at $q = 5$ and negative from then on. What does the strange notion of negative marginal revenue mean? That the firm is paying people to take its goods? Not at all. *Negative* MR *means that in order to sell additional units, the firm must decrease its price on earlier units so much that its total revenues decline.*

For example, when the firm sells 5 units, it gets

$$TR \text{ (5 units)} = 5 \times \$100 = \$500$$

Now say the firm wishes to sell an additional unit of output. Because it is an imperfect competitor, it can increase sales only by lowering price. So to sell 6 units, it lowers the price from $100 to $80. It gets $80 of revenue from the sixth unit, but it gets only $5 \times \$80$ on the first 5 units, yielding:

$$TR \text{ (6 units)} = 5 \times \$80 + 1 \times \$80$$
$$= \$400 + \$80 = \$480$$

Marginal revenue between 5 and 6 units is $480 − $500 = −$20. The necessary price reduction on the first 5 units was so large that, even after adding in the sale of the sixth unit, total revenue fell. This is what happens when *MR* is negative. To test your understanding, fill in the blanks in columns (2) to (4).

Note that even though *MR* is negative, *AR* or price is still positive. Do not confuse marginal revenue with average revenue or price. Table 9-3 shows that they are different. In addition, Figure 9-3(*a*) plots the demand (*AR*) curve and the marginal revenue (*MR*) curve. Scrutinize Figure 9-3(*a*) to see that the plotted rust-colored steps of *MR* definitely lie below the black *dd* curve of *AR*. In fact, *MR* turns negative when *AR* is halfway down toward zero.

To summarize:

With demand sloping downward,

$P > MR (= P -$ reduced revenue on all previous q)

Elasticity and Marginal Revenue. What is the relationship between the price elasticity of demand and marginal revenue?

Marginal revenue is positive when demand is elastic, zero when demand is unit-elastic, and negative when demand is inelastic.

This result is really a different way of stating the definition of elasticity that we used in Chapter 4. Recall that demand is elastic when a price decrease leads to a revenue increase. In such a situation, a price decrease raises output demanded so much that

revenues rise, so marginal revenue is positive. For example, in Table 9-3, as price falls in the elastic region from $P = \$180$ to $P = \$160$, output demanded rises sufficiently to raise total revenue, and marginal revenue is positive.

What happens when demand is unit-elastic? A price cut then just matches an increase in output, and marginal revenue is therefore zero. Can you see why marginal revenue is always negative in the inelastic range? Why is the marginal revenue for the perfect competitor's infinitely elastic demand curve always positive?

PROFIT-MAXIMIZING CONDITIONS

We are now ready to find the maximum-profit equilibrium of the monopolist. If a monopolist faces a given demand curve and wishes to maximize total profit (*TP*), what should it do? By definition, total profit equals total revenue minus total costs; in symbols, $TP = TR - TC = (P \times q) - TC$.

To maximize its profits, the firm must find the equilibrium price and quantity, P^* and q^*, that give the largest profit, or the largest difference between *TR* and *TC*. An important result is that *maximum profit will occur when output is at that level where the firm's marginal revenue is equal to its marginal cost.*

One way to determine this maximum-profit condition is by using a table of costs and revenues, such as Table 9-4. To find the profit-maximizing quantity and price, compute total profit in column (5). This column tells us that the monopolist's best quantity, which is 4 units, requires a price of $120 per unit. This produces a total revenue of $480, and, after subtracting total costs of $250, we calculate total profit to be $230. A glance shows that no other price-output combination has as high a level of total profit.

A second and equivalent way of arriving at the same answer is to compare marginal revenue, column (6), and marginal cost, column (7). As long as each additional unit of output provides more revenue than it costs—that is to say, as long as *MR* is greater than *MC*—the firm's profit will increase. So the firm should continue to increase its output as long as *MR* is greater than *MC*. By contrast, suppose that at a given level of output *MR* is less than *MC*. This means that increasing output would lead to a lower level of profits, so the profit-maximizing firm should at that point cut back on output. Clearly, the

(1)	(2)	(3)	(4)	(5)	(6)	(7)
Quantity q	Price P ($)	Total revenue TR ($)	Total cost TC ($)	Total profit TP ($)	Marginal revenue MR ($)	Marginal cost MC ($)

Summary of Firm's Maximum Profit

Quantity q	Price P ($)	Total revenue TR ($)	Total cost TC ($)	Total profit TP ($)	Marginal revenue MR ($)	Marginal cost MC ($)	
0	200	0	145	−145	+200	34	
					+180	30	MR > MC
1	180	180	175	+5	+160	27	
					+140	25	
2	160	320	200	+120	+120	22	
					+100	20	
3	140	420	220	+200	+80	21	
					+60	30	
4*	**120**	**480**	**250**	**+230**	+40	40	MR = MC
					+20	50	
5	100	500	300	+200	0	60	
					−20	70	
6	80	480	370	+110	−40	80	
					−60	90	
7	60	420	460	−40	−80	100	
					−100	110	MR < MC
8	40	320	570	−250			

*Maximum-profit equilibrium.

TABLE 9-4. Equating Marginal Cost to Marginal Revenue Gives Firm's Maximum-Profit q and P

Total and marginal costs of production are now brought together with total and marginal revenues. The maximum-profit condition is where $MR = MC$, with $q^* = 4$, $P^* = \$120$, and maximum $TP = \$230 = (\$120 \times 4) − \$250$. (For convenience, the light MR and MC numbers are put in to give the smoothed values at each q point.)

best-profit point comes at the point where marginal revenue exactly equals marginal cost, as is shown by the data in Table 9-4. The rule for finding maximum profit is therefore:

The maximum-profit price and quantity of a monopolist come where the firm's marginal revenue equals its marginal cost:

$$MR = MC, \text{ at the maximum-profit } P^* \text{ and } q^*$$

These examples show the logic of the $MC = MR$ rule for maximizing profits, but we always want to understand the intuition behind the rules. Look for a moment at Table 9-4 and suppose that the monopolist is producing $q = 2$. At that point, its MR for producing 1 full additional unit is +$100, while its MC is $20. Thus, if it produced 1 additional unit, the firm would make additional profits of $MR − MC = \$100 − \$20 = \$80$. Indeed, column (5) of Table 9-4 shows that the extra profit gained by moving from 2 to 3 units is exactly $80.

Thus, when MR exceeds MC, additional profits can be made by increasing output; when MC exceeds MR, additional profits can be made by decreasing q. Only when $MR = MC$ can the firm maximize profits, because there are no additional profits to be made by changing its output level.

Monopoly Equilibrium in Graphs

Figure 9-4 on page 166 shows the monopoly equilibrium. Part (a) combines the firm's cost and revenue curves. The maximum-profit point comes at that output where MC equals MR, which is given at their intersection at E. The monopoly equilibrium, or maximum-profit point, is at an output of $q^* = 4$. To find the profit-maximizing price, we run vertically up from E to the DD curve at G, where $P = \$120$. The fact that average revenue at G lies above average cost at F guarantees a positive profit. The actual amount of profit is given by the rust shaded area in Figure 9-4(a).

(a) Profit Maximization

(b) Total Cost, Revenue, and Profit

The same story is told in part (b) with curves of total revenue, cost, and profit. Total revenue is dome-shaped. Total cost is ever rising. The vertical difference between them is total profit, which begins negative and ends negative. In between, TP is positive, reaching its maximum of $230 at $q^* = 4$. At the maximum-profit output, the black slopes of TR and TC (which are MR and MC at those points) are parallel and therefore equal. If the slopes were pointing outward in a nonparallel fashion (as at $q = 2$), the firm would gain extra profit by expanding q. At $q^* = 4$, marginal cost and marginal revenue are balanced. At that point total profit (TP) reaches its maximum, as an additional unit adds exactly equal amounts to costs and revenues.

A monopolist will maximize its profits by setting output at the level where $MC = MR$. Because the monopolist has a downward-sloping demand curve, this means that $P > MR$. Because price is above marginal cost for a profit-maximizing monopolist, the monopolist reduces output below the level that would be found in a perfectly competitive industry.

Perfect Competition as a Polar Case of Imperfect Competition

Although we have applied the MC and MR rule to monopolists who desire to maximize profits, this rule is actually applicable far beyond the present analysis. A little thought shows that the $MC = MR$ rule applies with equal validity to a profit-maximizing perfect competitor. We can see this in two steps:

FIGURE 9-4. Profit-Maximizing Equilibrium Can Be Shown Using Either Total or Marginal Curves

(**a**) At E, where MC intersects MR, the equilibrium position of maximum profit is found. Any move from E will lose some profit. Price is at G, above E; and since P is above AC, the maximized profit is a positive profit. (Can you explain why the rust-colored shaded rectangle measures total profit? And why the gray triangles of shading on either side of E show the reduction in total profit that would come from a departure from $MR = MC$?) Panel (**b**) tells the same story of maximizing profit as does (**a**), but it uses total concepts rather than marginal concepts. Total profit (TP) is given by the vertical distance from TC up to TR. TP is at a maximum where its thin black slope is zero. At the maximum-profit point, the total revenue and total cost curves have equal and parallel slopes, $MR = MC$.

1. **MR** *for a perfect competitor.* The first question is, What is *MR* for a perfect competitor? For a perfect competitor, the sale of extra units will never depress price, and the "lost revenue on all previous *q*" is therefore equal to zero. Price and marginal revenue are identical for perfect competitors.

   Under perfect competition, price equals average revenue equals marginal revenue ($P = MR = AR$). A perfect competitor's *dd* curve and its *MR* curve coincide as horizontal lines.

2. **MR = P = MC** *for a perfect competitor.* In addition, we can see that the logic of profit maximization for monopolists applies equally well to perfect competitors, but the result is a little different. Economic logic requires that profits are maximized at that output level where *MC* equals *MR*. But by step 1 above, for a perfect competitor, *MR* equals *P. Therefore,* the *MR = MC* profit-maximization condition becomes the special case of *P = MC* that we derived above for a perfect competitor:

   Because a perfect competitor can sell all it wants at the market price, $MR = P = MC$ at the maximum-profit level of output.

You can see this result visually by redrawing Figure 9-4(a). If the graph applied to a perfect competitor, the *DD* curve would be horizontal at the market price, and it would coincide with the *MR* curve. The profit-maximizing *MR = MC* intersection would also come at *P = MC*. We see then how the general rule for profit maximization applies to perfect as well as imperfect competitors.

THE MARGINAL PRINCIPLE: LET BYGONES BE BYGONES

We close this chapter with a more general point about the use of marginal analysis in economics. While economic theory will not necessarily make you fabulously wealthy, it does introduce you to some new ways of thinking about costs and benefits. *One of the most important lessons of economics is that you should look at the marginal costs and marginal benefits of decisions and ignore past or sunk costs.* We might put this as follows:

Let bygones be bygones. Don't look backward. Don't cry over spilt milk or moan about yesterday's losses.

Make a hard-headed calculation of the extra costs you'll incur by any decision, and weigh these against its extra advantages. Make a decision based on marginal costs and marginal benefits.

This is the **marginal principle**, which means that people will maximize their incomes or profits or satisfactions by counting only the marginal costs and marginal benefits of a decision. There are countless situations in which the marginal principle applies. We have just seen that the marginal principle of equating marginal cost and marginal revenue is the rule for profit maximization by firms. Another example is investment decisions. When deciding about whether to invest in a company or sell a house, forget about past gains or losses and decide only on the basis of marginal returns and costs. The marginal principle is one of the central lessons of economics.

MONOPOLISTS OF THE GILDED AGE

Because abstract concepts like marginal cost and deadweight loss hide the human drama of monopoly, we close this section by recounting one of the most colorful periods of American business history. Because of changing laws and customs, monopolies in today's America bear little resemblance to the brilliant, inventive, unscrupulous, and often dishonest robber barons of the Gilded Age (1870–1914). Legendary figures like Rockefeller, Gould, Vanderbilt, Frick, Carnegie, Rothschild, and Morgan were driven by visions that created entire industries like railroads, oil, and steel, provided their finance, developed the western frontier, destroyed their competitors, and passed on fabulous fortunes to their heirs.

The robber barons of the last century were sometimes ingenious tricksters. Daniel Drew was a cattle rustler, horse trader, and railroader who mastered the trick of "watering the stock." This practice involved depriving his cattle of water until they reached the slaughterhouse; he then induced a great thirst with salt and allowed the beasts to engorge themselves on water just before being weighed. Later, tycoons would "water their stock" by inflating the value of their securities.

The railroaders of the American frontier west were among the most unscrupulous entrepreneurs on record. The transcontinental railroads were funded with vast federal land grants, aided by bribes and stock gifts to numerous members of Congress and the cabinet. Shortly after the Civil War, the wily railroader Jay Gould attempted to corner the entire gold supply of the United States, and with it the nation's money supply. Gould later promoted his railroad by describing the route of his northern railroad—snowbound much of the year—as a tropical paradise, filled with orange groves, banana plantations, and monkeys. By century's end, all the bribes, land grants, watered stock, and fantastic promises had led to the greatest rail system in the world.

The story of John D. Rockefeller epitomizes the nineteenth-century monopolist. Rockefeller saw visions of riches in the fledgling oil industry and began to organize oil refineries. He was a meticulous manager and sought to bring "order" to the quarrelsome wildcatters. He bought up competitors and consolidated his hold on the industry by persuading the railroads to give him deep and secret rebates and supply information about his competitors. When competitors stepped out of line, Rockefeller refused to ship their oil and even spilled it on the ground. By 1878, John D. controlled 95 percent of the pipelines and oil refineries in the United States. Prices were raised and stabilized, ruinous competition was ended, and monopoly was achieved.

Rockefeller devised an ingenious new device to ensure control over his alliance. This was the "trust," in which the stockholders turned their shares over to "trustees" who would then manage the industry to maximize its profits. Other industries imitated the Standard Oil Trust, and soon trusts were set up in kerosene, sugar, whiskey, lead, salt, and steel. This practice so upset agrarians and populists that the nation soon passed antitrust laws (see Chapter 17). Indeed, in 1910, the Standard Oil Corporation was dissolved in the first great victory by the Progressives against "Big Business."

Great monopolies produced great wealth. Whereas the United States had three millionaires in 1861, there were 4000 of them by 1900 ($1 million at the turn of the century was equivalent to about $100 million in today's dollars).

Great wealth in turn begot conspicuous consumption (a term introduced into economics by Thorstein Veblen in *The Theory of the Leisure Class*, 1899). Like European popes and aristocrats of an earlier era, American tycoons wanted to turn their fortunes into lasting monuments. The wealth was spent in constructing princely palaces such as the "Marble House," which can still be seen in Newport, Rhode Island; in buying vast art collections, which form the core of the great American museums like New York's Metropolitan Museum of Art; and in launching foundations and universities such as those named after Stanford, Carnegie, Mellon, and Rockefeller. Long after their private monopolies were broken up by the government or overtaken by competitors, and long after their wealth was largely dissipated by heirs and overshadowed by later generations of entrepreneurs, the philanthropic legacy of the robber barons continues to shape American arts, science, and education.

SUMMARY

A. Patterns of Imperfect Competition

1. Most market structures today fall somewhere on a spectrum between perfect competition and pure monopoly. Under imperfect competition, a firm has some control over its price, a fact seen as a downward-sloping demand curve for the firm's output.

2. Important kinds of market structure are (*a*) monopoly, where a single firm produces all the output in a given industry; (*b*) oligopoly, where a few sellers of a similar or differentiated product supply the industry; (*c*) monopolistic competition, where a large number of small firms supply related but somewhat differentiated products; and (*d*) perfect competition, where a large number of small firms supply an identical prod-

uct. In the first three cases, firms in the industry face downward-sloping demand curves.

3. Economies of scale, or decreasing average costs, are the major source of imperfect competition. When firms can lower costs by expanding their output, the situation tends to destroy perfect competition because a few companies can produce the industry's output most efficiently. When the minimum efficient size of plant is large relative to the national or regional market, cost conditions produce imperfect competition.

4. In addition to declining costs, other forces leading to imperfections are barriers to entry in the form of legal restrictions (such as patents or government regulation), high entry costs, advertising, and product differentiation.

B. Marginal Revenue and Monopoly

5. We can easily derive a firm's total revenue curve from its demand curve. From the schedule or curve of total revenue, we can then derive marginal revenue, which denotes the change in revenue resulting from an additional unit of sales. For the imperfect competitor, marginal revenue is less than price because of the lost revenue on all previous units of output that will result when the firm is forced to drop its price in order to sell an extra unit of output. That is, with demand sloping downward,

   $$P = AR > MR = P - \text{lost revenue on all previous } q.$$

6. A monopolist will find its maximum-profit position where $MR = MC$, that is, where the last unit it sells brings in extra revenue just equal to its extra cost. This same $MR = MC$ result can be shown graphically by the intersection of the MR and MC curves or by the equality of the slopes of the total revenue and total cost curves. In any case, *marginal revenue = marginal cost* must always hold at the equilibrium position of maximum profit.

7. For perfect competitors, marginal revenue equals price. Therefore, the profit-maximizing output for a competitor comes where $MC = P$.

8. Economic reasoning leads to the important *marginal principle*. In making decisions, count marginal future advantages and disadvantages, and disregard sunk costs that have already been paid.

CONCEPTS FOR REVIEW

Patterns of Imperfect Competition

perfect vs. imperfect competition
monopoly, oligopoly, monopolistic competition
product differentiation

barriers to entry (government and economic)

Marginal Revenue and Monopoly

marginal (or extra) revenue, MR

$MR = MC$ as the condition for maximizing profits
$MR = P$, $P = MC$, for perfect competitor
natural monopoly
the marginal principle

QUESTIONS FOR DISCUSSION

1. List the distinguishing features of perfect and imperfect competition. What are the main varieties of imperfect competition? In which category would you place General Motors? Your local water company? Sears? Farmer Sam? Your college or university?

2. Explain why each of the following statements is false. For each, write the correct statement.
   a. A monopolist maximizes profits when $MC = P$.
   b. The higher the price elasticity, the higher is a monopolist's price above its MC.
   c. Monopolists ignore the marginal principle.
   d. Monopolists will maximize sales. They will therefore produce more than perfect competitors and their price will be lower.

3. What is MR's numerical value when dd has unitary elasticity? Explain.

4. Figure 9-4 shows the maximum-profit equilibrium position. Explain in detail how it really shows two different ways of describing exactly the same fact: namely, that a firm will stop expanding its production where the extra cost of further output just balances its extra revenue.

5. Redraw Figure 9-4(*a*) for a perfect competitor. Why is *dd* horizontal? Explain why the horizontal *dd* curve coincides with MR. Then proceed to find the profit-maximizing MR and MC intersection. Why does this yield the competitive condition $MC = P$? Now redraw Figure 9-4(*b*) for a perfect competitor. Show that the slopes of *TR* and *TC* must still match at the maximum-profit equilibrium point for a perfect competitor.

6. Banana Computer Company has fixed costs of production of $100,000, while each unit costs $600 of labor and $400 of materials and fuel. At a price of $3000, consumers would buy no Banana computers, but for each $10 reduction in price, sales of Banana computers increase by 1000 units. Calculate marginal cost and marginal revenue for Banana Computer, and determine its monopoly price and quantity.

7. Show that a profit-maximizing monopolist will never operate in the price-inelastic region of its demand curve.

8. Explain the error in the following statement: "A firm out to maximize its profits will always charge the highest price that the traffic will bear." State the correct result, and use the concept of marginal revenue to explain the difference between the correct and the erroneous statement.

CHAPTER 10
OLIGOPOLY AND MONOPOLISTIC COMPETITION

Putnam (Braniff): **Do you have a suggestion for me?**
Crandall (American): **Yes. I have a suggestion for you. Raise your [expletive deleted] fares 20% and I'll raise mine the next morning.**
Putnam: **Robert, we . . .**
Crandall: **You'll make more money and I will too.**
Putnam: **We can't talk about pricing.**
Crandall: **Oh [expletive deleted], Howard. We can talk about any [expletive deleted] thing we want to talk about.**

A tape-recorded conversation between Howard Putnam, head of Braniff Airlines, and Robert Crandall, head of American Airlines

Earlier chapters analyzed the market structures of perfect competition and complete monopoly. If you look out the window at the American economy, however, you'll find that such polar cases are rare; you are more likely to see varieties of imperfect competition between these two extremes. Most industries are populated by a small number of firms competing with each other.

What are the key features of these intermediate types of imperfect competitors? How do they set their prices? And why do their practices lead to inefficiencies? To answer these questions, this chapter begins with a close look at what happens under oligopoly and monopolistic competition, paying special attention to the role of concentration and strategic interaction. The next section then focuses on large corporations, since these are the predominant form of economic organization in the modern capitalist economy. We end the chapter with a comparison of the economic costs and benefits of imperfect competition.

A. BEHAVIOR OF IMPERFECT COMPETITORS

Look back at Table 9-1, which shows the following kinds of market structures: (1) *Perfect competition* is found when a large number of firms produce an identical product—so many firms, indeed, that none of them can affect the market price. This market structure thrives mainly on farms and in financial markets such as the market for foreign currencies or bonds. (2) *Monopolistic competition* occurs when a large number of firms produce slightly differentiated products, while (3) *oligopoly* is an intermediate form of imperfect competition in which an industry is dominated by a few firms. The most concentrated market structure is (4) *monopoly*, in which a single firm produces the entire output of an industry.

In many situations—such as deciding whether government should intervene in a market or whether a firm has abused its monopoly position—economists need a quantitative measure of the extent of market power. **Market power** signifies the degree of control that a single firm or a small number of firms has over the price and production decisions in an industry. The most common measure of market power is the *concentration ratio* for an industry, illustrated in Figure 10-1 on page 172. The **four-firm concentration ratio** is defined as the percent of total industry output (or shipments) that is accounted for by the largest four firms. Similarly, the eight-firm concentration ratio is the percent of output shipped by the top eight firms. In a pure monopoly, the four- or eight-firm concentration ratio would be 100 percent, while for perfect competition, both ratios would be close to zero.

How concentrated is American manufacturing? For 1992, data show that 19 percent of manufacturing output takes place in highly concentrated industries (those with four-firm concentration ratios above 60 percent), while 16 percent resides in unconcentrated industries (those with four-firm concentration ratios less than 20 percent). Historical studies indicate that the measured degree of concentration has been decreasing in recent years.

 Warning on concentration measures: Although traditional concentration measures are still widely used in economics and in law, they are becoming obsolete because of international competition and structural change. Conventional concentration measures include only domestic production and exclude imports. Because imports and import competition have risen sharply over the last two decades, the actual concentration or market power probably declined even more sharply than is indicated by these measures. As a result, in those industries that are exposed to international competition, concentration ratios will overstate the extent of market power. For example, the conventional concentration measure shown in Figure 10-1 indicates that the top four automotive firms had 84 percent of the market. But if imports are included in sales, these same four firms had only 67 percent of the market.

In addition, these concentration measures also ignore the growing impact of competition from other industries. For example, concentration ratios are typically calculated for a narrow industry definition, such as paired-wire telephone services. Sometimes, however, strong competition can come from other quarters. Cellular telephones provide a major threat to conventional paired-wire local telephone service even though the two are in different industries. Care must always be taken to interpret quantitative indexes of market power appropriately.

THE NATURE OF IMPERFECT COMPETITION

In analyzing the determinants of concentration, economists have found that three major factors are present in imperfectly competitive markets. These factors are costs, barriers to entry, and strategic interaction:

- *Costs.* When the minimum efficient size of operation for a firm occurs at a sizable fraction of industry output, only a few firms can profitably survive and oligopoly is likely to result.
- *Barriers to competition.* When there are large economies of scale or government restrictions to entry, they will limit the number of competitors in an industry.
- *Strategic interaction.* When only a few firms operate in a market, they will soon recognize their interdependence. **Strategic interaction**, which is a genuinely new feature of oligopoly that has inspired the field of game theory, occurs when each firm's business plans depend upon the behavior of its rivals.

Why are economists particularly concerned about industries characterized by imperfect competition? The answer is that such industries behave in certain ways that are inimical to the public interest. For example, imperfect competition generally leads to prices that are above marginal costs; this results in an inefficient allocation of resources.

As a result of high prices, oligopolistic industries often (but not always) have supernormal profits. The profitability of the highly concentrated tobacco and pharmaceutical industries has been the target of political attacks on numerous occasions. Careful studies show, however, that concentrated industries tend to have only slightly higher rates of profit than unconcentrated ones. This is a surprising finding, and it has especially perplexed critics of big business, who expected to find the biggest companies earning enormous profits.

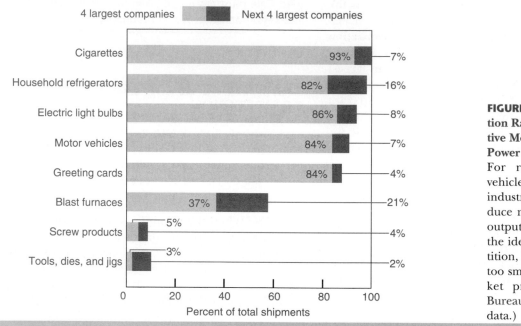

Concentration Measured by Value of Shipments in Manufacturing Industries, 1992

4 largest companies   Next 4 largest companies

Industry	
Cigarettes	93% — 7%
Household refrigerators	82% — 16%
Electric light bulbs	86% — 8%
Motor vehicles	84% — 7%
Greeting cards	84% — 4%
Blast furnaces	37% — 21%
Screw products	5% — 4%
Tools, dies, and jigs	3% — 2%

Percent of total shipments

FIGURE 10-1. Concentration Ratios Are Quantitative Measures of Market Power

For refrigerators, motor vehicles, and many other industries, a few firms produce most of the domestic output. Compare this with the ideal of perfect competition, in which each firm is too small to affect the market price. (Source: U.S. Bureau of the Census, 1992 data.)

Another point concerns research and development (R&D). Industries with high levels of concentration sometimes have high levels of R&D spending per dollar of sales as they try to get a technological edge over their rivals. By contrast, there's no sense in a small farmer or tiny bakery setting up a scientific laboratory. The high levels of R&D are generally regarded favorably by economists, and this is seen as one of the major mitigating features of imperfect competition.

THEORIES OF IMPERFECT COMPETITION

While the concentration of an industry is important, it does not tell the whole story. Indeed, to explain the behavior of imperfect competitors, economists have developed a field called *industrial organization.* We cannot cover this vast area here. Instead, we will focus on three of the most important cases of imperfect competition—collusive oligopoly, monopolistic competition, and small-number oligopoly.

Collusive Oligopoly

The degree of imperfect competition in a market is influenced not just by the number and size of firms but by how they behave. When only a few firms operate in a market, they see what their rivals are doing and react. For example, if there are two airlines operating along the same route and one raises its fare, the other must decide whether to match the increase or to stay with the lower fare, undercutting its rival. *Strategic interaction* is a term that describes how each firm's business strategy depends upon its rivals' business behavior.

When there are only a small number of firms in a market, they have a choice between *cooperative* and *noncooperative* behavior. Firms act noncooperatively when they act on their own without any explicit or implicit agreement with other firms. That's what produces price wars. Firms operate in a cooperative mode when they try to minimize competition between themselves. When firms in an oligopoly actively cooperate with each other, they engage in **collusion**. This term denotes a situation in which two or more firms jointly set their prices or outputs, divide the market among themselves, or make other business decisions jointly.

During the early years of American capitalism, before the passage of effective antitrust laws, oligopolists often merged or formed a trust or cartel (recall Chapter 9's discussion of the Golden Age, pages 167–68). A **cartel** is an organization of independent firms, producing similar products, that work together to raise prices and restrict output. Today, with only a few exceptions, it is strictly illegal in the United States and most other market economies for companies to collude by jointly setting prices or dividing markets. (The antitrust laws pertaining to such behavior are discussed in Chapter 17.)

Nonetheless, firms are often tempted to engage in tacit collusion, which occurs when they refrain from competition without explicit agreements. When firms tacitly collude, they often quote identical (high) prices, pushing up profits and decreasing the risk of doing business. A recent examination found that about 9 percent of major corporations have admitted to or been convicted of illegal price fixing. In recent years, makers of infant formula, scouring pads, and kosher Passover products have been investigated for price fixing, while universities, art dealers, the airlines, and the telephone industry have been accused of collusive behavior.

The rewards of successful collusion can be great. Imagine a four-firm industry—call the firms A, B, C, and D—where all the rivals have tired of ruinous price wars. They tacitly agree to charge the same price and not undercut each other. In such a situation, firms may seek the **collusive oligopoly** equilibrium by finding the price which maximizes their joint profits. Figure 10-2 illustrates oligopolist A's situation. A's demand curve, $D_A D_A$, is drawn assuming that the other firms all follow firm A's lead in raising and lowering prices. Thus the firm's demand curve has the same elasticity as the industry's DD curve. Firm A will get one-fourth of the shared market as long as all firms charge the same price.

The maximum-profit equilibrium for the collusive oligopolist is shown in Figure 10-2 at point E, the intersection of the firm's MC and MR curves. Here, the appropriate demand curve is $D_A D_A$, which recognizes that the other firms will charge the same price as A. The optimal price for the collusive oligopolist

FIGURE 10-2. Collusive Oligopoly Looks Much Like Monopoly

After experience with disastrous price wars, firms will surely recognize that each price cut is canceled by competitors' price cuts. So oligopolist A may estimate its demand curve $D_A D_A$ by assuming that others will be charging similar prices. When firms collude to set a jointly profit-maximizing price, the price will be very close to that of a single monopolist. Can you see why profits are equal to the gray rectangle?

is shown at point G on $D_A D_A$, just above point E. This price is identical to the monopoly price: it is well above marginal cost and earns the colluding oligopolists a handsome monopoly profit.

When oligopolists can collude to maximize their joint profits, taking into account their mutual interdependence, they will produce the monopoly output and price and earn the monopoly profit.

Although many oligopolists would be delighted to earn such high profits, in reality many obstacles hinder effective collusion. First, collusion is illegal. Second, firms may "cheat" on the agreement by cutting their price to selected customers, thereby increasing their market share. Secret price cutting is particularly likely in markets where prices are secret, where goods are differentiated, where there is more than a handful of firms, or where the technology is changing rapidly. Third, the growth of international trade means that many companies face intensive competition from foreign firms as well as domestic companies.

Indeed, experience shows that it's hard to put together a successful cartel which lasts very long today, whether it's explicit or tacit.

Two notable failures at collusion can be cited. Since 1973, the Organization of Petroleum Exporting Countries (OPEC) has attempted to set up an oil cartel. That strategy worked from 1973 to 1975, when prices skyrocketed. But a successful cartel requires that members curtail their production to keep prices high. Sometimes OPEC succeeds, but every few years price competition breaks out, as one or more OPEC countries exceed their quota for production. This happened in a spectacular way in 1986, when Saudi Arabia drove oil prices from $28 per barrel down to below $10. It is particularly hard to enforce a cartel agreement among parties that hate each other or even—as with Iraq, Iran, and Kuwait—are fighting real wars as well as price wars.

The airline industry is another example of a market with a history of repeated—and failed—attempts at collusion. It would seem a natural candidate for collusion. There are only a few major airlines, and on many routes there are only one or two rivals. But just look at the quote at the beginning of the chapter, an apparent attempt at collusion. Since then, Braniff has gone bankrupt twice, and American Airlines and other airlines, while successful in the mid-1980s, lost more than $10 billion between 1990 and 1993. If collusion exists, it clearly has not raised profits. Indeed, the evidence shows that the only time an airline can boost fares is when it has a near-monopoly on all flights to a city.

Monopolistic Competition

At the other end of the spectrum from collusive oligopolies is **monopolistic competition**. Monopolistic competition resembles perfect competition in three ways: there are many buyers and sellers, entry and exit are easy, and firms take other firms' prices as given. The distinction is that products are identical under perfect competition, while products are differentiated under monopolistic competition.

Monopolistic competition is very common—just scan the shelves at any supermarket, and you'll see a dizzying array of different brands of breakfast cereals, shampoos, and frozen foods. Within each product group, products or services are different, but close enough to compete with each other. Here are some other examples of monopolistic competition: There may be several grocery stores in a neighborhood, each carrying the same goods but at different locations. Gas stations, too, all sell the same product, but they compete on the basis of location and brand name. The several hundred magazines on a newsstand rack are monopolistic competitors, as are the fifty or so competing brands of personal computers. The list is endless.

For our analysis, the important point is that product differentiation means each seller has some freedom to raise or lower prices, more so than in a perfectly competitive market. *Product differentiation leads to a downward slope in each seller's demand curve.* Figure 10-3 might represent a monopolistically competitive fishing magazine which is in short-run equilibrium at *G*. The firm's *dd* demand curve shows the

FIGURE 10-3. Monopolistic Competitors Produce Many Similar Goods

Under monopolistic competition, numerous small firms sell differentiated products and therefore have downward-sloping demand. Each firm takes its competitors' prices as given. Equilibrium has *MR = MC* at *E*, and price is at *G*. Because price is above *AC*, the firm is earning a profit, area *ABGC*.

Monopolistic Competition Before Entry

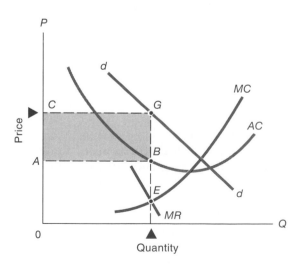

relationship between sales and its price when other magazine prices are unchanged; its demand curve slopes downward since this magazine is a little different from everyone else's because of its special focus. The profit-maximizing price is at *G*. Because price at *G* is above average cost, the firm is making a handsome profit represented by area *ABGC*.

But our magazine has no monopoly on writers or newsprint or insights on fishing. Firms can enter the industry by hiring an editor, having a bright new idea and logo, locating a printer, and hiring workers. Since the fishing magazine industry is profitable, entrepreneurs bring new fishing magazines into the market. With their introduction, the demand curve for the products of existing monopolistically competitive fishing magazines shifts leftward as the new magazines nibble away at our magazine's market.

The ultimate outcome is that fishing magazines will continue to enter the market until all economic profits (including the appropriate opportunity costs for owners' time, talent, and contributed capital) have been beaten down to zero. Figure 10-4 shows the final long-run equilibrium for the typical seller. In equilibrium, the demand is reduced or shifted to the left until the new *d'd'* demand curve just touches (but never goes above) the firm's *AC* curve. Point *G'* is a long-run equilibrium for the industry because profits are zero and no one is tempted to enter or forced to exit the industry.

This analysis is well illustrated by the personal computer industry. Originally, such computer manufacturers as Apple and Compaq made big profits. But the personal computer industry turned out to have low barriers to entry, and numerous small firms entered the market. Today, there are dozens of firms, each with a small share of the computer market but no economic profits to show for its efforts.

The monopolistic competition model provides an important insight into American capitalism: The rate of profit will in the long run be zero in this kind of imperfectly competitive industry as firms enter with new differentiated products.

In the long-run equilibrium for monopolistic competition, prices are above marginal costs but economic profits have been driven down to zero.

Some critics believe that monopolistic competition is inherently inefficient, even though profits are zero in the long run. They argue that monopolistic competition breeds an excessive number of new products and that eliminating unnecessary product differentiation could really cut costs and lower prices. To understand their reasoning, look back at the long-run equilibrium price at *G'* in Figure 10-4. At that point, price is above marginal cost; hence, output is reduced below the ideal competitive level.

This argument against monopolistic competition has considerable appeal. It takes real ingenuity to demonstrate the gains to human welfare from adding Apple Cinnamon Cheerios to Honey Nut Cheerios and Whole Grain Cheerios. It is sometimes hard to see the reason for gasoline stations on every corner of an intersection. But there is strong logic to the incredible variety we find in the American economy. Reducing the number of monopolistic competitors, while cutting costs, might well end up lowering consumer welfare because it would reduce the diversity of available goods and services. Centrally planned

FIGURE 10-4. Free Entry of Numerous Monopolistic Competitors Wipes Out Profit

The typical seller's original profitable *dd* curve in Fig. 10-3 will be shifted downward and leftward to *d'd'* by the entry of new rivals. Entry ceases only when each seller has been forced into a long-run, no-profit tangency such as at *G'*. At long-run equilibrium, price remains above *MC*, and each producer is on the left-hand declining branch of its long-run *AC* curve.

Monopolistic Competition After Entry

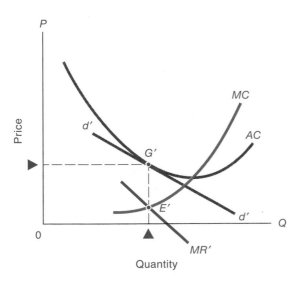

socialist countries tried to standardize output on a small number of varieties, and this left their consumers highly dissatisfied. People will pay a great deal to be free to choose.

Rivalry Among the Few

For our third example of imperfect competition, we turn back to markets in which only a few firms compete. This time, instead of focusing on collusion, we consider the fascinating case where firms have a strategic interaction with each other. Strategic interaction is found in any market which has relatively few competitors. Like a tennis player trying to outguess her opponent, each business must ask how its rivals will react to changes in key business decisions. If Wrigley, which controls 50 percent of the chewing-gum markets, cuts its prices, how will its competitors react? If GE introduces a new model of refrigerator, what will Whirlpool, its principal rival, do? If American Airlines lowers its transcontinental fares, how will United react?

Consider as an example the market for air shuttle services between New York and Washington, currently served by Delta and USAir. This market is called a *duopoly* because it is served by two firms. Suppose that Delta has determined that if it cuts fares 10 percent, its profits will rise as long as USAir does not match its cut, but its profits will fall if USAir does match its price cut. If they cannot collude, Delta must make an educated guess as to how USAir will respond to its price moves. Its best approach would be to estimate how USAir would react to each of its actions and then to maximize profits *with strategic interaction recognized*. This analysis is the province of game theory, to which we turn shortly.

Similar strategic interactions are found in many large industries: in television, in automobiles, even in economics textbooks. Unlike the simple approaches of monopoly and perfect competition, it turns out that there is no simple theory to explain how oligopolists behave. Different cost and demand structures, different industries, even different temperaments on the part of the firms' managers will lead to different strategic interactions and to different pricing strategies. Sometimes, the best behavior is to introduce some randomness into the response simply to keep the opposition off balance.

Competition among the few introduces a completely new feature into economic life: It forces firms to take into account competitors' reactions to price and output deviations and brings strategic considerations into their markets.

Game Theory

To analyze the outcome of strategic interactions, economists rely upon a fascinating area of economic theory known as *game theory*. This is the analysis of situations involving two or more decision makers who have conflicting objectives. Game theory was originated in the 1940s by John von Neumann and Oskar Morgenstern in their pathbreaking work, *The Theory of Games and Economic Behavior*.[1] Game theory has been used by economists to study the interaction of duopolists, union-management disputes, countries' trade policies, international environmental agreements, reputations, and a host of other situations. In the area of imperfect competition, some of the important results are the following:

- As the number of noncooperative or competing oligopolists becomes large, industry price and quantity tend toward the output of the perfectly competitive market.
- If firms decide to collude rather than compete, the market price and quantity will be close to those generated by a monopoly. But experiments suggest that as the number of firms increases, collusive agreements are more difficult to police, and the frequency of cheating and noncooperative behavior increases.
- In many situations, there is no stable equilibrium for oligopoly. Strategic interplay may lead to unstable outcomes as firms threaten, bluff, start price wars, capitulate to stronger firms, punish weak opponents, signal their intentions, or simply exit from the market.

Game theory offers insights for politics, warfare, and everyday life as well. For example, it suggests that in some circumstances a carefully chosen random pattern of behavior may be the best strategy. A security guard should make rounds at random, not in a set routine. And you should occasionally bluff at poker, not simply to win a pot with a weak hand but also to ensure that other players do not drop out when you bet high on a good hand. The next chapter explores the theory of games in greater depth.

---

[1] 3d ed. (Princeton University Press, Princeton, N.J., 1953).

B. CONTROL, INNOVATION, AND INFORMATION

The world of imperfect competition contains many different species, from huge corporations to tiny vendors on the information superhighway. The largest corporations like GE and IBM are qualitatively different from competitive firms. They possess enormous resources, and they operate globally in many markets simultaneously. Their survival depends not just on pricing but also on developing new commodities, new technologies, and new markets that can pay off for years to come.

In this section we examine two of the crucial features of imperfect competition. We begin by analyzing the structure of large firms. We will see that there is a divergence of interest between owners and managers that suggests that big firms may have other objectives besides maximizing profits. We then examine the issues raised by the increasing importance of information as an economic commodity. We look at the significant role of large firms in the innovation of new products and processes—an argument first made by Joseph Schumpeter—and then discuss the novel issues raised by the Internet and the growing problem of intellectual property rights.

DIVORCE OF OWNERSHIP AND CONTROL IN THE LARGE CORPORATION

The first step in understanding the behavior of large corporations is to realize that they are mostly "publicly owned." Corporate shares can be bought by anyone, and ownership is spread among many investors. Take a company like AT&T. In 1996, more than 2.3 million people owned its shares, which were worth almost $100 billion. But no single person owned as much as 1 percent of the total. Such dispersed ownership is typical of our large publicly owned corporations. While pension funds and mutual funds hold growing blocks of shares in many companies, each one still owns only a small share of the total.

Because the stock of large companies is so widely dispersed, ownership is typically divorced from control. Individual owners cannot easily affect the actions of large corporations. And while the stockholders of a company elect its board of directors—a group of insiders and knowledgeable outsiders—most often it is the salaried management that makes the major decisions about corporate strategy and day-to-day operations. The managers have acquired special training and management skills, and they are much more intimately acquainted with the details of the company.

In most situations, there is no clash of goals between the management and stockholders. Higher profits benefit everyone. But there are three important potential conflicts of interest between managers and stockholders. First, insiders may vote themselves large salaries, expense accounts, bonuses, and generous retirement pensions at the stockholders' expense. Nobody is arguing that managers should work for the minimum wage, but in recent years some top executives at poorly performing companies have received salaries and bonuses totaling $50 million or more.

A second conflict of interest may arise in connection with paying out dividends. The managers of a company have an understandable tendency to hold on to profits and use them to expand the size of the company instead of paying them out as dividends. But there may be situations where the profits that are plowed back into a company could be more profitably invested outside the company. In some cases, shareholders would benefit if the company would agree to be taken over by another corporation or to simply liquidate itself and pay out the proceeds. But few are the occasions when management gladly votes itself out of jobs and the firm out of business.

The third conflict of interest comes about because managers are often primarily interested in maintaining the smooth operation of the organization rather than running major risks and making revolutionary changes. If firms avoid worthwhile but risky investments because their managers fear the possibility of large losses, the pace of invention and innovation could be slowed. On an economywide basis, excessive managerial aversion to risk could retard productivity growth and thereby hurt a nation's living standard. Some economists believe that this is an important reason why the U.S. economy has fared poorly in recent years.

These conflicts of interest all grow worse the bigger the company is. As soon as a firm gains some market power, it begins to have the ability to seek objectives beyond pure profit maximization. A monopolist can divert profits to uneconomic purposes without going bankrupt. The eminent British economist J. R. Hicks wrote, "The best of all monopoly profits is the quiet life." This saying captures the notion that market power allows managers to pursue alternative goals which may not maximize profits.

However, the decisions of managers cannot diverge too far from profit maximization. If a firm is reckless in making its cost, revenue, and profit decisions, market forces will eventually eliminate that firm, or its managers, from the scene. That has been especially true in recent years, as more and more companies face true competition from foreign rivals. Hence, to survive, a firm must pay some attention to the profitability of its actions. Perhaps firms do not always make optimal, profit-maximizing decisions, but they cannot cast around randomly either.

 Rationality and rules of thumb: Economists often write of optimizing behavior in which consumers maximize utility and firms maximize profits. But in the real world, people have limited resources and information and are therefore forced to make decisions based on incomplete information or analysis. Searching for the absolute maximum of profits or utility would take too much time. Consumers cannot spend all day looking for the lowest-priced head of lettuce; a firm cannot spend millions of dollars hiring econometricians to study the price elasticity for each one of its thousand products. Instead, as Nobel Prize–winning economist Herbert Simon has emphasized, firms or consumers often exhibit *bounded rationality*. This means that they usually strive to make a good decision, rather than waste resources hunting for the best decision.

In some situations the use of a "rule of thumb"—or simplified decision rule—is an economical way of making choices. For example, it is common practice for companies—especially ones in imperfectly competitive markets—to set prices on a "cost-plus-markup" basis. This is how it works: Instead of setting prices by an *MR* and *MC*

comparison, companies take the calculated average cost of a product and mark it up by adding a fixed percentage—say, 20 percent of the average cost. This cost-plus-markup figure then becomes the selling price. Note that if all goes as planned, the price will cover all direct and overhead costs and earn the firm a solid profit.

Does markup pricing indicate that firms do not maximize profits? To some extent, yes. But a better explanation would be that markup pricing is a useful rule of thumb that economizes on scarce managerial resources in a world of bounded rationality. Managers have many tasks other than setting prices. So while markup pricing does not maximize profits to the last decimal point, it comes reasonably close to maximum profits given the other demands on management time.

INFORMATION, INNOVATION, AND SCHUMPETERIAN ECONOMICS

Economic theory tends to glorify perfect competition as the most efficient market structure. Imperfect competitors, by contrast, set prices too high, earn supernormal profits, and neglect product quality. This dismal view of monopoly was challenged by one of the great economists of this century, Joseph Schumpeter. He argued that the essence of economic development is innovation and that monopolists in fact are the wellsprings of innovation in a capitalist economy.

Joseph Schumpeter: Economist as romantic. Born in the Austrian Empire, Joseph Schumpeter (1883–1950) was a legendary scholar who ranged widely in the social sciences and led a flamboyant private life. His three ambitions were to be the world's greatest economist, Austria's greatest horseman, and Vienna's greatest lover—although he is reported to have said that there were too many fine horsemen in Austria for him to succeed in all his aspirations.

He began studying law, economics, and politics at the University of Vienna—then one of the world centers of economics and home of the "Austrian School" that today reveres laissez-faire capitalism. He became the youngest professor in the Austrian Empire and was both the bane and the champion of his students. Six months into his teaching career at the University of Czernowitz (on the

Russian border of the waning Austrian Empire), he charged into the library and scolded the librarian for not allowing his students to have free use of the books. After trading insults, the librarian challenged Schumpeter to a duel which, thanks to his aristocratic training, Schumpeter won by nicking the librarian on the shoulder. After that, his students had unlimited access to the needed books.

Between duels, insulting the stodgy faculty by showing up at faculty meetings in riding pants, and carousing, Schumpeter devoted himself to introducing economic theory on the European continent, founding the Econometric Society, and traveling to England and America. At the end of World War I, he had a disastrously short career as Austrian state secretary of finance. Because he was a monarchist believer in free-enterprise capitalism, Schumpeter ran into trouble when he undermined the left-wing government's program of socializing industry. He was soon thrown out of the government when he challenged the program of union (*Anschluss*) with Germany. He later moved to Harvard, where he eventually became embittered as the theories of his great rival, John Maynard Keynes, swept the profession and his students and the war ravaged his homeland.

Schumpeter's writings covered much of economics, sociology, and history, but his first love was economic theory. His magisterial *History of Economic Analysis* (published posthumously in 1954) has never been surpassed as a survey of the emergence of modern economics. His "popular" book, *Capitalism, Socialism, and Democracy* (1942), laid out the *Schumpeterian hypothesis* on the technological superiority of monopoly and developed the theory of competitive democracy which later grew into public-choice theory. He ominously predicted that capitalism would wither away because of disenchantment among the elites. While this prophesy has not been borne out, he might well join in the conservative complaint today that the welfare state drains the economic vitality of the market economy.[2]

Schumpeter's early classic, *The Theory of Economic Development* (1911), broke with the traditional static analysis of that time by emphasizing the importance of the entrepreneur or innovator, the person who introduces "new combinations," in the form of new products or methods of organization. Innovations result in temporary supernormal innovational profits, which are eventually eroded away by imitators. Ever the romantic, Schumpeter saw in the entrepreneur the hero of capitalism, the person of "superior qualities of intellect and will," motivated by the will to conquer and the joy of creation.

This vision of capitalism as a dynamic process has inspired a new generation of growth theorists, such as Stanford's Paul Romer, who have developed a Schumpeterian theory of induced innovation to supplement the more traditional neoclassical growth theory. Modern interpretations of the Schumpeterian vision emphasize the special economic problems involved in the **economics of information.** Information is a fundamentally different commodity from normal goods. *Because information is costly to produce but cheap to reproduce, markets in information are subject to severe market failures.*

Consider the production of a software program, such as Windows 95. This program took several years and cost Microsoft about $1 billion to develop. Yet you can buy a legal copy for about $100 or even purchase a pirated copy in Beijing for $5. The same phenomenon is at work in publishing, pharmaceuticals, entertainment, and other areas where goods have high information content. In each of these areas, the actual conception and development of the product may be a laborious process that takes years or even a lifetime. But once the work is recorded on paper, in a computer, on a tape or compact disc—at that point, it can be reproduced and used by a second person with virtually no resource cost.

The inability of firms to capture the full monetary value of their inventions is called **inappropriability**. Case studies by Edwin Mansfield and others have found that the social return to invention (that is, the value of inventions to all consumers and producers) is around 3 times the appropriable private return to the inventor (that is, the monetary value of the invention to the inventor).

To the extent that the rewards to invention are inappropriable, we would expect private research and development to be underfunded, with the most significant underinvestment in basic research. The inappropriability and high social returns on research lead most governments to subsidize basic research in health and science and to promise special incentives for creative activities.

---

[2] Of the many biographies of Schumpeter, one by a former student captures the drama of his life particularly effectively. See Robert Loring Allen, *Opening Doors: The Life and Work of Joseph Schumpeter* (Transaction, New Brunswick, N.J., 1991).

Intellectual Property Rights and the Dilemma of the Internet. Because the rewards to producing valuable information like inventions are reduced by imitation, governments take steps to create **intellectual property rights**. These are special laws governing patents, copyrights, trade secrets, and, most recently, electronic media. The purpose of intellectual property rights is to give the owner special protection against the material being copied and used by others without compensation to the owner or original creator.[3]

One of the earliest forms of intellectual property rights was the **patent**, which is a monopoly over the use of an invention conveyed by a government for a limited period of time, currently 20 years. Why would governments actually *create* monopolies? By allowing the creators monopolies on intellectual property, the government increases the degree of appropriability and thereby increases the incentives for people to invent useful new products, write books, compose songs, and write computer software. Examples of successful patents include those on the telephone, the Xerox machine, and the Polaroid camera. Patent protection is particularly valuable in the creation of new drugs.

The growth of electronic storage, access, and transmission of information highlights the dilemma of providing incentives for creating new information. With the low and decreasing cost of electronic information systems like the Internet, it is technologically possible to make most information available to everyone, everywhere, at essentially zero resource cost.

This prospect raises the conflict between efficiency and incentives. On the one hand, all information might be provided free—databases, economics textbooks, movies, performances. This would appear to be economically efficient because the price would be set at the marginal cost of zero. On the other hand, this regime of zero returns on intellectual property would reduce or destroy the profit incentives to produce new data, books, performances, or other information because creators would reap no reward from their creative activity.

Society has struggled with this dilemma in the past. But with reproduction costs so much cheaper for electronic information than for traditional information—ever more expensive to produce and ever cheaper to reproduce—finding sensible public policies and enforcing intellectual property rights is becoming ever more difficult.

Experts emphasize that intellectual property rights are imperfect. Recently, the United States got into a trade dispute with China because that country was condoning the illegal copying of American movies, recordings, and software. Appropriability is increased by strengthening intellectual property rights. It is also increased when the innovating firm has a large share of the product market. If Microsoft sells 90 percent of the operating systems for personal computers, it will naturally benefit substantially from research in that area. By contrast, small firms have less ability to appropriate the value of their inventions, particularly if intellectual property rights are weak. If I invent a new programming language and cannot protect it with a patent or other means, I have such a small share of the computer market that I will probably not benefit at all.

It was just this view that led Joseph Schumpeter to advance his bold hypothesis:

> The modern standard of life of the masses evolved during the period of relatively unfettered "big business." If we list the items that enter the modern workman's budget and, from 1899 on, observe the course of their prices, . . . we cannot fail to be struck by the rate of the advance which, considering the spectacular improvement in qualities, seems to have been greater and not smaller than it ever was before. . . .
>
> Nor is this all. As soon as we . . . inquire into the individual items in which progress was most conspicuous, the trail leads not to the doors of those firms that work under conditions of comparatively free competition but precisely to the doors of the large concerns—which, as in the case of agricultural machinery, also account for much of the progress in the competitive sector—and a shocking suspicion dawns upon us that big business may have had more to do with creating that standard of life than keeping it down.[4]

How well has the bold Schumpeterian hypothesis survived a half-century of scrutiny? The facts are

---

[3] For an entry point into economics on the web, you can go to the excellent source by Bill Goffe of the University of Southern Mississippi, "Resources for Economists on the Internet," which is found at http://econwpa.wustl.edu:80/EconFAQ. Starting there, you can find a wide variety of different sources of data and information.

---

[4] J. A. Schumpeter, *Capitalism, Socialism and Democracy* (Harper, New York, 1942), p. 81.

Industrial R&D Performance by Size of Company			
Size of company (number of employees)	R&D-sales ratio (percent)		Total company R&D (billions of dollars)
	1983	1993	1993
Fewer than 500	2.2	3.6	13.9
500 to 999	na	2.7	3.0
1,000 to 4,999	2.0	2.4	12.2
5,000 to 9,999	1.3	2.7	8.3
10,000 to 24,999	2.3	2.5	12.6
25,000 or more	3.4	3.6	45.7

TABLE 10-1. Research and Development by Size of Firm
Large firms do most of the research and development (R&D). In the last decade, however, small firms have forged ahead in the invention business and now have larger R&D-sales ratios than all but the largest industrial corporations. (Source: National Science Foundation, *Science and Engineering Indicators: 1996.*)

much more complex than this simple hypothesis would suggest. To begin with, this view might have had greater validity a century ago, when large firms were tiny by today's standards and most firms had great difficulty raising capital to promote their innovations. Moreover, it is surely true that our corner grocery store today does little R&D.

But careful studies indicate that individuals and small firms play a vital role in the inventive process. Table 10-1 shows the amount of R&D performed by different firm classes as well as the ratio of R&D to sales for each. In earlier years, most R&D was indeed undertaken by large firms. But in the last decade, particularly with the cottage-industry approach of the computer industry, research in small firms has grown rapidly and they now finance more than one-fifth of all R&D.

Moreover, studies indicate that small firms are responsible for a disproportionate share of major inventions and innovations. When John Jewkes and

his colleagues traced the history of the most important inventions of this century, they found that less than half came from the laboratories of large corporations. The importance of small inventors has been confirmed in recent years as major new products seem to arise from nowhere—every day we seem to receive an advertisement for a new software package developed by some unheard-of start-up firm.

The relationship between innovation and market power is complex. Because large firms have made a major contribution to research and innovation, we should be cautious about claims that bigness is unmitigated badness. At the same time, we must recognize that small businesses and individuals have made some of the most revolutionary technological breakthroughs and are performing an ever-larger share of industry-financed R&D. To promote rapid innovation, a nation must preserve a variety of approaches and organizations.

C. A BALANCE SHEET ON IMPERFECT COMPETITION

Politicians like to extol "small business" and the "family farm" while disparaging "big businesses" with their "obscene profits." Does economic analysis justify this romantic picture? In this section we assess the economic impact of imperfect competition on today's economy. We begin by showing how imper-

fect competition distorts resource allocation. Then we provide quantitative estimates of the waste due to imperfect competition. We conclude by examining the policy measures that governments can use to control the damage from imperfect competition.

ECONOMIC COSTS OF IMPERFECT COMPETITION

The Cost of Inflated Prices and Insufficient Output

Our analysis has shown how imperfect competitors reduce output and raise price, thereby producing less than would be forthcoming in a perfectly competitive industry. This can be seen most clearly for monopoly, which is the most extreme version of imperfect competition. To see how and why monopoly keeps output too low, imagine that all dollar votes are distributed properly and that all industries other than one are perfectly competitive, with MC equal to P and no externalities. In this world, price is the correct economic standard or measure of scarcity: price measures both the marginal utility of consumption to households and the marginal cost of producing goods by firms.

Now Monopoly Inc. enters the picture. A monopolist is not a wicked firm—it doesn't rob people or force its goods down consumers' throats. Rather, Monopoly Inc. exploits the fact that it is the sole seller of a good or service. By keeping its output a little scarce, Monopoly Inc. raises its price above marginal cost. Hence society does not get as much of the monopolist's output as it wants in terms of the good's marginal cost and marginal value to consumers. The same is true for oligopoly and monopolistic competition, as long as companies can hold prices above marginal cost.

Measuring the Waste from Imperfect Competition

We can depict the efficiency losses from imperfect competition by using a simplified version of our monopoly diagram, here shown in Figure 10-5. If the industry could be competitive, then the equilibrium would be reached at the point where $MC = P$, at point E. Under universal perfect competition, this industry's quantity would be 6 with a price of 100.

Now consider the impact of monopoly—perhaps one gained by a tariff, perhaps by a foreign-trade quota, or perhaps because government prevented entry by regulation or allowed a labor union to monopolize the labor in the industry. Whatever the source, the monopolist would set its MC equal to MR (not to industry P), displacing the equilibrium

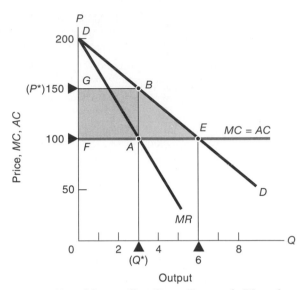

FIGURE 10-5. Monopolists Cause Economic Waste by Restricting Output

Monopolists make their output scarce and thereby drive up price and increase profits. If industry were competitive, equilibrium would be at point E, where social MC equals social MU and welfare is maximized.

At the monopolist's output at point B (with $Q = 3$ and $P = 150$), social MU is above social MC, and consumer surplus is lost. Adding together all the consumer-surplus losses between $Q = 3$ and $Q = 6$ leads to economic waste from monopoly equal to the gray shaded area ABE. In addition, the monopolist has monopoly profits given by the rust-colored shaded region $GBAF$.

to $Q = 3$ and $P = 150$ in Figure 10-5. The rust-colored area $GBAF$ is the monopolist's profit, which compares with a zero-profit competitive equilibrium.

We can measure the inefficiency from monopoly by using the tools of consumer surplus (see Chapter 5). Economists measure the economic harm from inefficiency in terms of the **deadweight loss**; this term signifies the loss in real income that arises because of monopoly, tariffs and quotas, taxes, or other distortions. Recall that for each unit of output reduction below E, the efficiency loss is the vertical distance between the demand curve and the MC curve. The total deadweight loss from the monopolist's output restriction is the sum of all such losses, represented by the gray triangle ABE in Figure 10-5.

To see this, recall that the DD curve represents the good's marginal value to consumers at each level of output, while the *MC* curve represents the opportunity cost of devoting production to this good rather than to other industries. For example, at $Q = 3$, the vertical difference between *B* and *A* represents the difference between the value and the cost of a small increase in the output of *Q*. Adding up all these differences from $Q = 3$ to $Q = 6$ gives the shaded region *ABE*.

The technique of measuring the costs of market imperfections by "little triangles" of deadweight loss, such as the one in Figure 10-5, can be extended to other areas. Similar analysis applies to foreign-trade tariffs and quotas, taxes and subsidies, and externalities.

EMPIRICAL STUDIES OF COSTS OF MONOPOLY

Economists have applied the analysis of deadweight loss to measure the overall costs of imperfect competition in the United States. In essence, these studies estimate the deadweight loss of consumer surplus in *ABE* of Figure 10-5 for all industries. Early studies set the total deadweight loss from monopoly at less than 0.1 percent of GDP. In today's economy, it would total only about $7 billion. One economist quipped that economists might make a larger social contribution fighting fires and eradicating termites than attempting to curb monopolies.

More recent studies have calculated that the deadweight welfare loss attributable to monopolistic resource misallocation in the United States lies somewhere between 0.5 and 2 percent of gross national product.[5] Some critics believe that the efficiency losses may be compounded as the higher prices pile on top of each other as goods cascade from one stage of production to the other.

The most important reservation about this approach is that it ignores the impact of market structure upon technological advance or "dynamic efficiency." The deadweight loss measured in Figure 10-5 assumes that the cost curves are the same for perfect competitors and for imperfect competitors. But some economists point out that according to the Schumpeterian hypothesis, discussed in the previous section, imperfect competition actually pro-

motes invention and technological change and reduces costs. This suggests that the gains from invention may offset the efficiency losses from too high prices.

But not everyone accepts this argument. Some skeptical economists retort that monopolists mainly promote the quiet life, poor quality, and uncivil service. Indeed, a common complaint about companies with a dominant market position is that they pay little attention to quality of product. When AT&T had a monopoly on telephone equipment, consumers had to be satisfied with plain black phones for many years. Once competitors entered, there was a sharp increase in the variety of colors, styles, and ancillary equipment (such as answering machines). In the automobile industry as well, foreign competition forced U.S. automakers to produce more reliable and safer cars.

INTERVENTION STRATEGIES

In discussing the problem of imperfect competition, Milton Friedman, a Nobel Prize winner and perhaps the leading conservative economist of the modern age, wrote: "There is only a choice among three evils: private unregulated monopoly, private monopoly regulated by the state, and government operation." In this final subsection, we examine the six major approaches that governments in market economies can use to deal with imperfect competition. The first three policy measures form the core of modern policies toward big business. The next three have been tried but are seldom used in modern market economies like the United States.

1. The major method for combating market power is the use of *antitrust policy*. Antitrust policies are laws that prohibit certain kinds of behavior (such as firms' joining together to fix prices) or curb certain market structures (such as pure monopolies and highly concentrated oligopolies). This important policy approach will be explored in detail in Chapter 17.
2. More generally, anticompetitive abuses can be avoided by *encouraging competition* whenever possible. There are many government policies that can promote vigorous rivalry even among large firms. It is particularly crucial to reduce barriers to entry into all lines of business. That means

---

[5] F. M. Scherer and David Ross, *Industrial Market Structure and Economic Performance*, 3d ed. (Houghton Mifflin, Boston, 1990), p. 667.

encouraging small businesses and not walling off domestic markets from foreign competition.

3. Over the last 100 years, American government has evolved a new tool for government control of industry: *regulation*. Economic regulation allows specialized regulatory agencies to oversee the prices, outputs, entry, and exit of firms in regulated industries such as public utilities and transportation. Unlike antitrust policies, which tell businesses what *not* to do, regulation tells businesses what to do and how to price products. It is, in effect, government control without government ownership. This important tool for containing monopoly is used particularly for local natural monopolies. It will be discussed in detail in Chapter 17 in our survey of government's role in curtailing market power.

4. *Government ownership* of monopolies has been an approach widely used outside the United States. For some natural monopolies such as water, gas, and electricity distribution, it is thought that efficient production requires a single seller. In such cases, the real dilemma is whether to impose government ownership or government regulation on such firms. Most market economies have chosen the regulatory route, and in recent years many governments have "privatized" industries that were in former times public enterprises.

5. *Price controls* on most goods and services have been used in wartime, partly as a way of containing inflation, partly as a way of keeping down prices in concentrated industries. Studies indicate that these controls are a very blunt instrument: they lead to numerous distortions and subterfuges that undermine the economy's efficiency. During the most recent experience with price controls in the United States, in the 1970s, there were long lines for gasoline when its price was set too low, and shortages also cropped up for beef, natural gas, and even toilet paper. Placing the entire economy under price controls to curtail a few monopolists is like poisoning the entire garden to kill a few chinch bugs.

6. *Taxes* have sometimes been used to alleviate the income-distribution effects. By taxing monopolies, a government can reduce monopoly profits, thereby softening some of the socially unacceptable effects of monopoly. But if taxation over-

comes the objections to monopoly based on equity, it does little to reduce the distortion of output. A nondistorting tax drains profits but has no effect on output. If the tax increases marginal cost, it is likely to push the monopolist even further from the efficient level of output—raising price and lowering output even more.

The Bottom Line. What is the bottom line on the advantages and disadvantages of imperfect competition? To begin with, the question of "monopoly vs. competition" is too simple to be useful—it is much like asking whether big animals are more beautiful or more efficient than small animals. As the survey above emphasizes, there is a vast array of species of imperfect competition. Most have evolved to handle the special characteristics of the market they deal with—automobile firms are large publicly owned companies because they need to raise capital to gain the efficiencies of mass production; lawyers are organized in partnerships because of the need to pool skills and enhance trust among clients; colleges are nonprofit organizations because profits and teaching are hard to mix; farms are operated by families because of the need to perform a wide variety of activities in sparsely populated regions.

In virtually all cases, as Milton Friedman states in his quote on page 183, governments are choosing among different evils when they curb excessive market power. After two centuries of observing different market structures, many economists have concluded that *promoting vigorous competition among unregulated firms is almost always the least of these evils*. Removing barriers to entry and exit and ensuring strong prohibitions against collusion are the surest formula for preventing monopoly pricing and encouraging rapid innovation. The keys to this strategy might be summarized in the following rules:

Remove government constraints to competition.
Remember that "the tariff is the mother of monopoly."
Promote vigorous competition from foreign firms.
Use auctions and competitive bidding whenever possible.
Don't try to second-guess future technological trends.
Encourage small businesses to challenge established firms.

⌂

SUMMARY

A. Behavior of Imperfect Competitors

1. Recall the four major market structures: (*a*) *Perfect competition* is found when no firm is large enough to affect the market price. (*b*) *Monopolistic competition* occurs when a large number of firms produce slightly differentiated products. (*c*) *Oligopoly* is an intermediate form of imperfect competition in which an industry is dominated by a few firms. (*d*) *Monopoly* comes when a single firm produces the entire output of an industry.

2. Measures of concentration are designed to indicate the degree of market power in an imperfectly competitive industry. Industries which are more concentrated tend to have higher levels of R&D expenditures, but their profitability is not higher on average.

3. High barriers to entry and complete collusion can lead to collusive oligopoly. This market structure produces a price and quantity relation similar to that under monopoly.

4. Another common structure is the monopolistic competition that characterizes many retail industries. Here we see many small firms, with slight differences in the quality of products (such as different kinds of gasoline or groceries). The existence of product differentiation leads each firm to face a downward-sloping *dd* demand curve. In the long run, free entry extinguishes profits as these industries show an equilibrium in which firms' *AC* curves are tangent to their *dd* demand curves. In this tangency equilibrium, prices are above marginal costs but the industry exhibits greater diversity of quality and service than under perfect competition.

5. A final situation recognizes the strategic interplay when an industry has but a handful of firms. Where a small number of firms compete in a market, they must recognize their strategic interactions. Competition among the few introduces a completely new feature into economic life: It forces firms to take into account competitors' reactions to price and output deviations and brings strategic considerations into these markets. Game theory explores the way firms choose strategies that try to anticipate the reactions of their opponents.

B. Control, Innovation, and Information

6. As public corporations grow, and their owners become numerous and dispersed, we see the phenomenon of the separation of ownership from control. Such a trend can introduce conflicts of interest between shareholders and managers—such as when managers shun risk or pay themselves overly generous compensation.

7. A careful study of the actual behavior of oligopolists shows certain kinds of behavior at variance with standard economic assumptions about profit maximization. One limit on profit maximization is bounded rationality. This principle recognizes that it is costly to make decisions, so managers may make less-than-perfect decisions, often employing rules of thumb, to economize on search and decision time. An important example of rule-of-thumb behavior is markup pricing—where prices are set by adding a percentage increase on top of costs of production.

8. Schumpeter emphasized the importance of the innovator, who introduces "new combinations" in the form of new products or methods of organization and is rewarded by temporary entrepreneurial profits. The Schumpeterian hypothesis holds that traditional monopoly theory ignores the dynamics of technological change. According to this view, monopolies and oligopolies are the chief source of innovation and growth in living standards—to turn large firms into perfect competitors would risk raising prices in the long run as the fragmentation of industry slows technological progress.

9. Today, the economics of information emphasizes the difficulties involved in efficient production and distribution of new and improved knowledge. Information is different from normal goods because it is expensive to produce but cheap to reproduce. The inability of firms to capture the full monetary value of their inventions is called inappropriability. To increase appropriability, governments create intellectual property rights governing patents, copyrights, trade secrets, and electronic media. The rise of electronic information systems like the Internet raises, in heightened form, the dilemma of the efficient pricing of information services.

C. A Balance Sheet on Imperfect Competition

10. Exercise of monopoly power leads to economic inefficiency when price rises above marginal cost, and deterioration in quality may also occur. Empirical studies indicate that the deadweight or efficiency losses from imperfect competition are small relative to national output.

11. To curb the abuses of imperfect competition, governments in an earlier age sometimes used taxation, price controls, and nationalization. These are little used

today in most market economies. The three major tools in American industrial policy today are regulation, antitrust laws, and the encouragement of competition. Of these, the most important is to ensure vigorous rivalry by lowering the barriers to competition whenever possible.

CONCEPTS FOR REVIEW

Models of Imperfect Competition

concentration
market power
strategic interaction
tacit and explicit collusion
imperfect competition:
    collusive oligopoly
    monopolistic competition
    small-number oligopoly
no-profit equilibrium in monopolistic
    competition
inefficiency of $P > MC$

Aspects of Imperfect Competition

separation of ownership from control
limits on profit maximization:
    bounded rationality
    markup pricing
Schumpeterian hypothesis
economics of information:
    inappropriability
    protection of intellectual prop-
        erty rights
    dilemma of efficient production
        of knowledge

deadweight losses
older approaches:
    taxation
    price controls
    nationalization
current approaches:
    regulation
    antitrust policy
    pro-competitive policies

QUESTIONS FOR DISCUSSION

1. Review the first two theories of imperfect competition analyzed in the first section of this chapter. Draw up a table that compares perfect competition, monopoly, and the two theories with respect to the following characteristics: (*a*) number of firms; (*b*) extent of collusion; (*c*) price vs. marginal cost; (*d*) price vs. long-run average cost; (*e*) efficiency.

2. The market shares in the U.S. airline industry for 1995 are shown in Table 10-2. Calculate the four-firm and six-firm concentration ratios. What would be the change in these indexes if Delta merged with United?

3. "The tragedy of most industries characterized by monopolistic competition is not at all excessive profits. Rather, there are no profits, and prices are excessive as resources are frittered away in low levels of production." Explain what this writer might mean in terms of the long-run equilibrium shown in Figure 10-4. Defend monopolistic competition by showing how it might lead to greater diversity of products.

4. "It is naive to try to break up monopolies into even a few effectively competing units, because the basic cause of monopoly is the law of decreasing cost with mass production. Moreover, if there are even a few firms, the price is likely to be close to marginal cost." Discuss both parts of this statement.

5. A recent interesting study of the Internet by two economists states, "Traditional pricing schemes are not appropriate [for information services]. If you buy a table we like, we generally have to go to the manufacturer to buy one for ourselves; we can't simply copy yours. With information goods, the pricing-by-replication breaks down. Once the sunk costs of software are invested, replication costs are essentially zero. This is a much greater problem [with electronic information] than that which publishers face from unauthorized photocopying, since the cost of replication is essentially zero."[6]

Analyze this quotation in terms of the issues concerning the economics of information. Explain why appropriability is an issue for a book or page on the Internet but not for a chair or gallon of gasoline. Why might high charges for photocopying material or access to the Internet impede efficiency? Relate this question to the Schumpeterian hypothesis.

TABLE 10-2.

(Source: U.S. Department of Transportation, *Air Carrier Financial Statistics Quarterly*, 1995.)

Firm	Market share (%)	Firm	Market share (%)
American	13	USAir	8
Delta	13	Continental	5
United	12	Southwest	4
Northwest	11	America West	2

---

[6] This is slightly condensed from Jeffrey K. MacKie-Mason and Hal Varian, "Economic FAQs about the Internet," *Journal of Economic Perspectives* (Summer 1994), p. 92. Further information can be obtained on the Internet under the heading "intellectual property" or at the authors' home pages.

6. Explain the following statements:
   a. In the retail drugstore business, each store has a little market power but fails to earn any economic profit on its activities.
   b. According to the theory of bounded rationality, it is truly efficient for GE not to adjust the price of its refrigerators so that $MC = MR$ each and every day.
7. The government decides to tax a monopolist at a constant rate of $x per unit. Show the impact upon output and price. Is the posttax equilibrium closer to or further from the ideal equilibrium of $P = MC$?
8. Firms often lobby for tariffs or quotas to provide relief from import competition.
   a. Suppose that the monopolist shown in Figure 10-5 has a foreign competitor that will supply output perfectly elastically at a price slightly above the monopolist's $AC = MC$. Show the impact of the foreign competitor's entry into the market.
   b. What would be the effect on the price and quantity if a prohibitive tariff were levied on the foreign good? (A prohibitive tariff is one that is so high as to effectively wall out all imports.) What would be the effect of a small tariff? Use your analysis to explain the statement, "The tariff is the mother of monopoly."
9. Explain in words and with the use of diagrams why a monopolistic equilibrium leads to economic inefficiency relative to a perfect competitor. Why is the condition $MC = P = MU$ of Chapter 8 critical for this analysis?

FIGURE 10-6. Perfect Competition

10. In long-run equilibrium, both perfectly competitive and monopolistically competitive markets achieve a tangency between the firm's *dd* demand curve and its *AC* average cost curve. Figure 10-4 shows the tangency for a monopolistic competitor, while Figure 10-6 displays the tangency for the perfect competitor. Discuss the similarities or differences in the two situations with respect to:
   a. The elasticity of the demand curve for the firm's product
   b. The extent of divergence between price and marginal cost
   c. Profits
   d. Economic efficiency

CHAPTER 11
UNCERTAINTY AND GAME THEORY

Risk varies inversely with knowledge.

Irving Fisher, **The Theory of Interest** *(1930)*

Life is full of uncertainty and strategic behavior. A capsule history of exploring for oil in Russia will illustrate this point. During the turmoil of the early 1990s, oil production in Russia declined sharply, and Russia fell from being the world's largest oil producer to number three. Western oil companies were invited to participate in investing in and modernizing the Russian oil fields.

Suppose that you are in charge of a Texaco joint venture in Siberia. What obstacles would you face? You would of course face the normal risks that plague oil producers everywhere—the risks of a price plunge, of embargoes, or of an attack on your tankers by some hostile regime. Added to these are the uncertainties of operating in a new area: you are unfamiliar with the geological formations, with the terrain for getting the oil to the market, with the success rate on drilling wells, and with the skills of the work force.

In addition to these uncertainties is a set of political risks involved in dealing with a divided central government in Moscow, with autonomous regions, with localities, and with the Russian "mafia" in a country where property rights, bribes, and taxation are subject to haggling and the rule of bureaucracy rather than the rule of law.

The dilemmas of the Texaco joint venture show that economic activity often raises complexities that are not captured in our elementary theories. One complication arises because of the vast uncertainties involved in economic life. Our oil company must deal with the uncertainties of drilling, of costs, of prices, and of marketing. Households must contend with uncertainty about future wages or employment and about the return on their investments in education or in financial assets. Occasionally, people suffer from misfortunes such as devastating hurricanes or the mighty Mississippi overrunning its banks. Firms must also contend with uncertainties about the prices of their products and inputs, political turmoil when they produce abroad, taxes and interest rates, the course of technological change in their industry, and the strength of rivalry from domestic and foreign competitors. The study of this first area is called the *economics of uncertainty.*

A second complication arises because much of economic life involves haggling, bargaining, and strategizing. In perfectly competitive markets, all parties take prices as given and need not worry about others' reactions to their actions. In a wide variety of circumstances, however, strategic considerations are of the essence. Our oil company must worry about whether a big oil find will simply be expropriated by the Russians. Closer to home, in an oligopolistic industry, each firm must worry about how other firms will react to price or output decisions. Will a price cut lead to a price war? Will the price war lead to bankruptcy? Most large firms engage in collective bargaining with a union to determine wages and conditions of work. Will too tough a position lead to a crippling strike?

We often see elements of bargaining in economic policy-making. When governments make decisions about taxes and expenditures, these often result from intricate bargaining between political parties, or between the President and Congress, or among the many power brokers in Congress. The struggle between President Clinton and the Republicans after the big Republican congressional victory in 1994 involved an intricate series of bargains and threats over shutting down the government, and at one point the Republicans threatened to cause a default on the national debt. Even family life involves subtle elements of strategy and bargaining about the allocation of chores or the division of the family's income. No sphere of the economy is exempt from strategizing about *what, how,* and *for whom.*

The study of the economic games people, firms, and nations play is known as *game theory.* No study of the realities of economic life is complete without a thorough study of the fascinating interplay of uncertainty and strategy.

A. ECONOMICS OF RISK AND UNCERTAINTY

Our analysis of markets presumed that costs and demands were known for certain and that each firm could foresee how other firms would behave. In reality, business life is teeming with risk and uncertainty. Let's return briefly to our Russian oil investment and examine how risk clouds the picture. Let's say that you have decided to drill a well. To begin with, you might plan on costs of $100 million for the well, but this is just a guess because you don't know how deep you need to drill to find oil, or whether your equipment will break down and need to be replaced, or how long your crew will need to be on the job. In addition, you cannot know about the revenues from the well because of price and output uncertainty. Price uncertainty comes because oil prices fluctuate widely—they have been as low as $10 a barrel and as high as $38 a barrel over the last 15 years. Output uncertainty is undoubtedly the major worry, for your well may be dry, or it may yield too little to be worth operating, or it may be a lucrative gusher.

These problems are not confined to the oil business. Virtually all firms find that output prices will fluctuate from month to month; input prices of labor, land, machines, and fuel are often highly volatile; the behavior of competitors cannot be forecast in advance. The essence of business is to invest now in order to make profits in the future, in effect putting fortunes up as hostage to future uncertainties. Economic life is a risky business.

Modern economics has developed useful tools to incorporate uncertainty into the analysis of business and household behavior. This section examines the role of markets in spreading risks over space and time, presents the theory of individual behavior under uncertainty, and provides the essential theory underlying insurance markets. These topics are but a brief glimpse into the fascinating world of risk and economic life.

SPECULATION: SHIPPING GOODS ACROSS SPACE AND TIME

We begin by considering the role of speculative markets. **Speculation** is the activity which involves making profits from the fluctuations in prices. Generally, a speculator buys a commodity with an eye to selling it later for a profit when the price has risen. The commodity might be grain, oil, eggs, or foreign currencies. Speculators are not interested in using the product or making something with it. Rather, they want to buy low and sell high. The last thing they want is to see the egg truck roll up to their door!

Why might speculation be beneficial to society? The economic function of speculators is to "move" goods from periods of abundance to periods of scarcity—where the "move" will be across space, time, or uncertain states of nature. Even though speculators never once see a barrel of oil or a truckload of eggs, they may help even out the price differences of these commodities among regions or over time. They do this by buying at a time or place when goods are abundant and prices are low and selling when goods are scarce and prices are high.

Arbitrage and Geographical Price Patterns

The simplest case is one in which speculative activity reduces or eliminates regional price differences by buying and selling the same commodity. This activity is called **arbitrage**, which is the purchase of a good or asset in one market for immediate resale in another market in order to profit from a price discrepancy.

Let's say that the price of wheat is 50 cents per bushel higher in Chicago than in Kansas City. Further, suppose that the costs of insurance and transportation are 10 cents per bushel. Then an *arbitrager* (someone engaged in arbitrage) can purchase wheat in Kansas City, ship it to Chicago, and make a profit of 40 cents per bushel. As a result of market arbitrage, the differential must be reduced so that the price differential between Chicago and Kansas City can never exceed 10 cents per bushel. *More generally, as a result of arbitrage, the price difference between markets will generally be less than the cost of moving the good from one market to the other.*

The frenzied activities of arbitragers—talking on the phone simultaneously to several brokers in several markets, searching out price differentials, trying to eke out a tiny profit every time they can buy low and sell high—tend to align the prices of identical products in different markets. Once again, we see the invisible hand at work—the lure of profit acts to smooth out price differentials across markets and make markets function more efficiently.

Speculation and Price Behavior Over Time

Forces of speculation will tend to establish definite patterns of prices over time as well as over space. But the difficulties of predicting the future make this pattern less perfect: We have an equilibrium that is constantly being disturbed but is always in the process of re-forming itself—rather like a lake's surface under the play of the winds.

Consider the simplest case of a crop like corn that is harvested once a year and can be stored for

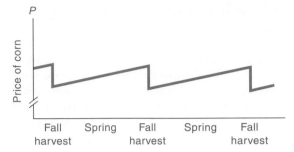

FIGURE 11-1. Speculators Even Out the Price of a Commodity over Time

When a good is stored, the expected price rise must match holding costs. In equilibrium, price is lowest at harvest time, rising gently with accumulated storage, insurance, and interest costs until the next harvest. This flexible pattern tends to even out consumption over the seasons. Otherwise, a harvest glut would cause very low autumn price and sky-high spring price.

future use. To avoid shortages, the crop must last for the entire year. Since no one passes a law regulating the storage of corn, how does the market bring about an efficient pattern of pricing and use over the year? The equilibrium is set by the activities of speculators trying to make a profit.

A well-informed corn speculator realizes that if all the corn is thrown on the market after the autumn harvest, it will fetch a very low price because there will be a glut on the market. Several months later, when corn is running short, the price will tend to skyrocket. In this case, speculators can make a profit by (1) purchasing some of the autumn crop while it is cheap, (2) putting it into storage, and (3) selling it later when the price has risen.

As a result of the speculative activities, the autumn price increases, the spring supply of corn increases, and the spring price declines. The process of speculative buying and selling tends to even out the supply and therefore the price over the year.

Moreover, if there is brisk competition among well-informed speculators, none of them will make excess profits. The returns to speculators will include the interest on invested capital, the appropriate earnings for their time, plus a risk premium to compensate them for whatever risks they incur with their funds. The speculators will probably never touch a kernel of corn, nor need they know anything about the technology of storage or delivery. They merely buy and sell pieces of paper.

There is one and only one monthly price pattern that will result in zero profits for competitive speculators. A little thought will show that it will not be a pattern of constant prices. Rather, the competitive speculative price pattern will produce the lowest prices after the autumn harvest, followed by a gradual price rise until the peak is reached just before the new corn is harvested. The price would normally rise from month to month to compensate for the storage and interest costs of carrying the crop. Figure 11-1 shows the behavior of prices over an idealized yearly cycle.

Speculation reveals the invisible-hand principle at work. By leveling out supplies and prices, speculation actually increases economic efficiency. By moving goods over time from periods of abundance to periods of scarcity, the speculator is buying where the price and marginal utility of the good are low and selling where the price and marginal utility are high. By pursuing their private interests (profits), speculators are at the same time increasing the public interest (total utility).

Shedding Risks through Hedging

One important function of speculative markets is to allow people to shed risks through hedging. **Hedging** consists of reducing the risk involved in owning a commodity by making a counteracting sale of that commodity. Let's see how it works. Consider someone who owns a corn warehouse. She buys 2 million bushels of Kansas corn in the fall, stores it for six months, and sells it in the spring. She makes her living by storing corn, charging 10 cents per bushel of storage. With a full warehouse, she would earn $200,000 before expenses, which is sufficient to cover all costs.

The problem is that corn prices tend to fluctuate. If the price of corn rises, she makes a large windfall gain. But if the price falls sharply, the decrease could completely wipe out her storage profits or even drive her into bankruptcy. The warehouse owner wants to earn her living by storing corn and wants to avoid speculating on the price of corn. What can she do to accomplish this?

The answer is that she can avoid all the corn-price risk by hedging her investments. The owner hedges by selling the corn the moment it is bought

from the farmers rather than waiting until it is shipped 6 months later. Upon buying 2 million bushels of corn in September, she sells the corn immediately for delivery in the future at an agreed-upon price that will just yield a 10-cents-per-bushel storage charge. She thereby protects herself against all corn-price risk. *Hedging by making the counterpart sale allows businesses to insulate themselves from the risk of price changes.*

The Economic Impacts of Speculation

But who buys the corn, and why? Here is where the speculator and the speculative market enter: The speculator agrees to buy the warehouse owner's corn now for future delivery. This moves the risks from the original owner to the speculator. You might wonder exactly why the speculator agreed to take on the corn-price risk. Perhaps the speculator believed that corn prices were rising and that he would make a supernormal return on the investment; perhaps he sold the futures contract to buyers (possibly a bakery chain which desired to reduce the risk of input prices for its bread) who wished to lock in the price of corn before it rose; perhaps he sold it to investors who put a small corn position in their portfolios. The point is that someone, somewhere, had an economic incentive to take on the risk of corn-price fluctuations.

Speculative markets serve to improve the price and allocation patterns across space and time as well as to help transfer risks. These tasks are performed by speculators who, spurred on by the desire to profit from price changes, in fact show the invisible hand at work, reallocating goods from times of feast (when prices are low) to times of famine (when prices are high).

Our discussion has suggested that ideal speculative markets can increase economic efficiency. Let's see how. Say that identical consumers have utility schedules in which satisfaction in one year is independent of that in every other year. Now suppose that in the first of 2 years there is a big crop—say, 3 units per person—while the second year has a small crop of only 1 unit per person. If this crop deficiency could be foreseen perfectly, how should the consumption of the 2-year, 4-unit total be spread over the 2 years? Neglecting storage, interest, and insurance costs, *total utility and economic efficiency for the 2 years together will be maximized only when consumption is equal in each year.*

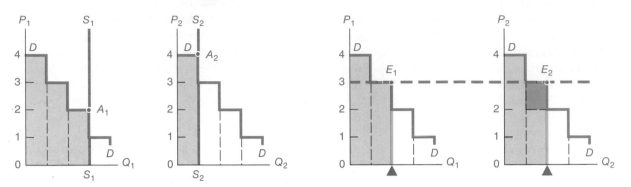

FIGURE 11-2. Speculative Storage Can Improve Efficiency

The gray areas measure total utility enjoyed each year. Carrying 1 unit to the second year equalizes Q and also P and MU and increases total utility by the amount of the dark rust block. This diagram will apply equally well to a number of situations.

It could be labeled "**(a)** Without Arbitrage across Regional Markets" and "**(b)** With Arbitrage across Markets." We can also use this diagram to illustrate risk aversion if we label it "**(a)** With a Risky Gamble" and "**(b)** Without a Risky Gamble." Insurance then serves to move people from **(a)** to **(b)** by spreading the risks across many independent potential gambles.

Why is uniform consumption better than any other division of the available total? Because of the law of diminishing marginal utility. This is how we might reason: "Suppose I consume more in the first year than in the second. My marginal utility (MU) in the first year will be low, while it will be high in the second year. So if I carry some crop over from the first to the second year, I will be moving consumption from low-MU times to high-MU times. When consumption levels are equalized, MUs will be equal and I will be maximizing my total utility."

A graph can illuminate this argument. If utility could be measured in dollars, with each dollar always denoting the same marginal utility, the demand curves for the risky commodity would look just like the marginal utility schedule of Figure 5-1 on page 82. The two curves of Figure 11-2(*a*) show what would happen if there were no carryover—with price determined first at A_1, where S_1S_1 intersects DD, and second at A_2, where the lower supply S_2S_2 intersects DD. Total utility of the gray shaded areas would add up to only $(4 + 3 + 2) + 4$, or \$13.

But with optimal carryover of 1 unit to the second year, as shown in Figure 11-2(*b*), Ps and Qs will be equalized at E_1 and E_2, and the total utility of the

shaded areas will add up to $(4 + 3) + (4 + 3)$, or \$14 per head. A little analysis can show that the gain in utility of \$1 is measured by Figure 11-2(*b*)'s dark rust block, which represents the excess of the second unit's marginal utility over that of the third. This shows why the equality of marginal utilities, which is achieved by ideal speculation, is optimal.

Ideal speculation serves the important function of reducing the variation in consumption. In a world with individuals who display diminishing marginal utility, speculation can increase total utility and allocational efficiency.

RISK AND UNCERTAINTY

Why do people try to shed economic risks? What institutions in a market economy help individuals pool risks or spread them to the broader community? Why do markets fail to provide insurance in some circumstances? We turn now to these issues.

Whenever you drive a car, own a house, store corn, make an investment, or work on a risky job, you are risking life, limb, or fortune. How do people behave in the face of risks? We generally find that people want to avoid uncertainties about their income and consumption. When we desire to avoid risk and uncertainty, we are "risk-averse."

A person is **risk-averse** when the displeasure from losing a given amount of income is greater than the pleasure from gaining the same amount of income.

For example, suppose that we are offered a risky coin flip in which we will win $1000 if the coin comes up heads and lose $1000 if the coin comes up tails. This bet has an *expected value* of 0 (equal to a probability of $\frac{1}{2}$ times $1000 and a probability of $\frac{1}{2}$ times −$1000); a bet which has a zero expected value is called a fair bet. If we turn down all fair bets, we are risk-averse.

In terms of the utility concept that we analyzed in Chapter 5, risk aversion is the same as *diminishing marginal utility of income*. Being risk-averse implies that the gain in utility achieved by getting an extra amount of income is less than the loss in utility from losing the same amount of income. For a fair bet (such as flipping a coin for $1000), the expected dollar value is zero. But in terms of utility, the expected utility value is negative because the satisfaction you stand to win is less than the satisfaction you stand to lose.

We can use Figure 11-2 to illustrate the concept of risk aversion. Say that situation (*b*) is the initial position, in which you have equal amounts of consumption in states 1 and 2, consuming 2 units in both states. A "risk lover" comes to you and says, "Let's flip a coin for 1 unit." The risk lover is in effect offering you the chance to move to situation (*a*), where you would have 3 units of consumption if the coin came up heads and 1 unit if tails. By careful calculation, you see that if you refuse the bet and stay in situation (*b*), the expected value of utility is 7 utils (= $\frac{1}{2} \times 7$ utils + $\frac{1}{2} \times 7$ utils), whereas if you accept the bet, the expected value of utility is $6\frac{1}{2}$ utils (= $\frac{1}{2} \times 9$ utils + $\frac{1}{2} \times 4$ utils). This example shows that if you are risk-averse, with diminishing marginal utility, you will avoid actions that increase uncertainty without some expectation of gain.

Say that I am a corn farmer. While I clearly must contend with the natural hazards of farming, I do not also want to bear corn-price risks. Suppose that the expected value of the corn price is $4 per bushel, where this expectation arises from two equally likely outcomes with prices of $3 and $5 per bushel. Unless

I can shed the price risk, I am forced into a lottery where I must sell my 10,000-bushel crop for either $30,000 or $50,000 depending upon the flip of the corn-price coin.

But by the principle of risk aversion and diminishing marginal utility, I would prefer a sure thing. That is, I would prefer to hedge my price risk by selling my corn for the expected-value price of $4, yielding a total of $40,000. Why? Because the prospect of losing $10,000 is more painful than the prospect of gaining $10,000 is pleasant. If my income is cut to $30,000, I will have to cut back on important spending, such as college tuition or a roof repair. On the other hand, the extra $10,000 might be less critical, yielding only some jewelry or a new 100-horsepower, eight-speed, air-conditioned lawn mower.

People are generally risk-averse, preferring a sure thing to uncertain levels of consumption—that is, people prefer outcomes with less uncertainty and the same average values. For this reason, activities that reduce the uncertainties of consumption lead to improvements in economic welfare.

INSURANCE AND RISK SPREADING

Risk-averse individuals want to avoid risks. But risks cannot simply be buried. When a house burns down, when someone is killed in an automobile accident, or when a hurricane tears through Florida—someone, somewhere, must bear the cost.

Markets handle risks by **risk spreading**. This process takes risks that would be large for one person and spreads them around so that they are but small risks for a large number of people. The major form of risk spreading is **insurance**, which is a kind of gambling in reverse.

For example, in buying fire insurance on a house, homeowners seem to be betting with the insurance company that the house will burn down. If it does not, the owners forfeit the small premium charge. If it does burn down, the company must reimburse the owners for the loss at an agreed-upon rate. What is true of fire insurance is equally true of life, accident, automobile, or any other kind of insurance.

The insurance company is spreading risks by pooling many different risks: it may insure millions of houses or lives or cars. The advantage for the insurance company is that what is unpredictable for an individual is highly predictable for a population. Say that the Inland Fire Insurance Company insures 1 million homes, each worth $100,000. The chance that a house will burn down is 1 in 1000 per year. The expected value of losses to Inland is then .001 × $100,000 = $100 per house per year. It charges each homeowner $100 plus another $100 for administration and for reserves.

Each homeowner is faced with the choice between the *certain* loss of $200 for each year or the *possible* 1-in-1000 catastrophic loss of $100,000. Because of risk aversion, the household will choose to buy insurance that costs more than the expected value of the household's loss in order to avoid the small chance of a catastrophic loss. Insurance companies can set a premium that will earn the company a profit and at the same time produce a gain in expected utility of individuals. Where does the economic gain come from? It arises from the law of diminishing marginal utility.

We see therefore how insurance, which appears to be just another form of gambling, actually has exactly the opposite effect. Whereas nature deals us risks, insurance helps to lessen and spread risks.

Capital Markets and Risk Sharing

Another form of risk sharing takes place in the capital markets because the *financial* ownership of *physical* capital can be spread among many owners through the vehicle of corporate ownership.

Take the example of investment to develop a new commercial aircraft. A completely new design, including research and development, might require $2 billion of investment spread over 10 years. Yet there is no guarantee that the plane will find a large enough commercial market to repay the invested funds. Few people have the wealth or inclination to undertake such a risky venture.

Market economies accomplish this task through publicly owned corporations. A company like Boeing is owned by millions of people, none of whom owns a major portion of the shares. In a hypothetical case, divide Boeing's ownership equally among 10 million individuals. Then the $2 billion investment becomes $200 per person, which is a risk that many would be willing to bear if the returns on Boeing stock appear attractive.

The principle of risk spreading extends into the international dimension as well. The risks of large-scale investment and production are shared with investors from Japan, Britain, Germany, and other countries when they buy shares of American corporations. And, just as an insurance company reduces its risks by insuring houses in different cities, so investors can reduce the riskiness of their portfolios by holding shares in companies operating around the world.

By spreading the ownership of capital or of individual risky investments among a multitude of owners, capital markets can spread risks and allow much larger investments and risks than would be tolerable for individual owners.

The Troubling Rise in Gambling

Speculation must be distinguished from gambling, which has spread rapidly in recent years. While ideal speculative activity increases economic welfare, gambling raises serious economic issues. To begin with, aside from recreational value, gambling does not create goods and services. In the language of game theory described in the second half of this chapter, it is a "zero-sum game" for society. Indeed, in lotteries and professionally run casinos, it is a "negative-sum game" in which the customers are (almost) sure to lose in the long run. In addition, by its very nature, gambling increases income inequality. People who sit down to the gambling table with the same amount of money go away with widely different amounts. A gambler's family must expect to be on top of the world one week only to be living on crumbs and remorse when luck changes.

Given the substantial economic case against gambling, how can we understand the recent trend to legalize gambling and operate lotteries? One reason is that when states are starved for tax revenues, they look under every tree for new sources; they rationalize lotteries and casinos as a way to channel private vices to the public interest by skimming off some of the revenues. In addition, by bringing gambling above ground, legal gambling may drive out illegal numbers rackets and take some of the profitability out of organized crime. Notwithstanding these rationales, many observers raise questions about an activity in which the state profits by promoting irrational behavior among those who can least afford it.

MARKET FAILURES IN INFORMATION

Our analysis up to now has assumed that investors and consumers are well informed about the risks they face and that speculative and insurance markets function efficiently. In reality, markets involving risk and uncertainty are plagued by market failures. Two of the major failures are adverse selection and moral hazard. When these are present, markets may give the wrong signals, incentives may get distorted, and sometimes markets may simply not exist. In such cases, governments may decide to step in and offer social insurance.

Moral Hazard and Adverse Selection

While insurance is undoubtedly a useful device for spreading risks across the population, the fact is that we cannot buy insurance for all the risks of life, and sometimes the price of insurance makes it too unattractive to buy. The reason behind the incompleteness of insurance markets is that these markets can thrive only under limited conditions.

What are the conditions for the functioning of efficient insurance markets? First, there must be a large number of events. Only then will companies be able to pool different events and spread the risks so that what is a large risk to an individual will become a small risk to many people. Moreover, the events must be relatively independent. No prudent insurance company would sell all its fire-insurance policies in the same building or sell only earthquake insurance in San Francisco. Rather, insurance companies strive to spread their coverage around to different and independent risks. Additionally, there must be sufficient experience regarding such events so that insurance companies can reliably estimate the losses. Finally, the insurance must be relatively free of moral hazard. **Moral hazard** is at work when insurance reduces a person's incentive to avoid or prevent the risky event and thereby changes the probability of loss.

When these ideal conditions are met—when there are many risks, all more or less independent, and the probabilities can be accurately gauged and are not contaminated by individual gain—private insurance markets can function efficiently.

In many situations moral hazard is unimportant. Few people will tempt fate simply because they have a generous life-insurance policy—partly because life is precious and additionally because you can't take the proceeds with you into the grave. In other areas, moral hazard is severe. Studies indicate that the presence of full medical insurance has a major impact upon the amount of cosmetic surgery and the utilization of long-term care such as nursing homes, and most medical-insurance policies consequently exclude these services.

As another example, say that students tried to buy "grade insurance." This would compensate them for the income loss from poor grades. Can you see why no sane insurance company would offer such coverage? The reason is that grades depend so much on individual effort. We would say that the presence of moral hazard in cosmetic surgery and student grades leads to incomplete or missing markets in the sense that supply and demand intersect at zero or very low levels of insurance.

In addition, sometimes private insurance is unavailable or is priced at unfavorable terms because of adverse selection. **Adverse selection** arises when the people with the highest risk are the most likely ones to buy the insurance. Let's take the case where the population is equally divided between two kinds of people—healthy people and the terminally ill. The healthy families average $2000 of medical care each year; the terminally ill—faced with a terrible illness and long hospitalization—have costs averaging $8000. If both kinds of people were included, the average cost would be $5000 per year.

Say that Blue Cross set a uniform price for all insured. This might be the case because government required *nondiscrimination* among insured people. Or it might occur because of *asymmetric information*, where people know about their health status but the insurance company does not. In any case, the ill would gladly buy the Blue Cross policy; by contrast, on looking at that price, a healthy family might decide to run the risk of remaining uninsured rather than to pay the high premiums. The insurance company is therefore left with only the high-cost people, and the price must rise to $8000 to cover the costs. Indeed, in New York, a family of four pays over $8000 for Blue Cross coverage in part because of adverse selection.

We see here that uniform and voluntary pricing of medical insurance has led to adverse selection, raising the price, limiting the coverage, and producing an incomplete market. Similar market failures are important factors in automobile insurance, in disability insurance, and in long-term-care insurance.

Social Insurance

When market failures are so severe that the private market cannot provide adequate coverage, there may be a role for **social insurance**, which is mandatory insurance provided by the government. In these circumstances, the government may choose to step in and provide broad and universal coverage. The taxing and regulatory powers of government, plus the ability to avoid adverse selection through universal coverage, can make government insurance a welfare-improving measure.

One important example of social insurance is unemployment insurance. This is an example of a private market that cannot function because so many of the requirements for private insurance are violated. Insurance companies do not provide unemployment insurance because the moral hazard is so high (people may decide to become unemployed if benefits are generous), because of severe adverse

selection (those who often lose jobs are more likely to participate), and because spells of unemployment are not independent (they tend to occur together during business-cycle recessions). At the same time, countries feel that people should have a safety net under them should they lose their job. As a result, governments often step in to provide unemployment insurance. The government cannot remove the problem of moral hazard, but adverse selection is avoided by universal coverage.

Another important example of cases where governments step in is health insurance for the elderly. We noted above the problems of adverse selection that arise when healthy people decline coverage and leave insurers to cover only high-cost individuals. Adverse selection is particularly serious for the aged because medical costs in the last year of life are almost 20 percent of all health-care costs. Today, to avoid adverse selection, the U.S. government offers universal health coverage for the elderly, Medicare, paid for through premiums and through taxes on active workers.

B. GAME THEORY

Strategic thinking is the art of outdoing an adversary, knowing that the adversary is trying to do the same to you.

Avinash Dixit and Barry Nalebuff, **Thinking Strategically** *(1991)*

Economic life is full of situations in which people or firms or countries jockey for dominance. The oligopolies that we analyzed in the last chapter sometimes break out into economic warfare. Such rivalry was seen in the last century when Vanderbilt and Drew cut and recut shipping rates on their parallel railroads. In recent years, Continental Airlines tried to lure customers from its bigger rivals by offering fares far under prevailing levels. When larger airlines such as American and United were deciding how to react, they also had to take into account how Continental would react when they reacted, and so forth. These situations typify an area of economic analysis known as "game theory."

Game theory analyzes the way that two or more players or parties choose actions or strategies that jointly affect each participant. This theory, which may sound frivolous in its terminology, is in fact fraught with significance and was largely developed by John von Neumann (1903–1957), a Hungarian-born mathematical genius. We will sketch the major concepts involved in game theory and discuss some important economic applications.[1]

---

[1] A witty and readable introduction to game theory, filled with examples from economics and daily life, is contained in Avinash Dixit and Barry Nalebuff, *Thinking Strategically* (Norton, New York, 1991).

Let's begin by analyzing the dynamics of price cutting. You are the head of Berney, a New York–based department store, whose motto is "We will not be undersold." Your arch-rival, Sax Fifth Avenue, runs an advertisement, "We sell for 10 percent less." Figure 11-3 shows the dynamics. The vertical rust arrows show Sax's price cuts; the horizontal rust arrows show Berney's responding strategy of matching each price cut.

By tracing through the pattern of reaction and counterreaction, you can see that this kind of rivalry will end in mutual ruin at a zero price. Why? Because the only price compatible with both strategies is a price of zero: 90 percent of zero is zero.

Sax finally realizes that when it cuts its price, Berney will match the price cuts. Only if you are shortsighted will you think you can undercut your rival for long. You will then start to ask what Sax will do if you charge price A, price B, and so forth. *Once you begin to consider how others will react to your actions, you have entered the realm of game theory.*

BASIC CONCEPTS

We will illustrate the basic concepts of game theory by analyzing a **duopoly price war.** This is a situation where the market is supplied by two firms that are deciding whether to engage in economic warfare of ruinously low prices. For simplicity, we assume that each firm has the same cost and demand structure. Further, each firm can choose whether to charge its normal price or lower its price below marginal costs and try to drive its rival into bankruptcy. The novel element in the duopoly game is that the firm's profits will depend on its rival's strategy as well as on its own.

A useful tool for representing the interaction between two firms or people is a two-way **payoff table**. A payoff table is a means of showing the strategies and the payoffs of a game between two players. Figure 11-4 on page 198 shows the payoffs in the duopoly price game for our two stores. In the payoff table, a firm can choose between the strategies listed in its rows or columns. For example, Sax can choose between its two columns and Berney can choose between its two rows. In this example, each firm decides whether to charge its normal price or to start a price war by choosing a low price.

Combining the two decisions of each duopolist gives four possible outcomes, which are shown in the four cells of the table. Cell A, at the upper left, shows the outcome when both firms choose the normal price; D is the outcome when both choose a price war; and B and C result when one firm has a normal price and one a war price.

The numbers inside the cells show the **payoffs** of the two firms; that is, these are the profits earned by each firm for each of the four outcomes. The rust number in the lower left shows the payoff to the player on the left (Berney); the black entry in the upper right shows the payoff to the player at the top (Sax). Because the firms are identical, the payoffs are mirror images.

Alternative Strategies

Now that we have seen the basic structure of a game, consider how you should behave as a player in the duopoly or any other game. In economics, we assume that firms maximize profits and consumers maximize utility. The new element in game theory is to think through the goals and actions of your opponent and to make your decisions based on your opponent's goals and actions. But you must always remember that your opponent will also be trying to outwit you.

FIGURE 11-3. What Happens When Two Firms Insist on Undercutting Each Other?
Trace through the steps by which dynamic price cutting leads to ever-lower prices for two rivals.

FIGURE 11-4. A Payoff Table for a Price War

The payoff table shows the payoffs associated with different strategies. Berney has a choice between two strategies, shown as its two rows. Sax can choose between its two strategies, shown as two columns. The entries in the cells show the profits for the two players. For example, in cell C, Berney plays "price war" and Sax plays "normal price." The result is that Berney has rust profit of −$100 while Sax has black profit of −$10. Thinking through the best strategies for each player leads to the dominant equilibrium in cell A.

The guiding philosophy in game theory is the following: Pick your strategy by asking what makes most sense for you assuming that your opponent is analyzing your strategy and acting in his or her best interest.

Let's apply this maxim to the duopoly example. First, note that our two firms have the highest joint profits in outcome A. Each firm earns $10 when both follow a normal-price strategy. At the other extreme is the price war, where each cuts prices and runs a big loss.

In between are two interesting strategies where only one firm engages in the price war. In outcome C, for example, Sax follows a normal-price strategy while Berney engages in a price war. Berney takes most of the market but loses a great deal of money because it is selling below cost. Sax is actually better off selling at normal prices rather than responding.

Dominant Strategy. In considering possible strategies, the simplest case is that of a **dominant strategy**. This situation arises when one player has a best strategy *no matter what strategy the other player follows.*

In our price-war game, for example, consider the options open to Berney. If Sax conducts business as usual with a normal price, Berney will get $10 of

profit if it plays the normal price and will lose $100 if it declares economic war. On the other hand, if Sax starts a war, Berney will lose $10 if it follows the normal price but will lose even more if it also engages in economic warfare. You can see that the same reasoning holds for Sax. Therefore, no matter what strategy the other firm follows, each firm's best strategy is to have the normal price. *Charging the normal price is a dominant strategy for both firms in the price-war game.*

When both (or all) players have a dominant strategy, we say that the outcome is a **dominant equilibrium**. We can see that in Figure 11-4, outcome A is a dominant equilibrium because it arises from a situation where both firms are playing their dominant strategies.

Nash Equilibrium. Most interesting situations do not have a dominant equilibrium, and we must therefore look further. We can use our duopoly example to explore this case. In this example, which we call the *rivalry game,* each firm considers whether to have its normal price or to raise its price toward the monopoly price and try to earn monopoly profits.

The rivalry game is shown in Figure 11-5. The firms can stay at their normal-price equilibrium, which we found in the price-war game. Or they can raise their price in the hopes of earning monopoly

The Rivalry Game

* Nash equilibrium

FIGURE 11-5. Should a Duopolist Try the Monopoly Price?
In the rivalry game, each firm can earn $10 by staying at its normal price. If both raise price to the high monopoly level, their joint profits will be maximized. However, each firm's temptation to "cheat" and raise its profits ensures that the normal-price Nash equilibrium will prevail in the absence of collusion.

profits. It is interesting that our two firms have the highest *joint* profits in cell A, where they earn a total of $300 when each follows a high-price strategy. Situation A would surely come about if the firms could collude and set the monopoly price. At the other extreme is the competitive-style strategy of the normal price, where each rival has profits of $10.

In between are two interesting strategies where one firm chooses a normal-price and one a high-price strategy. In cell C, for example, Sax follows a high-price strategy but Berney undercuts. Berney takes most of the market and has the highest profit of any situation, while Sax actually loses money. In cell B, Berney gambles on high price, but Sax's normal price means a loss for Berney.

In this example of the rivalry game, Berney has a dominant strategy; it will profit more by choosing a normal price no matter what Sax does. On the other hand, Sax does not have a dominant strategy, because Sax would want to play normal if Berney plays normal and would want to play high if Berney plays high.

Sax has an interesting dilemma. Should it play high and hope that Berney will follow suit? Or play safe by playing normal? By thinking through the payoffs, it becomes clear that Sax should play normal price. The reason is simple. Sax should start by putting itself in Berney's shoes. You can see that Berney will play normal price no matter what Sax

does because that is Berney's dominant strategy. Therefore, Sax should find its best action by assuming that Berney will follow Berney's best strategy, which immediately leads to Sax's playing normal. This illustrates the basic rule of game theory: you should set your strategy on the assumption that your opponent will act in his or her best interest.

The solution that we have discovered is actually a very general one which is called the **Nash equilibrium** after mathematician John Nash, who won the Nobel Prize in economics for his contributions to game theory. *A Nash equilibrium is one in which no player can improve his or her payoff given the other player's strategy.* That is, given player A's strategy, player B can do no better, and given B's strategy, A can do no better. Each strategy is a best response against the other player's strategy.[2]

The Nash equilibrium is also sometimes called the **noncooperative equilibrium**, because each party chooses that strategy which is best for itself—without collusion or cooperation and without regard for the welfare of society or any other party.

---

[2] More precisely, suppose that firm A picks strategy S_A while firm B picks strategy S_B. The pair of strategies (S_A^*, S_B^*) is a Nash equilibrium if neither player can find a better strategy to play under the assumption that the other player sticks to his or her original strategy. That is, as long as A plays strategy S_A^*, B cannot do better than to play strategy S_B^*, and the analogous rule holds for A.

The Invisible-Hand Game

		Billy's strategy		
		Competitive output		Low output

Competitive output / Low output table (Betsy's strategy rows):

	Competitive output	Low output
Betsy's strategy: Competitive output	A* $0 $0 *NI* = $5000	B† −$100 $800 *NI* = $4400
Betsy's strategy: Low output	C† $600 −$50 *NI* = $4500	D‡ $300 $250 *NI* = $4000

* Competition
† Unilateral low output
‡ Monopolistic collusion

FIGURE 11-6. Under Perfect Competition, Private Profit Seeking Leads to Social Efficiency
Under perfect competition, each competitor can decide on its competitive output (where $MC = P$) or lower its output to secure some monopoly profits. Consider two out of many competitors, Billy and Betsy. If either lowers output, his or her own profits go down from the zero-profit level. The table also shows in the lower right of each cell the total national income (NI), which is a measure of total social utility. National income declines if competitors depart from the efficient Nash equilibrium. This demonstrates the invisible-hand principle that, under perfect competition, social utility is maximized when each firm behaves in a noncooperative or Nash manner to maximize its own profits.

If all the Billies and Betsies successfully collude, they might move to the monopolistic collusion equilibrium in the lower right cell. Note that their joint profits are maximized and that national income declines under monopoly. What prevents collusive monopoly in most circumstances is that each competitor has a powerful incentive to defect and behave in a noncooperative manner, moving the market back to the competition in the upper left cell.

We can verify that the starred strategies in Figure 11-5 are Nash equilibria. That is, neither Sax nor Berney can improve its payoffs from the (normal, normal) equilibrium as long as the other doesn't change its strategy. If Berney moves to its high-price strategy, its profits go from $10 to −$20, while if Sax raises its price from the normal-price Nash equilibrium, its profits go from $10 to −$30. (Verify that the dominant equilibrium shown in Figure 11-4 is also a Nash equilibrium.)

SOME IMPORTANT EXAMPLES OF GAME THEORY

The Invisible-Hand Game

We can use game theory to illustrate some of the important principles of microeconomics. Begin with the *invisible-hand game* shown in Figure 11-6. We have shown two perfect competitors, Billy and Betsy. They are just two of many competitors in the auction mar-

ket for identical computer chips. Consider Billy's strategy. He might follow the textbook rule for a competitor and produce up to the point where marginal cost equals price. This is the competitive strategy.

Then a poor strategist comes to Billy and says, "Why don't you lower your output to get a little monopoly going?" Billy decides to try the low-output strategy, lowering output in the hope that his competitors will do the same, thereby raising the market price. Billy knows that if the competitors do not lower their output, his profits will fall from 0 to minus $100. Nonetheless, he gives it a try.

Alas, this strategy is foolish and doomed, as Billy would have seen if he had looked at the payoff table in Figure 11-6. The reason is that Betsy's dominant strategy is to follow the competitive-output rule. Whether Billy has competitive or low output, Betsy will still do best by setting output at the level where $MC = P$. The profit incentives in a perfectly competitive market will lead firms to the efficient noncooperative equilibrium; the competitive equilibrium is a Nash or noncooperative equilibrium.

Note also that total social utility is maximized when each firm behaves noncooperatively. This point recalls Adam Smith's doctrine of the invisible hand: "By pursuing [an individual's] own interest, he frequently promotes that of society more effectually than when he really intends to promote it." The paradox of the invisible hand is that, even though each person is behaving in a noncooperative manner, the economic outcome is socially efficient. Moreover, the competitive equilibrium is a Nash equilibrium in the sense that no individual would be better off by changing strategies if all other individuals hold firm to their strategies.

In an ideal, perfectly competitive economy, non-cooperative behavior produces the socially desirable state of economic efficiency.

The Collusion Game

Why don't the firms collude to raise their profits? Remember Adam Smith's maxim: "People of the same trade seldom meet together . . . but the conversation ends . . . in some contrivance to raise prices." They might form a cartel or persuade the government to limit entry into the industry.

Figure 11-6 shows what happens if the firms collude or behave in a cooperative manner. A **cooperative equilibrium** comes when the players act in unison to find strategies that will maximize their joint payoffs. The cooperative equilibrium comes at the collusive monopoly prices in the lower right cell of Figure 11-6, where both Billy and Betsy have low outputs. Although joint profits are maximized at the cooperative equilibrium, total social utility is definitely lower than it would be at the competitive equilibrium.

What are the impediments to the cooperative monopoly solution? To begin with, cartels and collusion in restraint of trade are illegal in most market economies. But the highest hurdle is self-interest. As is illustrated in Figure 11-6, each firm has a powerful incentive to cheat on the agreement and move toward the noncooperative equilibrium. If Billy defects, his profits go up from $300 to $600. Soon after Billy defects, Betsy would notice that her profits had declined sharply from $250 to −$50. She would reassess her strategy, probably conclude that the cartel had come unglued, and return to a competitive strategy. If the cooperative equilibrium was not enforceable, the firms would probably gravitate to the noncooperative or Nash equilibrium in the upper left cell of Figure 11-6.

To summarize:

In a perfectly competitive economy, noncooperative behavior of many independent firms produces an efficient allocation of resources. Cooperation and collusion on low outputs and high prices lead to economic losses to consumers. This suggests why governments want to enforce antitrust laws that contain harsh penalties for those who collude to fix prices or divide up the markets.

The Pollution Game

You definitely should not conclude from the invisible-hand game, however, that all attempts at cooperation are antisocial. In many circumstances, noncooperative behavior leads to economic inefficiency or social misery. One important economic example is the *pollution game* shown in Figure 11-7 on page 202. Consider an economy with externalities such as pollution. In this world of unregulated firms, each profit-maximizing firm would prefer to pollute rather than install expensive pollution-control equipment. Moreover, any firm which behaves altruistically and cleans up its wastes will have higher production costs, higher prices, and fewer customers. If its costs are high enough, the firm may even go bankrupt. The pressures of Darwinian competition will drive all firms to the starred Nash equilibrium in cell D in Figure 11-7; here neither firm can improve its profits by lowering pollution.

The pollution game is an example of a situation in which the invisible-hand mechanism of efficient perfect competition breaks down. *This is a situation in which the noncooperative or Nash equilibrium is inefficient.* When markets or decentralized equilibria become dangerously inefficient, governments may step in. By setting efficient regulations or emissions charges, government can induce firms to move to outcome A, the "low-pollute, low-pollute" world. In that equilibrium, the firms make the same profit as in the high-pollution world, and the earth is a healthier place to live in.

Deadly Arms Races

Game theory has wide applications in political science, military strategy, and evolutionary biology. A

The Pollution Game

* Nash equilibrium

FIGURE 11-7. Noncooperative Behavior Leads to More Pollution
In the deadly pollution game, each unregulated profit-maximizing steel firm emits pollution into streams and air. If a single firm tries to clean up its production, it raises prices, loses business, and suffers a decline in profits. The noncooperative Nash equilibrium in D leads to the high-pollution solution at bottom right. Government can overcome this by enforcing the cooperative equilibrium in A, where profits are the same and the environment has been cleaned up.

particularly dangerous game with an inefficient non-cooperative equilibrium is the *arms race*. Say you are superpower A facing hostile superpower R. You want to make sure that you have sufficient nuclear weapons to deter aggression. Since you are not sure about your opponent's intentions, you play it safe by having a modest weapons superiority over your opponent. This is, your generals tell you, just prudent policy.

Now put yourself in the shoes of R, which is watching you engage in a military buildup. R does not know *your* intentions. Its generals also counsel a strategy of prudent superiority. So A wants 10 percent more bombs than R, and R wants 10 percent more bombs than A. This triggers an explosive arms race. Nor is this a fanciful example. The noncooperative arms race between the United States and the Soviet Union over the 1945–1991 period led to massive military spending and an arsenal of almost 100,000 nuclear warheads, many of which are still floating around the remnants of the Soviet empire.

Some people fear that easy availability of guns in America may lead to a domestic arms race as people arm themselves out of fear of other people's guns.

These situations call for cooperative solutions in which the parties get together to reduce the armaments. Arms-control agreements move the outcome

from an inefficient noncooperative equilibrium to a less inefficient cooperative outcome. In doing so, they can increase the security and welfare of all participants.

Winner-Take-All Society?

Is it possible that economic life is increasingly becoming a giant tournament—the civilian equivalent of an arms race?

Ask yourself what all of the following have in common: best-sellers, patents, Olympic swimmers, supermodels, victorious lawsuits, and the President of the United States. These are all outcomes of **winner-take-all games,** situations in which the payoffs are determined primarily by relative merit rather than absolute merit. There is only one gold medalist in the 400-meter dash, only one winner to a lawsuit, and only one book at the top of the best-seller list. Compare such situations with factory workers, whose earnings are determined by absolute marginal productivity rather than relative marginal productivity.

A second feature of such contests is that the rewards are heavily concentrated at the very top. A top fashion model like Claudia Schiffer might be paid $25,000 for a fashion show, while most models make nothing. Best-selling authors like Stephen King

The Winner-Take-All Game

		Winner	
		Work in standard industry	Work in winner-take-all industry
Runner-Up	Work in standard industry	A* $50 $50 NI = $100	B† $300 $50 NI = $350
	Work in winner-take-all industry	C $50 $200 NI = $250	D‡ $300 $0 NI = $300

Note: Earnings in thousands.
* Dull
† Efficient
‡ Overcrowded

FIGURE 11-8. When Too Many People Enter Contests, National Income Can Fall
In the winner-take-all game, Winner at top prevails in professional sports or best-selling books. Runner-Up at left is lured into the winner-take-all market by the possibility of a large gain. Like too many fishing boats chasing the same fish, winner-take-all markets are overcrowded with people ultimately getting low earnings. Total incomes would rise if Runner-Up stayed in a standard, absolute-reward industry.

or Danielle Steel are paid up to $60 million for the rights to their books, while surveys indicate that the average writer makes not much more than the minimum wage. A few movie superstars like Mel Gibson or Kevin Costner get millions of dollars per film. By contrast, in a recent year, only one-tenth of the members of the actors' guild were actually paid for appearing in films, while hopefuls kept the wolf from the door with activities such as driving taxis and waiting on tables.

Figure 11-8 shows the winner-take-all game. Lucky or talented Winner has a powerful incentive to participate in the winner-take-all tournament; she ultimately prevails and gets income of $300,000. Runner-Up has the choice of working in an absolute-return industry like manufacturing or joining the tournament in entertainment, athletics, or law. If Runner-Up thinks he has an even chance of prevailing, he enters the race because he estimates that his expected earnings are $100,000 in winner-take-all industries and $50,000 in conventional occupations.

The equilibrium comes in the "overcrowded" equilibrium at the lower right, where both people enter the tournament. National income is higher here than in the dull equilibrium, where there are no exciting contests, but lower than in the efficient outcome, where Runner-Up does not enter the contest. An inefficient winner-take-all equilibrium generates the highest inequality of earnings of all.

A fascinating study by Robert Frank and Philip Cook explores the consequences of what they call a "winner-take-all society." The following quote suggests how game theory has illuminated this important part of economic life:

> Whereas free marketeers maintain that market incentives lead to socially efficient results, our claim is that winner-take-all markets attract too many contestants, result in inefficient patterns of consumption and investment, and often degrade our culture. . . . The explosion of top salaries has stemmed largely from the growing prevalence of winner-take-all markets.[3]

Frank and Cook argue the need for "positional arms control" (such as reforming the legal system) and progressive taxes on consumption as a way of reducing the waste from excessive competition for large prizes in entertainment, athletics, and business.

Games, Games, Everywhere . . .
The insights of game theory pervade economics, the social sciences, business, and everyday life. In

---

[3] Robert H. Frank and Philip J. Cook, *The Winner-Take-All Society* (Free Press, New York, 1995), pp. 6, 19. Many examples in this section are drawn from their study.

economics, for example, game theory can explain trade wars as well as price wars (some illuminating examples are provided in the questions at the end of this chapter).

Game theory can also suggest why foreign competition may lead to greater price competition. What happens when Japanese firms enter a U.S. market where firms had tacitly colluded on a price strategy that led to a high oligopolistic price? The foreign firms may "refuse to play the game." They did not agree to the rules, so they may cut prices to gain market shares. Collusion may break down.

A key feature in many games is the attempt of players to build *credibility*. You are credible if you are expected to keep your promises and carry out your threats. But you cannot gain credibility with simple promises. Credibility must be consistent with the incentives of the game.

How can you get credibility? Here are some examples: Central banks earn reputations for being tough on inflation by adopting politically unpopular policies. Even greater credibility comes when the central bank's rules are written into law or the nation's constitution. Businesses make credible promises by writing contracts that inflict penalties if they do not perform as promised. A more paradoxical approach is for an army to burn its bridges behind it. Because there is no retreat, the threat to fight to the death is a credible one.

These few examples provide a small tasting from the vast harvest produced by game theorists over the last half-century. This area has been enormously useful in helping economists and other social scientists think about situations where small numbers of people are well informed and try to outwit each other in markets, politics, or military affairs.

SUMMARY

A. Economics of Risk and Uncertainty

1. Economic life is full of uncertainty. Consumers face uncertain incomes and employment patterns as well as the threat of catastrophic losses; businesses have uncertain costs and their revenues contain uncertainties about price and production.

2. In well-functioning markets, arbitrage, speculation, and insurance help smooth out the unavoidable risks. Speculators are people who buy and sell commodities with an eye to making profits on price differentials across markets. They move goods across regions from low-price to high-price markets, across time from periods of abundance to periods of scarcity, and even across uncertain states of nature to periods when chance makes goods scarce.

3. The profit-seeking action of speculators and arbitragers tends to create certain equilibrium patterns of price over space and time. These market equilibria are zero-profit outcomes where the marginal costs and marginal utilities in different regions, times, or uncertain states of nature are in balance. To the extent that speculators moderate price and consumption instability, they are part of the invisible-hand mechanism that performs the socially useful function of reallocating goods from fat times (when prices are low) to lean times (when prices are high).

4. Speculative markets allow individuals to hedge against unwelcome risks. The economic principle of risk aversion, which derives from diminishing marginal utility, implies that individuals will not accept risky situations with zero expected value. Risk aversion implies that people will buy insurance to reduce the disastrous declines in utility from fire, death, or other calamities.

5. Insurance and risk spreading tend to stabilize consumption in different states of nature. Insurance takes large individual risks and spreads them so broadly that they become acceptable to a large number of individuals. Insurance is beneficial because, by helping to equalize consumption across different uncertain states, it raises the expected level of utility.

6. The conditions for operation of efficient insurance markets are stringent: there must be large numbers of independent events, with little chance of moral hazard or adverse selection. When market failures arise, prices can become distorted or markets may simply not exist. If private insurance markets fail, the government may step in to provide social insurance. Even in the most laissez-faire of advanced market economies today, governments insure against unemployment and health risks in old age.

B. Game Theory

7. Economic life contains many situations of strategic interaction among firms, households, governments, or others. Game theory analyzes the way that two or more parties, who interact in an arena such as a market,

choose actions or strategies that jointly affect each participant.

8. The basic structure of a game includes the players, who have different actions or strategies, and the payoffs, which describe the profits or other benefits that the players obtain in each outcome. The key new concept is the payoff table of a game, which shows the strategies and the payoffs or profits of the different players.

9. The key to choosing strategies in game theory is for players to think through both their own and their opponent's goals, never forgetting that the other side is doing the same. When playing a game in economics or any other field, assume that your opponent will choose his or her best option. Then pick your strategy so as to maximize your benefit, always assuming that your opponent is similarly analyzing your options.

10. Sometimes a dominant strategy is available, one that is best no matter what the opposition does. More often,

we find the Nash equilibrium (or noncooperative equilibrium) most useful. A Nash equilibrium is one in which no player can improve his or her payoff given the other player's strategy. Sometimes, parties can collude or cooperate, which produces the cooperative equilibrium.

11. A Nash equilibrium produces an efficient outcome in Adam Smith's invisible-hand game. Here, noncollusive firms produce at prices equal to marginal costs, and the noncooperative equilibrium is efficient. In such situations, cooperation leads to inefficient production.

12. Sometimes, however, noncooperative behavior leads to social ruin, as when competitors pollute the planet or engage in dangerous arms races. Winner-take-all games, such as lawsuits or athletic contests, can induce the entry of too many contestants and increase the inequality of incomes. In these cases, regulation or taxation may enhance economic efficiency by harnessing private competition to the public interest.

CONCEPTS FOR REVIEW

Risk and Uncertainty

spatial P equality
ideal seasonal price pattern
speculation, arbitrage, hedging
risk aversion and diminishing marginal utility
consumption stability vs. instability
insurance and risk spreading

market failure in information
moral hazard, adverse selection
social insurance

Game Theory

players, strategies, payoffs
payoff table
dominant strategy and equilibrium

Nash or noncooperative equilibrium
cooperative or collusive equilibrium
important games:
   invisible hand
   collusion
   pollution
   winner-take-all
credibility

QUESTIONS FOR DISCUSSION

1. Suppose an honest friend offers to flip a fair coin, with you paying your friend $100 if it comes up heads and your friend paying you $100 if it comes up tails. Explain why the expected dollar value is $0. Then explain why the expected utility value is negative if you are risk-averse. Can you see why your friend must be a risk lover (someone with increasing marginal utility of income)?

2. Consider the example of grade insurance (see page 195). Suppose that under grade insurance, students would be compensated $5000 a year for each point that their grade point average fell below the top grade (this figure might be an estimate of the impact of grades on future earnings). Explain why the presence of grade insurance would produce moral hazard and adverse selection. Why would moral hazard and adverse selection make insurance companies reluctant

to sell grade insurance? Are you surprised that you cannot buy grade insurance?

3. List some important differences between private and social insurance. Explain why it might be sensible for social insurance to provide universal health care for the elderly or unemployment insurance for workers but not fire insurance for homeowners.

4. In the early nineteenth century, little of the nation's agricultural output was sold in markets, and transportation costs were very high. What would you expect to have been the degree of variation of prices across regions compared with today?

5. Assume that a firm is making a risky investment (say, spending $1 billion developing a new commercial aircraft). Can you see how the widely diversified ownership of this firm could allow near-perfect risk spreading on the aircraft investment?

FIGURE 11-9. Countries Gain from Trade but Lose from Trade War
Japan and the United States can agree to the cooperative equilibrium at A in which they reduce all tariffs and quotas and enjoy the benefits of free trade. Each would, however, be tempted to "cheat" by putting trade restrictions on imports, thus gaining income at home while hurting total world income, moving to B or C. Retaliation would lead to the worst of all worlds, at D.

6. In the late 1980s, "arbs" (arbitragers) who became rich upon the illegal use of inside information gave a bad name to speculation and arbitrage. Suppose that speculation and arbitrage are made a criminal offense (as was the case until recently in Russia). Explain the economic damage that could result.

7. Explain the logic behind the invisible-hand game. Explain why a Nash or noncooperative equilibrium is efficient in the invisible-hand game and inefficient in the pollution game.

8. "In a world with no spillovers or externalities, collusion harms the public interest. In a world full of pollution, arms races, and winner-take-all markets, cooperation is essential." Interpret this statement in light of your understanding of game theory.

9. Consider the dilemma of maintaining free trade shown in the payoff table in Figure 11-9, which gives total real national incomes (in billions) for two countries as a function of foreign-trade policies. Each country can have a policy of either free trade with no tariffs or quotas or protectionism with tight quotas on imported goods and services. The payoffs are the real incomes in each country.
    a. List the four outcomes, and calculate each region's national income and world income.
    b. Show how countries acting noncooperatively (without agreements and in their own selfish national interest) will be led to a trade war at the Nash equilibrium in cell D. What is the effect of the trade war on total world income?

    c. What is the impact on incomes of a trade agreement that abolishes all trade restrictions and produces free trade?
    d. Is there an incentive for each country to "cheat" on the trade agreement? What happens if the cheating leads to retaliation and to the high-tariff outcome?

10. **Advanced problem:** We can modify Figure 11-2 to show the gains from insurance. Redraw Figure 11-2 by labeling the left-hand pair in (a) "Individual Does Not Buy Insurance," while the right-hand set in (b) can be titled "Individual Buys Insurance." Then, from left to right, label the four states of the world as "No fire and no insurance," "Fire and no insurance," "No fire with insurance less premiums," and "Fire with insurance reimbursement."

    By purchasing insurance, people can remove the risks of fire and thereby equalize the amount of consumption in each state of nature. In new panel (a), note that the no-fire state of nature has very high consumption while the fire state of nature has low consumption. In new panel (b), by paying insurance premiums, the individual lowers consumption a little if no fire occurs but gains greatly if a fire strikes. Because of diminishing marginal utility, people gain greatly by paying a fair insurance premium to ensure the same level of housing (or cars or health) no matter how the dice of life turn up.

PART THREE

FACTOR MARKETS: LAND, LABOR, CAPITAL, AND INCOME DISTRIBUTION

CHAPTER 12
HOW MARKETS DETERMINE INCOMES

You know, Ernest, the rich are different from us.

F. Scott Fitzgerald

Yes, I know. They have more money than we do.

Ernest Hemingway

Earlier chapters examined product markets: the way that markets determine *what* should be produced under different market structures like perfect competition and monopoly. We are also vitally concerned with the *for whom* question of the incomes that people earn from their labor and other sources of income. In Part Three, we turn to the functioning of factor markets along with the **theory of income distribution,** which examines the determination of income in a society. This chapter lays out the basic principles, while the next two chapters apply these principles to the markets for labor, land, and capital.

A. INCOME AND WEALTH

America is a land of extremes of income and wealth. If you are one of the 400 richest Americans, you are a 63-year-old white male with a degree from an Ivy League school and a net worth of $750 million. You probably made your fortune in manufacturing or real estate. Your voyage to the top was as much the product of birth as of brains, for your family is likely to have given you a nice head start with at least a few million dollars in the family business. You might also have succeeded by blazing new trails in computer software or discount stores for small towns.

At the other extreme are forgotten people who never make the cover of *Forbes* or *People* magazine. Listen to the story of Robert Clark, homeless and unemployed. A roofer and Vietnam veteran, he came to Miami from Detroit looking for work in 1992. He slept on the city streets on a piece of cardboard covered by a stolen sheet. Every day he and other homeless men crept out of the culverts into the daylight to work for temporary employment firms. These firms charged clients $8 to $10 an hour, paid the men the minimum wage, and then took most of the money back for transportation and tools. Clark's pay stub showed earnings of $31.28 for 31 hours of work.

How can we understand these extremes of income and wealth? Why are some people paid $1 million a year, while others net only $1 an hour? Why

Type of income	Amount ($, billion)	Share of total (%)	Examples
Labor income:			
Wages and salaries	3,634	58.1	Autoworker's wages; teacher's salary
Benefits and other labor income	793	12.7	Company contribution to pension fund
Property income:			
Proprietors' income	520	8.3	Proceeds from owner-run business; lawyer's share of partnership earnings
Net rent	146	2.3	Landlord's rental from apartments, after expenses and depreciation
Corporate profits	736	11.8	Microsoft's profits
Net interest	425	6.8	Interest paid on savings account
Total	**6,254**	**100.0**	

TABLE 12-1. Division of National Income, 1996
National income includes all the incomes paid to factors of production. Three-quarters consists of wages and other kinds of compensation of labor, while the rest is divided among rents, corporate profits, and the incomes of proprietors. (Source: U.S. Department of Commerce, *Survey of Current Business.*)

is real estate in Tokyo or Manhattan worth thousands of dollars a square foot, while land in the desert may sell for but a few dollars an acre? And what is the source of the billions of dollars of profits earned by giant enterprises like Exxon or Toyota?

The questions about the distribution of income are among the most controversial in all economics. Some people argue that high incomes are the unfair result of past inheritance and luck while poverty stems from discrimination and lack of opportunity. Others believe that people get what they deserve and that interfering with the market distribution of income would injure an economy's efficiency and make almost everyone worse off. In the broad middle are those who believe that the government should ensure that a social "safety net" catches those who fall below some minimum standard of living.

INCOME

In measuring the economic status of a person or a nation, the two yardsticks most often used are income and wealth. **Income** refers to the total receipts or cash earned by a person or household during a given time period (usually a year). The aggregate of all incomes is *national income*, the components of which are shown in Table 12-1. The biggest share of national income goes to labor, either as wages or salaries or as fringe benefits. The remainder goes to the different types of *property income*: rent, net interest, corporate profits, and proprietors' income. This last category basically includes the returns to the owners of small businesses.

The proceeds from a market economy are distributed to the owners of the economy's factors of production in the form of wages, profits, rent, and interest.

About three-quarters of national income goes to labor, while the rest is distributed as some form of returns to capital. The last quarter-century has been a turbulent one. What has been the impact of oil-price shocks, the computer revolution, globalization, and corporate downsizing on labor's share of the total income pie? Looking at Figure 12-1, we can see that the share of national income going to labor has changed very little in recent decades. This is one of the remarkable features of the income distribution in the United States.

Role of Government

How does government fit into this picture? Federal, state, and local governments are the major

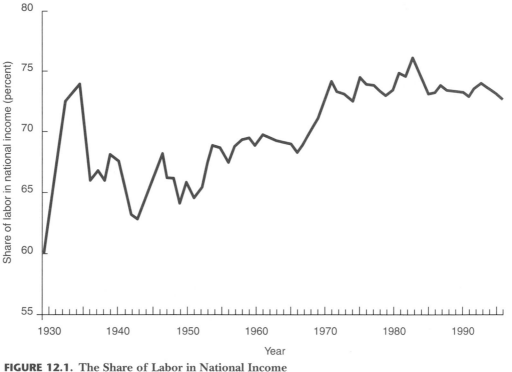

FIGURE 12.1. The Share of Labor in National Income
The share of labor income increased gradually from 1929 to 1970. Since then, it has been remarkably stable at around 75 percent of national income. The remainder of income is distributed among rents, interest, corporate profits, and proprietors' income. The share of property-type income is 100 minus the labor share. (Source: U.S. Department of Commerce.)

source of income for millions of people. They employ about 16 percent of the work force, paying about $641 billion in wages and salaries annually. In 1996, governments paid almost $189 billion in interest to holders of government bonds and other debt. Moreover, governments rent millions of square feet of office space and are responsible, directly and indirectly, for billions in profits to corporations which do business with them. All these direct payments to factors of production are reflected in Table 12-1.

Yet government also has a direct role in incomes that does not show up in Table 12-1. To begin with, the government collects a sizable share of national income through taxation and other levies. In 1996 about 32 percent of gross domestic product was collected by federal, state, and local governments as various types of taxes, including personal income taxes, corporate-profit taxes, and social security taxes.

But what the government taketh, it also giveth away. Governments at all levels provide incomes in the form of **transfer payments,** which are direct dollar payments from government to individuals that are not made in return for current goods or services. The biggest single category of transfer payments is social security for older Americans, but transfer payments also include veterans' benefits, farm subsidies, and welfare payments. Whereas Americans derived almost none of their incomes from governments in 1929, fully 17 percent of personal incomes in 1996 came from government transfer payments.

Personal income equals market income plus transfer payments. Most market income comes from wages and salaries; a small, prosperous minority derives its market income from earnings on property. The major component of government transfers is social security payments to the elderly.

Factor Incomes vs. Personal Incomes
It is important to understand the distinction between factor incomes and personal incomes.

What American Households Own, 1989		
Type of asset	Amount of assets ($, billion)	Percentage held by richest 1% of households
Tangible:		
Own home	6,415	8.4
Other real estate	2,907	43.0
Motor vehicle	773	7.6
Business investment	3,719	67.7
Other tangible assets	815	39.2
Financial:		
Checking, savings, and money market accounts	2,630	19.9
Stocks and bonds	2,056	54.5
Other financial assets (such as life insurance)	772	35.0
Total	**20,092**	**32.8**
Average dollar value of assets per household, 1989	216,043	

TABLE 12-2. Tangible and Financial Assets of Households

Households own tangible assets (such as houses and cars) as well as financial assets (such as savings accounts and stocks). Even though the average assets per household totaled more than $216,000, much of this was concentrated in a few hands. (Source: Arthur Kennickell and R. Louise Woodburn, "Estimation of Household Net Worth," April 1992.)

Table 12-1 reports the distribution of factor income—how much is paid in wages, in profits, and so on. But the same person may own many different factors of production. For example, someone might receive a salary, earn interest on money in a savings account, get dividends from shares in a mutual fund, and collect rent on a real-estate investment. In economic language, we observe that a person's market income is simply the quantities of factors of production sold by that person times the earnings of each factor. In addition, many people, particularly retirees on social security, receive transfer payments from the government.

WEALTH

We see that some income comes from interest or dividends on holdings of bonds or stocks. This brings us to the second important economic concept: **Wealth** consists of the net dollar value of assets owned at a given point in time. Note that wealth is a *stock* (like the volume of a lake) while income is a *flow* per unit of time (like the flow of a stream). A household's wealth includes its tangible items (houses, cars and other consumer durable goods, and land) and its financial holdings (such as cash, savings accounts, bonds, and stocks). All items that are of value are called *assets,* while those that are owed are called *liabilities.* The difference between total assets and total liabilities is called wealth or *net worth.*

Table 12-2 presents a breakdown of the asset holdings of Americans. The single most important asset of the majority of households is the family home: 64 percent of families own houses, as compared with 55 percent a generation ago. Most households own a modest amount of financial wealth in savings accounts and corporate stocks. But it turns out that a large proportion of the nation's financial wealth is concentrated in the hands of a small fraction of the population. About one-third of all wealth is owned by the richest 1 percent of American households.

△
B. INPUT PRICING BY MARGINAL PRODUCTIVITY
▽

Why do different people have such different incomes? We begin by observing that the theory of income distribution is a special case of the theory of prices. When we look for the price of labor, we look for wages; similarly, the price for using land is land rent. The prices of factors of production are set by the interaction between supply and demand for different factors—just as the prices of goods are determined by the supply and demand for goods.

But pointing to supply and demand is just the first step on the road to economic understanding. It leaves unanswered important questions: Why are Americans paid 5 times as much as Mexicans? Why are women paid only two-thirds of the average wage of men? What determines the profit rate on capital? Why are land prices so much higher in the city than in the desert?

The key to these questions is the marginal-productivity theory of incomes. By applying the production theory of earlier chapters, we will see that the demands for factors of production can be expressed in terms of the revenues earned on their marginal products. This key finding on demand, combined with supplies of factors, will determine the prices and quantities of factors and thereby market incomes.

THE NATURE OF FACTOR DEMANDS

The demand for factors differs from that for consumption goods in two important respects: (1) Factor demands are derived demands, and (2) factor demands are interdependent demands.

Demands for Factors Are Derived Demands

Let's consider the demand for office space by a firm which produces computer software. A software company will rent office space for its programmers, customer service representatives, and other workers. Similarly, other companies like pizza shops or banks will need space for their activities. In each region, there will be a downward-sloping demand curve for

office space linking the rental being charged by landlords to the amount of office space desired by companies—the lower the price, the more space companies will want to rent.

But there is an essential difference between ordinary demands by consumers and the demand by firms for inputs. Consumers demand final goods like computer games or pizzas because of the direct enjoyment or utility these consumption goods provide. By contrast, a business does not pay for inputs like office space because they yield direct satisfaction. Rather, it buys inputs because of the production and revenue that it can gain from employment of those factors.

Satisfactions are in the picture for inputs—but at one stage removed. The satisfaction that consumers get from playing computer games determines how many games the software company can sell, how many order takers it needs, and how much office space it must rent. The more successful its software, the more the demand curve for office space shifts to the right. An accurate analysis of the demand for inputs must, therefore, recognize that consumer demands do *ultimately* determine business demands for office space.

This analysis is not limited to office space. Consumer demands determine the demand for all inputs, including farmland, oil, pizza ovens, and even college professors!

The firm's demand for inputs is derived indirectly from the consumer demand for its final product.

Economists therefore speak of the demand for productive factors as a **derived demand.** This means that when firms demand an input, they do so because that input permits them to produce a good which consumers desire now or in the future. Figure 12-2 on page 214 shows how the demand for a given input, such as fertile cornland, must be regarded as derived from the consumer demand curve for corn. In the same way, the demand for office space is derived from the consumer demand for software and all the other products and services provided by the companies that rent office space.

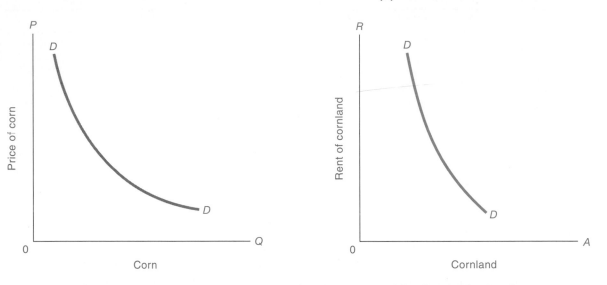

FIGURE 12-2. Demand for Factors Is Derived from Demand for Goods They Produce
The rust curve of derived demand for cornland comes from the black curve of commodity demand for corn. Shift the black curve out, and out goes the rust curve. If the black commodity curve becomes more inelastic, the same tends to happen to the rust input demand curve.

Demands for Factors Are Interdependent

Production is a team effort. A chain saw by itself is useless to me if I want to cut down a tree. A worker with empty hands is equally worthless. Together, the worker and the saw can cut the tree very nicely. In other words, the productivity of one factor, such as labor, depends upon the amount of other factors available to work with.

That means it is generally impossible to say how much output has been created by a single input taken by itself. The different inputs interact with one another. Sir William Petty put the matter in this striking way: Labor is the father of product and land the mother. We cannot say which is more essential in producing a baby—a mother or a father. So, too, it is generally impossible to say how much output has been created by any one of the different inputs taken by itself.

It is this *interdependence* of productivities of land, labor, and capital goods that makes the distribution of income a complex topic. Suppose we had to distribute at one time the entire output of a nation. If land had by itself produced so much, and labor had alone produced so much, and machinery had by itself produced the rest, distribution might be easy. Under supply and demand, if each factor produced a certain amount by itself, it could enjoy the undivided fruits of its own work.

But reread the above paragraph and underline such words as "by itself produced" and "had alone produced." They refer to a fantasy world of independent productivities which simply does not exist in reality. When an omelette is produced by chef's labor and chicken's eggs and cow's butter and land's natural gas, how can you unscramble the separate contributions of each input?

To find the answer, we must look to the interaction of marginal productivities (which affect demand) and factor supplies—both of which determine the competitive price and quantity.

REVIEW OF PRODUCTION THEORY

The fundamental point to understand is that *the demands for the various factors of production are derived from the revenues that each factor yields on its marginal product.* Before showing this result, we will review the essentials of Chapter 6's production theory.

(1)	(2)	(3)	(4)	(5)
		Marginal Revenue Product		
Units of labor (workers)	Total product (bushels)	Marginal product of labor (bushels per worker)	Price of output ($ per bushel)	Marginal revenue product of labor ($ per worker)
0	0			
		20,000	3	60,000
1	20,000			
		10,000	3	30,000
2	30,000			
		5,000	3	15,000
3	35,000			
		3,000	3	9,000
4	38,000			
		1,000	3	3,000
5	39,000			

TABLE 12-3. Calculation of Marginal Revenue Product for Perfectly Competitive Firm

The marginal product of labor is shown in column (3). Marginal revenue product of labor shows how much additional revenue the firm receives when an additional unit of labor is employed. It equals the marginal product in column (3) times the competitive output price in column (4).

The theory of production begins with the notion of the production function. The *production function* indicates the maximum amount of output that can be produced, with a given state of technical knowledge, for each combination of factor inputs. The production-function concept provides a rigorous definition of marginal product. Recall that the *marginal product* of an input is the extra product or output added by 1 extra unit of that input while other inputs are held constant.[1] The first three columns of Table 12-3 provide a review of the way marginal products are calculated.

As a final element of review, recall the *law of diminishing returns*. Column (3) of Table 12-3 shows that each successive unit of labor has a declining marginal product. "Declining marginal product" is another name for diminishing returns. Moreover, we can interchange land for labor, varying the amount of land while holding constant labor and other inputs, and we would generally observe the law of diminishing returns at work for land as well as for labor.

---
[1] Note that the marginal product of a factor is expressed in *physical* units of product per unit of additional input. So economists sometimes use the term "marginal physical product" rather than "marginal product," particularly when they want to avoid any possible confusion with a concept we will soon encounter called "marginal revenue product." For brevity, we will skip the word "physical" and abbreviate marginal product as *MP*.

Marginal Revenue Product

We can use the tools of production theory to devise a key concept in distribution theory, *marginal revenue product (MRP)*. Suppose we are operating a giant shirt factory. We know how many shirts each additional worker produces. But the firm wants to maximize profits measured in dollars, for it pays salaries and dividends with money, not with shirts. We therefore need a concept that measures the additional *dollars* each additional unit of input produces. Economists give the name "marginal revenue product" to the money value of the additional output generated by an extra unit of input.

The **marginal revenue product** of input A is the additional revenue produced by an additional unit of input A.

Competitive Case. It is easy to calculate marginal revenue product when product markets are perfectly competitive. In this case, each unit of the worker's marginal product (MP_L) can be sold at the competitive output price (P). Moreover, since we are considering perfect competition, the output price is unaffected by the firm's output, and price therefore equals marginal revenue (MR). If we have an MP_L of 10,000 bushels and a price and MR of $3, the dollar value of the output produced by the last worker—the marginal revenue product of labor

(MRP_L)—is \$30,000 (equal to 10,000 × \$3). This is shown in column (5) of Table 12-3. Hence, under perfect competition, each worker is worth to the firm the dollar value of the last worker's marginal product; the value of each acre of land is the marginal product of land times the output price; and so forth for each factor.

Imperfect Competition. What happens in the case of imperfect competition, where the individual firm's demand curve is downward-sloping? Here, the marginal revenue received from each extra unit of output sold is less than the price because the firm must lower its price on previous units to sell an additional unit. Each unit of marginal product will be worth $MR < P$ to the firm.

To continue our previous example, say that the MR is \$2 while the price is \$3. Then the MRP of the second worker in Table 12-3 would be \$20,000 (equal to the MP_L of 10,000 × the MR of \$2), rather than the \$30,000 of the competitive case.

To summarize, the additional revenue gained by a firm from an additional unit of input is called the marginal revenue product. It is measured in dollar terms by the marginal revenue multiplied by the marginal product of the input.

Marginal revenue product represents the additional revenue a firm earns from employment of an additional unit of an input, with other inputs held constant. It is defined as the marginal product of the input multiplied by the marginal revenue obtained from selling an extra unit of output. This holds for labor (L), land (A), and other inputs:

Marginal revenue product of labor
$$(MRP_L) = MR \times MP_L$$

Marginal revenue product of land
$$(MRP_A) = MR \times MP_A$$

and so forth.

Under conditions of perfect competition, because $P = MR$:

Marginal revenue product
$$(MRP_i) = P \times MP_i$$

for each input.

THE DEMAND FOR FACTORS OF PRODUCTION

Having analyzed the underlying concepts, we now turn to the determinants of the demand for inputs.

We then show how profit-maximizing firms decide upon the optimal combination of inputs, which allows us to derive the demand for inputs.

Factor Demands for Profit-Maximizing Firms

Where did the demand for cornland shown in Figure 12-2 come from? For that matter, what determines the demand for any factor of production? To understand these issues, we must analyze how a profit-oriented firm chooses its optimal combination of inputs.

Imagine that you are a profit-maximizing farmer. In your area, you can hire all the farmhands you want at \$20,000 per year. Your accountant hands you a spreadsheet with the data in Table 12-3. How would you proceed?

You could try out different possibilities. If you hire one worker, the additional revenue (the MRP) is \$60,000 while the marginal cost of the worker is \$20,000, so your extra profit is \$40,000. A second worker gives you an MRP of \$30,000 for an additional profit of \$10,000. The third worker produces extra output yielding revenue of only \$15,000 but costs \$20,000; hence, it is not profitable to hire the third worker. Table 12-3 shows that the maximum profit is earned by hiring two workers. We have by trial and error found an interesting rule:

A firm will maximize profits by hiring a factor of production as long as the MRP of that input exceeds the extra cost of that input.

By using this reasoning, we can derive the rule for choosing the optimal combination of inputs: To maximize profits, inputs should be added as long as the marginal revenue product of the input exceeds the marginal cost or price of the input.

For perfectly competitive factor markets, the rule is even simpler. Recall that under competition the marginal revenue product equals price times marginal product ($MRP = P \times MP$).

The profit-maximizing combination of inputs for a perfectly competitive firm comes when the marginal product times the output price equals the price of the input:

Marginal product of labor × output price
= price of labor = wage rate
Marginal product of land × output price
= price of land = rent

and so forth.

We can understand this rule by the following reasoning: Say that inputs into corn production (or any competitive industry) are bundled into $1 units—$1 units of labor, $1 units of land, and so forth. The firm will want to hire that quantity of $1 units of each input which will cause the revenue earned on the last unit to also be just $1. The incremental revenue is the corn *MP* of the input times the corn price, *P*. When inputs have been added so that the $MP \times P$ just reaches $1, the $1 of additional input cost just equals the $1 of additional revenue.

Least-Cost Rule. We can restate the condition much more generally in a way that applies to both perfect and imperfect competition in product markets (as long as factor markets are competitive). Reorganizing the basic conditions shown above, we have

$$\frac{\text{Marginal product of labor}}{\text{Price of labor}} = \frac{\text{marginal product of land}}{\text{price of land}} = \cdots$$

$$= \frac{1}{\text{marginal revenue}}$$

Suppose that you own a cable television monopoly in Denver. If you want to maximize profits, you will want to choose the best combination of workers, land easements for your cables, trucks, and testing equipment to minimize costs. If a month's truck rental costs $8000 while monthly labor costs per worker are $800, costs are minimized when the marginal products *per dollar of input* are the same. Since trucks cost 10 times as much as labor, truck *MP* must be 10 times labor *MP*.

Least-cost rule: Costs are minimized when the marginal product per dollar of input is equalized for each input. This holds for both perfect and imperfect competitors in product markets.

Marginal Revenue Product and the Demand for Factors

Having derived the *MRP* for different factors, we can now understand the demand for factors of production. We just saw that a profit-maximizing firm would choose input quantities such that the price of each input equaled the *MRP* of that input. This means that from the *MRP* schedule for an input, we can immediately determine the relationship

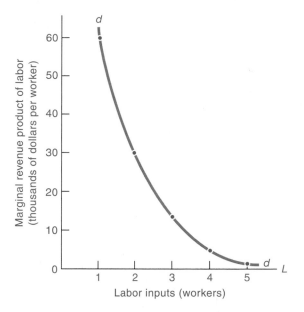

FIGURE 12-3. Demand for Inputs Derived through Marginal Revenue Products

The demand for labor is derived from the marginal revenue product of labor. This figure uses the data for the competitive firm displayed in Table 12-3.

between the price of the input and the quantity demanded of that input. This relationship is what we call the demand curve.

Glance back at Table 12-3 on p. 215. This table shows in the last column the *MRP* of labor for our corn farm. By the profit-maximizing condition, we know that at a wage of $60,000 the firm would choose 1 unit of labor; at a $30,000 wage, 2 units of labor would be sought; and so forth.

The *MRP* schedule for each input gives the demand schedule of the firm for that input.

We have used this result in Figure 12-3 to draw a labor demand curve for our corn farm using the data shown in Table 12-3. We have in addition drawn a smooth curve through the individual points to show how the demand curve would appear if fractional units of labor could be purchased.

Substitution Rule. A corollary of the least-cost rule is the **substitution rule:** If the price of one factor rises while other factor prices remain fixed, the firm will profit from substituting more of the other inputs for the more expensive factor. A rise in labor's price, P_L, will reduce MP_L/P_L. Firms will respond by reducing employment and increasing land use until equality of marginal products per dollar of input is restored—thus lowering the amount of needed L and increasing the demand for land acres. A rise in land's price, P_A, alone will, by the same logic, cause labor to be substituted for more expensive land. Like the least-cost rule, the substitution rule and the derived demand for factors apply to both perfect and imperfect competition in product markets.

SUPPLY OF FACTORS OF PRODUCTION

A complete analysis of the determination of factor prices and of incomes must combine both the demand for inputs just described and the supplies of different factors. The general principles of supply vary from input to input, and this topic will be explored in depth in the next two chapters. At this point we provide a few introductory comments.

In a market economy, most factors of production are privately owned. People "own" their labor in the sense that they control its use; but this crucial "human capital" can today only be rented, not sold. Capital and land are generally privately owned by households and by businesses.

Decisions about *labor* supply are determined by many economic and noneconomic factors. The important determinants of labor supply are the price of labor (i.e., the wage rate) and demographic factors, such as age, gender, education, and family structure. The quantity of *land* and other natural resources is determined by geology and cannot be significantly changed, although the quality of land is affected by conservation, settlement patterns, and improvements. The supply of *capital* depends upon past investments made by businesses, households, and governments. In the short run, the stock of capital is fixed like land, but in the long run the supply of capital is sensitive to economic factors such as risks and rates of return.

Can we say anything about the elasticity of supply of inputs? Actually, the supply curve may slope positively or be vertical and might even have a negative slope. For most factors, we would expect that the supply responds positively to the factor's price in the long run; in this case, the supply curve would slope upward and to the right. The supply of land is usually thought

to be unaffected by price, and in this case the supply of land will be perfectly inelastic, with a vertical supply curve. In some special cases, when the return to the factor increases, owners may supply less of the factor to the market. For example, if people feel they can afford to work fewer hours when wages rise, the supply curve for labor might bend backward at high wage rates, rather than slope upward.

The different possible elasticities for the supply of factors are illustrated by the *SS* supply curve shown in Figure 12-4.

DETERMINATION OF FACTOR PRICES BY SUPPLY AND DEMAND

A full analysis of the distribution of income must combine the supply and demand for factors of production. Earlier parts of this section provided the underpinnings for analysis of demand and gave a brief description of supply. We showed that, for given factor prices, profit-maximizing firms would choose input combinations according to their marginal revenue products. As the price of land falls, each farmer would substitute land for other inputs such as labor, machinery, and fertilizer. Each farmer therefore would show a demand for cornland inputs like that in Figure 12-2(*b*).

How do we obtain the *market demand* for inputs (whether cornland, unskilled labor, or computers)? We add together the individual demands of each of the firms. Thus at a given price of land, we add together all the demands for land of all the firms at that price; and we do the same at every price of land. In other words, *we add horizontally all the demand curves for land of the individual firms to obtain the market demand curve for land.* We follow the same procedure for any input, summing up all the derived demands of all the businesses to get the market demand for each input. And in each case, the derived demand for the input is based on the marginal revenue product of the input under consideration.[2] Figure 12-5 shows a general demand curve for a factor of production as the *DD* curve.

How do we find the overall market equilibrium? *The equilibrium price of the input in a competitive market*

---

[2] Note that this process of adding factor demand curves horizontally is exactly the same procedure that we followed in obtaining market demand curves for consumers in Chapter 5.

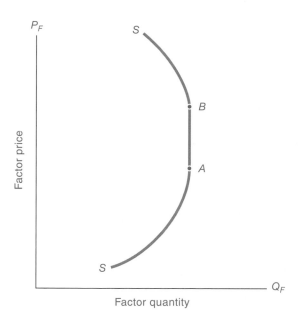

FIGURE 12-4. Supply Curve for Factors of Production
Supplies of factors of production depend upon character-istics of the factors and the preferences of their owners. Generally, supplies will respond positively to price, as in the region below A. For factors that are fixed in supply, like land, the supply curve will be perfectly inelastic, as from A to B. In special cases where a higher price of the factor increases the income of its owner greatly, such as for labor or oil, the supply curve may bend backward, as in the region above B.

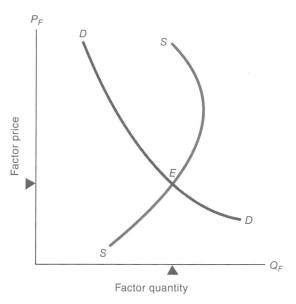

FIGURE 12-5. Factor Supply and Derived Demand Inter-act to Determine Factor Prices and Income Distribution
Factor prices are determined by the interaction of factor supply and demand. If the demand for an inelastically sup-plied factor such as land rises, that factor's total income will rise. Similarly, supplies and demands for trucks or computer programmers or office buildings will affect their prices and quantities sold. At what point will an increase in demand decrease both quantity supplied and total income of this factor?

comes at that level where the quantities supplied and demanded are equal. This is illustrated in Figure 12-5, where the derived demand curve for a factor inter-sects its supply curve at point E. Only at that price will the amount that owners of the factor willingly supply just balance the amount that the buyers will-ingly purchase.

Of Slicers and Flippers. We can apply these concepts to two factor markets to see why disparities in incomes are so high. Figure 12-6 on page 220 shows the markets for two kinds of labor—surgeons and fast-food workers. The supply of surgeons is severely limited by the need for medical licensing and the length and cost of education and training; as a result, there are but 50,000 practicing surgeons in the United States. Demand for surgery is growing rapidly along with other health-care services. The

result is that surgeons earn $245,000 a year on average. Moreover, an increase in demand will result in a sharp increase in earnings with little increase in output.

At the other end of the earnings scale are fast-food workers. These jobs have no skill or educational requirements and are open to virtually everyone. The supply is highly elastic, and employment has grown from 1.5 million workers in 1970 to 2.5 mil-lion workers in 1993. Wages are close to the mini-mum wage because of the ease of entry into this mar-ket, and the average full-time employee makes $12,000 a year. What is the reason for the vast differ-ence in earning power of surgeons and hamburger flippers? It is mainly the quality of labor, not the quantity of hours.

The Rich and the Rest. If you are one of the richest Americans, you might have $50 million of interest, dividends, and other property income, while the median household earns less than $1000 a year on its financial wealth. Figure 12-7 explains this difference. The rate of return on stocks or bonds is not that much higher for the richest than for the middle class. Rather, the rich have a much bigger wealth base to earn on. The shaded rectangles in Figure 12-7 show the capital earnings of the two groups. Make sure you understand that it is the amount of wealth rather than the rate of return that makes the rectangle of the top wealth holders so large.

These two examples show that factor prices and people's incomes are not determined solely by chance. Rather, the forces of supply and demand operate to create high returns to factors that have either limited supply or high demand as reflected in high marginal revenue product. If a factor such as surgeons becomes scarcer, say, because training requirements are tightened, the price of this factor will rise and surgeons will enjoy higher incomes. However, if demand decreases in some field like psy-

chiatry—perhaps because insurance companies decide to cut back on psychiatric coverage, or close substitutes like social workers and psychologists lure away patients, or people stop wanting so much counseling—psychiatrists' incomes will fall. Competition giveth, and competition taketh away.

THE DISTRIBUTION OF NATIONAL INCOME

With our new understanding of marginal-productivity theory, we can now come back to the question raised at the beginning of the chapter. In a world of intense competition, how do markets allocate national output among two or more factors of production?

A simplified theory of factor-income distribution was first proposed around the turn of the century by John Bates Clark, a distinguished economist at Columbia University. It can be applied to competitive markets for any number of final products and

FIGURE 12-6. The Markets for Surgeons and Fast-Food Workers
In (**a**), we see the impact of a limited supply of surgeons: small output and high earnings per surgeon. What would be the effect on total earnings of surgeons and on the price of an operation if a rising share of elderly led to increases in the demand for surgeons?

In (**b**), open entry and low skill requirements imply a highly elastic supply of fast-food workers. Wages are beaten down and employment is high. What would be the effect on wages and employment if more teenagers look for jobs?

(a) Market for Surgeons

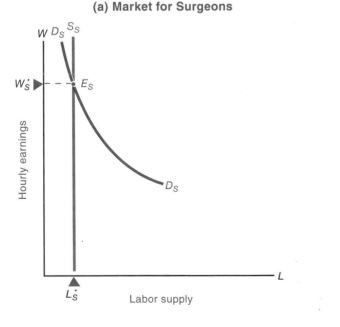

(b) Market for Fast-Food Workers

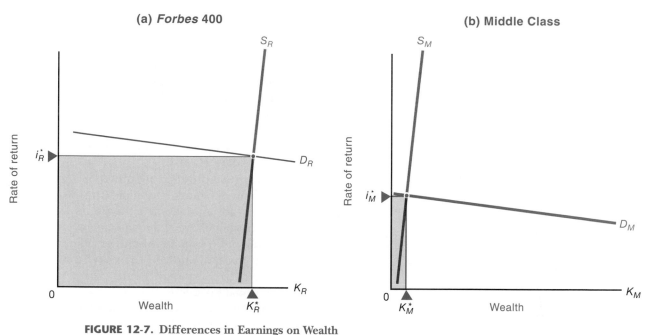

FIGURE 12-7. Differences in Earnings on Wealth

The top wealth holders in (**a**) bring vastly more wealth to the market. Because they invest in riskier areas, their investments have slightly higher returns than those of the middle class. Shaded rectangles are the product of wealth and rate of return and give annual property income.

The middle class in (**b**) has little property and invests it conservatively. Total property income is modest in comparison with (**a**).

factor inputs. But it is most easily grasped if we consider a simplified world with only one product in which all accounts are kept in real terms. The product could be corn or a basket of goods, but we will call it Q. Moreover, by setting the price equal to 1, we can conduct the entire discussion in real terms, with the value of output being Q and with the wage rate being the real wage in terms of goods or Q. In this situation, a production function tells how much Q is produced for each quantity of labor-hours, L, and for each quantity of acres of homogeneous land, A. Note that because $P = 1$, under perfect competition $MRP = MP \times P = MP \times 1 = MP$ and the wage = MP_L.

Clark reasoned as follows: A first worker has a large marginal product because there is so much land to work with. Worker 2 has a slightly smaller marginal product. But the two workers are alike, so they must get exactly the same wage. The puzzle is, which wage? The MP of worker 1, or of worker 2, or the average of the two?

Under perfect competition, the answer is clear: Landlords will not hire a worker if the market wage exceeds that worker's marginal product. So the demand curve for labor will ensure that *all* the workers receive a wage rate equal to the marginal product of the last worker.

But now there is a surplus of total output over the wage bill because earlier workers had higher MPs than the last worker. What happens to the excess MPs produced by all the earlier workers? The excess stays with the landlords as their residual earnings, which we will later call *rent*. Why, you might ask, do the landlords, who may be sipping their martinis thousands of miles away, earn anything on the land? The reason is that each landowner is a participant in the competitive market for land and rents the land for its best price. Just as worker competes with worker for jobs, landowner competes with landowner for workers. There are no conspiracies, no employer associations, and no unions in Clark's competitive world—just the operation of supply and demand.

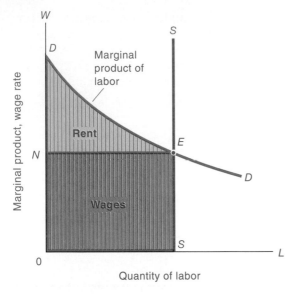

FIGURE 12-8. Marginal Product Principles Determine Factor Distribution of Income

Each vertical slice represents the marginal product of that unit of labor. Total national output 0*DES* is found by adding all the vertical slices of *MP* up to the total supply of labor at *S*.

The distribution of output is determined by marginal product principles. Total wages are the lower rectangle (equal to the wage rate 0*N* times the quantity of labor 0*S*). Land rents get the residual upper triangle *NDE*.

We have therefore determined the total wages paid to labor. Figure 12-8 shows that the marginal product curve of labor gives the demand curve of all employers in terms of real wages. Labor-supply factors determine the supply of labor (shown as *SS*). The equilibrium wage comes at *E*. The total wages paid to labor are given by $W \times L$ (for example, if $W = 5$ and $L = 1$ million, total wages = 5 million); this is shown by the dark area of the rectangle, 0*SEN*.

Surprisingly, we can also calculate the rent income of land. The light rust rent triangle *NDE* in Figure 12-8 measures all the surplus output which was produced but was not paid out in wages. The size of the rent triangle is determined by how much the *MP* of labor declines as additional labor is added—that is, by the extent of diminishing returns. If there are a few high-quality plots, additional units of labor will show sharp diminishing returns and rent's share will be large. If, by contrast, there is a great deal of homogeneous frontier land

just waiting to be cleared, there may be little tendency to diminishing returns and land's rent triangle will be very small.

We have drawn Figure 12-8 so that labor's wages are about 3 times larger than property's rents. This 3-to-1 relationship reflects the fact that labor earnings constitute about three-quarters of national income.

Marginal-Productivity Theory with Many Inputs

The marginal-productivity theory is a great step forward in understanding the pricing of different inputs. Note additionally that the positions of land and labor could be reversed to get a complete theory of distribution. To switch the roles of labor and land, hold labor constant and add successive units of variable land to fixed labor. Calculate each successive acre's marginal product.

Then draw a demand curve showing how many acres labor owners will demand of land at each rent rate. In the new version of Figure 12-8 that you draw, find a new E' point of equilibrium. Identify land's rectangle of rent as determined by rent × quantity of land. Identify labor's residual wage triangle. Finally, note the complete symmetry of the factors. This new graph shows that we should think of the distributive shares of each and every factor of production as being simultaneously determined by their interdependent marginal products.

That is not all. Instead of labor and land, suppose the only two factors were labor and some versatile capital goods. Suppose a smooth production function relates Q to labor and capital with the same general properties as in Figure 12-8. In this case, you can redraw Figure 12-8 and get an identical picture of income distribution between labor and capital. Indeed, we can perform the same operation for three, four, or any number of factors.

In competitive markets, the demand for inputs is determined by the marginal products of factors. In the simplified case where factors are paid in terms of the single output, we get

Wage = marginal product of labor
Rent = marginal product of land

and so forth for any factor. This distributes 100 percent of output, no more and no less, among all the factors of production.

We see, then, that the aggregate theory of the distribution of income is compatible with the competitive pricing of any number of goods produced by any number of factors. This simple but powerful theory shows how the distribution of income is related to productivity in a competitive market economy.

Now that we are armed with the general principles underlying the pricing of factors of production and the determination of the distribution of income, we can turn to a detailed discussion of the special features in the three major factor markets—land, labor, and capital.

SUMMARY

A. Income and Wealth

1. Distribution theory is concerned with the basic question of *for whom* economic goods are to be produced. In examining how the different factors of production—land, labor, and capital—get priced in the market, distribution theory considers how supplies and demands for these factors are linked and how they determine all kinds of wages, rents, interest rates, and profits.

2. Income refers to the total receipts or cash earned by a person or household during a given time period (usually a year). Income consists of labor earnings, property income, and government transfer payments.

3. National income consists of the labor earnings and property income generated by the economy in a year. Government takes a share of that national income in the form of taxes and gives back part of what it collects as transfer payments. The posttax personal income of an individual includes the returns on all the factors of production—labor and property—that the individual owns, plus transfer payments from the government, less taxes.

B. Input Pricing by Marginal Productivity

4. To understand the demand for factors of production, we must analyze the theory of production and the derived demand for factors. The demand for inputs is a derived demand: We demand pizza ovens and wheatland not for their own sake but for the pizzas and bread that they can produce for consumers. Factor demand curves are derived from commodity demand curves. An upward shift in the final demand curve causes a similar upward shift in the derived factor demand curve; greater inelasticity in commodity demand produces greater inelasticity of derived factor demand.

5. We met in earlier chapters the concepts of the production function and marginal products. The demand for a factor is drawn from its marginal revenue product (MRP), which is defined as the extra revenue earned from employing an extra unit of a factor. In any market, MRP equals the marginal revenue earned by the sale of an additional unit of the product times the marginal product of an input ($MRP = MR \times MP$). For competitive firms, because price equals marginal revenue, this simplifies to $MRP = P \times MP$.

6. A firm maximizes profits (and minimizes costs) when it sets the MRP of each factor equal to that factor's marginal cost, which is the factor's price. This can be stated equivalently as a condition in which the MRP per dollar of input is equalized for each input. This must hold in equilibrium because a profit-maximizing employer will hire any factor up to the point where the factor's marginal product will return in dollars of marginal revenue just what the factor costs.

7. To obtain the market demand for a factor, we add horizontally all firms' demand curves. This, along with the particular factor's own supply curve, determines the supply-and-demand equilibrium. At the market price for the factor of production, the amounts demanded and supplied will be exactly equal—only at equilibrium will the factor price have no tendency to change.

8. The marginal-productivity theory of income distribution analyzes the way total national income gets distributed among the different factors. Competition of numerous landowners and laborers drives factor prices to equal their marginal products. That process will allocate exactly 100 percent of the product. Any factor, not just labor alone, can be the varying factor. Because each unit of the factor gets paid only the MP of the last unit hired, there is a residual surplus of output left over from the MPs of early inputs. This residual is exactly equal to the incomes of the other factors under marginal productivity pricing. Hence, the marginal-productivity theory of distribution, though simplified, is a logically complete picture of the distribution of income under perfect competition.

CONCEPTS FOR REVIEW

income distribution
income, wealth
national income
transfer payments
personal income
marginal product, marginal revenue
    product, derived demand

marginal revenue product of input i
    $= MRP_i = MR \times MP_i = P \times MP_i$
    for competitive firm
aggregate distribution theory
MP rectangle, residual rent triangle

factor demands under competition:
    $MP_i \times P =$ factor price$_i$, which
    gives least-cost rule:

$$\frac{MP_L}{P_L} = \frac{MP_A}{P_A} = \cdots$$

$$= \frac{1}{\text{marginal revenue}}$$

QUESTIONS FOR DISCUSSION

1. Over the last century, hours of work per lifetime have declined about 50 percent while real wages have increased about 8 times. Assuming that the main change was an increase in the marginal-productivity-of-labor schedule, draw supply-and-demand diagrams for labor in 1895 and 1995 that will explain this trend. In your diagrams, put the number of hours worked per lifetime on the horizontal axis and the real wage rate on the vertical axis. What key factor about the supply of labor must you invoke to explain this historical trend?

2. For each of the following factors, name the final output for which the item is a derived demand: wheatland, gasoline, barber, machine tool for basketballs, wine press, economics textbook.

3. Study Figure 12-6. Assume that as the population ages, demand moves away from hamburgers and toward medical care. Draw the new demand curves and the new equilibria. Describe the outcome in terms of the wages, employment, and total income of surgeons and fast-food workers.

4. Why is each of the following incorrect? State the correct proposition.
    a. Marginal revenue product is calculated as total revenue earned per worker.
    b. Distribution theory is simple. You simply figure out how much each factor produces and then give the factor its share of output.
    c. Under competition, workers get paid the total output produced minus the costs of raw materials.

5. Figure 12-1 shows that the share of labor in national income changed little from 1935 to 1996 even though total national output rose by 700 percent. Draw a set of economywide curves like those in Figure 12-8 which can explain these two facts.

6. Labor leaders used to say, "Without any labor there is no product. Hence labor deserves *all* the product." Apologists for capital would reply, "Take away all capital goods, and labor scratches a bare pittance from the earth; practically all the product belongs to capital."

    Analyze the flaws in these arguments. If you were to accept the arguments, show that they would allocate 200 or 300 percent of output to two or three factors, whereas only 100 percent can be allocated. How does Clark's marginal-productivity theory resolve this dispute?

7. Draw the supply and demand curves for the oil market. Now suppose that a workable electric car shifts demand away from oil. Draw the new demand curve and the new equilibrium. Describe the outcome in terms of the price of oil, the quantity consumed, and the total income of the oil producers.

8. Consider the marginal product distribution theory in Figure 12-8. If immigration increases labor supply, the economy moves down the labor demand curve. Will labor's wage fall? (Show that the answer is yes.) Will the residual earnings of land, capital, and other factors rise? (Again, show that the answer is yes.) Can you tell what will happen to the absolute total of labor's rectangle as well as the share of labor income in the total? (Show that the answers are both no.)

9. In the marginal-productivity theory shown in Figure 12-8, let land rather than labor be the varying input. Draw a new figure and explain the theory with this new diagram. What is the residual factor?

CHAPTER 13
THE LABOR MARKET

Work is the curse of the drinking class.

Oscar Wilde

Workers are more than abstract factors of production. The economy, after all, is a method for organizing society whose purpose is to serve people both as consumers and as workers. It is for that reason that we worry about the quality and quantity of jobs, that the unemployment rate is a central social concern, and that the labor market is a constant source of controversy, social strife, and political ferment. The last century has witnessed pitched battles between labor and capital over wages, working conditions, and the right to organize; today, women and minorities struggle for good jobs and pay equity.

This chapter explores how wages are set in a market economy. Section A reviews the supply of labor and the determination of wages under competitive conditions. This is followed by a survey of labor unions, which are one means by which workers can collectively control their labor supply. We close with a review of the thorny problem of racial and gender discrimination in labor markets.

A. FUNDAMENTALS OF WAGE DETERMINATION

THE GENERAL WAGE LEVEL

In analyzing labor earnings, economists tend to look at the average **real wage**, which represents the purchasing power of an hour's work, or the money wages divided by the cost of living.[1] By that measure, American workers today are far better off than they

were 100 years ago. Figure 13-1 on page 226 shows the average hourly wage, adjusted for inflation, along with the average length of workweek.

The same powerful gains for workers are found in every industrial country. Across Western Europe, Japan, and the rapidly industrializing countries of East Asia, there has definitely been a steady, long-term improvement in the average worker's ability to buy food, clothing, and housing, as well as in the health and longevity of the population. In Europe and the United States, these gains began in earnest

---

[1] In this chapter, we will generally use the term "wages" as a shorthand expression for "wages, salaries, and other forms of compensation."

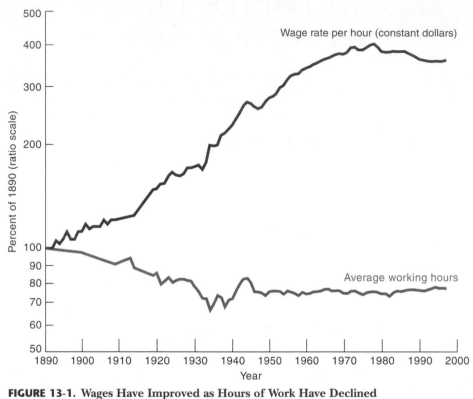

FIGURE 13-1. Wages Have Improved as Hours of Work Have Declined
With advancing technology and improved capital goods, American workers enjoy higher wages while working shorter hours. Slower growth in productivity in the last two decades has led to slower growth in real wages.

in the early 1800s, with the advent of the technological and social changes associated with the Industrial Revolution. By comparison, before that time real wages meandered up and down, with few long-term gains.

That is not to say that the Industrial Revolution was an unmitigated benefit to workers, especially in the laissez-faire days of the 1800s. In point of fact, a Dickens novel could hardly do justice to the dismal conditions of child labor, workplace dangers, and poor sanitation in early-nineteenth-century factories. A workweek of 84 hours was the prevailing rule, with time out for breakfast and sometimes supper. A good deal of work could be squeezed out of a 6-year-old child, and if a woman lost two fingers in a loom, she still had eight left.

Was it a mistake for people to leave the farms for the rigors of the factory? Probably not. Modern historians emphasize that even with the demanding conditions in the factories, living standards were nevertheless greatly improved over those in the earlier centuries of agrarian feudalism. The Industrial Revolution was a giant step forward for the working class, not a step back. The idyllic picture of the healthful, jolly countryside peopled by stout yeomen and happy peasantry is a historical myth unsupported by statistical research.

DEMAND FOR LABOR

We begin our examination of the general wage level by examining the factors underlying the demand for labor. The basic tools were provided in the last chapter, where we saw that the demand for a factor of production reflects the marginal productivity of that input.

Figure 13-2 illustrates the marginal-productivity theory. At a given time and with a given state of tech-

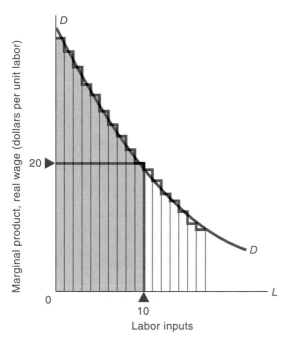

FIGURE 13-2. Demand for Labor Reflects Marginal Productivity

The demand for labor is determined by its marginal productivity in producing national output. The light gray vertical slices represent the extra output produced by the first, second, . . . unit of labor. The competitively determined general wage level at 10 units of labor is $20 per unit, equal to the marginal productivity of the tenth unit. The labor demand curve shifts up and out over time with capital accumulation, technological advance, and improvements in labor quality.

nology, there exists a relationship between the quantity of labor inputs and the amount of output. By the law of diminishing returns, each additional unit of labor input will add a smaller and smaller slab of output. In the example shown in Figure 13-2, at 10 units of labor, the competitively determined general wage level will be $20 per unit.

But probe deeper and ask what lies behind the marginal product. To begin with, the marginal productivity of labor will rise if workers have more or better capital goods to work with. Compare the productivity of a ditchdigger using a bulldozer with that of a similar digger using a hand shovel, or the copying capabilities of the medieval scribes with those of modern secretaries. Second, marginal productivity

of better-trained or better-educated workers will generally be higher than that of workers with less "human capital."

These reasons explain much of why wages and living standards have risen so much over the last century. Wages are high in the United States and other advanced countries because these nations have accumulated substantial capital stocks: dense networks of roads, rails, and communications; substantial amounts of plant and equipment for each worker; and adequate inventories of spare parts. Even more important are the vast improvements in technologies compared to those of an earlier era. Over the last century we have seen light bulbs replace oil lamps, airplanes replace horses, xerography replace quill and ink, and computers replace abacuses. Just imagine how productive the average American would be today with the technologies of 1897.

The quality of labor inputs is another factor determining the general wage level. By any measure—literacy, education, or training—the U.S. labor force of 1997 is vastly superior to the one of 1897. Years of education are necessary to produce an engineer capable of designing precision equipment. A decade of training must precede the ability to perform successful brain surgery. Overall, the proportion of adults who have completed college rose from 6 percent in 1950 to 22 percent in 1995. Such accumulations of human capital provide a substantial boost to the productivity of labor.

International Comparisons

The same reasoning explains why wage levels differ so dramatically across the world. Look at Table 13-1 on page 228, which gives the average wages plus benefits in manufacturing industries for eight countries. Wages are more than 10 times higher in the United States than in Mexico, 4 times higher in Japan than in South Korea, and almost 20 times higher in Great Britain than in India. We also see that compensation levels in Germany and Japan have pushed ahead of those in North America.

What accounts for the enormous differences? It's not that governments in India and Mexico are suppressing wage increases, though government policies do have some impact on the minimum wage and other aspects of the labor market. Rather, real

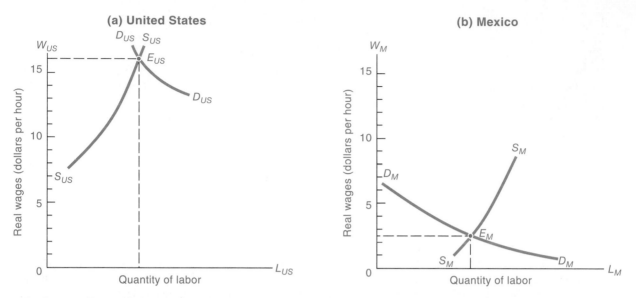

FIGURE 13-3. Favorable Resources, Skills, Management, Capital, and Technology Explain High U.S. Wages
Supply and demand determine a higher competitive wage in the United States than in Mexico. The major forces leading to high U.S. wages are a better-educated and more skilled work force, a larger stock of capital per worker, and modern technologies.

wages differ among countries primarily because of the operation of the supply and demand for labor. Look at Figure 13-3. Suppose that Figure 13-3(a) represents the state of affairs in the United States while Figure 13-3(b) describes Mexico. In Figure 13-3(a), the supply of U.S. workers is shown by the supply curve, $S_{US}S_{US}$, while the demand for workers is represented by $D_{US}D_{US}$. The equilibrium wage will settle at the level shown at E_{US}. If the wage were lower than E_{US}, shortages of labor would occur and employers would bid up wages to E_{US}, restoring the equilibrium. Similar forces determine E_M, the Mexican wage.

We see that the Mexican wage is lower than the U.S. wage principally because the Mexican demand curve for labor is far lower as a result of the low marginal productivity of labor in Mexico. Compared to the United States, a country like Mexico has much less capital to work with: many of the roads are unpaved, few computers and fax machines are in use, and much of the equipment is old or poorly maintained. In addition, the average educational levels in Mexico fall far short of the American standard, with a substantial fraction of the population still illiterate. All these factors make labor's marginal productivity low.

TABLE 13-1. General Wage Levels Vary Enormously across Countries
Western European nations, Japan, and the United States are high-wage countries, while Indian hourly wages are a tiny fraction of American levels. General wage levels are determined by supply and demand, but behind supply and demand lies the relative abundance of labor, capital, and resources, along with levels of skill and technology. (Source: U.S. Bureau of Labor Statistics *Monthly Labor Review,* 1996.)

Region	Wages and fringe benefits in manufacturing ($ per hour, 1995)
Western Germany	31.88
Japan	23.66
United States	17.20
Italy	16.48
Great Britain	13.77
South Korea	5.25
Mexico	1.51
India	0.71

This analysis can also help explain why wages are rising rapidly in East Asian countries like Hong Kong, South Korea, and Thailand. These countries are devoting a sizable share of their outputs to educating their population, investing in new capital goods, and importing the latest productive technologies. As a result, real wages in these countries have doubled over the last 20 years, while wages have stagnated in countries whose investments and economic policies are less well designed.

THE SUPPLY OF LABOR

Determinants of Supply

So far we have focused on the demand side of the labor market. Now we turn to the supply side of the labor market. *Labor supply* refers to the number of hours that the population desires to work in gainful activities. The three key elements for labor supply are hours per worker, labor-force participation, and immigration.

Hours Worked. While some people have jobs with flexible hours, most Americans work between 35 and 40 hours a week, without much leeway to increase or cut back their weekly hours. However, most people have a lot of control over how many hours they work over the course of their lifetimes. The decisions to go to college, to retire early, and to work part-time rather than full-time—all of these can reduce the number of total lifetime hours worked. On the other hand, the decision to moonlight and take on a second job will increase the lifetime hours worked.

Suppose that wages rise. Will that increase or decrease the lifetime hours of work? Look at the supply curve of labor in Figure 13-4. Note how the supply curve rises at first in a northeasterly direction; then at the critical point *C*, it begins to bend back in a northwesterly direction. How can we explain why higher wages may first increase and then decrease the quantity of labor supplied?

Put yourself in the shoes of a worker who has just been offered higher hourly rates and is free to choose the number of hours to be worked. You are tugged in two different directions. On the one hand, you are affected by the *substitution effect*, which tempts you to work longer hours because each hour of work is now better paid. Each hour of leisure has

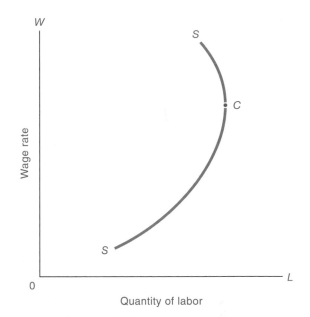

FIGURE 13-4. As Wages Rise, Workers May Work Fewer Hours

Above the critical point *C*, raising the wage rate reduces the amount of labor supplied as the income effect outweighs the substitution effect. Why? Because at higher wages workers can afford more leisure even though each extra hour of leisure costs more in wages forgone.

become more expensive, and you have an incentive to substitute extra work for leisure.

But acting against the substitution effect is the *income effect*.[2] With the higher wage, your income is higher. With a higher income, you will want to buy more goods and services, and, in addition, you will want more leisure time. You can afford to take a week's vacation in the winter or an extra week in the summer or to retire earlier than you otherwise would.

Which will be more powerful, the substitution effect or the income effect? There is no single correct answer; it depends upon the individual. In the case shown in Figure 13-4, for all wage rates up to point *C*, labor supplied increases with a higher wage: the substitution effect outweighs the income effect. But from point *C* upward, the income effect outweighs the substitution effect, and labor supplied declines as wage rates climb higher.

---

[2] See Chapter 5 for a discussion of substitution and income effects in connection with consumption.

Labor-Force Participation. One of the most dramatic developments in recent decades has been the sharp influx of women into the work force. The labor-force participation rate of women (i.e., the fraction of women over 15 employed or actively looking for jobs) has jumped from 34 percent in 1950 to 60 percent today. In part this can be explained by rising real wages, which have made working more attractive for women. However, a change of this magnitude cannot be explained by economic factors alone. To understand such a significant alteration in working patterns, one must look outside economics to changing social attitudes toward the role of women as mothers, homemakers, and workers.

At the same time that more women have entered the labor force, the participation rate of older men has fallen sharply, especially for men over 65. The most important reason for this change is probably the increased generosity of federal health and retirement benefits, which has made it possible for many people to retire rather than keep working.

Immigration. The role of immigration in the labor-force supply has always been important in the United States. Whereas only 5 percent of the U.S. population was foreign-born in 1970, by 1990 the number had risen to almost 10 percent.

The flow of legal immigrants is controlled by an intricate quota system which favors skilled workers and their families, as well as close relatives of U.S. citizens and permanent residents. In addition, there are special quotas for political refugees. In recent years, the biggest groups of legal immigrants have come from places like Mexico, the Philippines, Vietnam, and some of the Central American and Caribbean countries.

The major change in immigration in recent decades has been a change in the characteristics of immigrants. In the 1950s, Germany and Canada were the major sources, while in the 1980s Mexico and the Philippines were the dominant sources. As a result, recent immigrants have been relatively much less skilled and educated than those of an earlier age.

From the point of view of labor supply, the overall effect of recent immigration has been an increase in the supply of low-skilled workers in the United States relative to high-skilled workers. Studies have estimated that this change in supply has contributed to a sharp decline in the wages of less-educated groups relative to the college-educated.

TABLE 13-2. Empirical Estimates of Labor-Supply Responses
Economists have devoted careful study to the response of labor supply to real wages. For males, the supply curve looks firmly backward-bending, while teenagers and adult females generally respond positively to wages. For the economy as a whole, the labor supply curve is close to completely inelastic or vertical. [Source: U.S. Department of Labor, *Employment and Earnings* (May 1997).]

Labor-Supply Patterns		
Group of workers	Labor-force participation rate (% of population) 1960 / 1997	Response of labor supply to increase in real wages
Adult males	86 / 77	Supply curve found to be backward-bending in most studies. Thus income effect dominates substitution effect. Supply elasticity is relatively small, in the order of -0.1 to -0.2; this implies that a 10% increase in real wages would lead to a 1% to 2% reduction in labor supplied.
Adult females	38 / 60	Most studies find positive effect of labor supplied in response to higher real wages.
Teenagers	46 / 52	Highly variable response.
Entire population 16 years and over	59 / 67	Elasticity of total labor supply is close to zero, with income effects just balancing out substitution effects. Estimated labor-supply elasticity for entire population is in the range from 0 to 0.2.

Empirical Findings

Theory does not tell us whether the labor supply of a group will react positively or negatively to a wage change. Will an income-tax increase on high-income workers—which reduces their after-tax wages—cause them to reduce their work effort? Will subsidizing the wages of the working poor reduce or increase their hours worked? These vital questions must be considered by the President and legislators as they weigh issues of equity and efficiency. We often need to know the exact shape or elasticity of the labor supply curve.

Table 13-2 presents a summary of numerous studies of the subject. This survey shows that the labor supply curve for adult males appears to be slightly backward-bending, while the response of other demographic groups looks more like a conventional upward-sloping supply curve. For the population as a whole, labor supply appears to respond very little to a change in real wages.

WAGE DIFFERENTIALS

While analysis of the general wage level is important for comparing different countries and times, we often want to understand *wage differentials*. In practice, wage rates differ enormously. The average wage is as hard to define as the average person. An auto executive may earn $4 million a year at the same time that a clerk earns $15,000 and a farmhand $12,000. A doctor may earn 15 or 20 times more than a lifeguard even though both are saving lives. In the same factory, a skilled machinist may earn $500 a week, while an unskilled janitor gets $200. Women may be paid $300 a week at the same time that equally qualified men earn $400.

In addition, there is a wide range of wage rates among broad industry groups. Table 13-3 shows that smaller, nonunionized sectors such as farming or retail trade tend to pay low wages, while the larger firms in manufacturing pay twice as much. But within major sectors there are large variations that depend on worker skills and market conditions—

fast-food workers make much less than doctors even though they all provide services.

How can we explain these wage differentials? Let's consider first a *perfectly competitive labor market*, one in which there are large numbers of workers and employers, none of which has the power to affect wage rates appreciably.[3] If all jobs and all people are identical in a perfectly competitive labor market, competition will cause the hourly wage rates to be exactly equal. No employer would pay more for the work of one person than for that person's identical twin or for another person who possessed identical skills.

This means that to explain the pervasive wage differences across industries or individuals, we must look to either differences in jobs, differences in people, or imperfect competition in labor markets.

Differences in Jobs: Compensating Wage Differentials

Some of the tremendous wage differentials observed in everyday life arise because of differences in the quality of jobs. Jobs differ in their attractive-

---

TABLE 13-3. Wages in Different Sectors

Average annual wages and salaries by broad industry groups range from a high of $44,200 in mining to a low of $17,500 in farming. Among industry groups, we see that average hourly earnings vary by a factor of 4 between computer programmers and fast-food workers. [Source: U.S. Department of Labor, *Employment and Earnings* (May 1997); U.S. Bureau of Economic Analysis.]

Compensation by Industry		
Industry	**Average wages per full-time employee, 1996 ($ per year)**	**Average hourly earnings, January 1997 ($ per hour)**
Farming	18,709	—
Mining	48,329	16.05
Manufacturing	37,165	13.02
Retail trade	18,821	8.23
Eating and drinking places	—	5.93
Services	29,935	12.25
Computer programming	—	22.74
Financial and real estate	44,629	13.16
Government	35,300	—

---

[3] Few labor markets are perfectly competitive in reality, but some (such as a large city's market for inexperienced teenagers or clerical workers) approach the competitive concept reasonably closely.

ness; hence wages may have to be raised to coax people into the less attractive jobs.

Wage differentials that serve to compensate for the relative attractiveness, or nonmonetary differences, among jobs are called **compensating differentials.**

Window washers must be paid more than janitors because of the risks of climbing skyscrapers. Workers often receive 5 percent extra pay on the 4 P.M. to 12 P.M. "swing shift" and 10 percent extra pay for the 12 midnight to 8 A.M. "graveyard shift." For hours beyond 40 per week or for holiday and weekend work, 1½ to 2 times the base hourly pay is customary. Jobs that involve hard physical labor, tedium, low social prestige, irregular employment, seasonal layoff, or physical risk all tend to be less attractive. No wonder, then, that companies must pay $50,000 to $80,000 a year to recruit people to work at dangerous and lonely jobs on offshore oil platforms or in northern Alaska. Similarly, for jobs that are especially pleasant or psychologically rewarding, such as those of park rangers and the clergy, pay levels tend to be modest.

To test whether a given difference in pay between two jobs is a compensating differential, ask people who are well qualified for both jobs: "Would you take the higher-paying job in preference to the lower?" If they are not eager to take the higher-paying job, the pay difference is probably a compensating differential that reflects the nonmonetary differences between the jobs.

Differences in People: Labor Quality

We have just seen that some wage differentials serve to compensate for the differing degrees of attractiveness of different jobs. But look around you. Garbage collectors make much less than lawyers, yet surely the legal life has higher prestige and much more pleasant working conditions. We see countless examples of high-paying jobs that are more pleasant rather than less pleasant than low-paying work. We must look to factors beyond compensating differentials to explain the reason for most wage differences.

One key to wage disparities lies in the tremendous qualitative differences among people, differences traceable to differences in innate mental and

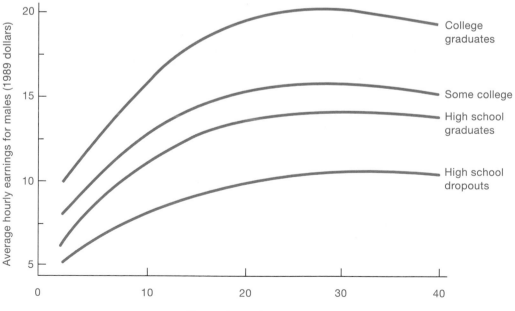

FIGURE 13-5. Earnings Benefit from Education and Experience
Earnings profiles of men show that earnings rise with both education and years of experience. [Adapted from Kevin M. Murphy and Finis Welch, "The Structure of Wages," *Quarterly Journal of Economics* (February 1992).]

physical abilities, upbringing, education and training, and experience. A biologist might classify all of us as members of the species *homo sapiens,* but a personnel officer would insist that people differ enormously in their abilities to contribute to a firm's output.

While many of the differences in labor quality are determined by noneconomic factors, the decision to accumulate human capital can be evaluated economically. The term **human capital** refers to the stock of useful and valuable skills and knowledge accumulated by people in the process of their education and training. Doctors, lawyers, and engineers invest many years in their formal education and on-the-job training. They spend large sums on tuition and wages forgone, investing $100,000 to $200,000 in college and graduate training, and often work long hours. Part of the high salaries of these professionals should be viewed as a return on their investment in human capital—a return on the education that makes these highly trained workers a very special kind of labor.

Economic studies of incomes and education show that human capital is a good investment on average. Figure 13-5 shows the income profiles for different groups as a function of their education and experience. Groups with higher education start out with higher incomes and enjoy more rapid growth in incomes than do less educated groups.

Figure 13-6 shows the ratio of the hourly earnings of college graduates to those of high school graduates. Relative earnings rose sharply during the 1980s as the "price of skill" rose. Studies by labor economists have shown that individuals who have high quantitative abilities or computer skills have an economic advantage in today's labor market.

The return to investments in human capital: What is an investment in human capital? When a student goes to college, each year he or she might pay $10,000 in tuition and $15,000 in oppor-

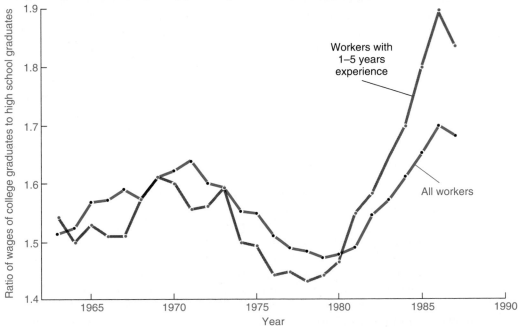

FIGURE 13-6. Relative Income Gains Have Been Dramatic for College Graduates
Income profiles changed dramatically during the turbulent 1980s. Incomes of college graduates rose sharply relative to those of high school graduates, and the largest gains were among the young. [Adapted from Lawrence F. Katz and Kevin M. Murphy, "Changes in Relative Wages: 1963–87," *Quarterly Journal of Economics* (February 1992).]

tunity costs of earnings forgone. That would mean a 4-year outlay of $100,000.

Does college actually pay off? The evidence suggests that it does. In return for this substantial investment, the earnings of the college graduate might exceed those of a high school graduate by $10,000 or more per year. Moreover, the returns to a college education have soared dramatically over the last 15 years. Whereas a college graduate earned 45 percent more than a high school graduate with the same background in the late 1970s, a decade later the earnings differential had widened to 85 percent (see Figure 13-6). More and more, in today's service economy, companies are processing information rather than raw materials. In the information economy, the skills learned in college are a prerequisite for a high-paying job. A high school dropout is generally at a severe disadvantage in the job market.

Even if you have to borrow for your education, put off years of gainful employment, live away from home, and pay for food and books, your lifetime earnings in the occupations that are open only to college graduates will probably more than compensate you for the costs. Recent data show that an 18-year-old male who graduates from college will earn about $4.5 million (at 1996 price and income levels) before the age of 65. A member of the same generation who graduates only from high school will earn about $2.7 million. Someone who does not finish high school will earn an average of only $1.8 million.

Often, people point to the role of luck in determining economic circumstances. But, as Louis Pasteur remarked, "Chance favors the prepared mind." In a world of rapidly changing technologies, education prepares people to understand and profit from new circumstances.

Differences in People: The "Rents" of Unique Individuals

For the lucky few, fame has lifted incomes to astronomical levels. Entertainers like Bill Cosby, basketball stars like Michael Jordan, singers like Whitney Houston, and even academic scribblers who served as advisers to presidents earn fabulous sums for their services.

These extremely talented people have a particular skill that is highly valued in today's economy. Outside their special field, they might earn but a small fraction of their high incomes. Moreover, their labor supply is unlikely to respond perceptibly to wages that are 20 or even 50 percent higher or lower. Econ-

omists refer to the excess of these wages above those of the next-best available occupation as a *pure economic rent*; these earnings are logically equivalent to the rents earned by fixed land.

Some economists have suggested that technological changes are making it easier for a small number of top individuals to serve a larger share of the market (recall our discussion of "winner-take-all markets" in Chapter 11). Top entertainers or athletes can now give a single performance that reaches a billion people via television and recordings—something that was not possible just a few years ago. If this trend continues, and labor rents rise further, the income gap between the winners and the runners-up may widen even further in the years ahead.

Segmented Markets and Noncompeting Groups

Even in a perfectly competitive world where people could move easily from one occupation to another, substantial wage differentials would appear. These differences would be necessary to reflect differences in the costs of education and training or in the unattractiveness of certain occupations or to indicate rewards for unique talents.

But even after taking into account all these reasons for wage differentials, we still find a large disparity in wage rates. The major reason for the difference is that labor markets are segmented into *noncompeting groups*.

A moment's thought will suggest that, instead of being a single factor of production, labor is many different, but closely related, factors of production. Doctors and mathematicians, for example, are noncompeting groups because it is difficult and costly for a member of one profession to enter into the other. Just as there are many different kinds of houses, each commanding a different price, so are there many different occupations and skills that compete only in a general way. Once we recognize the existence of many different submarkets of the labor market, we can see why wages may differ greatly among groups.

Why is the labor market divided into so many noncompeting groups? The major reason is that, for professions and skilled trades, it takes a large investment of time and money to become proficient. If coal mining declines because of environmental restrictions, the miners can hardly hope to land jobs

Summary of Competitive Wage Determination	
Labor situation	**Wage result**
1. People are all alike—jobs are all alike.	No wage differentials.
2. People are all alike—jobs differ in attractiveness.	Compensating wage differentials.
3. People differ, but each type of labor is in unchangeable supply (noncompeting groups).	Wage differentials that reflect supply and demand for segmented markets.
4. People differ, but there is some mobility among groups (partially competing groups).	General-equilibrium pattern of wage differentials as determined by general demand and supply (includes 1 through 3 as special cases).

TABLE 13-4. Market Wage Structure Shows Great Variety of Patterns under Competition

teaching environmental economics overnight. Once people specialize in a particular occupation, they become part of a particular labor submarket. They are thereby subject to the supply and demand for that skill and will find that their own labor earnings rise and fall depending upon events in that occupation and industry. Because of this segmentation, the wages for one occupation can diverge substantially from the wages in other areas.

The job choice of new immigrants is a classic case of noncompeting groups. Rather than go into the open job market, new immigrants from a particular country tend to cluster in certain occupations. For example, in many cities, such as Los Angeles and New York, a large number of grocery stores tend to be owned by Koreans. The reason is that the Koreans can get advice and support from friends and relatives who also own grocery stores. As immigrants get more experience and education in the United States and become more fluent in English, their job choice widens and they become part of the overall labor supply.

In addition, the theory of noncompeting groups helps us understand labor market discrimination. We will see in the next section of this chapter that much discrimination arises because workers are separated by gender, race, or ethnic background into noncompeting groups as a result of custom, law, or prejudice.

While the theory of noncompeting groups highlights an important aspect of labor markets, we must recognize that in the longer run entry and exit will reduce differentials. It is true that copper miners are unlikely to become computer programmers when computers and fiber optics displace rotary dials and copper wires. Consequently, we may see wage differentials arise between the two kinds of labor. But in the longer run, as more young people study computer science rather than work in copper mines, competition will tend to reduce some of the differentials of these noncompeting groups.

Table 13-4 summarizes the different forces at work in determining wage rates in competitive conditions.

B. THE AMERICAN LABOR MOVEMENT

So far we have looked at competitive labor markets. But for the 16 million Americans who belong to labor unions, some of the labor-supply decisions are made collectively. Unions negotiate collective bargaining agreements which often specify who can fill different jobs, what they will be paid, and what the

work rules are. And unions can decide to go on strike—withdraw their labor supply completely—in order to win a better deal from the employer.

The study of unions is an important part of understanding the dynamics of the U.S. labor market. For one thing, about one-seventh of the work force still belongs to unions, although that percentage reflects a significant decrease during recent years. Furthermore, in negotiating collective bargaining contracts, unions raise issues which are important to all workers, such as pensions, health-care benefits, and working hours.

HISTORY AND PRACTICE OF LABOR UNIONS

How did American labor unions begin? Although the first stirrings of American labor unions predate the Civil War, it was not until the last third of the nineteenth century that labor began to revolt against big business. In 1881, the present-day labor movement began to take shape with the founding of the American Federation of Labor (AFL). For almost half a century, until his death in 1924, Samuel Gompers dominated this organization and gave the movement its characteristic pattern.

Gompers' strategy was simple: Because he believed that no movement opposed to capitalism would flourish on American soil, he insisted on *business unionism.* Under this principle, American unions were engaged primarily in improving the economic status of workers—the struggle for higher wages, shorter hours, more vacations, better working conditions, and improved fringe benefits. American unions were the opposite of the labor movements in many European countries; abroad, unions have sometimes dominated major political parties and waged a class struggle to alter the form of government or to promote socialism.

At the beginning, labor was organized as *craft unions,* in which workers were grouped on the basis of a particular skill, such as carpentry or bricklaying. This strategy prevented the organization of huge mass-production industries into a single union. By the 1930s, astute union advocates began to see the handwriting on the wall: *industrial unions* (those organizing an entire industry, such as steel or coal) were the wave of the future. Industrial unions were introduced in 1935 with the formation of the Congress of Industrial Organizations (CIO). Today, American labor unions are organized into the AFL-CIO, which is the major national labor organization in the United States.

The wages and fringe benefits of unionized workers are determined by **collective bargaining.** This is the process of negotiation between representatives of firms and of workers for the purpose of establishing mutually agreeable conditions of employment. We have all heard of the last-minute, all-night sessions before a labor agreement is reached. What is actually in this agreement? The central part, of course, is the *economic package.* This includes the basic wage rates for different job categories, along with the rules for holidays and coffee breaks. In addition, the agreement will contain provisions for fringe benefits such as a pension plan, coverage for health care, and similar items. During periods of high inflation the agreement will generally contain a cost-of-living-adjustment (COLA) clause, which adjusts wages upward when consumer prices rise rapidly.

A second important and often controversial subject is *work rules.* These concern work assignments and tasks, job security, and workloads. Particularly in declining industries, the staffing requirements are a major issue because the demand for labor is falling. In the railroad industry, for example, there were decades of disputes about the number of people needed to run a train.

Collective bargaining is a complicated business, a matter of give-and-take. Much effort is spent negotiating purely economic issues, dividing the pie between wages and profits. Sometimes agreements get hung up on issues of management prerogatives, such as the ability to reassign workers or change work rules. In the end, both workers and management have a large stake in ensuring that workers are satisfied and productive on their jobs.

Government and Collective Bargaining

The history of labor unions reminds us that the legal framework is an important determinant of economic organization. Two hundred years ago, when labor first tried to organize in England and America, common-law doctrines against "conspiracy in restraint of trade" were used against union members. Well into this century, unions and their members were convicted by courts, fined, jailed, and harassed by various injunctive procedures. The Supreme Court repeatedly struck down acts designed to improve working conditions for women and children and other reform legislation on hours and wages.

It was only after the pendulum swung toward support of unions and collective bargaining that the explosive growth of unions began. A major landmark was the Clayton Act (1914), hailed as "labor's Magna Carta" and designed to remove labor from antitrust prosecution. The Fair Labor Standards Act (1938) barred child labor, called for time-and-a-half pay for weekly hours over 40, and set a federal minimum wage for most nonfarm workers.

The most important labor legislation of all was the National Labor Relations (or Wagner) Act of 1935. This law stated: "Employees shall have the right to . . . join . . . labor organizations, to bargain collectively . . . , and to engage in concerted activities." Spurred by pro-labor legislation, union membership rose from under one-tenth of the labor force in the 1920s to one-quarter of the work force by the end of World War II. Since the early 1970s, with deregulation of many industries and increasing international competition, union monopolies have been undermined, and the fraction of the labor force belonging to unions in the United States has steadily declined.

HOW UNIONS RAISE WAGES

How can labor unions raise the wages and improve the working conditions of their members? *Unions gain market power by obtaining a legal monopoly on the provision of labor services to a particular firm or industry.* Using this monopoly, they compel firms to provide wages, benefits, and working conditions that are above the competitive wage. For example, if nonunion plumbers earn $15 per hour in Alabama, a union might bargain with a large construction firm to set the wage at $25 per hour for that firm's plumbers.

Such an agreement is, however, valuable to the union only if the firm's access to alternative labor supplies can be restricted. Hence, under a typical collective bargaining agreement, firms agree not to hire nonunion plumbers, not to contract out plumbing services, and not to subcontract to nonunion firms. Each of these provisions helps prevent erosion of the union's monopoly lock on the supply of plumbers to the firm. In some industries, like steel and autos, unions will even try to unionize the entire industry so that firm A's unionized workers need not compete with firm B's nonunion workers. All these steps are necessary to protect high union wage rates.

Figure 13-7 shows the impact of agreed-upon high standard wages, where the union forces

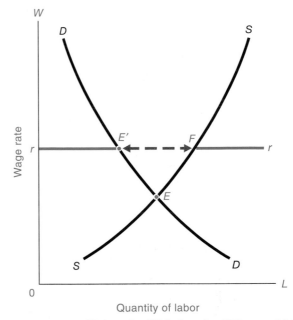

FIGURE 13-7. Unions Set High Standard Wage and Limit Employment

Raising the standard wage to rr increases wages and decreases the employment in the unionized labor market. Because of supply and demand imbalance, workers from E' to F cannot find employment in this market.

If unions push real wages too high for an entire economy, firms will demand E', while workers will supply F. Thus the black arrow from E' to F represents the amount of classical unemployment. This source of unemployment is particularly important when a country cannot affect its price level or exchange rate, and it differs from the unemployment caused by insufficient aggregate demand.

employers to pay wages at the standard rate shown by the horizontal line rr. The equilibrium is at E', where rr intersects the employers' demand curve. Note that the union has not directly reduced supply when it sets high standard wage rates. How does the market operate when wages are set above the market-clearing level? At the high wage rates, employment is limited by the firms' demand for labor. The number of workers who seek employment exceeds the demand by the segment $E'F$. These excess workers might be unemployed and waiting for vacancies in the high-paying union sector, or they might become discouraged and look for jobs in other sectors. The workers from E' to F are as effectively excluded from jobs as they would be if the union had directly limited entry.

The need to prevent nonunion competition also explains many of the political goals of the national labor movement. It explains why unions want to limit immigration; why unions support protectionist legislation to limit imports of foreign goods, which are goods made by workers who are not members of American unions; why quasi unions like medical associations fight to restrict the practice of medicine by other groups; and why unions sometimes oppose deregulation in industries such as trucking, communications, and airlines.

Theoretical Indeterminacy of Collective Bargaining.

In most collective bargaining negotiations, the workers press for higher wages while management holds out for lower compensation costs. This is a situation known as *bilateral monopoly*—where there is but one buyer and one seller. The outcome of bilateral monopoly cannot be predicted by economic forces of costs and demands alone; it depends as well on psychology, politics, and countless other intangible factors.[4]

EFFECTS ON WAGES AND EMPLOYMENT

The advocates of labor unions claim that unions have raised real wages and have benefited workers. Critics argue that the result of raising wages is high unemployment, inflation, and distorted resource allocation. What are the facts?

Has Unionization Raised Wages?

Let's start by reviewing the effects of unions on relative wages. Economists have estimated the economic impacts of unions by examining wages in unionized and nonunionized industries. On the basis of these analyses, economists have concluded

that union workers receive on average a 10 to 15 percent wage differential over nonunion workers. The differential ranges from a negligible amount for hotel workers and barbers to 25 to 30 percent higher earnings for skilled construction workers or coal miners. The pattern of results suggests that where unions can effectively monopolize labor supply and control entry, they will be most effective in raising wages.

Another approach examines the wages of individual workers, correcting for worker characteristics and taking into account whether the worker is in a union or nonunion job. Orley Ashenfelter of Princeton University examined a panel of workers over the period of 1967 to 1975. Correcting for the influence of each worker's sex, race, education, and other personal characteristics, he found that the workers who belonged to unions had wages 16 percent above those of nonunion workers. In addition, Ashenfelter found that black males who belonged to unions obtained even higher wage differentials than other groups: 23 percent higher wages as compared to 16 percent for white males. Since 1975, there has been relatively little change in the wages of union members relative to nonunionized workers, but the overall share of union workers in the labor force has declined.

Overall Impacts.   Granted that unions raise the wages of union members, we might ask whether unions bootstrap the entire economy to a higher real wage. Most economists now believe that unions redistribute income not from capital to labor but from nonunion labor to union labor. Put differently, if unions succeed in raising their wages above competitive levels, their gains come at the expense of the wages of nonunion workers.

This analysis is supported by empirical evidence showing that the share of national income going to labor has changed little over the last six decades. Once cyclical influences on labor's share are removed, we can see no appreciable impact of unionization on the share of wages in the United States (see Figure 12-1 on page 211). The evidence from heavily unionized European countries suggests that when unions succeed in raising money wage rates, they sometimes trigger an inflationary wage-price spiral with little or no permanent effect upon real wages.

---

[4]   Situations like labor-management bargains are the subject of game theory, analyzed in Chapter 11. The theoretical indeterminacy of collective bargaining stems from the following result from game theory: A two-person noncooperative game does not generally have a unique outcome. Rather, as with wars or strikes, the outcome depends on many factors, such as bargaining power, prestige, bluffing ability, and even each side's perception of the strength of its opponent.

Effects on Employment

If unions do not affect overall real wage levels, this suggests that their impact lies primarily upon *relative* wages. That is, wages in unionized industries would rise relative to those in nonunionized industries. Moreover, employment would tend to be reduced in unionized and expanded in nonunionized industries.

When powerful unions raise real wages to artificially high levels, the result is an excess supply of labor and what is called *classical unemployment*. This case is also illustrated by Figure 13-7. Assume that unions raise wages above the market-clearing wage at E to a higher real wage at rr. Then, if the supply and demand for labor in general are unchanged, the arrow between E' and F will represent the number of workers who want to work at wage rr but cannot find work. This is called *classical unemployment* because it results from too high real wages.

Economists often contrast classical unemployment with the unemployment that occurs in business cycles, often called Keynesian unemployment, which results from insufficient aggregate demand. The effects of too high real wages were seen after the economic unification of Germany in 1990. The economic union fixed East German wages at a level estimated to be at least twice as high as could be justified by labor's marginal revenue product. The result was a sharp decline in employment in eastern Germany after unification.

This analysis suggests that when a country or region gets locked into real wages that are too high, high levels of unemployment may result. The unemployment will not respond to the traditional macroeconomic policy of increasing aggregate spending but, rather, will require remedies that lower real wages.

 Declining unionism in the United States: One of the major trends in American labor markets has been the gradual erosion of labor unions since World War II. Whereas unions had organized one-quarter of the labor force in 1955, the fraction has fallen sharply since 1980. The share of workers in manufacturing has shrunk dramatically in the last two decades; only in the public sector are unions still a powerful force.

One of the reasons for the decline in unions is the waning power of the strike, which is the ultimate threat in collective bargaining. In the 1970s U.S. labor unions used that weapon regularly, averaging almost 300 strikes per year. More recently, though, strikes have become relatively uncommon; in fact, they have virtually disappeared from the American labor market. The reason for the decline is that strikes have often backfired on workers. In 1981, the striking air-traffic controllers were all fired by President Reagan. When the professional football players went on strike in 1987, they were forced back to work when the football owners put on the games with replacement players. In 1992, workers striking Caterpillar Inc., a huge maker of heavy equipment, had to end their 6-month strike when Caterpillar threatened to fill their jobs with permanent replacements. The inability to hurt firms through strikes has led to a significant weakening in the overall power of labor unions in the last two decades.

You might wonder if the declining power of unions would reduce labor compensation. Economists generally hold that a decline in union power will lower the relative wages of union workers rather than lower the overall share of labor. Look back at Figure 12-1 to examine the share of labor in national income. Can you determine any effect of the declining power of unions after 1980 on labor's share? Most economists believe not.

The Lump-of-Labor Fallacy

We close our analysis of wage theory by examining an important fallacy that often motivates labor market policies. Whenever unemployment is high, people often think that the solution lies in spreading existing work more evenly among the labor force. For example, Europe in the 1990s suffered extremely high unemployment, and many labor leaders and politicians suggested that the solution was to reduce the workweek so that the same number of hours would be worked by all the workers. This view—that the amount of work to be done is fixed—is called the **lump-of-labor fallacy.**

To begin with, we note the grain of truth in this viewpoint. For a particular group of workers, with special skills and stuck in one region, a reduction in the demand for labor may indeed pose a threat to their incomes. If wages adjust slowly, these workers may face prolonged spells of unemployment. The lump-of-labor fallacy may look quite real to these workers.

But from the point of view of the economy as a whole, the lump-of-labor argument implies that there is only so much remunerative work to be done, and this is indeed a fallacy. A careful examination of economic history in different countries shows that an increase in labor supply can be accommodated by higher employment, although that increase may require lower real wages. Similarly, a decrease in the demand for a particular kind of labor because of technological shifts in an industry can be adapted to—lower relative wages and migration of labor and capital will eventually provide new jobs for the displaced workers.

Work is not a lump that must be shared among the potential workers. Labor market adjustments can adapt to shifts in the supply and demand for labor through changes in the real wage and through migration of labor and capital. Moreover, in the short run, when wages and prices are sticky, the adjustment process can be lubricated by appropriate macroeconomic policies.

C. DISCRIMINATION BY RACE AND GENDER

Some earnings differentials arise from differences in education, work experience, and other factors; earnings disparities are inevitable in a market economy. But even after correction for such differences, a gap remains between the wages of white males and those of other groups. African-American and Hispanic citizens in the United States have long experienced a measurably lower level of income and wealth than other groups. And a woman will typically end up earning 20 percent less than a man with the same amount of schooling, the same test scores, and the same social background. In this section, we see how discrimination affects labor markets and incomes.

THE ECONOMICS OF DISCRIMINATION

When differences in earnings arise simply because of an irrelevant personal characteristic, such as race, gender, sexual orientation, or religion, we call this **discrimination.**

The history of black Americans illustrates how social processes depressed their wages and social status. After slavery was abolished, the black population of the American south fell into a caste system of peonage under "Jim Crow" legislation. Even though legally free and subject to the laws of supply and demand, black workers had earnings far below those of whites. Why? Because they had inferior schooling and were excluded from the best jobs by trade unions, local laws, and customs. They were consequently shunted into menial, low-skilled occupations that were effectively noncompeting groups.

Supply and demand can illustrate how exclusion lowers the incomes of groups that are targets of discrimination. Under discrimination, certain jobs are reserved for the privileged group, as is depicted in Figure 13-8(*a*). In this labor market, the supply of privileged workers is shown by S_pS_p, while the demand for such labor is depicted as D_pD_p. Equilibrium wages occur at the high level shown at E_p.

Meanwhile, Figure 13-8(*b*) shows what is happening for low-paid unskilled jobs. Minority workers live in areas with poor schools and cannot afford private education, so they do not receive training for the high-paying jobs. With low levels of skills, they have low marginal revenue products in the low-skilled jobs, so their wages are depressed to the low-wage equilibrium at E_m.

Note the differential between the two markets. Because minorities are excluded from good jobs, market forces have decreed that they earn much lower wages than the privileged workers. Someone might even argue that minorities "deserve" lower wages because their competitive marginal revenue products are lower. But this rationalization overlooks the root of the wage differentials, which is that wage differences arose because certain groups were excluded from the good jobs by their inability to obtain education and training and by the force of custom, law, or collusion.

Statistical Discrimination

Discrimination is particularly harmful when it distorts incentives for visible groups to work hard and invest in human capital. This occurs under **sta-**

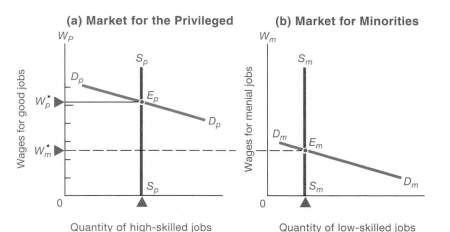

FIGURE 13-8. **Discrimination by Exclusion Lowers the Wage Rates of Excluded Minorities**
Discrimination is often enforced by excluding certain groups from privileged jobs. If minorities are excluded from good jobs in market (**a**), they must work in inferior jobs in (**b**). The privileged group enjoys high wage rates at E_p, while minorities earn low wage rates at E_m in market (**b**).

tistical discrimination, in which individuals are treated on the basis of the average behavior of members of the group to which they belong.

One common example arises when an employer screens employees on the basis of their college. Experience has shown that people who graduate from better schools are *on average* more productive; in addition, grade point averages are often difficult to evaluate because of differences in grading standards at schools. Employers therefore often hire people on the basis of their college rather than on their grades. A more careful screening process would show that there are many highly qualified workers from the less well-known schools. We see here a common form of statistical discrimination on the basis of average quality of schooling.

Statistical discrimination becomes pernicious because it reinforces stereotypes and reduces the incentives of individual members of a group to develop skills and experience. Consider someone who goes to a less well known school. She knows that she will be largely judged by the quality of her schooling credentials. The grade point average, the difficulty of the courses taken, the actual learning, and on-the-job experience may be ignored. The result is that, when subject to statistical discrimination, individuals have greatly reduced incentives to invest in activities that will improve skills and make better workers.

Statistical discrimination is seen in many areas of society. Life insurance and automobile insurance generally average the risks of people who are careful with those who live dangerously; this tends to reduce the incentive to behave cautiously and leads to a decrease in the average amount of caution in the population. Women were traditionally excluded from quantitatively oriented professions like engineering; as a result, women were more likely to choose humanities and social sciences, thereby reinforcing the stereotype that women were uninterested in engineering.

Statistical discrimination not only stereotypes individuals on the basis of group characteristics; it also reduces the incentives of individuals to make investments in education and training and thereby tends to reinforce the original stereotype.

Gary Becker: Economics as a tool for understanding social issues. The economics of discrimination was pioneered by Gary Becker of the University of Chicago in his doctoral dissertation. He pointed out that even if some employers are biased against a group of workers, their bias is not sufficient to reduce that group's incomes. Suppose that a group of firms in a competitive market decides to pay blue-eyed workers more than equally productive brown-eyed workers. Nondiscriminating firms could enter the market, undercut the costs and prices of the discriminating firms by hiring mainly brown-eyed workers, and drive the discriminating firms out of business. This theory does not deny the existence of economic discrimination; rather, it points to the importance of nonmarket forces like exclusion, educational barriers, and caste systems as important factors in maintaining discrimination.

Becker, who won the Nobel Prize in economics in 1992, has been a leading advocate of the idea that economic reasoning applies to a wide range of social issues. Becker was a pioneer in the theory of human capital, arguing that utility-maximizing people make educational decisions as investments—just as a profit-maximizing company selects its best combination of plant and equipment. He also studied the economics of crime and punishment and the way that economic forces influence the choice of family size, marriage, and divorce.

ECONOMIC DISCRIMINATION AGAINST WOMEN

The largest group to suffer from economic discrimination is women. Even year-round, full-time female workers on average earn only 80 percent as much as men of comparable education and background.

The pattern of earnings is clear. Female college graduates earn about the same amount as male high school graduates. Although white males generally receive increases in annual earnings as they grow older, income profiles show that women in their late twenties earn as much on average as do older women.

What lies behind the income differentials between men and women? The causes are complex, grounded in social customs and expectations, statistical discrimination, and economic factors such as education and work experience. In general, women are not paid less than men for the same job. Rather, the lower pay of women arose because women were excluded from certain high-paying professions, such as engineering, construction, and coal mining. In addition, women tended to interrupt their careers to have children and perform household duties. Also, economic inequality of the sexes was maintained because, until recently, few women were elected to the boards of directors of large corporations, to senior partnerships in major law firms, or to tenured professorships in top universities.

Like minority groups, then, women are often found in low-paying noncompeting groups. The extent of labor market segmentation is detailed in Table 13-5, which shows the fraction of women in selected high-paying and low-paying occupations. To understand discrimination, we should avoid simple explanations like the idea that employers simply beat down the wage demands of women or African-Americans or Hispanics. Rather, discrimination involves subtle exclusionary processes that prevent certain groups from participating fully in all occupations, as well as the stubborn persistence of stereotypes and perverse incentives due to statistical discrimination.

Empirical Evidence

Having analyzed the mechanisms by which the political process and the market economy enforce discrimination against women and minority groups, let's examine the size of earnings differentials. Table 13-6 shows the ratio of total annual earnings of males and females of different minority groups relative to those of white males. On average, earnings differentials are substantial for women and for minorities. Note that women are generally penalized in the labor market only once; many minority women show earnings close to those of white women.

TABLE 13-5. Many High-Paid Occupations Are Reserved for Men

Discrimination today seldom occurs because women get lower wages for the same job. Rather, women have been limited to lower-paying occupations. Overall, for full-time workers, the median weekly earnings are only 75 percent of those of men. (Source: U.S. Department of Labor, Bureau of Labor Statistics.)

Labor Market Segmentation, 1996	
Occupation	**Percentage female**
High-paid occupations:	
Engineers	8.5
Physicians	26.4
Lawyers	29.5
Low-paid occupations:	
Child-care workers	97.1
Secretaries	98.6
Nurses' aides	88.4

Earnings Differentials, 1990		
	Earnings of group (as % of earnings of white males of European ancestry)	
Group	Males	Females
White		
European (except Spain)	100	67
Hispanic	73	57
Asian	94	71
Black	73	56
Native American	71	53

TABLE 13-6. Minorities and Women Earn Substantially Less Than White Males
How do different ethnic groups and sexes fare in the marketplace? Data were examined on the total annual earnings of full-time, year-round workers in different groups in the United States. These data do not correct for education, labor-force status, or previous work experience. The most disadvantaged minority-group males earn only 71 percent of white male earnings. Females earn even less. (Source: 1990 Census. Compiled by Ann Green of the Yale Stat Lab using the Explorer program of the 1990 Public Use Sample, available on the Internet.)

Economists have found that earnings differentials among different groups are not entirely due to discrimination. The first section of this chapter noted that there are differences in quality of labor. African-American workers have historically received less education than have whites; women customarily spend more time out of the labor force than do men. Since both education and continuing work experience are linked to higher pay, it is not surprising that some earnings differentials exist.

Economists in recent years have conducted numerous empirical studies that attempt to separate the earnings differentials due to measurable characteristics (such as education, labor market experience, absenteeism, and long-term career plans) from those due to discrimination and other factors. Studies indicate that one-half to three-quarters of the male-female wage gap can be explained by differences in education and job experience. This leaves one-quarter to one-half to be explained by discrimination and other nonmeasured sources.

REDUCING LABOR MARKET DISCRIMINATION

Over the last 25 years, governments have taken numerous steps to end discriminatory practices. But even today, the United States has been unable to eradicate discrimination based on race, gender, and other characteristics.

What approaches are available to combat discrimination? The major steps were legal landmarks, such as the Civil Rights Act of 1964 (which outlaws discrimination in hiring, firing, and employment) and the Equal Pay Act of 1963 (which requires employers to pay men and women equally for the same work).

Such laws helped dismantle the most blatant discriminatory practices, but more subtle barriers remain. To counter them, more aggressive and controversial policies have been introduced, including measures such as *affirmative action*. This requires employers to show that they are taking extra steps to locate and hire underrepresented groups. Studies indicate that this approach, labeled by critics as "reverse discrimination," has had a modest positive effect on the hiring and wages of women and minorities.

Often, discrimination can be combated by encouraging employers to pay more attention to personal performance. If statistical discrimination tends to harm women and minority groups and reduce incentives to invest in human capital, discrimination will be reduced if employers look at measures of personal skills such as school grades as well as teacher and employer recommendations. It is instructive to note that in those industries where individual performances are more easily measured—such as athletics and entertainment—women and minorities are relatively more highly paid than in those sectors where skills and marginal products are harder to measure and there is consequently more room for statistical and personal discrimination.

Uneven Progress
Discrimination is a complex social and economic process. It is rooted in social customs and was enforced by laws that denied disadvantaged groups a decent education and good jobs. Even after equality was established by law, separation of races and sexes perpetuated social and economic stratification.

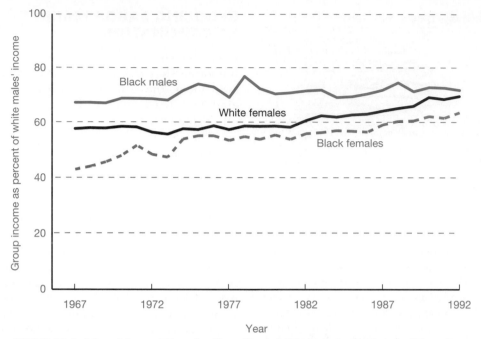

FIGURE 13-9. Minorities and Females Show Uneven Progress in Closing the Wage Gap
The wage gap between white males and other groups closed significantly in the last half-century. Black females have gained parity with white females, but females and black males earn significantly less than white males. [Source: G. D. Jaynes and R. M. Williams Jr., eds., *A Common Destiny: Blacks and American Society* (National Academy Press, Washington, 1989), p. 295, updated by authors.]

Progress is being made, but the results are uneven. In recent years, members of disadvantaged groups have entered the best educational institutions and the highest-paying professions in large numbers. For example, among those under 35 years of age, women now constitute 41 percent of mathematicians and computer scientists, 29 percent of lawyers and judges, and half of managerial and professional workers. Figure 13-9 shows the slow progress toward closing the earnings gap between nonwhite and white members of the population.

But substantial differences in incomes, wealth, and jobs persist. The deteriorating social order in central cities, the disintegration of the traditional nuclear family, cuts in government social programs, a backlash against many antidiscrimination programs, and the declining relative wages of the unskilled have led to declining living standards for many minority groups. Women and minorities have succeeded at the ballot box, but they continue to have lagging incomes in the marketplace.

SUMMARY

A. Fundamentals of Wage Determination

1. The demand for labor, as for any factor of production, is determined by labor's marginal product. A country's general wage level tends to be higher when its workers

are better trained and educated, when it has more and better capital to work with, and when it uses more advanced production techniques.

2. For a given population, the supply of labor depends on three key factors: population size, average number of hours worked, and labor-force participation. For the United States, immigration has been a major source of new workers in recent years, increasing the proportion of relatively unskilled workers.

3. As wages rise, there are two opposite effects on the supply of labor. The substitution effect tempts each worker to work longer because of the higher pay for each hour of work. The income effect operates in the opposite direction because higher wages mean that workers can now afford more leisure time along with other good things of life. At some critical wage, the supply curve may bend backward. The labor supply of very gifted, unique people is quite inelastic: their wages are largely pure economic rent.

4. Under perfect competition, if all people and jobs were exactly alike, there would be no wage differentials. The equilibrium wage rates determined by supply and demand would all be equal. But once we drop unrealistic assumptions concerning the uniformity of people and jobs, we find substantial wage differentials even in a perfectly competitive labor market. Compensating wage differentials, which compensate for nonmonetary differences in the quality of jobs, explain some of the differentials. Differences in the quality of labor explain many of the other differentials. In addition, the labor market is made up of innumerable categories of noncompeting and partially competing groups.

B. The American Labor Movement

5. Labor unions occupy an important but diminishing role in the American economy, in terms of both membership and influence. Management and labor representatives meet together in collective bargaining to negotiate a contract. Such agreements typically contain provisions for wages, fringe benefits, and work rules. Unions affect wages by bargaining for standard rates. However, in order to raise real wages above prevailing market-determined levels, unions generally must prevent entry or competition from nonunion workers.

6. According to economic theory, there is no unique outcome of a collective bargaining session. Bilateral monopoly or management-union bargaining (like war or two-person games) has a theoretically indetermi-

nate solution. Empirical studies find that unions have raised the wages of union members relative to those of nonunionized workers. Studies estimate that, on average, union workers have earned wages 10 to 30 percent higher than nonunion workers with the same characteristics. This union differential may have eroded in the last decade's period of competition from nonunion and foreign labor.

7. While unions may raise the wages of their members, they probably do not increase a country's real wages or labor's share of national income. They are likely to increase unemployment among union members who would prefer to wait for recall from layoff of their high-paid jobs rather than move or take low-paying jobs in other industries. And in a nation with inflexible prices, real wages that are too high may induce classical unemployment.

C. Discrimination by Race and Gender

8. By an accident of history, a tiny minority of white males in the world has enjoyed the greatest affluence. Even a century after the abolition of slavery, inequality of opportunity and economic, racial, and gender discrimination can be shown, by the tools of competitive supply and demand, to lead to loss of income by underprivileged groups.

9. There are many sources of discrimination. An important mechanism is the establishment and maintenance of noncompeting groups. By segmenting labor markets, reserving managerial and professional positions for white men while relegating women and minorities to menial, dead-end jobs, an economy can allow inequality of earnings to persist for decades. In addition, statistical discrimination occurs when individuals are treated on the basis of the average behavior of members of the group to which they belong. This subtle form of discrimination stereotypes individuals on the basis of group characteristics, reduces the incentives of individuals to engage in self-improvement, and thereby reinforces the original stereotype.

10. Steps to reduce labor market discrimination have been taken in many directions. Early approaches focused on outlawing discriminatory practices, while later steps mandated policies such as affirmative action.

CONCEPTS FOR REVIEW

Wage Determination under Perfect Competition

elements in demand for labor:

labor quality
technology
quality of other inputs

elements in supply of labor:
    hours
    labor-force participation

immigration
income effect vs. substitution effect
compensating differentials in wages
rent element in wages
segmented markets and noncompet-
　　ing groups

Impact of Unions

collective bargaining
unions as monopolies
control of entry by unions
effect of unions on real wages
classical unemployment

Discrimination in Labor Markets

discrimination
earnings differentials: quality differ-
　　ences vs. discrimination
statistical discrimination
antidiscrimination policies

QUESTIONS FOR DISCUSSION

1. What steps could be taken to break down the segmented markets shown in Table 13-5?

2. Explain, both in words and with a supply-and-demand
diagram, the impact of each of the following upon the
wages and employment in the affected labor market:
   a. *Upon union bricklayers:* The bricklayers' union
   negotiated a lower standard work rule, from 26
   bricks per hour to 20 bricks per hour.
   b. *Upon airline pilots:* After the deregulation of the
   airlines, nonunion airlines like Continental
   increased their market share by 20 percent.
   c. *Upon M.D.s:* Many states begin to allow nurses to
   be given more of the physicians' responsibilities.
   d. *Upon American autoworkers:* Japan agreed to limit its
   exports of automobiles to the United States.

3. Explain what would happen to wage differentials as a
result of each of the following:
   a. An increase in the cost of going to college
   b. Free migration among the nations of Europe
   c. Introduction of free public education into a country where education had previously been private
   and expensive
   d. Through technological change, a large increase in
   the number of people reached by popular sports
   and entertainment programs.

4. Discrimination occurs when disadvantaged groups like
women or African-Americans are segmented into low-
wage markets. Explain how each of the following practices, which prevailed in some cases until recently,
helped perpetuate discriminatory labor market segmentation:
   a. Many state schools would not allow women to
   major in engineering.
   b. Many top colleges would not admit women.
   c. Nonwhites and whites received schooling in separate school systems.

   d. Elite social clubs would not admit women, African-
   Americans, or Catholics.
   e. Employers refused to hire workers who had
   attended inner-city schools because the average
   productivities of workers from there were low.

5. Recent immigration has increased the number of low-
skilled workers with little impact upon the supply of
highly trained workers. A recent study by George Bor-
jas, Richard Freeman, and Lawrence Katz estimated
that the wages of high school dropouts declined by 4
percent relative to the wages of college graduates in
the 1980s as a result of immigration and trade. This
problem shows how to understand the reasons.
   a. To see the impact of *immigration*, turn back to Figure 12-6 in the last chapter. Redraw these diagrams, labeling part (*a*) "Market for Skilled Workers" and part (*b*) "Market for Unskilled Workers."
   Then let immigration increase the supply of
   unskilled labor down and to the right while leaving the supply of skilled workers unchanged. What
   would happen to the relative wages of the skilled
   and unskilled and to the relative levels of employment as a result of immigration?
   b. Next analyze the impact of *international trade* on
   wages and employment. Suppose that lower trade
   barriers increased the demand for skilled workers
   in (*a*) while reducing the demand for domestic
   unskilled workers in (*b*). Show that this would
   tend to increase the inequality between skilled
   and unskilled workers.

6. In periods of high unemployment, people often think
that a solution lies in spreading the existing amount
of work more evenly. In Europe during the 1990s, for
example, many governments proposed that the workweek be reduced to spread the declining employment
among more workers—this being the lump-of-labor

fallacy. Use diagrams to explain the impact of a reduced workweek in a competitive market as well as in a market with classical unemployment.

7. People often worry that high tax rates would reduce the supply of labor. Consider the impact of higher taxes with a backward-bending supply curve as follows: Define the before-tax wage as W, the posttax wage as W_p, and the tax rate as t. Explain the relationship $W_p = (1 - t)W$. Draw up a table showing the before-tax and posttax wages when the before-tax wage is $20 per hour for tax rates of 0, 15, 25, and 40 percent. Next add a supply-and-demand diagram to Figure 13-4. For the regions above and below point C, show the impact of a lower tax rate upon labor supplied. In your table, show the relationship between the tax rate and the government's tax revenues.

CHAPTER 14
LAND AND CAPITAL

> In the first stone which [a person] flings at the wild animal he pursues, in the first stick that he seizes to strike down the fruit which hangs above his reach, we . . . discover the origin of capital.
>
> *Robert Torrens*, An Essay on the Production of Wealth *(1821)*

The United States is a "capitalist" economy. By this, we mean that capital, land, and assets are largely privately owned. In 1995, the net stock of capital in the United States was $70,000 per capita, of which 68 percent was owned by private corporations, 14 percent by private persons, and 19 percent by governments. Moreover, the ownership of the nation's wealth was highly concentrated in the portfolios of the richest Americans.

By contrast, in socialist countries, like Russia before 1991 or China today, most of the land and capital is owned by government, and there are no super-rich families like the du Ponts or the Gettys. Under capitalism, individuals and private firms do most of the saving, own most of the wealth, and get most of the profits on these investments.

The difference between poor and rich countries comes in large measure from the ability to generate large flows of savings and invest those savings in high-return capital. But a nation's nonhuman assets include much beyond its plant and equipment. We would also want to count its land, natural resources like oil and minerals, and environmental assets like clean air and healthy drinking water.

In this chapter we will study the workings of the factor markets for the major nonlabor inputs, land and capital. Both are durable assets that are privately owned, can be bought and sold in markets, and can be "rented" out for a period of time. We will start by looking at the market for land, which is a nonproduced factor. Then we will turn to the crucial questions of the supply and demand for capital, which is an output of the economy as well as an input. This will give us a much deeper understanding of some key features of a market economy.

A. LAND AND RENT

Rent as Return to Fixed Factors

Unless you are planning to run your company from a balloon, land is an essential factor of production for any business. The essential feature of land is that its quantity is fixed and completely unresponsive to price.[1] Will Rogers put this nicely when he

---

[1] Sometimes natural resources are included along with land. We postpone our analysis of the economics of natural resources until Chapter 18.

quipped, "Land is a good investment: they ain't making it no more."

The price of using a piece of land for a period of time is called its **rent** or, sometimes, **pure economic rent.** Rent is calculated as dollars per unit of time. The notion of paying rent applies not only to land but to any factor that is fixed in supply. For example, da Vinci's portrait *Mona Lisa* is unique; if you could get it for an exhibition, you would be paying rent for its temporary use.

Rent is the payment for the use of factors of production that are fixed in supply.

Market Equilibrium. The supply curve for land is completely inelastic—that is, vertical—because the supply of land is fixed. In Figure 14-1, the demand and supply curves intersect at the equilibrium point *E.* It is toward this factor price that the rent of land must tend. Why?

FIGURE 14-1. Fixed Land Must Work for Whatever It Can Earn
Perfectly inelastic supply characterizes the case of rent, sometimes also called pure economic rent. We run up the *SS* curve to the factor demand curve to determine rent. Aside from land, we can apply rent considerations to rich oil and gold properties, 7-foot basketball players, and anything else in fixed supply.

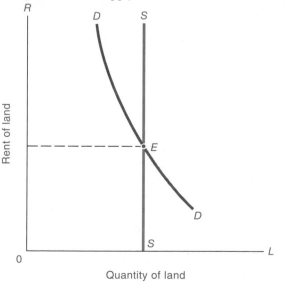

If rent were above the equilibrium price, the amount of land demanded by all firms would be less than the existing amount that would be supplied. Some property owners would be unable to rent their land at all; they would have to offer their land for less and thus bid down its rent. By similar reasoning, the rent could not remain below the equilibrium intersection for long. If it did, the bidding of unsatisfied firms would force the factor price back up toward the equilibrium level. Only at a competitive price where the total amount of land demanded exactly equals the fixed supply will the market be in equilibrium.

Suppose the land can be used only to grow corn. If the demand for corn rises, the demand curve for corn-land will shift up and to the right, and the rent will rise. This leads to an important point about land: The price of land is high because the price of corn is high. This is a fine example of the fact that the demand for factors is a derived demand—derived from the demand for the product produced by the factor.

Because the supply of land is inelastic, land will always work for whatever competition gives it. Thus the value of the land derives entirely from the value of the product, and not vice versa.

Taxing Land

The fact that the supply of land is fixed has a very important consequence. Consider the land market in Figure 14-2 on page 250. Suppose the government introduces a 50 percent tax on all land rents, taking care to ensure that there is no tax on buildings or improvements, because that certainly would affect the volume of construction activity. All that is being taxed is the income or rent on the fixed supply of agricultural and urban land sites.

After the tax, the total demand for the land's services will not have changed. At a price (*including* tax) of $200 in Figure 14-2, people will continue to demand the entire fixed supply of land. Hence, with land fixed in supply, the market rent on land services (including the tax) will be unchanged and must be at the original market equilibrium at point *E.*

What will happen to the rent received by the landowners? Demand and quantity supplied are unchanged, so the market price will be unaffected by the tax. Therefore, the tax must have been completely paid out of the landowner's income.

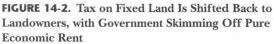

FIGURE 14-2. Tax on Fixed Land Is Shifted Back to Landowners, with Government Skimming Off Pure Economic Rent

A tax on fixed land leaves prices paid by users unchanged at *E* but reduces rent retained by landowners to *E′*. What can the landowners do but accept a lower return? This provides the rationale for Henry George's single-tax movement, which aimed to capture for society the increased land values that result from urbanization.

The situation can be visualized in Figure 14-2. What the farmer pays and what the landlord receives are now two quite different things. As far as the landlords are concerned, once the government steps in to take its 50 percent share, the effect is just the same as it would be if the net demand to the owners had shifted down from *DD* to *D′D′*. Landowners' equilibrium return after taxes is now only *E′*, or only half as much as *E*. *The whole of the tax has been shifted backward onto the owners of the factor in inelastic supply.*

Landowners will surely complain. But under perfect competition there is nothing they can do about it, since they cannot alter the total supply and the land must work for whatever it can get. Half a loaf is better than none.

You might at this point wonder about the effects of such a tax on economic efficiency. The striking result is that *a tax on rent will lead to no distortions or economic inefficiencies.* Why not? Because a tax on pure economic rent does not change anyone's economic

behavior. Demanders are unaffected because their price is unchanged. The behavior of suppliers is unaffected because the supply of land is fixed and cannot react. Hence, the economy operates after the tax exactly as it did before the tax—with no distortions or inefficiencies arising as a result of the land tax.

A tax on pure economic rent will lead to no distortions or inefficiencies.

Henry George's single-tax movement:
The theory of pure economic rent was the basis for the single-tax movement of the late 1800s. At the time, America's population was expanding rapidly as people migrated here from all over the world. With the growth in population and the expansion of railroads into the American west, land rents soared, creating handsome profits for those who were lucky or farsighted enough to buy land early.

Why, some people asked, should lucky landowners be permitted to receive these "unearned land increments"? Henry George (1839–1897), a journalist who thought a great deal about economics, crystallized these sentiments in his best-selling book *Poverty and Progress* (1879). His book called for financing government principally through property taxes on land, while cutting or eliminating all other taxes on capital, labor, and the improvements on the land. George believed that such a tax could improve the distribution of income without harming the productivity of the economy.

While the U.S. economy obviously never went very far toward the single-tax ideal, many of George's ideas were picked up by subsequent generations of economists. In the 1920s, the English economist Frank Ramsey asked the natural sequel to George's exploration: What are the most efficient kinds of taxes? This led to the development of efficient or Ramsey tax theory. This analysis shows that taxes are least distortionary if levied on sectors whose supplies or demands are highly price-inelastic.

The reasoning behind Ramsey taxes is essentially the same as that shown in Figure 14-2: If a commodity is highly inelastic in supply or demand, a tax on that sector will have very little impact on production and consumption, and the distortion will be relatively small.

⬦

B. CAPITAL AND INTEREST
⬦

You can have your cake and eat it too: Lend it out at interest.

Anonymous

BASIC CONCEPTS

Economic analysis traditionally divides factors of production into three categories: land, labor, and capital. The first two of these are called *primary* or *original factors* of production, whose supplies are determined largely outside the marketplace. To them we add a *produced factor* of production, capital.

Capital (or capital goods) consists of those durable produced goods that are in turn used as productive inputs for further production. Some capital goods might last a few years, while others might last for a century or more. But the essential property of a capital good is that it is both an input and an output.

There are three major categories of capital goods: structures (such as factories and homes), equipment (consumer durable goods like automobiles and producer durable equipment like machine tools and computers), and inventories of inputs and outputs (such as cars in dealers' lots).

Prices and Rentals on Capital Goods

Capital goods are bought and sold in capital-goods markets. For example, IBM sells computers to businesses; these computers are used by firms to help improve the efficiency of their payroll systems or production management. When sales occur, we observe the *prices of capital goods.*

Most capital goods are owned by the firm that uses them. Some capital goods, however, are rented out by their owners. Payments for the temporary use of capital goods are called *rentals.* An apartment that is owned by Ms. Landlord might be rented out for a year to a student—the monthly payment of $400 constitutes a rental. We distinguish rent on fixed factors like land from rentals on durable factors like capital.

Rate of Return on Capital Goods

One of the most important tasks of any economy, business, or household is to allocate its capital across different possible investments. Should a country devote its investment resources to heavy manufacturing like steel or to information technologies like the Internet? Should Intel build a $4 billion factory to produce the next generation of microprocessors? Should Farmer Jones, hoping to improve his record keeping, buy a customized accounting program or go with one of the popular varieties available for around $100? All these questions involve costly investments—laying out money today to obtain a return in the future.

In deciding upon the best investment, we need a measure for that yield or return on capital. One important measure is the **rate of return on capital,** which denotes the net dollar return per year for every dollar of invested capital.

Let's consider the example of a rental car company. Ugly Duckling Rental Company buys a used Ford for $10,000 and rents it out for $2500 per year. After calculating all expenses (maintenance, insurance, depreciation,[2] etc.), and ignoring any change in car prices, Ugly Duckling earns a net rental of $1200 each year. We say, then, that the rate of return on the Ford is 12 percent per year (= $1200 ÷ $10,000). Note also that the rate of return is a pure number per unit of time. That is, it has the dimensions of (dollars per period)/(dollars) and is usually calculated as percent per year.

---

[2] *Depreciation* is an estimate of the loss in dollar value of a capital good due to obsolescence or wear and tear during a period of time.

You might be considering different investments: rental cars, oil wells, apartments, education, and so forth. Your financial advisers tell you that you do not have sufficient cash to invest in everything, so how can you decide which investments to make?

One useful approach is to compare the rates of return on capital of the different investments. For each one, you first calculate the dollar cost of the capital good. Then estimate the net annual dollar receipts or rentals yielded by the asset. The ratio of the annual net rental to the dollar cost is the rate of return on capital: It tells you the amount of money you get back for every dollar invested, measured as dollars per year per dollar of investment.

The rate of return on capital is the annual net return (rentals less expenses) per dollar of invested capital. It is a pure number—percent per year.

Of Wine, Trees, and Drills. Here are some examples of rates of return on investments:

- I buy grape juice for $10 and sell it a year later as wine for $11. If there are no other expenses, the rate of return on this investment is $1/$10, or 10 percent per year.
- I plant a pine tree with labor cost of $100. At the end of 25 years the grown tree sells for $430. The rate of return on this capital project is then 330 percent per quarter-century, which, a calculator will show, is equivalent to a return of 6 percent per year. That is, $100 \times (1.06)^{25} = 429.2$.
- I buy a $20,000 piece of oil-drilling equipment. For 10 years it earns annual rentals of $30,000, but I incur annual expenses of $26,000 for fuel, insurance, and maintenance. The $4000 net return covers interest and repays the principal of $20,000 over 10 years. What is the rate of return on the drill? Amortization tables show that the rate of return is 15 percent per year.

Financial Assets and Interest Rates

We have spoken so far of capital goods like computers. But where do the resources needed to produce capital come from? Someone must be saving, or abstaining from current consumption, to provide real resources for buying the capital goods. In a modern market economy like the United States, households and firms channel funds into capital goods by saving money in various financial assets. People buy bonds and stocks; they put money in savings accounts; they put dollars away for retirement in their pension funds. All these are vehicles that carry funds from savers to the investors who actually buy capital goods.

When people save, they expect a return. This is the **interest rate,** or the financial return on funds, or the annual return on borrowed funds. The yield you get when you put your money in a time deposit at a commercial bank is an example of an interest rate. Say that the interest rate for 1998 is 5 percent per year. If you deposit $1000 on January 1, 1998, you will end up with $1050 on January 1, 1999.

You will usually see interest rates quoted as x percent per year. This is the interest that would be paid if the sum were borrowed for an entire year; for shorter or longer periods, the interest payment is adjusted proportionately.

There are many varieties of interest rates. There are long-term and short-term interest rates, depending on the duration of the loan or the bond; there are fixed-interest-rate loans and variable-interest-rate loans; there are interest rates on super-safe bonds (like U.S. government securities); and there are interest rates on highly risky "junk bonds."

To summarize:

Households and other savers provide financial resources or funds to those who want to purchase physical capital goods. The rate of interest represents the price that a bank or other financial intermediary pays a lender for the use of the money for a period of time; interest rates are quoted as a certain percent yield per year.

Real vs. Nominal Interest Rates

The interest rates just discussed are measured in dollar or *nominal* terms and not in terms of trees or wine or cars. Interest is the yield on an investment measured in dollars per year per dollar of investment. But dollars can become distorted yardsticks. The prices of fish, trees, wine, and other goods change from year to year as the general price level rises due to inflation.[3] We therefore need to find a

---

[3] The *rate of inflation* is defined as the rate of change of prices from one period to the next. If the general price level is 100 in 1997 and 103.5 in 1998, the rate of inflation is 3.5 percent per year.

real return on capital, one that measures the quantity of goods we get tomorrow for goods forgone today.

As an example, say that you invested 1000 pesos in a Mexican bond in 1995. Because you were offered a 70 percent interest rate, you might have looked forward to getting a hefty return, ending up with 1700 pesos at the end of the year. But when you later took your money out to buy some consumer goods, you found that prices had risen 65 percent during 1995. In terms of the real quantity of goods, you could actually buy only 3 percent more (1.030 = 1.70/1.65) than you could have bought at the start of the year. In other words, if you were to lend 1000 market baskets of goods at the beginning of 1995, you could obtain only 1030 market baskets of goods the following year. The difference between real and nominal interest rates is particularly dramatic during periods of high inflation.

We call the real yield on funds the **real interest rate,** as opposed to the **nominal interest rate,** which is the dollar return on dollars invested. For low rates of interest and inflation, the real interest rate is very close to the nominal interest rate minus the rate of inflation.[4]

The real interest rate is the return on funds in terms of goods and services; we generally calculate the real interest rate as the nominal interest rate minus the rate of inflation.

Table 14-1 shows nominal interest rates on different instruments over the last three decades. (Using the formula, you can obtain real interest rates by taking into account that inflation averaged 4 percent per year over this period.)

PRESENT VALUE OF ASSETS

Capital goods are durable assets that produce a stream of rentals or receipts over time. If you own an apartment building, you will collect rental payments over the life of the building, much as the owner of a fruit orchard will pick fruit from the trees each season.

Suppose you become weary of tending the building and decide to sell it. To set a fair price for the

---

[4] In other words, let π be the inflation rate, i the nominal interest rate, and r the real interest rate. The exact calculation of the real interest rate is $1 + r = (1 + i)/(1 + \pi)$. For small values of i and π, however, $r = i - \pi$.

U.S. financial instrument	Nominal rate of return, 1967–1996 (% per year)
State and local bonds:	
High grade, tax free	3.5
Federal government bonds:	
Short term	4.1
Long term	5.2
Corporate bonds:	
Safe (Aaa)	4.5
Risky (< Baa)	6.0
Consumer loans:	
Mortgages	4.8
Credit cards	10.8
New-car loans	15.8

TABLE 14-1. Interest Rates on Selected Financial Instruments

Nominal interest rates depend upon risk, inflation, and tax treatment. The lowest interest rates are on tax-free and safe state and local securities, followed by taxable federal government obligations. New-car loans carry high interest rates because of default risks. Foreign debt from risky countries with high sovereign risk and high inflation can be many times higher. (Source: Federal Reserve Board.)

building, you would need to determine the value today of the entire stream of future income. The value of that stream is called the present value of the capital asset.

The **present value** is the dollar value today of a stream of income over time. It is measured by calculating how much money invested today would be needed, at the going interest rate, to generate the asset's future stream of receipts.

Let's start with a very simple example. Let's say somebody offers to sell you a bottle of wine that matures in exactly 1 year and can then be sold for exactly $11. Assuming the market interest rate is 10 percent per year, what is the present value of the wine—that is, how much should you pay for the wine today? Pay exactly $10, because $10 invested today at the market interest rate of 10 percent will be worth $11 in 1 year. So the present value of next year's $11 wine is today $10.

Present Value for Perpetuities

We present the first way of calculating present value by examining the case of a *perpetuity*, which is an asset like land that lasts forever and pays $N each year from now to eternity. We are seeking the present value (V) if the interest rate is i percent per year, where the present value is the amount of money invested today that would yield exactly $N each year. This is simply

$$V = \frac{\$N}{i}$$

where V = present value of the land ($)
    N = permanent annual receipts ($ per year)
    i = interest rate in decimal terms (e.g., 0.05, or $\frac{5}{100}$ per year)

This says that if the interest rate is always 5 percent per year, an asset yielding a constant stream of income will sell for exactly 20 (= 1 ÷ $\frac{5}{100}$) times its annual income. In this case, what would be the present value of a perpetuity yielding $100 every year? At a 5 percent interest rate its present value would be $2000 (= $100 ÷ 0.05).

General Formula for Present Value

Having seen the simple case of the perpetuity, we move to the general case of the present value of an asset with an income stream that varies over time. The main thing to remember about present value is that future payments are worth less than current payments and they are therefore *discounted* relative to the present. Future payments are worth less than current payments just as distant objects look smaller than nearby ones. The interest rate produces a similar shrinking of time perspective.

Let's take a fantastic example. Say that someone proposes to pay $100 billion to your heirs in 999 years. How much should you pay for this today? According to the general rule for present value, to figure out the value today of $P payable t years from now, ask yourself how much must be invested today to grow into $P at the end of t years. Say the interest rate is 6 percent per annum. Applying this each year to the growing amount, a principal amount of $P grows in t years proportionally to $P \times \$(1 + 0.06)^t$. Hence, we need only invert this expression to find present value: the present value of $P payable t years from now is only $P/(1 + 0.06)^t$. Using this formula, we determine that the present value of $100 billion paid in 999 years is $0.0000000000000052.[5]

---

[5] Question 9 at the end of this chapter asks about the present value of the real estate of Manhattan when it was purchased by the Dutch.

In most cases, there are several terms in an asset's stream of income. In present-value calculations, each dollar must stand on its own feet. Evaluate the present value of each part of the stream of future receipts, giving due allowance for the discounting required by its payment date. Then simply add together all these separate present values. This summation will give you the asset's present value.

The exact formula for present value is the following:

$$V = \frac{N_1}{1 + i} + \frac{N_2}{(1 + i)^2} + \cdots + \frac{N_t}{(1 + i)^t} + \cdots$$

In this equation, i is the one-period market interest rate (assumed constant). Further, N_1 is the net receipts (positive or negative) in period 1, N_2 the net receipts in period 2, N_t the net receipts in period t, and so forth. Then the stream of payments (N_1, N_2, ..., N_t, ...) will have the present value, V, given by the formula.

For example, assume that the interest rate is 10 percent per year and that I am to receive $1100 next year and $2662 in 3 years. The present value of this stream is

$$V = \frac{1100}{(1.10)^1} + \frac{2662}{(1.10)^3} = 3000$$

Figure 14-3 shows graphically the calculation of present value for a machine that earns steady net annual rentals of $100 over a 20-year period and has no scrap value at the end. Its present value is not $2000 but only $1157. Note how much the later dol-

FIGURE 14-3. Present Value of an Asset

The lower rust area shows the present value of a machine giving net annual rentals of $100 for 20 years with an interest rate of 6 percent per year. The upper gray area has been discounted away. Explain why raising the interest rate increases the gray area and therefore depresses the market price of an asset.

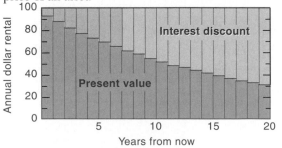

lar earnings are scaled down or discounted because of our time perspective. The total area remaining after discounting (the rust shaded area) represents the machine's total present value—the value today of the stream of all future incomes.

Acting to Maximize Present Value

The present-value formula tells us how to calculate the value of any asset once we know the earnings. But note that an asset's future receipts usually depend on business decisions: Shall we use a truck 8 or 9 years? Overhaul it once a month or once a year? Replace it with a cheap, nondurable truck or an expensive, durable one?

There is one rule that gives correct answers to all investment decisions: Calculate the present value resulting from each possible decision. Then always act so as to maximize present value. In this way you will have more wealth to spend whenever and however you like.

PROFITS

In addition to wages, interest, and rent, economists often talk about a fourth category of income called *profits*. What are profits? How do they differ from interest and the returns on capital more generally?

Reported Profit Statistics

Accountants define **profits** as the difference between total revenues and total costs. To calculate profits, start with total revenues from sales. Subtract all expenses (wages, salaries, rents, materials, interest, excise taxes, and the rest). What is left over is the residual called profits.[6]

Determinants of Profits

What determines the rate of corporate profits in a market economy? Profits are in fact a combination

of different elements, including the implicit returns on owners' capital, reward for risk bearing, and innovational profits.

Profits as Implicit Returns. To the economist, business profits are a hodgepodge of different elements. Much of reported business profits is primarily the return to the owners of the firm for the capital and labor provided by the owners, that is, for factors of production supplied by them.

For example, some profits are the return on the personal work provided by the owners of the firm—such as the doctor or lawyer who works in a small professional corporation. Part is the rent return on self-owned natural resources. In large corporations, most profits are the opportunity costs of invested capital. These returns are called *implicit returns*, which is the name given to the opportunity costs of factors owned by firms.

Thus some of what is ordinarily called profit is really nothing but rentals, rents, and wages under a different name. "Implicit rentals," "implicit rent," and "implicit wages" are the names economists give to the earnings on factors that the firm itself owns.

Profits as Reward for Risk Bearing. Profits also include an element of reward for risk bearing. In analyzing the reward for risk bearing, however, we would not want to include default risk or insurable risk. A provision for *default risk* would cover the possibility that a loan or investment could not be paid, say, because the borrower went bankrupt. *Insurable risks*, such as those analyzed in Chapter 11, would include fires or hurricanes, which could be covered through purchase of insurance. Default and insurable risks are the normal costs of doing business and should be counted as costs.

A kind of risk that must be considered in profit calculations is the *uninsurable* or *systematic risk of investments*. A company may have a high degree of sensitivity to business cycles, which means that its earnings fluctuate a great deal when aggregate output goes up or down. Because investors are averse to risky situations, they require a risk premium on this uncertain investment to compensate for their risk aversion. Developing countries are subject to *sovereign risk*, which occurs when the government defaults on its obligations and (because the government is "sovereign" and exercises ultimate legal authority) there is no recourse in the legal system.

---

[6] In analyzing profits, it is important to distinguish *business profits* from *economic profits*. Business profits are the residual income, equal to sales less costs, measured by accountants. Business profits include an implicit return on the capital owned by firms. Economic profits are the earnings after all costs—both money and implicit or opportunity costs—are subtracted. In large corporations, therefore, economic profits would equal business profits less an implicit return on the capital owned by the firm along with any other costs (such as unpaid management time) not fully compensated at market prices.

Corporate profits are a risky component of national income, so corporate capital must contain a significant risk premium to attract investors. Empirical studies that we will review later in this chapter (see Table 14-2 on page 260) suggest that between 3 and 6 percentage points of the annual return on corporate stocks is the risk premium necessary to attract people to hold this risky investment.

Profits as Reward for Innovation. A third kind of profits consists of the returns to innovation and invention. A modern economy is constantly producing new products—from software programs to exotic materials to jet skis. These new products are the result of research, development, and marketing. We call the person who brings a new product or process to market an *innovator* or *entrepreneur.*

What do we mean by "innovators"? Innovators are people who have the vision, originality, and daring to introduce new ideas in business. History has seen great inventors like Alexander Graham Bell (the telephone), Thomas Edison (the light bulb), and Chester Carlson (xerography). Some inventors amass great fortunes from their entrepreneurship. The modern age has seen Steven Jobs launch Apple Computers, while Bill Gates' Microsoft dominates the software business with innovative operating systems and software.

Every successful innovation creates a temporary pool of monopoly. We can identify *innovational profits* (sometimes called *Schumpeterian profits*) as the temporary excess return to innovators or entrepreneurs. For a short time, innovational profits are earned. These profit earnings are temporary and are soon competed away by rivals and imitators. But just as one source of innovational profits is disappearing, another is being born. Innovational profits will continue to exist as long as the economy produces technological change.

Review

Let's review the terms we have learned before turning to apply them:

- A modern industrial economy has accumulated large stocks of *capital,* or capital goods. These are the machines, buildings, and inventories that are so vital to an economy's productivity.

- The annual dollar earnings on capital are called *rentals.* When we divide the net earnings (rentals less costs) by the dollar value of the capital generating the rentals, we obtain the *rate of return on capital* (measured in percent per year).
- Capital is financed by savers who lend funds and hold financial assets. The dollar yield on these financial assets is the *interest rate,* measured in percent per year.
- Capital goods and financial assets generate a stream of income over time. This stream can be converted into a *present value,* i.e., the value that the stream of income would be worth today. This conversion is made by asking what quantity of dollars today would be just sufficient to generate the asset's stream of income at going market interest rates.
- *Profits* are a residual income item, equal to total revenues minus total costs. Profits contain elements of implicit costs (such as return on owners' capital), return for risk bearing, and innovational profits.

THE THEORY OF CAPITAL AND INTEREST

Now that we have surveyed the major concepts, we turn to an analysis of the *classical theory of capital.* This approach was developed independently by the Austrian E. V. Bohm-Bawerk, the Swede Knut Wicksell, and Yale's Irving Fisher in the United States.

Roundaboutness

In Chapter 2, we noted that investment in capital goods involves indirect or *roundabout* production. Instead of catching fish with our hands, we find it ultimately more worthwhile first to build boats and make nets—and then to use the boats and nets to catch many more fish than we could by hand.

Put differently, investment in capital goods involves forgoing present consumption to increase future consumption. Consuming less today frees labor for making nets to catch many more fish tomorrow. In the most general sense, capital is productive because by forgoing consumption today we get more consumption in the future.

To see this, imagine two islands that are exactly alike. Each has the same amount of labor and natural

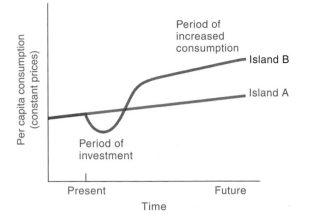

FIGURE 14-4. Investments Today Yield Consumption Tomorrow

Two islands begin with equal endowments of labor and natural resources. Spendthrift Island A invests nothing and shows a modest growth in per capita consumption. Thrifty Island B devotes an initial period to investment, forgoing consumption, and then enjoys the harvest of much higher consumption in the future.

resources. Island A uses these primary factors directly to produce consumption goods like food and clothing; it uses no produced capital goods at all. By contrast, thrifty Island B sacrifices current consumption and uses its resources and labor to produce capital goods, such as plows, shovels, and looms. After this temporary sacrifice of current consumption, B ends up with a large stock of capital goods.

Figure 14-4 shows the way that Island B forges ahead of A. For each island, measure the amount of consumption per person that can be enjoyed while maintaining the existing capital stock. Because of its thrift, Island B, using roundabout, capital-intensive methods of production, will enjoy more future consumption than Island A. B gets more than 100 units of future-consumption goods for its initial sacrifice of 100 units of present consumption.

By sacrificing current consumption and building capital goods today, societies can increase their consumption in the future.

Diminishing Returns and the Demand for Capital

What happens when a nation sacrifices more and more of its consumption for capital accumulation as production becomes more and more roundabout or indirect? We would expect the law of diminishing returns to set in. Let's take the example of computers. The first computers were expensive and used intensively. Three decades ago, scientists would eke every last hour of time from an expensive mainframe computer that had less power than today's personal computer. By the late 1990s, the nation's stock of computers had millions of times more computational and storage capacity. But the marginal product of computer power—the value of the last calculation or the last byte of storage—had diminished greatly as computer inputs increased relative to labor, land, and other capital. More generally, as capital accumulates, diminishing returns set in and the rate of return on the investments tends to fall.

Unless offset by technological change, the diminishing returns from rapid investment will drive down the rate of return on investment. Surprisingly, the rate of return on capital has not fallen markedly over the course of the last 150 years, even though our capital stocks have grown manyfold. Rates of return have remained high because innovation and technological change have created profitable new opportunities as rapidly as past investment has annihilated them. Even though computers are thousands of times more powerful than they were three decades ago, new applications in every corner of society from electronic mail to medical diagnostics continue to make investments in computers profitable.

Determination of Interest and the Return on Capital

We can use the classical theory of capital to understand the determination of the rate of interest. Households *supply* funds for investment by abstaining from consumption and accumulating saving over time. At the same time, businesses *demand* capital goods to combine with labor, land, and other inputs. In the end, a firm's demand for capital is driven by its desire to make profits by producing goods.

Or as Irving Fisher put the matter at the beginning of this century:

> The quantity of capital and the rate of return on capital are determined by the interaction between (1) people's *impatience* to consume now rather than accumulate more capital goods for future consumption (perhaps for old-age retirement or for that proverbial rainy day); and (2) *investment opportunities* that yield higher or lower returns to such accumulated capital.

To understand interest rates and the return on capital, consider an idealized case of a closed economy with perfect competition and without risk or inflation. In deciding whether to invest, a profit-maximizing firm will always compare its cost of funds with the rate of return on capital. If the rate of return is higher than the market interest rate at which the firm can borrow funds, it will undertake the investment. If the interest rate is higher than the rate of return on investment, the firm will not invest.

Where will this process end? Eventually, firms will undertake all investments whose rates of return are higher than the market interest rate. Equilibrium is then reached when competition among firms beats down the return on investment to the level of the market interest rate.

In a competitive economy without risk or inflation, the competitive rate of return on capital would be equal to the market interest rate. The market interest rate serves two functions: It rations out society's scarce supply of capital goods for the uses that have the highest rates of return, and it induces people to sacrifice current consumption in order to increase the stock of capital.

Graphical Analysis of the Return on Capital

We can illustrate capital theory by concentrating on a simple case in which all physical capital goods are alike. In addition, assume that the economy is in a steady state with no population growth or technological change.

In Figure 14-5, *DD* shows the demand curve for the stock of capital; it plots the relationship between the quantity of capital demanded and the rate of return on capital. Recall from Chapter 12 that the demand for a factor like capital is a "derived demand"—the demand comes from the *marginal product of capital*, which is the extra output yielded by additions to the capital stock.

The law of diminishing returns can be seen in the fact that the demand-for-capital curve in Figure 14-5 is downward-sloping. When capital is very scarce, the most profitable roundabout projects have a very high rate of return. Gradually, as the community exploits all the high-yield projects by accumulating capital, with total labor and land fixed, diminishing returns to capital set in. The community must

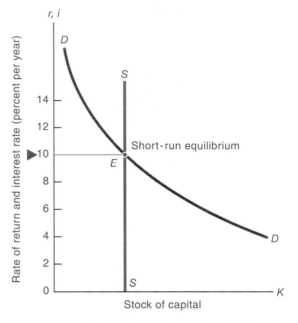

FIGURE 14-5. Short-Run Determination of Interest and Returns

In the short run, the economy has inherited a given stock of capital from the past, shown as the vertical *SS* supply-of-capital schedule. Intersection of the short-run supply curve with the demand-for-capital schedule determines the short-run return on capital, and the short-run real interest rate, at 10 percent per year.

then invest in lower-yield projects as it moves down the demand-for-capital curve.

Short-Run Equilibrium. We can now see how supply and demand interact. In Figure 14-5, past investments have produced a given stock of capital, shown as the vertical short-run supply curve, *SS*. Firms will demand capital goods in a manner shown by the downward-sloping demand curve, *DD*.

At the intersection of supply and demand, at point *E*, the amount of capital is just rationed out to the demanding firms. At this short-run equilibrium, firms are willing to pay 10 percent a year to borrow funds to buy capital goods. At that point, the lenders of funds are satisfied to receive exactly 10 percent a year on their supplies of capital.

Thus, in our simple, riskless world, the rate of return on capital exactly equals the market interest rate. Any higher interest rate would find firms unwilling to borrow for their investments; any lower

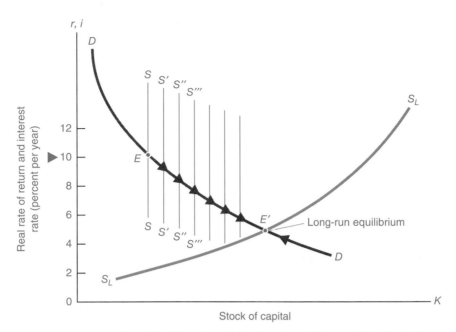

FIGURE 14-6. Long-Run Equilibration of the Supply and Demand for Capital

In the long run, society accumulates capital, so the supply curve is no longer vertical. As pictured here, the supply of wealth is responsive to higher interest rates. At the original short-run equilibrium at E there is net investment, so the economy moves down the DD demand curve as shown by the black arrows. Long-run equilibrium comes at E', where net saving ceases.

interest rate would find firms clamoring for the too scarce capital. Only at the equilibrium interest rate of 10 percent are supply and demand equilibrated. (Recall that these are *real* interest rates because there is no inflation.)

But the equilibrium at E is sustained only for the short run: At this high interest rate, people will want to go on saving. At the short-run equilibrium, people desire to accumulate more capital, i.e., to continue saving. This means that the capital stock increases. However, because of the law of diminishing returns, the rate of return and the interest rate move downward. As capital increases—while other things such as labor, land, and technical knowledge remain unchanged—the rate of return on the increased stock of capital goods falls to ever-lower levels.

This process is shown graphically in Figure 14-6. Note that capital formation is taking place at point E. So each year, the capital stock is a little higher as net investment occurs. As time passes, the community moves slowly down the DD curve as shown by the black arrows in Figure 14-6. You can actually see a series of very thin short-run supply-of-capital curves in the figure—S, S', S'', S''', ... These curves show how the short-run supply of capital increases with capital accumulation.

Long-Run Equilibrium. Where does long-run equilibrium occur? It comes at E' in Figure 14-6; this is where the long-run supply of capital (shown as $S_L S_L$) intersects with the demand for capital. The long-run equilibrium is attained when the interest rate has fallen to the point where the capital stock held by firms has expanded so as to match the amount of wealth that people desire to supply. At the long-run equilibrium, net saving stops, net capital accumulation is zero, and the capital stock is no longer growing.

The long-run equilibrium stock of capital comes at that real interest rate and rate of return on capital where the value of assets that people want to hold exactly matches the amount of capital that firms want for production.

APPLICATIONS OF CLASSICAL CAPITAL THEORY

We have completed our survey of the classical theory of interest and capital. But capital theory needs some amplifications and qualifications to account for important realistic features of economic life.

Taxes and Inflation

Investors always keep a sharp eye out for inflation and taxes. Recall that inflation tends to reduce the quantity of goods you can buy with your dollars. Therefore, we want to calculate the real interest rate or the real return to our investments, removing the effect of the changing yardstick of money. Another important feature is taxes. Part of our incomes go to the government to pay for public goods and other government programs. Therefore, investors will want to focus on the posttax return on investments.

Technological Disturbances

A deeper complexity involves technological change. Historical studies show that inventions and discoveries raise the return on capital and thereby affect equilibrium interest rates. Indeed, the tendency toward falling interest rates via diminishing returns has been just about canceled out by inventions and technological progress.

Some economists (such as Joseph Schumpeter) have likened the investment process to a plucked violin string: In a world of unchanging technology, the string gradually comes to rest as capital accumulation drives down returns on capital. But before the economy has settled into a steady state, an outside event or invention comes along to pluck the string and set the forces of investment in motion again.

Uncertainty and Expectations

The final qualification concerns the risks that exist in investment decisions. In real life no one has a crystal ball to read the future. All investments, resting as they do on estimates of future earnings, must necessarily be guesses about future costs and payoffs. Our discussion assumed that there were no risks. But in fact almost any loan or investment has an element of risk. Machines break down; an oil well may turn out to be a dry hole; your favorite computer company may go belly up. Investments differ in their degree of risk, but no investment is completely risk-free.

Investors are generally averse to holding risky assets. They would rather hold an asset that is sure to yield them 10 percent than an asset that is equally likely to yield 0 or 20 percent. Investors must therefore receive an extra return, or *risk premium*, to induce them to hold investments with high systematic or uninsurable risk.

EMPIRICAL FINDINGS

Returns on Different Assets

What are the actual real returns on investments in different forms? Table 14-2 shows a summary of recent studies on the return to capital in different fields. The rates of return on assets like corporate capital, farmland, and real estate have averaged around 6 percent over the last three decades. Because these assets can be packaged and sold as stocks and bonds, they tend to have lower returns

TABLE 14-2. Real Rates of Return on Different Assets

The real returns to tangible capital, land, and human capital vary widely depending upon country and risk. Because consumers cannot pool risks on their investments and often are liquidity-constrained, consumer investments have the highest returns. [Source: Tabulation by the authors from a variety of sources, including Roger G. Ibbotson and Gary P. Brinson, *Investment Markets* (McGraw-Hill, New York, 1987); United Nations Development Program; World Bank; and scholarly studies.]

Asset class	Period	Real rate of return (% per year)
Corporate capital (U.S.):		
Posttax return	1959–1996	5.4
Pretax return	1959–1996	9.3
Real estate	1960–1984	5.5
Farmland	1947–1984	5.5
Human capital:		
United States	1980s	6–12
Developing countries	1970s–1980s	13–26
Consumer durables	1970s–1980s	48
Energy conservation	1970s–1980s	19
Nonresidential capital stock (7 major industrial countries)	1975–1990	15

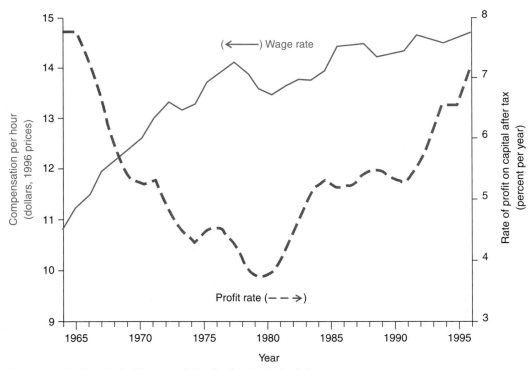

Figure 14-7. Trends in Wages and Profits in the United States

How have the returns to labor and capital varied in recent years? Real wages (including fringe benefits) grew sharply in the period after World War II and then slowed after the 1970s. After falling in the turbulent 1970s, the post-tax rate of profit on American business capital doubled since 1980. Explanations of the reversal of fortunes include the trend toward deregulation, greater openness to trade, and the information revolution. (Source: U.S. Departments of Commerce and Labor with profit data from James Poterba, "Recent Developments in Corporate Profitability: Patterns and Explanations," March 1997.)

than riskier, nondiversified assets like human capital, venture capital, consumer durables, and developing-country capital. These riskier investments have returns ranging from around 10 percent upward.

Returns to Labor and Capital

A final comparison, shown in Figure 14-7, shows the trends in labor and capital returns in the United States over the last 35 years. We see that labor's earnings grew sharply but then stagnated after the early 1970s. The rate of profit on capital, by contrast, has skyrocketed in recent years, with a near-doubling of the after-tax rate of return to nonfinancial corporate capital since 1980. This trend led one commentator to the conclusion that this is a good time to be a capitalist in the United States.

What were the forces that lay behind the sharp reversal of fortunes of workers and capitalists over the last two decades? While economists are just beginning to sort out the reasons, the following are among the leading possibilities:

- Since the 1980s, the conservative and pro-market political movement has led to a deregulation of many industries, allowing capital to pursue fields of highest profitability. This trend is seen most dramatically for electric utilities, where the capital intensity of production has declined sharply as former monopolies have faced increasing competition in the electricity market.
- A sharp increase in trade with developing countries means that U.S. workers—particularly unskilled workers—must compete with the vast army of workers in the rest of the world. By contrast, domestic management and capital are scarce factors in the world, and we would expect

to see their return rise with the opening of markets at home and abroad.

- One intriguing possibility is that technological change in the last decade has become "capital-saving" as compared with the "labor-saving" technological change that characterized most of the period since the Industrial Revolution. In an earlier era, new technologies used power looms to replace textile workers. Today, computers and other informational capital form an ever-larger share of investment. Informational capital can be capital-saving because it helps airlines schedule aircraft and passengers, allows oil companies to run refineries and find oil rather than just drill blindly, and helps all companies keep their inventories down.

People will be watching wage and profit trends carefully to see if the divergent trends continue.

VALEDICTORY THOUGHTS ON FACTOR PRICES, EFFICIENCY, AND DISTRIBUTION

The recent reversal of fortune of labor and capital—with capital earnings rising rapidly over the last two decades as wages stagnated—raises questions about the fairness as well as the efficiency of the distribution of income in a market economy. Economists emphasize that a free market in capital and land will promote high rates of saving and investment, rapid economic growth, and healthy productivity growth. In the political arena, people worry that this same free market will lead the rich to become richer while the poor are falling behind. We would offer three final thoughts on these debates:

1. People's market incomes are determined by rents, interest, and wages. We may or may not like the competitive distribution of income, but we must recognize that competitive pricing helps solve the question of *how* goods are to be produced in an efficient manner. Getting the prices right is crucial to ensuring efficient selection of inputs in the production process.

    Consider, for example, how different relative proportions of land and labor are reflected in different countries. Compare America, with plentiful land and scarce labor, with Hong Kong,

where land is precious and labor abundant. As a result of supply and demand, wages are high relative to rents in America while the opposite is true in Hong Kong. Because these relative scarcities are transmitted by factor prices, markets help ensure that the efficient land-labor combinations are used. Americans have huge farms and use labor sparingly, while land in Hong Kong is reserved for industry and housing rather than for land-intensive agriculture.

2. The debates about profits tend to obscure the basic point about the role of capital in a market economy. The accumulation of capital and its return are driven by two fundamental forces. On the one hand, the demand for capital results from the fact that indirect or roundabout production processes are productive; by abstaining from consumption today, society can raise consumption in the future. On the other hand, people must be willing to abstain from consumption in order to accumulate financial assets, lending funds to firms that will make the productive investments in roundabout productive processes. These two forces of technology and impatience are brought into balance by the interest rate, which ensures that society's accumulation of capital just matches the amount that people are willing to hold back from consumption in the form of saving.

3. Finally, we must remember that the factor prices of wages, rents, interest, and profits are not carved in granite. They are subject to government policies. As Henry George's approach emphasizes, if society dislikes the inequality brought about by high land rents or fabulous wages of unique individuals, taxes on these factors can reduce inequality without inducing great inefficiencies. Well-designed taxes on high incomes and inheritance, efficient wage subsidies to low-wage workers, and transfer programs to help the truly needy can reduce the worst inequalities of a market economy without impairing the ability of factor prices to guide markets to efficient allocations or unduly reducing saving, investment, and economic growth.

With well-designed tax and transfer programs, a country can have its cake of growing productivity and share the cake more fairly among its citizens.

SUMMARY

A. Land and Rent

1. The return to fixed factors like land is called pure economic rent, or rent for short. Since the supply curve for land is vertical and totally inelastic, the rent will be price-determined rather than price-determining.

2. A factor like land that is inelastically supplied will continue to work the same amount even though its factor reward is reduced. For this reason, Henry George pointed out that rent is in the nature of a surplus rather than a reward necessary to coax out the factor's effort. This provides the basis for his single-tax proposal to tax the unearned increment of land value, without shifting the tax forward to consumers or distorting production. Modern tax theory extends this proposition by showing that inefficiencies are minimized by taxing goods that are relatively inelastic in supply or demand.

B. Capital and Interest

3. A third factor of production is capital, a produced durable good that is used in further production. In the most general sense, investing in capital represents deferred consumption. By postponing consumption today and producing buildings or equipment, society increases consumption in the future. It is a technological fact that roundabout production yields a positive rate of return.

4. Recall the definitions:
   Capital goods: durable produced goods used for further production
   Rentals: net annual dollar returns on capital goods
   Rate of return on capital: net annual receipts on capital divided by dollar value of capital (measured as percent per year)
   Interest rate: yield on funds, measured as percent per year
   Real interest rate: yield on funds corrected for inflation, also measured as percent per year
   Present value: value today of a stream of future returns generated by an asset
   Profits: a residual income item equal to revenues minus costs

5. Assets generate streams of income in future periods. By calculating the present value, we can convert the stream of returns into a single value today. This is done by asking what amount of dollars today will generate the stream of future returns when invested at the market interest rate.

6. The exact present-value formula is as follows: Each dollar payable t years from now is a present value (V) of $\$1/(1 + i)^t$. So for any net receipt stream (N_1, N_2, . . . , N_t, . . .) where N_t is the dollar value of receipts t years in the future, we have

$$V = \frac{N_1}{1 + i} + \frac{N_2}{(1 + i)^2} + \cdots + \frac{N_t}{(1 + i)^t} + \cdots$$

7. Interest is a device that serves two functions in the economy. As a motivating device, it provides an incentive for people to save and accumulate wealth. As a rationing device, interest allows society to select only those investment projects with the highest rates of return. However, as more and more capital is accumulated, and as the law of diminishing returns sets in, the rate of return on capital and the interest rate will be beaten down by competition. Falling interest rates are a signal to society to adopt more capital-intensive projects with lower rates of return.

8. Saving and investment involve waiting for future consumption rather than consuming today. Such thrift interacts with the net productivity of capital to determine interest rates, the rate of return on capital, and the capital stock. The funds or financial assets needed to purchase capital are provided by households that are willing to sacrifice consumption today in return for larger consumption tomorrow. The demand for capital comes from firms that have a variety of roundabout investment projects. In long-run equilibrium, the interest rate is thus determined by the interaction between the net productivity of capital and the willingness of households to sacrifice consumption today for consumption tomorrow.

9. Important qualifications of classical capital theory include the following: Technological change shifts the productivity of capital; imperfect foresight means that capital's return is highly volatile; and investors must consider the impact of taxes and inflation.

10. Profits are revenues less costs. Reported business profits are chiefly corporate earnings. Economically, we distinguish three categories of profits. (*a*) An important source is profits as implicit returns. Firms generally own many of their own nonlabor factors of production—capital, natural resources, and patents. In these cases, the implicit return on unpaid or owned inputs is part of profits. (*b*) Another source of profits is uninsurable risk, particularly that associated with the business cycle or sovereign risk. (*c*) Finally, innovational profits will be earned by entrepreneurs who introduce new products or innovations.

CONCEPTS FOR REVIEW

Land

rent
inelastic supply of land
taxation of fixed factors

Capital and interest

capital, capital goods

rentals, rate of return on capital,
    interest rate, profits
investment as abstaining from con-
    sumption
real vs. nominal interest rate
present value

twin elements in interest determina-
    tion: returns to roundaboutness
    and impatience
source of profits:
    implicit returns
    uninsurable risks
    innovation

QUESTIONS FOR DISCUSSION

1. Define "pure economic rent."
    a. Show that an increase in supply of the rent-earn-
        ing factor will depress its rent and lower the prices
        of goods that use much of it.
    b. Explain the following statement from rent theory:
        "It is not true that the price of corn is high because
        the price of land is high. Rather, the reverse is
        closer to the truth: The price of cornland is high
        because the price of corn is high." Illustrate with a
        diagram.
    c. Consider the quotation in (**b**). Why is this correct
        for the market as a whole but incorrect for the
        individual farmer? Explain the fallacy of composi-
        tion that is at work here.
2. Reread the section on "winner-take-all markets" in
    Chapter 11. Some observers have suggested that tax-
    ing the highest incomes would reduce income
    inequality. What would you expect to be the result of
    such a tax on the work efforts of top rock stars or bas-
    ketball players?
3. Calculate the real interest rates for each financial
    instrument in Table 14-1 if the inflation rate was 4 per-
    cent during the 1967–1996 period.
4. Contrast the following four returns on durable assets:
    (*a*) rent on land, (*b*) rental of a capital good, (*c*) rate
    of return on a capital good, and (*d*) real interest rate.
    Give an example of each.
5. Using the supply-and-demand analysis of interest,
    explain how each of the following would affect interest
    rates in capital theory:
    a. An innovation that increased the marginal prod-
        uct of capital at each level of capital
    b. A decrease in the desired wealth holdings of
        households
    c. A 50 percent tax on the return on capital (in the
        short run and the long run)
6. Looking back to Figures 14-5 and 14-6, review how the
    economy moved from the short-run equilibrium inter-

est rate at 10 percent per year to the long-run equilibrium. Now explain what would occur in both the long
run and the short run if innovations shift up the
demand-for-capital curve. What would happen if the
government debt became very large and a large part of
people's supply of capital was siphoned off to holdings
of government debt?

7. Explain the rule for calculating the present dis-
    counted value of a perpetual income stream. At 5 per-
    cent, what is the worth of a perpetuity paying $100 per
    year? Paying $200 per year? Paying $*N* per year? At 10
    or 8 percent, what is the worth of a perpetuity paying
    $100 per year? What does doubling the interest rate do
    to the capitalized value of a perpetuity—say, a perpet-
    ual bond?

8. Recall the algebraic formula for a convergent geomet-
    ric progression:

$$1 + K + K^2 + \cdots = \frac{1}{1 - K}$$

for any fraction K less than 1. If you set $K = 1/(1 + i)$,
can you verify the present-value formula for a permanent income stream, $V = \$N/i$? Provide an alternative
proof using common sense. What would be the value
of a lottery that paid you and your heirs $5000 per year
forever at an interest rate of 6 percent per year?

9. The value of land in Manhattan was in 1997 around
    $60 billion. Imagine that it is 1626 and you are the eco-
    nomic adviser to the Dutch when they are considering
    whether to buy Manhattan. Further, assume that the
    relevant interest rate for calculating the present value
    is 4 percent per year. Would you advise the Dutch that
    a purchase price of $24 is a good deal or not? How
    would your answer change if the interest rate were 6
    percent? 8 percent? (*Hint:* For each interest rate, cal-
    culate the present value in 1626 of the land value as of
    1997. Then compare that with the purchase price in
    1626.)

CHAPTER 15
MARKETS AND ECONOMIC EFFICIENCY

> A market economy . . . is the only natural economy, the only kind that makes sense, the only one that can lead to prosperity, because it is the only one that reflects the nature of life itself. The essence of life is infinitely and mysteriously multiform, and therefore it cannot be contained or planned for, in its fullness and variability, by any central intelligence.
>
> *Václav Havel,* **Summer Meditations** *(1993)*

By the end of the 1980s, socialist Eastern Europe and the Soviet empire were in ruins, with long lines for bread and other necessities in the stores, low and declining living standards, outdated technologies, and deteriorating environmental conditions. This large and once-prosperous region had been laid low, not by war or pestilence, but by an ambitious social experiment called *socialist central planning,* devised by Vladimir Lenin and his communist followers. When the communists were thrown out of office in 1989–1991, the new leaders of the affected countries, people like the playwright-turned-president Václav Havel of Czechoslovakia, decided without hesitation that introducing a market economy was the first step toward regaining economic health.

Why did the leaders of these centrally planned economies turn to the market? As Havel's quotation at the beginning of this chapter states, they were convinced that a market economy, based on principles of decentralized supply and demand, was the surest route to economic health. They had seen West Germany become the powerhouse of Europe while East Germany stagnated; they lived in a Czechoslovakia poisoned by toxic wastes, while southern neighbor Austria, with its mixed capitalist system, was a rural idyll. They were reading the lessons of history.

How well does the market perform, and what are its shortcomings? Our analysis of the basic properties of a market economy—of both product and factor markets—concludes in this chapter with an explanation of the remarkable efficiency properties of competitive capitalism. The chapter then identifies some market failures, those areas where the market fails to provide the proper signals and leads to inefficiencies.

A. THE EFFICIENCY OF PERFECT COMPETITION

Two centuries ago, Adam Smith proclaimed that, through the workings of the invisible hand, those who pursue their own self-interest in a competitive economy would most effectively promote the public interest. This concept—that the rough-and-tumble of market competition is a potent force for raising output and living standards—is one of the most profound and powerful ideas in history.

265

One of the great achievements of modern economics has been understanding the exact meaning of Adam Smith's argument. Over the last two centuries, economists have refined the notion of "public interest" and today understand its logic and limitations. Efficiency, as economists define it, is a process by which society squeezes the maximum amount of consumer satisfaction out of the available resources. More precisely, **allocative efficiency** (sometimes called **Pareto efficiency,**[1] or just *efficiency* for short) occurs when there is no way to reorganize production or consumption so that it will increase the satisfaction of one person without reducing the satisfaction of another person. Or, to put it another way, an efficient situation is one where no one can be made better off without making someone else worse off.

Today, we know the following:

Under limited conditions, including perfect competition, a market economy will display allocative efficiency, In such a system, the economy as a whole is efficient, and no one can be made better off without making someone else worse off.

This is truly an astounding statement about the power of competition to produce beneficial results. It means that, given the resources and technology of the society, even the most skilled planner cannot come along with a computer or an ingenious reorganization scheme and find a solution superior to the competitive marketplace; no reorganization can make everyone better off. And this result is true whether the economy has one or two or two million competitive markets for goods and factors.

A GENERAL EQUILIBRIUM OF ALL MARKETS

Having stated the fundamental proposition about competitive markets, we will explore the reasons behind this remarkable result. Let's review first what we have learned in earlier chapters about the behavior of individual markets:

1. Competitive supply and demand operate to determine prices and quantities in individual markets.
2. Market demand curves are derived from the marginal utilities of different goods.

3. The marginal costs of different commodities lie behind their competitive supply curves.
4. Firms calculate marginal costs of products and marginal revenue products of factors and then choose inputs and outputs so as to maximize profits.
5. These marginal revenue products, summed for all firms, provide the derived demands for the factors of production.
6. These derived demands for land, labor, or capital goods interact with their market supplies to determine factor prices such as rent, wages, and interest rates.
7. The factor prices and quantities determine incomes, which then close the circle back to steps 1 and 2 by helping to determine the demand for different commodities.

All these statements are the result of **partial-equilibrium analysis,** which involves the behavior of a single market, household, or firm, taking the behavior of all other markets and the rest of the economy as given. In this chapter, we are concerned with **general-equilibrium analysis,** which examines how (and how successfully) all the households, firms, and markets interact simultaneously to solve the questions of *how*, *what*, and *for whom*.

Interaction of All Markets in General Equilibrium

It is the interconnectedness of economic life that makes it so intricate and complex. How was it that a revolution in Iran in 1979 led to a worldwide oil-price increase, lowering the demand for automobiles and causing thousands of steelworkers to lose their jobs? How did the reunification of Germany in 1990 lead to higher interest rates in Germany, thereby producing stagnation in the rest of Europe, and then to a currency crisis and a breakdown of the European Monetary System? These and countless other economic impacts take place through the general-equilibrium interactions of the seven steps outlined above.

Notice how our list of steps follows a logical progression from step to step. The textbook chapters follow in almost the same order. But in real life, which comes first? Is there an orderly sequence that determines prices in single markets on Monday, evaluates consumer preferences on Tuesday, and reckons

---

[1] It is so-called after Vilfredo Pareto (1848–1923), the Italian economist who first proposed the concept.

business costs on Wednesday and marginal products on Thursday? Obviously not. *All these partial-equilibrium processes are going on simultaneously.*

That is not all. These different activities do not go on independently, each in its own little groove, careful not to get in the way of the others. All the processes of supply and demand, of cost and preference, of factor productivity and demand are really different aspects of one vast, simultaneous, interdependent process.

A Circular Flow. Like an invisible web, the markets for inputs and outputs are connected in an interdependent system that we call a general equilibrium. Figure 15-1 depicts the general structure of a general equilibrium. The outer loops show the

FIGURE 15-1. Inputs, Production, Outputs, and Consumption Form the Circular Flow of Economic Life
The general equilibrium of an economy links together the supplies and demands of a vast number of factors and products. Observe how profit-maximizing firms and utility-maximizing households interact in product markets at *A* and in factor markets at *E*. Also, note that the flow of money inside the circular flow moves in the opposite direction from the flow of goods and factors.

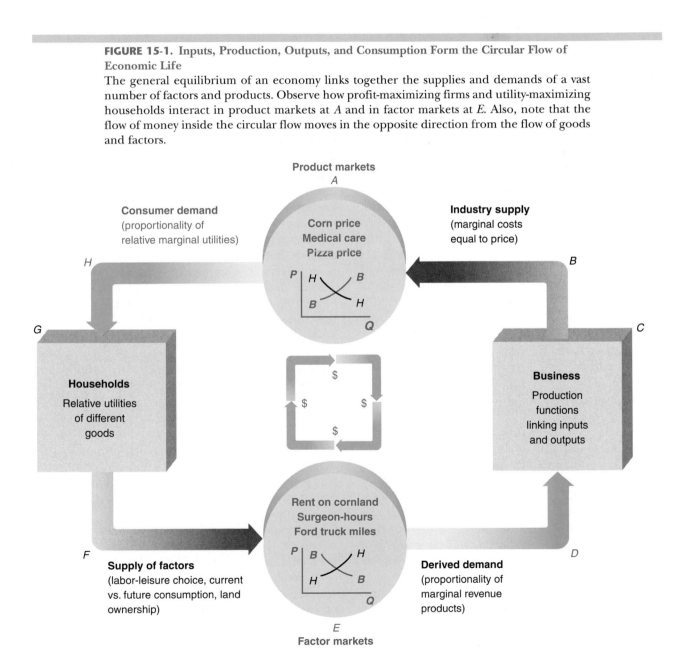

demands and supplies of all goods and factors. We speak here not of a single good or factor but of *all* different products (corn, medical care, pizzas, etc.), which are made by a vast array of factors of production (cornland, surgeons, trucks, etc.).

Each good or factor is exchanged in a market, and the equilibrium of supply and demand determines the price and quantity of the item. That marriage of supply and demand is occurring millions of times every day, for all kinds of commodities from abacuses to zwieback. Note in Figure 15-1 that the upper loop carries the supplies and demands for products, while the lower loop matches it with the supplies and demands for factors of production. See how consumers demand products and supply factors; indeed, households buy their consumption goods with the incomes they earn from the factors they supply. Similarly, businesses buy factors and supply products, paying out factor incomes and profits with the revenues from the products that they sell.

Thus we see a logical structure behind the millions of markets determining prices and outputs: (1) Households, which want to maximize their satisfactions, supply factors and buy products while (2) firms, guided by the lure of profits, transform factors bought from households into products sold to households. The logical structure of a general-equilibrium system is complete.

Properties of a Competitive General Equilibrium

Not surprisingly, analyzing a general-equilibrium system is more complicated than using partial-equilibrium analysis, which deals with only a single market. A general-equilibrium system represents a whole economy, rather than just part of one. It may contain many different kinds of labor, machines, and land, all of which are serving as inputs to produce dozens of different kinds of computers, hundreds of different specifications of automobiles, thousands of different items of clothing, and so on. It contains services like cellular connections, college courses, and vacations to Disneyland, as well as goods like heavy construction equipment, pizzas, and cellular telephones.

How can we possibly know that a competitive market economy is efficient? In answering this question, we proceed as follows: We first describe the assumptions of our general economic equilibrium.

We then describe in a summary fashion the properties of a general equilibrium. Next, in a more technical discussion, we sketch the properties of a general equilibrium in more detail. Finally, we show why a perfectly competitive general equilibrium will be efficient.

The Basic Principles. What assumptions do we make in analyzing a competitive economy? We assume that all markets are perfectly competitive—that is, they are subject to the relentless competition of many buyers and sellers. Each price, whether for an input or an output, moves flexibly enough to equilibrate supply and demand at all times. Firms maximize profits, while consumers choose their most preferred market baskets of goods. Each good is produced under conditions of constant or decreasing returns to scale. No pollution, externalities, entry-limiting regulations, or monopolistic labor unions mar the competitive landscape. Consumers and producers are well informed about prices and economic opportunities. These conditions are obviously an idealized situation. But were such an economy to exist, it would be one in which Adam Smith's invisible hand could rule without any impediment from externalities or imperfect competition.

For this economy, we can describe consumer behavior and producer behavior and then show how they dovetail to produce an overall equilibrium. First, consumers will allocate their incomes across different goods in order to maximize their satisfactions. They choose goods such that the marginal utilities per dollar of expenditure are equal for the last unit of each commodity.

What are the conditions for the profit maximization of producers? In product markets, each firm will set its output level so that the marginal cost of production equals the price of the good. Since this is the case for every good and every firm, it follows that the competitive market price of each good reflects society's marginal cost of that good.

Putting together these two statements yields the conditions for a competitive equilibrium. For each consumer, the marginal utility of consumption for each good is proportional to that good's marginal cost. Hence, the marginal utility per last dollar spent on each good is equalized for every good.

An example will clarify this result. Say that we have two individuals, Ms. Smith and Mr. Ricardo, and two kinds of goods, pizza and clothing. Set the utility scale so that 1 util equals $1.[2] In the consumer equilibrium, Ms. Smith buys pizza and clothing until her *MU* per dollar of each good is 1 (Smith) util. Similarly, Mr. Ricardo distributes his income so that he gets 1 (Ricardo) util per dollar of spending. The pizza and clothing producers set their output levels such that price equals marginal cost, so a dollar-bundle of pizza will have a marginal cost of production of $1 for each producer, as will a dollar-bundle of clothing. If society were to produce one more dollar-bundle of pizza, the cost to society would be exactly 1 dollar's worth of a bundle of scarce labor, land, and capital resources.

Putting these conditions together, we see that each extra dollar of consumption, by either Smith or Ricardo, yields exactly 1 extra util of subjective satisfaction, whether that extra spending is on clothing or on food. Similarly, each extra unit of spending will have a marginal or additional cost to society of 1 extra dollar of resources, and this is so whether that extra dollar is spent by Smith or Ricardo or on food or clothing. *The general equilibrium of markets therefore determines prices and outputs so that the marginal utility of each good to consumers equals the marginal cost of each good to society.*

Detailed Analysis of General Equilibrium[3]

Let us look more closely at the *conditions of a competitive general equilibrium.* These conditions fall naturally into two categories; the first, relating to consumers, corresponds to the upper loop of Figure 15-1 on page 267, while the second, concerning production, corresponds to the lower loop.

1. *Consumer Equilibrium.* Our analysis of consumer behavior in Chapter 5 showed that, when choosing among goods, consumers would maximize their utility by equalizing the marginal utility per

dollar of spending. This rule implies the following condition:

$$\frac{MU_1}{MU_2} = \frac{P_1}{P_2}$$

In words, the ratio of the marginal utilities of two goods is equal to the ratio of their prices. This condition must hold for any individual consumer who buys the two goods in question.

2. *Producer Equilibrium.* The behavior of profit-maximizing firms leads to an analogous but somewhat more complex set of conditions, covered in Chapters 6 through 8. In those chapters we found that competitive firms choose input and output levels as follows:

a. The *output condition* for producers is that the level of output is set so that the price of each good equals the marginal cost of that good. By rearranging terms in this equation, we then find:

$$\frac{MC_1}{MC_2} = \frac{P_1}{P_2}$$

This equation says that, in a competitive economy, the ratio of the marginal costs of two final products is equal to their price ratio. The equality holds for all goods that are produced and for all firms that produce these goods. We can also interpret the ratio of marginal costs as the slope of the production-possibility frontier, which gives the rate at which society can transform one good into another. If a pizza's *MC* is $1 and a haircut's *MC* is $10, then, by transferring resources from barbers to farmers, society can transform one haircut into 10 units of pizza.

The fundamental point to understand about a competitive economy is that the competitive prices reflect social costs or scarcities. We just noted that the ratio of marginal costs tells us the rate at which society can transform one good into another. But because the ratio of marginal costs equals the price ratio, it follows that relative prices reflect the rate at which society can transform one good into another. It is just this essential result—that competitive prices provide an accurate signal of the relative scarcity of different goods—that shows how perfectly competitive markets contribute to allocative efficiency.

---

[2] To simplify the analysis, we have adopted a "money metric" for utility. This means that we adjust our utility yardstick so that the marginal utility of an additional hour of leisure is always constant and has a value of $1. We can then express all prices in these dollar-units of leisure, so a "util" is a unit of utility in this money metric.

[3] This section is relatively technical and can be skipped in short courses.

b. Competition also leads to certain *input conditions* for producers. We have seen that profit-maximizing firms choose the amount of each input so that the value of its marginal product is equal to its price. Hence:

Marginal product of land in good 1
× price of good 1 = rent on land

Marginal product of land in good 2
× price of good 2 = rent on land

Marginal product of labor in good 1
× price of good 1 = wage of labor

and so forth.

These relationships have several important implications. First, because each firm in a given industry faces the same prices for inputs and outputs, the marginal product of input A is the same for each firm in that industry.

By rearranging the terms in the above equations, we can see that the ratio of marginal revenue products of inputs is equal to the ratio of their prices:

$$\frac{\text{Marginal revenue product of land in good 1}}{\text{Marginal revenue product of labor in good 1}} = \frac{\text{price of land}}{\text{price of labor}}$$

In addition, this relationship holds for all firms that use land and labor to produce good 1. Moreover, it holds for all factors of production (capital, oil, unskilled labor, etc.) and for all produced goods.

The input conditions are important because they imply that the ratios of marginal products of factors are the same for all inputs and all firms in all uses. If labor is scarce relative to land in the American southwest, land rents will be low relative to labor wages. The low rent-wage ratio will signal farms to spread their labor thinly across large farms and will lead to large houses, wide roads, and shorter commuting times. In Manhattan, with much higher ratios of land prices to labor wages, we see more high-rise apartments and longer commuting times, and farms are found only in the dreams of rural life.

To summarize:

In competitive general equilibrium, with utility-maximizing consumers and profit-maximizing firms:

- The ratios of marginal utilities of goods for all consumers are equal to the relative prices of those goods.
- The ratios of marginal costs of goods produced by firms are equal to the relative prices of those goods.
- The relative marginal revenue products of all inputs are equal for all firms and all goods and are equal to those inputs' relative prices.

THE EFFICIENCY OF COMPETITIVE MARKETS

Now that we have seen the way a competitive economy allocates resources, we can understand why a competitive economy is efficient.

A general-equilibrium market system will display allocative efficiency when there is perfect competition, with well-informed producers and consumers and no external effects. In such a system, each good's price is equal to its marginal costs and each factor's price is equal to the value of its marginal product. When each producer maximizes profits and each consumer maximizes utility, the economy as a whole is efficient. No one can be made better off without making someone else worse off.

What is the reason for this surprising coincidence between public welfare and private interest? We can easily see the logic by using an example. Suppose some economic wizard comes forth and says, "I have found a way of reorganizing the perfectly competitive economy to make everyone better off. We are producing too few pizzas. Simply give everyone more pizzas and fewer shirts and everyone will be better off."

But the self-proclaimed wizard is mistaken. Suppose the current price of shirts is $15, while the price of pizzas is $5. On the consumer's side, each individual has allocated his or her budget so that the marginal utility of the last pizza is just one-third of the marginal utility of the last shirt. So consumers would certainly not want to have more pizzas and fewer shirts unless they could get more than three pizzas for each shirt given up.

Can the economy squeeze out more than three pizzas for each forgone shirt? Not if it is competitively organized. Under perfect competition, the ratio of the price of shirts to the price of pizzas is the ratio of the marginal costs of the two goods. Hence, if their price ratio is $15/$5 = 3, producers can squeeze out only three more pizzas for each shirt not produced. Indeed, if the production-possibility frontier is bowed out, producers will actually get somewhat less than three pizzas for every shirt forgone.

So we see why our wizard is wrong. Consumers are willing to eat more pizzas and have fewer shirts only if they can improve their satisfactions, which means that they must get more than three pizzas for every shirt forgone. But this is not possible because profit-maximizing producers cannot get more than three pizzas by producing one less shirt. Therefore the proposed reorganization will not improve everybody's economic satisfaction.

The reasoning, of course, extends far beyond pizzas and shirts. With a little thought, you can see that it works as well for all consumer goods. With a little more work, you can even see how it will extend to include reorganizations of inputs and production across firms. And it is easy to see that it would apply to trade among nations as well as trade within a nation.

The basic point to see is that, because prices serve as signals of economic scarcity for producers and social utility for consumers, a competitive price mechanism allows the best mix of goods and services to be produced from a society's resources and technology.

A Graphic Demonstration

These points can be shown neatly using a device known as the *utility-possibility frontier* (or the *UPF*). This curve shows the outer limit of utilities or satisfactions that an economy can attain. Such a concept is very similar in spirit to the production-possibility frontier. The major difference is that the *UPF* places utilities or levels of satisfaction on the two axes, as is shown in Figure 15-2. The *UPF* slopes downward to indicate that, on the frontier, as one person's satisfaction increases, the other person's must decrease.

Note that the *UPF* is drawn somewhat wavy. This shape indicates that the scale of the individual util-

FIGURE 15-2. Efficient Allocations Are on the Utility-Possibility Frontier

Economic efficiency occurs when no one's satisfaction can be improved without hurting someone else. This means that efficient outcomes are on society's utility-possibility frontier (*UPF*). Moving from outcome *A* to outcome *C* improves Smith's welfare only by hurting Jones; both are efficient allocations. Point *B* is inside the *UPF* and is inefficient because Jones, Smith, or both can be made better off without hurting anyone else.

ity measure is arbitrary; however, the inability to measure and compare individual utilities is completely unimportant for analyzing efficiency. All that matters here is that a person's level of satisfaction rises as the utility index increases. Because of this positive relation between utility and desired levels of consumption, we are guaranteed that each person will want to move out as far as possible on his or her utility axis.

Now comes the important point: An efficient economy is one that is on the frontier of its utility-possibility curve. One such efficient (or Pareto-efficient) point is shown at *A* in Figure 15-2. Why is point *A* Pareto-efficient? Because there is no feasible economic reorganization that makes anyone better off without making someone else worse off. We can, of course, move to point *C*. Such a move would certainly delight Smith, whose consumption and satisfaction are increased. But Smith's gain comes only at Jones' expense. When all possible gains to Smith must come at Jones' expense, the economy is on its *UPF* and is operating efficiently.[4]

An economy is efficient when it is on the utility-possibility frontier.

Efficient International Trade

The general principles laid out here can be used to illustrate one of the most important propositions of all economics: the efficiency of free international trade and the harms from tariffs and other trade barriers. A free-trade system is one in which there are no tariffs, quotas, or other barriers to imports and exports. In a free-trade regime, the costs of importing foreign goods would involve only the true marginal costs and not artificial costs imposed by governments to "protect" domestic firms and workers.

International trade is no different from trade within a nation, which means that *in a free-trade situation the world would be on its utility-possibility frontier.* The efficiency of free trade is illustrated in Figure 15-3. We have divided the world into two countries, America and Japan, and have shown the satisfactions of the consumers of the two countries on the two axes. Point *A* represents an efficient, perfectly competitive, free-trade equilibrium.

Now suppose that an American politician enters and says, "We need to protect our automobile and computer workers from unfair competition. Let's limit imports of cars and computer chips." These measures would distort prices and push the economy inside the world *UPF*. If the trade barriers were well crafted, America might improve the economic position of its consumers, say, by moving to point *B* in Figure 15-3. This is clearly a "beggar-thy-neighbor" policy in which America wins at the expense of Japan.

FIGURE 15-3. Free Trade vs. Managed Trade

Free and open international trade among perfectly competitive economies secures the efficient equilibrium at point *A*. If America manages trade through tariffs or other trade barriers, it might move the equilibrium to *B*, which improves America's position at the expense of Japanese consumers. If Japan retaliates or restricts its exports, however, both countries may lose as restrictions on trade raise prices and lower real incomes everywhere at point *C*.

The diagram can also show the gains from trade. Countries with no trade might start at point *C*. After opening economy to free trade, the utilities of both countries must improve, as illustrated by the free-trade point at *A*.

More likely is that the measures will end up hurting both countries. A Japanese bureaucrat might respond by saying, "If you feel threatened by our automobile industry, let us ration out the exports among our firms." The result would be that Japan would in effect exercise market power, raise the prices of its exports, and lower the welfare of American consumers. Another possibility is that Japan might retaliate by putting tariffs on American imports. Such dismal outcomes would be illustrated by point *C*, where interferences with free trade have ended up hurting both countries.

We can also use this discussion to illustrate the gains from trade. The basic idea is that isolated communities or nations can improve their consumption possibilities by engaging in trade with others. Without trade, each group can consume only what it produces.

---

[4] The text discussion has analyzed the first theorem of competitive systems. In addition, a second theorem is the converse of the first theorem. Consider an economy in which preferences and technology are "regular"—that is, one with diminishing marginal utilities of consumption and no increasing returns in production. Under these and a few other conditions, any efficient allocation of resources can be reached by some perfectly competitive equilibrium. Put differently, if the government wishes to reach some particular efficient outcome, such as point *A* in Fig. 15-2, in principle it can do so by redistributing initial incomes (say, by ideal lump-sum taxes and transfers) and then allowing the invisible hand to guide the economy to the desired point. In such regular economies, a combination of efficient income redistribution plus competition is enough to reach any efficient allocation of resources on the *UPF*.

Free international trade allows each country to improve its living standards. The potential improvement in income and consumption from allowing free and open interchange is called the **gains from trade.**

The reason why countries gain from trade is a simple corollary of the efficiency of competitive markets. Boundaries are irrelevant for the invisible-hand principle. In the idealized conditions, competitive markets are efficient in Houston, in Texas, in the United States, in North America, and in the world. The maximum consumption possibilities are attained when there are no interferences with the free flow of products. This point is easily seen in Figure 15-3. Say that point C is the utilities of the two countries without trade. Then borders are opened to free trade. We know that in a competitive economy, the equilibrium must move to the northeast, such as to point A. The difference between points A and C represents the gains from trade.

To summarize:

Under free trade, the world economy can attain its highest consumption and utility levels. The increase in consumption from opening borders to trade is the gains from trade. Interferences with the free international flow of goods push the economy inside its *UPF* and lowers potential consumption.

 Searching for the truth in the invisible-hand doctrine: A careful reader might now ask: "Are you sure that the supply-and-demand equations will lead to a complete and consistent set of supply-and-demand equilibria for all inputs and outputs?" A further question is, "Do we know that a competitive market is efficient?" Although Adam Smith understood the essence of competitive markets more than two centuries ago, it required some of the most powerful minds of mathematics and economics to provide a rigorous answer to these issues.

Economists have pondered these profound questions for almost a century. Léon Walras, a French economist of the nineteenth century, is usually credited with discovery of the theory and equations of general equilibrium. He was, however, unable to provide a rigorous proof that there is an equilibrium of the competitive system. Only in the middle third of the twentieth century was a complete proof of the existence of a competitive equilibrium given, using high-powered mathematical tools such as topology and set theory, by mathematical genius John von Neumann and American Nobel Prize–winning economists Kenneth Arrow and Gerard Debreu. This revolutionary discovery showed that under certain limited conditions there will always exist at least one set of prices that will exactly balance the supplies and demands for all inputs and outputs—even if there are millions of inputs and outputs, in many different regions, and even if goods are produced and sold at different times.

A giant step into the computer age occurred when Herbert Scarf developed the first method of actually calculating a general economic equilibrium—thus giving rise to the new field of computable general-equilibrium models.

The idea of efficiency of a competitive equilibrium was understood in an intuitive way by the physiocrats and Adam Smith. The decisive breakthrough in actually proving the efficiency of competitive economies came first with the introduction of the concept of efficiency by Vilfredo Pareto and then with a rigorous proof of efficiency by Arrow and Debreu. Today, economists tend to emphasize the dynamic advantages of competition—that competition breaks the bread of custom and spurs innovation and the adoption of best-practice technologies. Historical studies point to rapidly growing East Asian countries as examples of how competition not only "gets the prices right" but also leads to robust investment and rapid technological change.

B. QUALIFICATIONS

This chapter has spoken of the remarkable efficiency properties of competitive markets. But be warned: Economies do not live on markets alone. The United States has a mixed economy, which combines private markets with elements of government intervention. Why do market-oriented countries still rely on government interventions? There are two reasons. First, efficiency may be hard to achieve in many real-world situations when pollution or other externalities are present or when there is imperfect competition. Second, the outcomes of competitive markets, even when they are efficient, may not be socially desirable or acceptable.

Let's review, then, the two major qualifications of efficiency of markets: market failures and unacceptable income distribution.

MARKET FAILURES

A number of market failures spoil the idyllic picture assumed in our discussion of efficient markets: imperfect competition, externalities, and imperfect information. We have explored these issues in earlier chapters and will return to them in our analysis of government's role in economic life.

Imperfect Competition. When a firm has market power in a particular market (say it has a monopoly because of a patented drug or a local electricity franchise), the firm can raise the price of its product above its marginal cost. Consumers buy less of such goods than they would under competition, and consumer satisfaction is reduced. This kind of reduction of consumer satisfaction is typical of the inefficiencies created by imperfect competition.

Externalities. A second market failure is externalities. Recall that externalities arise when some of the side effects of production or consumption are not included in market prices. For example, a utility might pump sulfurous fumes into the air, causing damage to neighboring homes and to people's health. If the utility does not pay for these impacts, pollution will be inefficiently high and consumer welfare will suffer.

Not all externalities are harmful. Some are beneficial, such as the externalities that come from knowledge-generating activities. For example, when Chester Carlson invented xerography, he became a millionaire; but he still received only a tiny fraction of the benefits when the world's secretaries and students were relieved of billions of hours of drudgery. Another positive externality arises from public-health programs, such as inoculation against smallpox, cholera, or typhoid; an inoculation protects not

only the inoculated person but also others whom that person might infect.

Imperfect Information. A third important market failure is imperfect information. The invisible-hand theory assumes that buyers and sellers have full information about the goods and services they buy and sell. Firms are assumed to know about all the blueprints for operating in their industry. Consumers are presumed to know about the quality and prices of goods—such as which cars are lemons or the safety and efficacy of pharmaceuticals and angioplasty.

Clearly, reality is far from this idealized world. The critical question is, How damaging are departures from perfect information? In some cases, the loss of efficiency is slight. I will hardly be greatly disadvantaged if I buy a chocolate ice cream that is slightly too sweet or if I don't know the exact temperature of the beer that flows from the tap. In other cases, the loss is severe. Take the case of steel mogul Eben Byers, who early in this century took Radithor, sold as an aphrodisiac and cure-all, to relieve his ailments. Later analysis showed that Radithor was actually distilled water laced with radium. Byers died a hideous death when his jaw and other bones disintegrated. This kind of invisible hand we don't need.

Luckily, few products are as poorly understood as Radithor. One of the important tasks of the government is to identify those areas where informational deficiencies are significant and then to find appropriate remedies.

Economics in a Vacuum?

We have already encountered many examples of market failure or the breakdown of competition. We have seen that wages are often rigid in contrast to the minute-to-minute flexibility of competitive auction prices seeking their equilibria. We have seen that two equally skilled people may work for different wage rates at similar jobs. We have seen how oligopolies and monopolies can restrain quantities to raise prices and profits. In later chapters, we will examine environmental problems like the greenhouse effect and informational deficiencies that muddy the market for medical care.

After reading this list of qualifications, you may wonder about the relevancy of the competitive theory. Taken literally, no one could believe that a perfect and absolutely efficient competitive mechanism has ever existed. But the insights of the competitive theory still retain a great deal of validity.

The perfectly competitive world of the economist is like the frictionless vacuum of the physicist. Even though engineers know that they can never create a perfect vacuum, they still find the analysis of behavior in a vacuum extremely valuable for illuminating many complex problems. So it is with our competitive model. In the long run, many imperfections turn out to be transient as monopolies are eroded by competing technologies. While oversimplified, the competitive model points to many important hypotheses about economic behavior, and these hypotheses appear especially valid in the long run.

Suppose, for example, that a revolution in the Middle East greatly reduces the supply of oil to world markets. Competitive analysis says that the price of oil will rise and that the quantity demanded will fall. Sophisticated analysts of n-person game theory will quarrel with that conclusion, arguing that the world oil market is not perfectly competitive and that no hard-and-fast conclusions can be drawn. But put your money with the competitive model, betting that oil prices will rise in the short run but eventually fall as supply responds, and you will probably end up wealthier than the sophisticated skeptics.

THE DISTRIBUTION OF INCOME

Let us for the moment close our eyes to the many market failures. What do ideal competitive markets mean for the distribution of income? Is there an invisible hand in the marketplace that ensures that the most deserving people will obtain their just rewards? Or that those who toil long hours will receive a decent standard of living? No. In fact, competitive markets do not guarantee that income and consumption will necessarily go to the neediest or most deserving. Rather, the distribution of income and consumption in a market economy reflects initial endowments of inherited talents and wealth along with a variety of factors such as race, gender, location, effort, health, and luck.

Laissez-faire competition might lead to massive inequality, to malnourished children who grow up to produce more malnourished children, and to the perpetuation of inequality of incomes and wealth for generation after generation. Those who

tout the wonders of the market point to the major gains in efficiency that have come with the deregulation, privatization, reduced trade barriers, and decline in unions over the last two decades. *But the movement toward greater market competition has been accompanied by greater inequality of incomes in countries as different as the United States, Sweden, and Russia.* In many "winner-take-all" markets, the rewards have gone predominantly to a tiny group of superstars who won lawsuits, elections, or athletic races by a hair's breadth.

In short, Adam Smith was not wholly justified in asserting that an invisible hand successfully channels individuals who selfishly seek their own interests into promoting the "public interest"—if the public interest includes a fair distribution of income and property. Smith proved nothing of this kind, nor has any economist since 1776.

MARKETS AND ECONOMIC POLICY

We have now concluded our basic analysis of the functioning of markets. In Part Four, we will be confronting some of the major ethical and political issues of modern society. We will consider whether government should impose expensive controls to curb pollution, whether the tax system should redistribute income from rich to poor, and whether the government should override the market in the health-care industry. In examining these issues, we will continue to use the supply-and-demand framework along with the refined analyses of contemporary economists.

But economics cannot have the final word on these controversial problems. For underlying all these issues are normative assumptions and value judgments about what is good and right and just. What an economist does, therefore, is try very hard to keep positive science cleanly separated from normative judgments—to keep a distance between the economic calculations of the head and the human feelings of the heart.

But keeping description separate from prescription does not mean that the professional economist must turn into a bloodless robot. Economists are as divided in their political philosophies as is the rest of the population. Conservative economists argue strenuously for reducing the scope of government and ending programs to redistribute income. Liberal economists are often passionate advocates for extending health coverage to the uninsured or using macroeconomic policies to combat unemployment.

Economic science cannot in the end tell us which political point of view is right or wrong. But it can arm us for the great debate.

SUMMARY

A. The Efficiency of Perfect Competition

1. Under certain conditions, including perfect competition, a market economy will display allocative efficiency. Allocative efficiency (sometimes called Pareto efficiency) signifies that no one person can be made better off without someone else being made worse off.

2. This surprising result can be shown by analyzing the *general equilibrium* of all markets. The general equilibrium of all markets is interrelated in a circular flow by a web of price connections. Households supply factors of production and demand final goods; businesses buy factors of production and transform and sell them as final goods.

3. The central result of general-equilibrium analysis is this: Because prices serve as signals of economic scarcity for producers and social utility for consumers, a competitive price mechanism allows the maximum output and satisfaction to be produced from a society's resources and technology. Under idealized perfect competition, the economy is on both its production-possibility frontier and its utility-possibility frontier.

4. The efficiency of competitive markets can be fruitfully applied to international trade. Free trade allows the world economy to attain the highest consumption and utility levels. The increases in consumption from opening borders to trade are called the gains from trade. Interferences with the free international flow of goods create inefficiency and lower potential consumption.

B. Qualifications

5. There are exacting limits on the conditions under which an efficient competitive equilibrium can be attained: There can be no externalities and no imperfect competition; and consumers and producers must have complete information. The presence of imperfections leads to a breakdown of the *price ratio = marginal cost ratio = marginal utility ratio* conditions, and hence to inefficiency.

6. Even if the ideal conditions for efficient perfect competition were to hold, one major reservation about the outcome of competitive laissez-faire would remain. We have no reason to think that income under laissez-faire will be fairly distributed. The outcome might be one with enormous disparities in income and wealth that persist for generations. In most market economies, governments act to reduce the sting of poverty.

CONCEPTS FOR REVIEW

partial equilibrium vs. general
   equilibrium
allocative (or Pareto) efficiency
utility-possibility frontier (*UPF*)
invisible-hand theory: in Adam
   Smith's doctrine and in today's
   general-equilibrium theory

key conditions in efficient general
   equilibrium:
   *MU*s proportional to *P*s
   *MC*s proportional to *P*s
   ∴ *MU*s proportional to input *MC*s
two theorems about competitive
   economies

gains from international trade
qualifications to the invisible-hand
   doctrine:
   market failures (imperfect
     competition, externalities,
     imperfect information)
   arbitrary distribution of income

QUESTIONS FOR DISCUSSION

1. Summarize how a competitive pricing system solves the three fundamental economic problems.

2. List the qualifications to the invisible-hand theory. Illustrate each qualification with an example from your own experience or reading.

3. List the conditions for competitive general equilibrium described in the text under "Detailed Analysis of General Equilibrium." State each condition in a sentence or two. Explain why monopoly or a pollution externality would lead to a failure of one of these conditions.

4. State carefully the two theorems about competitive economies. How would they apply to the following quotations?

   a. "Perfect competition affords the ideal condition for the distribution of wealth." (Francis Walker, 1892)

   b. "The invisible hand, if it is to be found anywhere, is likely to be found picking the pockets of the poor." (Edward Nell, 1982)

   c. Adam Smith's quotation on the invisible hand (see Chapter 2, page 29).

   d. "Pareto . . . suggested that competition brought about a state in comparison to which no consumer's satisfaction can be made higher, within the limitations of available resources and technological know-how, without at the same time lowering at least one other consumer's satisfaction level." (Tjalling Koopmans, 1957)

   e. "Perfect competition can achieve anything that can be obtained under socialism."

5. The analysis of the efficiency of competitive economies assumes that there is no technological advance. Recall the Schumpeterian hypothesis from Chapter 10. How does this elaboration qualify the view of economic efficiency of the competitive mechanism? What kind of market failure is exemplified by invention? In a world of rapid potential technological advance, use production-possibility curves to illustrate how in the long run an innovative economy with imperfect competition might produce higher consumption than an efficient but technologically stagnant competitive economy.

6. **Advanced problem:** "The second theorem about competitive economies (page 272, footnote 4) means that all the debates about socialism versus capitalism are vacuous. Anything that can be done by ideal, centrally planned socialism can, by the second theorem, be done by competitive markets plus the proper dose of redistributive taxation." Comment on the logic behind this statement. State whether you agree or not, and defend your position.

PART FOUR
GOVERNMENT'S ROLE IN THE ECONOMY

CHAPTER 16
GOVERNMENT TAXATION AND EXPENDITURE

> The spirit of a people, its cultural level, its social structure, the deeds its policy may prepare, all this and more is written in its fiscal history. . . . He who knows how to listen to its messenger here discerns the thunder of world history more clearly than anywhere else.
>
> *Joseph Schumpeter*

The scope of government control over the economy has been a political battleground for centuries. Today, liberals want government to correct flaws in the market mechanism and alleviate social problems for the poor and disadvantaged. Conservatives demand that governments "get off our backs" so that markets can work their miracles in raising everybody's living standards. What are the flaws and social problems that liberals worry about, and is it true that governments can improve things? How can a government of the people, by the people, and for the people be on the backs of the people? These are some of the questions that economic analysis must soberly address in the continuing examination of the government's role in economic life.

Markets have over the last two centuries proved to be a mighty engine for powering the economies of industrial countries. Nonetheless, about a century ago, governments in virtually all countries of Europe and North America began to intervene in economic activity to correct the perceived market failures and imbalances of economic power. The increase of government involvement has brought a vast increase in the influence of the state over economic life, both in the share of national income devoted to transfers and income-support payments and in the legal and regulatory controls over economic activity.

Government encroachment on the private sector has not been continuous; rather, following the cycle of politics, market economies take two steps forward, then one step backward, on the road to greater government involvement. Not too long ago, we witnessed the *reemergence of the market* in both capitalist and socialist countries. The crusade for reduced government involvement, launched during the Reagan and Bush administrations in the United States during 1981–1992, was joined by governments in many other countries. Then, starting in 1993 the Clinton administration attempted to find the "vital center" in which vital government programs were retained while the size of government and the budget deficit were reduced. Throughout, the electorate has remained divided on the proper role of government. Some people want to continue expanding the scope of government; others take up the banner of the conservative revolution and strive to cut taxes and reduce government's role.

As economists, we want to go beyond the partisan debates and analyze the functions of government—government's comparative advantage in the mixed economy. In some countries, such as the former socialist countries that are adopting market systems, government has been withdrawing from much of the economy. At the same time, the major industrialized countries have still been funneling one-third to one-half of their national output into government spending. All countries across the world are grappling to find the appropriate balance between state and market.

The chapters in Part Four, then, are devoted to many of the key issues of our age. The first chapter examines the role of government in an advanced industrialized economy. What are the appropriate goals for economic policy in a market economy, and what instruments are available to carry them out? The chapter then takes a close look at government taxation and spending.

The next chapter investigates the tools that government has to promote vigorous competition: antitrust policies and regulation. Chapter 18 examines the emerging issue of protecting the environment. Finally, Chapter 19 addresses one of the most divisive economic issues where the realities of the market butt heads squarely with the forces of compassion. The unfettered market creates extremes of poverty and deprivation that a humane society wants to cushion. Yet attempts to redistribute income from the rich to the poor reduce some of the incentives that make a market economy thrive. This dilemma lies at the heart of the effort in the United States and other countries to redefine the welfare state.

A. GOVERNMENT CONTROL OF THE ECONOMY

Debates about the role of government often take place on bumper stickers such as "No new taxes" or "Balance the budget." These simplistic phrases cannot capture the serious business of government economic policy. Say the populace decides that it wants to devote more resources to improving public health or reducing famine; or that the country needs to mobilize when the armies of a foreign dictator overrun a friendly country and attack our ships; or that protecting our precious environment for future generations is a key national priority; or that more resources should be devoted to educating the young; or that the rich are getting too large a slice of the national pie and more resources should flow to the poor; or that unemployment in a deep recession should be reduced. The market cannot automatically solve these problems. Each of these objectives can be met if and only if the government changes its taxes, spending, or regulations. The thunder of world history is heard in fiscal policy because taxing and spending are such powerful instruments for social change.

THE TOOLS OF GOVERNMENT POLICY

In a modern industrial economy, no sphere of economic life is untouched by the government. We can identify three major instruments or tools that government uses to influence private economic activity. These are

1. *Taxes* on incomes and goods and services. These reduce private income, thereby reducing private expenditures (on automobiles or restaurant food) and providing resources for public expenditure (on tanks and school lunches). The tax system also serves to discourage certain activities which are taxed more heavily (such as smoking cigarettes) while encouraging lightly taxed sectors (such as owner-occupied housing).
2. *Expenditures* on certain goods or services (such as tanks, education, or police protection), along with *transfer payments* (like social security and health-care subsidies) that provide resources to individuals.
3. *Regulations* or controls that direct people to perform or refrain from certain economic activities. Examples include rules that limit the amount firms can pollute, or that divide up the radio spectrum, or that mandate testing the safety of new drugs.

Fiscal History

When Schumpeter wrote of the thunder of fiscal history, he referred to the drama over government budgets and their impacts on the economy. For more than a century, national income and production have been rising in all industrial economies. At the same time, in most countries, government expenditures have been rising even faster. Each period of emergency—depression, war, or concern over social problems such as poverty or pollution—expanded the activity of government. After the crisis passed, government controls and spending never returned to their previous levels.

Before World War I, the combined federal, state, and local government expenditures or taxation amounted to little more than one-tenth of our entire national income. The war effort during World War II compelled government to consume about half the nation's greatly expanded total output. In the mid-1990s, expenditures of all levels of government in the United States ran around 35 percent of GDP.

Figure 16-1 shows the trend in taxes and expenditures for all levels of government in the United States. The rising curves indicate that the shares of government taxes and spending have grown steadily upward over the course of this century.

Government's expansion has not occurred without opposition; each new spending and tax program provoked a fierce reaction. For example, when social security was first introduced in 1935, opponents denounced it as an ominous sign of socialism. But with the passage of time, political attitudes evolve. The "socialistic" social security system was defended by conservative President Ronald Reagan in the 1980s as part of the "safety net." The radical doctrines of one era become accepted gospel of the next.

Figure 16-2 on page 284 shows how government spending as a percent of GDP varies among countries. High-income countries tend to tax and spend a larger fraction of GDP than do poor countries. Can we discern a pattern among wealthy countries? Within the high-income countries, no simple law relating tax burdens and the citizenry's well-being

FIGURE 16-1. Government's Share of the Economy Has Grown Sharply in This Century

Government expenditures include spending on goods, services, and transfers at the federal, state, and local levels. Note how spending grew rapidly during wartime but did not return to prewar levels afterward. The difference between spending and taxes is the government deficit or surplus. (Source: U.S. Department of Commerce.)

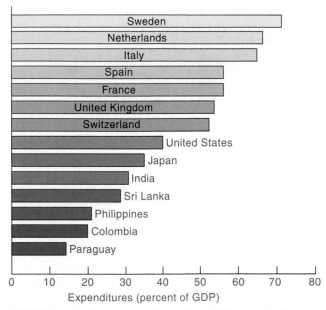

FIGURE 16-2. Government Spending Is Highest in High-Income Lands

Governments of poor countries tax and spend relatively little of national income. With affluence come greater demands for public goods and redistributional taxation to aid low-income families. (Source: International Monetary Fund.)

can do justice to the true diversity of the fiscal facts of nations.[1] For example, financing for the education and health-care systems, two of the largest components of government spending, is organized very differently across countries.

The Growth of Government Controls and Regulation

The increase in collective expenditures is only part of the story. In addition to the rapid growth in spending and taxing, there has also been a vast

expansion in the laws and regulations governing economic affairs.

Nineteenth-century America came as close as any economy has come to being a pure laissez-faire society—the system that the British historian Thomas Carlyle labeled "anarchy plus the constable." This philosophy permitted people great personal freedom to pursue their economic ambitions and produced a century of rapid material progress. But critics saw many flaws in this laissez-faire idyll. Historians record periodic business crises, extremes of poverty and inequality, deep-seated racial discrimination, and poisoning of water, land, and air by pollution. Muckrakers and progressives called for a bridle on capitalism so that the people could steer this wayward beast in more humane directions.

Beginning in the 1890s, the United States gradually turned away from the belief that "government governs best which governs least." Presidents Theodore Roosevelt, Woodrow Wilson, Franklin Roosevelt, and Lyndon Johnson—in the face of strenuous opposition—pushed out the boundaries of federal control over the economy, devising new regulatory and fiscal tools to combat the ailments of the day.

Constitutional powers of government were interpreted broadly and used to "secure the public interest" and to "police" the economic system. In 1887, the federal Interstate Commerce Commission (ICC) was established to regulate rail traffic across state boundaries. Soon afterward, the Sherman Antitrust Act and other laws were aimed against monopolistic combinations in "restraint of trade."

During the 1930s, a whole set of industries came under *economic regulation*, in which government sets the prices, conditions of exit and entry, and safety standards. Regulated industries since that time have included the airlines, trucking, and barge and water traffic; electric, gas, and telephone utilities; financial markets; and oil and natural gas, as well as pipelines.

In addition to regulating the prices and standards of business, the nation attempted to protect health and safety through increasingly stringent *social regulation*. Following the revelations of the muckraking era of the early 1900s, pure food and drug acts were passed. During the 1960s and 1970s, Congress passed a series of acts that regulated mine safety and then worker safety more generally; regulated air and water pollution; authorized safety standards for automobiles and consumer products; and

---

[1] Figs. 16-1 and 16-2 show the total expenditures of governments. Such expenditures include purchases of goods and services (like missiles and teachers) as well as transfer payments (like social security payments and interest on the government debt). Purchases of goods and services are called "exhaustive" because they make a direct claim upon the production of a country; transfer payments, by contrast, increase people's income and allow individuals to purchase goods and services but do not directly reduce the quantity of goods and services available for private consumption and investment.

regulated strip mining, nuclear power, and toxic wastes. More recent legislation was aimed at reducing the threats to the international environment from ozone-depleting chemicals.

Over the last two decades, the tide of government economic regulation has ebbed. Economists argued persuasively that many economic regulations were impeding competition and keeping prices up rather than down. Indeed, the first major federal regulatory agency, the Interstate Commerce Commission, was abolished shortly after its hundredth birthday. In the area of social regulations, economists have emphasized the need to ensure that the benefits of regulations outweigh their costs.

Still, there is no likelihood of a return to the laissez-faire era. When conservative Republicans captured Congress in 1994, they attempted to roll back the welfare state and many environmental laws. They did succeed in ending the entitlement to welfare benefits by poor families. In other areas, such as the attempt to dismantle environmental laws, they retreated after a storm of popular protest. Government constraints have changed the very nature of capitalism. Private property is less and less wholly private. Free enterprise has become progressively less free. Irreversible evolution is part of history.

THE FUNCTIONS OF GOVERNMENT

We are beginning to get a picture of how government directs and interacts with the economy. What are the appropriate economic goals for government action in a modern mixed economy? Let's examine the four major functions:

1. Improving economic efficiency
2. Improving the distribution of income
3. Stabilizing the economy through macroeconomic policies
4. Conducting international economic policy

Improving Economic Efficiency

A central economic purpose of government is to assist in the socially desirable allocation of resources. This is the *microeconomic* side of government policy; it concentrates on the *what* and *how* of economic life. Microeconomic policies differ among countries according to customs and political philosophies. Some countries emphasize a hands-off, laissez-faire approach, leaving most decisions to the market. Other countries lean toward heavy government regulation, or even ownership of businesses, in which production decisions are made by government planners.

The United States is fundamentally a market economy. On any microeconomic issue, most people presume that the market will solve the economic problem at hand. But sometimes there is good reason for government to override the allocational decisions of market supply and demand.

The Limits of the Invisible Hand. Chapter 15 explained how the invisible hand of perfect competition would lead to an efficient allocation of resources. But this invisible-hand result holds only under very limited conditions. All goods must be produced efficiently by perfectly competitive firms. All goods must be private goods like loaves of bread, the total of which can be cut up into separate slices of consumption for different individuals, so that the more I consume out of the total, the less you consume. There can be no externalities like air pollution. Consumers and firms must be fully informed about the prices and characteristics of the goods they buy and sell.

If all these idealized conditions were met, the invisible hand could provide perfectly efficient production and distribution of national output, and there would be no need for government intervention to promote efficiency.

Yet even in this case, if there were to be a division of labor among people and regions, and if a price mechanism were to work, government would have an important role. Courts and police forces would be needed to ensure fulfillment of contracts, nonfraudulent and nonviolent behavior, freedom from theft and external aggression, and the legislated rights of property.

Inescapable Interdependencies. Laissez-faire with minimal government intervention might be a good system if the idealized conditions listed above were truly present. In reality, each and every one of the idealized conditions enumerated above is violated to some extent in all human societies. Most production takes place in units too large for truly perfect competition. Unregulated factories do tend to pollute the air, water, and land. Often, contagious diseases break out and private markets have little incentive to develop effective public-health programs. Consumers are sometimes poorly informed about the characteristics of the goods they buy. The market is not ideal. There are market failures.

In other words, government often deploys its weapons to correct important market failures, of which the most important are the following:

- *The breakdown of perfect competition.* When monopolies or oligopolies collude to reduce rivalry or drive firms out of business, government may apply antitrust policies or regulation.
- *Externalities and public goods.* The unregulated market may produce too much air pollution and too little investment in public health or knowledge. As we will see in Chapter 18, government may use its influence to control harmful externalities or to fund programs in science and public health. Government can levy taxes on activities which impose external public costs (such as cigarette smoking), or it can subsidize activities which are socially beneficial (such as education or prenatal health care).
- *Imperfect information.* Unregulated markets tend to provide too little information for consumers to make well-informed decisions. In an earlier era, hucksters hawked snake oil remedies that would just as easily kill you as cure you. This led to food and drug regulations that require pharmaceutical companies to provide extensive data on the safety and efficacy of new drugs before they can be sold. Because of inadequate information, the government requires companies to provide information on energy efficiency of major household appliances like refrigerators and water heaters. In addition, government may use its spending power to collect and provide needed information itself, as it does with automobile crash-and-safety data.

Clearly, there is much on the agenda of possible allocational problems for government to handle.

Improving the Distribution of Income

Even when the invisible hand works and is marvelously efficient, it may at the same time produce a very unequal distribution of income. Under laissez-faire, people end up rich or poor depending on their inherited wealth, on their talents and efforts, on their luck in finding oil or owning land in the right place, and on their gender or the color of their skin. To some people, the distribution of income arising from unregulated competition looks as arbitrary as the Darwinian distribution of food and plunder among animals in the jungle.

In the poorest societies, there is little excess income to take from the better-off and provide to the unfortunate. But as societies become more affluent, they can devote more resources to providing services for poor people; this activity—income redistribution—is the second major economic function of government. The welfare states of North America and Western Europe now devote a significant share of their revenues to maintaining minimum standards of health, nutrition, and income.

Income redistribution is usually accomplished through taxation and spending policies, though regulation sometimes plays a role as well. Most advanced countries now rule that children shall not go hungry because of the economic circumstances of their parents; that the poor shall not die because of insufficient money for needed medical care; that the young shall receive free public education; and that the old shall be able to live out their years with a minimum level of income. In the United States, these government activities are provided primarily by transfer programs, such as food stamps, Medicaid, and social security.

But attitudes about redistribution evolve as well. With rising tax burdens and government budget deficits, along with rising costs of income-support programs, taxpayers increasingly resist redistributive programs and progressive taxation. Sweden, which took the welfare state to its extreme and collects 70 percent of national income as taxes, is today struggling to trim spending while maintaining the most important redistributive programs.

Stabilizing the Economy Through Macroeconomic Policies

Early capitalism was prone to financial panics and bouts of inflation and depression, and the traumatic memory of the Great Depression of the 1930s is still vivid among older Americans. Today government has the responsibility of preventing such calamitous business depressions by the proper use of monetary and fiscal policy, as well as close regulation of the financial system. In addition, government tries to smooth out the ups and downs of the business cycle, in order to avoid either large-scale unemployment at the bottom of the cycle or raging price inflation at the top of the cycle. More recently, government has become concerned with finding economic policies which boost long-term economic growth. These questions are considered at length in the branch of economics called macroeconomics.

Conducting International Economic Policy

In recent years, international trade and finance have become far more important to the United States than they were in the past. Government now plays a critical role representing the interests of the nation on the international stage and negotiating beneficial agreements with other countries on a wide range of issues. We can group the international issues of economic policy into four main areas:

- *Reducing trade barriers.* An important part of economic policy involves harmonizing laws and reducing trade barriers so as to encourage fruitful international specialization and division of labor. In recent years, nations have negotiated a series of trade agreements to lower tariffs and other trade barriers on agricultural products, manufactured goods, and services (recall from Chapter 15 how competitive free trade puts countries on the world utility-possibility frontier).

    Such agreements are often contentious. They sometimes harm certain groups, as when removing textile tariffs reduces employment in that industry. In addition, international agreements may require giving up national sovereignty as the price of raising incomes. Suppose that one country's laws protect intellectual property rights, such as patents and copyrights, while another country's laws allow free copying of books, videos, and software. Whose laws shall prevail?

- *Conducting assistance programs.* Rich nations have numerous programs designed to improve the lot of the poor in other countries. These involve direct foreign aid, disaster and technical assistance, the establishment of institutions like the World Bank to give low-interest-rate loans to poor countries, and concessionary terms on exports to poor nations.

- *Coordinating macroeconomic policies.* Nations have found that their increased economic interdependence means that macroeconomic policies must be coordinated to combat inflation and unemployment. Exchange rates (which are the relative prices of the currencies of different nations) do not manage themselves; establishing a smoothly functioning exchange-rate system is a prerequisite for efficient international trade. Nations have seen that fiscal and monetary policies of other nations can affect domestic economic conditions. When the United States raised interest rates to fight inflation in 1979, the tight money led to a world recession and an international debt crisis in the 1980s. Particularly in tightly integrated regions, like Western Europe, countries work to coordinate their fiscal, monetary, and exchange-rate policies, or even adopt a common currency, so that inflation or unemployment in one country does not spill over to hurt the entire area.

- *Protecting the global environment.* The most recent facet of international economic policy is to work with other nations to protect the global environment in cases where several countries contribute to or are affected by spillovers. The most active areas historically have been protecting fisheries and water quality in rivers. More recently, as scientists have raised concerns about ozone depletion, deforestation, global warming, and species extinction, nations have begun to consider ways to protect our global resources. Clearly, international environmental problems can be resolved only through the cooperation of many nations.

Even the staunchest conservatives agree that government has a major role to play in representing the national interest in the anarchy of nations.

PUBLIC-CHOICE THEORY

For the most part, our analysis has concentrated on the *normative* theory of government—on the appropriate policies that the government *should follow* to increase the welfare of the population. But economists are not starry-eyed about the government any more than they are about the market. Governments can make bad decisions or carry out good ideas badly. Indeed, just as there are market failures such as monopoly and pollution, so are there "government failures" in which government interventions lead to waste or redistribute income in an undesirable fashion.

These issues are the domain of **public-choice theory,** which is the branch of economics and political science that studies the way that governments make decisions. Public-choice theory examines the way different voting mechanisms can function and shows that there are no ideal mechanisms to sum up individual preferences into social choices. This approach also analyzes government failures, which arise when state actions fail to improve economic efficiency or when the government redistributes income unfairly. Public-choice theory points to issues such as short time horizons of elected representatives, the lack of a hard budget constraint, and the role of money in financing elections as sources of government failures. A careful study of government failures is crucial for understanding the limitations of government and ensuring that government programs are not excessively intrusive or wasteful.

 The economics of politics: Since the time of Adam Smith, economists have focused most of their energy on understanding the workings of the marketplace. But serious thinkers have also pondered the government's role in society. Joseph Schumpeter pioneered public-choice theory in *Capitalism, Socialism, and Democracy* (1942), and Kenneth Arrow's Nobel Prize–winning study on social choice brought mathematical rigor to this field. The landmark study by Anthony Downs, *An Economic Theory of Democracy* (1957), sketched a powerful new theory which held that politicians set economic policies in order to be reelected. Downs showed how parties tend to move toward the center of the political spectrum, and he posed the "voting paradox," which holds that it is irrational for people to vote given the small likelihood of any individual's affecting the outcome.

Further studies by James Buchanan and Gordon Tullock in *The Calculus of Consent* (1959) defended checks and balances and advocated the use of unanimity in political decisions—arguing that unanimous decisions do not coerce anyone and therefore impose no costs. For this and other works, Buchanan received the Nobel Prize in 1986. Public-choice economics received careful study by conservative politicians during the early 1980s. It was applied to such areas as farm policy, regulation, and the courts, and it formed the theoretical basis for a proposed constitutional amendment to balance the budget.

B. GOVERNMENT EXPENDITURES

Nowhere can the changes in government's role be seen more clearly than in the area of government spending. Look back at Figure 16-1 on page 283. It shows the share of national output going for government spending, which includes things like purchases of goods, salaries of government workers, social security and other transfers, and interest on the government debt. You can see that government's share has been steadily rising for the last 60 years, with temporary bulges during wartime.

FISCAL FEDERALISM

While we have been referring to government as if it were a single entity, in fact Americans face three levels of government: federal, state, and local. This reflects a division of fiscal responsibilities among the different levels of government—a system known as *fiscal federalism.* The boundaries are not always clear-cut, but in general the federal government directs activities that concern the entire nation—paying for defense, space, and foreign affairs. Local governments educate children, police streets, and remove garbage. States build highways, run university systems, and administer welfare programs.

The amounts of spending by the different government levels are shown in Table 16-1. The dominance of the federal role is a comparatively recent phenomenon. Before the twentieth century, local government was by far the most important of the three levels. The federal government did little more than support the military, pay interest on the national debt, and finance a few public works. Most of its tax collection came from liquor and

Level of government	Total spending, 1994* ($, billion)
Federal	1,412
State	550
Local (including counties)	710

*Outlays exclude transfers to lower levels.

TABLE 16-1. Government Spending at Different Levels

In the early days of the Republic, most spending was at the state and local levels. Today, more than half of total government outlays are federal. (Source: Bureau of the Census.)

tobacco excises and import tariffs. But the combination of two hot world wars and one cold war—along with the rise of transfer programs such as social security and Medicare—boosted spending, while the advent of the national income tax in 1913 provided a source of funds that no state or locality could match.

To understand fiscal federalism, economists emphasize that spending decisions should be allocated among the levels of government according to the spillovers from government programs. In general, localities are responsible for *local public goods*, activities whose benefits are largely confined to local residents. Since libraries are used by townspeople and streetlights illuminate city roads, decisions about these goods are appropriately made by local residents. Many federal functions are *national public goods*, which provide benefits to all the nation's citizens. For example, an AIDS vaccine would benefit people from every state, not just those living near the laboratory where it is discovered; similarly, when the U.S. Army waged war in the Persian Gulf, oil supplies were protected for the entire country. What about global public goods like protecting the ozone layer or slowing global warming? These are *international public goods* because they transcend the boundaries of individual countries.

An efficient system of fiscal federalism takes into account the way the benefits of public programs spill over political boundaries. The most efficient arrangement is to locate the tax and spending decisions so that the beneficiaries of programs pay the taxes and can weigh the tradeoffs.

Federal Expenditures

Let's look now at the different levels of government. The U.S. government is the world's biggest enterprise. It buys more automobiles and steel, meets a bigger payroll, and handles more money

TABLE 16-2. Federal Spending Is Dominated by Defense and Entitlement Programs

About one-third of federal spending is for defense and interest or pensions due to past wars. More than half today is for rapidly growing entitlement programs—income security, social security, and health. Note how small is item 10's traditional cost of government. (Source: Office of Management and Budget, *Budget of the U.S. Government, Fiscal Year 1998.*)

Federal Expenditures, Fiscal Year 1998	Budget ($, billion)	Percentage of total
1. Social security	384.3	22.8
2. National defense, veterans, and international affairs	315.3	18.7
3. Health and Medicare	345.3	20.5
4. Income security	247.5	14.7
5. Interest on government debt	249.9	14.8
6. Education, training, employment, and social service	56.2	3.3
7. Transportation, commerce, and housing	42.6	2.5
8. Energy, natural resources, and environment	24.6	1.5
9. Science, space, and technology	16.5	1.0
10. General government	12.9	0.8
11. Agriculture	12.3	0.7
12. Miscellaneous and offsetting receipts	−19.9	−1.2
Total	**1,687.5**	**100.0**

than any other organization anywhere. The numbers involved in federal finance are astronomical—in the billions and trillions of dollars. The federal budget for 1998 is projected to be in the neighborhood of $1.7 trillion; this enormous number amounts to roughly $6300 for each American or approximately 2.5 months of total national output (gross domestic product, or GDP).

Table 16-2 on page 289 lists the major categories of federal expenditure for fiscal year 1998. (The federal fiscal year 1998 covers October 1, 1997, through September 30, 1998.)

The most rapidly expanding items in the last two decades have been *entitlement programs*, which provide benefits or payments to any persons who meet certain eligibility requirements set down by law. The major entitlements are social security (old-age, survivors, and disability insurance), health programs (including Medicare for those over 65 and Medicaid for indigent families), and income security programs (including subsidies for food and unemployment insurance). In fact, virtually the entire growth in federal spending in recent years can be

accounted for by entitlement programs, which increased from 28 percent of the budget in 1960 to 59 percent in 1994.

State and Local Expenditures

Although the battles over the federal budget command the headlines, state and local units provide many of the essential functions in today's economy. Figure 16-3 illustrates the way states and localities spend their money. By far the largest item is education because most of the nation's children are educated in schools financed primarily by local governments. By attempting to equalize the educational resources available to every child, public education helps level out the otherwise great disparities in economic opportunity.

In recent years, the fastest-growing categories of spending for states and localities have been health care and prisons. In the 1980s the number of prisoners in state prisons tripled, as the United States fought a war on crime partly by using longer prison sentences, especially for drug offenders. At the same time, state and local governments were forced to absorb their share of rising health-care costs.

CULTURAL AND TECHNOLOGICAL IMPACTS

Government programs have subtle impacts on the country beyond the dollar spending. The federal government has changed the landscape through the interstate highway system. By making automotive travel much faster, this vast network lowered transportation costs, displaced the railroads, and brought goods to every corner of the country. It also helped accelerate urban sprawl and the growth of the suburban culture. Similarly, the social security system, by raising the income of senior citizens, gave older Americans the financial ability to pick up roots and move. Thus were created retirement havens in Florida and Arizona.

The government has put the United States on the map in many areas of science and technology. Government support gave a powerful running start to the budding U.S. electronics industries. The development of the transistor by Bell Labs, for example, was partially funded by the U.S. military, anxious for better radar and communications. And accord-

FIGURE 16-3. State and Local Governments Concentrate on Local Public Goods

State and local programs include providing education, financing hospitals, and maintaining the streets. In the division of labor among governments, cities pave their streets and states construct highways between cities, while the federal government pays for 90 percent of interstate highways. Do you see a pattern of fiscal federalism here? (Source: U.S. Bureau of the Census, *Government Finances in 1989–1990.*)

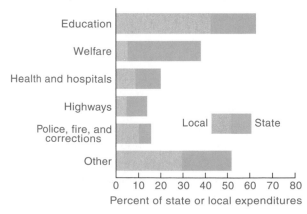

ing to some economists, the government's role went much further:

> It was not just R&D grants that greased the electronics industries' wheels, but the prospect of ensured government markets. *All* of the early semiconductor production of Western Electric, Bell's manufacturing affiliate, went to military shipments. From 1956 to 1964, the Pentagon consumed over 70 percent of the industry's output, particularly in the Minuteman missile program.[2]

Today's healthy computer and airplane industries were boosted in their early years by strong government support.

Because of the weight of its spending power, the government has an enormous voice in the development of science and technology. Throughout the 1980s and early 1990s, federal funds have continued to support about half of all research and development. In recent years, federal funding for health-care research has more than doubled, helping spawn the booming biotechnology industry. Often, if you follow a successful invention upstream to its source, you will find that government subsidized the education, supported basic university research in biology or physics, and purchased prototype versions for defense. Economic studies indicate that these funds were well spent, moreover, for the rates of return to education and research are estimated to compare favorably with those in other areas.

C. ECONOMIC ASPECTS OF TAXATION

Taxes are what we pay for a civilized society.

Justice Oliver Wendell Holmes

Governments must pay for their programs. The funds come mainly from taxes, and any shortfall is a deficit that is borrowed from the public.

But in economics we always need to pierce the veil of monetary flows to understand the flow of real resources. Behind the dollar flows of taxes, what the government really needs is the economy's scarce land, labor, and capital. When the nation fights a war in the desert, it appears to tax and borrow to pay for the war; but what really happens is that people are diverted from their civilian jobs, airplanes transport troops rather than tourists, and oil goes to tanks rather than cars. When the government gives out a grant for biotechnology research, its decision really means that a piece of land that might have been used for an office building is now being used for a laboratory.

In taxing, government is in reality deciding how to draw the required resources from the nation's households and businesses for public purposes. The money raised through taxation is the vehicle by which real resources are transferred from private goods to collective goods.

PRINCIPLES OF TAXATION

Benefit vs. Ability-to-Pay Principles

Once the government has decided to collect some amount of taxes, it has a bewildering array of possible taxes available to it. It can tax income, tax profits, or tax sales. It can tax the rich or tax the poor, tax the old or tax the young. Are there any guidelines that can help construct a fair and efficient tax system?

Indeed there are. Economists and political philosophers have proposed two major principles for organizing a tax system:

- The **benefit principle,** which holds that different individuals should be taxed in proportion to the benefit they receive from government programs. Just as people pay private dollars in proportion to their consumption of private bread, a person's

---

[2] Ann Markusen and Joel Yudken, *Dismantling the Cold War Economy* (Basic, New York, 1992), p. 48.

taxes should be related to his or her use of collective goods like public roads or parks.
- The **ability-to-pay principle,** which states that the amount of taxes people pay should relate to their income or wealth. The higher the wealth or income, the higher the taxes. Usually tax systems organized along the ability-to-pay principle are also *redistributive*, meaning that they raise funds from higher-income people to increase the incomes and consumption of poorer groups.

For instance, if the construction of a new bridge is funded by tolls on the bridge, that's a reflection of the benefit principle, since you pay for the bridge only if you use it. But if the bridge is funded out of income-tax collections, that would be an example of the ability-to-pay principle.

Horizontal and Vertical Equity

Whether they are organized along benefit or ability-to-pay lines, most modern tax systems also attempt to incorporate modern views about fairness or equity. One important principle is that of **horizontal equity,** which states that those who are essentially equal should be taxed equally.

The notion of equal treatment of equals has deep roots in Western political philosophy. If you and I are alike in every way except the color of our eyes, all principles of taxation would hold that we should pay equal taxes. In the case of benefit taxation, if we receive exactly the same services from the highways or parks, the principle of horizontal equity states that we should therefore pay equal taxes. Or if a tax system follows the ability-to-pay approach, horizontal equity dictates that people who have equal incomes should pay the same taxes.

A more controversial principle is **vertical equity,** which concerns the tax treatment of people with different levels of income. Abstract philosophical principles provide little guidance in resolving the issues of fairness here. Imagine that A and B are alike in every respect except that B has 10 times the property and income of A. Does that mean that B should pay the same absolute tax dollars as A for government services such as police protection? Or that B should pay the same percentage of income in taxes? Or, since the police spend more time protecting the property of well-to-do B, is it perhaps fair for B to pay a larger fraction of income in taxes?

Be warned that general and abstract principles cannot determine the tax structure for a nation. When Ronald Reagan campaigned for lower taxes, he did so because he thought high taxes were unfair to those who had worked hard and saved for the future. A decade later, Bill Clinton said, "We now have real fairness in the tax code with over 80 percent of the new tax burden being borne by those who make over $200,000 a year." What looks fair to the goose seems foul to the gander.

Pragmatic Compromises in Taxation

How have societies resolved these thorny philosophical questions? Governments have generally adopted pragmatic solutions that are only partially based on benefit and ability-to-pay approaches. Political representatives know that taxes are highly unpopular. After all, the cry of "taxation without representation" helped launch the American Revolution. Modern tax systems are an uneasy compromise between lofty principles and political pragmatism. As the canny French finance minister Colbert wrote three centuries ago, "Raising taxes is like plucking a goose: you want to get the maximum number of feathers with the minimum amount of hiss."

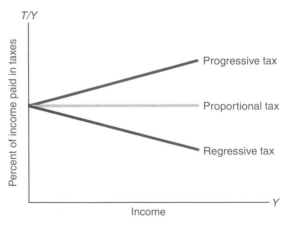

FIGURE 16-4. Progressive, Proportional, and Regressive Taxes

Taxes are progressive if they take a larger fraction of income as income rises; proportional if they are a constant fraction of income; and regressive if they place a larger relative burden on low-income families than on high-income families.

What practices have emerged? Often, public services primarily benefit recognizable groups, and those groups have no claim for special treatment by virtue of their average incomes or other characteristics. In such cases, modern governments generally rely on benefit taxes.

Thus, local roads are usually paid for by local residents. "User fees" are charged for water and sewage treatment, which are treated like private goods. Taxes collected on gasoline may be devoted (or "earmarked") to roads.

Progressive and Regressive Taxes.

Benefit taxes are a declining fraction of government revenues. Today, advanced countries rely heavily on **progressive income taxes.** With progressive taxes, a family with $50,000 of income is taxed more than one with $20,000 of income. Not only does the higher-income family pay a larger income tax, but it in fact pays a higher fraction of its income.

This progressive tax is in contrast to a strictly **proportional tax,** in which all taxpayers pay exactly the same proportion of income. A **regressive tax** takes a larger fraction of income in taxes from poor families than it does from rich families.

A tax is called *proportional, progressive,* or *regressive* depending on whether it takes from high-income people the same fraction of income, a larger fraction of income, or a smaller fraction of income than it takes from low-income people.[3]

The different kinds of taxes are illustrated in Figure 16-4. What are some examples? A personal income tax that is graduated to take more and more out of each extra dollar of income is progressive. A cigarette tax is regressive because spending on cigarettes takes a larger fraction of income from low-income groups.

Direct and Indirect Taxes.

Taxes are classified as direct or indirect. **Indirect taxes** are ones that are levied on goods and services and thus only "indirectly" on individuals. Examples are excise and sales taxes, cigarette and gasoline taxes, tariff duties on imports, and property taxes. By contrast, **direct taxes** are levied directly upon individuals or firms. Examples of direct taxes are personal income taxes, social security or other payroll taxes, and inheritance and gift taxes. Direct taxes have the advantage of being easier to tailor to fit personal circumstances, such as size of family, income, age, and more generally the ability to pay. By contrast, indirect taxes have the advantage of being cheaper and easier to collect, since they can be taxed at the retail or wholesale level.

FEDERAL TAXATION

Let us now try to understand the principles by which the federal system of taxation is organized. Table 16-3 provides an overview of the major taxes collected by the federal government and shows whether they are progressive, proportional, or regressive.

The Individual Income Tax

Our discussion will concentrate on the individual income tax, which is the most complex and controversial part of the tax system. The income tax is a direct tax, and it is the tax which most clearly reflects the ability-to-pay principle.

The individual income tax arrived late in our nation's history. The Constitution forbade any direct

---

TABLE 16-3. Income and Payroll Taxes Are the Main Federal Revenue Sources

Progressive taxes are still the leading source of federal revenues, but proportional payroll taxes are closing fast. (Source: Office of Management and Budget, *Budget of the U.S. Government, Fiscal Year 1998.*)

Federal Tax Receipts, Fiscal Year 1998	Receipts (% of total)
Progressive:	
Individual income taxes	44.1
Death and gift taxes	1.2
Corporate income taxes	12.1
Proportional:	
Payroll taxes	35.6
Regressive:	
Excise taxes	3.9
Other taxes and receipts	3.1
Total	**100.0**

---

[3] It should be noted that the words "progressive" and "regressive" are technical economic terms relating to the proportions that taxes bear to different incomes.

tax that was not apportioned among the states according to population. This was changed in 1913, when the Sixteenth Amendment to the Constitution provided that "Congress shall have power to lay and collect taxes on income, from whatever source derived."

How does the federal income tax work? The principle is simple, although the forms are complicated. You start by calculating your income; you next subtract certain expenses, deductions, and exemptions, to obtain taxable income. You then calculate your taxes on the basis of your taxable income.

Table 16-4 shows a calculation of individual taxes for a family of four at different levels of income. Column (1) shows different levels of *adjusted gross income*—that is, wages, interest, dividends, and other income earned by the household. Assuming that our household has four people and takes certain deductions, column (2) shows the tax due. Note that the tax is negative for those with wage incomes of $5000, $10,000, and $20,000 because of the *earned-income tax credit*; in this income range, the government is actually transferring income to low-income families.

Column (3) shows the **effective** or **average tax rate,** which is equal to total taxes divided by total income. From this calculation, we see just how progressive the personal-income-tax code really is. A $50,000-a-year family is made to bear a relatively heavier burden than a $20,000-a-year family—the former pays 9 percent of income in taxes, while the latter has a negative rate of minus 2 percent. Someone earning $1 million each year is made to bear a still heavier relative burden.

Column (4) introduces a new and significant concept. The **marginal tax rate** is the extra tax that is paid per dollar of additional income. We have met the term "marginal" before, and it always means "extra." If you must pay $30 of additional taxes for every $100 of extra income, your marginal tax rate is 30 percent. Under current law, the marginal tax rate is minus 34 percent for poor families and rises to 15 percent for those just entering the positive tax system.

For incomes above $250,000, the marginal tax rate from the federal income tax is about 41 percent. If you live in New York City, you would add 8 percent for New York state and city taxes and 2.5 percent of health insurance for a total marginal tax rate on labor earnings of close to 50 percent. This may seem like a high rate, but the top rate today is far below the top rate of 94 percent during World

TABLE 16-4. Federal Income Tax for a Family of Four, 1996

The table shows incomes, taxes, and tax rates for a representative family of four in 1996. Because of the earned-income tax credit, low-income workers get a tax rebate—this is a "negative income tax" on wages. Marginal tax rates are initially negative, are zero at around $10,000 of income, then rise to 41 percent of income for top taxpayers. Average or effective rates are always less than marginal rates because the income tax is progressive. (Source: Derived from *TurboTax* computerized tax program. Table assumes that deductions are the greater of the standard deduction or 20 percent of income.)

(1) Adjusted gross income (before exemptions and deductions) ($)	(2) Individual income tax ($)	(3) Average tax rate (%) (3) = [(2) ÷ (1)] × 100	(4) Marginal tax rate (= tax on extra dollar) (%)	(5) Disposable income ($) (5) = (1) − (2)
5,000	−1,709	−34	−34	6,709
10,000	−2,152	−22	0	12,152
20,000	−338	−2	31	20,338
50,000	4,474	9	15	45,526
100,000	14,338	14	28	85,662
150,000	27,300	18	33	122,700
250,000	60,900	24	35	189,100
1,000,000	302,279	30	41	697,721
10,000,000	3,260,399	33	41	6,739,601

War II. Figure 16-5 shows the history of the highest marginal tax rate in the United States.

The notion of marginal tax rates is extremely important in modern economics. Remember the "marginal principle": People should be concerned only with the extra costs or benefits that occur; they should "let bygones be bygones." Under this principle, the major effect of any tax on incentives comes from the marginal tax rate. This notion has formed the intellectual core of supply-side economics.

Column (5) shows the amount of *disposable income after taxes*. Note that it always pays to get more income: Even when a rock star makes another million dollars, she still has $590,000 of disposable income left over [= $1,000,000 − (41% × $1,000,000)].

Social Insurance Taxes

Virtually all industries now come under the Social Security Act. Workers receive retirement benefits that depend on their earnings history and past social security taxes. The social insurance program also funds a disability program and health insurance for the poor and elderly.

To pay for these benefits, employees and employers are charged a *payroll tax*. In 1996, this consisted of a total of 15.4 percent of all wage income below a ceiling of about $57,600 a year per person, with an additional 2.9 percent of annual wage income between $57,600 and $135,000. The tax is split between employer and employee.

Table 16-3 shows the payroll tax as a proportional tax because it taxes a fixed fraction of employment earnings. It does have some regressive features, however, because it exempts property income and is higher on low wages than on high wages.

The payroll tax is the fastest-growing source of federal revenues, rising from zero in 1929, to 18 percent of revenues in 1960, to 37 percent in 1996.

Other Taxes

The Federal government collects a wide variety of other taxes, some of which are shown in Table 16-3. The *corporate income tax* is a tax on the profits of corporations. The top federal corporation tax rate in 1996 was set at 35 percent of corporate profits. The corporation income tax is heavily criticized among economists. Some oppose this tax, arguing that the corporation is but a legal fiction and should not be

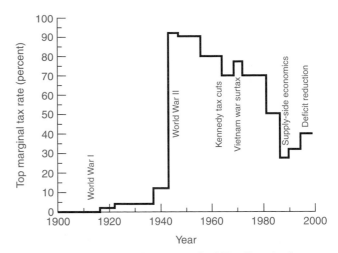

FIGURE 16-5. History of Top Marginal Tax Rate in the United States

The marginal tax rate is the extra tax that is paid per dollar of additional income. The top marginal tax rate on individual incomes reached 94 percent during World War II, was reduced in steps to a low of 28 percent during the Reagan years, and was raised to 40 percent in the 1993 Clinton economic package. (Source: U.S. Department of the Treasury.)

taxed. By taxing first corporate profits and then the dividends paid by corporations and received by individuals, the government subjects corporations to double taxation. Because of double taxation, corporate production is the most heavily taxed sector of the economy, a fact that may discourage investment in this dynamic sector.

The United States has no national sales tax, although there are a number of *federal excise taxes* on specific commodities such as cigarettes, alcohol, and gasoline. Sales and excise taxes are generally regressive, because consumption in general, and purchase of these items in particular, takes a larger fraction of income from a poor family than from a rich one.

Many economists and political leaders have argued that the United States should rely more heavily on sales or consumption taxes than it has up till now. One proposal, widely used outside the United States, is the *value-added tax*, or VAT. The VAT is like a sales tax, but it collects taxes at each stage of production. Thus, if a VAT were levied on bread, it would be collected from the farmer for wheat production, from the miller for flour production, from the baker at the dough stage, and from the grocer at the delivered-loaf stage.

Sales taxes and VATs are part of a more general class of *consumption taxes.* Their advocates argue that the country is currently saving and investing less than is necessary for future needs and that by substituting consumption taxes for income taxes, the national savings rate would increase. Critics of consumption taxes respond that such a change is undesirable because sales taxes are more regressive than today's income tax. One recent tax-reform proposal is the *flat tax,* which is a highly simplified system of personal consumption taxation. This approach would set all marginal tax rates at a uniform low rate (around 20 percent) and eliminate most deductions and tax-exempt fringe benefits, such as for health care and mortgage interest (see Question for Discussion 9). After a flurry of enthusiasm for flat taxes, the administration and Congress instead chose the "Christmas-tree" approach in the 1997 Taxpayer Relief Act. This bill introduced much greater complexity into the tax code by giving tax breaks to property income earned as capital gains, promoting a number of complicated new devices to encourage retirement saving, and helping students and their families through education tax credits and deductibility of interest on student loans. While the total annual impact on revenues will be small—about 0.3 percent of GDP—the increased complexity will make tax-related decisions more difficult and provide full employment for tax specialists for a long time to come.

STATE AND LOCAL TAXES

Under the U.S. system of fiscal federalism, state and local governments rely on a very different set of taxes than does the federal government. Figure 16-6 illustrates the main sources of funds that finance state and local expenditures.

Property Tax

The *property tax* is levied primarily on real estate—land and buildings. Each locality sets an annual tax rate which is levied on the assessed value of the land and structures. In many localities, the assessed value may be much smaller than the true market value. The property tax accounts for about 30 percent of the total revenues of state and local finance. Figure 16-6 shows that localities are the main recipient of property taxes.

Because about one-fourth of property values are from land, the property tax has elements of a capital tax and elements of a Henry George–type land tax. Economists believe that the land component of the property tax has little distortion, while the capital component will drive investment from high-tax central cities out to the low-taxed suburbs.

Whatever the views of economists, the property tax became controversial during the housing boom of the 1970s, when housing valuations and taxes skyrocketed. Across the country, taxpayers revolted. In Massachusetts, voters passed "Proposition $2\frac{1}{2}$," limiting tax payments to $2\frac{1}{2}$ percent of market value. Today, almost half the states have limitations on property or other taxes; these limits prevent state and local taxes from rising as rapidly as they did in the 1970s. During recessions, the tax limits sometimes push cities and states into fiscal crises as the governments run out of tax funds and are forced to cut services.

Other Taxes

Most other state taxes are closely related to the analogous federal taxes. States get most of their rev-

FIGURE 16-6. Property and Sales Taxes Dominate at State and Local Levels

Cities rely heavily on property taxes because houses and land cannot easily flee to the next town to avoid a city's tax. (Source: U.S. Bureau of the Census, *Government Finances in 1989–1990.*)

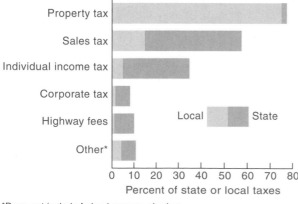

*Does not include federal revenue sharing.

enues from *general sales taxes* on goods and services. Each purchase at the department store or restaurant incurs a percentage tax (food and other necessities are exempt in some states). States tax the net income of corporations. Forty-five states imitate the federal government, on a much smaller scale, by taxing individuals according to the size of their incomes.

There are other miscellaneous revenues. Many states levy "highway user taxes" on gasoline. A growing source of revenue is lotteries and legalized gambling, in which the states benefit from encouraging people to impoverish themselves.

TAXES AND EFFICIENCY

Taxes affect both economic efficiency and the distribution of income. In recent years, the impacts on efficiency have become a principal concern of tax policy as economists and policymakers study the effect of incentives upon individual and business behavior. In tax policy, this involves primarily the question of how people respond to different levels of marginal tax rates.

An important political movement was the rise of *supply-side economics* in the 1980s. This program, championed by Republican President Ronald Reagan, pursued a macroeconomic policy directed toward long-run economic growth rather than business-cycle management; followed a budget policy that bolstered defense, cut civilian programs, and gave little weight to fiscal deficits; launched a regulatory program to reduce the burden of federal regulations, especially those pertaining to health, safety, and the environment; and, most important, lowered tax rates and tax burdens.

The major legacy of this period was the tax reforms of 1981 and 1986. These acts lowered marginal tax rates dramatically, broadened the tax base, and completely overhauled the individual income tax. The fiscal programs of these periods also led to a major increase in the federal budget deficit and to a government debt that grew sharply relative to national output.

How do high tax rates affect economic behavior? In the area of labor supply, the impacts are mixed. As we saw in Chapter 13, the impact of tax rates on hours worked is unclear because the income and substitution effects of wage changes work in opposite directions. As a result of progressive taxes, some

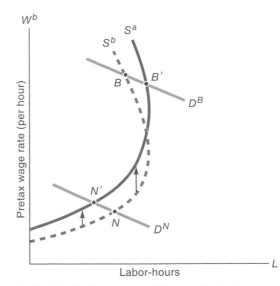

FIGURE 16-7. Response of Work to Taxes Depends on Shape of Supply Curve

Supply and demand plots labor supplied against pretax wage. Before-tax supply curve of labor (S^b) shifts vertically upward to after-tax supply (S^a) after imposition of a 25 percent income tax on labor earnings. If demand for labor intersects supply in the normal region at bottom, we see an expected decline in labor supplied from N to N'. If the labor supply is backward-bending, as at top, the labor supplied actually rises with the tax increase, going from B to B'.

people may choose more leisure over more work. Other people may work harder in order to make their millions. Many high-income doctors, artists, celebrities, and business executives, who enjoy their jobs and the sense of power or accomplishment that they bring, will work as hard for $800,000 after tax as for $1,000,000 after tax. Moreover, high taxes on winner-take-all activities may reduce the supply of talent to those overcrowded areas. Figure 16-7 shows how an increase in the tax rate on labor will affect labor supply; note the paradox that work effort may actually decline after a tax-rate cut if the labor supply curve is backward-bending.

In the area of saving and investment, taxes clearly have major impacts upon economic activity. When taxes are high in one sector, resources will flow into more lightly taxed areas. For example, because corporate capital is double-taxed, people's savings will flow out of the corporate sector and into lightly taxed sectors like oil and gas or into vacation homes financed by tax-deductible interest payments. If risky investments are taxed unfavorably, investors may prefer safer investments. The inefficiency comes as much from the divergence of taxes across sectors as from the existence of high taxes.[4]

Efficiency vs. Fairness

Economists have long been concerned with the impact of taxes on economic efficiency. Recall from Chapter 14 that Henry George argued that a tax on land will have little impact on efficiency because the supply of land is completely inelastic. The modern theory of efficient taxation puts forth the *Ramsey tax rule*, which states that the government should levy the heaviest taxes on those inputs and outputs that are most price-inelastic in supply or demand.[5] The rationale for the Ramsey tax rule is that if a commodity is very price-inelastic in supply or demand, a tax on the commodity will have little impact upon consumption and production. In some circumstances, Ramsey taxes may constitute a way of raising revenues with a minimum loss of economic efficiency.

But economies and politics do not run on efficiency alone. While stiff taxation of land rents or food might be efficient, many would think them unfair. A sober reminder of the dilemma was the proposal to introduce a poll tax in Britain in 1990. A *poll tax* is a *lump-sum tax*, or a fixed tax per person. The advantage of this tax is that, like a land tax, it would induce no inefficiencies. After all, people are unlikely to decamp to Russia or commit harikari to avoid the tax, so the economic distortions would arguably be minimal.

Alas, the British government underestimated the extent to which the populace felt this tax to be unfair. The poll tax is highly regressive because it places a much higher proportional burden on low-income people than on high-income people. Criticism of the poll tax played a key role in bringing down the Thatcher government after 11 years in power. This illustrates clearly the difficult choice between efficiency and fairness in taxes and other areas of economic policy.

---

[4] One interesting example of the interaction of efficiency and taxes is the Laffer curve, which is discussed in question 8 at the end of this chapter.

[5] Recall Chapter 14's discussion of Henry George's single tax and the extension to efficient or Ramsey taxes.

Taxing "Bads" Rather Than "Goods": Green Taxes

While poll taxes have been little advocated by economists, economists have favored an approach wherein the tax system would weigh more heavily on "bads" than on "goods." The main source of inefficiency is that taxes generally tax "goods"—economic activities like working, investing in capital, saving, or risk taking—and thereby discourage these activities. An alternative approach is to tax "bads." Traditional taxes on bads include "sin taxes": taxes on alcohol, cigarettes, and other substances that have harmful health effects.

A new approach to taxation is to tax pollution and other undesirable externalities; such taxes are called *green taxes* because they are designed to help the environment as well as to raise revenues. Say that the nation decides to help slow global warming by levying a "carbon tax," which is a tax on carbon-dioxide emissions from power plants and other sources. By standard economic reasoning we know that the tax will lead firms to lower their carbon-dioxide emissions, thereby improving the environment. In addition, of course, this green tax will provide revenues, which the government can use either to finance its activities or to reduce tax rates on beneficial activities like working or saving. So green taxes are doubly effective: The state gets revenue, and the environment is improved because the taxes discourage harmful externalities.

THE THORNY PROBLEM OF TAX INCIDENCE

Who actually ends up paying all these taxes that governments levy? We should not assume that the people or firms that send the tax revenues to the government will end up paying that tax. Just because the oil company sends the gasoline-tax receipts to the Treasury does not mean that the taxes come out of the profits of the oil company. Businesses may be able to shift the tax "forward" onto their customers by raising their price by the amount of the tax. Or they may shift the tax "backward" onto their suppliers (owners of labor, land, and other factors), who find themselves with lower wages, rents, and other factor prices than they would have enjoyed had there been no tax.

The question of shifting of taxes concerns **tax incidence.** This concept involves the way the tax burden ultimately is borne and its total effects on prices, quantities, and the composition of production and consumption.

Tax-incidence questions include these: Did the 4.3-cent-a-gallon tax on fuels passed in 1993 raise the price at the pump by 4.3 cents so that the incidence was on the consumer? Or did it lower the price of crude oil so that the incidence was on the oil producers? Or was the incidence somewhere in between? Did it change coal prices? And did the tax kill off oil production, so it had incidence effects beyond those which show up in money prices and wages and even beyond the burdens that you can allocate among the different citizens?

Microeconomics provides some important tools for analyzing tax incidence. In earlier chapters, we saw the incidence of a gasoline tax. In such simple cases, involving only supply of and demand for a single commodity, incidence analysis is straightforward. In other cases, the effects cascade through the economy, making analysis extremely complex and sometimes requiring general-equilibrium approaches.

We might want to know the *fiscal incidence* of the government tax and transfer system as a whole. Fiscal incidence examines the impact of both tax and expenditure programs on the incomes of the population. Fiscal incidence concerns the overall degree of progressivity or regressivity of government programs. It is estimated by allocating all taxes and transfer payments to different groups. Such a study is only approximate, since no one is sure how much the corporation tax or the property tax gets shifted.

The conceptual experiment we want to make is

- to measure incomes without taxes and transfers,
- then to measure incomes with taxes and transfers,
- and finally to measure *incidence* as the difference between these two situations.

Of course, economists are not magicians who can make such controlled experiments, but they take careful measurements and use good judgment to estimate the effects of taxes and spending.

Incidence of Federal Taxes and Transfers

Figure 16-8 shows the results of a recent study of the incidence of all U.S. taxes and cash transfers; in

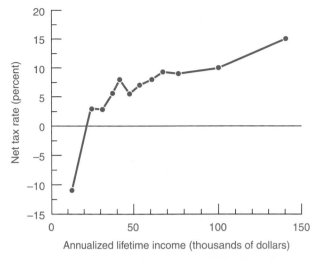

FIGURE 16-8. Who Pays the Taxes and Who Benefits from Transfers?

How does the modern welfare state affect the income of its citizens over their entire life cycle? Fullerton and Rogers estimate the impact on a household's lifetime income of all federal, state, and local taxes and cash transfers that were in place in 1984. The tax and transfer system is progressive at almost every income category. Note that the system actually transfers income to the lowest group while the highest group has a net tax rate of 15 percent. [Source: Don Fullerton and Diane Lim Rogers, *Who Bears the Lifetime Tax Burden?* (Brookings Institution, Washington, D.C., 1993), p. 123. The data have been updated to 1993 incomes, and the lifetime incomes were converted into annualized incomes using a 5 percent real interest rate.]

this figure, transfers are treated as negative taxes and are measured in the negative direction. The interesting contribution of this approach is that it examines *lifetime income and taxes* rather than looking at only a single year. Thus it takes into account important changes that occur over a lifetime (e.g., people go in and out of the labor market, and they pay social security taxes when young and then receive the taxes as benefits when retired). The study also takes into account the incredible complexity of our tax system, as described above.

The results indicate that the tax system is generally progressive from the top to the bottom, with the lowest group receiving net transfers while the top group has the highest average tax rate. A closer look at the structure of the tax and transfer system indicates that its progressive structure, particularly at the bottom, comes primarily from transfers rather than from taxes.

This pattern of net fiscal impact is similar to that found in most advanced market economies today. As one survey of fiscal incidence in high-income countries concluded:

> The evidence for almost all countries suggests that the tax system overall has almost no effect on income distribution. . . . This results from the progressive impact of income taxes being offset by regressive taxes, notably employers' social security contributions and indirect taxes. . . . When tax, transfer, and expenditure programs are viewed together, it is apparent that public expenditure programs, particularly the provision of cash transfers, have been almost totally responsible for the changes in income distribution which governments have brought about.[6]

FINAL WORD

Our introductory survey of government's role in the economy is a sobering reminder of the responsibilities and shortcomings of collective action. On the one hand, governments must defend their borders, stabilize their economies, protect the public health, and regulate pollution. On the other hand, many policies designed to benefit the public interest suffer from inefficiencies and inconsistencies.

Does this mean we should abandon the visible hand of government for the invisible hand of markets? Economics cannot answer such deep political questions; all it can do is examine the strengths and weaknesses of both collective and market choices, and point to mechanisms (such as green taxes or subsidies to research and development) by which a mended invisible hand may be more efficient than the extremes of either pure laissez-faire or unbridled bureaucratic rule making.

SUMMARY

A. Government Control of the Economy

1. The economic role of government has increased sharply over the last century. The government influences and controls private economic activity by using taxes, expenditures, and direct regulation.

2. A modern welfare state performs four economic functions: (*a*) It remedies market failures; (*b*) it redistributes income and resources; (*c*) it establishes macroeconomic stabilization policy to stabilize the business cycle and promote long-term economic growth; and (*d*) it manages international economic affairs.

3. Public-choice theory analyzes how governments actually behave. Just as the invisible hand can break down, so there are government failures, in which government interventions lead to waste or redistribute income in an undesirable fashion.

B. Government Expenditures

4. The American system of public finance is one of fiscal federalism. The federal government concentrates its spending on issues of national concern—on national public goods like defense and space exploration.

States and localities generally focus on local public goods—those whose benefits are largely confined within state or city boundaries.

5. Government spending and taxation today take approximately one-third of total national output. Of this total, 70 percent is spent at the federal level, and the balance is divided between state and local governments. Only a tiny fraction of government outlays is devoted to traditional functions like police and the courts.

C. Economic Aspects of Taxation

6. Notions of "benefits" and "ability to pay" are two principal theories of taxation. A tax is progressive, proportional, or regressive as it takes a larger, equal, or smaller fraction of income from rich families than it does from poor families. Direct and progressive taxes on incomes are in contrast to indirect and regressive sales and excise taxes.

7. More than half of federal revenues come from personal and corporation income taxes. The rest comes from taxes on payrolls or consumption goods. Local governments raise most of their revenue from property taxes, while sales taxes are most important for states.

8. The individual income tax is levied on "income from whatever source derived," less certain exemptions and

---

6 Peter Saunders, "Evidence on Income Redistribution by Governments," OECD, Economics and Statistics Department, Working Papers, no. 11 (January 1984).

deductions. The marginal tax rate, denoting the fraction paid in taxes for every dollar of additional income, is key to determining the impact of taxes on incentives to work and save. Marginal tax rates were lowered sharply during the 1980s, but top rates were then raised in President Clinton's fiscal package of 1993.

9. The fastest-growing federal tax is the payroll tax, used to finance social security. This is an "earmarked" levy, with funds going to provide public pensions and health and disability benefits. Because there are visible benefits at the end of the stream of payments, the payroll tax has elements of a benefit tax.

10. Economists point to the Ramsey tax rule, which emphasizes that efficiency will be promoted when taxes are levied more heavily on those activities that are relatively price-inelastic. A new approach is green taxes, which levy fees on environmental externalities, reducing harmful activities while raising revenues that would otherwise be levied on goods or productive inputs. But in all taxes, equity and political acceptability are severe constraints.

11. The incidence of a tax refers to its ultimate economic burden and to its total effect on prices, outputs, and other economic magnitudes. Those who pay a tax can often pass its burden forward to consumers or backward to factors of production. The current U.S. tax and transfer system is moderately progressive.

CONCEPTS FOR REVIEW

Functions of Government

three tools of government economic control:
    taxes
    expenditures
    regulation
market failures vs. government failures
public-choice theory

four functions of government:
    efficiency
    distribution
    stabilization
    international representation

Government Expenditures and Fiscal Incidence

fiscal federalism and local vs. national public goods

economic impact of government spending
benefit and ability-to-pay principles
horizontal and vertical equity
direct and indirect taxes
progressive, proportional, and regressive taxes
tax and transfer incidence and shifting
Ramsey and green taxes

QUESTIONS FOR DISCUSSION

1. Recall Justice Oliver Wendell Holmes' statement, "Taxes are what we pay for a civilized society." Interpret this statement, remembering that in economics we always need to pierce the veil of monetary flows to understand the flow of real resources.

2. In considering whether you want a pure laissez-faire economy or government regulation, discuss whether there should be government controls over prostitution, addictive drugs, heart transplants, assault weapons, and alcohol. Discuss the relative advantages of high taxes and prohibition for such goods (recall the discussion of drug prohibition in Chapter 5).

3. Critics of the U.S. tax system argue that it harms incentives to work, save, and innovate and therefore reduces long-run economic growth. Can you see why "green taxes" might promote economic efficiency and economic growth? Consider, for example, taxes on sulfur or carbon-dioxide emissions or on leaky oil tankers. Construct a list of taxes that you think would increase efficiency, and compare their effects with the effects of taxes on labor or capital income.

4. Tax economists often speak of lump-sum taxes, which are levied on individuals without regard to their economic activity. Lump-sum taxes like poll taxes have no distortion or inefficiencies because they have no effect on incentives; in other words, they impose zero marginal tax rates on all inputs and outputs. Assume that the government imposes a lump-sum tax of $200 on each individual. Show in a supply-and-demand diagram why this will have no effect on either wages or labor supplied. (Recall Henry George's analysis of land taxes.)

    In a lifetime framework, we could think of the dynamic equivalent of the lump-sum tax as an "endowment tax," which would tax individuals on the basis of their potential labor incomes. Fullerton and Rogers (op. cit., page 299) find that a perfectly efficient proportional endowment tax would increase average lifetime incomes by 1.3 percent. Would you favor such a change? Describe some of the difficulties in implementing an endowment tax.

5. Make a list of different federal taxes in order of their progressiveness. If the federal government were to trade in income taxes for consumption or sales taxes, what would be the effect in terms of overall progressiveness of the tax system?

6. Some public goods are local, spilling out to residents of small areas; others are national, benefiting an entire nation; some are global, affecting all nations. A private good is one whose spillover is negligible. Give some examples of purely private goods and of local, national, and global public goods or externalities. For each, indicate the level of government that could design policies most efficiently, and suggest one or two appropriate government actions that could solve the externality.

7. Some incidence questions that can be answered using supply and demand:

   a. In the 1993 Budget Act, Congress raised federal gasoline taxes by 4.3 cents a gallon. Assuming the wholesale price of gasoline is determined in world markets, what is the relative impact of the tax on American producers and consumers?

   b. Social insurance taxes are generally levied on labor earnings. What is their incidence if labor supply is perfectly inelastic? If labor supply is backward-bending?

   c. If firms must earn a posttax rate of return on investment determined in world capital markets, what is the incidence of a tax on corporate income in a small open economy?

8. An interesting question involves the *Laffer curve*, named for California economist and sometime senatorial candidate Arthur Laffer. In Figure 16-9, the Laffer curve shows how revenues rise as *tax rates* are increased, reach a maximum at point *L*, and then decline to zero at a 100 percent tax rate as activity is completely discouraged. The exact shape of the Laffer curve for different taxes is highly controversial.

   A common mistake in discussing taxes is the post hoc fallacy (see Chapter 1's discussion of this). Proponents of lower taxes often invoke the Laffer curve in their arguments. They point to tax cuts of the 1960s to suggest that the economy is to the right of the peak of Mt. Laffer, say at *B*. They say, in effect, "After the Kennedy-Johnson tax cuts of 1964, federal revenues actually rose from $110 billion in 1963 to $133 billion in 1966. Therefore, cutting taxes raises revenues." Explain why this does not prove that the economy was to the right of *L*. Further explain why this is an example of the *post hoc* fallacy. Give a correct analysis.

9. A popular tax reform proposal of the 1990s was the "flat tax," developed by economists Robert Hall and Alvin Rabushka of Stanford University. The idea of the flat tax is to tax all personal and corporate income only once at a low constant rate. Table 16-5 shows how such a flat tax might work. Compare the average and marginal tax rates of the flat tax with the tax schedule shown in Table 16-4 in the text. List advantages and disadvantages of both. Which is more progressive?

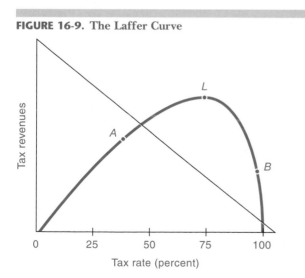

FIGURE 16-9. The Laffer Curve

TABLE 16-5.

(1) Adjusted gross income ($)	(2) Deductions and exemptions ($)	(3) Taxable income ($)	(4) Individual income tax ($)
5,000	20,000	0	0
10,000	20,000	0	0
20,000	20,000	0	0
50,000	20,000	30,000	6,000
100,000	20,000	80,000	16,000
1,000,000	20,000	980,000	196,000

CHAPTER 17
CURBING MARKET POWER

Both theoretical and empirical research question the extent to which regulation can achieve the goals for which it has been promulgated.

Stephen Breyer and Paul MacAvoy,
Regulation and Deregulation (1987)

Before studying economics, many people think that the government needs to be a watchdog to prevent monopolistic abuses and price gouging. A little learning might easily lead students to reverse this view, for the invisible-hand theory teaches that the forces of profit seeking themselves serve as guarantees against excess profits. If a firm enjoys profits above the normal rate of return, these profits will lure in new competitors, raise output, and lower prices and profits. For the most part, then, governments in market economies rely on the force of rivalry and competition—the carrot of profits and the stick of bankruptcy—to stimulate the private sector to behave efficiently.

But the forces of competition cannot work effectively when competitors are absent or feeble. When businesses have market power, they can raise prices above the competitive level for a long time. When there is excessive market power, government can take steps to promote competition.

Moreover, the government steps in to help ameliorate a whole range of perceived market failures.

Sometimes people may not have the information or the capability to protect themselves. So the government requires drug companies to demonstrate the safety and efficacy of new drugs or monitors the safety performance of airlines. The government also regulates industries like banking and electricity, tries to protect consumers from false advertising and financial misrepresentation, and engages in zoning decisions which control the economic use of land.

How can governments deal with market failures and the excesses of monopoly power without obstructing the powerful efficiency gains of unfettered market competition and rivalry? This has proved to be a mighty dilemma. Sometimes, the public interest compels regulation in a limited domain; at other times, economic regulation creates more problems than it solves, and governments are advised to deregulate a sector. Governments also attempt to promote competition and prevent monopoly abuses by banning certain kinds of anticompetitive practices; this area of government activity, antitrust policy, is the subject of the second half of this chapter.

A. BUSINESS REGULATION: THEORY AND PRACTICE

Federal regulation of American industry goes back more than a century to the founding of the Interstate Commerce Commission (ICC) in 1887. The ICC was designed as much to prevent price wars and to guarantee service to small towns as it was to control monopoly. Later, federal regulation spread to banks in 1913, to electric power in 1920, and to communications, securities markets, labor, trucking, and air travel during the 1930s. In recent years, as we will see, the federal government has changed its course by deregulating many industries.

In attempting to control economic activity, governments can use commands or market incentives. Historically the main form of regulation has been a direct approach, where governments issue *command-and-control orders*. In this approach, governments command people to undertake or desist from certain activities through government regulation. For example, the government might require that businesses locate only in commercial areas or that they do not pour chemicals in the river. Government commands today cover a wide variety of areas, including not only pollution and zoning but also informational reporting, labor standards on wages and hours, and many regulations specific to particular industries such as those using pesticides, producing new drugs, or engaged in international trade.

Recently, economists have been instrumental in convincing government to try a brand-new form of regulation: relying on *market incentives*. The best example of market incentives is the 1990 Clean Air Act, discussed in the next chapter. This bill set up markets for buying and selling "tradeable emissions permits"—in essence, licenses to pollute. Such harnessing of market forces has the possibility of achieving regulatory goals much more efficiently than command-and-control methods.

Regulation consists of government rules or market incentives designed to control the price, sale, or production decisions of firms.

TWO BRANDS OF REGULATION

It is customary to distinguish between two forms of regulation. **Economic regulation** involves the control of prices, entry and exit conditions, and standards of service in a particular industry. Prominent examples are regulation of public utilities (telephone, electricity, natural gas, and water) as well as regulations in other industries (transportation, radio, and TV). The financial industry has been heavily regulated since the 1930s, with strict rules specifying what banks, brokerage firms, and insurance companies can and cannot do.

In addition, there is a newer form of regulation, known as **social regulation**, which is used to protect the environment along with the health and safety of workers and consumers. Its rules are aimed at correcting a wide variety of side effects or externalities that result from economic activity. Programs to clean our air and water or to ensure the safety of nuclear power or drugs or cars are the most prominent examples of social regulation. Because of its importance, we will study environmental regulation in detail in the next chapter.

WHY REGULATE INDUSTRY?

Regulation restrains the unfettered market power of firms. What are the legitimate reasons why governments might choose to override the decisions made in free markets? There are three major *public-interest justifications* of regulation. The first is to regulate firm behavior to prevent abuses of market power by monopolies or oligopolies. A second major reason is to correct negative externalities like pollution—this is the subject of social regulation, studied in the next chapter. A third reason is to remedy informational failures, such as occur when consumers have inadequate information about the characteristics of important products like drugs or energy-using appliances.

Containing Market Power

The traditional public-interest view of economic regulation is normative: that regulatory measures should be taken to reduce excessive market power. More specifically, government should regulate industries where there are too few firms to ensure vigorous rivalry. Government should regulate industries particularly in the extreme case of natural monopoly, especially where the monopoly occurs for necessities that have a low price elasticity of demand.

An important example of a natural monopoly is local water distribution. The cost of gathering water, building a water-distribution system, and piping water into every home is sufficiently great that it would not pay to have more than one firm provide local water service, so this is a natural monopoly. Sometimes water service is provided by the government; more often, it is provided by a regulated privately owned water company.

Another type of natural monopoly can occur when an industry has *economies of scope*, which arise when a number of different products can be produced more efficiently together than by separate firms. For example, transport-equipment firms show economies of scope—a firm producing cars and trucks has a cost advantage in producing buses and tanks. Why? Because specialized knowledge and machinery are shared across the different products. These firms have economies of scope in production of ground-based transport systems.

We know from our discussion of declining costs in Chapter 7 that pervasive economies of scale are inconsistent with perfect competition; we will see oligopoly or monopoly in such cases. But the point here is even more extreme: *When there are such powerful economies of scale or scope that only one firm can survive, we have a natural monopoly.*

Why do governments regulate natural monopolies? They do so because a natural monopolist, enjoying a large cost advantage over its potential competitors and facing price-inelastic demand, can jack up its price sharply, obtain enormous monopoly profits, and create major economic inefficiencies. In recent years, cable television companies have exploited their local monopolies in providing multiple channels with high-quality pictures by raising prices sharply. This provoked Congress and several states to enact legislation regulating the prices set by companies. Studies indicated that this price regulation was ineffective and may actually have raised prices in some categories. Consequently, in the 1995 Communications Act, Congress changed its mind and lifted price and entry controls with the idea that greater competition would be more beneficial for consumers than price controls.

In earlier times, regulation was justified on the dubious grounds that it was needed to prevent cutthroat or destructive competition. This was one argument for continued control over railroads, trucks, airlines, and buses, as well as for regulation of the level of agricultural production. Economists today have little sympathy for this argument. After all, competition with increased efficiency and low prices is exactly what an efficient market system is designed to ensure.

Remedying Information Failures

Another reason for regulation is that consumers have inadequate information about products. For example, testing pharmaceutical drugs is expensive and scientifically complex. The government regulates drugs by allowing the sale of only those drugs which are proved "safe and efficacious." Government also prohibits false and misleading advertising. In both cases, the government is attempting to correct for the market's failure to provide information efficiently.

Much of the regulation of the financial industry serves the purpose of increasing the quantity and quality of information so that markets can work better. For example, when a company sells stocks or bonds in the United States, it is required to issue copious documentation of its current financial condition and future prospects. This helps protect investors from fraudulent claims about the value of the company's securities. Government requirements are sometimes reinforced by the private sector: companies which list on the New York Stock Exchange must comply with an even tougher set of accounting regulations. Financial regulations are less stringent in other countries, with the consequence that investors often find themselves bilked when companies inflate profits or hide damaging information. Paradoxically, tough reporting standards are beneficial to financial markets because they reduce informational asymmetries between buyers and sellers.

Safety regulation in the workplace, too, helps cure informational deficiencies. Remember from Chapter 13 that the theory of compensating differentials says that more hazardous jobs should entail premium wages. The problem is that many hazards may not be obvious, and companies clearly have an interest in not publicizing problems in their workplaces. For this reason it may be efficient for the government to set minimum standards for worker safety, so that an individual worker does not have to undertake a costly investigation of the safety record of every company where he or she is applying for a job.

Dealing with Externalities

Government regulation can also be justified when there are externalities. The classic example of regulation of this type, which we analyze in the next chapter, is antipollution measures. But there are other interesting cases. One pervasive example is local zoning regulation, which limits how landowners can use their land. Most zoning regulations specify whether a plot of land can be used for residences, stores, or industry and how big the buildings can be.

What is the justification for zoning regulation? Allowing a junkyard in a quiet residential area, for instance, would generate externalities that might harm everyone in the neighborhood. Similarly, a 50-story office building in a neighborhood of 2-story homes might overwhelm the local transportation system and other neighborhood services.

The economic impact of zoning can be huge. Being able to build a 50-story building on a plot of land, as opposed to a 2-story one, can dramatically affect the value of the land. That's why zoning is perhaps the most important type of regulation done at the local level of government.

Interest-Group Theories of Regulation

So far we have been looking at the normative public-interest justifications for government regulation. We should recognize, however, that regulation redistributes income and thereby creates interest groups that have vested interests in the regulatory outcomes. Sometimes, because of the interaction between regulation and politics, regulation has the perverse result of restricting entry into the regulated industry, which actually *raises prices and profits* for established companies.[1] Hence, a regulated industry may actually lobby in favor of continued regulation, in order to keep out competitors and keep profits high.

Economists who emphasize the anticompetitive aspect of regulation argue, "You say that regulation is in the interest of consumers and workers. Don't believe it. Rather, regulation is designed to boost the incomes of producers by limiting entry and preventing competition in the regulated industry. Any gains to consumers or workers are purely incidental."

The historical record shows that there is much truth to this view. For example, numerous economic studies of regulation have shown that regulation often keeps prices *high*. For many years, trucking companies and airlines had to get permission before lowering prices or entering new markets. Other types of regulation also have the effect of limiting competition. For example, high standards for new drugs means that the process of getting regulatory approval is lengthy and expensive. That keeps out many smaller companies which cannot afford the years of testing that a new drug requires.

The most recent example of a regulatory program benefiting the industry at the expense of taxpayers came in the savings and loan industry. The federal program of deposit insurance was established in the 1930s to help restore confidence and

FIGURE 17-1. Cost Curves for a Natural Monopolist
For a natural monopolist, the *AC* curve is still falling at the point where it cuts the industry's *DD* curve. Thus efficient production requires output to be concentrated in a single firm. (Can you estimate from the diagram how much more expensive it would be if Q^* were to be produced by two firms, each producing $\frac{1}{2} Q^*$?)

[1] The germinal work in this area was by George Stigler of the University of Chicago, who won a Nobel Prize for this and other contributions. The Chicago School has been highly influential in its view that government intervention in the economy often does more harm than good.

prevent bank panics. By the early 1980s, however, it became clear that the program was poorly designed. It provided a government guarantee on bank deposits without ensuring that banks behaved prudently with the insured deposits. As a result, many banks could pay high interest rates to attract deposits and then use the money to make risky loans and investments and to pay high salaries to their executives. When the banks began going bankrupt, the government had to pick up the tab; losses mounted to the hundreds of billions of dollars. Because of intense lobbying and generous campaign contributions, appropriate government action to stop the wasteful practices was delayed for years until Congress acted to curb the worst abuses in 1989. Who were the major beneficiaries of the corrupt regulatory regime in the banking industry? Primarily bankers, banks, and bank stockholders. Who were the losers? The taxpayers.

PUBLIC-UTILITY REGULATION OF NATURAL MONOPOLY

A traditional economic argument for regulation is to prevent monopoly pricing by natural monopolists. Let us see exactly how regulators control excessive price increases of monopolists. Recall that a natural monopoly is an industry in which the most efficient way of organizing production is through a single firm. Figure 17-1 shows the way the AC, MC, and industry demand curve might look for a natural monopoly. Note that the industry demand curve (DD) intersects the firm's MC curve where AC is falling. If two similar firms were to produce the

FIGURE 17-2. Ideal and Practical Regulation of Monopolists
Maximum-profit equilibrium for the unregulated monopolist is at M, directly above the intersection of MR and long-run MC, with price above MC.

Public-utility commissions customarily require prices to be equal to average cost at R, where the demand curve intersects the long-run average cost curve. This wipes out excess profit and brings price down closer to marginal cost. Ideally, price should be forced all the way down to I, where price = MC and hence marginal social costs and marginal benefits are appropriately balanced. At point I, there is no efficiency loss from price being above marginal cost.

industry output, the average cost for the two firms would be well above that of a single firm.

Suppose that the legislature decides to impose *public-utility regulation* on a particular industry. How would it proceed? It would first set up a public-utility commission to oversee prices, service, and entry into and exit from the industry. The most important decision would be to determine the pricing of the monopoly firm.

Traditionally, regulation imposes *average cost pricing* on regulated firms. For example, an electric utility would take all its costs (fixed as well as variable) and distribute them to each product sold (say, electricity and steam). Then each class of customer would be charged the *fully distributed average cost* of that type of service.

Figure 17-2 illustrates public-utility regulation. Point M (associated with output Q_M) is the unregulated profit-maximizing output of the monopolist we examined in Chapter 9. Here we find high price, reduced quantity, and handsome profits (as shown by the shaded region in Figure 17-2).

In traditional regulation, the monopolist is allowed to charge a price only high enough to cover average cost. In this case, the firm will set its price where the demand curve DD intersects the AC curve. Hence, the equilibrium is at point R, with output Q_R.

How good is the solution? Economically speaking, it might represent an improvement over unregulated monopoly. First, the owners of the monopoly are presumably no more deserving than the consumers. So there is no reason to allow them to extract monopoly profits from consumers.

Second, in making the monopolist cut its price from P_M to P_R, the regulators have reduced the discrepancy between price and marginal cost. This change improves economic efficiency because the additional output is worth more to consumers in marginal utility than it costs society in terms of the marginal cost. Only when price is equal to marginal cost in all sectors is society using its resources most efficiently.

Ideally Regulated Pricing. If $P = MC$ is such a good thing, why shouldn't the regulators force the monopolist to lower price until it equals marginal cost at the intersection point of the DD and MC curves (at I)?

Actually, *marginal-cost pricing* where $P = MC$ is the ideal target for economic efficiency. But it presents a serious practical obstacle: if a firm with declining average cost sets price equal to marginal cost, it will incur a chronic loss. The reason is that if AC is falling, then $MC < AC$, so setting $P = MC$ implies having $P < AC$. When price (or average revenue) is less than average cost, the firm is losing money. To see this point visually, examine the ideal regulatory solution at point I in Figure 17-2. At that point, price equals marginal cost, but MC is less than average cost. When average cost is greater than price, the firm is losing money. Since firms will not operate at a loss for long, and governments are reluctant to subsidize monopolists, the ideal regulatory solution is rarely pursued.

In an alternative approach, pricing is based on *two-part tariffs*. The firm charges a fixed fee (say, a few dollars a month) to cover the overhead costs and then adds a variable cost (per phone call, unit of electricity, or whatever the commodity is) to cover the marginal cost. This approach can come even closer to the ideal marginal-cost pricing than does traditional average cost pricing.

 Economic innovations: price-cap regulation. As we saw above, under traditional rate-of-return regulation, prices are determined as the cost of production plus an authorized rate of return on invested capital. This approach has very weak incentives to economize and is biased toward capital-intensive production techniques. The incentives are actually perverse because if price equals average cost, firms can actually increase profits by raising costs. As one economist noted, this is the only market where you can profit by putting a fancy Oriental carpet in your office!

A radical new approach that can improve incentives is performance-based regulation. Under this approach, firms are regulated on performance rather than on inputs, usually by use of a *price cap*. One formula is that regulated prices should move with "inflation minus *X*." Under this approach, the maximum price would be raised each year by an amount equal to the inflation rate ("inflation") less a normative annual efficiency improvement ("*X*"). The attractiveness of this approach is that it mimics a competitive market. Firms become price-takers, and any cost reduction flows directly into profits. The perverse incentives of conventional regulation are removed. Well-designed price-cap regulation encourages utilities to reduce costs, allows the introduction of competition, and reduces uneconomical cross subsidization.

This novel technique has been employed in several industries over the last decade. One of the early examples occurred with the deregulation of the electricity industry in Britain (discussed below). While price caps provide superior incentives for efficiency, they are not without flaws. The major disadvantage of this approach is uncertainty about the appropriate X rate. X should represent the target rate of cost reduction relative to the economy as a whole. When British electricity regulators set X, they were extremely conservative and chose $X = 0$, implicitly assuming that there would be no differential productivity improvement in the electricity industry. If X is set incorrectly for too long, the system will either degenerate into a state of chronic losses or earn large windfall monopoly profits. In setting $X = 0$, the British appear to have been more averse to losses than to excess profits. Economists and regulators are monitoring the experience with performance-based regulation closely to see whether it lives up to its promise.

THE COSTS OF REGULATION

Economists have studied the impact of regulation to weigh its costs and benefits. The results of a recent survey are shown in Table 17-1 on page 310. The effects of regulation include both efficiency gains or losses (such as those that come when inefficiently high levels of pollution are curbed) and income redistribution (as occurs when high trucking prices redistribute income from consumers to truckers). Most studies suggest that the main effects of economic regulation are losses in efficiency and large amounts of income redistribution. The record of social regulation is mixed, with some cases showing significant benefits and others having large costs with few benefits. The costs of both social and economic regulation (including the restrictions on international trade) are estimated to have been around 3.3 percent of net domestic product as of 1988.

Decline of Economic Regulation

For the last two decades, many economists have argued that most economic regulation was actually creating monopoly power rather than curbing it. This idea is partially based on the interest-group view of regulation analyzed above. In addition, observers noted that economic regulation had spread far beyond the local natural monopolies. By the mid-1970s, regulators were issuing their orders to railroads and trucks, airlines and buses, radio and TV broadcasting, oil and natural gas, pecans and milk, and virtually all financial markets. Many of these regulated industries were closer to the pole of perfect competition than to natural monopoly, as Figure 17-3 on page 311 suggests.

Pioneering Deregulation in the Airline Industry

Since 1975, the federal government has partially or totally deregulated many industries, including petroleum, airlines, trucking, railroad, stockbroking, long-distance telephone service, banking, communications, and natural gas. Each of these industries has structural characteristics that are favorable to competition because their markets are large relative to the efficient size of individual firms.

The airline industry provides a dramatic example of the dilemmas of deregulation. Since its creation in the 1930s, the Civil Aeronautics Board (CAB) viewed its role as deterring competition. No major new air carriers were allowed to enter the interstate market from 1938 to 1978. When innovative low-cost and no-frills airfares were proposed, the CAB slapped these proposals down. The CAB was (as the interest-group view of regulation predicted) devoted to keeping airfares up, not down.

In 1977, President Carter appointed Alfred Kahn chairman of the CAB. A distinguished economist and critic of regulation, Kahn set out to allow more competition through entry and fare flexibility. Shortly thereafter, Congress passed legislation allowing free entry and exit on all domestic air routes. Airlines were free to set whatever fares the traffic would bear.

Many people worried that there would be massive layoffs and loss of service without regulation. However, after almost two decades of experience with deregulation, the airline industry employs 65 percent more people and logs 70 percent more domestic passenger-miles. Studies indicate that (after correcting for inflation) average fares fell sharply over the years after deregulation; that utilization of aircraft has increased; and that airlines have become extraordinarily innovative in their pricing strategies. The competition has been so intense

The Impact of Regulation, U.S., 1988*				
	Efficiency gains or losses			Income redistribution ($, billion)
	Benefits ($, billion)	Costs ($, billion)	Net benefits ($, billion)	
Economic regulation:				
Telecommunications	0.0	14.1	−14.1	42.3
Agriculture	0.0	6.7	−6.7	18.4
Airline	0.0	3.8	−3.8	7.7
Rail	0.0	2.3	−2.3	6.8
Milk	0.0	0.7	−0.7	2.2
Natural gas	0.0	0.3	−0.3	5.0
Credit	0.0	0.3	−0.3	0.8
Barge	0.0	0.3	−0.3	0.8
Davis-Bacon Act	0.0	0.2	−0.2	0.5
Ocean	0.0	0.1	−0.1	0.2
Postal rates	0.0	na	0.0	8.0
Social regulation:				
Environment	58.4	66.5	−8.1	na
Nuclear power	na	6.5	na	na
Occupational safety	0.0	8.8	−8.8	na
Highway safety	35.6	7.7	27.9	na
Pharmaceuticals	na	2.3	na	na
Equal opportunity	na	0.9	na	na
Consumer products	na	0.03	na	na
Other:				
International trade	0.0	17.3	−17.3	98.1
Total, all regulations and trade:†				
Billions of dollars	**94**	**139**	**−35**	**191**
As percent of gross domestic product	**2.1**	**3.2**	**−0.8**	**4.4**

*All estimates are in 1988 dollars; na = not available.

† Note that the na's are set at zero. This is likely to understate benefits slightly and to underestimate the total amount of redistribution.

TABLE 17-1. Regulation Affects Efficiency and Redistributes Income

Studies of the impact of economic and social regulation show that economic regulations have few benefits, cause substantial efficiency losses, and redistribute much income. Social regulations have benefits, although they are often extremely difficult to measure. (Source: Robert W. Hahn and John A. Hird, "The Costs and Benefits of Regulation: Review and Synthesis," *Yale Journal on Regulation*, vol. 8, 1991, pp. 233–287. Where a range of estimates is given, the midpoint is taken.)

that the airline industry has shown very low profitability over the last decade, and bankruptcies are quite common. New airlines like Southwest Airlines have started up to replace bankrupt old ones. By most measures, the industry has operated more efficiently since deregulation.

The success of airline deregulation encouraged economists and noneconomists around the world to trust an unregulated market to make allocational decisions even in industries where firms have the potential for significant market power.

Deregulating the Electricity Industry

The most recent battleground for deregulation has been the electricity industry. Electricity has traditionally been one of the most heavily regulated industries. Many countries have regulated electricity through government ownership of major facilities,

FIGURE 17-3. Degree of Natural Monopoly in Different Industries

This figure displays several regulated and unregulated industries by their degree of natural monopoly or of perfect competition. In perfectly competitive industries, the efficient level of output is tiny relative to the market, while the average cost for a natural monopoly continues to decline even when the firm produces total industry output. Agriculture and mining are inherently quite competitive, while highways and local network utilities such as for water are close to polar natural monopolies. The asterisk (*) indicates industries that have historically been heavily regulated or even operated by governments.

while others have used traditional rate-of-return public-utility regulation to control the prices and markets of electric utilities. The electricity industry in the United States is populated predominantly by vertically integrated local monopolies supplying relatively large areas.

Electricity has been heavily regulated because it was typically cast as a natural monopoly. It is useful to divide the electricity industry into three parts: generation, transmission, and distribution. Until recently, it was commonly assumed that because of the high transmission costs and significant economies of scale in generation, the entire industry should be treated as a local natural monopoly. In the last decade, this view has been challenged, and only the transmission and small-customer distribution networks are now commonly viewed as having major elements of natural monopoly. The shift in viewpoint has come partly because of the successful breakup of vertically and horizontally integrated telecommunications networks and partly because of the exhaustion of the economies of scale in generation. Most independent specialists today hold that, while the generation segment is technically complex, the optimal scale of plant is sufficiently small so that reasonably competitive markets can emerge among alternative generators.

These theoretical presumptions have been strengthened by experience around the world in the actual deregulation of electricity markets—particu-larly the British case. Before deregulation, the British system consisted of two vertically integrated state-owned segments—one for generation and one for transmission. The British government decided to break up and privatize the industry. The generation segment was divided into two private companies. The transmission segment was to remain a regulated monopoly, National Grid.

One of the most radical features of the British reforms was the establishment of a "spot market" to coordinate generation. Many systems coordinate electricity generation by a centralized "pool" system whereby a central dispatcher brings power stations on line in increasing order of their marginal production costs. Under the British spot market, each generator must declare its offers of quantities and prices of supply for each half-hour of the following day. The National Grid Company ranks these offers on the basis of costs, and, together with estimates of demand, sets up a plan for least-cost operations for the coming day. This also generates a series of spot (or short-term) prices, which have proved highly variable (as is appropriate for an industry in which the marginal cost varies so greatly depending upon the load).

No conclusive evaluation of the British reforms is possible at this time, but a few tentative conclusions can be reached on the basis of evidence to date. First, the system as a whole appears to have been a major success and to be functioning relatively smoothly. Second, by opening up the generation market and separating generation from transmission, the British reforms have induced significant new entry. Third, the use of inflation-minus-X or price-cap regulation has been a technical success, although there have been no noticeable price benefits of deregulation to consumers.

The United States is currently considering similar deregulation proposals, emphasizing the deregulation of electricity generation. There continue to be major vested interests opposing full deregulation, however. An important issue concerns the fate of $100 billion worth of "stranded assets." These are electricity-generation plants, built under the inefficient cost-plus pricing system, whose production costs are so high that they would lose money under deregulation. The fairness issues rasied by these stranded assets have been a major roadblock to electricity deregulation in the United States.

A Cautionary Word

As regulation loosens its grip on industries like the airlines, electricity, and banking, it is important to remember the broader role of government in economic life. Just because price regulation has often been poorly designed does not imply that all government programs are wasteful. In the banking industry, economists worry that inadequate regulation will lead to bank failures and potential macroeconomic disturbances. In the airlines, people became concerned that intense competition was leading airlines to cut corners on maintenance. A similar concern was raised as increased competition in the electricity industry induced some nuclear power plants to curtail their safety investments. These incidents were a sober reminder that regulation is not an either/or situation—that government oversight includes much more than telling firms what to produce and at what price.

B. ANTITRUST POLICY

Now we will examine in detail one of the oldest and most important forms of government oversight of business, antitrust policy. This branch of microeconomic policy is designed to promote vigorous competition and rivalry in markets and to prevent monopolistic abuses.

Review of Imperfect Competition

Chapters 9 and 10 discussed the way that imperfect competitors set their prices and quantities. Let's begin by reviewing the major elements of the economic theory that relate to government antimonopoly policies:

- Imperfect competitors are inefficient because they set prices above marginal cost. The consumers in the monopolistic or oligopolistic industry are consuming less of its goods than would be the case if the goods were efficiently supplied.
- Many industries have technologies that exhibit significant economies of scale. It would be unrealistic to try to produce the output of such industries with perfectly competitive firms, for that would require that firms be inefficiently small. In

rare cases, the technology in an industry can be efficiently produced only by a single firm; we call this a "natural monopoly."

- In the long run, most economic progress comes from technological change. According to the Schumpeterian hypothesis, large firms with considerable market power are responsible for much invention and technological change. Government policies should be especially careful not to harm the incentives for innovation.
- The major abuses in markets—either too high a price or poor product quality—come when an industry is effectively monopolized. A good rule of thumb is that an industry behaves like a monopolist when a single firm or colluding group of firms produces more than three-quarters of the output in an industry.
- The government has taken on the responsibility of preventing monopolization from occurring and of regulating monopolies when they are inevitable. Antitrust policies attempt to prevent monopolization or anticompetitive abuses; economic regulation is used to control the exercise of monopoly power in natural monopolies.

With the decline of economic regulation as a major tool for preventing monopolistic abuses, governments increasingly focus on promoting competition and on applying antitrust policy as the major weapons for encouraging economic efficiency in markets. In this section we discuss antitrust policies, which attack anticompetitive abuses in two different ways. First, they prohibit certain kinds of *business conduct,* such as price fixing, that restrain competitive forces. Second, they restrict some market structures, such as monopolies, that are thought most likely to restrict commerce and abuse their economic power in other ways.

The framework for antitrust policy was set by a few key legislative statutes and by a century of court decisions. In recent years, under the prodding of economists, antitrust policy has been evolving away from the "big is bad" philosophy and toward the *economic approach to antitrust.* Emphasizing the intrinsic rivalry of oligopolists, the economic approach holds that the most powerful incentives for large business to reduce prices and improve product quality occur in a deregulated world in which barriers to entry are low and markets are open to domestic and foreign competition. In this view, antitrust policy should be reserved for the worst abuses of market power.

THE FRAMEWORK STATUTES

Antitrust law is like a huge forest that has grown from a handful of seeds. The statutes on which the law is based are so concise and straightforward that they can be quoted in Table 17-2; it is astounding how much law has grown from so few words.

Sherman Act (1890)

Monopolies had long been illegal under the common law, based on custom and past judicial deci-

---

TABLE 17-2. American Antitrust Law Is Based on a Handful of Statutes

The Sherman, Clayton, and Federal Trade Commission acts laid the foundation for American antitrust law. Interpretation of these acts has fleshed out modern antitrust doctrines.

The Antitrust Laws

Sherman Antitrust Act (1890, as amended)

§1. Every contract, combination in the form of trust or otherwise, or conspiracy, in restraint of trade or commerce among the several States, or with foreign nations, is declared to be illegal.

§2. Every person who shall monopolize, or attempt to monopolize, or combine or conspire with any other person or persons, to monopolize any part of the trade or commerce among the several States, or with foreign nations, shall be deemed guilty of a felony. . . .

Clayton Antitrust Act (1914, as amended)

§2. It shall be unlawful . . . to discriminate in price between different purchasers of commodities of like grade and quality . . . where the effect of such discrimination may be substantially to lessen competition or tend to create a monopoly in any line of commerce. . . . *Provided,*

That nothing herein contained shall prevent differentials which make only due allowance for differences in the cost. . . .

§3. That it shall be unlawful for any person . . . to lease or make a sale or contract . . . on the condition, agreement, or understanding that the lessee or purchaser thereof shall not use or deal in the . . . commodities of a competitor . . . where the effect . . . may be to substantially lessen competition or tend to create a monopoly in any line of commerce.

§7. No [corporation] . . . shall acquire . . . the whole or any part . . . of another [corporation] . . . where . . . the effect of such an acquisition may be substantially to lessen competition, or to tend to create a monopoly.

Federal Trade Commission Act (1914, as amended)

§5. Unfair methods of competition . . . and unfair or deceptive acts or practices . . . are declared unlawful.

sions. But the body of laws proved ineffective against the mergers and trusts[2] that began to grow in the 1880s. Populist sentiments then led to passage of the Sherman Act in 1890.

The Sherman Act made it illegal to "monopolize trade" and outlawed any "combination or conspiracy in restraint of trade." But beyond an antipathy toward "monopolizing" there is no evidence that anyone had clear notions about which actions were to be regarded as legal or illegal.

Clayton Act (1914)

The Clayton Act was passed to clarify and strengthen the Sherman Act. It outlawed *tying contracts* (in which a customer is forced to buy product B if she wants product A); it ruled *price discrimination* and exclusive dealings illegal; it banned *interlocking directorates* (in which some people would be directors of more than one firm in the same industry) and *mergers* formed by acquiring common stock of competitors. These practices were not illegal per se (meaning "in themselves") but only when they might substantially lessen competition. The Clayton Act emphasized prevention as well as punishment.

Another important element of the Clayton Act was that it specifically provided antitrust immunity to labor unions.

Federal Trade Commission

In 1914 the Federal Trade Commission (FTC) was established to prohibit "unfair methods of competition" and to warn against anticompetitive mergers. In 1938, the FTC was also empowered to ban false and deceptive advertising. To enforce its powers, the FTC can investigate, hold hearings, and issue cease-and-desist orders.

BASIC ISSUES IN ANTITRUST: CONDUCT AND STRUCTURE

While the basic antitrust statutes are straightforward, it is not easy in practice to decide how to apply them to specific situations of market structure or conduct. Actual law has evolved through an interaction of economic theory and actual case law.

---

[2] A *trust* is a group of firms, usually in the same industry, that combine together by a legal agreement to regulate production, prices, or other industrial conditions.

Illegal Conduct

Some of the earliest antitrust decisions concerned illegal behavior. The courts have ruled that certain kinds of collusive behavior are illegal per se; there is simply no defense that will justify these actions. The offenders cannot defend themselves by pointing to some worthy objective (such as product quality) or mitigating circumstance (such as low profits).

The most important class of per se illegal conduct is agreements among competing firms to fix prices, restrict output, or divide markets. Such actions have the effect of raising prices and lowering output. Even the severest critics of antitrust policy can find no redeeming virtue in price fixing.

Other forms of conduct are also limited by antitrust laws. These include:

- *Predatory pricing*, in which a firm sells its goods for less than production costs (usually interpreted as marginal cost or average variable cost). The argument against predatory pricing is that a big company can use its financial resources to cut prices and drive smaller rivals out of business, and then it can jack up prices. In recent years, some giant discount chains have been accused of predatory pricing by smaller local competitors.
- *Tying contracts* or arrangements, whereby a firm will sell product A only if the purchaser buys product B.
- *Price discrimination,* in which a firm sells the same product to different customers at different prices for reasons not related to cost or meeting competition.

Note that the practices on this list relate to a firm's *conduct.* It is the acts themselves that are illegal, not the structure of the industry in which the acts take place. Perhaps the most celebrated example is the great electric-equipment conspiracy. In 1961, the electric-equipment industry was found guilty of collusive price agreements. Executives of the largest companies—such as GE and Westinghouse—conspired to raise prices and covered their tracks like characters in a spy novel by meeting in hunting lodges, using code names, and making telephone calls from phone booths. Although the top executives in these companies were apparently unaware of what the vice presidents just below them were doing, they had put much pressure on their vice presidents for increased sales. The companies agreed to pay extensive damages to their customers for overcharges, and some executives were jailed for their antitrust violations.

Recent Price-Fixing Cases. Recent cases involve some interesting features of law and economics. One case involved Archer Daniels Midland (ADM), a large food-processing company. The company engaged in price fixing of lysine, an additive that makes pigs grow properly. In 1996, the company was fined $100 million—the largest antitrust fine in history—indicating that price fixing not only is illegal but also is not a profitable business practice. In addition, the government relied on game theory by using a "prisoner's dilemma" strategy on ADM executives. Each was told that if he confessed to price fixing, he would have a reduced sentence, while if he did not, he would be treated harshly. One unanticipated side effect of this strategy was that one executive actually manufactured evidence against his own employer!

An interesting academic case involved an investigation by the Justice Department of the way that colleges and universities set tuition and scholarship aid. The government claimed that a small group of educational institutions conspired to reduce scholarship competition for top students by agreeing to award scholarships only on the basis of financial need and by comparing prospective aid awards to commonly admitted applicants. One of the defendants, the Massachusetts Institute of Technology (MIT), fought the government in the courts, arguing that nonprofit institutions should meet a different standard than profit-maximizing businesses. MIT prevailed on appeal in court, but this case raised novel issues about the manner in which antitrust law and regulations will be applied to activities of educational and other nonprofit institutions.

Structure: Is Bigness Badness?

While price fixing and other illegal activities are important, the most visible antitrust cases concern the structure of industries rather than the conduct of companies. They consist of attempts to *break up* large firms as well as preventive *antimerger* proceedings against proposed mergers of large firms.

The first surge of antitrust activity under the Sherman Act focused on dismantling existing monopolies. In 1911, the Supreme Court ordered that the American Tobacco Company and Standard Oil be broken up into many separate companies. In condemning these flagrant monopolies, the Supreme Court enunciated the important "rule of reason": Only *unreasonable* restraints of trade (mergers, agreements, and the like) came within the scope of the Sherman Act and were considered illegal.

The rule-of-reason doctrine virtually nullified the antitrust laws' attack on monopolistic mergers, as shown by the U.S. Steel case (1920). J. P. Morgan had put this giant together by merger, and at its peak it controlled 60 percent of the market. But the Supreme Court held that size alone was no offense. In that period, as today, courts focused more on anticompetitive *conduct* than on pure monopoly *structure.*

The high-water mark of antitrust activity against bigness was the Alcoa case in 1945. Alcoa had gained a 90 percent market share in aluminum, by means that were not in themselves illegal. It had installed capacity in anticipation of the growth of demand and kept prices low to prevent potential competition. It had attempted to maintain its large market share by keeping entry unprofitable rather than by engaging in anticompetitive acts. The Court nonetheless found that Alcoa had violated the Sherman Act, holding that monopoly power, even if lawfully acquired, could constitute an economic evil and should be condemned. During this period, the courts came to emphasize market structure along with market conduct: *Monopoly power, even without otherwise illegal conduct, was declared illegal.*

Recent Developments. The most important antitrust cases of recent years involved three giant firms in two vitally important industries—telecommunications and computers. A review of the three cases reveals the flavor of modern thinking about antitrust policy.

The AT&T case. Until 1983 AT&T had a virtual monopoly on the telecommunications market. It handled more than 95 percent of all long-distance calls, provided 85 percent of all local lines, and sold most of the nation's telephone equipment. The complex of companies owned by AT&T—often called the Bell System—included Bell Telephone Labs, Western Electric Company, and 23 Bell operating companies.

In 1974, the Department of Justice filed a far-reaching suit. It contended that AT&T had (1) prevented competing long-distance carriers (like MCI) from connecting to local exchanges and (2) obstructed other equipment manufacturers from selling telecommunications equipment to subscribers or to Bell operating companies. The government's central legal and economic argument was that Bell had used its regulated natural monopoly in the local telephone market to create monopoly power in the long-distance and telephone-equipment markets.

Bell took two lines of defense. First, it denied many factual charges or rebutted their relevance. Second, it claimed that the U.S. telephone system was the best in the world precisely *because* Bell owned and operated most of that system. In a line of argument similar to the Schumpeterian hypothesis (see Chapter 10), AT&T argued that the size and scope of the Bell System promoted rapid technological change and made its monopoly a reasonable and efficient way to conduct the telephone business.

The bizarre ending of the case astonished everyone. Fearful that the case might end unfavorably, Bell's management settled with the government in a consent decree that met every point of the government's proposed remedy. Bell's local telephone operating companies were divested (or legally separated) from AT&T and, in 1984, were regrouped into seven large regional telephone holding companies. AT&T retained its long-distance operations as well as Bell Labs (the research organization) and Western Electric (the equipment manufacturer). The net effect was an 80 percent reduction in the size and sales of the Bell System.

The dismantling of the Bell System set off a breathtaking revolution in the telecommunications industry. This revolution was completed when Congress passed the 1995 Communications Act, which essentially took the gloves off all the players—including AT&T. Today, telephone companies are free to buy equipment from anyone and are entering joint ventures in cellular telephone, cable television, data services, and Internet provision, as well as traditional telephone service.

More significant is the explosion of new technologies that are invading the traditional communications markets. Cellular phone systems are breaking the natural monopoly of Alexander Graham

Bell's twisted copper wires; telephone companies are joining forces to bring television signals into homes; fiber-optic lines are beginning to function as data superhighways, carrying massive amounts of data around the country and the world. The Internet is linking people and places together in ways that were unimagined a decade ago. No one can say whether these technologies would have come as far and as fast had the Bell System not been broken up, but it is clear that monopoly is not necessary for rapid technological change.

The IBM case. A second set of antitrust cases in recent years involved computer companies. The first case was an attempt by the government to dismember IBM. Filed in 1969, the suit charged that IBM "has attempted to monopolize and has monopolized . . . general purpose digital computers." The government charged that IBM had a dominant market share, with 76 percent of the market in 1967. Moreover, the government claimed that IBM had used many devices to prevent others from competing; the alleged anticompetitive steps included tie-in pricing, excessively low prices to discourage entry, and introduction of new products that tended to reduce the attractiveness of the products of other companies.

IBM contested the government case with tenacity and vigor. IBM's major defense was that the government was penalizing success rather than anticompetitive behavior. The fundamental dilemma in such cases had been crisply stated in the Alcoa case: "The successful competitor having been urged to compete must not be turned on when he wins." IBM claimed that the government was punishing the firm that had accurately foreseen the enormous potential in the computer revolution and had dominated the industry through its "superior skill, foresight, and industry."

The case dragged along inconclusively until the Reagan administration's antitrust chief, William Baxter, decided in 1982 to dismiss the case as "without merit." The government's reasoning was that, unlike the telecommunications industry, the computer industry was unregulated and subject to the full force of market competition. Baxter held that this industry was intrinsically competitive and that government attempts to restructure the computer market were more likely to harm than promote economic efficiency.

The Microsoft case. The most recent major cases of market structure have involved government investigation of the giant software company Microsoft. In the early 1990s, the government investigated claims that Microsoft was monopolizing the market for operating systems. In that period, more than 80 percent of the world's computers were running on Microsoft operating systems like MS-DOS and Windows. The government made a number of complaints about Microsoft's behavior. Most involved the possibility that Microsoft would project its market power in operating systems into the market for applications. This could occur because Microsoft would bundle its applications or network services with its operating system. Another concern was that Microsoft was engaging in predatory pricing of its operating systems by charging computer companies for Windows even when they didn't install it. Microsoft defended itself vigorously. In 1994, the government and Microsoft agreed on a consent decree in which Microsoft agreed to change its pricing practices but would continue to be able to develop applications. But the government has continued to monitor Microsoft's activities closely, including criticizing Microsoft's attempt to purchase another large software firm. The latest concern has been that Microsoft might displace Netscape as the leading web browser. Too much commercial success is apparently a mixed blessing.

Lessons from the Structural Cases.
What lessons have economists drawn from the large structural cases we have reviewed? It is ironical that breaking up large companies appears to have benefited not only consumers but even the companies themselves. The remnants of the Bell System have in fact prospered, while the once-mighty IBM has fallen sharply in terms of both market share and market value. Since 1983, IBM share prices have fallen more than 20 percent, while the total value of all the parts of the former Bell System has risen over 200 percent. Some industrial-organization specialists hold that the forced dismantling of the Bell System may have been just what the doctor ordered, bringing more vitality and competition to that industry as the information revolution picked up speed.

By contrast, leaving IBM intact allowed the company to make a series of blunders that left it a weakened and discouraged organization. What brought IBM down? IBM was unable to capitalize on the revolution in personal computers and watched that technology gradually displace the mainframe computers that IBM dominated. According to one critic, it was "IBM's fear of risk, its civil-service mentality, its brainwashing of employees, its failure to make innovative products that anticipate customers' desires, its inability to adapt its work force quickly enough."[3] IBM survived the antitrust wars only to be humbled because it could not adapt to a changing marketplace. Many industrial-organization economists are wondering how the government's scrutiny of Microsoft will affect that company's innovative vigor.

Mergers: Law and Practice
Companies can gain market power through growth (plowing back earnings and building new plants). But a much easier way to gain market share, or simply to get bigger, is to merge with another company. The 1980s saw a tremendous growth in merger activity.

Horizontal mergers—in which companies in the same industry combine—are forbidden under the Clayton Act when the merger is likely to reduce competition in the industry substantially. Case law and the Department of Justice's 1982, 1984, and 1992 merger guidelines clarified the meaning of the vague statutory language. Under these guidelines, industries are divided into three groups: unconcentrated, moderately concentrated, and highly concentrated. Mergers in the latter two types of industries will be challenged even in cases where the firms involved have small market shares. For example, in a highly concentrated industry, if a firm with a market share of 10 percent acquires one with a share of 2.5 percent or more, the Department of Justice is likely to challenge the merger.

Vertical mergers occur when two firms at different stages of the production process come together. In recent years, the courts took a hard line toward vertical mergers. They worried about the potential restriction of competition through exclusive dealings if two independent firms merged. Courts tended to pay relatively little heed to the potential efficiencies of joint operations in vertical mergers.

---

[3] Paul Carroll, *Big Blues: The Unmaking of IBM* (Crown, New York, 1993).

As part of its campaign to reduce government intervention, the Reagan administration changed the guidelines on mergers. The new guidelines greatly relaxed enforcement with respect to both vertical and horizontal mergers. Many economists believe that these changes brought on the great wave of mergers and acquisitions of the 1980s.

A third kind of combination, called **conglomerate mergers**, joins together unrelated businesses. In a conglomerate merger, a chemical or steel company might buy an oil company. The critics of conglomerates make two points. First, they note that the absolute size of the largest corporations is awesome. The largest 200 corporations control almost $2.5 trillion of assets. The largest corporations therefore have great economic and political power. Increasingly, many observers worry more about the way that large organizations can buy favors in the political process than about how they abuse their market power.

The second point made by the critics of conglomerates is that many of these combinations serve no economic purpose. They are, it is argued, simply a brand of "boardroom poker" to entertain managers bored with supervising their tiresome steel or chemical operations. And, indeed, there is a point here: What does the airplane business have in common with meat-packing? Or typewriters with birth-control pills? Or computer leasing with passenger-bus operations?

Conglomerates are not without defenders. Some economists argue that these mergers bring good modern management to backward firms and that takeovers, like bankruptcy, represent the economy's way of eliminating deadwood in the economic struggle for survival. But there is no consensus on the merits or demerits of conglomerate mergers. No study has found major gains or costs, so perhaps the best policy is to keep a watchful eye.

ANTITRUST LAWS AND EFFICIENCY

Economic and legal views toward regulation and antitrust have changed dramatically over the last two decades. During the period, industries were deregulated, and antitrust law abandoned its mission "to put an end to great aggregations of capital because of the helplessness of the individual before them" (to quote from the 1945 Alcoa decision). Increasingly, both these instruments were directed toward the goal of improving economic efficiency. If big is efficient, big shall reign.

What has prompted the changing attitude toward antitrust policy? First, it grew out of technical developments in economic research. Economists found that performance was not always closely associated with structure. Some large firms (Intel, Microsoft, and Boeing, for example) and some highly concentrated markets (microprocessors, telecommunications, and aircraft manufacture) proved to be among the industries with the highest performance with respect to innovation and productivity growth. Whereas economic theory held that monopoly keeps prices high, historical experience indicated that highly concentrated industries often had rapidly declining prices relative to less concentrated industries. At the same time, some unconcentrated industries, such as agriculture and financial services, exhibited outstanding performance. No iron law has been found to link structure and performance.

How can we explain this paradox? Some economists invoke the Schumpeterian hypothesis. Firms in concentrated industries collect monopoly profits, to be sure. But the size of the market also means that large firms can appropriate much of the return on research and development (R&D) investments, and this explains the high levels of R&D and the rapid technological change in concentrated industries. If, as Schumpeter claimed, technological change originates in large firms, it would be foolish to slay these giant geese who lay such golden eggs. This view has been well expressed by Lester Thurow, former dean of the MIT Sloan School of Management: "The millions spent on the IBM [antitrust] case would have been better spent if they had been plowed back into research and development on keeping America No. 1 in computers."

A second thrust of the new approach to regulation and antitrust arose from revised views of the nature of competition. Considering both experimental evidence and observation, many economists have come to believe that intense rivalry will spring up even in oligopolistic markets as long as collusion is strictly prohibited. Indeed, in the words of Richard Posner, formerly a law professor and currently a federal judge:

> The only truly unilateral acts by which firms can get or keep monopoly power are practices like commit-

ting fraud on the Patent Office or blowing up a competitor's plant, and fraud and force are in general adequately punished under other statutes.[4]

In this view, the only valid purpose of the antitrust laws should be to replace existing statutes with a simple prohibition against *agreements*—explicit or tacit—that unreasonably restrict competition.

Third, the swing of the pendulum against strict antitrust enforcement came from the increasing emphasis on market forces and market-based incentives. This position was inspired by proponents of the Chicago School, which held that most monopoly power derives from government interventions. According to this view, the major pools of monopoly power lie in areas protected by government fiat. Important examples include economic regulations and rules (see Table 17-1) in such diverse areas as foreign trade, the exemption of labor unions from antitrust laws, monopoly protection conveyed by the patent laws, barriers to entry into the professions, and restrictions in medical care. Advocates of the laissez-faire view argue that reducing government regulation would enhance competition.

A final reason for the reduced activism in antitrust has been the increase in import competition. As more foreign firms gain a foothold in the American economy, they tend to compete vigorously for market share and often upset established sales patterns and pricing practices. As the sales of Japanese automakers increased, the cozy coexistence of the Big Three American auto firms dissolved. Many economists believe that the threat of foreign competition is a much more powerful tool for enforcing market discipline than are antitrust laws.

What is the future of antitrust? No one can predict the direction of future attitudes toward big business. Nonetheless, the views supporting the efficiency-oriented approach are shared by economists and lawyers across the political spectrum, and the intensity of foreign competition is unlikely to change, so a return to the trust-busting fervor of earlier years appears unlikely in the near future.

SUMMARY

A. Business Regulation: Theory and Practice

1. Regulation consists of government rules commanding firms to alter their business conduct. Economic regulation involves the control of prices, production, entry and exit conditions, and standards of service in a particular industry; social regulation consists of rules aimed at correcting information failures and externalities, particularly those that impinge on health and safety and the environment.

2. The normative view of regulation is that government intervention is appropriate when there are major market failures. These include excess market power in an industry, inadequate supply of information to consumers and workers, and externalities such as pollution. Economists have developed a positive theory of regulation in which regulation often serves the purpose of actually benefiting regulated firms, whose interests are furthered by exclusion of potential rivals.

3. The strongest case for economic regulation comes in regard to natural monopolies. Natural monopoly occurs when average costs are falling for every level of output, so the most efficient organization of the industry requires production by a single firm. Few industries come close to this condition today—perhaps only local utilities like water and electricity.

4. In conditions of natural monopoly, governments regulate the price and service of private companies. Traditionally, government regulation of monopoly has required that price be set at the average cost of production. The ideal regulation would require price to be set equal to marginal cost, but this approach is impractical because it requires that government subsidize the monopolist. A new approach is performance-based regulation, such as price caps, which provide superior incentives to regulated firms to reduce costs and improve productivity.

5. Given the strength of competitive forces, particularly from the global marketplace, the case for economic regulation holds for few industries today. The deregu-

---

[4] Richard A. Posner, *Antitrust Law: An Economic Prospectus* (University of Chicago Press, Chicago, 1976), p. 212. The writings of Posner—along with those of Robert Bork, William Baxter, and William Landes—have been highly influential in determining the new climate of antitrust thinking.

lation movement of the 1970s reduced the extent of economic regulation markedly, producing gains in industries such as the airlines.

B. Antitrust Policy

6. Antitrust policy, prohibiting anticompetitive conduct and preventing monopolistic structures, is the primary way that public policy limits abuses of market power by large firms. This policy grew out of legislation like the Sherman Act (1890) and the Clayton Act (1914). The primary purposes of antitrust are (*a*) to prohibit anticompetitive activities (which include agreements to fix prices or divide up territories, price discrimination, and tie-in agreements) and (*b*) to break up monopoly structures. In today's legal theory, such structures are those that have excessive market power (a large share

of the market) and also engage in anticompetitive acts.

7. In addition to limiting the behavior of existing firms, antitrust law prevents mergers that would lessen competition. Today, horizontal mergers (between firms in the same industry) are the main source of concern, while vertical and conglomerate mergers tend to be tolerated.

8. Antitrust policy has been significantly influenced by economic thinking during the last two decades. As a result, antitrust policy now focuses almost exclusively on improving efficiency, while it ignores earlier populist concerns with bigness itself. Moreover, in today's economy—with intense competition from foreign producers and deregulated rivals—many believe that antitrust policy should concentrate primarily on preventing collusive agreements like price fixing.

CONCEPTS FOR REVIEW

Regulation

two kinds of regulation:
  economic vs. social regulation
old-style (command-and-control) vs.
  new (economic-incentive)
  regulation
natural monopoly

reasons for regulation:
  market power
  externalities
  information failures

Antitrust Policy

Sherman, Clayton, and FTC acts

per se prohibitions vs. the "rule of
  reason"
mergers:
  vertical
  horizontal
  conglomerate
efficiency-oriented antitrust policy

QUESTIONS FOR DISCUSSION

1. What are the major weapons that government has to restrain monopoly power? Describe the strengths and weaknesses of each policy.

2. Review the three pricing outcomes in Figure 17-2. Can you think of the difficulties of implementing the ideal regulated price? (*Hint:* Where does the country get the revenues? Is *MC* easy to measure?) Similarly, can you think of reasons why many economists would prefer the unregulated to the regulated outcome? (*Hint:* What if P_M is not much above P_R? What if you worried about the interest-group theory of regulation?)

3. Explain why price-cap or inflation-minus-*X* price regulation has better incentives than average cost price regulation. Explain why the latter is better able to prevent monopoly profits.

4. "Microsoft, the large software company, is not bad just because it is big." Discuss, particularly with reference to the application of antitrust laws to large companies.

5. Examine the cost and demand curves in Figure 17-1. Using those curves, draw in the monopoly price and output. Compare these with the ideal regulated output and price. Describe the difference.

6. Two important approaches to antitrust are *structure* and *conduct*. The former looks only at the structure of the industry (such as the concentration of firms); the latter, at firm conduct (e.g., price fixing).
   a. Review the various statutes and cases to see which are related to conduct and which to structure. What about the merger guidelines of the 1980s?
   b. What are the advantages and disadvantages of each approach?

7. Make a list of the industries that you feel are candidates for the title "natural monopoly." Then review the different strategies for intervention to prevent exercise of monopoly power. What would you do about each industry on your list?

8. Show that a profit-maximizing, unregulated monopolist will never operate in the price-inelastic region of its demand curve. Show how regulation can force the monopolist onto the inelastic portion of its demand curve. What will be the impact of an increase in the regulated price of a monopolist upon revenues and profits when it is operating on (*a*) the elastic portion of the demand curve, (*b*) the inelastic portion of the demand curve, and (*c*) the unit-elastic portion of the demand curve?

CHAPTER 18
PROTECTING THE ENVIRONMENT

Growth for the sake of growth is the ideology of the cancer cell.

Edward Abbey

Clean air, clean water, unspoiled land—all of us would agree that these are desirable goals. But how much are we willing to pay to achieve them? And what is the threat to humanity if we do not respect the limits of our natural environment?

At one pole is an environmentalist philosophy of confines and perils. In this view, human activities threaten to disrupt the intricate web of natural ecosystems, unintended consequences threaten to overwhelm human ingenuity, and we must be ever vigilant lest the dikes break and we are inundated by the angry seas. The environmentalist point of view is well expressed in the bleak warning from the distinguished Harvard biologist E. O. Wilson:

> Environmentalism . . . sees humanity as a biological species tightly dependent on the natural world. . . . Many of Earth's vital resources are about to be exhausted, its atmospheric chemistry is deteriorating, and human populations have already grown dangerously large. Natural ecosystems, the wellsprings of a healthful environment, are being irreversibly degraded. . . . I am radical enough to take seriously the question heard with increasing frequency: Is humanity suicidal?[1]

Believers in this dismal picture argue that humans must practice "sustainable" economic growth and learn to live with the limitations of our scarce natural resources or we will suffer dire and irreparable consequences.

At the other pole are "cornucopians," who believe that we are far from exhausting either natural resources or the capabilities of technology. In this optimistic view, we can look forward to limitless economic growth and rising living standards, with human ingenuity well able to cope with any environmental problems. If oil runs out, there is plenty of coal and uranium. If those don't pan out, then new technologies will be induced by rising prices. In this view, technology, economic growth, and market forces are the saviors, not the villains.

In fact, humans have been encroaching on the environment for ages. Historically, the major interventions occurred when humans moved into settlements, converted forests into farms, and began to breed domestic plants and animals. But this qualitative transformation pales beside today's massive bioengineering, deforestation, and extraction of mineral and plant resources from the earth.

All these points raise the fundamental concerns voiced by Wilson and others. Generally, economists tend to lie between the environmentalist and the cornucopian extremes, pointing to the importance of a wise combination of market forces and government intervention as key to both environmental survival and continued improvements in living standards.

---

[1] Edward O. Wilson, "Is Humanity Suicidal?" *New York Times Magazine*, May 30, 1993, p. 27.

A. POPULATION AND RESOURCE LIMITATIONS

MALTHUS AND THE DISMAL SCIENCE

Fear of the voracious appetite of a fast-growing human population lies at the heart of many worries about the environment, as the quotation from Wilson at the start of this chapter suggests. Consider the following editorial from the world's leading scientific journal:

> First of all, it is important to identify the main villain as overpopulation. In the good old days, . . . in truth there were famine, starvation, horses and buggies that contributed to pollution, fireplaces that spewed forth soot from burning soft coal, and water contaminated with microorganisms. The humans were so few, and the land so vast, that these insults to nature could be absorbed without serious consequences. This is no longer true.[2]

Half of this proposition concerns the sources of pollution and other environmental problems, a topic which is taken up in Section C. The other half concerns the behavior of human populations, which we take up here.

Economic analysis of population dates back to the Reverend T. R. Malthus. He first developed his views while arguing at breakfast against his father's perfectionist opinion that the human race was always improving. Finally the son became so agitated that he wrote *An Essay on the Principle of Population* (1798). This was an instantaneous best-seller and since then has influenced the thinking of people all over the world about population and economic growth.

Malthus began with the observation of Benjamin Franklin that in the American colonies, where resources were abundant, population tended to double every 25 years or so. He then postulated a universal tendency for population—unless checked by limited food supply—to grow exponentially, or by a geometric progression. Eventually, a population which doubles every generation—1, 2, 4, 8, 16, 32, 64, 128, 256, 512, 1024, . . . —becomes so large that there is not enough space in the world for all the people to stand.

Economics at work: Compound interest and exponential growth. Exponential growth and compound interest are important tools in economics. Exponential (or geometric) growth occurs when a variable increases at a constant proportional rate from period to period. Thus, if a population of 200 is growing at 3 percent per year, it would equal 200 in year 0, 200×1.03 in year 1, $200 \times 1.03 \times 1.03$ in year 2, $200 \times (1.03)^3$ in year 3, . . . , $200 \times (1.03)^{10}$ in year 10, and so on.

When money is invested continuously, it earns compound interest, meaning that interest is earned on past interest. Money earning compound interest grows geometrically. An intriguing calculation is to determine how much the $24 received by the Indians for Manhattan Island would, if deposited at compound interest, be worth today. Say that this fund was placed in an endowment that earned 6 percent each year from 1626. It would be worth $60 billion in 1997.

A useful rule about compound interest is the **rule of 70**, which states that a magnitude growing at a rate of r per year will double in $(70/r)$ years. For example, a human population growing at 2 percent a year will double in 35 years, whereas if you invest your funds at 7 percent per year, the funds will double in value every 10 years.

After invoking compound interest, Malthus had one further card to play. At this point he unleashed the devil of diminishing returns. He argued that because land is fixed while labor inputs keep growing, food would tend to grow by an arithmetic progression and not by a geometric progression. (Compare 1, 2, 3, 4, . . . , with 1, 2, 4, 8, ...) Malthus concluded gloomily:

> As population doubles and redoubles, it is as if the globe were halving and halving again in size—until finally it has shrunk so much that the supply of food falls below the level necessary for life.

When the law of diminishing returns is applied to a fixed supply of land, food production tends not to keep up with a population's geometric-progression rate of growth.

---

[2] *Science*, Sept. 10, 1993, p.1371.

Now, Malthus did not say that population necessarily would increase at a geometric rate. This was only its tendency if unchecked. He described the checks that operate, in all times and places, to hold population down. In his first edition, he stressed the "positive" checks that increase the death rate: pestilence, famine, and war. Later, he backed down from this gloomy doctrine, holding out hope that population growth could be slowed by "moral restraint" such as abstinence and postponed marriages.

This important application of diminishing returns illustrates the profound effects a simple theory can have. Malthus' ideas had wide repercussions. His book was used to support a stern revision of the English poor laws. Under the influence of Malthus' writings, people argued that poverty should be made as uncomfortable as possible. His opinions also bolstered the argument that trade unions could not improve the welfare of workers— since any increase in their wages would allegedly only cause workers to reproduce until all were reduced to a bare subsistence.

Even today, the ghost of Malthus reappears in "doomsday" economics, such as a famous computer study called *The Limits to Growth* and its 1992 sequel *Beyond the Limits*.[3] The predictions of this modern-day Malthusianism were even more dismal than the original gospel:

> If present growth trends in world population, industrialization, pollution, food problems, and resource depletion continue unchanged, the limits to growth on this planet will be reached within the next one hundred years. The most probable results will be a rather sudden and uncontrollable decline in both population and industrial capacity.[4]

Flawed Prophecies of Malthus. Despite Malthus' careful statistical studies, demographers today think that his views were oversimplified. In his discussion of diminishing returns, Malthus never fully anticipated the technological miracle of the Industrial Revolution. Nor did he foresee that after 1870 population growth in most Western nations would begin to decline just as living standards and real wages grew most rapidly.

In the century following Malthus, technological advance shifted out the production-possibility frontiers of countries in Europe and North America. Indeed, technological change occurred so quickly that output far outpaced population, resulting in a rapid rise in real wages. Nevertheless, the germs of truth in Malthus' doctrines are still important for understanding the population behavior of India, Ethiopia, Nigeria, and other parts of the globe where the race between population and food supply continues today.

POPULATION, POLLUTION, AND LIVING STANDARDS

There is no doubt that growing human populations are not healthy for the trees, wolves, and marsh weeds that are pushed aside to make way for cities and other forms of human settlement. But is it also true, as modern-day Malthusians suggest, that those areas that are most heavily populated are also the most miserable? Are economic growth and industrialization the road to environmental ruin?

No such simple conclusion can be read from the historical record. Figure 18-1 shows population density and per capita income along with the line that best fits the data for 72 major countries. In fact, those areas with higher population density tend to have higher, not lower, living standards.

What about population and human health? On the whole, studies by the World Bank clearly indicate that human health is highly correlated with per capita income and, moreover, that the most important indicators of environmental degradation, such as poor sanitation and unsafe drinking water, are found in the poorest countries. One of the most thoughtful students of the relationship between population, economic development, and pollution is Oxford's Wilfred Beckerman, who summarized his findings as follows:

> The important environmental problems for the 75% of the world's population that live in developing countries are local problems of access to safe drinking water or decent sanitation, and urban degradation. Furthermore, there is clear evidence that . . . in the end the best—and probably the only—way to attain a decent environment in most countries is to become rich.[5]

---

[3] Donella H. Meadows, Dennis L. Meadows, and Jørgen Randers, *The Limits to Growth* (Potomac, Wash., 1972) and *Beyond the Limits* (Chelsea Green Publishing, Post Mills, Vt., 1992).

[4] *The Limits to Growth*, p. 23.

[5] Wilfred Beckerman, "Economic Growth and the Environment," *World Development*, vol. 20, no. 4, 1992, p. 482.

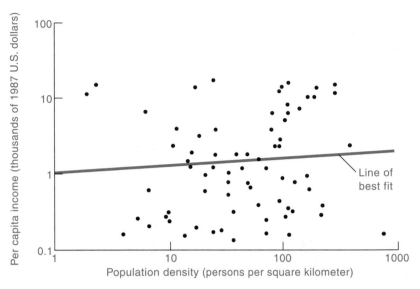

FIGURE 18-1. Population Density and Incomes

Is it true that living standards decline as population increases? Since the golden age of Athens, per capita incomes have generally been weakly but positively associated with population density. This scatter diagram shows the relation in 72 major countries for 1987. (Source: World Bank.)

What about the environment and alternative economic systems? You might think that a centrally planned economy would avoid the problems of a market economy by incorporating the externalities of population and environment into decisions. Experience reveals, ironically, that the socialist economies of Eastern Europe and the Soviet Union left a legacy of filth and far worse environmental problems than exist in the market economies. Under communism, for example, much of East Germany's power was provided by highly polluting brown coal, which poisoned the air with soot and sulfur dioxide. For East Germans, the switch to a market economy promises not only a boost in living standards but also an improved environment.

B. NATURAL-RESOURCE ECONOMICS

RESOURCE CATEGORIES

What are the important natural resources? They include land, water, and the atmosphere. This trio produces a variety of useful goods and services. The land gives us food and wine from fertile soils, as well as oil and other minerals from the earth's mantle. Our waters give us fish, recreation, and a remarkably efficient medium for transportation. The precious atmosphere yields breathable air, beautiful sunsets, and space for airplanes to fly in. Natural resources and the environment are in one sense just another set of factors of production, like labor and capital. They serve humans because we derive output or satisfaction from the services of natural resources.

Appropriable vs. Inappropriable Resources

In analyzing natural resources, economists make two key distinctions. The most important is whether the resources are appropriable or inappropriable. Recall that a commodity is called **appropriable** when firms or consumers can capture its full economic value. Appropriable natural resources include land (whose fertility can be captured by the farmer who sells wheat or wine produced on the land), mineral resources like oil and gas (where the owner can sell the value of the mineral deposit on markets), and trees (where the owner can sell the land or the trees to the highest bidder). In a well-functioning competitive market, we would expect that appropriable natural resources would be efficiently priced and allocated.

But we must be careful not to push these results too far. A second class of natural resources, known as **inappropriable** resources, can definitely cause economic problems. An inappropriable resource is one whose use is free to the individual but costly to society. In other words, inappropriable resources are ones involving externalities. Recall that *externalities* are those situations in which production or consumption imposes uncompensated costs or benefits on other parties.

Goods with externalities can be compared with normal economic goods. Market transactions involve voluntary exchange in which people exchange goods for money. When a firm uses a scarce appropriable resource like land, oil, or trees, it buys the good from its owner, who is fully compensated for the incremental costs of production of the good. But many interactions take place outside markets. Firm A dumps a toxic chemical into a stream and fouls the water for people who fish or swim downstream. Firm A has used the scarce, clean water without paying people whose water is fouled and has generated an external diseconomy.

Examples of inappropriable resources are found in every corner of the globe. Take the example of fish. A school of tuna not only provides food for the dinner table but also stock for breeding future generations of tuna. Yet this breeding potential is not captured or appropriated by markets; no one buys or sells the mating behavior of dog-toothed tuna. Consequently, when a fishing boat pulls out a tuna, it does not compensate society for the depletion of future breeding potential. Therefore, when unregulated, fisheries tend to be overfished.

This leads to the fundamental result of the economics of resources and the environment:

When resources are inappropriable, showing externalities, markets provide incorrect signals. Generally, markets produce too much of goods that generate external diseconomies and too little of goods that produce external economies.

Renewable vs. Nonrenewable Resources

Techniques for managing resources depend on whether the resources are renewable or nonrenewable. A **nonrenewable resource** is one whose services are essentially fixed in supply and which is not regenerated quickly enough to be economically relevant. Important examples are the fossil fuels, which were laid down millions of years ago and can be treated as fixed for human civilizations, and nonfuel mineral resources, such as copper, silver, gold, stone, and sand.

A second category is **renewable resources**, whose services are replenished regularly and which, if properly managed, can yield useful services indefinitely. Solar energy, agricultural land, river water, forests,

TABLE 18-1. Resource Classification

Resources are classified as inappropriable or appropriable according to whether there are significant externalities involved in their production or consumption. In addition, for nonrenewable resources, like oil and natural gas, the economic question is how to allocate the finite resource over space and time. For renewable resources, like timber or fisheries, the key issue is prudent management so that the yield maximizes the value of the resource.

	Renewable	Nonrenewable
Appropriable	Timber, agricultural land, solar energy	Oil, natural gas, copper
Inappropriable	Fisheries, air quality, mountain views	Climate, radioactive wastes

Sector	Value added, 1987* ($, billions)	Percent of gross domestic product, 1987
Renewable-resource industries:		1.8
Farming	59.8	
Forestry, timber cut	1.5	
Fisheries	3.7	
Hydroelectric-power generation	15.1	
Nonrenewable-resource industries:		2.2
Oil and natural gas	71.8	
Coal	13.3	
Other nonfuel minerals:		
Geologically scarce+	3.7	
Geologically superabundant‡	1.9	
Stone, clay, sand, etc.	7.8	

*Total sales less puchases of materials; includes profit, wages, interest, rent, depreciation, and taxes.

+ Includes 17 minerals such as copper, gold, silver, and vanadium.

‡Includes minerals such as iron and aluminum.

TABLE 18-2. Production from Different Resources, 1987
A wide variety of products are based on natural resources of both the renewable and non-renewable variety. Estimates of total output or sales include not only the economic value of the natural resource but also the returns to capital and labor. [Source: "Annual Input-Output Accounts of the U.S. Economy: 1987," *Survey of Current Business* (April 1992), pp. 55–71; Robert Gordon et al., *Toward a New Iron Age?* (Yale University Press, New Haven, 1989).]

and fisheries are among the most important categories of renewable resources.

The principles of efficient management of these two classes of resources present quite different challenges, as we will see below. Efficient use of a nonrenewable resource entails the distribution of a finite quantity of the resource over time: Should we use our low-cost natural gas for this generation or save it for the future? By contrast, prudent use of renewable resources involves ensuring that the flow of services is efficiently maintained, say, through appropriate forest management, protection of breeding grounds of fish, or regulation of pollution into rivers and lakes.

Table 18-1 shows this fundamental division of resources along with major examples of each.

ALLOCATION OF APPROPRIABLE NATURAL RESOURCES

We begin our survey with appropriable resources—those for which the underlying resource is privately owned or managed and where the major costs and benefits of production and consumption are captured in the marketplace. What are the most important natural-resource industries? Table 18-2 shows the value added in each of the major industries as measured in the national income and product accounts. The total of all marketed natural-resource industries constituted 4 percent of total output in 1987; two industries, farming and oil and gas, accounted for three-quarters of the economic output of the marketed natural resources.

Even though the share of resources in total income is low, it would be foolish to be complacent and assume that resources are unimportant for economic growth. Might we not someday exhaust some essential natural resource, like energy, and find ourselves devoting much effort to finding replacement power? Nothing would plunge a modern industrial economy into chaos and poverty more quickly than exhausting the fuel for energy-using factors like the internal combustion engine, central heating and cooling, electric motors, and electronics. This is worrisome because 90 percent of American energy consumption today comes from finite, nonrenewable sources like oil, gas, and coal. Should we be taking steps to limit the use of these most precious stocks of society's capital so that they will still be available for our grandchildren?

Economists answer this question in two ways. First, they point out that fossil fuels like oil and gas are finite but not "essential." An *essential* resource is one, like oxygen, for which there are no substitutes. Substitutes exist for all the energy resources. We can substitute coal for oil and gas in most uses; we can liquefy or gasify coal where liquid or gas fuels are needed; when coal runs out, we can use higher-cost solar energy, nuclear fission, and perhaps someday even nuclear fusion. These last three are superabundant in the sense that when we run out of solar energy, the earth will already be uninhabitable.

A second point concerns the relative productivity of different assets. Many environmentalists argue that energy and other natural resources like wilderness areas and old-growth forests are very special kinds of capital that need to be preserved so that we can maintain "sustainable" economic growth. Economists tend to disagree. They look at natural resources as yet another capital asset that society possesses—along with fast computers, human capital in an educated work force, and technological knowledge in its patents, scientists, and engineers. Both economists and environmentalists agree that this generation should leave an adequate stock of capital assets for future generations; but economists worry less about the exact form of capital than about its productivity. Economists ask, Would future generations benefit more from larger stocks of natural capital such as oil, gas, and coal or from more produced capital such as additional scientists, better laboratories, and libraries linked together by information superhighways?

The substitutability of natural capital and other kinds of capital is shown by the production indifference curve or "isoquant" in Figure 18-2. We show there the amounts of the two kinds of capital that would be required to attain a certain level of output in the future (Q^*), holding other inputs constant. That output can be produced at point C with a conservationist policy that emphasizes reducing energy use today, leaving much oil and gas and relatively little human capital for the future. Or it might be produced with a low-energy-price and high-education strategy at B. Either of these is feasible, and the more desirable one would be the one that has a higher consumption both now and in the future.

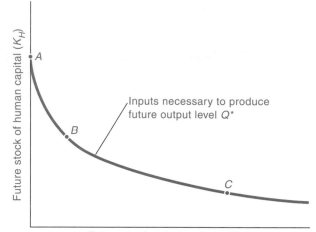

FIGURE 18-2. Natural Capital and Produced Capital Are Substitutes in Production

Output can be produced with either natural capital (K_N) or human capital (K_H). This equal-product curve shows the combination of inputs that will yield a given amount of output in the future (Q^*). Environmentalists urge conserving natural capital so that future stocks are large, as at C. Economists emphasize the need to ensure that scarce capital goes to sectors with the highest yield. If natural capital is abundant, it would be more efficient to go to point B by consuming stocks of natural capital today while building up stocks of human capital and improving technology through research and development.

Note as well that the isoquant hits the vertical axis at point A, indicating that we can produce future output level Q^* *with no oil and gas.* How is this possible? With the greater scientific and technical knowledge represented by point A, society can develop and introduce substitute technologies like clean coal or solar energy to replace the exhausted oil and gas. The curve hits the axis to indicate that in the long run, oil and gas are not essential.

Resource Price Trends

In 1973, following a war and an embargo in the Mideast, the price of oil skyrocketed, and many other resource prices also moved sharply upward. Many people feared that the world was on the verge of running out of its key nonrenewable resources.

Twenty-five years later, the price of oil was in fact only $20 per barrel. Adjusting for overall inflation, that means the price of oil is barely higher now than it was when the oil-price shocks of the 1970s occurred. Surprisingly, the same is true for almost

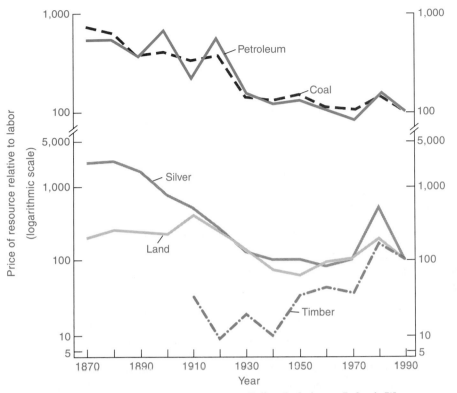

FIGURE 18-3. Prices of Most Resources Have Fallen Relative to Labor's Wage

For most natural resources, productivity and new discoveries have offset depletion, so their market prices have fallen relative to wage rates. The only major exception to this rule is timber. (Source: W. D. Nordhaus, "Lethal Model II: The Limits to Growth Revisited," *Brookings Papers on Economic Activity*, no. 2, 1992, pp. 24, 26.)

every natural resource—prices have been dropping rather than rising in the long run. Figure 18-3 shows the price trends of a number of resources compared to the price of labor. For all major appropriable natural resources except timber, the real price has fallen over the last century.

Looking at this issue from another vantage point, if the resource pessimists were correct, we might expect more and more of our national output to be devoted to resource sectors. Actually, the share of resource industries in the total economy has been declining. Figure 18-4 on page 330 shows the percentage of total national output in agriculture, forestry, fisheries, mining, and resource utilities. These industries formed about 14 percent of the economy in the late 1940s but declined to 6 percent of the economy by the early 1990s. Most of the decline came in agriculture, for reasons that we described in Chapter 4. The impact of the oil crises

of the 1970s is shown as bumps in Figure 18-4, as oil and gas prices and their share of the national economy spiked upward.

What lies behind these trends? The answer parallels our discussion of Malthus, above. In reality, the price-reducing influence of technological change and new discoveries has offset the price-increasing effect of depletion. For example, copper telephone wires are being replaced by fiber-optic cables, which use much cheaper and more plentiful raw materials. This same effect is happening in most of the natural-resource sectors.

The resource wager: In 1980 Julian Simon, an economist and a leading advocate of the cornucopian school, issued a challenge to the environmental pessimists. Offering to let them pick any natural resources they wanted, Simon, who believed that tech-

FIGURE 18-4. Appropriable Natural Resources Have Declining Share of Economy

Over the last half-century, agriculture has shrunk while other marketed natural resources have kept their share of national economy. (Source: "All" includes gross domestic product originating in agriculture, forestry, fisheries, mining, and water, gas, and electric utilities from U.S. Commerce Department.)

nology could find substitutes for any depleted resources, was willing to bet that the prices of the chosen resources would fall, and not rise.

Simon's challenge was taken up by Paul Ehrlich, a noted biologist and environmentalist. Ehrlich first came to fame in 1968 as author of *The Population Bomb,* in which he predicted imminent famines across the world. In a later book, he forecast shortages of key raw materials by 1985. Not surprisingly, Ehrlich found Simon's offer irre-

sistible. Ehrlich bet $1000 that the prices of five metals—chrome, copper, nickel, tin, and tungsten—-would rise by 1990, after adjustment for inflation.

Simon won hands down. After adjusting for inflation, the prices of all five metals dropped sharply over the decade (see Figure 18-3 for the general trend). Ehrlich not only overlooked the long-term relative trend in resource prices but had the bad fortune to pick a decade in which the business cycle reinforced longer-term forces.

C. CURBING EXTERNALITIES: ENVIRONMENTAL ECONOMICS

The task of saving the Earth's environment must and will become the central organizing principle of the post-cold-war world.

Albert J. Gore Jr., vice president of the United States (1993–)

During the 1992 presidential campaign, vice-presidential candidate Albert Gore spoke of the need to recognize the potentially catastrophic implications

of unchecked economic growth, pointing to present problems such as the Antarctic ozone hole as well as future problems like global warming. President

George Bush derided Gore, saying, "You know why I call him Ozone Man? This guy is so far off in the environmental extreme, we'll be up to our necks in owls and out of work for every American."

This political debate mirrors a deep division between those who see injury piled on top of damage as nations neglect their pressing environmental problems and others who believe that environmental problems can be easily handled with modern technology and pale beside the serious problems of war, joblessness, pestilence, drugs, and poverty. In this section we explore the nature of environmental externalities, describe why they produce economic inefficiencies, and analyze potential remedies.

In the first section of this chapter, we divided natural resources into appropriable and inappropriable resources, where an inappropriable resource is one which has externalities. An externality occurs when production or consumption inflicts involuntary costs or benefits on others. More precisely, an externality is an effect of one economic agent's behavior on another's well-being where that effect is not reflected in market transactions.

Externalities come in many guises. Some are positive (external economies), while others are negative (external diseconomies). Thus when I dump a barrel of acid into a stream, it kills fish and plants. Because I don't pay anyone for this damage, an external diseconomy occurs. When you discover a better way to clean up oil spills, the benefit will extend to many people who do not pay you for it. This is an external economy.

Some externalities are pervasive, while others have only small spillover components. When a carrier of bubonic plague entered a town during the Middle Ages, the entire population could be felled by the Black Death. On the other hand, when you chew an onion at a football stadium on a windy day, the external impacts are hardly noticeable.

Public vs. Private Goods

To illustrate the concept of external effects, consider the extreme example of a *public good*, which is a commodity that can be provided to everyone as easily as it can be provided to one person.

The case par excellence of a public good is national defense. Nothing is more vital to a society than its security. But national defense, as an economic good, differs completely from a private good

like bread. Ten loaves of bread can be divided up in many ways among individuals, and what I eat cannot be eaten by others. But national defense, once provided, affects everyone equally. It matters not at all whether you are hawk or dove, pacifist or militarist, old or young, ignorant or learned—you will receive the same amount of national security from the Army as does every other resident of the country.

Note therefore the stark contrast: The decision to provide a certain level of a public good like national defense will lead to a number of submarines, cruise missiles, and tanks to protect each of us. By contrast, the decision to consume a private good like bread is an individual act. You can eat four slices, or two, or a whole loaf; the decision is purely your own and does not commit anyone else to a particular amount of bread consumption.

The example of national defense is a dramatic and extreme case of a public good. But when you think of a smallpox vaccine, a park concert, a dam upstream on a river that prevents flood damage downstream, or many similar government projects, you generally find elements of public goods involved. In summary:

Public goods are ones whose benefits are indivisibly spread among the entire community, whether or not individuals desire to purchase the public good. **Private goods**, by contrast, are ones that can be divided up and provided separately to different individuals, with no external benefits or costs to others. Efficient provision of public goods often requires government action, while private goods can be efficiently allocated by markets.

In addition to public goods, we often see public "bads," which are public goods that impose costs uniformly across a group. These are unintended by-products of consumption or production activities. Later in this chapter, we will review the debate about the greenhouse effect, in which combustion of fossil fuels threatens global climate change. Other examples include the air and water pollution that results from chemical production, energy production, and use of automobiles; acid rain, which comes from long-distance transportation of sulfur emissions from power plants; radioactive exposure from atmospheric tests of nuclear weapons or from accidents like that at the Ukrainian plant in Chernobyl; and depletion of the ozone layer from buildup of chlorofluorocarbons. Note that in all these cases, those who caused the external effect did not desire to hurt any-one. The externalities were the unintentional but harmful side effects of economic activity.

MARKET INEFFICIENCY WITH EXTERNALITIES

Abraham Lincoln said that government is "to do for the people what needs to be done, but which they cannot, by individual effort, do at all, or do so well, for themselves." Pollution control satisfies this guide-line since the market mechanism does not provide an adequate check on polluters. Firms will not vol-untarily restrict emissions of noxious chemicals, nor will they always abstain from dumping toxic wastes in landfills. Pollution control is therefore generally held to be a legitimate government function.

Analysis of Inefficiency

Why do external diseconomies like pollution lead to economic inefficiency? Take a hypothetical coal-burning electric utility. Dirty Light & Power gen-erates an external diseconomy by spewing out tons of noxious sulfur dioxide fumes. Some of the sulfur harms the utility, requiring more frequent repaint-ing and raising the firm's medical bills. But most of the damage is "external" to the firm, settling throughout the region, harming vegetation and buildings, and causing various kinds of respiratory ailments and even premature death in people.

Being a sound profit-maximizing enterprise, Dirty Light & Power must decide how much pollu-tion it should emit. With no pollution cleanup, its workers and plant will suffer. Cleaning up every mol-ecule, on the other hand, will require heavy expenses for low-sulfur, cleaner fuels, recycling sys-tems, scrubbing equipment, and so forth. A com-plete cleanup would cost so much that Dirty Light & Power could not hope to survive in the marketplace.

The managers therefore decide to clean up just to the point where the benefits to the firm from addi-tional *abatement* or pollution removal (marginal pri-vate benefits) are equal to the extra cost of cleanup (marginal cost of abatement). The firm's accountants estimate that the marginal private benefits are $10 per ton of sulfur dioxide. Further, the firm's engi-neers tell management that removing 50 of the 400 tons normally emitted will have a marginal cost of $10 per ton. The firm has found its private optimal level

of pollution abatement of 50 tons, at which the mar-ginal private benefit to the firm just equals the mar-ginal private cost of abatement. Put differently, when Dirty Light & Power produces electricity in a least-cost manner, weighing only private costs and benefits, it will set its pollution at 350 tons and remove 50 tons.

Suppose, however, that a team of environmental scientists and economists is asked to examine the overall impacts on society rather than the impacts affecting only Dirty Light & Power. In examining the total impacts, the auditors find that the marginal *social* benefits of pollution control—including improved health and increased property values in neighboring regions—are 10 times the marginal pri-vate benefits. The impact from each extra ton on Dirty Light & Power is $10, but the rest of society suf-fers an additional impact of $90 per ton of *external costs*. Why doesn't Dirty Light & Power include the $90 of additional social benefits in its calculations? The $90 is excluded because these benefits are exter-nal to the firm and have no effect on its profits.

We now see how pollution and other externalities lead to inefficient economic outcomes: In an unreg-ulated environment, firms will determine their most profitable pollution levels by equating the marginal private benefit from abatement with the marginal pri-vate cost of abatement. When the pollution spillovers are significant, the private equilibrium will produce inefficiently high levels of pollution and too little cleanup activity.

Socially Efficient Pollution. Given that pri-vate decisions on pollution control are inefficient, is there a way of finding a better solution? Should pol-lution be completely prohibited? Should we require the damaged parties to negotiate with the polluters or allow them to sue for damages? Is there an engi-neering solution?

In general, economists look to determine the socially efficient level of pollution by balancing social costs and benefits. More precisely, *efficiency requires that the marginal social benefits from abatement equal the marginal social costs of abatement*. This equality occurs when the marginal benefits to the nation's health and property of reducing pollution by 1 unit just equal the marginal costs of that reduction.

How might an efficient level of pollution be determined? Economists recommend an approach known as *cost-benefit analysis*, in which efficient standards are set by balancing the marginal costs of an action against the marginal benefits of that action. In the case of Dirty Light & Power, suppose that experts study the cost data for abatement and environmental damage. They determine that marginal social costs and marginal social benefits are equalized when the amount of abatement is increased from 50 tons to 250 tons. At the efficient pollution rate, they find that the marginal cost of abatement is $40 per ton, while the marginal social benefits from the last unit removed are also $40 per ton.

Why is it efficient for the firm to emit 150 tons rather than 400 tons? Because at this emissions rate the net social value of production is maximized. If Dirty Light & Power were to emit more than 150 tons of pollution, the extra environmental damage would outweigh the cost savings from lower abatement. On the other hand, if pollution were to be cut below 150 tons, the marginal cost of pollution cleanup would be greater than the marginal benefit from cleaner air. Here again, as in many areas, we find the most efficient outcome by equating marginal cost and marginal benefit of an activity.

Cost-benefit analysis will show why extreme "no-risk" or "zero-discharge" policies are generally wasteful. Reducing pollution to zero would generally impose astronomically high cleanup costs, while the marginal benefits of reducing the last few grams of pollution may be quite modest. In some cases, it may even be impossible to continue to produce with zero emissions, so a no-risk philosophy might require closing down the computer industry or banning all vehicular traffic. Generally, economic efficiency calls for a compromise, balancing the extra value of the industry's output against the extra damage from pollution.

An unregulated market economy will generate levels of pollution (or other externalities) at which the marginal *private* benefit of abatement equals the marginal private costs of abatement. Efficiency requires that marginal *social* benefit equals marginal social abatement cost. In an unregulated economy, there will be too little abatement and too much pollution.

Valuing Damages

One of the major problems in conducting economic studies of the environment arises because many of the benefits are not priced in the market. Reaching the efficient level of regulation generally requires that regulators be able to put a dollar value on the externality. For example, if emissions fees are set to equate marginal social costs with marginal benefits, we clearly must be able to calculate social damages from pollution. In cases where the impacts are on marketed goods and services, the measurement is relatively straightforward. If a warmer climate reduces wheat yields, we can measure the damage by the net value of the wheat. Or if a new road requires tearing down someone's house, we can calculate the market value of a replacement dwelling.

But many types of environmental damage, particularly in nonmarket sectors, are much harder to value. For example, in the late 1980s and the early 1990s environmentalists called for a halt to logging across a wide swathe of the northwest in order to preserve the habitat of the spotted owl. That would cost thousands of logging jobs. How would we value the continued existence of the spotted owl? Or to take another example, the *Exxon Valdez* oil spill in Prince William Sound, Alaska, damaged beaches and killed wildlife. How much is the life of a sea otter worth? Even more controversial is the value of a human life. How much should society pay to reduce illness or life-shortening effects of air pollution?

Economists have developed several approaches for estimating damages which do not show up directly in market prices. Valuation is easiest in those cases in which environmental problems directly harm users. A polluted river or lake will discourage fishing and swimming, and the value of the lost recreational opportunities can be estimated by looking at its opportunity cost—how much people would pay for an equivalent form of recreation.

But what about the value of a spotted owl? Most people will never see a spotted owl, just as they will never see a whooping crane or actually visit Prince William Sound. But they may place a value on these natural resources nevertheless. Some environmental economists use a technique called *contingent valuation*, which involves asking people how much they would be willing to pay in a hypothetical situation, say, to keep some natural resource undamaged. In the case of the *Exxon Valdez* spill, people from around the country were surveyed to help find out how people who had never visited Prince William Sound valued preserving and restoring its pristine environment. The study placed a value of $3 billion on the cost of the accident.

The contingent-valuation methodology has stirred a bitter controversy. Its critics argue that the answers are not believable because people are being asked to value something they don't understand and have never experienced, like asking people how much they would pay to eat green cheese produced on the moon. Critics add that since people never actually have to pay the money, and because they feel good when they offer to pony up lots of hypothetical dollars for a worthy cause, their estimates will be unrealistically high and should be ignored.

Few would doubt that an unspoiled environment has a significant value to many Americans, but valuing the nonmarket components is an elusive business.

Graphical Analysis of Pollution

We can illustrate these points with the help of Figure 18-5. The upward-sloping market *MC* is the marginal cost of abatement. The downward-sloping curves are the marginal benefits of reducing pollution, with the upper solid *MSB* line being the marginal social benefit from less pollution while the lower *MPB* line is the marginal private benefit of abatement to the polluter.

Warning on graphing pollution: In analyzing pollution, it is useful to think of pollution control or abatement as a "good." In the graphs, we therefore measure marginal costs and benefits on the vertical axis and the abatement or pollution removed on the horizontal axis. The trick here is to remember that because pollution removal is a good, it is measured positively on the horizontal axis. You can also think of pollution as measured negatively from the far-right point of 400. So abatement of zero is pollution of 400, while abatement of 400 means zero pollution.

The unregulated market solution comes at point *I*, where the marginal private costs and benefits are equated. At this point, only 50 tons are removed, and the marginal private costs and benefits are $10 per ton. But the unregulated market solution is inefficient. We can see this by performing an experiment that increases abatement by 10 tons; this is represented by the thin slice to the right of point *I*. For this additional removal, the marginal benefits are given by the total area of the slice under the *MSB*

curve, while the marginal costs are given by the area under the *MC* curve. The net benefits are that part of the slice shown by the shaded area between the two curves.

The efficient level of pollution comes at point *E*, where marginal social benefits are equated to marginal cost of abatement. At that point, both *MSB* and *MC* are equal to $40 per ton. Also, because *MSB* and *MC* are equal, the experiment of increasing abatement by a tiny amount will find that there is no difference between the curves, so there is no net benefit from additional pollution control. We can also measure the net benefits of the efficient solution relative to the unregulated market by taking all the little slices of net benefits from the shaded slice to point *E* of Figure 18-5. This calculation shows that the area *ISE* represents the gains from efficient removal of pollutants.

As a final experiment, consider the impact of a rule which said that every bit of pollution had to be removed; this could be called a zero-risk philosophy and would require 400 units of pollution removal. For this action, the marginal social benefits are zero while the marginal costs are at point *Z*, so there are large excess costs of removal. By adding up all the little slices to the right of the efficient point, we can see that the net costs of a zero-risk approach are given by the area *EZB*.

POLICIES TO CORRECT EXTERNALITIES

What are the weapons that can be used to combat inefficiencies arising from externalities? The most visible activities are government antipollution programs that use either direct controls or financial incentives to induce firms to correct externalities. More subtle approaches use enhanced property rights to give the private sector the instruments for negotiating efficient solutions. We survey these approaches in this section.

Government Programs

Direct Controls. For almost all pollution, as well as other health and safety externalities, governments rely on direct regulatory controls; these are often called *social regulations* (see Chapter 17). For example, the 1970 Clean Air Act reduced allowable emissions of three major pollutants by 90 percent. In

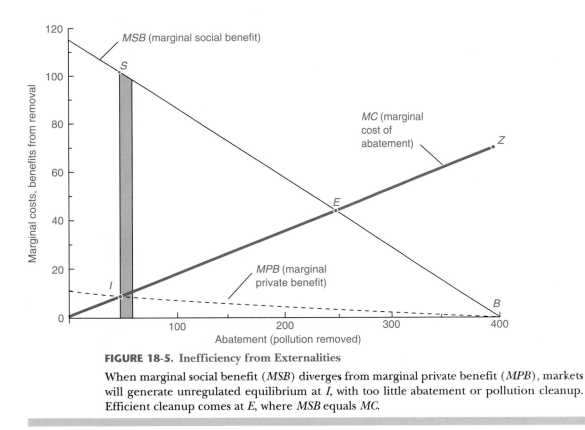

FIGURE 18-5. Inefficiency from Externalities

When marginal social benefit (*MSB*) diverges from marginal private benefit (*MPB*), markets will generate unregulated equilibrium at *I*, with too little abatement or pollution cleanup. Efficient cleanup comes at *E*, where *MSB* equals *MC*.

1977, utilities were told to reduce sulfur emissions at new plants by 90 percent. In a series of regulations over the last decades, firms were told they must phase out ozone-depleting chemicals. And so it goes with regulation.

How does the government enforce a pollution regulation? To continue our example of Dirty Light & Power, the state Department of Environmental Protection might tell Dirty Light & Power to increase its abatement to 250 tons of particulate matter. Under *command-and-control regulations*, the regulator would simply order the firm to comply, giving detailed instructions on what pollution-control technology to use and where to apply it. There would be little scope for novel approaches or tradeoffs within the firm or across firms. *If* standards are appropriately set—a very big "*if*"—the outcome might approach the efficient pollution level described in the previous part of this section.

While it is possible that the regulator might choose pollution-control edicts in a way that guarantees economic efficiency, in practice that is not very

likely. Indeed, much pollution control suffers from extensive government failures. For example, pollution regulations are often set without comparisons of marginal costs and marginal benefits, and without such comparisons there is no way to determine the most efficient level of pollution control. Indeed, for some regulatory programs, the law specifically prohibits cost-benefit comparison as a way of setting standards.

In addition, standards are inherently a very blunt tool. Efficient pollution reduction requires that the marginal cost of pollution be equalized across all sources of pollution. Command-and-control regulations generally do not allow differentiation across firms, regions, or industries. Hence, regulations are usually the same for large firms and small firms, for cities and rural areas, and for high-polluting and low-polluting industries. Even though firm A might be able to reduce a ton of pollution at a tiny fraction of the cost to firm B, both firms will be required to meet the same standard; nor will there be any incentives for the low-cost firm to reduce pollution more than the standard even though it would be economical to do just that. Study after study has confirmed that our environmental goals have proved unnecessarily costly because we have used command-and-control regulation.

Market Solution: Emissions Fees. In order to avoid some of the pitfalls of direct controls, many economists have suggested that environmental policy rely more on economic incentives than on government commands. One approach is the use of *emissions fees*, which would require that firms pay a tax on their pollution equal to the amount of external damage. If Dirty Light & Power were imposing external marginal costs of $35 per ton on the surrounding community, the appropriate emissions charge would be $35 per ton. This is in effect *internalizing* the externality by making the firm face the social costs of its activities. In calculating its private costs, Dirty Light & Power would find that, at point *E*, an additional ton of pollution would cost it $5 of internal costs to the firm plus $35 in emissions fees, for an overall marginal cost of $40 per ton of pollution. By equating the new marginal *private* benefit (private benefit plus emissions fee) with the marginal abatement cost, the firm would curb its pollution back to the efficient level. *If* the emissions fee were correctly calculated—another big "if"—profit-minded firms would be led as if by a mended invisible hand to the efficient point where marginal social costs and marginal social benefits of pollution are equal.

The alternative approaches are shown graphically in Figure 18-6, which is similar to Figure 18-5 except we have simplified it by removing the marginal private benefit curve. With the direct-control approach, the government simply instructs the firm to remove 250 tons of pollutants (or to emit no more than 150 tons). This would in effect place the standard at the heavy vertical line. If the standard were set at the right level, the firm would undertake the socially efficient level of abatement. Hence, with efficient regulation, the firm will choose point *E*, with *MSB* equal to *MC*.

What about the case of emissions fees? Say that the government charges the firm $35 per ton. In effect, this means that the marginal private benefit of abatement would go from $5 to $40 per ton. Faced with this incentive, the firm would again choose efficient point *E* in Figure 18-6.

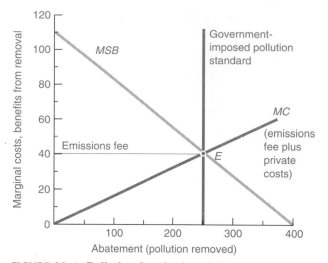

FIGURE 18-6. Pollution Standards and Emissions Fees

When government sets the pollution limitation at 150, or requires removal of 250, this standard will lead to efficient pollution at point *E*. The same result can be achieved with pollution fees of $35 per ton: at $35 per ton fee plus $5 per ton of marginal private damage, the sum will equal marginal cost and lead to efficient abatement at point *E*.

Market Solution: Tradeable Emissions Permits. A new approach that does not require the government to legislate taxes is the use of tradeable emissions permits. With this approach, instead of telling firms that they must pay $x per unit of pollution and then allowing firms to choose the level of pollution, the government chooses the level of pollution and allocates the appropriate number of permits. The price of permits, which represents the level of the emissions fee, is then set by supply and demand in the market for permits. Assuming the cost schedule is known, the tradeable permits approach has the same outcome as the emissions fee approach. One major difference between the two approaches is that the government often allocates emissions permits to firms to win their political support. This means that industry gets the revenues from the permits while the government gets the revenues from emissions fees.

 Economic innovations: Trading pollution permits. Most environmental regulations use a command-and-control approach that limits the emissions from individual sources, such as power plants or automobiles. This approach cannot cap overall emissions. More importantly, it virtually guarantees that the overall program is extremely inefficient because it does not satisfy the condition that emissions from all sources must have equal marginal costs of abatement.

In 1990, the United States introduced a radical new approach to environmental control in its program on control of sulfur dioxide, which is one of the most harmful environmental pollutants. Under the 1990 Clean Air Act amendments, the government issues a certain number of permits to emit sulfur dioxide each year for the entire country. By the end of the decade, emissions are scheduled to be reduced by 50 percent relative to 1990 levels. The innovative aspect of the plan is that the permits will be freely tradeable. Electric utilities receive pollution permits and are allowed to buy and sell them with each other just like pork bellies or wheat. Those firms which can reduce their sulfur emissions most cheaply do so and sell their permits; other firms which need additional permits for new plants or have no leeway to reduce emissions find it economical to buy permits rather than install expensive antipollution equipment or shut down.

Environmental economists believe that the enhanced incentives allow the ambitious targets to be met at a much lower cost than would be paid under traditional command-and-control regulation. Studies by economist Tom Tietenberg of Colby College in Maine have determined that the traditional approaches cost 2 to 10 times as much as would cost-effective regulations like emissions trading.

The behavior of this market has produced a big surprise. Originally, the government projected that permits in the early years would sell for around $300 per ton of sulfur dioxide. By 1997, however, the market price had fallen to between $60 and $80 per ton. One reason for the success was that the program gave strong incentives for firms to innovate, and firms found that low-sulfur coal could be used much more easily and cheaply than had earlier been anticipated. This important experiment has given powerful support to economists who argue for market-based approaches to environmental policy.

Private Approaches

Not all solutions involve direct government action. Two private approaches may provide a moderately efficient outcome: private negotiations and liability rules.

Negotiation and the Coase Theorem. Let's say that the government decides not to intervene. A startling analysis by Chicago's Ronald Coase suggested that voluntary negotiations among the affected parties would in some circumstances lead to the efficient outcome.

The conditions under which this might occur arise when there are well-defined property rights and the costs of negotiations are low. Suppose, for example, that I am spilling chemicals upstream from your fish ponds and killing many of your fish. Further, say that you can sue me for damage to your fish. In such a case, Coase argued, the two of us would have a powerful incentive to get together and agree on the efficient level of dumping. And this incentive would exist without any government antipollution program.

Some have tried to take Coase's suggestion even further, arguing that efficient bargains *will* occur. But this conclusion is surely too optimistic. Saying that there is room for an efficient, cost-saving bargain does not mean that a deal will always be struck—as the history of war, labor-management disputes, and the theory of games amply demonstrate.[6]

Nevertheless, Coase's analysis does point to certain cases where private bargains may help alleviate externalities—namely, where property rights are well defined and where there are only a few affected parties who can get together and negotiate an efficient solution.

Liability Rules. A second approach relies on the legal framework of liability laws or the tort system rather than upon direct government regulations. Here, the generator of externalities is legally liable for any damages caused to other persons.

----

[6] Those who have studied Chapter 11 will recognize that the theory of games can be fruitfully applied to the bargaining situations involved in this kind of an externality. What lessons emerge? Often, games can end up with an equilibrium that displays a distinctly inefficient outcome. Chapter 11 described the case of the "pollution game," in which polluters' private interests lead them to high levels of soot and waste. This occurred when firms pursued the competitive or noncooperative approach (this outcome is called a Nash equilibrium). Game theorists have found no theorem proving that an invisible hand will lead two or more bargainers to the Pareto-efficient level of pollution. Coase never proved such a result, nor has anyone else.

In some areas, this doctrine is well established. Thus, in most states, if you are injured by a negligent driver, you can sue for damages. Or if you are injured or become ill from a defective product, the company can be sued for product liability.

Returning to our example, how would a perfect liability system contain the externality? If Dirty Light & Power caused $35 of external damages per ton of pollution, the victims would recover these damages through the courts. Thus the liability faced by the firm would be $35 per ton just as if there were a $35-per-ton emissions fee; such costs would give firms strong incentives to reduce pollution back toward the efficient level.

Liability rules are in principle an attractive means of internalizing the nonmarket costs of production. In practice, liability rules are quite limited in their applicability. They usually involve high litigation costs, which adds an additional cost to the original externality. In addition, many harms cannot be litigated because of incomplete property rights (such as those involving clean air) or because of the large number of companies who contribute to the externality (as in the case of chemicals flowing into a stream).

CLIMATE CHANGE: TO SLOW OR NOT TO SLOW

Of all the environmental issues, none is so worrisome to scientists as the threat of global warming from the greenhouse effect. Climatologists and other scientists warn that the accumulation of gases like carbon dioxide (CO_2), largely produced by the combustion of fossil fuels, is likely to lead to global warming and other significant climatic changes over the next century. On the basis of climate models, scientists project that if current trends continue, the earth may warm 4 to 8° Fahrenheit over the next century. This would take the earth's climate out of the range experienced during the entire period of human civilization.

The greenhouse effect is the granddaddy of public-good problems; actions today will affect the climate for all people in all countries for centuries to come. The costs of reducing CO_2 emissions come in the near term as countries cut back their use of fossil fuels by conserving energy and using alternative energy sources (solar energy or perhaps nuclear

power), plant trees, and take other measures. In the short run, that means we will have to accept more expensive energy, lower living standards, and lower consumption levels. The benefits of emissions reductions will come many years in the future, when lower emissions reduce future climate-induced damages—with less disruption to agriculture, seacoasts, and ecosystems.

Economists have begun to study the economic impacts of climate change in order to understand how nations might undertake sensible strategies. To begin with, economists point out that in the long march of economic development, technology has increasingly insulated humans and economic activity from the vagaries of climate. Today, thanks to modern technology, humans live and thrive in virtually every climate on earth. For the bulk of economic activity, variables like wages, unionization, labor-force skills, and political factors swamp climatic considerations.

In general, those sectors of the economy that depend heavily on unmanaged ecosystems—that is, on naturally occurring rainfall, runoff, or temperatures—will be most sensitive to climate change. Agriculture, forestry, outdoor recreation, and coastal activities fall into this category. Countries like Japan and the United States are relatively insulated from climate change, while developing countries like India and Brazil are more vulnerable. Economic studies suggest that the total cost of climate change in the United States by the end of the next century is likely to be at most a few percent of total output. Outside the United States, it might be beneficial for countries like Russia with cold climates, but it could easily be catastrophic for low-lying island countries.

An efficient strategy for containing climate change requires weighing the marginal costs of reducing CO_2 emissions against the marginal benefits. Figure 18-7 shows schematically the marginal cost of reductions as *MC* and the marginal social benefit as *MSB*. The vertical axis measures costs and benefits in dollars, while the horizontal axis measures emissions reductions in percent reduction of carbon dioxide. Point *E* in the graph represents the efficient point at which marginal abatement costs equal marginal benefits from slowing climate change. This is the point which maximizes the present value of future human consumption. By contrast, the pure-market solution comes with emissions

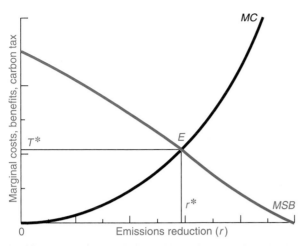

FIGURE 18-7. Carbon Taxes Can Slow Harmful Climate Change

Slowing climate change efficiently requires setting "carbon taxes" on harmful carbon dioxide emissions to balance marginal cost of reductions with marginal benefits of reducing damages from sea-level rise and other impacts of climate change.

reductions at 0, where *MSB* is far above the zero *MC*. An extreme environmentalist solution, which attempts to avoid any disruption to natural ecosystems, comes at the right-hand edge of the graph, where *MC* far exceeds *MSB*.

How can point *E*, the efficient level of CO_2 reduction, be achieved? Since CO_2 emissions come from burning carbon-containing fuels, some have suggested a "carbon tax" on the carbon content of fuels. Fuels which contain more carbon, like coal, would be taxed more heavily than low-carbon fuels like natural gas. Economists have calculated that the efficient carbon tax would be in the range of $5 to $10 per ton of carbon and would rise gradually over the next hundred years. At the higher level, a carbon tax would raise electricity bills by only 2 percent and gasoline prices by only 2 cents per gallon. This level of carbon tax would still allow considerable climate change. Therefore, environmentalists have proposed a much higher carbon tax—on the order of $100 per ton—which would have a larger impact on humans, in order to prevent significant future climate change.

Still, economists and environmentalists may not be as far apart as this analysis makes them seem. Cli-

mate change poses great difficulties for policymakers because its effects are so uncertain and stretch so far into the future. What are some of the major uncertainties? Scientists raise the specter of shifting currents turning Europe's climate into that of Alaska, of continental drying transforming grain belts into deserts, of great rivers drying up as snow packs disappear, of severe storms wiping out whole populations of low-lying regions, of northward migration of old or new tropical pests and diseases decimating the temperate regions, and of environmentally induced migration leading people to overrun borders in search of livable land.

Faced with this dilemma, economists rely upon the techniques of utility theory under uncertainty, surveyed in Chapter 11, to analyze different strategies. In this approach, a reasoned decision process involves listing the events that may occur, estimating the consequences of the events, judging the probability of the occurrence of each event, weighing the expected value of the consequences against the expected costs under different courses of action, and choosing the action that maximizes the expected value or utility of the outcome.

Preliminary studies suggest that because the uncertainties are so one-sided, with a small probability of very substantial damages, it might be rational to pay a "risk premium" in terms of taking additional steps today to slow climate change. Just as individuals find it rational to sacrifice a little income today to buy fire detectors to lower the chance of a catastrophic fire, so might societies find it prudent to sacrifice some of their national incomes today to reduce the chance of catastrophic global warming in the centuries to come.

We began this chapter with gloomy questions about the future of humanity. Having surveyed the field, how should we conclude? Depending on one's perspective, it is easy to become either optimistic or pessimistic about our ability to understand and cope with threats to our global environment. On the one hand, it is true that we are moving into uncharted waters, depleting many resources while altering others in an irreversible manner, and gambling with our universe in more ways than we know. Humans seem just as quarrelsome as they were at the dawn of recorded history, and they have devised weapons that are awesomely effective at avenging their quarrels. At the same time, our powers of observation and analysis are also orders of magnitude more formidable. The combination of monitoring, measuring, analyzing, and computing is growing even faster than our ability to emit wastes, cut trees, and produce yet more people.

What will prevail in this race between our tendency to quarrel and pollute and our power to reason and compute? Are there enough resources to allow the poor to enjoy the consumption standards of today's high-income countries, or will today's rich pull the ladder up behind them? There are no final answers to these deep questions, but many economists believe that if we manage our environmental resources wisely, *homo sapiens* can not only survive but also thrive for a long time to come.

SUMMARY

A. Population and Resource Limitations

1. Malthus' theory of population rests on the law of diminishing returns. He contended that population, if unchecked, would tend to grow at a geometric (or exponential) rate, doubling every generation or so. But each member of the growing population would have less land and natural resources to work with. Because of diminishing returns, income could grow at an arithmetic rate at best; output per person would tend to fall so low as to stabilize population at a subsistence level of near-starvation.

2. Over the last century and a half, Malthus and his followers have been criticized on several grounds. Among the major criticisms are that Malthusians ignored the possibility of technological advance and overlooked the significance of birth control as a force in lowering population growth.

3. Studies of the relationship between pollution, population, and income have determined that the demand for environmental quality rises rapidly with per capita income, so for most indicators environmental quality improves rather than deteriorates as per capita income rises.

B. Natural-Resource Economics

4. Natural resources are nonrenewable when they are essentially fixed in supply and cannot regenerate quickly. Renewable resources are ones whose services are replenished regularly and which, if properly managed, can yield useful services indefinitely.

5. From an economic point of view, the crucial distinction is between appropriable and inappropriable resources. Natural resources are appropriable when firms or consumers can capture the full benefits of their services; examples include vineyards or oil fields.

Natural resources are inappropriable when their costs or benefits do not accrue to the owners; in other words, they involve externalities. Examples include air quality and climate, which have externalities that are affected by such activities as the burning of fossil fuels.

6. Important examples of appropriable, nonrenewable natural resources are fossil fuels such as oil, gas, and coal. Economists argue that because private markets can efficiently price and allocate their services, such natural resources should be treated the same as any other capital asset.

C. Curbing Externalities: Environmental Economics

7. A major market failure that is increasing in importance is externalities. These occur when the costs (or benefits) of an activity spill over to other people, without those other people being paid (or paying) for the costs (or benefits) incurred (or received).

8. The most clear-cut example of an externality is the case of public goods, like defense, where all consumers in a group share equally in the consumption and cannot be excluded. Less obvious examples like public health, inventions, parks, and dams also possess public-good properties. These contrast with private goods, like bread, which can be divided and provided to a single individual.

9. Environmental problems arise because of externalities that stem from production or consumption. An unregulated market economy will produce too much pollution and too little pollution abatement. Unregulated firms decide on abatement (and other public goods) by comparing the marginal private benefits with the marginal private costs. Efficiency requires that marginal social benefits equal marginal social abatement costs.

10. There are numerous steps by which governments can internalize or correct the inefficiencies arising from externalities. Alternatives include decentralized solutions (such as negotiations or legal liability rules) and government-imposed approaches (such as pollution-emission standards or emissions taxes). Experience indicates that no approach is ideal in all circumstances, but many economists believe that greater use of marketlike systems would improve the efficiency of regulatory systems.

CONCEPTS FOR REVIEW

Population and Natural Resources

Malthusian population theory
renewable vs. nonrenewable
    resources
appropriable vs. inappropriable
    resources

Environmental Economics

externalities and public goods
private vs. public goods
inefficiency of externalities
internal vs. external costs, social vs.
    private costs

remedies for externalities:
    bargaining
    liability
    standards
    taxes
tradeable emissions permits

QUESTIONS FOR DISCUSSION

1. What is the difference between renewable and nonrenewable resources? Give examples of each.

2. What is meant by an inappropriable natural resource? Provide an example, and explain why the market allocation of this resource is inefficient. What would be your preferred way to improve the market outcome?

3. Many economists believe that the state should not interfere in a market where there are no important externalities—this being the "libertarian" or laissez-faire tradition. Are there externalities in population growth that would lead to positive or negative spillovers? Consider such items as education, national defense, roads, pollution, and the creation of geniuses like Mozart or Einstein.

4. A *geometric progression* is a sequence of terms $(g_1, g_2, \ldots, g_t, g_{t+1}, \ldots)$ in which each term is the same multiple of its predecessor: $g_2/g_1 = g_3/g_2 = \cdots = g_{t+1}/g_t = \beta$. If $\beta = 1 + i > 1$, the terms grow exponentially like compound interest. An arithmetic progression is a sequence $(a_1, a_2, a_3, \ldots, a_t, a_{t+1}, \ldots)$ in which the difference between each term and its predecessor is the same constant: $a_2 - a_1 = a_3 - a_2 \cdots = a_{t+1} - a_t = \cdots$. Give examples of each. Satisfy yourself that any geometric progression with $\beta > 1$ must eventually surpass any arithmetic progression. Relate this to Malthus' theory.

5. Recall that Malthus asserted that unchecked population would grow geometrically, while food supply—constrained by diminishing returns—would grow only arithmetically. Use a numerical example to show why per capita food production must decline if population is unchecked while diminishing returns lead food production to grow more slowly than labor inputs.

6. "Local public goods" are ones that mainly benefit the residents of a town or state—such as beaches or schools open only to town residents. Is there any reason to think that towns might act competitively to provide the correct amount of local public goods to their residents? If so, does this suggest an economic theory of "fiscal federalism" whereby local public goods should be locally supplied?

7. Decide whether each of the following externalities is serious enough to warrant collective action. If so, which of the four remedies considered in the chapter would be most efficient?
   a. Steel mills emitting sulfur oxides into the Birmingham air
   b. Smoking by people in restaurants
   c. Smoking by students without roommates in their own rooms
   d. Driving by persons under the influence of alcohol, involving 25,000 fatalities per year
   e. Driving by persons under 21 under the influence of alcohol

8. Get your classmates together to do a contingent-valuation analysis on the value of the following: Keeping Prince William Sound pristine; preventing the extinction of spotted owls for another 10,000 years; ensuring that there are at least 1 million spotted owls in existence for another 10,000 years; reducing the chance of dying in an automobile accident from 1 in 1000 to 1 in 2000 each year. How reliable do you think this technique is for gathering information about people's preferences?

9. **Advanced problem:** Global public goods pose special problems because no single nation can capture the benefits of its pollution-control efforts. To see this, redraw Figure 18-7, labeling it "Emissions Reduction for the United States." Label all the curves with "US" to indicate that they refer to costs and benefits for the United States alone. Next, draw a new *MSB* curve

which is everywhere 3 times higher than the MSB_{US} to indicate that the benefits to the world are 3 times those to the United States. Consider the "nationalistic" equilibrium at E in which the United States maximizes its own net benefits. Can you see why this is inefficient from the point of view of the entire globe? (*Hint:* The reasoning is exactly analogous to Figure 18-5.)

Consider this issue from the point of view of game theory. The Nash equilibrium would occur when each country chose the nationalistic equilibrium you have

just analyzed. Describe why this is exactly analogous to the inefficient Nash equilibrium in the pollution game of Chapter 11—only here the players are nations rather than firms. Now consider the cooperative game where nations get together to find the efficient equilibrium. Describe the efficient equilibrium in terms of global MC and MSB curves. Can you see why the efficient equilibrium would require a uniform carbon tax in each country?

CHAPTER 19

EFFICIENCY VS. EQUALITY: THE BIG TRADEOFF

[The conflict] between equality and efficiency [is] our biggest socioeconomic tradeoff, and it plagues us in dozens of dimensions of social policy. We can't have our cake of market efficiency and share it equally.

Arthur Okun (1975)

About a century ago, many Western governments introduced a wide variety of transfer programs, known as the "welfare state," as a bulwark against socialist pressures. In the industrial democracies of Europe and North America, governments now generally finance retirement and health care for the aged, provide food, health care, and housing assistance for the indigent, replace lost income for the unemployed and disabled, and channel incomes and wage subsidies to the poor. These programs have removed the sting of abject poverty.

But reducing poverty has not come without cost or controversy. A large and growing share of government budgets goes to income-support programs. Taxes have risen steadily over the last half-century. Attempts to

equalize incomes can cause adverse effects on incentives and efficiency. Today, people ask: How much of the economic pie must be sacrificed in order to divide it more equally? How should we redesign income-support programs to retain the objective of reducing want and inequality without bankrupting the nation?

The purpose of this chapter is to examine the distribution of income along with the dilemmas of policies to reduce inequality. These issues are among the most controversial economic questions of today. It is here that cool-headed economic analysis of facts and trends in poverty, as well as of the strengths and weaknesses of different programs, will have a large payoff in promoting both a sense of fairness and continued rapid growth of the mixed economy.

A. THE SOURCES OF INEQUALITY

To measure the inequality of control over economic resources, we need to concern ourselves with both income and wealth differences. Recall that by **personal income** we mean the total receipts or cash earned by a person or household during a given

time period (usually a year). The major components of personal income are labor earnings, property income (such as rents, interest, and dividends), and government transfer payments. **Disposable personal income** consists of personal income less any taxes

(1) Income class of households	(2) Income range	(3) Percentage of all households in this class	(4) Percentage of total income received by households in this class
Lowest fifth	Under $14,399	20.0	3.7
Second fifth	$14,400–$26,899	20.0	9.1
Third fifth	$26,900–$41,999	20.0	15.2
Fourth fifth	$42,000–$65,099	20.0	23.3
Highest fifth	$65,100 and over	20.0	48.7
Top 5 percent	$113,000 and over	5.0	21.0

TABLE 19-1. Distribution of Money Incomes of American Households, 1995

How was total income distributed among households in 1995? We group households into the fifth (or quintile) with the lowest income, the fifth with the second-lowest income, and so on. (Source: U.S. Bureau of the Census, *Money Income of Households, Families, and Persons in the United States: 1995*, Current Population Report, Series P-60, No. 184, September 1996.)

paid. **Wealth** or "net worth" consists of the dollar value of financial and tangible assets, minus the amount of money owed to banks and other creditors. You can refresh your memory about the major sources of income and wealth by reviewing Tables 12-1 and 12-2 (pages 210 and 212).

THE DISTRIBUTION OF INCOME AND WEALTH

Statistics show that in 1995 the median income of American families was $30,786—this means that half of all families received less than this figure while half received more. This number concerns the *distribution of income*, which shows the variability or dispersion of incomes. To understand the income distribution, consider the following experiment: Suppose one person from each household writes down the yearly income of his or her household on an index card. We can then sort these cards into *income classes*. Some of the cards will go into the lowest 20 percent, the group with under $14,400 of income. Some go into the next class. A few go into the top 5 percent of households, those with incomes of $113,00 and above.

The actual income distribution of American households in 1995 is shown in Table 19-1. Column (1) shows the different income-class fifths, or *quintiles*, plus the top 5 percent of households. Column (2) shows the range of household incomes in each income class. Column (3) shows the percentage of the households in each income class, while column (4) shows the percentage of total national income that goes to the households in an income class.

Table 19-1 enables us to see at a glance the wide spread of incomes in the U.S. economy. The poorest fifth of U.S. households have incomes less than $14,400, while households in the top fifth have incomes of $65,100 or more. About 5 percent of households have incomes over $113,000. Some people earn much more than that, but as you move further up the income pyramid, the numbers get smaller and smaller. If we made an income pyramid out of building blocks, with each layer portraying $500 of income, the peak would be far higher than Mount Everest, but most people would be within a few feet of the ground.

How to Measure Inequality Among Income Classes

How can we measure the degree of income inequality? At one pole, if incomes were absolutely equally distributed, there would be no difference between the lowest 20 percent and the highest 20 percent of the population: Each would receive exactly 20 percent of the total income. That's what absolute equality means.

The reality is far different. The lowest fifth, with 20 percent of the households, garners less than 4 percent of the total income. Meanwhile the situation is almost reversed for the top 5 percent of households, who get more than 20 percent of the income.

We can show the degree of inequality in a diagram known as the **Lorenz curve**, a widely used

(1)	(2) Percentage of total income received by households in this class	(3) Percentage of households in this class and lower ones	(4) Percentage of income received by this class and lower ones	(5)	(6)
Income class of households			Absolute equality	Absolute inequality	Actual distribution
		0	0	0	0.0
Lowest fifth	3.7	20	20	0	3.7
Second fifth	9.1	40	40	0	12.8
Third fifth	15.2	60	60	0	28.0
Fourth fifth	23.3	80	80	0	51.3
Highest fifth	48.7	100	100	100	100.0

TABLE 19-2. Actual and Polar Cases of Inequality

By cumulating the income shares of each quintile shown in column (2), we can compare in column (6) the actual distribution with polar extremes of complete inequality and equality. (Source: U.S. Bureau of the Census, *Money Income of Households, Families, and Persons in the United States: 1995,* Current Population Report, Series P-60, No. 184, September 1996.)

device for analyzing income and wealth inequality. Figure 19-1 is a Lorenz curve showing the amount of inequality listed in the columns of Table 19-2; that is, it contrasts the patterns of (1) absolute equality, (2) absolute inequality, and (3) actual 1995 American inequality.

Absolute equality is depicted by the gray column of numbers in column (4) of Table 19-2. When they are plotted, these become the diagonal dashed rust-colored line of Figure 19-1's Lorenz diagram.

At the other extreme, we have the hypothetical case of absolute inequality, where one person has all the income. Absolute inequality is shown in column (5) of Table 19-2 and by the lowest curve on the Lorenz diagram—the dashed, right-angled black line.

Any actual income distribution, such as that for 1995, will fall between the extremes of absolute equality and absolute inequality. The rust-colored column in Table 19-2 presents the data derived from the first two columns in a form suitable for plotting as an actual Lorenz curve. This actual Lorenz curve appears in Figure 19-1 as the solid rust-colored intermediate curve. The shaded area indicates the deviation from absolute equality, hence giving us a measure of the degree of inequality of income distribution. A quantitative measure of inequality that is often used is the *Gini coefficient*, which is 2 times the shaded area.

Distribution of Wealth

One source of the inequality of income is inequality of ownership of *wealth*, which is the net ownership

of financial claims and tangible property. Those who are fabulously wealthy—whether because of inheritance, skill, or luck—enjoy incomes far above the amount earned by the average household. Those without wealth begin with an income handicap.

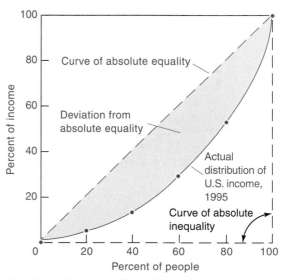

FIGURE 19-1. Lorenz Curve Shows Income Inequality

By plotting the figures from Table 19-2's column (6), we see that the solid rust-colored actual distribution-of-income curve lies between the two extremes of absolute equality and absolute inequality. The shaded area of this Lorenz curve (as a percentage of the triangle's area) measures relative inequality of income. (How would the curve have looked back in the roaring 1920s when inequality was greater? In a Utopia where all have equal inheritances and opportunities?)

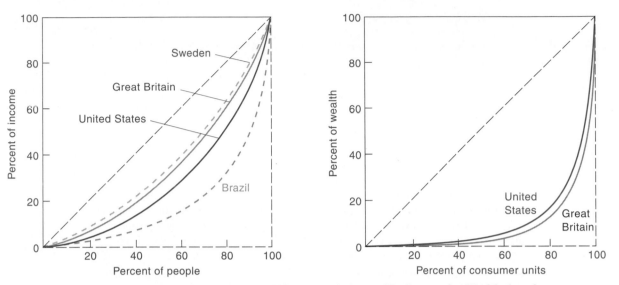

FIGURE 19-2. **Inequality Differs in Different Societies and Is Greater for Wealth than for Income**

(**a**) Advanced economies show less inequality of income distribution than do middle-income economies. Contrary to predictions of many socialists that the rich get richer and the poor get poorer under capitalism, the mixed economy shows increasing equality over time.
(**b**) Holdings of wealth tend to be more concentrated than do annual incomes. The United States and Great Britain have similar income distributions, but British wealth is somewhat more concentrated than America's. Socialist countries like China show much less concentration of private wealth. [Source: Federal Reserve Board, *Survey of Consumer Finances,* Washington, D.C., 1989; A. B. Atkinson and A. J. Harrison, "Trends in the Distribution of Wealth in Britain," in A. B. Atkinson (ed.), *Wealth, Income and Inequality* (Oxford University Press, London, 1980); *World Development Report 1993.*]

In market economies, wealth is much more un-equally distributed than is income, as Figure 19-2(*b*) shows. In the United States, 1 percent of the households own almost 40 percent of all assets. Studies by New York University's Edward Wolff show that the distribution of wealth has become much more unequal. Because of the booming stock market, the share of wealth held by the top 1 percent of people has doubled over the last two decades. Given the sharp and growing increases in wealth inequality, Wolff, along with legal scholars Bruce Ackerman and Anne Alstott, have proposed that the United States consider instituting a progressive wealth tax to go along with its progressive income tax.

The vast disparities in ownership of wealth have spurred radicals over the ages to propose heavy tax-ation of property income, wealth, or inheritance. Revolutionaries have agitated for expropriation by the state of great accumulations of property. In recent years, a more conservative political trend has muted the call for redistribution of wealth. Economists recognize that excessive taxation of property income and wealth dulls the incentives for saving and may reduce a nation's capital formation. Particularly in a world of open borders, countries with high tax rates on wealth may find that the wealth has fled across the borders to tax havens or Swiss bank accounts.

Inequality Across Countries

Countries show quite different income distribu-tions depending upon their economic and social

Country	Average income of poorest fifth as percent of top fifth
Brazil	3
Bolivia	5
Honduras	7
United Kingdom	11
United States	14
Sweden	22
Japan	23
Czech Republic	28

TABLE 19-3. Inequality in Different Countries, 1993

Inequality measured as the ratio of incomes of the bottom quintile to those of the top quintile is highest in middle-income countries with wealthy landowning and industrial elites. North America shows moderate levels of inequality. Greatest equality comes in countries with low immigration, homogeneous populations, and heavy welfare-state spending on redistributive policies. [Source: United Nations Development Program, *From Plan to Market: Human Development Report 1996* (Oxford University Press, Oxford, 1996).]

structure. Lorenz curves of four countries are shown in Figure 19-2(*a*). We see that Sweden has less income inequality than does the United States. The reason for this lies partly in the high levels of redistributive taxation in the European countries. In addition, the United States has growing numbers of single-parent families, who tend to have relatively low incomes. Among advanced market economies, the greatest income equality is found in Japan and Sweden; the most unequal income distributions come in the United States and Canada.

The experience of developing countries shows an interesting relationship. Inequality begins to rise as countries begin to industrialize, after which inequality then declines. The greatest extremes of inequality—with conspicuous opulence appearing alongside the most abject poverty—occur in middle-income countries, particularly Latin American countries like Peru, Brazil, and Venezuela.

Table 19-3 shows the ratio of the income of the bottom fifth of the population to that of the top fifth. Three groups of countries can be seen there: high-income countries with low inequality (such as Sweden or Japan), high-income countries with high

inequality (such as the United States), and middle-income countries with the highest inequality of all (such as Brazil).

INEQUALITY IN LABOR INCOME

What are the sources of inequality? The first place we would look for an answer is labor incomes, which account for about 75 percent of factor incomes. Even if property incomes were distributed equally, much inequality would remain. The forces that produce inequalities in earnings are differences in abilities and skills of labor, in intensities of work, in occupations, and in other factors.

Abilities and Skills

People vary enormously in their abilities—in physical, mental, and temperamental dimensions. However, these personal differences are of little help in explaining the puzzle of income dispersion. Physical traits (such as strength or height or girth) and measured mental traits (such as intelligence quotient or tone perception) explain relatively little of the difference among the earnings of people.

This is not to say that individual abilities matter little. The ability to hit a home run or charm an audience greatly enhances a person's earning potential. But the skills valued in the marketplace are varied and often difficult to measure. Markets tend to reward willingness to take risks, ambition, luck, strokes of engineering genius, good judgment, and hard work—none of which is easily measured in standardized tests. As Mark Twain might have said, "You don't have to be smart to make money. But you *do* have to know how to make money."

Intensities of Work

The intensity of work varies enormously among individuals. The workaholic may log 70 hours a week on the job, never take a vacation, and postpone retirement indefinitely. An ascetic might work just enough to pay for life's necessities. Differences in income might be great simply because of differences in work effort, yet no one would say that economic opportunity was therefore genuinely unequal.

Occupations

One important source of income inequality is people's occupations. At the low end of the scale we find domestic servants, fast-food personnel, and unskilled service workers. A full-time, year-round employee at McDonald's or at a car wash might earn $10,000 a year today.

At the other extreme are the high-earning professionals. What single profession seems to make the most money? In recent years it has without question been medical doctors. Physicians had average earnings of $156,000 in 1993, up almost 40 percent since 1986.

What is the source of such vast differences among occupations? Part of the disparity comes from the years of training needed to become a doctor. Abilities also play a role, for example, in limiting engineering jobs to those who have some quantitative skills. Some jobs pay more because they are dangerous or unpleasant. And when the supply of labor is limited in an occupation, say, because of union restrictions or professional licensing rules, the supply restrictions drive up the wages and salaries of that occupation.

In recent years the trend has been for pay in white-collar jobs to rise much faster than pay in blue-collar jobs. According to the Bureau of Labor Statistics, after adjusting for inflation, wages and salaries for white-collar jobs rose by 6.6 percent from 1981 to 1993, while pay in blue-collar jobs dropped by 4.1 percent over the same period. This has tended to increase the amount of income inequality in American society.

Other Factors

In addition to ability, intensity of work, and occupation, other factors affect the inequality of wage earnings. We saw in Chapter 13 that discrimination and exclusion from certain occupations have played an important role in keeping down the incomes of women and many minority groups.

In addition, the home life and community experience of children have a major impact on later earnings. Children of the affluent probably don't start life ahead of the poor, but they benefit from their environment at every stage. A child of poverty often experiences crowding, poor nutrition, run-down schools, and overworked teachers. The scales are tipped against many inner-city children before they are 10 years old.

Some economists believe that changing technology, immigration, international trade, and the increasing prevalence of winner-take-all markets are creating greater inequality. To take the first of these, recall Chapter 11's discussion of how technology is leveraging individual performance so that it reaches many more people. As a result, while talented athletes made little more than the average factory worker three decades ago, signing bonuses for basketball's free agents today are approaching $100 million. Similar trends are seen in other sports, in entertainment, and in salaries of corporate officers.

INEQUALITY IN PROPERTY INCOME

The greatest disparities in income arise from differences in inherited and acquired wealth. With few exceptions, the people at the very top of the income pyramid derive most of their money from property income. By contrast, the poor own few material goods and therefore earn no income on their nonexistent wealth. Let's examine the sources of differences in wealth—saving, entrepreneurship, and inheritance—and thus of inequalities in property income.

Sources of Wealth

While most people scrimp and save to put away a few dollars for their retirement, such thrift is probably not the major source of wealth in the United States. A study by Laurence Kotlikoff and Lawrence Summers suggests that only a small fraction of personal wealth, perhaps 20 percent, can be explained by life-cycle savings.

The difficulty of accumulating a large fortune by saving out of normal labor earnings can be illustrated using a realistic example. Suppose that the average middle-class family saved about $2000 annually (5 percent of its income) for 20 years. Further suppose that it was wise and managed to obtain a real return after tax of 5 percent each year. At the end of the period, total accumulated wealth would be $73,200—a sum equal to only one-quarter of average family net worth.

Entrepreneurship

Compared to thrift, entrepreneurship is a much more important road to riches. Table 19-4 displays the experience of the top 100 wealth holders in 1996. These data suggest that most of the richest people in America got that way by taking risks and creating profitable new businesses, such as computer software companies, television networks, and retail

America's 100 Richest People			
		Amount of net worth	
Source of wealth	Number of persons	Billions of dollars	Percent
Inheritance:	**24**	**58.0**	**22**
Oil	7	15.9	6
Retail	14	37.7	14
Other	3	4.4	2
Finance	**11**	**38.7**	**14**
Entrepreneurship:	**65**	**176.0**	**64**
Computers	10	51.7	19
Entertainment/communication	17	53.1	19
Oil	2	4.0	1
Real estate	5	8.8	3
Retailing	14	31.9	12
Other	17	26.5	10
Total	**100**	**272.7**	**100**

TABLE 19-4. How Did the Richest Americans Reach the Summit?

In 1996, 100 Americans had net worth of at least $1.1 billion, according to *Forbes* magazine. Most gained their wealth by entrepreneurship. Just under one-quarter are the beneficiaries of *earlier* entrepreneurship (like the Rockefellers). A small fraction gained wealth by shrewd financial investments. (Source: *Forbes,* Oct. 14, 1996.)

chains. The people who invented new products or services or organized the companies that brought them to market got rich on the "Schumpeterian profits" from these innovations. This group of wealthy individuals includes folk heroes like Bill Gates, who built software giant Microsoft, or Sam Walton, who founded Wal-Mart.

Inheritance

What about inheritance? About one-quarter of the 100 wealthiest individuals in 1996 got there by inheriting wealth rather than creating it, but that number may understate the importance of inheritance in determining the distribution of income. According to surveys, two-thirds of the top 1 percent of wealth holders in America inherited a substantial fraction of their property. It is this concentration of inherited wealth in a small number of hands which draws the most strenuous objections from people who are worried about the unequal distribution of wealth.

POVERTY IN AMERICA

Societies tend to define and concentrate on particular groups or problems. In the 1960s, the United

States declared "war on poverty" and launched ambitious health and nutrition programs to eradicate economic privation. Before we can analyze antipoverty programs, we must examine the definition of poverty, a surprisingly elusive concept.

What Is Poverty?

The word "poverty" means different things to different people. Clearly poverty is a condition in which people have inadequate incomes, but it is hard to draw an exact line between the poor and the nonpoor. Economists have therefore devised certain techniques which provide the official definition of poverty.

Poverty was officially defined in the 1960s in the United States as an income not adequate to maintain a subsistence level of consumption. This was calculated from family budgets and double-checked by examining the fraction of incomes that was spent on food. Since that time, the budget has been updated by the government's consumer price index to reflect changes in the cost of living. According to the standard definition, the subsistence cost of living for a family of four was $15,569 in 1995. This figure represents the "poverty line" or demarcation between

Poverty in Major Groups, 1995	
Population group	Percent of group in poverty
Total population	13.8
By racial and ethnic group:	
White	11.2
Black	29.3
Hispanic	30.3
By age:	
Under 18 years	20.8
18 to 64 years	11.4
65 years and over	10.5
By type of family:	
Married couple	6.8
Female-headed household,	
no spouse present	36.5
Unrelated subfamilies	46.4

TABLE 19-5. Incidence of Poverty in Different Groups

Whites, married couples, and the elderly have lower-than-average poverty rates. Blacks, Hispanics, and female-headed households have above-average poverty rates. (Source: U.S. Bureau of the Census, *Poverty in the United States: 1995,* Current Population Report, Series P-60, No. 194, September 1996.)

poor and nonpoor families. The poverty line also varies by family size.

While an exact figure for measuring poverty is helpful, scholars recognize that "poverty" is a relative term. The notion of a subsistence budget includes subjective questions of taste and social convention. Housing that is today considered substandard often includes household appliances and plumbing that were unavailable to the millionaires and robber barons of an earlier age. With these concerns in mind, a panel of experts of the National Academy of Sciences recommended in 1995 that the definition of poverty be changed to reflect *relative income status.* The panel recommended that a family be considered poor if its consumption is less than 50 percent of the median family's consumption of food, clothing, and housing. Poverty in the relative-income sense would decline when inequality decreased; poverty would be unchanged if the economy prospered with no change in the distribution of income and consumption. In this new world, a rising tide would lift all boats but not change the fraction of the population considered poor. This radical new approach is being weighed carefully by the government.

Who Are the Poor?

Poverty hits some groups harder than others. Table 19-5 shows the incidence of poverty in different groups for 1995. While close to 14 percent of the total population was counted as falling below the 1995 poverty line, the rate among black families was almost 3 times that of whites.

Perhaps the most ominous trend is that single-parent families headed by women are an increasingly large share of the poor population. In 1959, about 18 percent of poor families were headed by women raising children alone. By 1995, the poverty rate of that group was 37 percent. Social scientists worry that the children in these families will receive inadequate nutrition and education and will find it difficult to escape from poverty when they are adults.

No discussion of poverty would be accurate without an analysis of the position of minorities. Almost one-third of African-American, Hispanic, and Native American families have below-standard incomes.

Why are so many female-headed and minority families poor? What is the role of discrimination?[1] Experienced observers insist that blatant racial or gender discrimination in which firms simply pay minorities or women less is vanishing today. Yet the relative poverty of women and blacks is increasing. How can we reconcile these two apparently contradictory trends? The major factor at work is the increasing gap between earnings of highly educated and skilled workers and those of unskilled and less educated workers. Over the last 25 years, the wage differential between these two groups has grown sharply, as we will see in the next section. The growing wage gap has hit minority groups particularly hard.

Trends in Inequality

The history of inequality in the United States is shown in Figure 19-3. This shows the ratio of the incomes received by the top fifth of families to those received by the bottom fifth. We can see three distinct periods: falling inequality until World War II,

---

[1] The economics of discrimination in the workplace is analyzed in Chapter 13.

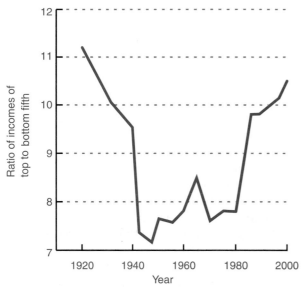

FIGURE 19-3. Trends in Inequality in the United States, 1929–1994

Another measure of inequality is the ratio of the incomes of the top fifth of the population to those of the bottom fifth. The share of top incomes declined after 1929 with the stock market collapse of the 1930s, the low unemployment and reduced barriers to women and minorities during World War II, and the migration from the farm to the city. Since about 1970, income inequality has grown sharply with higher immigration and decline of wages of the unskilled.(Source: U.S. Bureau of the Census, with historical series spliced together by authors.)

stable shares until 1970, then rising inequality over the last two decades. Since 1975, the ratio of upper- to lower-group incomes has increased by almost 50 percent.

Diminishing Inequality: 1929–1975. By any measure, in this period the poor enjoyed the fruits of economic growth along with more affluent groups. According to historical studies, the real income of the bottom fifth of the population rose steadily from the 1920s to the mid-1970s, growing slightly faster than the overall U.S. economy. As a result, the share of total income going to the poorest fifth of families rose from 3.8 percent to about 5 percent between 1929 and 1975. Over the same stretch, the poverty rate dropped so far that some people hoped that poverty could be eliminated completely.

Why did inequality narrow over this period?

Inequality declined in part because of the narrowing of wage inequality. With increasing education of poorer groups and unionization of the work force, the gap declined. Government policies like social security made a big difference for the elderly population, while programs like cash assistance and food stamps for the indigent and unemployment insurance boosted the incomes of other groups. Moreover, our progressive income-tax system, which taxed high incomes more heavily than low incomes, tended to reduce the degree of inequality.

Widening Gaps: 1975–1996. In the last two decades, several of these trends have reversed themselves. The share of total income going to the bottom quintile declined sharply in the 1980s, sinking from 5.4 percent in 1975 to 4.1 percent in 1995. Average real incomes for families in the bottom fifth are well below their peak. And the poverty rate is back up to 13.8 percent, in spite of the long boom that the U.S. economy enjoyed in the 1990s.

At the same time that the poor were falling further behind, the share of income going to the richest Americans soared. From 1979 to 1989, the share of total income going to the top 5 percent of households rose from 16.9 to 18.9 percent. Indeed, a recent study of high-income households indicates that most of the gains at the top were actually at the tip of the income pyramid, going to the top 0.1 percent of taxpayers.

Why did inequality suddenly start to rise again, after falling for so long? After intensely debating this question for years, economists have identified several causes of rising inequality. For one, government policies changed in the early 1980s: Welfare programs for the poor were cut, while the richest groups were helped by the supply-side tax cuts of the 1980s. But government actions are only part of the story. The last two decades saw sharp increases in the compensation of top executives and professionals, while the rising share of births going to single mothers sharply increased the number of female-headed households, which tend to have much higher rates of poverty.

Perhaps the most important cause of rising inequality is the fact that well-educated workers fared far better in the 1980s than their less educated counterparts. Economists have closely studied the *college–high school wage premium,* which is the pay differential between a worker with a college degree and a similar worker with only a high school diploma. Over the last decade the college–high school wage premium has grown sharply. According to the 1994 *Economic Report of the President,* in 1981 college graduates earned about 45 percent more than high school graduates. But by 1992, this difference had widened to almost 65 percent. Since college-educated workers were already paid more, the bigger pay differential had the effect of widening the gap between the top and bottom of the income distribution.

Why did the 1980s see increasing returns to education? One reason was a surge of immigration and competition from foreign imports. Both of these trends tend to hit hardest at less educated workers, who in earlier decades had been able to earn a good living working in factories making automobiles, steel, and other goods. In the 1980s these high-paying manufacturing jobs for workers without college educations began to dry up. In addition, the increasing deregulation and foreign competition tended to erode the market power of labor unions,

lowering the relative wages of highly paid union workers. At the same time, many of the new jobs that were being created called for relatively high levels of skills and education. The increasing prevalence of computers in the workplace places a high premium on literacy and analytical skills. All together, these trends have produced the sharp increase of inequality in the United States and most high-income countries.

We can point to at least one factor that did *not* lead to greater inequality: There was no decline in labor's share of national income. The fraction of total incomes coming from wages, salaries, and supplements in 1996 was virtually identical to what it had been a quarter-century earlier. This dog, at least, did not bite.

This concludes our description of the measurement and sources of inequality. In the next section, we turn to an analysis of government programs to combat poverty and reduce inequality. High-income democracies everywhere are rethinking these programs as they redefine the role of the state.

B. ANTIPOVERTY POLICIES

All societies take steps to provide for their poor citizens. But what is given to the poor must come from other groups, and that is undoubtedly the major point of resistance to redistributive programs. In addition, economists worry about the impact of redistribution upon the efficiency and morale of a country. These issues assume greater importance as budget deficits have increased and resistance to tax increases has stiffened. In this section, we review the rise of the welfare state, consider the costs of income redistribution, and survey the current system of income maintenance.

The Rise of the Welfare State

The early classical economists believed the distribution of income was unalterable. They argued that attempts to alleviate poverty by government interventions in the economy were foolish endeavors that

would simply end up reducing total national income. This view was contested by the English economist and philosopher John Stuart Mill. While cautioning against interferences with the market mechanism, he argued eloquently that government policies could reduce inequality.

A half-century later, at the end of the nineteenth century, political leaders in Western Europe took steps that marked a historic turning point in the economic role of government. Bismarck in Germany, Gladstone and Disraeli in Britain, followed by Franklin Roosevelt in the United States introduced a new concept of government responsibility for the welfare of the populace.

This marked the rise of the **welfare state**, in which government overrides market forces to protect individuals against specified contingencies and to guarantee people a minimum standard of living.

Important welfare-state policies include public pensions, accident and sickness insurance, unemployment insurance, health insurance, food and housing programs, family allowances, and income supplements for certain groups of people. These policies were introduced gradually from 1880 through to the modern era. The welfare state came late to the United States, being introduced in the New Deal of the 1930s with unemployment insurance and social security. Medical care for the aged and the poor was added in the 1960s. Many attempts to introduce universal health coverage in the United States failed however, with the latest being that of the Clinton administration in 1993–1994 (see Section C below).

THE COSTS OF REDISTRIBUTION

The basic purpose of the modern welfare state is to provide a safety net for those who are temporarily or permanently unable to provide adequate incomes for themselves. One reason for these policies is to promote greater equality.

What are the different concepts of equality? To begin with, democratic societies affirm the principle of equality of *political rights*—generally including the right to vote, trial by jury, and free speech and association. In the 1960s, liberal philosophers espoused the view that people should also have equal *economic opportunity*. In other words, all people should play by the same rules on a level playing field. All should have equal access to the best schools, training, and jobs. Then discrimination on the basis of race or gender or religion would disappear. Many steps were taken to promote greater equality, but inequalities of opportunity have proved very stubborn, and even America of the 1990s falls far short of the goal of equal economic opportunity.

A third, and the most far-reaching, ideal is equality of *economic outcome*. In this idealistic dream, people would have the same consumption whether they were smart or dull, eager or lazy, lucky or unfortunate. Wages would be the same for doctor and nurse, lawyer and secretary. "From each according to his abilities, to each according to his needs" was Karl Marx's formulation of this philosophy.

Today, even the most radical socialist recognizes that some differences in economic outcome are necessary if the economy is to function efficiently. With-

out some differential reward for different kinds of work, how can we ensure that people will do the unpleasant as well as the pleasant work, that they will work on dangerous offshore oil derricks as well as in pleasant parks? Insisting on equality of outcomes would severely hamper the functioning of the economy.

Equality vs. Efficiency

In taking steps to redistribute income from the rich to the poor, governments may harm economic efficiency and reduce the amount of national income available to distribute. On the other hand, if equality is a social good, it is one worth paying for.

The question of how much we are willing to pay in reduced efficiency for greater equity was addressed by Arthur Okun in his "leaky bucket" experiment. He noted that if we value equality, we would approve when a dollar is taken in a bucket from the very rich and given to the very poor. But suppose the bucket of redistribution has a leak in it. Suppose only a fraction—maybe one-half—of each dollar in taxes paid by the rich actually reaches the poor. Then redistribution in the name of equity has been at the expense of economic efficiency.[2]

Okun presented a fundamental dilemma. Redistributional measures like the progressive income tax, analyzed in Chapter 16, will probably reduce real output by reducing incentives to work and save. As a nation considers its income-distribution policies, it will want to weigh the benefit of greater equality against the impact of these policies on total national income.

Redistribution Costs in Diagrams. We can illustrate Okun's point by using the income-possibility curve of Figure 19-4. This graph shows the incomes available to different groups when government programs redistribute income.

We begin by dividing the population in half; the real income of the low-income group is measured on the vertical axis of Figure 19-4, while the income of the upper half is measured on the horizontal axis. At point *A*, which is the pre-redistribution point, no taxes are levied and no transfers are given, so people simply live with their market incomes. In a competi-

---

[2] Arthur M. Okun, *Equality and Efficiency: The Big Tradeoff* (Brookings Institution, Washington, D.C., 1975).

tive economy, point *A* will be efficient and the no-redistribution policy maximizes total national income.

Unfortunately, at laissez-faire point *A*, the upper-income group receives substantially more income than the lower half. People might strive for greater equality by tax and transfer programs, hoping to move toward the point of equal incomes at *E*. If such steps could be taken without reducing national output, the economy would move along the black line from *A* toward *E*. The slope of the *AE* line is −45°, reflecting the assumption about efficiency that the redistributive bucket has no leaks, so every dollar taken from the upper half increases the income of the lower half by exactly $1. Along the −45° line, total national income is constant, indicating that redistributional programs have no impact upon the total national income.

Most redistributive programs do affect efficiency. If a country redistributes income by imposing high tax rates on the wealthiest people, their saving and work effort may be reduced or misdirected, with a resulting lower total national output. They may spend more money on tax lawyers, save less for retirement, or invest less in high yielding but risky innovations. Also, if society puts a guaranteed floor beneath the incomes of the poor, the sting of poverty will be reduced and the poor may work less. All these reactions to redistributive programs reduce the total size of real national income.

In terms of Okun's experiment, we might find that for every $100 of taxation on the rich, the income of the poor increased by only $50, with the rest dissipated because of reduced effort or administrative costs. The bucket of redistribution has developed a large leak. Costly redistribution is shown by the *ABZ* curve in Figure 19-4. Here, the hypothetical frontier of real incomes bends away from the −45° line because taxes and transfers produce inefficiencies.

The experience of socialist countries exemplifies how attempts to equalize incomes by expropriating property from the rich can end up hurting everyone. By prohibiting private ownership of businesses, socialist governments reduced the inequalities that arise from large property incomes. But the reduced incentives for work, investment, and innovation crippled this radical experiment of "to each according to his needs" and impoverished entire countries. By

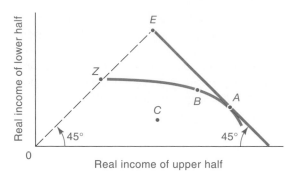

FIGURE 19-4. Redistributing Income May Harm Economic Efficiency

Point *A* marks the most efficient outcome, with maximal national output. If society could redistribute with no loss of efficiency, the economy would move toward point *E*. Because redistributive programs generally create distortions and efficiency losses, the path of redistribution might move along the rust-colored line *ABZ*. Society must decide how much efficiency to sacrifice to gain greater equality. Why would everyone want to avoid inefficient redistributional programs that take the economy to point *C*?

1990, comparisons of living standards in East and West had convinced many socialist countries that private ownership of business would benefit the living standards of workers as well as capitalists.

How Big Are the Leaks?

Okun characterized our redistributive system of taxes and transfers as a leaky bucket. But just how big are the leaks in the American economy? Is the country closer to Figure 19-4's point *A*, where the leaks are negligible? Or to *B*, where they are substantial? Or to *Z*, where the redistributive bucket is in fact a sieve? To find the answer, we must examine the major inefficiencies induced by high tax rates and by generous income-support programs: administrative costs, damage to work and savings incentives, and socioeconomic costs.

- The government must hire tax collectors to raise revenues and social security accountants to disburse them. These are clear inefficiencies or regrettable necessities, but they are small: the Internal Revenue Service spends only half a penny on administrative costs for each dollar of collected revenues.

- As the tax collector's bite grows larger and larger, might I not become discouraged and end up working less? Tax rates might conceivably be so high that total revenues are actually lower than they would be at more modest tax rates. Empirical evidence, however, suggests that the damage of taxes on work effort is limited. For a few groups, the labor supply curve may actually be backward-bending, indicating that a tax on wages might increase rather than decrease work effort. Most studies find a small impact of taxes on labor effort for middle-income and high-income workers. However, there may well be substantial impacts of the tax and transfer system on the behavior of poor people, a controversial topic to which we will turn shortly.

- Perhaps the most important potential leakage from the revenue bucket is the savings component. Some believe that current government programs discourage saving and investment. They worry that the nation's savings rate has declined sharply because of generous social programs—especially social security and Medicare—that reduce the need for people to save for old age and health contingencies. These economists point to the declining national savings rate over the last two decades as evidence of the impact of government programs. For most of the postwar period, the national savings rate averaged around 8 percent of total national product. That number has declined to around 3 percent in the last 5 years. Even economists who do not agree that government redistributive programs are the cause of the declining national savings rate today study how the government can take steps to reverse this trend.

- Some claim that the leaks cannot be found in the cost statistics of the economist; instead, the costs of equality are seen in attitudes rather than in dollars. Is the business ethic downplayed? Are young people so turned off by the prospect of high taxes that they turn on to drugs and idleness? Is the welfare system leading to a permanent underclass, a society of people who are trapped in a culture of dependency?

- Some people criticize the entire notion of costly redistribution, arguing as follows: Poverty is rooted in malnourishment in the early years, broken families, illiteracy at home, poor education, and lack of job training. Poverty begets poverty; the vicious cycle of malnutrition, poor education, drug dependency, low productivity, and low incomes leads to yet another generation of poor families. Programs providing health care and adequate food for poor families will increase productivity and efficiency rather than decrease output. By breaking the vicious cycle of poverty today, we will be raising the skills, human capital, and productivity of the children of poverty tomorrow. Programs to break the cycle of poverty are investments that require resources today to increase productivity tomorrow.

Adding Up the Leaks

When all the leaks are added up, how big are they? Okun argued that the leaks are small, particularly when funds for redistributive programs are drawn from the tap of a broad-based income tax. Others disagree strenuously, pointing to high marginal tax rates or overly generous transfer programs as confusing and destructive of economic efficiency.

What is the reality? While much research has been undertaken on the cost of redistribution, the truth has proved elusive. A cautious verdict is that there are but modest losses to economic efficiency from redistributional programs of the kind used in the United States today. The efficiency costs of redistribution appear small as compared to the economic costs of poverty in malnutrition, poor health, lost job skills, and human misery. But countries whose welfare-state policies have gone far beyond those in the United States see major inefficiencies. Egalitarian countries like Sweden or the Netherlands, which provide cradle-to-grave protection for their citizens, find declining labor-force participation, growing unemployment, and rising budget deficits.

Countries need to design their policies carefully to avoid the extremes of unacceptable inequality or great inefficiency.

ANTIPOVERTY POLICIES: PROGRAMS AND CRITICISMS

All societies provide for their aged, their young, and their sick. Sometimes, the support comes from families or religious organizations. Over the last century, nations have increasingly moved the source of

Federal Programs for the Poor, 1996		
Program	Amount ($, billion)	Percent of total federal spending
All income-security programs	**826.3**	**53.0**
General programs:	**592.7**	**38.0**
Social security	350.2	22.4
Medicare	174.2	11.2
Other (veterans, other retirement)	43.4	2.8
Unemployment compensation	24.9	1.6
Programs for the poor:	**233.6**	**15.0**
Medicaid	82.1	5.3
Other income security	64.3	4.1
Food and nutrition	40.4	2.6
Earned-income tax credit	24.3	1.6
Housing assistance	16.4	1.1
International development and aid	6.1	0.4

TABLE 19-6. **Most Federal Income-Security Dollars Go for General Programs Like Social Security**

Federal programs for income security are largely concentrated on the population as a whole, rather than the poor. Note as well the high cost of health programs for both the poor and the nonpoor. (Source: *Budget of the United States Government, 1998.* Earned-income tax credit figure includes both outlays and reduced tax revenues.)

income support for the needy to central governments. Yet, as governments have assumed larger responsibilities for more people, the fiscal burdens of transfer programs have grown steadily. Today, most high-income countries face the prospect of rising tax burdens to finance public health and retirement programs as well as income-support programs for poor families. This rising tax burden has provoked a sharp backlash against "welfare programs," particularly in the United States. Let's review the major antipoverty programs and recent reforms.

Income-Security Programs

What are the major income-security programs today? Let's look briefly at a few of the programs that have been established in the United States.

Most income-security programs are targeted at the elderly rather than the poor, as is shown in Table 19-6. The major programs are social security, which is a contributory federal retirement program, and Medicare, which is a subsidized health program for those over 65 years old. These two programs are the largest transfer programs in the United States and in most other high-income countries, and they are projected to be a source of continued spending growth over the coming decades.

Programs specifically targeted to poor households are a patchwork quilt of federal, state, and local programs. Some of these are cash assistance; some subsidize particular spending (such as the food-stamps program, which provides poor families with coupons that allow them to purchase food at a small fraction of its market cost); and others are transfers "in kind," such as Medicaid, which provides poor families with free health care. Most of the programs targeted to poor families have shrunk sharply over the last two decades.

The most controversial program was cash assistance to poor parents with small children. This program was drastically reformed in 1996, and we will discuss the reform below.

How much do all federal programs add up to in terms of budget expenditures? Table 19-6 shows the level of federal spending for income-security programs for both the general population and poor households. All federal poverty programs today amount to 15 percent of the total federal budget.

Incentive Problems of the Poor

One of the major obstacles faced by poor families is that the rules in most welfare programs severely reduce the incentives of low-income adults to seek work. If a poor person on welfare gets a job, the government will trim back food stamps, income-support payments, and rent subsidies, and the person might even lose medical benefits. We might say that poor people face high marginal "tax rates" (or, more accurately, "benefit-reduction rates") because welfare benefits are sharply reduced as earnings rise.

The following calculation for a family of three (mother and two children) living in Pennsylvania in the 1990s illustrates the problem. We choose the example of Pennsylvania because benefits in that state are close to the national average. If the mother did not have a job, the family would receive welfare benefits of $4584 and food stamps worth $1549, for a total disposable income of $6133. Suppose the parent takes a full-time job, earning $8000 a year. She would lose all the welfare benefits, but would retain $1306 worth of food stamps. After child-care and work-related expenses of $2400, disposable income would equal $6906.

The net gain from taking this $8000 job would be a gain in disposable income of $773 a year; the increase in disposable income is only 9.7 percent of the increase in earnings. If we consider benefit reductions as a kind of "tax," the tax rates on the working poor can easily reach 90 percent—far above the rate faced by the richest Americans and surely a major disincentive to the avid pursuit of work.

The Earned-Income Tax Credit

One popular and rapidly growing program for low-income workers is the *earned-income tax credit*. This credit applies to labor incomes and is in effect a wage supplement. In 1996, it amounted to a supplement to earned income of as much as 40 percent up to a maximum of $3556, and it was then phased out for incomes over $11,650. It is known as a "refundable" credit because it is actually paid to a taxpayer when the taxpayer owes no taxes.

Table 19-7 shows the impact of the earned-income tax credit for a family at different income levels. This example shows that the government can simultaneously support the poorest families and maintain an incentive for people to seek gainful employment.

Current Structure of Earned-Income Tax Credit, 1996		
Market earnings ($)	Algebraic tax (+ if tax; − if benefits received) ($)	Income after tax and credit ($)
0	0	0
4,000	−1,610	5,610
8,000	−3,210	11,210
12,000	−3,469	15,469
24,000	−941	24,941
28,000	−99	28,099

TABLE 19-7. Earned-Income Tax Credit Increases Reward for Work but Does Not Touch the Very Poorest

Under the current earned-income tax credit, labor earnings are increased by a supplement of up to 40 percent up to a maximum of $3,556, then phased out. This provides "negative taxes" for the very low-income wage earners. (Assumes two children.) (Source: U.S. Department of the Treasury.)

Compare this approach with that of the existing welfare system, examined above, to see how the current system destroys incentives while the negative income tax would motivate people to look for work.

THE BATTLE OVER WELFARE REFORM

The current welfare system has few defenders. Some want to dismantle it; others, to strengthen it. Some wish to devolve responsibility for income support to states, localities, or families; others, to strengthen the federal role. These disparate approaches reflect disparate views of poverty and lead to strikingly different policy proposals.

Two Views of Poverty

Social scientists put forth a wide variety of proposals to cure or alleviate poverty. The different approaches often reflect differing views of the roots of poverty. Proponents of strong government action see poverty as the result of social and economic conditions over which the poor have little control. They stress malnutrition, poor schools, broken families, discrimination, lack of job opportunities, and a dangerous environment as central determinants of the fate of the poor. If you hold this view, you might well believe that government bears a responsibility to alleviate poverty—either by providing income to the poor or by correcting the conditions that produce poverty.

A second view holds that poverty grows out of maladaptive individual behavior—behavior that is the responsibility of individuals and is properly cured by the poor themselves. In earlier centuries, laissez-faire apologists held that the poor were shiftless, lazy, or drunk; as a charity worker wrote almost a century ago, "Want of employment . . . is, as often as not, [caused by] drink." Sometimes the government itself is blamed for breeding dependency upon a patchwork of government programs that squelch individual initiative. Critics who hold these views advocate that the government should cut back on welfare programs so that people will develop their own resources.

The poverty debate was succinctly summarized by the eminent social scientist William Wilson:

> Liberals have traditionally emphasized how the plight of disadvantaged groups can be related to the problems of the broader society, including problems of discrimination and social class subordination. . . . Conservatives, in contrast, have traditionally stressed the importance of different group values and competitive resources in accounting for the experiences of the disadvantaged.[3]

Much of today's debate can be better understood if these two views and their implications are factored into the political equation.

Expanding the Federal Role: The Negative Income Tax

Contemplating the perverse effects of the current welfare system on economic efficiency and the social structure of the country, economists of varied political persuasions have concluded that the welfare system needs a fundamental reform. One important approach—proposed by conservatives like Milton Friedman of Chicago and liberals like James Tobin of Yale—is to consolidate all income-support programs into a single unified federal program of cash assistance.

This ambitious reform proposal is called the **negative income tax**. The basic notion is simple. When I

---

[3] William Julius Wilson, "Cycles of Deprivation and the Underclass Debate," *Social Service Review* (December 1985), pp. 541–559.

make $50,000 a year, I pay positive income taxes (as seen in Table 16-4). When I earn an extra thousand dollars, I pay extra taxes of $160, leaving me $840 of additional disposable income. Thus the incentive to earn more is preserved.

Next consider a poor family earning, say, $8000 in 1996. We might decide that such a family deserves an income above $8000, especially if it has earned its $8000 by work and if the family has small children to support. The government wants to provide further income support. Put differently, the family should not pay taxes on its income but should receive a *negative* income tax in the form of an income supplement.

The problem is how to continue to provide government income support without hurting the family's incentives to work. The way to do this is to provide a basic allowance and then permit the family to keep a significant portion of any earnings. A family might receive a basic allowance of $8000 and then get taxed 50 percent of any income. Just as people with high incomes can keep most of their earnings if they earn more money, similarly a poor family could keep much of its additional earnings if a family member gets a job.

In analyzing different systems for supplementing the incomes of the poor, the basic dilemma is whether to increase incentives for work or to increase the living standards of the very poor. The earned-income tax credit is one extreme, which gives nothing to those who do not work and supplements the earnings of those who do work. At the other pole is the current welfare system, which gives a generous allowance to poor families and then "taxes" back the earnings at a high rate. As noted above, such plans often have marginal tax rates on earnings near or even beyond 100 percent. The negative income tax lies between these two poles, retaining an incentive to work yet continuing to provide income to poor, nonworking families.

U.S. Welfare Reform: 1996 Style

In the battle over reforming welfare, the latest step came in 1996 with a radical reform of federal cash assistance. First enacted in the 1930s, the major cash assistance to poor families was Aid to Families with Dependent Children. This was a federal-state *entitlement program*, meaning that anyone who met certain qualifications could receive the benefits as a matter of law.

In 1996, an unusual alliance of a Democratic President who ran on the platform of "reforming welfare as we know it" and a sharply conservative Republican Congress completely changed the rules for cash assistance. The old program was replaced by the Temporary Assistance for Needy Families (TANF) Act of 1996. This act removed the federal entitlement to cash benefits and turned the program over to the 50 states.

The major provisions of the new program are the following:

- A "block grant," a fixed amount of federal funding, is given to the states to fund the federal part of cash benefits. This replaced an earlier system in which the federal government picked up 50 percent or more of state spending.
- The entitlement for federal cash assistance under TANF is removed.
- Each family is subject to a lifetime limit of 5 years of benefits under the federally supported program. After 5 years, TANF funds can no longer be used to support the family, even if it moves to a new state or has been off the welfare rolls for a number of years.
- Adults in the program must engage in work activities after 2 years of benefits.
- Legal immigrants may be excluded from TANF benefits.
- Other major low-income–support programs are largely unchanged.

Most economists agree that the 1996 welfare reform was a radical experiment in social policy that will have many unforeseen consequences in the years to come. The provisions will be implemented gradually over the next few years, and many features are at present poorly understood by both the government and welfare recipients. To the extent that the loss of benefits forces people to seek work, this will increase the supply of relatively uneducated and unskilled labor. This large increase in supply will tend to lower wages of the lowest paid workers and increase income inequality (much the same way that the recent sharp increase in immigration has contributed to lowering of wages of the unskilled in the last two decades). If equilibrium wages of some workers are driven down below the minimum wage, this may also lead to an increase in the unemployment rate of these groups.

One important feature of the new law is the *devolution* of responsibility for cash assistance to the states. This provision is one of the sharpest contrasts with the philosophy behind centralized income-support programs such as the negative income tax. Many economists believe that giving states "block grants" or lump-sum amounts and placing decision-making responsibility in the states for benefits of a mobile population will give strong incentives for states to trim welfare benefits to reduce the costs and the burden of the low-income population. This has been called a "race to the bottom" in which the equilibrium is for states to have the lowest possible benefits. It is unclear whether such an outcome was the intention of the 1996 welfare reform program, but it is likely to be a major force in welfare politics in the coming years.

C. HEALTH CARE: THE PROBLEM THAT WON'T GO AWAY

Each generation has its battleground for warring views of the welfare state. Earlier decades saw debates over the income tax, pensions for the elderly, and redistributive taxation. In the early 1990s, Americans engaged in a protracted struggle over the way that health care should be organized and financed. The Clinton administration bet its political fortunes in 1993 on passing uniform and comprehensive national health insurance. It lost the bet and was humiliated in the 1994 congressional elections, in which Republicans introduced *A Contract with America,* which argued for smaller government and private-sector health care.

Even as this debate took place, the health-care market was being transformed by a trend known as "managed competition." Under managed competition, people were increasingly joining health maintenance organizations, or HMOs, that exercised greater vigilance over costs and access to services and began to turn medical care into a profit-oriented business enterprise.

This final section surveys the economics of health care. This is an important sector of the economy as well as a fascinating area in itself. In addition, the analysis of health care will provide us with a laboratory for understanding the conflict between efficiency and equity and the importance of externalities and market failures such as inadequate information. We see here many of the issues that arise in deciding how far to extend government's role in the economy and how to redesign the welfare state.

GENESIS OF THE HEALTH-CARE DEBATE

What is the background of the debate about health care? In the United States, the health-care system is a partnership between the market system and the government. In recent years, this system has produced some remarkable accomplishments. Many terrible diseases, such as smallpox and polio, have been eradicated. Life expectancy, one of the key indexes of health, has improved in developing countries more from 1950 to 1990 than during the entire span of recorded history. Advances in medical technology, from arthroscopic knee surgery to sophisticated anticancer drugs, have enabled more people to live pain-free and productive lives.

Even with these great achievements, major health problems remained unsolved in the United States in the early 1990s. Infant mortality was higher than in many countries with lower incomes; 15 percent of Americans were without insurance coverage; great disparities in care existed between rich and poor; and communicable diseases like AIDS and tuberculosis were spreading.

The issue that most concerned the public, business community, and political leaders, however, was the exploding costs of health care. Health care rose from 4 percent of national output (GDP) in 1940 to 7 percent in 1970 and reached 14 percent in 1993. Virtually everyone agreed that the U.S. health system had contributed greatly to the nation's health, but many worried that it was becoming unaffordable.

Special Economic Features of Health Care

Good health is a crucial ingredient in economic welfare and one that tends to become more important to people as their incomes rise. The health-care system in the United States has three characteristics that have contributed to the rapid growth in that sector in recent years: a high income elasticity, rapid technological advance, and increasing insulation of consumers from prices.

Health care shows a high income elasticity, indicating that ensuring a long and fit life becomes increasingly important as people are able to pay for other essential needs. Goods with high income elasticities, other things constant, tend to take a growing share of consumer spending.

Coupled with a high income elasticity are the rapid developments in medical technology that have occurred during this century. Advances in fundamental biomedical knowledge, discovery and use of a wide variety of vaccines and pharmaceuticals, progress in understanding the spread of communicable diseases, and increasing public awareness of the role of individual behavior in areas such as smoking, drinking, and driving—all these have contributed to the remarkable improvement in the health status of Americans.

These advances have had the unusual consequence of stimulating spending in the health-care sector. The reason is that the new technologies have often been product inventions, that is, inventions that create new or improved products and therefore open up new markets. For example, when the antibiotic drug penicillin was discovered, it created a whole new market and stimulated spending in the health-care sector.

A third feature of the health-care industry that has stimulated rapid spending growth is the increasing insulation of the consumer from the prices of health care. Health-care coverage in the United

States is largely provided by employers as a tax-free fringe benefit.[4] Tax-free status is in effect a government subsidy. In 1960, most health-care expenses were paid directly by consumers; by 1990, only 23 percent of expenses were paid directly by consumers. Indeed, for hospital care, third parties like HMOs or the government pay 95 percent of costs, while the consumer pays only about 5 percent of the cost. This phenomenon is sometimes called the "third-party payment syndrome" to indicate that when a third party pays the bill, the consumer is often inattentive to the cost.

All these forces (high income elasticity, development of new technologies, and increasing scope of third-party payments) plus others (such as the aging of the population) contribute to the rapid growth of expenditures on medical care.

THE ROLE OF GOVERNMENT IN HEALTH CARE

A growing level of spending on health care is not sufficient to justify heavy government regulation, for it may simply indicate the economic vitality of the industry (as in computers). What are the reasons for government intervention in the health industry? In fact, both efficiency and equity considerations motivate government policy.

One set of concerns lies in the fact that control of communicable diseases and development of basic science are public goods that the market will not efficiently provide. Recall that *public goods* are ones whose benefits are indivisibly spread among the entire community, whether or not individuals choose to purchase the public good. *Private goods,* by contrast, are ones with no external costs or benefits. Eradication of smallpox benefited billions of potential victims, yet no firm could collect even a small fraction of the benefits. When one person stops smoking because of knowledge of its dangers, or when another person uses condoms on learning of the way AIDS is transmitted, these steps do not make such

activities less valuable to others. In such situations, government research and public-health programs can offset the market failures that arise when significant externalities and public goods are present.

A second set of market failures arises because of uncertainty and failure of insurance markets. One significant problem is the presence of *asymmetric information* among patients, doctors, and insurance companies. Medical conditions are often isolated occurrences for patients, so patients may be completely dependent upon doctors' recommendations regarding the appropriate level of health care. Sometimes, as when patients are wheeled into the operating room, they may be incapacitated and unable to choose treatment strategies for themselves, so demand depends upon the recommendations of suppliers. Special protection must be given to ensure that consumers do not unwittingly purchase unnecessary, poor-quality, or high-cost services.[5]

Another inefficiency arises because of informational asymmetries between the patient and the third-party payer, say, an insurance company. Insurance is usually priced on the basis of the average cost of service rather than the marginal cost. This leads to inefficiency because people generally know more about their medical condition than do insurance companies. Faced with average-cost premiums, the low-risk individual may choose not to buy insurance. This leads to *adverse selection*, increasing the average riskiness and the cost for those who participate. It is not surprising that healthy people in their twenties are the group most likely to be uninsured.

An additional complication for insurance arises because of *moral hazard*, which occurs when insurance reduces the incentives for individuals to avoid risk and expense through prudent behavior. A recent economic experiment measured the extent of moral hazard by providing one randomly selected

---

[4] The origin of the employer-provided system is instructive: During and after World War II, nonwage benefits were exempt from federal price and wage controls. This gave businesses the incentive to expand such benefits, and employer-provided medical coverage developed. This is a good example of "the law of unintended consequences," whereby a policy designed for one purpose has long-lasting and surprising consequences in other areas.

[5] Society has devised numerous mechanisms for dealing with situations where there are great informational asymmetries between buyer and seller. One mechanism is the brand name. When you buy relatively simple commodities like cars or soft drinks from Toyota or Coca-Cola, you are paying a premium for the quality control provided by those organizations. For more complicated areas like medical care or legal advice, there is no standard commodity or obvious remedy for informational asymmetries, and society relies on "the professional" to bridge the knowledge gap. By law and custom, professionals are put in positions of trust to provide appropriate services. Compare the amounts of confidence consumers put in the recommendations of doctors and used-car dealers.

Problem area	Current approach	Alternatives		
		Pure-market solution	Nationalized health service	Fedicare
Public goods (contagious diseases, basic science, and consumer information)	Through public-health expenditures where covered.	Does not provide public good.	Through public-health expenditures.	Through public-health expenditures.
Market failures:				
Moral hazard (third-party payment syndrome)	Major source of cost escalation and waste because of weak controls over costs.	None because consumer pays for service.	Very serious because all covered services are free. Can be alleviated through rationing and long waits for service.	Potentially serious if no charges for services. Can be alleviated if copayments and deductibles are on plans.
Adverse selection	Serious for uncovered population.	None because consumer pays for service.	Not a problem because of universal coverage.	Not a problem because of universal coverage.
Maldistribution of medical services	Uneven problem: employed, poor, and aged are covered; working poor and unemployed are vulnerable.	Very unequal: market-determined distribution of health care.	Universal and uniform.	Universal and uniform.

TABLE 19-8. Alternative Solutions for Health-Care Market Failures

The current system of health care in the United States experiences high cost because of large subsidies without a budget constraint yet fails to provide coverage for large numbers of people. Alternatives must find a path that rations health care efficiently and equitably while continuing to provide incentives for technological advance.

group of families full insurance and another group a plan with high levels of *coinsurance* (which denotes that the individual shares the costs with the insurer). The fully insured families used 30 percent more medical services, yet follow-up studies could determine no difference in the health status of the two groups after a 3- to 5-year period. The fact that a lower price increased quantity demanded is, of course, hardly surprising to economists; it simply reflects the law of downward-sloping demand.

A third concern of government policy is *equity*: to provide a minimum standard of medical care for the poor. In part, good health for all is increasingly viewed as a basic human right in wealthy countries. But good health for poor people is also a good social

investment. Inadequate health care is particularly harmful for poor people not only because they tend to be sicker than wealthier individuals but also because their incomes are almost entirely derived from their labor. A healthier population is a more productive population because healthy people have higher earnings and require less medical care. But nowhere is inadequate care more costly than with children. The medical condition of poor and minority children in the United States has in some dimensions actually worsened in recent years. Sick children are handicapped at the start: They are less likely to attend school, perform more poorly when they do attend, are more likely to drop out, and are less likely to get good jobs at high pay when they grow up. No

THE ROLE OF GOVERNMENT IN HEALTH CARE

country can prosper when a significant fraction of its children have inadequate medical care.

Alternative Approaches to Health-Care Reform

The combination of rising costs, a growing number of uninsured, and lagging health status has led to widespread calls for fundamental health-care reform in the United States. What are the major alternatives? At one extreme is the *pure-market* solution. With this approach, which was traditional in most countries until this century, each family pays 100 percent of its medical expenses and there are no government programs providing for public goods or shouldering the burden of medical care for the poor. As Table 19-8 indicates, the pure-market solution solves the market failures of adverse selection and moral hazard, but it does so at great cost to individuals with high medical expenses; more worrisome, a pure-market solution does not provide for public goods like basic science and prevention of communicable diseases. Given the adverse consequences of the pure-market model, it is not surprising that few economists or political figures endorse it.

At the other extreme is a *nationalized health service*, in which health care is publicly provided to all on an equal basis. This approach, used in the Medicare system for the elderly in the United States, solves many of the major market failures. Because health care is universal, there is no adverse selection, and government can provide the public goods of information and prevention. However, critics of nationalized health service point to a number of unattractive features. First, health care would be paid for in taxes or mandatory fees, increasing tax rates, raising business costs, and harming incentives to work and save. Second, since health care is free under this plan, moral hazard would be severe because consumers would have few incentives to limit their use of services; medical costs would grow ever more rapidly.

Nationalized systems have another problem as well, which arises because they limit costs by capping the fees and incomes of doctors and restricting the range of eligible services. The combination of price ceilings and subsidized service leads to chronic excess demand in many medical markets. By preventing market forces from operating in the medical market, shortages crop up, and demand must somehow be choked off. This phenomenon is known as nonprice rationing. *Nonprice rationing* usually takes the form of simply waiting for services. In other cases, the health provider rations the service by deciding which patient is most deserving. Examples of supplier rationing are seen in the British and Canadian national health services, in which there are generally long waits for elective surgery; similarly, because central-city emergency rooms in the United States provide much free care to low-income households, they are often crowded with patients who are there for routine care, even though few are in grave condition.[6] What is at work here? Because price is not allowed to rise to balance supply and demand, some other mechanism must be found to "clear the market."

Figure 19-5 on page 364 illustrates nonprice rationing in the medical market. There are only Q_0 units of medical care available. The market-clearing price would come at C, where quantities supplied and demanded are equal. However, the government pays 80 percent of all medical costs. Because the consumer pays only 20 percent of costs, the quantity demanded is Q_1. The segment from A to B is unsatisfied demand, which is subject to nonprice rationing; the greater the subsidy, the more nonprice rationing must be used.

Fedicare: Harnessing the Market

Virtually everyone agrees that the current system is wasteful and expensive—but few can agree on the appropriate reform. Rather than presenting a smorgasbord of different proposals, we focus here on a single plan which we call *Fedicare*. This is essentially a medical negative income tax, very similar to the neg-

---

[6] An interesting example of rationing comes in wartime, when medics employ *triage*. This practice derives from the French procedure in World War I of dividing the wounded into three categories: (1) those who would be helped by medical treatment, (2) those who would survive without attention, and (3) those who were likely to die no matter how much attention they received. Only the first category received most medical services. Can you see why this hard-headed strategy is "cost-effective" in that it maximizes the number of lives saved? Such a strategy has been proposed by the World Bank in its 1993 *World Development Report*. The World Bank recommends that countries focus on those medical treatments that show the greatest increase in the number of "disability-adjusted life years" per dollar of expenditure. This approach is similar to that of consumers maximizing utility or firms maximizing profits. Some states in the United States have proposed rationing medical care on a similar principle.

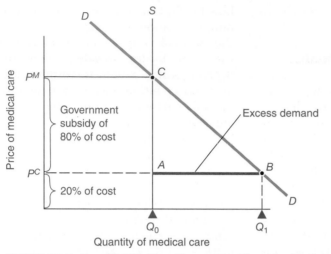

FIGURE 19-5. Free Health Care Guarantees Nonprice Rationing

When governments provide free or subsidized access to medical care, some way must be found to ration out the limited services. In the example of a government subsidy, when quantity demanded exceeds quantity supplied, excess demand *AB* is choked off by some mechanism other than price. Most often, people must wait for nonemergency services, sometimes for hours, sometimes for months.

ative income tax sketched in the last section except that it applies only to health care and not to all incomes.[7]

The basic idea under Fedicare is that the federal government ensures universal health care by providing subsidized medical insurance to all Americans. An important feature of the plan is to disconnect health insurance from employment, thus ending an accidental provision which has led to increasing numbers of uninsured people with the rise of casual and part-time employment. Under the Fedicare plan, the government defines a minimum package of medical benefits (hospital, physicians services, mental health, and so on). The plan could be relatively modest or quite generous depending upon the amount of the budget the country desired to allocate to subsidized medical care. For example, the standard package might cost $2000 per person annually.

The lowest-income family would pay nothing for its Fedicare insurance. However, as income rose, a family would pay an increasing fraction of the cost of

the plan. For example, a family of four might start paying for Fedicare when its income reached $10,000, with a "tax rate" of 20 percent. Hence, Fedicare would cost this family nothing at $10,000 of income, $1400 at $17,000 of income, $2000 at an income of $20,000, and so on. Under this plan, payment for health care would come from the government and individuals rather than out of wages.

Such a program would solve some of the problems of the current system without many of the disadvantages of either nationalized health care or a pure laissez-faire system. It would remove the problems of adverse selection and maldistribution of health services through universal coverage. If there were copayments and deductibles on health services, it would alleviate the third-party payment syndrome. And by continuing to encourage the private provision of medical care, it would promote the rapid technological advance that has been enjoyed over recent decades.

Depending upon the plan design, it might initially increase government health-care spending. The prospect, however, is that by explicitly limiting medical benefits and tax deductibility, the long-run costs might well be less than the cost of the current system.

---

[7] The proposal sketched here is similar to that proposed by the Bush administration in 1992 and was developed by Michael Graetz and James Tobin of Yale University.

In summary:

Health care is fundamentally no different from other goods and services in the economy. Physicians, nursing care, hospitalization, psychiatric care, and other services are limited in supply. The demands of the populace—summing up the critical, the reasonable, the marginal, and the ridiculous—far outstrip the available resources. But the resources must be somehow rationed out. Rationing according to the dollar votes of consumers is unacceptable because it does too much damage to the public health, leaves too many crucial demands unmet, and impoverishes too many. What should be the scope of the market, and what nonmarket mechanism should be used where the market is supplanted? These questions are the crux of the great debate about medical care.

REDEFINING GOVERNMENT'S ROLE AT CENTURY'S END

The last four chapters have reviewed the major debates about government's role in the mixed economy. We have seen that a modern mixed economy performs four economic functions: It combats market failures, redistributes income, stabilizes the economy, promotes long-term economic growth, and conducts international economic policy. Each of these is essential. No serious person today proposes to allow nuclear dumping, to let poor orphans starve in the streets, to sell off the central bank, and to shut down all foreign embassies.

As the mixed economy marks its centenary, how should its mission be redefined? The central lesson we read from America and Europe is the following: The critical role of the government also lends a special responsibility for government to operate efficiently. Every public dollar spent on wasteful programs could be used for promoting scientific research or alleviating hunger. Every private dollar wasted because of inefficient taxation reduces people's opportunity to improve their housing or go to college. The central premise of economics is that resources are scarce—and this applies equally to private funds and to government funds, which must be pried out of taxpayers.

SUMMARY

A. The Sources of Inequality

1. In the last century, the classical economists believed that inequality was a universal constant, unchangeable by public policy. This view does not stand up to scrutiny. Poverty made a glacial retreat over the early part of this century, and absolute incomes for those in the bottom part of the income distribution rose sharply. Since the early 1970s, this trend has reversed, and inequality has increased.

2. The Lorenz curve is a convenient device for measuring the spreads or inequalities of income distribution. It shows what percentage of total income goes to the poorest 1 percent of the population, to the poorest 10 percent, to the poorest 95 percent, and so forth.

3. Poverty is essentially a relative notion. In the United States, poverty was defined in terms of the adequacy of incomes in the early 1960s. By this standard of measured income, little progress has been made in the last decade.

4. The distribution of American income today appears to be less unequal than in the early part of this century or than in less developed countries now. But it still shows a considerable measure of inequality and increasing inequality over the last two decades. Wealth is even more unequally distributed than is income, both in the United States and in other capitalist economies.

5. To explain the inequality in income distribution, we can look separately at labor income and property income. Labor earnings vary because of differences in abilities and in intensities of work (both hours and effort) and because occupational earnings differ, due to divergent amounts of human capital, among other factors.

6. Property incomes are more unevenly distributed than labor earnings, largely because of the great disparities in wealth. Inheritance helps the children of the wealthy begin ahead of the average person; only a small fraction of America's wealth can be accounted for by life-cycle savings.

B. Antipoverty Policies

7. Political philosophers write of three types of equality: (*a*) equality of political rights, such as the right to vote; (*b*) equality of opportunity, providing equal access to

jobs, education, and other social systems; and (*c*) equality of outcome, whereby people are guaranteed equal incomes or consumptions. Whereas the first two types of equality are increasingly accepted in most advanced democracies like the United States, equality of outcome is generally rejected as impractical and too harmful to economic efficiency.

8. Equality has costs as well as benefits; the costs show up as drains from Okun's "leaky bucket." That is, attempts to reduce income inequality by progressive taxation or welfare payments may harm economic incentives to work or save and may thereby reduce the size of national output. Potential leakages are administrative costs and reduced hours of work or savings rates.

9. Major programs to alleviate poverty are welfare payments, food stamps, Medicaid, and a group of smaller or less targeted programs. As a whole, these programs are criticized because they impose high benefit-reduction rates (or marginal "tax" rates) on low-income families when families begin to earn wages or other income.

10. People are divided on how to improve the current income-support system. One proposal, called the negative income tax, would consolidate current programs into a unified federal cash income supplement. The supplement would be reduced (that is, income would be "taxed") at a moderate rate (say, one-third or one-half), so that low-income families would have a significant incentive to seek market employment. The United States has adopted a variant known as the earned-income tax credit, which provides a wage supplement to families with low earnings.

11. A second approach is reflected in the 1996 U.S. Temporary Assistance for Needy Families (TANF) program. This approach attempts to reduce long-term welfare dependency by putting time limits on benefits and devolving decisions to the states. Some believe this will result in a "race to the bottom" in which states compete to make themselves unattractive to potential beneficiaries by lowering benefits.

C. Health Care: The Problem That Won't Go Away

12. Health care is one of the largest and most rapidly growing sectors of the economy. It is characterized by multiple market failures that lead governments to intervene heavily. Health systems have major externalities, which include preventing communicable diseases and discovering new biomedical knowledge. In addition, there are market failures such as the asymmetric information between doctors and patients and between patients and insurance companies. These asymmetries lead to adverse selection in the purchase of insurance and to moral hazard (or the third-party payment syndrome) in excessive consumption of medical services. Finally, because health is so important to human welfare and to labor productivity, governments strive to provide a minimum standard of health care to the population.

13. The current health-care system in the United States has been criticized because of rising costs, a growing number of uninsured, and lagging health status, particularly of poor and minority groups. Few advocate returning to a pure-market system because of adverse effects on public health and on the generation of new biomedical knowledge. A nationalized system would provide universal coverage but ration health care by long waits for services. A promising new approach is Fedicare, or a medical negative income tax, which would provide a standard package of benefits. The price of the package would be zero for low-income families and would rise on a percentage basis with family income.

CONCEPTS FOR REVIEW

Inequality and Antipoverty Programs
trends of income distribution
Lorenz curve of income and wealth
labor and property income
relative roles of luck, life-cycle savings, risk taking, inheritance
college–high school wage premium
poverty
welfare state
Okun's "leaky bucket"

equality:
   political
   of opportunity
   of outcome
equality vs. efficiency
income-support programs
income-possibility curve: ideal and realistic cases
earned-income tax credit, negative income tax
1996 welfare reform (TANF)

Health-Care Economics
public goods of discovering new knowledge, preventing communicable diseases
insurance failures of moral hazard and adverse selection
alternative approaches to reform:
   pure market
   nationalized system
   medical negative income tax (Fedicare)

QUESTIONS FOR DISCUSSION

1. Let each member of the class anonymously write down on a card an estimate of his or her family's annual income. From these, draw up a frequency table showing the distribution of incomes. What is the median income? The mean income?

2. What effect would the following have on the Lorenz curve of after-tax incomes? (Assume that the taxes are spent by the government on a representative slice of GDP.)

   a. A proportional income tax (i.e., one taxing all incomes at the same rate)

   b. A progressive income tax (i.e., one taxing high incomes more heavily than low incomes)

   c. A sharp increase in taxes on cigarettes and food

   Draw four Lorenz curves to illustrate the original income distribution and the income distribution after each action, **a** to **c**.

3. Discuss the three different kinds of equality. Why might equality of opportunity not lead to equality of outcome? Should persons of different abilities be given the same access to jobs and education? What might be done to ensure equality of outcome? How might such steps lead to economic inefficiencies?

4. Consider two ways of supplementing the income of the poor: (*a*) cash assistance (say, $500 per month) and (*b*) categorical benefits such as subsidized food or medical care. List the pros and cons of using each strategy. Can you explain why the United States tends to use mainly strategy (*b*)? Do you agree?

5. Instead of using the Lorenz curve to measure inequality, calculate the area between the actual curve of inequality and the curve of equal incomes (i.e., the gray shaded region in Figure 19-1). Two times this ratio is called the Gini coefficient.

   What is the Gini coefficient for a society with absolute equality of income? For one in which one person gets all the income? Estimate the Gini coefficients for the different Lorenz curves in Figure 19-2.

6. In a country called Econoland, there are 10 people. Their incomes (in thousands) are $3, $6, $2, $8, $4, $9, $1, $5, $7, and $5. Construct a table of income quintiles like Table 19-2. Plot a Lorenz curve. Calculate the Gini coefficient defined in question 5.

7. Many people continue to argue about what form assistance for the poor should take. One school says, "Give people money and let them buy health services and the foods they need." The other school says, "If you give money to the poor, they may spend it on beer and drugs. Your dollar goes further in alleviating malnourishment and disease if you provide the services in kind. The dollar that you earn may be yours to spend, but society's income-support dollar is a dollar that society has the right to channel directly to its targets."

   The argument of the first school might rest on demand theory: Let each household decide how to maximize its utility on a limited budget. Chapter 5 shows why this argument might be right. But what if the parents' utility includes mainly beer and lottery tickets and no milk or clothing for the children? Might you agree with the second view? From your own personal experience and reading, which of these two arguments would you endorse? Explain your reasoning.

8. Long-term care for the elderly involves helping individuals with activities (such as bathing, dressing, and toileting) that they cannot perform for themselves. How were these needs taken care of a century ago? Explain why moral hazard and adverse selection make long-term-care insurance so expensive today that few people choose to buy it.

9. Table 19-9 shows illustrative calculations for a Fedicare system. Fill in the missing numbers. Compare this system with both a laissez-faire system and nationalized health care financed by a sales tax. What is the effect on the marginal tax rate at different income levels?

TABLE 19-9. Subsidized Premiums Can Provide Universal Health Coverage

Under an illustrative subsidized health-care system, a family of four would pay 20 cents for each dollar of income over $10,000. The maximum premium would be the insurance cost, assumed to be $8,000. Fill in the missing numbers.

Income ($)	Premiums for medical care package ($)	Income less premiums ($)
0	0	0
10,000	0	——
20,000	2,000	——
30,000	——	26,000
40,000	——	——
100,000	8,000	——

10. A policy is called "cost-effective" if it produces a given level of output at least cost or maximizes the level of output for a given amount of inputs. Assume there is a wartime situation with inadequate medical supplies. There are 100 units of health care (say, medication) and 400 patients equally divided into eight groups of 50. Table 19-10 gives the probabilities of survival with and without 1 unit of medical care.

You are charged with performing triage on the wounded. Your objective is to maximize the expected number of survivors (equal to the sum of the probability of survival times the number of patients, $p_1N_1 + \cdots + p_8N_8$, where p_i is the probability of survival with the medical treatment received and N_i is the number of patients).

a. Devise a triage rule based on the description in footnote 6 (page 363). Which two groups of patients fall into the triage category that receives treatment?

b. Calculate the expected number of surviving patients under your rule. Can you see why this strategy is cost-effective in the sense of maximizing the expected number of surviving patients?

c. Consider a rule that says treatment should go to the worst-off patients (the ones with the lowest probability of survival without care). Why is this not cost-effective?

d. Say that the number of units of medical care increased to 200. Why is your triage rule no longer appropriate? Can you determine the general rule for this example?

TABLE 19-10.

Patient group	Probability of Survival	
	With care	Without care
Tank and truck accidents:		
1. Broken legs	.99	.98
2. Severe burns	.41	.39
Shrapnel wounds:		
3. To limbs	.90	.30
4. To head	.05	.02
Bullet wounds:		
5. To limbs	.88	.85
6. To head	.10	.08
Infection:`		
7. Bacteriological	.98	.30
8. Unknown origin	.60	.59

PART FIVE

INTERNATIONAL TRADE AND THE WORLD ECONOMY

CHAPTER 20
INTERNATIONAL TRADE AND EXCHANGE RATES

The benefit of international trade—a more efficient employment of the productive forces of the world.

John Stuart Mill

As we go about our daily lives, it is easy to overlook the importance of international exchange. America ships enormous volumes of food, airplanes, computers, and construction machinery to other countries; and in return we get vast quantities of oil, VCRs, cars, kiwi fruits, and other goods and services. Even more important for most countries are the new products and services that have over the years derived from other regions. While we may produce most of our national output, it is sobering to reflect how much our consumption—including clocks, railroads, accounting, penicillin, radar, and the Beatles—originates in the ingenuity of long-forgotten people in faraway places.

What are the economic forces that lie behind international trade? Simply put, trade promotes specialization, and specialization increases productivity. Over the long run, increased trade and higher productivity raise living standards for all nations. Gradually, countries have realized that opening up their economies to the global trading system is the most secure road to prosperity.

In this final part, we survey the principles governing *international trade and finance*, which is the system by which nations export and import goods, services, and financial capital. International economics involves many of the most controversial questions of the day: Why does the United States benefit from importing almost one-quarter of its automobiles and half of its petroleum? What are the advantages to the

United States, Canada, and Mexico of a free-trade region? Is there wisdom in the European countries' adopting a common currency? And why has the United States become the world's largest debtor country in the last decade? The economic stakes are high in finding wise answers to these questions.

International vs. Domestic Trade

How does the analysis of international trade differ from that of domestic markets? There are three differences:

1. *Expanded trading opportunities.* The major advantage of international trade is that it expands trading horizons. If people were forced to consume only what they produced at home, the world would be poorer on both the material and the spiritual planes. Canadians could drink no wine, Americans could eat no bananas, and most of the world would be without jazz and Hollywood movies.

2. *Sovereign nations.* Trading across frontiers involves people and firms living in different nations. Each nation is a sovereign entity which regulates the flow of people, goods, and finance crossing its borders. This contrasts with domestic trade, where there is a single currency, trade and money flow freely within the borders, and people

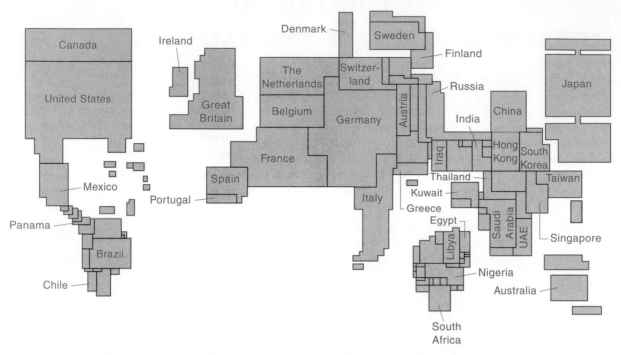

FIGURE 20-1. Countries of the World Scaled to Their International Trade

In this map, the area of each country is drawn proportional to its share of total world trade in 1991. Compare the size of the advanced industrial countries with that of Africa and Asia. [Adapted from Michael Kidron and Ronald Segal, *The New State of the World Atlas* (Simon and Schuster, New York, 1991), updated by authors.]

can migrate easily to seek new opportunities. Sometimes, political barriers to trade are erected when affected groups object to foreign trade and nations impose tariffs or quotas. This practice, called protectionism, is analyzed in the next chapter.

3. *Exchange rates.* Most nations have their own currencies. I want to pay for a Japanese car in dollars, while Toyota wants to be paid in Japanese yen. The international financial system must ensure a smooth flow of dollars, yen, and other currencies—or else risk a breakdown in trade.

A. ECONOMIC BASIS FOR INTERNATIONAL TRADE

TRENDS IN FOREIGN TRADE

We begin by examining the patterns of international trade. Figure 20-1 is a trade map, showing how the world would look if each country's geographical size were proportional to its share of world trade. Notice how large the United States, Western Europe, and Japan loom, while tiny Hong Kong appears larger than India.

An economy that engages in international trade is called an **open economy**. A useful measure of openness is the ratio of a country's exports or imports to its GDP. Figure 20-2 shows the trend in the shares of imports and exports for the United States. It shows the dip in the trade share during the trade wars of the 1930s, followed by the steady expansion of trade with lower trade barriers over the last three decades. Still, the United States is a relatively self-sufficient economy. Many nations, particularly in Western Europe and East Asia, are highly open economies and export and import more than 50 percent of their GDP.

The degree of openness is much higher in many U.S. industries, such as steel, textiles, consumer electronics, and autos, than it is for the U.S. economy as a whole. Table 20-1 on page 374 shows the commodity composition of U.S. foreign trade for 1996. These data reveal that despite being an advanced industrial economy, the United States exports surprisingly large amounts of primary commodities (such as food) and imports large quantities of sophisticated, capital-intensive manufactured goods (like automobiles and

telecommunications equipment). Moreover, we find a great deal of two-way, or intraindustry, trade. Within a particular industry, the United States both exports and imports at the same time because a high degree of product differentiation means that different countries tend to have niches in different parts of a market.

THE SOURCES OF INTERNATIONAL TRADE IN GOODS AND SERVICES

What are the economic factors that lie behind the patterns of international trade? Nations find it beneficial to participate in international trade for several reasons: because of diversity in the conditions of production, because of decreasing costs of production, and because of differences in tastes among nations.

FIGURE 20-2. Growing U.S. Openness

Like all major market economies, the United States has increasingly opened its borders to foreign trade over the last half-century. The result is a growing share of output and consumption involved in international trade. In the late 1980s, imports far outdistanced exports, causing the United States to become the world's largest debtor nation. (Source: U.S. Department of Commerce.)

U.S. Merchandise Trade, 1996		
	Share of each commodity as percent of total	
Commodity classification	Exports	Imports
Industrial supplies:		
Food and beverages	9	4
Petroleum and petroleum products	1	8
Other	22	15
Manufactures:		
Capital goods		
Computers and related equipment	7	7
Civilian aircraft and related equipment	5	1
Other capital goods	27	19
Automotive vehicles and parts	10	16
Consumer goods	11	21
Other	5	5
Total	100	100

TABLE 20-1. The United States Exports Surprising Amounts of Primary Goods and Imports Many Manufactures

The United States exports a large volume of primary commodities, especially food and coal, mainly because of its ample natural resources. At the same time, it imports many manufactured goods, like cars and cameras, because other countries specialize in different market niches and enjoy economies of scale. (Source: U.S. Department of Commerce.)

Diversity in Natural Resources

Trade may take place because of the diversity in productive possibilities among countries. In part, these differences reflect endowments of natural resources. One country may be blessed with a supply of petroleum, while another may have a large amount of fertile land. Or a mountainous country may generate large amounts of hydroelectric power which it sells to its neighbors, while a country with deep-water harbors may become a shipping center.

Differences in Tastes

A second cause of trade lies in preferences. Even if the conditions of production were identical in all regions, countries might engage in trade if their tastes for goods were different.

For example, suppose that Norway and Sweden produce fish from the sea and meat from the land in about the same amounts, but the Swedes have a great fondness for meat while the Norwegians are partial to fish. A mutually beneficial export of meat from Norway and fish from Sweden would take place. Both countries would gain from this trade; the sum of human happiness is increased, just as when Jack Sprat trades fat meat for his wife's lean.

Decreasing Costs

Perhaps the most important reason for trade is differences among countries in production costs. For example, manufacturing processes enjoy economies of scale; that is, they tend to have lower average costs of production as the volume of output expands. So when a particular country gets a head start in a particular product, it can become the high-volume, low-cost producer. The economies of scale give it a significant cost and technological advantage over other countries, which find it cheaper to buy from the leading producer than to make the product themselves.

Take consumer electronics as an example. No doubt a company such as GE or IBM could make a videocassette recorder (VCR) in the United States if it wanted to. But it could not make one cheap enough to compete with Japanese manufacturers like Sony, which have the advantages of enormous volumes and long experience in making consumer electronics. As a result, the United States imports almost all of its VCRs.

The shoe is on the other foot when it comes to civilian aircraft, where the United States dominates the world market. Boeing, the leading exporter in the United States, has two important advantages. First, Boeing has a long track record in building reliable and safe passenger jets. This is not an easy task for a competitor to match. Because modern planes are complicated and technologically sophisticated, it takes time and practice to learn how to build reliable planes at an affordable price.

Large scale is often an important advantage in industries with large research and development expenses. As the leading aircraft maker in the world, Boeing can spread the enormous cost of designing, developing, and testing a new plane over a large sales volume. That means it can sell planes at a lower price than competitors with a smaller volume. Boe-

ing's only real competitor, Airbus, got off the ground through large subsidies from several European countries to cover its research and development costs.

The example of decreasing cost helps explain the important phenomenon of extensive intra-industry trade shown in Table 20-1. Why is it that the United States both imports and exports computers and related equipment? The reason is that the United States has exploited the economies of scale in microprocessors and is specialized in that area, while Japan enjoys a cost advantage in memory chips and video screens for notebook computers and tends to specialize and export in that part of the market. Similar patterns of intraindustry specialization are seen with cars, steel, textiles, and many other manufactured products.

The next chapter synthesizes the different reasons for trade in the theory of comparative advantage.

B. THE DETERMINATION OF FOREIGN EXCHANGE RATES

FOREIGN EXCHANGE RATES

We are all familiar with domestic trade. When I buy Florida oranges or California shirts, I naturally want to pay in dollars. Luckily, the orange grower and the shirt manufacturer want payment in U.S. currency, so all trade can be carried out in dollars. Economic transactions within a country are simple.

But if I am interested in importing Japanese bicycles, the transaction becomes more complicated. The bicycle manufacturer needs to be paid in Japanese currency rather than in U.S. dollars. Therefore, in order to import the Japanese bicycles, I must first buy Japanese yen (¥) and use those yen to pay the Japanese manufacturer. Similarly, if the Japanese want to buy U.S. merchandise, they must first obtain U.S. dollars. This new complication involves foreign exchange.

Foreign trade involves the use of different national currencies. The **foreign exchange rate** is the price of one currency in terms of another currency. The foreign exchange rate is determined in the foreign exchange market, which is the market where different currencies are traded.

That little paragraph contains much information that will be explained in this section. To begin with, recall that all major countries have their own currencies—the U.S. dollar, the British pound, the Japanese yen, the German mark, the Mexican peso, and so forth. *We follow the convention of measuring exchange rates as the amount of foreign currency that can be bought with 1 unit of the domestic currency.* For example, the foreign exchange rate of the dollar might be 100 yen per U.S. dollar (¥100/$).

When we want to exchange one national money for another, we do so at a foreign exchange rate. For example, if you traveled to Canada in 1997, you would get about 1.4 Canadian dollars for 1 U.S. dollar. There is a foreign exchange rate between U.S. dollars and the currency of each and every other country. In mid-1997, the foreign exchange rate per U.S. dollar was 0.62 British pound, 1.8 German marks, 118 Japanese yen, and 7.97 Mexican pesos.

With foreign exchange, it is possible for me to buy a Japanese bicycle. Suppose its quoted price is 20,000 yen. I can look in the newspaper for the foreign exchange rate for yen. Suppose the rate is ¥100/$. I could go to the bank to convert my $200 into ¥20,000. With my Japanese money, I then can pay the exporter in the currency it needs for my bicycle.

You should be able to show what Japanese importers of American trucks have to do if they want to buy, say, a $36,000 shipment from an American exporter. Here yen must be converted into dollars. You will see that, when the foreign exchange rate is 100 yen per dollar, the truck shipment costs them ¥3,600,000.

Businesses and tourists do not have to know anything more than this for their import or export transactions. But the economics of foreign exchange rates cannot be grasped until we analyze the forces underlying the supply and demand for foreign currencies and the functioning of the foreign exchange market.

THE FOREIGN EXCHANGE MARKET

Foreign exchange rates, for the most part, are not fixed over time. Instead, like other prices, they vary from week to week and month to month according to the forces of supply and demand. The **foreign exchange market** is the market in which currencies of different countries are traded and foreign exchange rates are determined. Foreign currencies are traded at the retail level in many banks and firms specializing in that business. Organized markets in New York, Tokyo, London, and Zurich trade hundreds of billions of dollars worth of currencies each day.

We can use our familiar supply and demand curves to illustrate how markets determine the price of foreign currencies. Figure 20-3 shows the supply and demand for U.S. dollars in U.S. dealings with Japan.[1] The *supply* of U.S. dollars comes from people in the United States who need yen to purchase Japanese goods, services, or financial instruments. The *demand* for dollars comes from people in Japan who buy U.S. goods, services, or investments and who, accordingly, need to pay for these items in dollars. The price of foreign exchange—the foreign exchange rate—settles at that price where supply and demand are in balance.

Let us first consider the supply side. The supply of U.S. dollars to the foreign exchange market originates when Americans need yen to buy Japanese automobiles, cameras, and other commodities, to vacation in Tokyo, and so forth. In addition, foreign exchange is required if Americans want to purchase Japanese investments, such as shares in Japanese companies. In short, *Americans supply dollars when they purchase foreign goods, services, and assets.*

In Figure 20-3, the vertical axis is the crucial *foreign exchange rate,* e, *measured in units of foreign currency per unit of domestic currency* — that is, in yen per dollar, in Mexican pesos per dollar, and so forth. Make sure you understand the units here. The horizontal axis

---

FIGURE 20-3. Exchange-Rate Determination

Behind the supplies and demands for foreign exchange lie purchases of goods, services, and financial flows. Behind the demand for dollars is the Japanese desire for American goods and investments. The supply of dollars comes from Americans desiring Japanese goods and assets. Equilibrium comes at E. If the foreign exchange rate were above E, there would be an excess supply of dollars. Unless the government bought this excess supply for official reserves, market forces would push the foreign exchange rate back down to balance supply and demand at E.

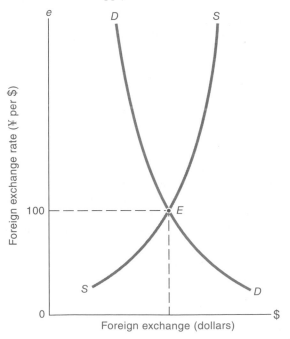

---

[1] This is a simplified example in which we consider only the bilateral trade between Japan and the United States.

shows the quantity of dollars transacted in the foreign exchange market.

The supply of U.S. dollars is represented by the upward-sloping SS curve. The central point here is that as the foreign exchange rate rises, the number of yen that can be bought per dollar increases. This means, other things being equal, that the prices of Japanese goods fall relative to those of American goods. Hence, Americans will tend to buy more Japanese goods, and the supply of U.S. dollars therefore increases. This shows why the supply curve slopes upward. Let's take the example of bicycles. If the foreign exchange rate were to rise from ¥100/$ to ¥200/$, the bicycle which cost ¥20,000 would fall in price from $200 to $100. If other things were unchanged, Japanese bicycles would be more attractive, and Americans would require more dollar foreign exchange to buy a larger quantity of bicycles. Hence, the quantity supplied of dollars would be higher at a higher exchange rate.

What lies behind the demand for dollars (represented in Figure 20-3 by the DD demand curve for dollar foreign exchange)? Foreigners demand U.S. dollars when they buy American goods, services, and assets. For example, suppose a Japanese student buys an American economics textbook or takes a trip to the United States. She will require U.S. dollars to pay for these items. Or when JAL buys a Boeing 767 for its fleet, this transaction increases the demand for U.S. dollars. In short, *foreigners demand U.S. dollars to pay for their purchases of American goods, services, and assets.*

The demand curve in Figure 20-3 slopes downward to indicate that as the dollar's value falls (and the yen therefore becomes more expensive), Japanese residents will want to buy more foreign goods, services, and investments. They will therefore demand more U.S. dollars in the foreign exchange market. Consider what happens when the foreign exchange rate on the dollar falls from ¥100/$ to ¥50/$. American computers, which had sold at $2000 × (¥100/$) = ¥200,000 now sell for only $2000 × (¥50/$) = ¥100,000. Japanese purchasers will therefore tend to buy more American computers, and the quantity demanded of U.S. foreign exchange will increase.

The purpose of the foreign exchange market is to equilibrate supply and demand. Market forces move the foreign exchange rate up or down to balance the supply and demand. The price will settle at the *equilibrium foreign exchange rate*, which is the rate at which the dollars willingly bought just equal the dollars willingly sold.

The balance of supply and demand for foreign exchange determines the foreign exchange rate of a currency. At the market exchange rate of 100 yen per dollar shown at point E in Figure 20-3, the exchange rate is in equilibrium and has no tendency to rise or fall.

We have discussed the foreign exchange market in terms of the supply and demand for dollars. But in this market, there are two currencies involved, so we could just as easily analyze the supply and demand for Japanese yen. To see this, you should sketch a supply-and-demand diagram with yen foreign exchange on the horizontal axis and the yen rate ($ per ¥) on the vertical axis. If ¥100/$ is the equilibrium looking from the point of view of the dollar, then $0.01/¥ is the *reciprocal exchange rate*. As an exercise, go through the analysis in this section for the reciprocal market. You will see that in this simple bilateral world, for every dollar statement there is an exact yen counterpart: supply of dollars is demand for yen; demand for dollars is supply of yen.

There is just one further extension necessary to get to actual foreign exchange markets. In reality, each country has its own currency. We therefore need to find the supplies and demands for each and every currency. And in a world of many nations, it is the many-sided exchange and trade, with demands and supplies coming from all parts of the globe, that determines the entire array of foreign exchange rates.

Exchange-Rate Systems

While this chapter is primarily devoted to laying out the basic tools for international economics, it is important to recognize that there are different approaches to managing a nation's exchange rates. The two systems most widely used today are flexible and fixed exchange rates. One system occurs when exchange rates are completely flexible and move purely under the influence of supply and demand. With this system, known as *flexible exchange rates* (or sometimes "floating" exchange rates), governments take a hands-off policy toward their exchange rate and do not try to set a particular rate. That is, in a flexible-exchange-rate system, the relative prices of currencies are determined in the marketplace through the buying and selling of households and businesses. The United States currently relies upon a flexible exchange rate.

The other major system is *fixed exchange rates*, where governments specify the rate at which their currency will be converted into other currencies. The gold standard was a fixed-exchange-rate system, as was the Bretton Woods system used by most countries after World War II. Over the last decade, many European countries have operated a fixed-exchange-rate system.

We will review the economic advantages and disadvantages of different exchange-rate systems in the last chapter of this book.

Terminology for Exchange-Rate Changes

Foreign exchange markets have a special vocabulary. By definition, a fall in the price of one currency in terms of one or all others is called a *depreciation*. A rise in the price of a currency in terms of another currency is called an *appreciation*. In our example above, when the price of the dollar rose from ¥100/$ to ¥200/$, the dollar appreciated. We also know that the yen depreciated.

In the supply-and-demand diagram for U.S. dollars, a fall in the foreign exchange rate (*e*) is a depreciation of the U.S. dollar, and a rise in *e* represents an appreciation.

The term "devaluation" is often confused with the term "depreciation." *Devaluation* is confined to situations in which a country has officially set or "pegged" its exchange rate relative to one or more other currencies. In this case, a devaluation occurs when the pegged rate or parity is changed by lowering the price of the currency. A *revaluation* occurs when the official price is raised.

For example, in December 1994 Mexico devalued its currency when it lowered the official price at which it was defending the peso from 3.5 pesos per dollar to 3.8 pesos per dollar. Mexico soon found it could not defend the new parity and "floated" its exchange rate. At that point, the peso fell, or depreciated, even further.

When a country's currency falls in value relative to that of another country, we say that the domestic currency has undergone a **depreciation** while the foreign currency has undergone an **appreciation**.

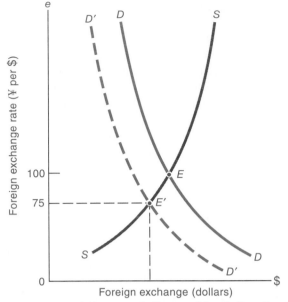

FIGURE 20-4. A Decrease in Demand for Dollars Leads to Dollar Depreciation

Suppose that a recession or deflation in Japan reduces the Japanese demand for dollars. This would shift the demand for dollars to the left from *DD* to *D'D'*. The exchange rate of the dollar depreciates, while the yen appreciates. Why would the new exchange rate discourage American purchases of Japanese goods?

When a country's official foreign exchange rate is lowered, we say that the currency has undergone a **devaluation**. An increase in the official foreign exchange rate is called a **revaluation.**

Effects of Changes in Trade

What would happen if there were changes in demand? For example, there might be a deep recession in Japan, or Japan might take protectionist measures by putting a quota on American goods.

In each of these cases, the demand for American dollars would decrease. The result is shown in Figure 20-4. The decline in purchases of American goods, services, and investments decreases the demand for dollars in the market. This change is represented by a leftward shift in the demand curve. The result will be a lower foreign exchange rate—that is, the dollar will depreciate and the yen will appreciate. At the lower exchange rate, the quantity of dollars supplied by Americans to the market will decrease because

Japanese goods are now more expensive. Moreover, the quantity of dollars demanded by the Japanese will decline because of the recession and protectionist measures. How much will exchange rates change? Just enough so that the supply and demand are again in balance. In the example shown in Figure 20-4, the dollar has depreciated from ¥100/$ to ¥75/$.

Purchasing-Power Parity and Exchange Rates

In the short run, market-determined exchange rates are highly volatile in response to monetary policy, political events, and changes in expectations. But over the longer run, economists believe, exchange rates are determined primarily by the relative prices of goods in different countries. An important implication is the *purchasing-power parity (PPP) theory of exchange rates.* Under this theory, a nation's exchange rate will tend to equalize the cost of buying traded goods at home with the cost of buying those goods abroad.

A special case is the *law of one price,* which states that (in the absence of transportation costs and trade barriers) identical goods must sell at the same price in all markets. The PPP theory can then be illustrated with a simple example. Suppose the price of a market basket of goods (automobiles, jewelry, oil, foods, and so forth) costs $1000 in the United States and 10,000 pesos in Mexico. At an exchange rate of 100 pesos to a dollar, this bundle would cost $100 in Mexico. Given these relative prices and the free trade between the two countries, we would expect to see American firms and consumers streaming across the border to buy at the lower Mexican prices. The result will be higher imports from Mexico, and an increased demand for Mexican pesos. That will cause the exchange rate of the Mexican peso to appreciate relative to the U.S. dollar, so you will need more dollars to buy the same number of pesos. As a result, the prices of the Mexican goods *in dollar terms* rise even though the prices in pesos have not changed.

Where would this process end? If the law of one price holds, with unchanged prices in the two countries the peso's exchange rate must fall to 10 pesos to the dollar. Only at this exchange rate would the price of the market basket of goods be equal in the two markets. At 10 pesos to the dollar, we say that the currencies have equal purchasing power in terms of the traded goods.

The PPP doctrine also holds that countries with high inflation rates will tend to have depreciating currencies. For example, if Country A's inflation rate is 10 percent while inflation in Country B is 2 percent, the currency of Country A will tend to depreciate relative to that of Country B by the difference in the inflation rates, that is, 8 percent annually. Alternatively, let's say that runaway inflation leads to a 100-fold rise of prices in Russia over the course of a year, while prices in the United States are unchanged. According to the PPP theory, the Russian ruble should depreciate by 99 percent in order to bring the prices of American and Russian goods back into equilibrium.

We should caution that the PPP theory is only an approximation and cannot predict the precise movement of exchange rates. The leeway in the PPP theory is seen in the relationship between the U.S. dollar and the Japanese yen over the last decade; this exchange rate has been as high as 168 yen to a dollar and as low as 85 yen to a dollar, even though most economists calculate the PPP level as being around 120 yen to a dollar. Trade barriers, transportation costs, and the presence of nontraded services allow prices to diverge significantly across countries. In addition, financial flows can overwhelm trade flows in the short run. So while the PPP theory is a useful guide to exchange rates in the long run, exchange rates can diverge from their PPP level for many years.

PPP and the size of nations: By any measure, the United States still has the largest economy in the world. But which country has the second largest? Is it Japan, Germany, Russia, or some other country? You'd think this would be an easy question to answer, like measuring height or weight. The problem, though, is that Japan totes up its national output in yen, while Germany's national output is given in marks, and America's is in dollars. To be compared, they all need to be converted into the same currency.

The customary approach is to use the market exchange rate to convert each currency into dollars, and by that yardstick Japan has the second-largest economy. However, there are two difficulties with using the market rate. First, because market rates can rise and fall sharply, the size of countries could easily change by 10 or 20 percent in a year. More-

	GDP using market exchange rates ($, billion)	GDP using PPP exchange rates ($, billion)
United States	6,648	6,648
Japan	4,591	2,802
China	522	2,473
Germany	2,046	1,558
India	294	1,174
France	1,330	1,117
United Kingdom	1,017	997
Indonesia	175	714
Russia	377	655
Mexico	377	635
Philippines	64	185
Malaysia	71	171
Nigeria	35	150
Hong Kong	132	128

TABLE 20-2. PPP Calculations Change the Relative Size of Nations, 1994

Using PPP exchange rates changes the economic ranking of nations. After correcting for the purchasing power of incomes, China moves from a middle-ranking country to an economic superpower. (Source: World Bank.)

over, using market exchange rates, many poor countries appear to have a very small national output.

Today, economists generally prefer to use PPP exchange rates to compare the living standards in different countries. The difference can be dramatic, as Table 20-2 shows. When market exchange rates are used, the outputs of low-income countries like China and India tend to be understated. This understatement occurs because a substantial part of their output comes in labor-intensive services, which are usually extremely inexpensive in low-wage countries. Hence, when we calculate PPP exchange rates including the prices of nontraded goods, the GDPs of low-income countries rise relative to those of high-wage countries. For example, when PPP exchange rates are used, China's GDP is 5 times the level calculated with market exchange rates. Furthermore, on the basis of PPP exchange rates, China leaps ahead of Germany to become the third-largest economy in the world.

C. THE BALANCE OF INTERNATIONAL PAYMENTS

BALANCE-OF-PAYMENTS ACCOUNTS

Economists keep score by looking at income statements and balance sheets. In the area of international economics, the key accounts are a nation's balance of payments. A country's **balance of international payments** is a systematic statement of all economic transactions between that country and the rest of the world. Its major components are the current account and the capital account. The basic structure of the balance of payments is shown in Table 20-3, and each element is discussed below.

Debits and Credits

Like other accounts, the balance of payments records each transaction as either a plus or a minus. The general rule in balance-of-payments accounting is the following:

I. **Current account**

Merchandise (or "trade balance")
Services
Investment income
Unilateral transfers

II. **Capital account**

Private
Government
  Official reserve changes
  Other

TABLE 20-3. Basic Elements of the Balance of Payments

The balance of payments has two fundamental parts. The current account represents the spending and receipts on goods and services along with transfers. The capital account includes asset purchases and sales. An important principle is that the two must always sum to zero.

If a transaction earns foreign currency for the nation, it is called a *credit* and is recorded as a plus item. If a transaction involves spending foreign currency, it is a *debit* and is recorded as a negative item. In general, exports are credits and imports are debits.

Exports earn foreign currency, so they are credits. Imports require spending foreign currency, so they are debits. How is the U.S. import of a Japanese camera recorded? Since we ultimately pay for it in Japanese yen, it is clearly a debit. How shall we treat interest and dividend income on investments received by Americans from abroad? Clearly, they are credit items like exports because they provide us with foreign currencies.

Details of the Balance of Payments

Balance on Current Account. The totality of items under section I in Table 20-3 is the **balance on current account**. This includes all items of income and outlay—imports and exports of goods and services, investment income, and transfer payments. The current-account balance is akin to the net income of a nation. It is conceptually similar to net exports in the national output accounts.

In the past, many writers concentrated on the **trade balance**, which consists of merchandise imports or exports. The composition of merchandise imports and exports was shown in Table 20-1; it consists mainly of primary commodities (like food and fuels) and manufactured goods. In an earlier era,

the mercantilists strove for a trade surplus (an excess of exports over imports), calling this a "favorable balance of trade." They hoped to avoid an "unfavorable trade balance," by which they meant a trade deficit (an excess of imports over exports). This point of view has carried over to today as many nations seek trade surpluses.

Today, economists avoid this language because a trade deficit is not necessarily harmful. Sometimes, a nation may have a trade deficit because the domestic productivity of capital is extremely high and borrowing to import capital equipment will in the long run raise national income.

In addition, *services* are increasingly important in international trade. Services consist of such items as shipping, financial services, and foreign travel. A third item in the current account is *investment income*, which includes the earnings on foreign investments (that is, earnings on U.S. assets abroad). One of the major developments of the last two decades has been the growth in services and investment income. A final element is transfers, which represent payments not in return for goods and services.

Table 20-4 on page 382 presents a summary of the U.S. balance of international payments for 1996. Note its two main divisions: current account and capital account. Each item is listed by name in column (a). Credits are listed in column (b), while column (c) shows the debits. Column (d) then lists the net credits or debits; it shows a credit if on balance the item added to our stock of foreign currencies or a debit if the total subtracted from our foreign-currency supply.

In 1996 our merchandise exports gave us credits of $612 billion. But our merchandise imports gave us debits of $803 billion. The *net* difference between credits and debits was a debit of $191 billion. This trade deficit is listed in column (d), on the first row. (Be sure you know why the algebraic sign is shown as − rather than as +.) From the table we see that services provided a surplus, while net investment income was close to zero. Our current-account deficit was thus $148 billion for 1996.

Capital Account. We have now completed analysis of the current account. But how did the United States "finance" its $148 billion current-account deficit in 1996? It must have either borrowed or reduced its foreign assets, for by definition that which you buy you must either pay for or owe for. This means that *the balance of international*

Section	(a) Items	(b) Credits (+)	(c) Debits (−)	(d) Net credits (+) or debits (−)
U.S. Balance of Payments, 1996 (Billions of Dollars)				
I.	Current account			−148
	a. Merchandise trade balance	612	−803	−191
	b. Services	237	−157	80
	c. Investment income	206	−204	3
	d. Unilateral transfers			−40
II.	Capital account [lending (−) or borrowing (+)]			148
	a. Private (including statistical discrepancy)			20
	b. Government			
	Official U.S. reserve changes			7
	Other foreign government changes			121
Sum of Current and Capital Account				0

TABLE 20-4. Basic Elements fo Balance of Payments

Source: U.S. Department of Commerce, *Survey of Current Business,* September 1997.

payments as a whole must by definition show a final zero balance.

Capital-account transactions are asset transactions between Americans and foreigners. They occur, for example, when a Japanese pension fund buys U.S. government securities or when an American buys stock in a Japanese firm.

It is easy to decide which items are credits and which are debits in the capital account if you use the following rule: Always think of the United States as exporting and importing stocks, bonds, or other securities—or, for short, exporting and importing IOUs in return for foreign currencies. *Then you can treat these exports and imports of securities like other exports and imports.* When we borrow abroad to finance a current-account deficit, we are sending IOUs (in the form of Treasury bills) abroad and gaining foreign currencies. Is this a credit or a debit? Clearly this is a credit because it brought foreign currencies into the United States.

Similarly, if U.S. banks lend abroad to finance a computer assembly plant in Mexico, the U.S. banks are importing IOUs from the Mexicans and the United States is losing foreign currencies; this is clearly a debit item in the U.S. balance of payments.

Line II shows that in 1996 the United States was a net *borrower*: we borrowed abroad more than we lent to foreigners. The United States was a net

exporter of IOUs (a net borrower) in the amount of $148 billion.[2]

Official Reserves. One part of the capital account is a special feature—the line showing the official-reserve changes. When all countries have purely market-determined exchange rates, the entry on line II(c) of Table 20-4 must be zero. When countries "intervene" in foreign exchange markets, they attempt to affect the exchange rate by buying and selling foreign currencies. This shows up in the balance of payments as changes in *official reserves.*

We will see that official reserves play a crucial role when countries have fixed exchange rates and defend the official exchange rates. When a country defends its official exchange rate, it does so by buying and selling foreign currencies. This leads to changes in official reserves. By contrast, when countries have market-determined (or flexible) exchange rates, there is little intervention and changes in official reserves are relatively small. In today's increas-

[2] As in all economic statistics, there are statistical errors (called the "statistical discrepancy" in the balance-of-payments accounts). These reflect the fact that many flows of goods and finance (from small currency transactions to the drug trade) are not recorded. We include the statistical discrepancy in the private capital account in line II(a) of Table 20-4.

ingly integrated capital markets, capital flows are dominated by private asset transactions.

Exchange Rates and the Balance of Payments

We can now see the connection between exchange rates and adjustments in the balance of payments. In the simplest case, assume that exchange rates are determined by supply and demand. Consider what happened after German unification when the German central bank decided to raise interest rates to curb inflation. After the monetary tightening, foreigners moved some of their assets into German marks to benefit from high German interest rates. This produced an excess demand for the German mark at the old exchange rate. In other words, at the old foreign exchange rate, people were, on balance, buying German marks and selling other currencies.

Here is where the exchange rate plays its role as equilibrator. As the demand for German marks increased, it led to an appreciation of the German mark and a depreciation of other currencies, like the U.S. dollar. The movement in the exchange rate continued until the capital and current accounts were back in balance. The equilibration for the current account is easiest to understand. Here, the appreciation of the mark made German goods more expensive and led to a decline in German exports and an increase in German imports. Both of these factors tended to reduce the German current-account surplus.

Exchange-rate movements serve as a balance wheel to remove disequilibria in the balance of payments.

LIFE CYCLE OF THE BALANCE OF PAYMENTS

A review of the economic history of industrialized countries reveals that they go through similar life cycles in their balance of payments as they grow from young debtor to mature creditor. This sequence is found, with variations related to their particular histories, in the advanced economies of North America, Europe, and Southeast Asia. We can illustrate the stages by recounting briefly the history of the balance of payments of the United States:

1. *Young and growing debtor nation.* From the Revolutionary War until after the Civil War, the United States imported on current account more than it exported. Europe lent the difference, which allowed the country to build up its capital stock. The United States was a typical young and growing debtor nation.

2. *Mature debtor nation.* From about 1873 to 1914, the U.S. balance of trade moved into surplus. But growth of the dividends and interest that were owed abroad on past borrowing kept the current account more or less in balance. Capital movements were also nearly in balance as lending just offset borrowing.

3. *New creditor nation.* During World War I, the United States expanded its exports tremendously. American citizens and the government lent money to allies England and France for war equipment and postwar relief needs. The United States emerged from the war a creditor nation.

4. *Mature creditor nation.* In the fourth stage, earnings on foreign capital and investments provided a large surplus on invisibles that was matched by a deficit on merchandise trade. This pattern was followed by the United States until the early 1980s. Countries like Japan today play the role of mature creditor nation as they enjoy large current-account surpluses which they in turn invest abroad.

The United States has entered an interesting new position in the last two decades. In this stage, the nation is again borrowing from abroad to finance its domestic investment. In part, the foreign borrowing is caused by low levels of U.S. domestic saving. In addition, capital is attracted to the United States because of the country's political stability, low inflation, and robust inventiveness. The counterpart of American dissaving is that foreigners, particularly Japanese investors, are purchasing substantial amounts of American assets.

Is this new stage of the U.S. balance of payments a transient period? Or does it mark the beginning of a long period of "structural" current-account deficits that will last for decades to come? No one can answer this question with certainty. Corrective forces in the 1990s appear to be shifting the U.S. current account back toward balance, but with a heavy foreign debt to service. When balance occurs, the United States will once again be a mature debtor nation, going back to stage 2, above.

SUMMARY

A. Economic Basis for International Trade

1. Specialization, division of labor, and trade increase productivity and consumption possibilities. The gains from trade hold among nations as well as within a nation. Engaging in international exchange is more efficient than relying only on domestic production.

2. Diversity is the fundamental reason that nations engage in international trade. Within this general principle, we see that trade occurs (*a*) because of differences in the conditions of production, (*b*) because of decreasing costs (or economies of scale), and (*c*) because of diversity in tastes.

B. The Determination of Foreign Exchange Rates

3. International trade involves the new element of different national currencies, which are linked by relative prices called foreign exchange rates. When Americans import Japanese goods, they ultimately need to pay in Japanese yen. In the foreign exchange market, Japanese yen might trade at ¥100/$ (or reciprocally, ¥1 would trade for $0.01). This price is called the foreign exchange rate.

4. In a foreign exchange market involving only two countries, the supply of U.S. dollars comes from Americans who want to purchase goods, services, and investments from Japan; the demand for U.S. dollars comes from Japanese who want to import commodities or financial assets from America. The interaction of these supplies and demands determines the foreign exchange rate. More generally, foreign exchange rates are determined by the complex interplay of many countries buying and selling among themselves. When trade or capital flows change, supply and demand shift and the equilibrium exchange rate changes.

5. A fall in the market price of a currency is a depreciation; a rise in a currency's value is called an appreciation. In a system where governments announce official foreign exchange rates, a decrease in the official exchange rate is called a devaluation, while an increase is a revaluation.

6. According to the purchasing-power parity (PPP) theory of exchange rates, exchange rates tend to move with changes in relative price levels of different countries. The PPP theory applies better to the long run than the short run. When this theory is applied to measure the purchasing power of incomes in different countries, it raises the per capita outputs of low-income countries.

C. The Balance of International Payments

7. The balance of international payments is the set of accounts that measures all the economic transactions between a nation and the rest of the world. It includes exports and imports of goods, services, and financial capital. Exports are credit items, while imports are debits. More generally, a country's credit items are transactions that make foreign currencies available to it; debit items are ones that reduce its holdings of foreign currencies.

8. The major components of the balance of payments are:
   I. Current account (merchandise trade, services, investment income, transfers)
   II. Capital account (private, government, and official-reserve changes)
   The fundamental rule of balance-of-payments accounting is that the sum of all items must equal zero: I + II = 0.

9. Historically, countries tend to go through stages of the balance of payments: from the young debtor borrowing for economic development, through mature debtor and young creditor, to mature creditor nation living off earnings from past investments. In the 1980s, the United States moved to a different stage where low domestic saving and attractive investment opportunities again led it to borrow heavily abroad and become a debtor nation.

CONCEPTS FOR REVIEW

Principles of International Trade

open economy
sources of trade:
   cost differences
   decreasing costs
   differences in tastes

Foreign Exchange Rates

foreign exchange rate, foreign
   exchange market
supply of and demand for foreign
   exchange
exchange rate terminology:
   appreciation and depreciation
   revaluation and devaluation

Balance of Payments

balance of payments (current
   account, capital account)
official-reserve changes
balance of payments components:
   I + II = 0
debits and credits
stages of balance of payments

QUESTIONS FOR DISCUSSION

1. Table 20-5 shows some foreign exchange rates (in units of foreign currency per dollar) as of early 1997. Fill in the last column of the table with the reciprocal price of the dollar in terms of each foreign currency, being especially careful to write down the relevant units in the parentheses.

2. Figure 20-3 shows the demand and supply for U.S. dollars in an example in which Japan and the United States trade only with each other.

   a. Describe and draw the reciprocal supply and demand schedules for Japanese yen. Explain why the supply of yen is equivalent to the demand for dollars. Also explain and draw the schedule that corresponds to the supply of dollars. Find the equilibrium price of yen in this new diagram and relate it to the equilibrium in Figure 20-3.

   b. Assume that Americans develop a taste for Japanese goods. Show what would happen to the supply and demand for yen. Would the yen appreciate or depreciate relative to the dollar? Explain.

3. Draw up a list of items that belong on the credit side of the balance of international payments and another list of items that belong on the debit side. What is meant by a trade surplus? By the balance on current account?

4. Construct hypothetical balance-of-payments accounts for a young debtor country, a mature debtor country, a new creditor country, and a mature creditor country.

5. Consider the situation for Germany described on page 383. Using a figure like Figure 20-3, show the supply and demand for German marks before and after the shock. Identify on your figure the excess demand for marks *before* the appreciation of the mark. Then show how an appreciation of the mark would wipe out the excess demand.

6. A Middle East nation suddenly discovers huge oil resources. Show how its balance of trade and current account suddenly turn to surplus. Show how it can acquire assets in New York as a capital account offset. Later, when it uses the assets for internal development, show how its current and capital items reverse their roles.

7. Consider the following quotation from the 1984 *Economic Report of the President*:

   > In the long run, the exchange rate tends to follow the differential trend in the domestic and foreign price level. If one country's price level gets too far out of line with prices in other countries, there will eventually be a fall in demand for its goods, which will lead to a real depreciation of its currency.

   Explain how the first sentence relates to the PPP theory of exchange rates. Explain the reasoning behind the PPP theory. In addition, using a supply-and-demand diagram like that of Figure 20-3, explain the sequence of events, described in the second sentence of the quotation, whereby a country whose price level is relatively high will find that its exchange rate depreciates.

8. A nation records the following data for 1994: exports of automobiles ($100) and corn ($150); imports of oil ($150) and steel ($75); tourist expenditures abroad ($25); private lending to foreign countries ($50); private borrowing from foreign countries ($40); official-reserve changes ($30 of foreign exchange bought by domestic central bank). Calculate the statistical discrepancy and include it in private lending to foreign countries. Create a balance-of-payments table like Table 20-4.

TABLE 20-5.

Currency	Price	
	Units of foreign currency per dollar	Dollars per unit of foreign currency
Zloty (Poland)	3.09 (zloty/$)	_____ ($/zloty)
Real (Brazil)	1.06	_____ (_____)
Renminbi (China)	8.33	_____ (_____)
Peso (Mexico)	7.97	_____ (_____)
Drachma (Greece)	268	_____ (_____)

CHAPTER 21

COMPARATIVE ADVANTAGE AND PROTECTIONISM

TO THE CHAMBER OF DEPUTIES: We are subject to the intolerable competition of a foreign rival, who enjoys such superior facilities for the production of light that he can inundate our national market at reduced price. This rival is no other than the sun. Our petition is to pass a law shutting up all windows, openings, and fissures through which the light of the sun is used to penetrate our dwellings, to the prejudice of the profitable manufacture we have been enabled to bestow on the country.
Signed: The Candle Makers

F. Bastiat

In his "Petition of the Candle Makers," the French economist Frederic Bastiat was satirizing the many solemn proposals to block out foreign goods that compete with domestic suppliers. Today, people often regard foreign competition with suspicion, and campaigns to "Buy American" sound patriotic.

Yet economists since the time of Adam Smith have marched to a different drummer. Economics teaches that international trade is beneficial to a nation. It encourages specialization and expands a nation's consumption possibilities. Japan sells America cameras; America sells computers to Australia; Australia closes the circle by selling coal to Japan. By specializing in its areas of greatest relative productivity, each nation can consume more than it could produce alone. This is the simple yet elusive essence of foreign trade which will be presented in this chapter.

A. COMPARATIVE ADVANTAGE AMONG NATIONS

THE PRINCIPLE OF COMPARATIVE ADVANTAGE

It is only common sense that countries will produce and export goods for which they are uniquely qualified. But there is a deeper principle underlying *all* trade—in a family, within a nation, and among nations—that goes beyond common sense. The *principle of comparative advantage* holds that a country can benefit from trade even if it is absolutely more efficient (or absolutely less efficient) than other countries in the production of every good. Indeed, trade according to comparative advantage provides mutual benefits to all countries.

Uncommon Sense

Say that the United States has higher output per worker (or per unit of input) than the rest of the world in making both computers and grain. But suppose the United States is relatively more efficient in computers than it is in grain. For example, it might be 50 percent more productive in computers and 10 percent more productive in grain. In this case, it would benefit the United States to export that good in which it is relatively more efficient (computers) and import that good in which it is relatively less efficient (grain).

Or consider a poor country like Mali. How could impoverished Mali, whose workers use handlooms and have productivity that is only a fraction of that of industrialized countries, hope to export any of its textiles? Surprisingly, according to the principle of comparative advantage, Mali can benefit by exporting the goods in which it is *relatively* more efficient (like textiles) and importing those goods which it produces *relatively* less efficiently (like turbines and automobiles).

The principle of **comparative advantage** holds that each country will benefit if it specializes in the production and export of those goods that it can produce at relatively low cost. Conversely, each country will benefit if it imports those goods which it produces at relatively high cost.

This simple principle provides the unshakable basis for international trade.

The Logic of Comparative Advantage

To explain the principle of comparative advantage, we begin with a simple example of specialization among people and then move to the more general case of comparative advantage among nations.

Consider the case of the best lawyer in town who is also the best typist in town. How should the lawyer spend her time? Should she write and type her own legal briefs? Or should she leave the typing to her secretary? Clearly, the lawyer should concentrate on legal activities, where her *relative* or *comparative* skills are most effectively used, even though she has *absolutely* greater skills in both typing and legal work.

Or look at it from the secretary's point of view. He is a fine typist, but his legal briefs are likely to lack sound legal reasoning and be full of errors. He is *absolutely* less efficient than the lawyer both in writing and in typing, but he is *relatively* or *comparatively* more efficient in typing.

In this scenario, the greatest efficiency will occur when the lawyer specializes in legal work and the secretary concentrates on typing. The most efficient and productive pattern of specialization occurs when people or nations concentrate on activities in which they are relatively or comparatively more efficient

than others; this implies that some people or nations may specialize in areas in which they are absolutely less efficient than others. But even though individual people or countries may differ in absolute efficiency from all other people and countries, each and every person or country will have a definite comparative advantage in some goods and a definite comparative disadvantage in other goods.

Ricardo's Analysis of Comparative Advantage

Let us illustrate the fundamental principles of international trade by considering America and Europe of a century ago. If labor (or resources, more generally) is absolutely more productive in America than in Europe, does this mean that America will import nothing? And is it economically wise for Europe to "protect" its markets with tariffs or quotas?

These questions were first answered in 1817 by the English economist David Ricardo, who showed that international specialization benefits a nation. He called this result the law of comparative advantage.

For simplicity, Ricardo worked with only two regions and only two goods, and he chose to measure all production costs in terms of labor-hours. We will follow his lead here, analyzing food and clothing for Europe and America.[1]

Table 21-1 on page 388 shows the illustrative data. In America, it takes 1 hour of labor to produce a unit of food, while a unit of clothing requires 2 hours of labor. In Europe the cost is 3 hours of labor for food and 4 hours of labor for clothing. We see that America has *absolute advantage* in both goods, for it can produce them with greater absolute efficiency than can Europe. However, America has *comparative advantage* in food, while Europe has comparative advantage in clothing, because food is relatively inexpensive in America while clothing is relatively less expensive in Europe.

From these facts, Ricardo proved that both regions will benefit if they specialize in their areas of comparative advantage—that is, if America specializes in the production of food while Europe specializes in the production of clothing. In this situation,

---

[1] An analysis of comparative advantage with many countries and many commodities is presented later in this chapter.

American and European Labor Requirements for Production		
	Necessary labor for production (labor-hours)	
Product	In America	In Europe
1 unit of food	1	3
1 unit of clothing	2	4

TABLE 21-1. Comparative Advantage Depends Only on Relative Costs

In a hypothetical example, America has lower labor costs in both food and clothing. American labor productivity is between 2 and 3 times Europe's (twice in clothing, thrice in food).

America will export food to pay for European clothing, while Europe will export clothing to pay for American food.

To analyze the effects of trade, we must measure the amounts of food and clothing that can be produced and consumed in each region (1) if there is no international trade and (2) if there is free trade with each region specializing in its area of comparative advantage.

Before Trade. Start by examining what occurs in the absence of any international trade, say, because all trade is illegal or because of a prohibitive tariff. Table 21-1 shows the real wage of the American worker for an hour's work as 1 unit of food or $\frac{1}{2}$ unit of clothing. The European worker earns only $\frac{1}{3}$ unit of food or $\frac{1}{4}$ unit of clothing per hour of work.

Clearly, if perfect competition prevails in each isolated region, the prices of food and clothing will be different in the two places because of the difference in production costs. In America, clothing will be 2 times as expensive as food because it takes twice as much labor to produce a unit of clothing as it does to produce a unit of food. In Europe, clothing will be only $\frac{4}{3}$ as expensive as food.

After Trade. Now suppose that all tariffs are repealed and free trade is allowed. For simplicity, further assume that there are no transportation costs. What is the flow of goods when trade is opened up? Clothing is relatively more expensive in America, and food is relatively more expensive in Europe. Given these relative prices, and with no tariffs or transportation costs, food will soon be shipped from America to Europe and clothing from Europe to America.

As European clothing penetrates the American market, American clothiers will find prices falling

and profits shrinking, and they will begin to shut down their factories. By contrast, European farmers will find that the prices of foodstuffs begin to fall when American products hit the European markets; they will suffer losses, some will go bankrupt, and resources will be withdrawn from farming.

After all the adjustments to international trade have taken place, the prices of clothing and food must be equalized in Europe and America (just as the water in two connecting pipes must come to a common level once you remove the barrier between them). Without further knowledge about the exact supplies and demands, we cannot know the exact level to which prices will move. But we do know that the relative prices of food and clothing must lie somewhere between the European price ratio (which is $\frac{3}{4}$ for the ratio of food to clothing prices) and the American price ratio (which is $\frac{1}{2}$). Let us say that the final ratio is $\frac{2}{3}$, so 2 units of clothing trade for 3 units of food. For simplicity, we measure prices in American dollars and assume that the free-trade price of food is $2 per unit, which means that the free-trade price of clothing is $3 per unit.

With free trade, the regions have shifted their productive activities. America has withdrawn resources from clothing and produces food, while Europe has contracted its farm sector and expanded its clothing manufacture. *Under free trade, countries shift production toward their areas of comparative advantage.*

The Economic Gains from Trade

What are the economic effects of opening up the two regions to international trade? America as a whole benefits from the fact that imported clothing costs less than clothing produced at home. Likewise, Europe benefits by specializing in clothing and consuming food that is less expensive than domestically produced food.

We can most easily reckon the gains from trade by calculating the effect of trade upon the real wages of workers. Real wages are measured by the quantity of goods that a worker can buy with an hour's pay. Using Table 21-1, we can see that the real wages after trade will be greater than the real wages before trade for workers in both Europe *and* America. For simplicity, assume that each worker buys 1 unit of clothing and 1 unit of food. Before trade, this bundle of goods costs an American worker 3 hours of work and a European worker 7 hours of work.

After trade has opened up, as we found, the price of clothing is $3 per unit while the price of food is $2 per unit. An American worker must still work 1 hour to buy a unit of food; but at the price ratio of 2 to 3, the American worker need work only $1\frac{1}{2}$ hours to produce enough to buy 1 unit of European clothing. Therefore the bundle of goods costs the American worker $2\frac{1}{2}$ hours of work when trade is allowed—this represents an increase of 20 percent in the real wage of the American worker.

For European workers, a unit of clothing will still cost 4 hours of labor in a free-trade situation, for clothing is domestically produced. To obtain a unit of food, however, the European worker need produce only $\frac{2}{3}$ of a unit of clothing (which requires $\frac{2}{3} \times 4$ hours of labor) and then trade that $\frac{2}{3}$ clothing unit for 1 unit of American food. The total European labor needed to obtain the bundle of consumption is then $4 + 2\frac{2}{3} = 6\frac{2}{3}$, which represents an increase in real wages of about 5 percent over the no-trade situation.

When countries concentrate on their areas of comparative advantage under free trade, each country is better off. Compared to a no-trade situation, workers in each region can obtain a larger quantity of consumer goods for the same amount of work when they specialize in the areas of comparative advantage and trade their own production for goods in which they have a relative disadvantage.

GRAPHICAL ANALYSIS OF COMPARATIVE ADVANTAGE

We can use the production-possibility frontier (*PPF*) to expand our analysis of comparative advantage. We will continue the numerical example based upon

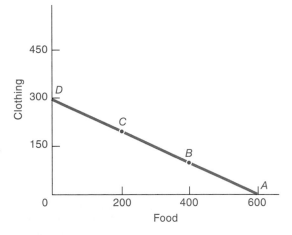

America's production-possibility schedule
(1-to-2 constant-cost ratio)

Possibilities	Food (units)	Clothing (units)
A	600	0
B	400	100
C	200	200
D	0	300

FIGURE 21-1. American Production Data

The constant-cost line *DA* represents America's domestic production-possibility frontier. America will produce and consume at *B* in the absence of trade.

labor costs, but the theory is equally valid in a competitive world with many different inputs.

America without Trade

Chapter 1 introduced the *PPF*, which shows the combinations of commodities that can be produced with a society's given resources and technology. Using the production data shown in Table 21-1, and assuming that both Europe and America have 600 units of labor, we can easily derive each region's *PPF*. The table that accompanies Figure 21-1 shows the possible levels of food and clothing that America can produce with its inputs and technology. Figure 21-1 plots the production possibilities; the rust line *DA* shows America's *PPF*. The *PPF* has a slope of $-\frac{1}{2}$, for this represents the terms on which food and clothing can be substituted in production; in competitive markets with no international trade, the price ratio of food to clothing will also be one-half.

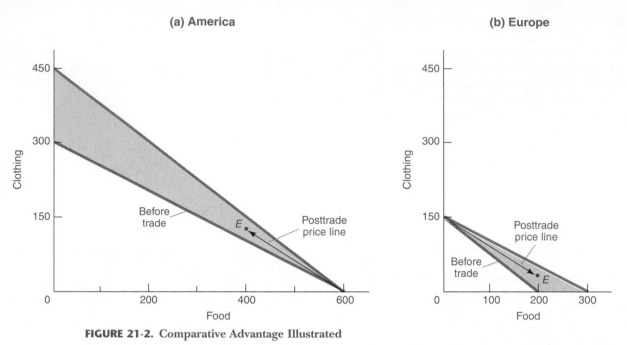

FIGURE 21-2. Comparative Advantage Illustrated

Through trade, both Europe and America improve their available consumption. If no trade is allowed, each region must be satisfied with its own production. It is therefore limited to its production-possibility curve, shown for each region as the line marked "Before trade." After borders are opened and competition equalizes the relative prices of the two goods, the relative-price line will be as shown by the arrow. If each region is faced with prices given by the arrows, can you see why its consumption possibilities must improve?

So far we have concentrated on production and ignored consumption. Note that if America is isolated from all international trade, it can consume only what it produces. Say that, for the incomes and demands in the marketplace, point *B* in Figure 21-1 marks America's production and consumption in the absence of trade. Without trade, America produces and consumes 400 units of food and 100 units of clothing.

We can do exactly the same thing for Europe. But Europe's *PPF* will look different from America's because Europe has different efficiencies in producing food and clothing. Europe's price ratio is ¾, reflecting Europe's relative productivity in food and clothing.

Opening Up to Trade

Now allow trade between the two regions. Food can be exchanged for clothing at some price ratio. We call the ratio of export prices to import prices

the **terms of trade**. To indicate the trading possibilities, we put the two *PPF*s together in Figure 21-2. America's rust *PPF* shows its domestic production possibilities, while Europe's black *PPF* shows the terms on which it can domestically substitute food and clothing. Note that Europe's *PPF* is drawn closer to the origin than America's because Europe has lower productivities in both industries; it has an absolute disadvantage in the production of both food and clothing.

Europe need not be discouraged by its absolute disadvantage, however, for it is the difference in *relative* productivities or *comparative* advantage that makes trade beneficial. The gains from trade are illustrated by the outer lines in Figure 21-2. If America could trade at Europe's relative prices, it could produce 600 units of food and move northwest along the outer black line in Figure 21-2(*a*)—where the black line represents the price ratio or terms of trade that are generated by Europe's *PPF*. Similarly, if

Europe could trade at America's prices, Europe could specialize in clothing and move southeast along the rust line in Figure 21-2(*b*)—where the rust line is America's pretrade price ratio.

This leads to an important and surprising conclusion: Small countries have the most to gain from international trade. They affect world prices the least and therefore can trade at world prices that are very different from domestic prices. From this, you can see why countries that are different from other countries gain much while large countries have the least to gain. (These points are raised in question 3 at the end of this chapter.)

Equilibrium Price Ratio.

Once trade opens up, some set of prices must hold in the world marketplace depending upon the overall market supplies and demands. Without further information we cannot specify the exact price ratio, but we can determine what the price range will be. The prices must lie somewhere between the prices of the two regions. That is, we know that the relative price of food and clothing must lie somewhere in the range between $\frac{1}{2}$ and $\frac{3}{4}$.

The final price ratio will depend upon the relative demands for food and clothing. If food is very much in demand, the food price would be relatively high. If food demand were so high that Europe produced food as well as clothing, the price ratio would be at Europe's relative prices, or $\frac{3}{4}$. On the other hand, if clothing demand were so strong that America produced clothing as well as food, the terms of trade would equal America's price ratio of $\frac{1}{2}$. If each region specializes completely in the area of its comparative advantage, with Europe producing only clothing and America producing only food, the price ratio will lie somewhere between $\frac{1}{2}$ and $\frac{3}{4}$. The exact ratio will depend on the strength of demand.

Assume now that the demands are such that the final price ratio is $\frac{2}{3}$, with 3 units of food selling for 2 units of clothing. With this price ratio, each region will then specialize—America in food and Europe in clothing—and export some of its production to pay for imports at the world price ratio of $\frac{2}{3}$.

Figure 21-2 illustrates how trade will take place. Each region will face a consumption-possibility curve according to which it can produce, trade, and consume. *The consumption-possibility curve begins at the region's point of complete specialization and then runs out*

FIGURE 21-3. America Before and After Trade

Free trade expands the consumption options of America. The rust-colored line *DA* represents America's production-possibility curve when America is able to trade freely at the price ratio $\frac{2}{3}$ and, in consequence, to specialize completely in the production of food (at *A*). The rust arrows from *S* to *B'* and *A* to *S* show the amounts exported (+) and imported (−) by America. As a result of free trade, America ends up at *B'*, with more of both goods available than if it produced what it consumed along *DA*.

at the world price ratio of $\frac{2}{3}$. Figure 21-2(*a*) shows America's consumption possibilities as a thin black arrow with slope of $-\frac{2}{3}$ coming out of its complete-specialization point at 600 units of food and no clothing. Similarly, Europe's posttrade consumption possibilities are shown in Figure 21-2(*b*) by the black arrow running southeast from its point of complete specialization with a slope of $-\frac{2}{3}$.

The final outcome is shown by the points *E* in Figure 21-2. At this free-trade equilibrium, Europe specializes in producing clothing and America specializes in producing food. Europe exports $133\frac{1}{3}$ units of clothing for 200 units of America's food. Both regions are able to consume more than they would produce alone; both regions have benefited from international trade.

Figure 21-3 illustrates the benefits of trade for America. The rust inner line shows the *PPF,* while the black outer line shows the consumption possibilities at the world price ratio of $\frac{2}{3}$. The rust arrows show the amounts exported and imported. America ends up at point *B'*. Through trade it moves along the black line *D'A* just as if a fruitful new invention had pushed out its *PPF*.

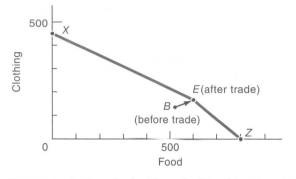

FIGURE 21-4. Free Trade Allows the World to Move to Its Production-Possibility Frontier

We show here the effect of free trade from the viewpoint of the world as a whole. Before trade is allowed, each region is on its own national *PPF*. Because the no-trade equilibrium is inefficient, the world is inside its *PPF*.

Free trade allows each region to specialize in the goods in which it has comparative advantage. As a result of efficient specialization, the world moves out to the efficiency frontier.

The lessons of this analysis are summarized in Figure 21-4. This figure shows the *world* production-possibility frontier. The world *PPF* represents the maximum output that can be obtained from the world's resources when goods are produced in the most efficient manner—that is, with the most efficient division of labor and regional specialization.

The world *PPF* is built up from the two regional *PPF*s in Figure 21-2 by determining the maximum level of world output that can be obtained from the individual regional *PPF*s. For example, the maximum quantity of food that can be produced (with no clothing production) is seen in Figure 21-2 to be 600 units in America and 200 units in Europe, for a world maximum of 800 units. This same point (800 food, 0 clothing) is then plotted in the world *PPF* in Figure 21-4. Additionally, we can plot the point (0 food, 450 clothing) in the world *PPF* by inspection of the regional *PPF*s. All the individual points in between can be constructed by a careful calculation of the maximum world outputs that can be produced if the two regions are efficiently specializing in the two goods.

Before opening up borders to trade, the world is at point *B*. This is an inefficient point—inside the world *PPF*—because regions have different levels of *relative* efficiency in different goods. After opening

the borders to trade, the world moves to the free-trade equilibrium at *E*, where countries are specializing in their areas of comparative advantage.

Free trade in competitive markets allows the world to move to the frontier of its production-possibility curve.

EXTENSIONS TO MANY COMMODITIES AND COUNTRIES

The world of international trade consists of more than two regions and two commodities. However, the principles we explained above are essentially unchanged in more realistic situations.

Many Commodities

When two regions or countries produce many commodities at constant costs, the goods can be arranged in order according to the comparative advantage or cost of each. For example, the commodities might be aircraft, computers, wheat, automobiles, wine, and shoes—all arranged in the comparative-advantage sequence shown in Figure 21-5. As you can see from the figure, of all the commodities, aircraft is least expensive in America relative to the costs in Europe. Europe has its greatest comparative advantage in shoes, while its advantage in wine is somewhat less than that in shoes.

We can be virtually certain that the introduction of trade will cause America to produce and export aircraft, while Europe will produce and export shoes. But where will the dividing line fall? Between wheat and automobiles? Or wine and shoes? Or will the dividing line fall on one of the commodities rather than between them—perhaps automobiles will be produced in both places.

You will not be surprised to find that the answer depends upon the demands and supplies of the different goods. We can think of the commodities as beads arranged on a string according to their comparative advantage; the strength of supply and demand will determine where the dividing line between American and European production will fall. An increased demand for aircraft and computers, for example, would tend to shift prices in the direction of American goods. The shift might lead America to specialize so much more in areas of its comparative advantage that it would no longer be profitable to produce in areas of comparative disadvantage, like automobiles.

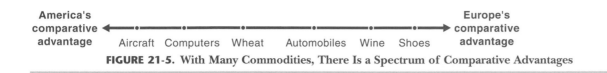

FIGURE 21-5. With Many Commodities, There Is a Spectrum of Comparative Advantages

Many Countries

What about the case of many countries? Introducing many countries need not change our analysis. As far as a single country is concerned, all the other nations can be lumped together into one group as "the rest of the world." The advantages of trade have no special relationship to national boundaries. The principles already developed apply between groups of countries and, indeed, between regions within the same country. In fact, they are just as applicable to trade between our northern and southern states as to trade between the United States and Canada.

Triangular and Multilateral Trade

With many countries brought into the picture, it will generally be beneficial to engage in *triangular* or *multilateral trade* with many other countries. *Bilateral* trade between two countries is generally unbalanced.

Consider the simple example of triangular trade flows presented in Figure 21-6, where the arrows show the direction of exports. America buys consumer electronics from Japan, Japan buys oil and primary commodities from developing countries, and developing countries buy machinery from America. In reality, trade patterns are even more complex than this triangular example.

The multilateral nature of trade shows the fallacy in arguments that focus on the bilateral balance between particular countries. In recent years, the large bilateral trade imbalance between the United States and Japan has fueled protectionist sentiment. On many occasions over the last two decades, the United States has threatened to impose trade sanctions on Japan. But the bilateral balance by itself has no economic significance. Even countries that have a zero current-account balance will run surpluses with some countries and deficits with others. What would happen if all nations signed bilateral trade agreements that balanced trade between each pair of countries? Trade would be sharply curbed;

imports would balance exports, but at the level of whichever was the smaller. The gains from trade would be severely reduced.

QUALIFICATIONS AND CONCLUSIONS

We have now completed our look at the elegant theory of comparative advantage. Its conclusions apply for any number of countries and commodities. Moreover, it can be generalized to handle many inputs, changing factor proportions, and diminishing returns. But we cannot conclude without noting two important qualifications of this elegant theory.

1. *Classical assumptions.* From a theoretical point of view, the major defect lies in its classical assumptions. The theory assumes a smoothly working competitive economy with flexible prices and wages and no involuntary unemployment. Would the theory still hold if autoworkers, laid off when the share of Japanese cars sold in the American market rises rapidly, cannot easily find new jobs? What if an overvalued foreign exchange rate

FIGURE 21-6. Triangular Trade Benefits All

Advantages of multilateral trade would be much reduced if bilateral balancing were required.

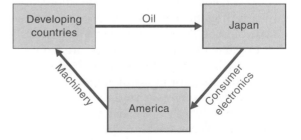

reduces the demand for manufacturing workers and these workers cannot find comparable jobs in other sectors? In such cases, trade might well push a nation *inside* its *PPF* as unemployment rises and GDP falls. When the economy is in depression or the price system malfunctions, we cannot be sure that countries will gain from trade or that the theory of comparative advantage will hold in every case.

Given this reservation, there can be little wonder that the theory of comparative advantage sells at a big discount during business downturns. In the Great Depression of the 1930s, as unemployment soared and real outputs fell, nations built high tariff walls at their borders and the volume of foreign trade shrank sharply. In every recession, underutilized labor and capital lobby to protect their markets from foreign competition. These periods of history remind us that the classical theory of comparative advantage is strictly valid only when exchange rates, prices, and wages are at appropriate levels and when macroeconomic policies banish major business cycles and trade dislocations from the economic scene.

2. *Income distribution.* A second proviso concerns the impact on particular people, sectors, or factors of production. We showed above that opening a country to trade will raise a country's national income. The country can consume more of all goods and services than would be possible if the borders were sealed to trade.

But this does not mean that every individual, firm, sector, or factor of production will benefit from trade. If free trade increases the supply of goods that are produced by particular factors of production or in particular regions, those factors or regions may end up with lower incomes than under restricted trade. Suppose that free trade increases the supply of cheap cotton shirts in the United States. We would not be surprised to learn that textile firms suffered losses and bankruptcies. Recent studies indicate that unskilled labor in high-income countries has in the last two decades suffered reductions in real wages because of the increased imports of goods in related industries from low-wage developing countries. Wage losses occurred because imports are produced by factors that are close substitutes for the unskilled labor in high-income countries.

The theory of comparative advantage shows that other sectors will gain more than the injured sectors will lose. Moreover, over long periods of time, those displaced from low-wage sectors eventually gravitate to higher-wage jobs. But those who are temporarily injured by international trade are genuinely harmed and are vocal advocates for protection and trade barriers.

Notwithstanding its limitations, the theory of comparative advantage is one of the deepest truths in all of economics. Nations that disregard comparative advantage pay a heavy price in terms of their living standards and economic growth.

B. PROTECTIONISM

The theory of comparative advantage shows how countries can benefit from specialization and international division of labor. Notwithstanding this established economic finding, legislatures are continuously besieged by groups lobbying for "protective" measures in the form of tariffs or import quotas. In the United States, Congress and the President struggle every year over whether to enact measures to protect domestic industries from inexpensive imports.

Is protectionism sound economic policy? Economists generally agree that it is not. They believe that free trade promotes a mutually beneficial division of labor among nations and that free and open trade allows *each* nation to expand its production and consumption possibilities, raising the world's living standard.

But many people disagree with this assessment. Just as Alexander Hamilton wanted to build tariff

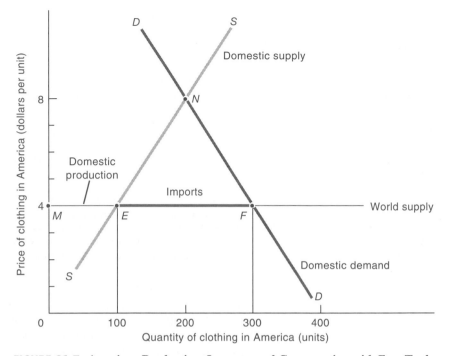

FIGURE 21-7. American Production, Imports, and Consumption with Free Trade

We see here the free-trade equilibrium in the market for clothing. America has a comparative disadvantage in clothing. Therefore, at the no-trade equilibrium at *N*, America's price would be $8, while the world price is $4.

Assuming that American demand does not affect the world price of $4 per unit, the free-trade equilibrium comes when America produces *ME* (100 units) and imports the difference between demand and domestic supply, shown as *EF* (or 200 units).

---

walls around our manufacturing industries in 1789, so today people argue that we need to protect our industries against foreign competition. This section reviews the economic impact of protectionism.

SUPPLY-AND-DEMAND ANALYSIS OF TRADE AND TARIFFS

Free Trade vs. No Trade

The theory of comparative advantage can be illuminated through the analysis of supply and demand for goods in foreign trade. Consider the clothing market in America. Assume, for simplicity, that America is a small part of the market and therefore cannot affect the world price of clothing. (This assumption will allow us to analyze supply and demand very easily; the more realistic case in which

a country can affect world prices will be considered later in this chapter.)

Figure 21-7 shows the supply and demand curves for clothing in America. The demand curve of American consumers is drawn as *DD* and the domestic supply curve of American firms as *SS*. We assume that the price of clothing is determined in the world market and is equal to $4 per unit. Although transactions in international trade are carried out in different currencies, for now we can simplify by converting the foreign supply schedule into a dollar supply curve by using the current exchange rate.

No-Trade Equilibrium. Suppose that transportation costs or tariffs for clothing were prohibitive (say, $100 per unit of clothing). Where would the no-trade equilibrium lie? In this case, the American market for clothing would be at the intersection

Commodity class	Average tariff rate, 1994 (%)	
	United States	Japan
Food	6.3	12.3
Beverages and tobacco	2.9	16.1
Crude materials, except fuels	0.3	1.3
Fuels	0.5	0.8
Chemicals	4.0	3.7
Manufactured goods	3.3	5.1
Machinery and transport equipment	1.9	0.1

TABLE 21-2. Average Tariff Rates for the United States and Japan

Tariff rates for industrial countries like the United States and Japan are generally low today. High tariffs or import quotas are found in politically sensitive sectors like agriculture in Japan and clothing in the United States. [Source: U.S. Department of Commerce and World Trade Organization.]

of *domestic* supply and demand, shown at point *N* in Figure 21-7. At this no-trade point, prices would be relatively high at $8 per unit, and domestic producers would be meeting all the demand.

Free Trade. Next, open up trade in clothing. In the absence of transport costs, tariffs, and quotas, the price in America must be equal to the world price. Why? Because if the American price were above the European price, sharp-eyed entrepreneurs would buy where clothing was cheap (Europe) and sell where clothing was expensive (America); Europe would therefore export clothing to America. Once trade flows fully adjust to supplies and demands, the price in America would equal the world price level. (In a world with transportation and tariff costs, the price in America would equal the world price adjusted for these costs.)

Figure 21-7 illustrates how prices, quantities, and trade flows will be determined under free trade in our clothing example. The horizontal line at $4 represents the supply curve for imports; it is horizontal, or perfectly price-elastic, because American demand is assumed to be too small to affect the world price of clothing.

Once trade opens up, imports flow into America, lowering the price of clothing to the world price of $4 per unit. At that level, domestic producers will supply the amount *ME,* or 100 units, while at that price consumers will want to buy 300 units. The difference, shown by the heavy line *EF,* is the amount of imports. Who decided that we would import just this

amount of clothing and that domestic producers would supply only 100 units? A European planning agency? A cartel of clothing firms? No, the amount of trade was determined by supply and demand.

Moreover, the level of prices in the no-trade equilibrium determined the direction of the trade flows. America's no-trade prices were higher than Europe's, so goods flowed into America. Remember this rule: *Under free trade, indeed in markets generally, goods flow uphill from low-price regions to high-price regions.* When markets are opened to free trade, clothing flows uphill from the low-price European market to the higher-price American market until the price levels are equalized.

Trade Barriers

For centuries, governments have used tariffs and quotas to raise revenues and influence the development of individual industries. Since the eighteenth century—when the British Parliament attempted to impose tariffs on tea, sugar, and other commodities on its American colonies—tariff policy has proved fertile soil for revolution and political struggle.

We can use supply-and-demand analysis to understand the economic effects of tariffs and quotas. To begin with, note that a **tariff** is a tax levied on imports. Table 21-2 lists tariff rates for major categories for the United States and Japan in 1994. To take an example, the United States has a 1.9 percent tariff on automobiles. If a foreign car costs $20,000, the domestic price including the tariff will be $20,380. A **quota** is a limit on the quantity of imports.

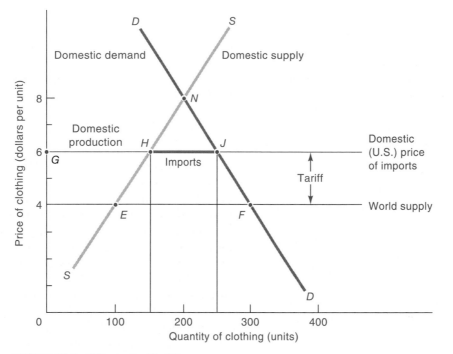

FIGURE 21-8. Effect of a Tariff

A tariff lowers imports and consumption, raises domestic production and price. Starting from the free-trade equilibrium in Fig. 21-7, America now puts a $2 tariff on clothing imports. The price of European clothing imports rises to $6 (including the tariff).

The market price rises from $4 to $6, so the total amount demanded falls. Imports shrink from 200 to 100 units, while domestic production rises from 100 to 150 units.

The United States has quotas on many products, including peanuts, textiles, and beef.

Prohibitive Tariff. The easiest case to analyze is a *prohibitive tariff*—one that is so high that it chokes off all imports. Looking back at Figure 21-7, what would happen if the tariff on clothing were more than $4 per unit (that is, more than the difference between America's no-trade price of $8 and the world price of $4)? This would be a prohibitive tariff, shutting off all clothing trade. Any importer who buys clothing at the world price of $4 would sell it in America at above the no-trade price of $8. But this price would not cover the cost of the good plus the tariff. Prohibitive tariffs thus kill off all trade.

Nonprohibitive Tariff. Lower tariffs (less than $4 per unit of clothing) would injure but not kill off trade. Figure 21-8 shows the equilibrium in the clothing market with a $2 tariff. Again assuming no transportation costs, a $2 tariff means that for-

eign clothing will sell in America for $6 per unit (equal to the $4 world price plus the $2 tariff).

The equilibrium result of a $2 tariff is that domestic consumption (or quantity demanded) is lowered from 300 units in the free-trade equilibrium to 250 units after the tariff is imposed, the amount of domestic production is raised by 50 units, and the quantity of imports is lowered by 100 units. This example summarizes the economic impact of tariffs:

A tariff will tend to raise price, lower the amounts consumed and imported, and raise domestic production.

Quotas. Quotas have the same qualitative effect as tariffs. A prohibitive quota (one that prevents all imports) is equivalent to a prohibitive tariff. The price and quantity would move back to the no-trade equilibrium at *N* in Figure 21-8. A less stringent quota might limit imports to 100 clothing units; this quota would equal the heavy line *HJ* in Figure 21-8.

A quota of 100 units would lead to the same equilibrium price and output as did the $2 tariff.

Although there is no essential difference between tariffs and quotas, some subtle differences do exist. A tariff gives revenue to the government, perhaps allowing other taxes to be reduced and thereby offsetting some of the harm done to consumers in the importing country. A quota, on the other hand, puts the profit from the resulting price difference into the pocket of the importers or exporters lucky enough to get a permit or import license. They can afford to use the proceeds to wine, dine, or even bribe the officials who give out import licenses.

Because of these differences, economists generally regard tariffs as the lesser evil. However, if a government is determined to impose quotas, it should auction off the scarce import-quota licenses. An auction will ensure that the government rather than the importer or the exporter gets the revenue from the scarce right to import; in addition, the bureaucracy will not be tempted to allocate quota rights by bribery, friendship, or nepotism.

Transportation Costs. What of transportation costs? The cost of moving bulky and perishable goods has the same effect as tariffs, reducing the extent of beneficial regional specialization. For example, if it costs $2 per unit to transport clothing from Europe to the United States, the supply-and-demand equilibrium would look just like Figure 21-8, with the American price $2 above the European price.

But there is one difference between protection and transportation costs: Transport costs are imposed by nature—by oceans, mountains, and rivers—whereas restrictive tariffs are squarely the responsibility of nations. Indeed, one economist called tariffs "negative railroads." Imposing a tariff has the same economic impact as throwing sand in the engines of vessels that transport goods to our shores from other lands.

The Economic Costs of Tariffs

What happens when America puts a tariff on clothing, such as the $2 tariff shown in Figure 21-8? There are three effects: (1) The domestic producers, operating under a price umbrella provided by the tariff, can expand production; (2) consumers are faced with higher prices and therefore reduce their consumption; and (3) the government gains tariff revenue.

Tariffs create economic inefficiency. When tariffs are imposed, the economic loss to consumers exceeds the revenue gained by the government plus the extra profits earned by producers.

Diagrammatic Analysis. Figure 21-9 shows the economic cost of a tariff. The supply and demand curves are identical to those in Figure 21-8, but three areas are highlighted. (1) Area B is the tariff revenue collected by the government. It is equal to the amount of the tariff times the units of imports and totals $200. (2) The tariff raises the price in domestic markets from $4 to $6, and producers increase their output to 150. Hence total profits rise by $250, shown by the area $LEHM$ and equal to $200 on old units and an additional $50 on the 50 new units. (3) Finally, note that a tariff imposes a heavy cost on consumers. The total consumer-surplus loss is given by the area $LMJF$ and is equal to $550.

The overall social impact is then a gain to producers of $250, a gain to the government of $200, and a loss to consumers of $550. The net social cost (counting each of these dollars equally) is therefore $100. We can reckon this as equal to areas A and C. The interpretation of these areas is important:

- Area A is the net loss that comes because domestic production is more costly than foreign production. When the domestic price rises, businesses are thereby induced to increase the use of relatively costly domestic capacity. They produce output up to the point where the marginal cost is $6 per unit instead of up to $4 per unit under free trade. Firms reopen inefficient old factories or work existing factories extra shifts. From an economic point of view, these plants have a comparative disadvantage because the new clothing produced by these factories could be produced more cheaply abroad. The new social cost of this inefficient production is area A, equal to $50.

- In addition, there is a net loss to the country from the higher price, shown by area C. This is the loss in consumer surplus that cannot be offset by business profits or tariff revenue. This area represents the economic cost incurred when

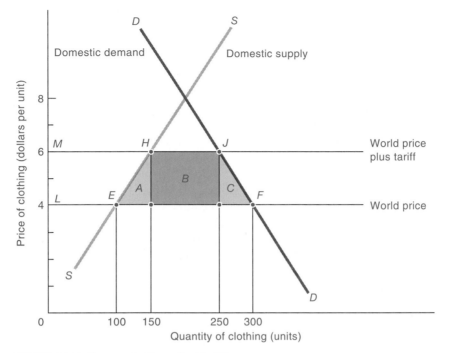

FIGURE 21-9. Economic Cost of a Tariff

Imposing a tariff raises revenues and leads to inefficiency. We see the impact of the tariff as three effects. Rectangle *B* is the tariff revenue gained by the government. Triangle *A* is the cost of the inefficiency in production induced by a higher domestic price. Triangle *C* is the net loss in consumer surplus from the inefficiently high price after subtracting both the tariff revenue and business profits from the lost consumer surplus. Areas *A* and *C* are the irreducible inefficiencies caused by the tariff.

consumers shift their purchases from low-cost imports to high-cost domestic goods. This area is also equal to $50.

Hence, the total social loss from the tariff is $100, calculated either way.

Figure 21-9 illustrates one feature that is important in understanding the politics and history of tariffs. When a tariff is imposed, part of the economic impact comes because tariffs redistribute income from consumers to the protected domestic producers and workers. In the example shown in Figure 21-9, areas *A* and *C* represent efficiency losses from inefficiently high domestic production and inefficiently low consumption, respectively. Under the simplifying assumptions used above, the efficiency losses sum up to $100. The redistribution involved is much larger, however, equaling $200 raised in tariff revenues levied upon consumers of the commodity plus

$250 in higher profits. Consumers will be unhappy about the higher product cost, while domestic producers and workers in those firms will benefit. We can see why battles over import restrictions generally center more on the redistributive gains and losses than on the issues of economic efficiency.

Imposing a tariff has three effects: It encourages inefficient domestic production; it induces consumers to reduce their purchases of the tariffed good below efficient levels; and it raises revenues for the government. Only the first two of these necessarily impose efficiency costs on the economy.

 The cost of textile protection: Let's flesh out this analysis by examining the effects of a particular tariff, one on clothing. Today, tariffs on imported textiles and apparel are among the highest

levied by the United States. How do these high tariffs affect consumers and producers?

To begin with, the tariff raises domestic clothing prices. Because of the higher prices, many factories, which would otherwise be bankrupt in the face of a declining comparative advantage in textiles, remain open. They are just barely profitable, but they manage to eke out enough sales to continue domestic production. Employment in textiles exceeds the free-trade situation, although—because of pressure from foreign competition—textile wages are among the lowest of any manufacturing industry.

From a national point of view, we are wasting resources in textiles. These workers, materials, and capital would be more productively used in other sectors—perhaps in producing computers or aircraft or financial services. The nation's productive potential is lower because it keeps factors of production in an industry in which it has lost its comparative advantage.

Consumers, of course, pay for this protection of the textile industry with higher prices. They get less satisfaction from their incomes than they would if they could buy textiles from Korea, China, or Indonesia at prices that exclude the high tariffs. Consumers are induced to cut back on their clothing purchases, channeling funds into food, transportation, and recreation, whose relative prices are lowered by the tariff.

Finally, the government gets revenues from tariffs on textiles. These revenues can be used to buy public goods or to reduce other taxes, so (unlike the consumer loss or the productive inefficiency) this effect is not a real social burden.

THE ECONOMICS OF PROTECTIONISM

Having examined the impact of tariffs on prices and quantities, we now turn to an analysis of the arguments for and against protectionism. The arguments for tariff or quota protection against the competition of foreign imports take many different forms. Here are the main categories: (1) noneconomic arguments that suggest it is desirable to sacrifice economic welfare in order to subsidize other national objectives, (2) arguments that are based on a misunderstanding of economic logic, and (3) analyses that rely on market power or macroeconomic imperfections. Many of these arguments are a century old;

others have been developed by a school known as "new international economics."[2]

Noneconomic Goals

If you are ever on a debating team given the assignment of defending free trade, you will strengthen your case at the beginning by conceding that there is more to life than economic welfare. A nation surely should not sacrifice its liberty, culture, and human rights for a few dollars of extra income.

The U.S. semiconductor industry provides a useful example here. In the 1980s, the Defense Department claimed that without an independent semiconductor industry, the military would become excessively dependent on Japanese and other foreign suppliers for chips to use in high-technology weaponry. This led to an agreement to protect the industry. Economists were skeptical about the value of this approach. Their argument did not question the goal of national security. Rather, it focused on the efficiency of the means of achieving the desired result. They thought that protection was more expensive than a policy targeted on the industry, perhaps a program to buy a minimum number of high-quality chips.

National security is not the only noneconomic goal in trade policy. Countries may desire to preserve their cultural traditions or environmental conditions. France recently has argued that its citizens need to be protected from "uncivilized" American movies. The fear is that the French film industry could be drowned by the new wave of stunt-filled, high-budget Hollywood thrillers. As a result, France has maintained strict quotas on the number of U.S. movies and television shows that can be imported, upholding its stance even in the face of strong pressure from the United States in the latest round of trade negotiations. In another example, the Swiss government chose to ban trucks passing through Switzerland in an effort to pre-

---

2 An official statement on trade policy is contained in the *Economic Report of the President,* 1991 (U.S. Government Printing Office, Washington, D.C., 1991). For a nontechnical account of the sources of the trade deficit and an account of new international economics as told by one of its leading practitioners, see Paul Krugman, *The Age of Diminished Expectations: U.S. Economic Policy in the 1990s* (MIT Press, Cambridge, Mass., 1990).

serve the tranquility and clean air of its mountain valleys.

Unsound Grounds for Tariffs

Mercantilism. To Abraham Lincoln has been attributed the remark, "I don't know much about the tariff. I do know that when I buy a coat from England, I have the coat and England has the money. But when I buy a coat in America, I have the coat and America has the money."

This reasoning represents an age-old fallacy typical of the so-called mercantilist writers of the seventeenth and eighteenth centuries. They considered a country fortunate which sold more goods than it bought, because such a "favorable" balance of trade meant that gold would flow into the country to pay for its export surplus.

The mercantilist argument confuses means and ends. Accumulating gold or other monies will not improve a country's living standard. Money is worthwhile not for its own sake but for what it will buy from other countries. Most economists today therefore reject the idea that raising tariffs to run a trade surplus will improve a country's economic welfare.

Tariffs for Special-Interest Groups. The single most important source of pressure for protective tariffs is powerful special-interest groups. Firms and workers know very well that a tariff on their particular products will help *them*, whatever its effect on some abstract goal like total economic welfare. Adam Smith understood this point well when he wrote:

> To expect freedom of trade is as absurd as to expect Utopia. Not only the prejudices of the public, but what is much more unconquerable, the private interests of many individuals, irresistibly oppose it.

If free trade is so beneficial to the nation as a whole, why do the proponents of protectionism continue to wield such a disproportionate influence in Congress? The few who benefit gain much from specific protection and therefore devote large sums to lobbying politicians. By contrast, individual consumers are only slightly affected by the tariff on one product; because losses are small and widespread, individuals have little incentive to spend resources expressing an opinion on every tariff case. A century ago, outright bribery was used to get the votes nec-

essary to pass tariff legislation. Today, powerful political action committees (PACs), financed by labor or business, round up lawyers and drum up support for tariffs or quotas on textiles, lumber, autos, steel, sugar, and other goods.

If political votes were cast in proportion to total economic benefit, nations would legislate most tariffs out of existence. But all dollars of economic interests do not always get proportional representation. It is much harder to organize the masses of consumers and producers to agitate for the benefits of free trade than it is to organize a few companies or labor unions to argue against "cheap Chinese labor" or "unfair Japanese competition." In every country, the tireless enemies of free trade are the special interests of protected firms and workers.

A dramatic case is the U.S. quota on sugar, which benefits a few producers while costing American consumers over $1 billion a year. The average consumer is probably unaware that the sugar quota costs $1\frac{1}{2}$ cents a day per person, so there is little incentive to lobby for free trade.

Competition from Cheap Foreign Labor. Of all the arguments for protection, the most persistent is that free trade exposes U.S. workers to competition from low-wage foreign labor. The only way to preserve high U.S. wages, so the argument goes, is to protect domestic workers by keeping out or putting high tariffs on goods produced in low-wage countries. An extreme version of this contention is that under free trade U.S. wages would converge to the low foreign wages. This point was trumpeted by presidential candidate Ross Perot during the debates over the North American Free Trade Agreement (NAFTA) when he argued:

> Philosophically, [NAFTA] is wonderful, but realistically it will be bad for our country. That thing is going to create a giant sucking sound in the United States at a time when we need jobs coming in, not jobs going out. Mexican wages will come up to $7\frac{1}{2}$ an hour and our wages will come down to $7\frac{1}{2}$ an hour.

This argument is superficially appealing, but it has a big flaw because it ignores the principle of comparative advantage. The reason American workers have higher wages is that they are on average more productive. If our equilibrium wage is 3 times that in Mexico, it is because we are on average roughly 5 times more productive in the production of tradable goods and services. Trade flows according to comparative advantage, not wage rates or absolute advantage.

Having shown that the nation gains from importing the goods produced by "cheap foreign labor" in which it has a comparative disadvantage, we should not ignore the costs that this strategy may temporarily impose on the affected workers and firms. If plants in a particular locality are unexpectedly shut down because production moves overseas, the local labor market may be inundated with job seekers. Older workers with outdated job skills may have trouble finding attractive jobs and will suffer a decline in their real incomes. The difficulties of displaced workers will be greater when the overall economy is depressed or when the local labor markets have high unemployment. Over the long run, labor markets will reallocate workers from declining to advancing industries, but the transition may be painful for many people.

In summary:

The economic answer to the cheap-foreign-labor argument rests on the comparative-advantage analysis. This shows that a country will benefit from trade even though its wages are far above those of its trading partners. High wages come from high efficiency, not from tariff protection.

Retaliatory Tariffs.
While many people would agree that a world of free trade would be the best of all possible worlds, they note that this is not the world we live in. They reason, "As long as other countries impose import restrictions or otherwise discriminate against our products, we have no choice but to play the protection game in self-defense. We'll go along with free trade only as long as it is fair trade. But we insist on a level playing field." On several occasions in the 1990s, the United States went to the brink of trade wars with Japan and China, threatening high tariffs if the other country did not stop some objectionable trade practice.

While this argument seems sensible, it is not well grounded in economic analysis or history. As we have seen, when another country increases its tariffs, doing so is akin to increasing its transportation costs. But if France decided to slow down trade by putting mines in its harbors, should we mine ours? Few would think so. Similarly, if China violated trade

agreements by pirating American CDs, how would the United States gain by putting 100 percent tariffs on Chinese silks and other textiles?

Those who advocate this approach argue that retaliation may help reform other countries' trade practices. This rationale was described in a 1982 analysis of protection in the *Economic Report of the President:*

> Intervention in international trade . . . , even though costly to the U.S. economy in the short run, may, however, be justified if it serves the strategic purpose of increasing the cost of interventionist policies by foreign governments. Thus, there is a potential role for carefully targeted measures . . . aimed at convincing other countries to reduce their trade distortions.

While potentially valid, this argument should be used with great caution. Just as building missiles leads to an arms race as often as to arms control, protectionist bluffs may end up hurting the bluffer as well as the opponent. Historical studies show that retaliatory tariffs usually lead other nations to raise their tariffs still higher and are rarely an effective bargaining chip for multilateral tariff reduction.

Import Relief.
In the United States and other countries, firms and workers who are injured by foreign competition attempt to get protection in the form of tariffs or quotas. Today, relatively little direct tariff business is conducted on the floor of Congress. Congress realized that tariff politics was too hot to handle and has set up specialized agencies to decide on complaints. Generally, a petition for relief is analyzed by the U.S. Department of Commerce and the U.S. International Trade Commission. Relief measures include the following actions:

- The *escape clause* was popular in earlier periods. It allows temporary import relief (tariffs, quotas, or export quotas negotiated with other countries) when an industry has been "injured" by imports. Injury occurs when the output, employment, and profits in a domestic industry have fallen while imports have risen.
- *Antidumping tariffs* are levied when foreign countries sell in the United States at prices below their average costs or at prices lower than those in the home market. When dumping is found, a "dumping duty" is placed on the imported good.

- *Countervailing duties* are imposed when foreigners subsidize exports to the United States. They became the most popular form of import relief and were pursued in hundreds of cases.

What is the justification for enacting such retaliatory measures or for protecting an industry threatened by imports? Import relief may sound reasonable, but it actually runs completely counter to the economic theory of comparative advantage. That theory says that an industry which cannot compete with foreign firms ought to be injured by imports. *Looking at this from an economic vantage point, less productive industries are actually being killed off by the competition of more productive domestic industries.*

This sounds ruthless indeed. No industry willingly dies. No region gladly undergoes conversion to new industries. Often the shift from old to new industries involves considerable unemployment and hardship. The weak industry and region feel they are being singled out to carry the burden of progress.

Potentially Valid Arguments for Protection

Finally, we can consider three arguments for protection that may have true economic merit:

- Tariffs may move the terms of trade in favor of a country.
- Temporary tariff protection for an "infant industry" with growth potential may be efficient in the long run.
- A tariff may under certain conditions help reduce unemployment.

The Terms-of-Trade or Optimal-Tariff Argument. One valid argument for imposing tariffs is that doing so will shift the terms of trade in a country's favor and against foreign countries. (Recall that the *terms of trade* are the ratio of export prices to import prices.) The idea is that when a large country levies tariffs on its imports, the tariffs will reduce the world price of its imports while increasing the prices of its exports. Such a change will be an improvement in the terms of trade. By shifting the terms of trade in its favor, the United States can export less wheat and fewer aircraft in order to pay for imports of oil and cars. The set of tariffs that maximizes our domestic real incomes is called the *optimal tariff.*

The terms-of-trade argument goes back 150 years to the free-trade proponent John Stuart Mill. It is the only argument for tariffs that would be valid under conditions of full employment and perfect competition. We can understand it by considering the simple case of an optimal tariff on oil. The optimal tariff on oil will raise the domestic price above the foreign price. But because our demand is curtailed as a result of the tariff, and because we are a significant part of the world demand for oil, the world market price of oil will be bid down. So part of the tariff really falls on the oil producer. (We can see that a very small country could not use this argument, since it cannot affect world prices.)

Have we not therefore found a theoretically secure argument for tariffs? The answer would be yes if we could forget that this is a "beggar-thy-neighbor" policy and could ignore the reactions of other countries. But other countries are likely to react. After all, if the United States were to impose an optimal tariff of 30 percent on its imports, why should the European Union and Japan not put 30 or 40 percent tariffs on their imports? In the end, as every country calculated and imposed its own domestic optimal tariff, the overall level of tariffs might spiral upward in the tariff version of an arms race.

Ultimately, such a situation would surely not represent an improvement of either world or individual economic welfare. When all countries impose optimal tariffs, it is likely that *everyone's* economic welfare will decline as the impediments to free trade become great. All countries are likely to benefit if all countries abolish trade barriers.

Tariffs for Infant Industries. In his famous *Report on Manufactures* (1791), Alexander Hamilton proposed to encourage the growth of manufacturing by protecting "infant industries" from foreign competition. According to this doctrine, which received the cautious support of free-trade economists like John Stuart Mill and Alfred Marshall, there are lines of production in which a country could have a comparative advantage if only they could get started.

Such infant industries would not be able to survive the rough treatment by larger bullies in the global marketplace. With some temporary nurturing, however, they might grow up to enjoy economies of mass production, a pool of skilled labor, inventions well adapted to the local economy, and the technological efficiency typical of many mature industries. Although protection will raise prices to the consumer at first, the mature industry would become so efficient that cost and price would actually fall. A tariff is justified if the benefit to consumers at that later date would be more than enough to make up for the higher prices during the period of protection.

This argument must be weighed cautiously. Historical studies have turned up some genuine cases of protected infant industries that grew up to stand on their own feet. And studies of successful newly industrialized countries (such as Singapore and South Korea) show that they have often protected their manufacturing industries from imports during the early stages of industrialization. But the history of tariffs reveals even more contrary cases like steel, sugar, and textiles in which perpetually protected infants have not shed their diapers after lo these many years.

 Brazil's tragic protection of its computer industry: Brazil offers a striking example of the pitfalls of protectionism. In 1984, Brazil passed a law actually banning most foreign computers. The idea was to provide a protected environment in which Brazil's own infant computer industry could develop. The law was vigorously enforced by special "computer police" who would search corporate offices and classrooms looking for illegal imported computers.

The results were startling. Technologically, Brazilian-made computers were years behind the fast-moving world market, and consumers paid 2 or 3 times the world price when they could get them. By one estimate, the law cost Brazilian consumers about $900 million each year. At the same time, because Brazilian computers were so expensive, they could not compete on the world market, so Brazilian computer companies could not take advantage of economies of scale by selling to other countries. The high price of computers hurt competitiveness in the rest of the economy as well. "We are effectively very backward because of this senseless nationalism," said Zelia Cardoso de Mello, Brazil's economy minister in 1990. "The computer problem effectively blocked Brazilian industry from modernizing."

The combination of pressure from Brazilian consumers and businesses and U.S. demands for open markets forced Brazil to drop the ban on imported comput-

ers in 1992. Within a year, electronics stores in São Paulo and Rio de Janeiro were filled with imported laptop computers, laser printers, and cellular telephones, and Brazilian companies could begin to exploit the computer revolution. Each country and each generation learns anew the lessons of comparative advantage.

Tariffs and Unemployment. Historically, a powerful motive for protection has been the desire to increase employment during a period of recession or stagnation. Protection creates jobs by raising the price of imports and diverting demand toward domestic production; Figure 21-8 demonstrates this effect. As domestic demand increases, firms will hire more workers and unemployment will fall.[3] This too is a beggar-thy-neighbor policy, for it raises domestic demand at the expense of output and employment in other countries.

However, while economic protection may raise employment, it does not constitute an effective program to pursue high employment, efficiency, and stable prices. Macroeconomic analysis shows that there are better ways of reducing unemployment than by imposing import protection. By the appropriate use of monetary and fiscal policy, a country can increase output and lower unemployment. Moreover, the use of general macroeconomic policies will allow workers displaced from low-productivity jobs in industries losing their comparative advantage to move to high-productivity jobs in industries enjoying a comparative advantage.

This lesson was amply demonstrated during the 1980s. From 1982 to 1987, the United States created 15 million net new jobs while maintaining open markets and low tariffs and sharply increasing its trade deficit; by contrast, the countries of Europe created virtually no new jobs while moving toward a position of trade surpluses.

---

[3] Those who have studied the chapters on macroeconomics can understand the mechanism by which tariffs increase employment in the short run. Recall that higher investment or government spending increases aggregate demand, output, and employment. By similar reasoning, greater protection or higher tariffs increase spending on domestic production and thereby increase aggregate demand. This expenditure switch will have multiplier effects in the short run much like those of investment or government spending on goods and services.

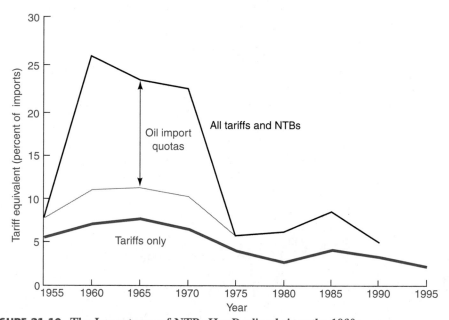

FIGURE 21-10. The Importance of NTBs Has Declined since the 1960s

Non-tariff barriers (NTBs) play a significant role in U.S. trade. The biggest trade barrier in the last four decades was a quota on imported oil. Even with NTBs included, however, barriers to trade have declined sharply and are far below those before World War II.

Tariffs and import protection are an inefficient way to create jobs or to lower unemployment. A more effective way to increase productive employment is through domestic monetary and fiscal policy.

Other Barriers to Trade

While this chapter has mainly spoken of tariffs, most points apply equally well to any other impediments to trade. Quotas have much the same effects as tariffs, for they prevent the comparative advantages of different countries from determining prices and outputs in the marketplace. In recent years, countries have negotiated quotas with other countries. The United States, for example, forced Japan to put "voluntary" export quotas on automobiles and negotiated similar export quotas on televisions, shoes, and steel.

We should also mention the so-called nontariff barriers (or NTBs). These consist of informal restrictions or regulations that make it difficult for countries to sell their goods in foreign markets. For example, American firms complained that Japanese regulations shut them out of the telecommunications, tobacco, and construction industries.

How important are the nontariff barriers relative to tariffs? Figure 21-10 shows estimates of the tariff equivalent of the most important nontariff barriers for the United States from 1955 through 1990. Nontariff barriers were actually more important than tariffs during the 1960s because of a quota on oil imports; in recent years, they have effectively doubled the protection found in the tariff codes.

MULTILATERAL TRADE NEGOTIATIONS

Given the tug-of-war between the economic benefits of free trade and the political appeal of protection, which force has prevailed? The history of U.S. tariffs, shown in Figure 21-11 on page 406, has been bumpy. For most of American history, the United States has been a high-tariff nation. The pinnacle came after the infamous Smoot-Hawley tariff of 1930, which was opposed by virtually every American economist, yet sailed through Congress.

The trade barriers erected during the Depression helped raise prices and exacerbated economic distress. In the trade wars of the 1930s, countries

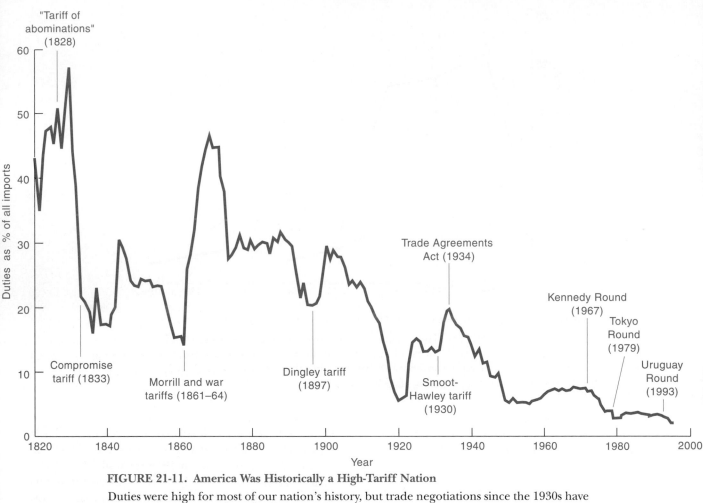

FIGURE 21-11. America Was Historically a High-Tariff Nation

Duties were high for most of our nation's history, but trade negotiations since the 1930s have lowered tariffs significantly.

attempted to raise employment and output by raising trade barriers at the expense of their neighbors. Nations soon learned that at the end of the tariff-retaliation game, all were losers.

Negotiating Free Trade

At the end of World War II, the international community established a number of institutions to promote peace and economic prosperity through cooperative policies. One of the most successful of these was the General Agreement on Tariffs and Trade (GATT), which became the World Trade Organization (WTO) at the beginning of 1995. Their charters speak of raising living standards through "substantial reduction of tariffs and other barriers to trade and the elimination of discrimina-

tory treatment in international commerce." The WTO currently has 130 member countries, which account for 90 percent of international trade.

Among the principles underlying the WTO are (1) countries should work to lower trade barriers; (2) all trade barriers should be applied on a nondiscriminatory basis across nations (i.e., all nations should enjoy "most-favored-nation" status); (3) when a country increases its tariffs above agreed-upon levels, it must compensate its trading partners for the economic injury; and (4) trade conflicts should be settled by consultations and arbitration.

The history of trade negotiations has proved to be one of the major successes in international economic cooperation. Every few years, representatives of major industrialized countries meet together to identify major trade barriers and negotiate their removal. In 1993 nations completed the "Uruguay Round." In addition to pursuing the traditional goal of reducing tariff and quota barriers, the new round undertook the ambitious goals of lowering trade barriers and subsidies in agriculture and removing quotas on textiles, and it has extended free trade to services and intellectual property. In addition, the WTO has substantially increased powers to enforce international-trade agreements.

Recent Steps. Over the last few years, governments have taken a number of steps to promote free trade or to broaden markets. Among the most important were the following:

- In 1987, the United States and Canada negotiated a set of principles for free trade between the two countries. This agreement was particularly significant because Canada is the largest trading partner of the United States, with total trade flows between the two of $276 billion in 1995. Canada's tariff rates were among the highest of the major industrial countries, and Canada curtailed foreign investment on nationalist grounds. Economists have estimated that the free-trade agreement will raise real incomes in Canada by 5 percent and those in the United States by 1 percent.
- The most controversial proposal for lowering trade barriers was the North American Free Trade Agreement (NAFTA), which was hotly debated and passed by Congress by a close vote in 1993. Mexico is the third-largest trading partner of the United States, and most U.S.-Mexico trade is in manufactured goods. NAFTA not only allows goods to pass tariff-free across the borders but also liberalizes regulations on investments by the United States and Canada in Mexico. Proponents of the plan argued that it would allow a more efficient pattern of specialization and would enable U.S. firms to compete more effectively against firms in other countries; opponents, par-

ticularly labor groups, argued that it would increase the supply of goods produced by low-skilled labor and thereby depress the wages of workers in the affected industries. Economists caution, however, that regional trading agreements like NAFTA can cause inefficiency if they exclude potential trading countries. They point to the stagnation in the Caribbean countries that followed the passage of NAFTA as a cautionary example of the dangers of the regional approach.
- The most far-reaching trade accord has been the movement toward a single market among the major European countries. The nations of the European Union (EU) are developing a common market with no or few barriers to international trade or movement of factors of production in the European area. The first step involved eliminating all internal tariff and regulatory barriers to trade and labor and capital flows. The second and more difficult step is to introduce a common currency for the core members of the European Union. The issues involving European monetary union (EMU) are analyzed in Chapter 22.

Appraisal

After World War II, policymakers around the world believed firmly that free trade was essential for world prosperity. These convictions translated into several successful agreements to lower tariffs, as Figure 21-11 shows. The free-trade conviction among economists and market-oriented policymakers has been severely tested by periods of high unemployment and exchange-rate disturbances. Nevertheless, most countries have continued the trend toward increased openness and outward orientation.

By most accounts, countries have benefited from more open trade in increased trade flows and higher living standards. But the struggle to preserve open markets is constantly tested as interest groups use new weapons and arguments in their tireless attempt to fell the mighty theory of comparative advantage.

SUMMARY

A. Comparative Advantage among Nations

1. Recall that trade occurs because of differences in the conditions of production or diversity in tastes. The foundation of international trade is the Ricardian

principle of comparative advantage. The principle of comparative advantage holds that each country will benefit if it specializes in the production and export of those goods that it can produce at relatively low cost.

Conversely, each country will benefit if it imports those goods which it produces at relatively high cost. This principle holds even if one region is absolutely more or less productive than another in all commodities. As long as there are differences in *relative* or *comparative* efficiencies among countries, every country must enjoy a comparative advantage or a comparative disadvantage in some goods.

2. The law of comparative advantage predicts more than just the geographical pattern of specialization and direction of trade. It also demonstrates that countries are made better off and that real wages (or, more generally, total national income) are improved by trade and the resulting enlarged world production. Prohibitive quotas and tariffs, designed to "protect" workers or industries, will lower a nation's total income and consumption possibilities.

3. Even with many goods or many countries, the same principles of comparative advantage apply. With many commodities, we can arrange products along a continuum of comparative advantage, from relatively more efficient to relatively less efficient. With many countries, trade may be triangular or multilateral, with countries having large bilateral (or two-sided) surpluses or deficits with other individual countries.

B. Protectionism

4. Completely free trade equalizes prices of tradeable goods at home with those in world markets. Under trade, goods flow uphill from low-price to high-price markets.

5. A tariff raises the domestic prices of imported goods, leading to a decline in consumption and imports along with an increase in domestic production. Quotas have very similar effects and may, in addition, lower government revenues.

6. A tariff causes economic waste. The economy suffers losses from decreased home consumption and from wasting resources on goods lacking comparative advantage. The losses generally exceed government revenues from the tariff.

7. Most arguments for tariffs simply rationalize special benefits to particular pressure groups and cannot withstand economic analysis. Three arguments that can stand up to careful scrutiny are the following: (*a*) The terms-of-trade or optimal tariff can in principle raise the real income of a large country at the expense of its trading partners. (*b*) In a situation of less-than-full employment, tariffs might push an economy toward fuller employment, but monetary or fiscal policies could attain the same employment goal with fewer inefficiencies than this beggar-thy-neighbor policy. (*c*) Sometimes, infant industries may need temporary protection in order to realize their true long-run comparative advantages.

8. The principle of comparative advantage must be qualified if markets malfunction because of unemployment or exchange market disturbances. Moreover, individual sectors or factors may be injured by trade if imports lower their returns.

CONCEPTS FOR REVIEW

Principles of International Trade

absolute and comparative advantage (or disadvantage)
principle of comparative advantage
economic gains from trade
triangular and multilateral trade
world vs. national *PPF*s

consumption vs. production possibilities with trade

Economics of Protectionism

price equilibrium with and without trade
tariff, quota

effects of tariffs on price, imports, and domestic production
mercantilist, cheap-foreign-labor, and retaliatory arguments
the optimal tariff, unemployment, and infant-industry exceptions
WTO and trade negotiations

QUESTIONS FOR DISCUSSION

1. State whether or not each of the following is correct and explain your reasoning. If the quotation is incorrect, provide a corrected statement.
   a. "We Mexicans can never compete profitably with the Northern colossus. Her factories are too efficient, she has too many computers and ma-

chine tools, and her engineering skills are too advanced. We need tariffs, or we can export nothing!"
   b. "If American workers are subjected to the unbridled competition of cheap Mexican labor, our real wages must necessarily fall drastically."

c. "The current account for a country need not balance bilaterally (i.e., with each country), but it must balance multilaterally (i.e., with all countries)."

d. "The principle of comparative advantage applies equally well to families, cities, and states as it does to nations and continents."

e. The quotation from Ross Perot on page 401.

2. Reconstruct Figure 21-1 and its accompanying table to show the production data for Europe; assume that Europe has 600 units of labor and that labor productivities are those given in Table 21-1.

3. What if the data in Table 21-1 changed from (1, 2; 3, 4) to (1, 2; 2, 4)? Show that all trade is killed off. Use this to explain the adage, *"Vive la différence!"* (freely translated as "Let diversity thrive!"). Why do the largest gains in trade flow to small countries whose pretrade prices are very different from prevailing world prices?

4. *Follow-up to question 3:* Suppose that the data in Table 21-1 pertain to a newly industrialized country (NIC) and America. What are the gains from trade between the two countries? Now suppose that NIC adopts American technology and has production possibilities identical to that in the American column of Table 21-1. What will happen to international trade? What will happen to NIC's living standards and real wages? What will happen to America's living standards? Is there a lesson here for the impact of converging economies on trade and welfare?

5. A U.S. senator wrote the following: "Trade is supposed to raise the incomes of all nations involved—or at least that is what Adam Smith and David Ricardo taught us. If our economic decline has been caused by the economic growth of our competitors, then these philosophers—and the entire discipline of economics they founded—have been taking us on a 200-year ride."

Explain why the first sentence is correct. Also explain why the second sentence does not follow from the first. Can you give an example of how economic growth of Country J could lower the standard of living in Country A? (*Hint:* The answer to question 4 will help uncover the fallacy in the quotation.)

6. New international economics developed theories that might support the following arguments for protecting domestic industries against foreign competition:

a. In some situations, a country could improve its standard of living by imposing protection if no one else retaliated.

b. If the marketplace is not working well and there is excessive unemployment, tariffs might lower the unemployment rate.

c. A country might be willing to accept a small drop in its living standard to preserve certain industries that it deems necessary for national security, such as supercomputers or oil, by protecting them from foreign competition.

d. Wages in Korea are but one-tenth of those in the United States. Unless we limit the imports of Korean manufactures, we face a future in which our trade deficit continues to deteriorate under the onslaught of competition from low-wage East Asian workers.

In each case, relate the argument to one of the traditional defenses of protectionism. State the conditions under which it is valid, and decide whether you agree with it.

7. The United States has had quotas on steel, shipping, automobiles, textiles, and many other products. Economists estimate that by auctioning off the quota rights, the Treasury would gain at least $10 billion annually. Use Figure 21-9 to analyze the economics of quotas as follows: Assume that the government imposes a quota of 100 on imports, allocating the quota rights to importing countries on the basis of last year's imports. What would be the equilibrium price and quantity of clothing? What would be the efficiency losses from quotas? Who would get revenue rectangle *C*? What would be the effect of auctioning off the quota rights?

CHAPTER 22
MANAGING THE GLOBAL ECONOMY

Before I built a wall I'd ask to know
What I was walling in or walling out . . .

Robert Frost

A history of the twentieth century shows two distinct periods. The period from 1914 to 1945 was characterized by destructive competition, hot and cold military and trade wars, despotism, and depression. From 1945 to the present, the world has enjoyed cooperation, widening trade linkages, an expansion of democracy, and rapid economic growth.

The stark contrast between the first and second halves of this century is a reminder of the high stakes in the wise management of our national and global economies. Economically, no nation is an island unto itself. When the bell tolls depressions or financial crisis, the sounds reverberate around the world.

What are the economic links among nations? The last two chapters surveyed the major economic mechanisms. We saw that international exchange takes place not by barter but through the medium of money. Trade occurs through the buying or selling of commodities for dollars or pesos or other currencies. Further, we saw that international trade allows nations to raise their standards of living by specializing in areas of comparative advantage, exporting goods in which they are relatively efficient and importing those in which they are relatively inefficient.

Yet the forces of comparative advantage are not the whole story. Some countries have managed their economies well, opening their economies, adapting to the evolving technologies and markets in the world economy, growing, and prospering. Others have fallen behind, either because they are trapped in the vicious cycle of poverty or because war, corruption, and the heavy hand of government regulation have snuffed out the flames of entrepreneurship and wrecked the best-laid plans.

Trade among nations sometimes seems a brutal Darwinian conflict for market shares, profits, and vital resources. But humans have in the second half of this century evolved beyond the red-in-tooth-and-claw struggle—they have built institutions that serve the common cause of growth and fairness in the international arena. These institutions include a system for managing international finance mechanisms, a system for coordinating monetary policies, and agreements for curbing trade restrictions. In this final chapter, we examine the major international economic problems and some of the cooperative institutions that have grown up to make international markets operate more smoothly.

410

A. THE INTERNATIONAL MONETARY SYSTEM

We start with an analysis of the **international monetary system**. This term denotes the institutions under which payments are made for transactions that reach across national boundaries. In particular, the international monetary system determines how foreign exchange rates are set and how governments can affect exchange rates.

 Reminder: The essence of foreign exchange. Chapter 20 explained that international trade involves the use of different national currencies, which are linked by relative prices called foreign exchange rates. In the foreign exchange market, the demand for American dollars comes from foreigners who want to purchase goods, services, and investments from America; the supply of American dollars comes from Americans who want to purchase foreign commodities or financial assets. The interaction of these supplies and demands determines the foreign exchange rate.

A fall in the market price of a currency is a depreciation; a rise in a currency's value is called an appreciation. In a system where governments have official foreign exchange rates, a decrease in the official exchange rate is called a devaluation while an increase is a revaluation.

The importance of the international monetary system was well described by economist Robert Solomon:

> Like the traffic lights in a city, the international monetary system is taken for granted until it begins to malfunction and to disrupt people's lives. . . . A well-functioning monetary system will facilitate international trade and investment and smooth adaptation to change. A monetary system that functions poorly may not only discourage the development of trade and investment among nations but subject their economies to disruptive shocks when necessary adjustments to change are prevented or delayed.[1]

---

[1] Robert Solomon, *The International Monetary System, 1945–1976: An Insider's View* (Harper & Row, New York, 1977), pp. 1, 7.

The central element of the international monetary system involves the arrangements by which exchange rates are set. In recent years, nations have used one of three major exchange-rate systems:

- A system of flexible or floating exchange rates, where exchange rates are entirely determined by market forces
- A system of fixed exchange rates
- A hybrid system of "managed" exchange rates, which involves some currencies whose values float freely, some currencies whose values are determined by a combination of government intervention and the market, and some that are pegged or fixed to one currency or a group of currencies

PURE FLEXIBLE EXCHANGE RATES

At one extreme is an international monetary system in which exchange rates are completely flexible and move purely under the influence of supply and demand. This system, known as **flexible exchange rates**, is one where governments neither announce an exchange rate nor take steps to enforce one. (Another term often used is "floating" exchange rates, which means the same thing.) In a flexible-exchange-rate system, the relative prices of currencies are determined by buying and selling among households and businesses.

Let us see how exchange rates are determined under flexible rates. In 1994, the peso was under attack in foreign exchange markets, and the Mexicans allowed the peso to float. At the original exchange rate of approximately 4 pesos per U.S. dollar, there was an excess supply of pesos. This meant that at that exchange rate, the supply of pesos by Mexicans to buy American and other foreign goods and assets outweighed the demand for pesos by Americans and others who wanted to purchase Mexican goods and assets.

What was the outcome? As a result of the excess supply, the peso depreciated relative to the dollar.

How far did the exchange rates move? Just far enough so that—at the depreciated exchange rate of about 6 pesos to the dollar—the quantities supplied and demanded were balanced.

What lies behind the equilibration of supply and demand? Two main forces are involved: (1) With the dollar more expensive, it costs more for Mexicans to buy American goods, services, and investments, causing the supply of pesos to fall off in the usual fashion. (2) With the depreciation of the peso, Mexican goods and assets become less expensive for foreigners. This increases the demand for pesos in the marketplace. (Note that this simplified discussion assumes that all transactions occur only between the two countries; a more complete discussion would involve the demands and supplies of currencies from all countries.)

Where is the government? In a freely flexible exchange-rate system, the government is on the sidelines. It allows the foreign exchange market to determine the value of the dollar, just as it allows markets to determine the value of lettuce, machinery, GM stock, or copper. Consequently, it is possible to get enormous swings in flexible exchange rates over relatively short periods.

FIXED EXCHANGE RATES: THE CLASSICAL GOLD STANDARD

At the other extreme is a system of **fixed exchange rates**, where governments specify the exact rate at which dollars will be converted into pesos, yen, and other currencies. Historically, the most important fixed-exchange-rate system was the **gold standard**, which was used off and on from 1717 until 1933. In this system, each country defined the value of its currency in terms of a fixed amount of gold, thereby establishing fixed exchange rates among the countries on the gold standard.[2]

The functioning of the gold standard can be seen easily in a simplified example. Suppose people

---

[2] Why was gold used as the standard of exchange and means of payment, rather than some other commodity? Certainly other materials could have been used, but gold had the advantages of being in limited supply, being relatively indestructible, and having few industrial uses. Can you see why wine, wheat, or cattle would not be a useful means of payment among countries?

everywhere insisted on being paid in bits of pure gold metal. Then buying a bicycle in Britain would merely require payment in gold at a price expressed in ounces of gold. By definition there would be no foreign-exchange-rate problem. Gold would be the common world currency.

This example captures the essence of the gold standard. Once gold became the medium of exchange or money, foreign trade was no different from domestic trade; everything could be paid for in gold. The only difference between countries was that they could choose different *units* for their gold coins. Thus, Queen Victoria chose to make British coins about $\frac{1}{4}$ ounce of gold (the pound) and President McKinley chose to make the U.S. unit $\frac{1}{20}$ ounce of gold (the dollar). In that case, the British pound, being 5 times as heavy as the dollar, had an exchange rate of $5/£1.

This was the essence of the gold standard. In practice, countries tended to use their own coins. But anyone was free to melt down coins and sell them at the going price of gold. So exchange rates were fixed for all countries on the gold standard. *The exchange rates (also called par values or parities) for different currencies were determined by the gold content of their monetary units.*

Hume's Adjustment Mechanism

The purpose of an exchange-rate system is to promote international trade while facilitating adjustment to shocks and disequilibria. Key to understanding international economics is to see how the *international adjustment mechanism* functions. What happens if a country's wages and prices rise so sharply that its goods are no longer competitive in the world market? Under flexible exchange rates, the country's exchange rate could depreciate to offset the domestic inflation. But under fixed exchange rates, equilibrium must be restored by deflation at home or inflation abroad.

Let's examine the international adjustment mechanism under a fixed-exchange-rate system with two countries, America and Britain. Suppose that American inflation has made American goods uncompetitive. Consequently, America's imports rise and its exports fall. It therefore runs a trade deficit with Britain. To pay for its deficit, America would have to ship gold to Britain. Eventually—if there were no adjustments in either America or Britain—America would run out of gold.

In fact, an automatic adjustment mechanism does exist, as was demonstrated by the British philosopher David Hume in 1752. He showed that the outflow of gold was part of a mechanism that tended to keep international payments in balance. His argument, though nearly 250 years old, offers important insights for understanding how trade flows get balanced in today's economy.

Hume's explanation rested in part upon the quantity theory of prices, which is a theory of the overall price level that is analyzed in macroeconomics. This doctrine holds that the overall price level in an economy is proportional to the supply of money. Under the gold standard, gold was an important part of the money supply—either directly, in the form of gold coins, or indirectly, when governments used gold as backing for paper money.

What would be the impact of a country's losing gold? First, the country's money supply would decline either because gold coins would be exported or because some of the gold backing for the currency would leave the country. Putting both these consequences together, a loss of gold leads to a reduction in the money supply. According to the quantity theory, the next step is that prices and costs would change proportionally to the change in the money supply. If the United States loses 10 percent of its gold to pay for a trade deficit, the quantity theory predicts that U.S. prices, costs, and incomes would fall 10 percent. In other words, the economy would experience a deflation. If gold discoveries in California increase America's gold supplies, we would expect to see a major increase in the price level in the United States.

The Four-Pronged Mechanism.

Now consider Hume's theory of international payments equilibrium. Suppose that America runs a large trade deficit and begins to lose gold. According to the quantity theory of prices, this loss of gold reduces America's money supply, driving down America's prices and costs. As a result, (1) America decreases its imports of British and other foreign goods, which have become relatively expensive; and (2) because America's domestically produced goods have become relatively inexpensive on world markets, America's exports increase.

The opposite effect occurs in Britain and other foreign countries. Because Britain's exports are growing rapidly, it receives gold in return. Britain's money supply therefore increases, driving up British prices and costs according to the quantity theory. At this point, two more prongs of the Hume mechanism come into play: (3) British and other foreign exports have become more expensive, so the volume of goods exported to America and elsewhere declines; and (4) British citizens, faced with a higher domestic price level, now import more of America's low-priced goods.

Figure 22-1 on page 716 illustrates the logic in Hume's mechanism. Make sure you can follow the logical chain from the original deficit at the top through the adjustment to the new equilibrium at the bottom.

The result of Hume's four-pronged gold-flow mechanism is an improvement in the balance of payments of the country losing gold and a worsening in that of the country gaining the gold. In the end, an equilibrium of international trade and finance is reestablished at new relative prices, which keep trade and international lending in balance with no net gold flow. This equilibrium is a stable one and requires no tariffs or other government intervention.

Adjustment with Fixed Exchange Rates.

Understanding the gold standard is important not only because of its historical role but also because it is a pure example of a fixed-exchange-rate system. The same analysis applies to all fixed-exchange-rate systems: If exchange rates are not free to move when the prices or incomes among countries get out of line, *domestic* prices and incomes must adjust to restore equilibrium. If Europe decides to adopt a common currency, the mechanism by which adjustments will occur is similar to that under a gold standard.

In Hume's mechanism, it is gold flows that move prices and wages and ensure equilibrium. In modern macroeconomic thinking, output and employment are also part of the international adjustment mechanism. We will see later in this chapter that *the necessity of having real output and employment adjust to ensure relative-price equilibrium among countries on a fixed exchange rate is a crucial dilemma faced by countries*

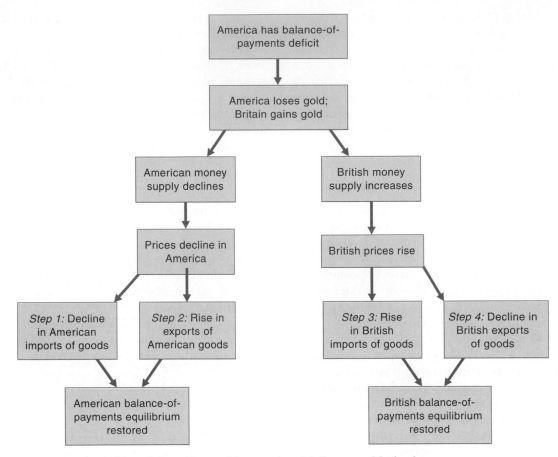

FIGURE 22-1. Hume's Four-Pronged International Adjustment Mechanism

Hume explained how a balance-of-payments disequilibrium would automatically produce equilibrating adjustment under a gold standard. Trace the lines from the original disequilibrium at the top through the changes in prices to the restored equilibrium at the bottom. This mechanism works in modified form under any fixed-exchange-rate system. Modern economics augments the mechanism in the fourth row of boxes by replacing the fourth row with "Prices, output, and employment decline in Amercia" and "Prices, output, and employment rise in Britain."

considering a fixed exchange rate. The same question arises in Europe's decision on whether to adopt a common currency.

MANAGED EXCHANGE RATES

Few countries today adopt either the extreme of absolutely fixed exchange rates or that of pure flexi-

ble exchange rates. Rather, the norm is the middle ground of **managed exchange rates**, meaning that exchange rates are basically determined by market forces but governments buy or sell currencies or change their money supplies to affect their exchange rates. Sometimes governments lean against the winds of private markets. At other times governments have "target zones" which guide their policy actions.

FIGURE 22-2. Governments Intervene to Defend Fixed Exchange Rate

Say the Mexican government announces a fixed exchange rate of 0.4 dollars per peso ($2\frac{1}{2}$ pesos per dollar). Initial equilibrium is at *A*. Deteriorating economic conditions—perhaps inflation or concerns over Mexico's political stability—lead to a decline in the demand for pesos. In a flexible-exchange-rate system, the new equilibrium would be at *B*, with an exchange rate of 0.2 dollars to the peso (or 5 pesos to the dollar). Central banks can reestablish official parity by buying *CA* worth of pesos, in effect shifting the demand back to the original demand curve, *D*. Alternatively, by raising Mexican interest rates, the governments can induce private investors to increase their demand for pesos by *CA*.

Intervention

Managing the exchange rate requires that governments intervene in foreign exchange markets. Government exchange-rate **intervention** occurs when the government buys or sells its own or foreign currencies to affect exchange rates. For example, the Japanese government on a given day might buy $1 billion worth of Japanese yen with U.S. dollars. This would cause a rise in value, or an appreciation, of the yen. In general, a government intervenes when it believes its foreign exchange rate is out of line with its currency's fundamental value.

Figure 22-2 illustrates the operation of a fixed-exchange-rate system. Suppose that Mexico decides to peg its exchange rate at $0.40 per peso (or $2\frac{1}{2}$ pesos per dollar). The initial equilibrium is shown as

point *A* in Figure 22-2. At an exchange rate of $0.40 per peso, the quantities of Mexican pesos supplied and demanded are equal.

Suppose that the demand for pesos falls, perhaps because inflation in Mexico is higher than in the United States. This produces a downward shift in the demand for pesos from *D* to *D'*. In a world of flexible exchange rates, the peso would depreciate and reach a new equilibrium at *B* in Figure 22-2.

Here is where the new wrinkle appears: Recall that Mexico is committed to maintaining the parity of $0.40 per peso. What can it do?

- One approach is to intervene by *buying the depreciating currency (pesos) and selling the appreciating currency (dollars)*. In this example, if the Mexican central bank buys the amount shown by the segment *CA*, this will increase the demand for pesos and maintain the official parity.
- An alternative would be to use monetary policy. The Mexican central bank could *induce the private sector to increase its demand for pesos* by raising Mexican interest rates. Say that Mexican interest rates rise relative to U.S. rates; this would lead investors to move funds into pesos and increase the private demand for pesos, in effect moving the private demand curve back toward the original *D* demand curve.

These two operations are not really so different as they sound. In effect, both involve monetary policies in Mexico. In fact, one of the complications of managing the open economy, as we will shortly see, is that the need to use monetary policies to manage the exchange rate can collide with the need to use monetary policy to stabilize the domestic business cycle.

To summarize:

A *freely flexible* exchange rate is one determined purely by supply and demand without any government intervention. A *fixed-exchange-rate* system is one where governments state official exchange rates, which they defend through intervention and monetary policies. A *managed-exchange-rate* system is a hybrid of fixed and flexible rates in which governments attempt to affect their exchange rates *directly* by buying or selling foreign currencies or *indirectly*, through monetary policy, by raising or lowering interest rates.

B. INTERNATIONAL INSTITUTIONS

In the early part of the twentieth century, even nations which were ostensibly at peace engaged in debilitating trade wars and competitive devaluations. After World War II, international institutions were developed to foster economic cooperation among nations. These institutions continue to be the means by which nations coordinate their policies and seek solutions to common problems. This section surveys the major international institutions and examines the issues raised by interdependencies among nations.

The United States emerged from World War II with its economy intact—able and willing to help rebuild the countries of friends and foes alike. The postwar international political system responded to the needs of war-torn nations by establishing durable institutions that facilitated the quick recovery of the international economy. The major international economic institutions of the postwar period were the General Agreement on Tariffs and Trade (rechartered as the World Trade Organization in 1995), the Bretton Woods exchange-rate system, the International Monetary Fund, and the World Bank. These four institutions stand as monuments to wise and farsighted statecraft.

The Bretton Woods System

The major economists of the 1940s, particularly John Maynard Keynes, were greatly affected by the economic crisis of the prewar period. They were determined to avoid the economic chaos and competitive devaluations that had occured during the Great Depression.

Under the intellectual leadership of Keynes, nations gathered in 1944 at Bretton Woods, New Hampshire, and hammered out an agreement that led to the formation of the major economic institutions. For the first time, nations agreed upon a system for regulating international financial transactions. Even though some of the rules have changed since 1944, the institutions established at Bretton Woods continue to play a vital role today.

Those who attended the Bretton Woods conference remembered well how the gold standard was too inflexible and served to deepen economic crises. To replace the gold standard, the **Bretton Woods system** established a parity for each currency in terms of both the U.S. dollar and gold. Currencies were defined in terms of both gold and the dollar, and exchange rates among currencies were determined in much the same way as they had been under the gold standard. For example, the parity of the British pound was set at £12.5 per ounce of gold. Given that the gold price of the dollar was $35 per ounce, this implied an official exchange rate between the dollar and the pound of $35/£12.5 = $2.80 per £1, which was thereby set as the official parity on the pound.

The revolutionary innovation of the Bretton Woods system was that exchange rates were *fixed but adjustable*. When one currency got too far out of line with its appropriate or "fundamental" value, the parity could be adjusted. The ability to adjust exchange rates when fundamental disequilibrium arose was the central distinction between the Bretton Woods system and the gold standard. Ideally, exchange-rate changes would be worked out among countries in a cooperative way.

By creating a fixed but adjustable system, the designers of Bretton Woods hoped to have the best of two worlds. They could maintain the *stability* of the gold standard, a world in which exchange rates would be predictable from one month to the next, thereby encouraging trade and capital flows. At the same time, they would simulate the *adjustment* of flexible exchange rates, under which persistent relative-price differences among countries could be adjusted to by exchange-rate changes rather than by the painful deflation and unemployment necessary under the gold standard.

The International Monetary Fund (IMF)

An integral part of the Bretton Woods system was the establishment of the International Monetary Fund (or IMF), which still administers the international monetary system and operates as a central bank for central banks. Member nations subscribe by lending their currencies to the IMF; the IMF then relends these funds to help countries in balance-of-payments difficulties. In recent years, the IMF has played a key role in organizing a cooperative response to the international debt crisis and in helping formerly communist countries make the transition to the market.

How would the IMF accomplish this objective? Suppose, for example, that Russia's transition to the market is in trouble because of a rapid inflation and an inability to raise funds in private markets. The country is having trouble paying interest and principal on its foreign loans. The IMF might send a team of specialists to pore over the country's books. The IMF team would come up with an austerity plan for Russia, generally involving reducing the budget deficit and tightening credit; these measures would slow inflation and increase confidence in the Russian ruble. When Russia and the IMF agree on the plan, the IMF would lend money to Russia, perhaps $5 billion, to "bridge" the country over until its balance of payments improved. In addition, there would probably be a debt restructuring, wherein banks would lend more funds and stretch out payments on existing loans.

If the IMF program was successful, Russia's balance of payments would begin to improve, and the country would resume economic growth.

The World Bank

Another international financial institution created after World War II was the World Bank. The Bank is capitalized by rich nations that subscribe in proportion to their economic importance in terms of GDP and other factors. The Bank makes low-interest loans to countries for projects which are economically sound but which cannot get private-sector financing. As a result of such long-term loans, goods and services flow from advanced nations to developing countries. In 1996, the World Bank made new loans of $21 billion.

If the projects are selected wisely, production in the borrowing lands will rise by more than enough to pay interest on the loans; wages and living standards generally will be higher, not lower, because the foreign capital has raised GDP in the borrowing countries. In addition, as the loans are being paid back, the advanced nations will gain by enjoying somewhat higher imports of useful goods.

Demise of the Bretton Woods System

For the first three decades after World War II, under the Bretton Woods arrangements, the U.S. dollar was the key currency. Most international trade and finance were carried out in dollars, and payments were most often made in dollars. Exchange-rate parities were quoted in dollar terms, and private and government reserves were kept invested in dollar securities. This was a period of unprecedented growth and prosperity. The industrial nations began to lower trade barriers and to make all their currencies freely convertible. The economies of Western Europe and East Asia recovered from war damage and grew at spectacular rates. During this period, the world was on a dollar standard. In essence, the U.S. dollar was the world currency because of its stability, convertibility, and widespread acceptability.

But recovery contained the seeds of its own destruction. U.S. trade deficits were fueled by an overvalued currency, budget deficits to finance the Vietnam war, and growing overseas investment by American firms. Dollars consequently began to pile up abroad as Germany and Japan developed trade surpluses. Dollar holdings abroad grew from next to nothing in 1945 to $50 billion in the early 1970s.

By 1971, the stock of liquid dollar balances had become so large that governments had difficulty defending the official parities. People began to lose confidence in the "almighty dollar." And the lower barriers to financial flows meant that billions of dollars could cross the Atlantic in minutes and threaten to overwhelm existing parities. On August 15, 1971, President Nixon formally severed the link between the dollar and gold, bringing the Bretton Woods era to an end. No longer would the United States automatically convert dollars into other currencies or into gold at $35 per ounce; no longer would the United States set an official parity of the dollar and then defend this exchange rate at all costs. As the United States abandoned the Bretton Woods system, the world moved into the modern era.

Today's Hybrid System

Unlike the earlier uniform system under either the gold standard or Bretton Woods, today's exchange-rate system fits into no tidy mold. Without anyone's having planned it, the world has moved to a hybrid exchange-rate system. The major features are as follows:

- A few countries allow their currencies to *float freely,* as the United States has for some periods in the last two decades. In this approach, a country allows markets to determine its currency's value and it rarely intervenes.
- Some major countries have *managed but flexible* exchange rates. Today, this group includes Canada, Japan, and more recently Britain. Under this system, a country will buy or sell its currency to reduce the day-to-day volatility of currency fluctuations. In addition, a country will sometimes engage in systematic intervention to move its currency toward what it believes to be a more appropriate level.
- Many countries, particularly small ones, *peg* their currencies to a major currency or to a "basket" of currencies. Sometimes, the peg is allowed to glide smoothly upward or downward in a system known as a *gliding* or *crawling peg.*
- Some countries join together in a *currency bloc* in order to stabilize exchange rates among themselves while allowing their currencies to move flexibly relative to those of the rest of the world. The most important of these blocs is the European Monetary System (discussed below).
- In addition, almost all countries tend to intervene either when markets become "disorderly" or when exchange rates seem far out of line with the "fundamentals," that is, with exchange rates that are appropriate for existing price levels and trade flows.

MACROECONOMIC INTERACTIONS

For much of the nation's history, economic policies in the United States have concentrated on domestic affairs, influenced largely by domestic inflation, unemployment, and elections. During the turbulent 1980s, the United States came of age as a mature leader in world economic affairs. It saw its domestic monetary and fiscal policies spill over to affect exchange rates and trade flows, and American unemployment and inflation were buffeted by trends in the world economy.

The central lesson of the last decade is clear: In a world where economies are increasingly linked by trade and finance, interdependence is unavoidable. No walls can insulate a country from global economic

forces. Isolationism is today no more feasible in economic affairs than it is in political or military affairs. We devote the remainder of this section to describing the major economic linkages among nations.

Economic Interaction

Domestic economic welfare depends upon the health of the entire international economy. This fact is captured in the old saying, "When America sneezes, Europe catches cold." To see why economic ailments can be contagious, let's examine the principal links in the interaction of nations' economic policies.

Multiplier Link: Net Exports and Multiplier Effects. The first link relates to the spillovers from business cycles in different regions. Suppose that income and output in America fall, perhaps because America decides to contract the economy to slow inflation or maybe simply because demand in the private sector is weak. We know that lower income in America will lead to lower imports from other countries. But American imports are other countries' exports, so Europe may find its exports declining, and the decrease tends to reduce Europe's aggregate demand, output, and employment. Therefore, any factor that reduces America's national output also tends to reduce output and employment abroad. The causation is summarized as

$$Y_A \downarrow \rightarrow Im_A \downarrow \rightarrow Ex_E \downarrow \rightarrow Y_E \downarrow$$

Here Y_A and Y_E are output in America and Europe, Im_A is America's imports, while Ex_E is Europe's exports.

This multiplier link is what governments have in mind when they try to persuade their trading partners to expand their economies. For example, in 1993, Lawrence Summers, an eminent Harvard economist serving as the U.S. undersecretary of the Treasury, pointed out to Japanese business leaders that if the Japanese government increased its fiscal outlays, boosting Japanese national income and imports from abroad, then jobs would be created abroad too:

> The extra demand that would be created by a return of the Japanese current account surplus to its historically average level of one and a half percent of GDP would be enough to create more than $60 billion in

additional exports from the rest of the world, which translates into an extra one to two million jobs.[3]

A Japanese fiscal expansion would stimulate production (and employment) in other nations; Summers' argument is an example of the multiplier link.

Monetary Link: Financial Markets and Interest-Rate Effects. While the multiplier link works through the current account, the monetary link operates through financial markets. Under flexible exchange rates, large countries have room to change their monetary policies. When central banks raise interest rates through a monetary tightening, the higher interest rates attract funds and the country's foreign exchange rate tends to appreciate. This in turn reduces exports, raises imports, lowers output, and slows inflation. Empirical studies on the United States have found that the international transmission mechanism for monetary policy (whereby interest rates affect exchange rates and net exports) is just as powerful as the domestic mechanism (whereby higher interest rates reduce domestic investment).

But here again we find that the domestic policy spills over to other nations. Consider what happens in Europe when America raises its interest rates. As America's interest rate (r_A) rises, investors sell European financial assets and buy American financial assets. This leads to an appreciation of the dollar $(e_\$\uparrow)$ and a depreciation of European currencies. It also tends to raise European interest rates (r_E).

There are a number of effects on America's trading partners. The higher interest rates tend to depress domestic investment in Europe and thereby to lower Europe's output and employment. However, the depreciated value of Europe's currency will tend to stimulate Europe's economy, as the increase in exports to America increases Europe's net exports. The overall effect for Europe is depressed domestic investment and increased exports, with an uncertain impact on total output and employment. This then is the monetary link among nations:

$$r_A \uparrow \to \begin{cases} e_\$ \uparrow \to Ex_E \uparrow \to Y_E \uparrow \\ r_E \uparrow \to I_E \downarrow \to Y_E \downarrow \end{cases}$$

---

[3] *Treasury News*, June 25, 1993, p. 4.

where I_E is Europe's domestic investment (other variables were defined under the equation in the multiplier link discussion).

In addition, note that the multiplier link comes into play here, as the economic contraction in America will also lower output in Europe through the direct effect on Europe's exports.

Savings and Investment Link. The first two linkages show how business-cycle shocks ripple through the world economy. We also want to understand the impact of changes in domestic saving and investment upon other countries. What would happen, for example, if the United States decides to balance its budget? Or if Japan has more saving than it can productively use at home?

Let's take the example of a U.S. fiscal tightening. Higher taxes and lower government spending increase public saving. The savings and investment mechanism is as follows:

$$(T-G)_A \uparrow \to \begin{cases} r_A \downarrow, \, e_\$ \downarrow \to X_A \uparrow \to I_A \uparrow \\ r_E \downarrow, \, e_\$ \downarrow \to X_E \uparrow \to I_E \uparrow \end{cases}$$

This equation shows the effect of a decrease in the U.S. budget deficit—an increase in $(T-G)_A$. The top line after the bracket states that the fiscal tightening will lower U.S. interest rates and lead to a depreciation of the dollar. This will increase both America's domestic investment (I_A) and American net exports or net foreign investment (X_A). The lower line shows how the American fiscal policy affects Europe. The lower U.S. interest rates also lower European interest rates. This will tend to increase European domestic investment in equipment and structures. Europe's net foreign investment is likely to decline, however, as its net exports to the United States decline as the counterpart of the higher U.S. net exports. Note that American net savings and national investment will increase because both components of investment rise. For Europe, the impact is uncertain because the two components of investment go in opposite directions. But we can see that the composition of Europe's saving and investment definitely changes as a result of American fiscal policy.

We can easily understand this policy looking from the point of view of the world as a whole. Because the world is a closed economy, a lower budget deficit in the United States increases world sav-

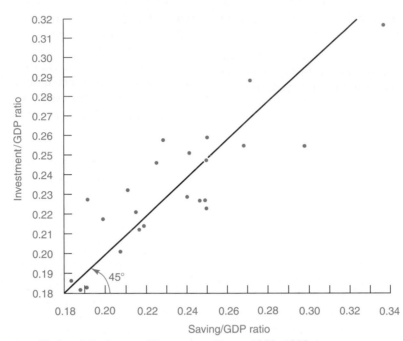

FIGURE 22-3. National Savings and Investment Rates, 1960–1986

Each point shows the average savings and investment rate of one of the 23 advanced industrial countries. For example, the point furthest out is Japan, with a ratio of saving to GDP of 34 percent and an investment-GDP ratio of 32 percent over the 1960–1986 period. Over the long run, higher savings rates tend to increase domestic investment rather than foreign investment. [Source: Adapted from Rudiger Dornbusch, "Comment," in B. Douglas Bernheim and John B. Shoven, *National Saving and Economic Performance* (University of Chicago Press, 1991).]

ing. This tends to lower world interest rates and raise total world investment.

Because of the complexity of the underlying relationships, economists have examined the actual pattern of investment and saving. It turns out that a nation's domestic savings rate tends to be highly correlated with its domestic investment rate. In other words, increases in a nation's savings rate are associated with almost equal increases in its investment rate. Figure 22-3 portrays this correlation for 23 industrialized nations over the 1960–1986 period.

This result is surprising because, if capital is highly mobile, saving would flow to the country with the highest productivity. A low savings rate in Canada would mean that Canada would borrow abroad whatever it needed to equate the cost of capital with capital's marginal productivity. If the investment rate in Canada is entirely determined by the productivity of capital in Canada, and foreign saving fills any

remaining gap left after domestic saving has done its job, the scatter of points in Figure 22-3 would be flat, with a slope of zero.

But the scatter in Figure 22-3 definitely has a positive slope, suggesting that there are substantial barriers to the free flow of capital. The reasons for this lack of capital mobility have puzzled economists. One possible reason is that deficit countries have trouble raising funds in international markets because foreign investors worry about getting back their investments. Another factor is that investors are averse to the risks of investing in other countries, so they tend to keep their funds at home. In addition, if corporations tend to finance their investments out of retained earnings rather than from the world capital market, this practice would directly link domestic saving and investment. All these factors may moderate in the future as countries become more integrated, and evidence suggests that the correlation between domestic saving and investment has declined in the last decade.

The limited mobility of capital has important implications for policy. The most important is that changes in domestic saving will primarily affect the domestic capital stock and the productivity of domestic workers. If budget deficits or other factors reduce domestic saving, in this view, nations cannot look to the saving of other nations to make up the shortfall.

In summary:

Three important factors link countries together: (1) The multiplier link means that output changes in one country are transmitted abroad. (2) The monetary link means that one country's monetary policy affects exchange rates and interest rates abroad. (3) The savings and investment link determines how changes in domestic saving differentially affect investment at home and abroad.

The Need for Coordination

Just because nations have economic problems does not necessarily mean that an international conclave of finance ministers is always a useful remedy. Some problems are largely domestic and must be addressed domestically. But other problems arise from the interaction among nations—because of spillovers, or a large oil-price increase, or a breakdown of the international monetary system. Such systemic problems generally require active or tacit cooperation among nations. Coordination can be fruitful when market failures, external constraints, or conflicting objectives produce counterproductive economic policies. Here are some specific examples:

• *Market failures.* A pervasive market failure comes from the lack of price and wage flexibility, which leads to business cycles and alternating periods of unemployment and inflation. A single economy cannot attain full employment with price stability; nor can all nations together. Nations will find it in their interests to cooperate in their pursuit of macroeconomic stability so that they do not export their unemployment or inflation.

• *External constraints.* Problems arise when governments lose credibility in financial markets. Private investors may believe that a nation will not

FIGURE 22-4. Cooperation Can Replace Beggar-Thy-Neighbor Policies

Nations may decide to improve their incomes through trade restrictions or macroeconomic policies that export inflation or unemployment. Such noncooperative policies move America from U to N_A and Europe from U to N_E. International cooperation looks for "win-win" policies, such as ones that move nations from U to C, making all countries better off.

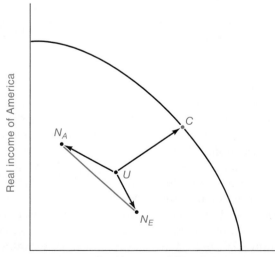

pay back its debts (as was the case for many Latin American countries in the 1980s and Mexico in 1994–1995) or that a nation is trying to defend an unrealistic exchange rate (as happened for country after country in Europe during the early 1990s). In these cases, a country may find that its currency is under speculative attack or, sometimes, that capital markets completely dry up. In effect, interest rates are sky-high and no longer reflect the true cost of funds or productivity of capital. In such cases, more liquid governments can step in and provide temporary loans until capital markets open up for the affected country. The United States did so for Mexico after the 1994 peso crisis, reducing the risk of a spiraling crisis of insolvencies and exchange-rate disruptions in other countries.

• *Conflicting objectives.* Sometimes, individual countries may act in their own national interests, adopting policies that increase domestic incomes and outputs at the expense of other countries. Nations may be tempted to depreciate their currencies to export their unemployment. Sometimes, nations engage in antisocial trade policies, giving valuable preferences to domestic over foreign production. A final facet of international coordination, therefore, is to bring nations together to agree on rules and standards that minimize the amount of antisocial economic activity.

The benefits of cooperation can be seen in the income-possibility curve in Figure 22-4 on page 723. Say that because of policy or exogenous shocks Europe and America find themselves stuck at point U with high unemployment and low incomes due to high interest rates, stubborn government deficits, and strong protectionist lobbies for domestic industries. America considers taking a *noncooperative policy,* perhaps introducing trade barriers, moving to its noncooperative optimum at point N_A. Europe might be weighing the same kind of noncooperative policy, restricting trade, depreciating its currency, or increasing purchases from within its borders—in effect moving to its noncooperative point at N_E. In pursuing these noncooperative policies along the rust $N_A N_E$ line, nations would not only beggar their neighbors but beggar themselves as well.

The alternative would be to find a cooperative approach that had positive rather than negative spillovers. This might involve lowering trade barriers, having a joint policy of monetary expansion, and tightening fiscal policies to increase saving and investment. If successfully designed and implemented, such a policy might move both America and Europe out to point C on the income-possibility curve in Figure 22-4.

International cooperation is designed to overcome the failures that prevent full utilization of resources as well as to promote the free and efficient flow of capital among nations.

C. INTERNATIONAL ECONOMIC ISSUES AT CENTURY'S END

In this final section, we apply the tools of international economics to examine three of the central issues that have concerned nations in recent years. We begin by examining the turbulent dollar "bubble" of the 1980s, showing the forces that led to the dollar overvaluation as well as the impacts of the overvaluation. One of the effects of the dollar's rise was a sharp deterioration in output in the U.S. tradeable sectors such as manufacturing, leading to the diagnosis that America was "deindustrializing." We will see that this raises the broader issue of the fundamental difference between competitiveness and

productivity. Finally, we will turn to one of the major issues of the late 1990s, the dilemma facing Europe as it moves toward monetary union.

THE RISE AND FALL OF THE DOLLAR

We have reviewed the rapid evolution of the international monetary system governing foreign exchange rates over the last half-century. Figure 22-5 shows the average exchange value of the dollar against major currencies. The dollar's exchange rate was quite stable until the Bretton Woods system broke down in

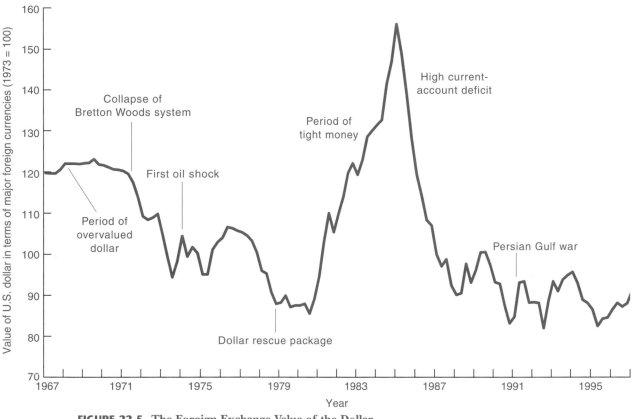

FIGURE 22-5. The Foreign Exchange Value of the Dollar

Before the collapse of the Bretton Woods system, the dollar's value was stable in exchange markets. Then, as the United States pursued its tight-money policies in the early 1980s, the high interest rates pulled up the dollar, decreased net exports, and led to large foreign debt. (Source: Federal Reserve System.)

1971. The dollar then depreciated sharply from 1971 to 1980.

The decade of the 1980s witnessed a dramatic cycle of dollar rise and fall—appreciation and depreciation. The rise of the dollar began in 1980 after a tight monetary policy and loose fiscal policy in the United States drove interest rates up sharply. This period witnessed high dollar interest rates, a conservative administration in the United States, a cut in U.S. tax rates, economic difficulties in continental Europe, socialism in France, and political unrest and a debt crisis in many Latin American countries. All these forces combined to attract mobile funds from other currencies to U.S. dollars.

Figure 22-5 shows the result: from 1979 to early 1985, the exchange rate on the dollar rose 80 percent. Many economists and policymakers became

convinced that the dollar was overvalued by 1985, and a swift decline soon followed. Over the next 6 years, the dollar fell more than it had risen in the early 1980s. This sequence has been called a speculative bubble by many.

The Overvalued Dollar

Many economists believed that the dollar was overvalued in the mid-1980s. An *overvalued currency* is one whose value is high relative to its long-run or sustainable level. The consequences of overvaluation were profound not only for the United States but for the entire world economy.

We examined the way tight monetary policies spill across national borders in our discussion of the monetary link earlier in this section. In this case, the first results came as the high interest rates

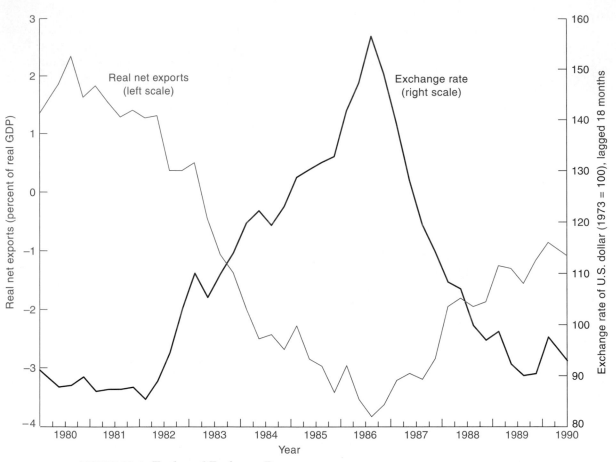

FIGURE 22-6. Trade and Exchange Rates

Real net exports react to exchange-rate changes, but with a time lag. The rising real exchange rate of the dollar during the early 1980s increased U.S. export prices and reduced prices of goods imported into the United States. As a result, real net exports (that is, exports minus imports, both measured in constant prices) fell sharply. When the dollar started to fall in 1985, real net exports began to react only after a considerable time lag. (Source: Real exchange rate is trade-weighted exchange rate corrected for differences in national price levels, from Federal Reserve Board; real net exports from U.S. Department of Commerce.)

in the United States reduced business and residential investment, thereby decreasing aggregate spending, slowing economic activity, and raising unemployment.

In addition, the high U.S. interest rates pulled up the interest rates of other major countries. These high interest rates reduced investment in other industrial economies and triggered a sharp slowdown in overall economic activity in the industrial world. This slowdown began in 1981 and continued through much of the 1980s. In addition, the high interest rates increased debt-service burdens in poor and middle-income countries and contributed to the international debt crisis.

The next effect came as a result of changing exchange rates. As the dollar rose, American export prices increased and the prices of goods imported into the United States fell. As a result, America's exports declined while its imports mounted sharply. From 1980 to 1985, the prices of imported goods and services fell by 6 percent, while the prices of our exports in foreign currencies rose over 80 percent. In response, the volume of imports rose 51 percent while export volumes rose only 2 percent.

The impact on the overall economy is measured by the changes in *real net exports,* which measure the trade balance in quantity terms; more precisely, real net exports are the quantity of exports minus the quantity of imports, where both are measured in constant prices. Figure 22-6 illustrates the dramatic effect of the rising exchange rate of the dollar on real net exports. From the peak in 1980 to the trough in 1986, real net exports declined by $158 billion, or 3 percent of 1983 GDP (all these figures are in 1992 prices).

Overall, the drop in real net exports had a contractionary effect upon domestic output and employment. When foreigners spent less here and Americans spent more abroad, the demand for American goods and services declined, real GDP fell, and unemployment rose. Economic studies indicate that the fall in real net exports was a major contributor to the deep recession in the early 1980s and tended to retard the growth of real GDP during much of the first half of the 1980s.

Dollar Correction and Economic Recovery

In economics, what goes up unsustainably sometimes comes crashing down. In the dollar's case, the dollar peaked in 1985 and began a sharp decline. The reversal was caused in part when governments intervened by selling dollars and buying other currencies, in part by speculators who believed that the dollar was overvalued, and in part by lower relative dollar interest rates. As can be seen in Figure 22-5, the dollar declined steadily for the next 6 years, and by 1991 it had lost all the ground gained between 1980 and 1985.

As the dollar depreciated, the recovery in U.S. net exports after 1985 was slow but steady. Figure 22-6 shows how U.S. real net exports gradually rose after the dollar bubble burst. The recovery in net exports contributed to the long expansion in economic activity from 1982 through 1990.

COMPETITIVENESS AND PRODUCTIVITY

"The Deindustrialization of America"

The roller-coaster ride of the dollar in the 1980s raised alarms about the fundamental performance of the American economy. The overvalued dollar produced severe economic hardships in many U.S. sectors exposed to international trade. Industries like automobiles, steel, textiles, and agriculture found the demand for their products shrinking as their prices rose relative to the prices of foreign competitors. Unemployment in the manufacturing heartland increased sharply as factories were closed, and the midwest became known as the "rust belt."

Many noneconomists interpreted U.S. trade problems as indicative of "America in decline." They fretted that America's technological leadership was eroding because of all sorts of factors, from lack of innovation to managerial sloth. They sometimes advocated economic protection against Japan and Western Europe; often, they argued for "industrial policies" for beleaguered industries to help stem the "deindustrialization of America." It was argued that Americans would be condemned to serving potato chips while others were manufacturing our computer chips.

Economists saw a different syndrome at work— the classic disease of an overvalued exchange rate. To understand the fundamentals, we must distinguish a nation's competitiveness from its productivity. *Competitiveness* refers to the extent to which a nation's goods can compete in the marketplace; this depends primarily upon the relative prices of domestic and foreign products. Competitiveness is, however, quite distinct from a nation's *productivity,* which is measured by the output per unit of input. Productivity is fundamental to the growth in living standards in a nation: it is roughly correct to state that the real income of a nation grows in step with its productivity growth.

It is true that U.S. competitiveness fell sharply during the 1980s. But the cause was not a deterioration in productivity growth. Rather, deteriorating competitiveness during the 1980s arose because the appreciation of the dollar raised American prices relative to those of its trading partners. In fact, there was no major change in the overall trend in productivity growth during the 1980s, and if anything, productivity probably grew more rapidly during that period than in the prior decade.

Make sure you understand this fundamental point about competitiveness: As the theory of comparative advantage demonstrates, nations are not inherently uncompetitive. Rather, they become uncompetitive when their prices move out of line with those of their trading partners because of an overvalued exchange rate. This point is indeed just a restatement of the law of comparative advantage, which shows that all nations can fruitfully engage in trade on the basis of their comparative advantage.

Trends in Productivity

The real story about U.S. real income is not about competitiveness—it concerns productivity. Recall that productivity measures the output per worker or per bundle of inputs. If American real incomes have stagnated over the last two decades, it is because productivity growth has slowed and not because America has become uncompetitive.

Competitiveness is important for trade but has no intrinsic relationship to the level or growth of real incomes. China has enjoyed a massive trade surplus in recent years at the same time that the United States ran a large trade deficit. But surely that does not mean that Americans would trade their living standards for those in China. Loss of competitiveness in international markets results from a nation's *prices* being out of line from those of its trading partners; it has no necessary connection with how a nation's *productivity* compares with other countries' productivity.

What are the recent trends in productivity? Despite the popular rhetoric, the growth of U.S. output, productivity, and consumption has changed little over the last quarter-century. Indeed, U.S. GDP per capita and output per hour worked still far exceed those of its major trading partners, Germany and Japan.

A particularly revealing study by the McKinsey Global Institute found that in 1990 manufacturing productivity in Japan was 17 percent below that in the United States while German productivity was 21 percent below U.S. levels.[4] Furthermore, the United States maintained a productivity lead in four of the nine manufacturing industries studied: computers, soaps and detergents, beer, and food. Japanese workers had higher productivity than U.S. workers in automobiles, auto parts, metalworking, steel, and consumer electronics production. In none of the industries surveyed were German workers the most productive, and indeed German productivity had declined relative to that in the United States during the 1980s.

The McKinsey study investigated the sources of productivity differences among the major countries in the nine industries studied. What emerged was surprising:

- Economies of scale and manufacturing technologies had a small role in some industries.
- Surprisingly, workers' skill levels and education were of little importance, being essentially the same in all three nations.
- Large differences in productivity exist within firms in the same industry. Managers could significantly improve productivity in *all* industries by adopting best-practice technologies.

One of the most striking findings of the McKinsey study was the importance of *globalization,* which denotes exposure to competition with the world leader in a particular industry. The study found that foreign direct investment by the most productive country (such as the Japanese auto transplants on American soil) has contributed to dramatic productivity improvements both through introducing leading-edge technologies and in stimulating competition.

This study provides further evidence that the surest route to high productivity and therefore to high living standards is to open markets to trade, capital, and ideas from the most advanced countries and to allow vigorous competition with companies that have adopted the most advanced technologies.

PARADISE LOST: THE SEARCH FOR STABLE EXCHANGE RATES

Fixed Exchange Rates and Monetary Policy

An ideal exchange-rate system is one that allows high levels of predictability of relative prices while ensuring smooth adjustment to economic shocks. In a well-functioning system, people can trade and invest in other countries without worrying that exchange rates will suddenly change and make their ventures unprofitable. This ideal seemed to be attained during most of the Bretton Woods era, when exchange-rate changes were infrequent yet output and trade grew rapidly. Outside of that period, the experience has been less satisfactory. The flexible-exchange-rate regime since 1973 has been one of great volatility as well as prolonged overvaluation and undervaluation. Fixed-exchange-

---

[4] McKinsey Global Institute, *Manufacturing Productivity* (Washington, D.C., 1993).

rate systems have sometimes been the subject of intense speculative attack, as occurred in Europe in 1992 and Mexico in 1994.

The difficulty in all fixed-exchange-rate systems is that they may impede economic adjustment if prices and trade among countries get too far out of line. The most ambitious attempt to curb exchange market fluctuations came in Europe with the creation in 1978 of a currency bloc known as the European Monetary System (or EMS). A group of West European countries, primarily Germany and France, designed this system along the lines of the Bretton Woods regime. As members of the EMS, nations commit to keeping their exchange rates within prescribed and narrow bands. These bands can be realigned periodically, but in between realignments each nation must take steps to ensure that member-country exchange rates remain inside the band.

Unfortunately, exchange-rate systems cannot operate in isolation from other macroeconomic policies. As we explained earlier in this chapter, keeping a currency at some prescribed level requires engaging in monetary policies through intervention or interest rates. In other words, adopting a fixed-exchange-rate system requires giving up control over domestic interest rates. If France has an exchange rate that is tightly tied to the German mark, free-market French interest rates cannot diverge significantly from those in Germany. A major divergence would lead to an avalanche of capital flows that would either overturn the exchange-rate system or drive interest rates together. (To see this, ask yourself if there can be major differences in the risk-free interest rates between Connecticut and California in the fixed-exchange-rate system of the United States.)

The exchange-rate system is an integral part of monetary policy. Nations which opt for open financial markets and a fixed exchange rate must devote their monetary policies to maintaining the exchange rate. In such a system, it is not possible to have independent monetary policies.

The Crisis of the European Monetary System

The loss of control over monetary policy by a bloc of countries operating a fixed exchange rate system would not be fatal during normal times, when the bloc's interest rates are close to those that would be desirable for the individual countries. But in times of crisis, the actual and desired monetary policies may diverge too much. That is exactly what happened in 1989–1993, and this divergence almost destroyed the European Monetary System.

The first key factor in the crisis of the EMS was the reunification of Germany in 1990. Following reunification, Germany's fiscal policy turned sharply expansionary as it subsidized East German industry. The expansion in western Germany led to an uptick in the German inflation rate. The German central bank (the Bundesbank) responded by raising German interest rates to dampen domestic demand. Here monetary policy was being used for domestic macroeconomic management, and the effects of the measures on Germany's trading partners were subordinated to domestic economic concerns.

Faced with rising German interest rates, other nations in the EMS had to raise their interest rates to prevent their currencies from depreciating against the German mark and moving outside the prescribed range. These interest-rate increases, along with a worldwide recession and a sharp decline in output from the collapsing communist bloc, pushed Europe, outside of Germany, into ever-deeper recession.

Speculative Attack! Eventually, the EMS was brought down by speculators who believed that countries would not tolerate unrealistic exchange rates and interest rates indefinitely. One by one, currencies came under attack—the Finnish mark, the Swedish crown, the Italian lira, the British pound, the Spanish peseta. In the end, only the inner sanctum of France and Germany withstood the speculative attacks.

If we sift through the rubble, we discover an important point: *A fixed exchange rate system is prone to devastating speculative attack if financial capital flows freely among countries.* The reason is the following: A fixed but adjustable exchange rate is susceptible to attack whenever speculators believe that changes are imminent. If a currency is likely to be devalued, speculators will quickly start selling that currency. The supply of the currency increases while demand drops.

At this point, central banks step in to defend the currency (recall Figure 22-2, above). But given the private resources available for speculative attacks—easily tens of billions of dollars in a few hours—the defender of a weak currency quickly runs out of reserves. Unless "hard-currency" countries are willing to provide unlimited lines of credit, the defending central bank will sooner or later give up and either devalue or allow the currency to float.

Toward a Common Currency: The Euro

The lesson of the 1992 crisis was, according to thoughtful scholars, that a country cannot simultaneously have (1) a fixed but adjustable exchange rate, (2) open capital markets, and (3) an independent domestic monetary policy. After three decades of integration, the major European countries have decided to resolve this dilemma by moving to a common currency. Under the Maastricht Treaty of 1991, European countries have decided to adopt a common currency (named the "Euro"). This process is called **monetary union**.

The basic philosophy behind monetary union is that it is necessary to complete European integration and that the full benefits of a single market require that countries adopt a common currency. This general belief is buttressed by the emerging view—sketched in the previous paragraph—that the fixed-exchange-rate system of multiple currencies would become increasingly unstable as the financial markets of European countries became increasingly open and integrated.

The monetary structure under a European monetary union would resemble that of countries like the United States. Monetary policy would be lodged in a European central bank (ECB), which would conduct monetary policy for countries in the European Union who adopt the common currency. The ECB would undertake open-market operations and determine interest rates of the Euro. As currently envisioned, the ECB would have price stability as its primary objective.

Those who endorse monetary union see important *benefits*. Under a common currency, exchange-rate volatility within Europe would be reduced to zero, so trade and finance would no longer have to contend with the uncertainties about prices induced by changing exchange rates. The primary result would be a reduction in transactions costs among countries. To the extent that national capital markets are segmented (recall the savings and investment link discussed above), moving to a common currency may allow a more efficient allocation of capital.

Many economists are skeptical and point to significant *costs* of monetary union. The dominant concern is the loss of the exchange rate as a tool for macroeconomic adjustment. The idea, going back to Robert Mundell, concerns the optimal currency area for Europe. An *optimal currency area* is one in which the differential shocks among nations are small or where labor mobility is sufficiently high to ensure rapid adjustment. Many economists worry that all of Europe is not an optimal currency area because of the rigidity of wage structures and the low degree of labor mobility among the different countries.

The fundamental problem arises because of inflexible wages and prices. When a shock occurs—such as the reunification of Germany, discussed above—inflexible wages and prices lead to rising inflation in the region with a demand increase and rising unemployment in the depressed region. In the United States, evidence suggests that differential regional shocks quickly lead to labor migration, so after a few years unemployment rates move back to preshock levels. Europe, by contrast, has much lower labor mobility, and unemployment differentials among nations tend to persist for many years. Monetary union will, in this view, condemn some regions and countries to persistent low growth and high unemployment.

Notwithstanding these reservations, Europeans are intent on moving to a single currency. Countries must satisfy certain *convergence criteria* before they will be allowed in the club. These include inflation and interest rates that are close to the lowest among the countries, along with severe limitations on government deficits and debts. The current timetable envisions that a core group of countries, including at least Germany and France, will irrevocably adopt the Euro on January 1, 1999—a prospect with a slightly millennial ring.

Monetary union in Europe is one of the great experiments of the twentieth century. Never before has such a large and powerful group of countries turned its economic fortunes over to a multinational body. Never before has a central bank been charged with containing the inflation and unemployment of a dozen nations with 300 million people producing $7 trillion of goods and services. Many economists worry that this experiment may lead to persistent stagnation and unemployment in large parts of Europe because of the lack of price and wage flexibility and insufficient labor mobility among countries.

FINAL ASSESSMENT

This survey of international economics must acknowledge a mixed picture, with some successes and some failures. But if we step back from the individual issues, an impartial jury of historians would surely rate the last half-century as one of unparalleled success for the countries of North America, Western Europe, and East Asia. The jury would point to the following:

- *Robust economic performance.* The period has seen the most rapid and sustained economic growth in recorded history. It is the only half-century since the Industrial Revolution that has avoided a deep depression, and none of the major industrial countries suffered from the cancer of hyperinflation.
- *The growth of trade.* Having learned the dangers of protectionism in the 1930s, nations have joined together in multinational trade treaties and agreements to desist from imposing trade restrictions. The latest of these was the Uruguay Round, completed in late 1993, which extended the principles of free and open trade to new sectors and new nations. The proof of the pudding in this area has been that international trade has grown faster than output for every major country.
- *The reemergence of free markets.* You often hear that imitation is the sincerest form of flattery. In economics, imitation occurs when a nation adopts another nation's system of organization in the hope that it will produce growth and stability. In the 1980s and 1990s, country after country threw off the shackles of communism and stifling central planning—not because the textbooks convinced them to do so but because they used their own eyes to see how the market-oriented countries of the West prospered while the command economies of the East collapsed. *For the first time, an empire collapsed simply because it could not produce sufficient butter along with its guns.*

Maintaining and strengthening the current international economic system is a worthy challenge for all.

SUMMARY

A. The International Monetary System

1. International trade and finance involve the use of different national currencies, which are linked by relative prices called foreign exchange rates. A well-functioning international economy requires a smoothly operating exchange-rate system, which denotes the institutions that govern financial transactions among nations. Three important exchange-rate systems are (*a*) the pure flexible-exchange-rate system, in which a country's foreign exchange rate is entirely determined by market forces of supply and demand; (*b*) the fixed-exchange-rate system (such as the gold standard or the Bretton Woods system), in which countries set and defend a given structure of exchange rates; and (*c*) the managed-exchange-rate system, in which government interventions and market forces interact to determine the level of exchange rates.

2. Classical economists like David Hume explained international adjustments to trade imbalances by the gold-flow mechanism. Under this process, gold movements would change the money supply and the price level. For example, a trade deficit would lead to a gold outflow and a decline in domestic prices that would (*a*) raise exports and (*b*) curb imports of the gold-losing country while (*c*) reducing exports and (*d*) raising imports of the gold-gaining country. This mecha-

nism shows that under fixed exchange rates, countries which have balance-of-payments problems must adjust through changes in domestic price and output levels.

B. International Institutions

3. After World War II, countries created a group of international economic institutions to organize international trade and finance. These included the International Monetary Fund (IMF), which oversees exchange-rate systems and helps countries with balance of payment difficulties; the World Bank, which lends money to low-income countries; and the Bretton Woods exchange-rate system. Under the Bretton Woods system, countries "pegged" their currencies to the dollar and to gold, providing fixed but adjustable exchange rates. When official parities deviated too far from fundamentals, countries could adjust parities and achieve a new equilibrium without incurring the hardships of inflation or recession.

4. When the Bretton Woods system broke down in 1971, it was replaced by today's hybrid system. Some large countries or regions allow their currencies to float independently; most small countries peg their currencies to the dollar or to other currencies; and many European countries adhere to the European Monetary System (EMS), which is a close cousin of the Bretton Woods system. Governments often intervene when their currencies get too far out of line from fundamentals or when exchange markets become disorderly.

5. Nations are interdependent through the multiplier and monetary links, wherein changes in output or monetary policy spill over to the output and investment of other countries. Countries are also linked through saving and investment. Sometimes, however, the uncoordinated activities of individual nations lead to inefficient outcomes—macroeconomic outcomes with high unemployment, or trade wars, or governments' loss of credibility in financial markets. International cooperation is designed to overcome the failures that prevent full utilization of resources and free and efficient flow of capital among nations.

6. Because of the increasing interdependence of national economies, countries often attempt to coordinate their economic policies. Important policy issues are the following:

    a. National trade policies affect the output and employment of other countries. A policy of protecting one's own industries by trade barriers is a beggar-thy-neighbor approach, in essence exporting unemployment and trade deficits.

    b. Foreign exchange rates can affect relative prices and net exports. A rise in a nation's foreign exchange rate will depress that nation's net exports and output, while a fall in a nation's foreign exchange rate will increase net exports and output. Because of the significant impact of exchange rates on national economies, countries have entered into agreements on international monetary arrangements.

    c. In recent years, countries have often coordinated their macroeconomic policies, trying to increase their national outputs or to lower their national inflation rates. By cooperating on fiscal or monetary policies, countries can take advantage of the expansionary or contractionary impacts that inevitably spill over the borders when output changes.

C. International Economic Issues at Century's End

7. When exchange rates get too far out of line, adverse consequences can occur. The United States experienced an overvalued currency in the mid-1980s as a result of tight money, loose fiscal policy, and speculative forces. The result was a severe contraction of those sectors exposed to international trade—particularly manufacturing—and this contraction deepened an already serious recession.

8. Popular analysis saw "deindustrialization" in the dollar overvaluation in the 1980s. But these discussions overlook the important distinction between productivity and competitiveness. Competitiveness refers to how well a nation's goods can compete in the global marketplace and is determined primarily by relative prices. Productivity denotes the level of output per unit of input. Real incomes and living standards depend primarily upon productivity, whereas the trade and current-account positions depend upon competitiveness. There is no close linkage between competitiveness and productivity.

9. European countries are moving toward monetary union, which involves a common currency and a unitary central bank. A common currency is appropriate when a region forms an optimal currency area. Those who favor European monetary union point to the improved predictability, lower transactions costs, and potential for better capital allocation. Skeptics worry that a common currency—like any irrevocably fixed-exchange-rate system—will require flexible wages and prices to promote adjustment to macroeconomic shocks. In an area with relatively low labor mobility, monetary union may doom major regions or countries to long periods of slow growth and high unemployment.

CONCEPTS FOR REVIEW

international monetary system
exchange-rate systems:
   flexible
   fixed rates
   managed flexible
managing exchange rates (intervention, monetary policy)

gold standard
international adjustment mechanism
Hume's four-pronged gold-flow
   mechanism
World Bank and IMF
Bretton Woods system, European
   Monetary System

international linkages:
   multiplier link
   monetary link
   savings and investment link
competitiveness vs. productivity
monetary union

QUESTIONS FOR DISCUSSION

1. James Tobin has written, "A great teacher of mine, Joseph Schumpeter, used to find puzzling irony in the fact that liberal devotees of the free market were unwilling to let the market determine the prices of foreign currencies." For what reasons might economists allow the foreign exchange market to be an exception to a general inclination toward free markets?

2. In the Louvre accord in 1987, major countries agreed to keep their currencies within "reference zones." Say that the United States and Germany agree to keep the German mark in the range of 1.60 to 1.80 marks to the dollar. Show with the help of a supply-and-demand diagram how the governments could implement this policy.

3. Consider two situations:
   a. Real incomes in America and Japan are growing at 1 percent per annum.
   b. Real incomes in America are growing at 2 percent, while real incomes in Japan are growing at 4 percent.
   Would you as an American prefer **a** or **b**? Defend your answer. Relate the question to the difference between absolute and relative incomes.

4. Consider the following three exchange-rate systems: the classical gold standard, freely flexible exchange rates, and the Bretton Woods system. Compare and contrast the three systems with respect to the following characteristics:
   a. Role of government vs. that of market in determining exchange rates
   b. Degree of exchange-rate volatility
   c. Method of adjustment of relative prices across countries
   d. Need for international cooperation and consultation in determining exchange rates
   e. Potential for establishment and maintenance of severe exchange-rate misalignment

5. The text states that a country cannot simultaneously have (*a*) a fixed but adjustable exchange rate, (*b*) open capital markets, and (*c*) an independent domestic monetary policy. Explain this statement. Apply it to the European monetary crisis of 1992. Why is there not a problem for the fixed-exchange-rate system between "California dollars" and "Texas dollars."

6. Consider the proposed European monetary union. List the pros and cons. How do you come down on the question of the advisability of monetary union? Would your answer change if the question concerned the United States?

VALEDICTION

We have now finished our tour of the exciting world of introductory economics. For us, the authors, this marks the fiftieth anniversary of our pilgrimage. Through sixteen editions, we have seen economics transformed into one of the most exciting and innovative of all the sciences.

For you, the introductory student, this marks the end of your first serious study of economics and the beginning of your life as a practicing economist. In this tour through the wonders of the world of economics you have discovered the realm of the qualified invisible hand, the promises and pitfalls of macroeconomic policy, and the opportunities to use market tools to preserve our precious environment. The market economy has been our major focus. We have seen that markets can be mighty engines of prosperity, but that they can also dish out great inequalities.

One of the extraordinary results of a careful study of economic principles is that you view the world through different eyes. You see the pattern in economic life—instead of the raw data of the upticks of the stock market and the downsizings of the labor market.

This golden anniversary provides the occasion for us to pause to reflect upon the evolution of economics and the economy. In designing this book, we try to be mindful of the fact that the principles learned here must serve the reader for the *next* five decades. We continually ask ourselves: What will the American and the global economies look like once we have crossed into the twenty-first century? What vital problems and cruel dilemmas will arise when today's students are running tomorrow's businesses, governments, and central banks?

One surprise about economics is how little the maladies change from decade to decade. As one old alum complained, "In economics, it's not the questions that change—it's the answers." The core problems of the 1990s differ little from those of the 1960s or the 1930s. We worry today as we did then about growth, stability, and distribution. Is our economic growth satisfactory? Are inflation and unemployment under control? Are the fruits of economic growth distributed fairly among the populace?

Central to all these questions is the perennial issue of how we should use our material gains to improve our personal and civic life. A striking analysis of this question was given by this century's greatest economist, John Maynard Keynes, in 1930. Keynes mused about the long-run prospects of the capitalist system and had these startling reflections:

> Suppose that a hundred years hence we are eight times better off than today. Assuming no important wars and no important increase in population, the *economic problem* may be solved. This means that the eco-

432

nomic problem is not—if we look into the future—*the permanent problem of the human race.*

Why, you may ask, is this so startling? It is startling because the economic problem, the struggle for subsistence, always has been hitherto the primary, most pressing problem of the human race—not only of the human race, but of the whole of the biological kingdom from the beginnings of life in its most primitive forms.

Thus we have been expressly evolved by nature—with all our impulses and deepest instincts—for the purpose of solving the economic problem. If the economic problem is solved, mankind will be deprived of its traditional purpose. I think with dread of the readjustment of the habits and instincts of the ordinary man, bred into him for countless generations, which he may be asked to discard within a few decades.

Must we not expect a general "nervous breakdown"? Thus for the first time since his creation man will be faced with his real, his permanent problem—how to use his freedom from pressing economic cares, how to occupy the leisure, which science and compound interest will have won for him, to live wisely and agreeably and well.

There are changes in other spheres too which we must expect to come. When the accumulation of wealth is no longer of high social importance, there will be great changes in the code of morals. The love of money as a possession—as distinguished from the love of money as a means to the enjoyments and realities of life—will be recognized for what it is, a somewhat disgusting morbidity, one of those semi-criminal, semi-pathological propensities which one hands over with a shudder to the specialists in mental disease. . . .

But beware! The time for all this is not yet. For at least another hundred years we must pretend to ourselves and to everyone that fair is foul and foul is fair; for foul is useful and fair is not. Avarice and usury and precaution must be our gods for a little longer still.[1]

We close with these fascinating thoughts because they remind us that great affluence has indeed not brought about a slackening of economic ambition in America. Even though our average real incomes are more than 4 times their levels at the beginning of this century, our society has become more competitive in the struggle for profits and jobs and markets. Markets are more pervasive, more intrusive. The growing orientation toward the market has accompanied widespread desire for smaller government, less regulation, and lower taxes.

Ours is the "ruthless economy." People are increasingly judged on their current productivities rather than past contributions. Old-fashioned loyalty to firm or community counts for little. Suppose a firm finds it profitable to lay off 1000 workers, or moves from New England to the Sunbelt, or moves from the United States to Mexico. It is likely to move in the relentless pursuit of profits . . . and as a protection against another firm gaining a competitive advantage.

Market-oriented economists will tell you that inequality is the price we pay for invention—that you can't make an omelette without breaking eggs. This hardheaded focus on efficiency pays no mind to the incomes of laid-off workers, of bankrupt firms, of crumbling cities, or of nations or regions which lose their comparative advantage.

But a closer look finds a silver lining behind this ruthlessness. With increased foreign competition, deregulation of many industries, and labor unions at their weakest since the Great Depression, labor and product markets have nowadays become increasingly competitive. With more vigorous competition, America's macroeconomic performance has perceptibly improved. Compared to a decade ago, the United States produces $1.5 trillion more output and has provided 17 million net new jobs. Money wage growth and price inflation have remained low and stable even as the unemployment rate fell below what most economists thought was its lowest sustainable rate. The labor force in our ruthless economy may feel cowed and anxious. But, from a macroeconomic point of view, meekness is a virtue because it keeps inflation low, allows a lower overall unemployment rate, and, most significantly, shields the least skilled workers from being frozen out of any employment at all.

Europe—the cradle of the welfare state—models itself as the "compassionate economy" and is a stark contrast. European workers of the 1990s are "protected" by strong unions, generous income-support systems, high minimum wages, and many restraints on hiring and firing. But weakening of market forces has led to hardening of the economic arteries as microeconomic generosity led to macroeconomic inefficiency. With growing inflexibility of its welfare

---

[1] John Maynard Keynes, "Economic Possibilities for Our Grandchildren," reprinted in his *Essays in Persuasion* (Macmillan, London, 1933), with minor editing.

and labor market institutions, the lowest sustainable unemployment rate in Europe has climbed steadily over the last three decades. By 1997, the European unemployment rate was twice that in the United States. Many European politicians are asking themselves whether they should in some degree emulate the ruthless competitiveness of the American model.

But before applauding the American successes too loudly, recall that competitive markets not only giveth much but also taketh away. Not everybody can be the "master of the universe" in the competitive Darwinian economy. The growing inequality of income in America—and the large numbers of people who are locked into dead-end jobs and living in run-down neighborhoods—is a sober reminder of the harsh inequalities possible in a market economy.

In the end, we render two cheers for the market, but not three. The last cheer is reserved for that day when everyone has the opportunity for a good job, an adequate income, and a safe environment. These are worthy goals for economics and for economists in the next 50 years!

GLOSSARY OF TERMS[1]

A

Ability-to-pay principle (of taxation). The principle that one's tax burden should depend upon the ability to pay as measured by income or wealth. This principle does not specify *how much* more those who are better off should pay.

Absolute advantage (in international trade). The ability of Country A to produce a commodity more efficiently (i.e., with greater output per unit of input) than Country B. Possession of such an absolute advantage does not necessarily mean

that A can export this commodity to B successfully. Country B may still have the comparative advantage.

Accelerator principle. The theory that a change in the rate of output induces a change in the demand for investment in the same direction.

Actual, cyclical, and structural budget. The **actual budget** deficit or surplus is the amount recorded in a given year. This is composed of the **structural budget**, which calculates what government revenues, expenditures, and deficits would be if the economy were operating at potential output, and the **cyclical budget**, which measures the effect of the business cycle on the budget.

Adaptive expectations. See **expectations**.

Adjustable peg. An exchange-rate system in which countries maintain a fixed or "pegged" exchange rate with respect to other currencies. This exchange rate is subject to periodic adjustment, however, when it becomes too far out of line with fundamental forces. This system was used for major currencies during the Bretton Woods period

from 1944 to 1971 and is called the **Bretton Woods system**.

Administered (or **inflexible**) **prices.** A term referring to prices which are set and kept constant for a period of time and over a series of transactions. (In contrast, refer to **price flexibility**.)

Adverse selection. A type of market failure in which those people with the highest risk are most likely to buy insurance. More broadly, adverse selection encompasses situations in which sellers and buyers have different information about a product, such as in the market for used cars.

Aggregate demand. Total planned or desired spending in the economy during a given period. It is determined by the aggregate price level and influenced by domestic investment, net exports, government spending, the consumption function, and the money supply.

Aggregate demand (*AD*) curve. The curve showing the relationship between the quantity of goods and services that people are willing to buy and the aggregate price level, other things equal. As with any demand curve, important variables lie behind the aggregate demand

---

[1] Words in bold type within definitions appear as separate entries in the glossary. For a more detailed discussion of particular terms, the text will provide a useful starting point. More complete discussions are contained in Douglas Greenwald, ed., *The McGraw-Hill Encyclopedia of Economics* (McGraw-Hill, New York, 1994); David W. Pearce, *Macmillan Dictionary of Modern Economics,* rev. ed. (Macmillan, London, 1992); *International Encyclopedia of the Social Sciences* (Collier and Macmillan, New York, 1968); and John Eatwell, Murray Milgate, and Peter Newman, *The New Palgrave: A Dictionary of Economics* (Macmillan, London, 1987), four volumes.

435

curve, e.g., government spending, exports, and the money supply.

Aggregate supply. The total value of goods and services that firms would willingly produce in a given time period. Aggregate supply is a function of available inputs, technology, and the price level.

Aggregate supply (*AS*) curve. The curve showing the relationship between the output firms would willingly supply and the aggregate price level, other things equal. The *AS* curve tends to be vertical at potential output in the very long run but may be relatively flat in the short run.

Allocative efficiency. A situation in which no reorganization or trade could raise the utility or satisfaction of one individual without lowering the utility or satisfaction of another individual. Under certain limited conditions, perfect competition leads to allocative efficiency. Also called **Pareto efficiency**.

Antitrust legislation. Laws prohibiting monopolization, restraints of trade, and collusion among firms to raise prices or inhibit competition.

Appreciation (of a currency). See **depreciation** (of a currency).

Appropriable. Describes a resource for which the owner can capture the full economic value. In a well-functioning competitive market, appropriable resources are usually priced and allocated efficiently. Also refer to **inappropriable**.

Arbitrage. The purchase of a good or asset in one market for immediate resale in another market in order to profit from a price discrepancy. Arbitrage is an important force in eliminating price discrepancies, thereby making markets function more efficiently.

Asset. A physical property or intangible right that has economic value. Important examples are plant, equipment, land, patents, copyrights, and financial instruments such as money or bonds.

Asset demand for money. See **demand for money**.

Automatic (or **built-in**) **stabilizers.** The property of a government tax and spending system that cushions income changes in the private sector. Examples include unemployment compensation and progressive income taxes.

Average cost. Refer to **cost, average**.

Average cost curve, long-run (*LRAC*, or *LAC*). The graph of the minimum average cost of producing a commodity for each level of output, assuming that technology and input prices are given but that the producer is free to choose the optimal size of plants.

Average cost curve, short-run (*SRAC*, or *SAC*). The graph of the minimum average cost of producing a commodity, for each level of output, using the given state of technology, input prices, and existing plant.

Average fixed cost. Refer to **cost, average fixed**.

Average product. Total product or output divided by the quantity of one of the inputs. Hence, the average product of labor is defined as total product divided by the amount of labor input, and similarly for other inputs.

Average propensity to consume. See **marginal propensity to consume**.

Average revenue. Total revenue divided by total number of units sold—i.e., revenue per unit. Average revenue is generally equal to price.

Average variable cost. Refer to **cost, average variable**.

B

Balance of international payments. A statement showing all of a nation's transactions with the rest of the world for a given period. It includes purchases and sales of goods and services, gifts, government transactions, and capital movements.

Balance of trade. The part of a nation's balance of payments that deals with merchandise (or visible) imports or exports, including such items as foodstuffs, capital goods, and automobiles. When services and other current items are included, this measures the **balance on current account**.

Balance on current account. See **balance of trade**.

Balance sheet. A statement of a firm's financial position as of a given date, listing **assets** in one column, **liabilities** plus **net worth** in the other. Each item is listed at its actual or estimated money value. Totals of the two columns must balance because net worth is defined as assets minus liabilities.

Balanced budget. Refer to **budget, balanced**.

Bank, commercial. A financial intermediary whose prime distinguishing feature until recently was that it accepts checkable deposits. All financial institutions that hold savings and checkable deposits are called depository institutions.

Bank money. Money created by banks, particularly the checking accounts (part of M_1) that are generated by a multiple expansion of bank reserves.

Bank reserves. Refer to **reserves, bank**.

Barriers to entry. Factors that impede entry into a market and thereby reduce the amount of competition or the number of producers in an industry. Important examples are legal barriers, regulation, and product differentiation.

Barter. The direct exchange of one good for another without using anything as money or as a medium of exchange.

Benefit principle (of taxation). The principle that people should be taxed in proportion to the benefits they receive from government programs.

Bond. An interest-bearing certificate issued by a government or corporation, promising to repay a sum of money (the principal) plus interest at specified dates in the future.

Break-even point (in macroeconomics). For an individual, family, or community, that level of income at which 100 percent is spent on consumption (i.e., the point where there is neither saving nor dissaving). Positive saving begins at higher income levels.

Bretton Woods system. See **adjustable peg**.

Broad money. A measure of the money supply (also known as M_2) that includes transactions money (or M_1) as well as savings accounts in banks and similar assets that are very close substitutes for transactions money.

Budget. An account, usually for a year, of the planned expenditures and the expected receipts. For a government, the receipts are tax revenues.

Budget, balanced. A budget in which total expenditures just equal total receipts (excluding any receipts from borrowing).

Budget constraint. See **budget line**.

Budget deficit. For a government, the excess of total expenditures over total receipts, with borrowing not included among receipts. This difference (the deficit) is ordinarily financed by borrowing.

Budget, government. A statement showing, for the government in question, planned expenditures and revenues for some period (typically 1 year).

Budget line. A line indicating the combination of commodities that a consumer can buy with a given income at a given set of prices. Also sometimes called the **budget constraint**.

Budget surplus. Excess of government revenues over government spending; the opposite of budget deficit.

Built-in stabilizers. See **automatic stabilizers**.

Business cycles. Fluctuations in total national output, income, and employment, usually lasting for a period of 2 to 10 years, marked by widespread and simultaneous expansion or contraction in many sectors of the economy. In modern macroeconomics, business cycles are said to occur when actual GDP rises relative to potential GDP (expansion) or falls relative to potential GDP (contraction or recession).

C

$C + I$, $C + I + G$, or $C + I + G + X$ **schedule.** A schedule showing the planned or desired levels of aggregate demand for each level of GDP, or the graph on which this schedule is depicted. The schedule includes consumption (C), investment (I), government spending on goods and services (G), and net exports (X).

Capital (capital goods, capital equipment). (1) In economic theory, one of the triad of productive inputs (land, labor, and capital). Capital consists of durable produced goods that are in turn used in production. (2) In accounting and finance, "capital" means the total amount of money subscribed by the shareholder-owners of a corporation, in return for which they receive shares of the company's stock.

Capital consumption allowance. See **depreciation** (of an asset).

Capital deepening. In economic-growth theory, an increase in the capital-labor ratio. (Contrast with **capital widening**.)

Capital gains. The rise in value of a capital asset, such as land or common stocks, the gain being the difference between the sales price and the purchase price of the asset.

Capital markets. Markets in which financial resources (money, bonds, stocks) are traded. These, along with **financial intermediaries**, are institutions through which saving in the economy is transferred to investors.

Capital-output ratio. In economic-growth theory, the ratio of the total capital stock to annual GDP.

Capital widening. A rate of growth in real capital stock just equal to the growth of the labor force (or of population), so that the ratio between total capital and total labor remains unchanged. (Contrast with **capital deepening**.)

Capitalism. An economic system in which most property (land and capital) is privately owned. In such an economy, private markets are the primary vehicles used to allocate resources and generate incomes.

Cardinal utility. See **ordinal utility**.

Cartel. An organization of independent firms producing similar products that work together to raise prices and restrict output. Cartels are illegal under U.S. antitrust laws.

Central bank. A government-established agency (in the United States, the Federal Reserve System) responsible for controlling the nation's money supply and credit conditions and for supervising the financial system, especially commercial banks and other depository institutions.

Change in demand vs. change in quantity demanded. A change in the quantity buyers want to purchase, prompted by any reason other than a change in price (e.g., increase in income, change in tastes, etc.), is a "change in demand." In graphical terms, it is a shift of the demand curve. If, in contrast, the decision to buy more or less is prompted by a change in the good's price, then it is a "change in quantity demanded." In graphical terms, a change in quantity demanded is a movement along an unchanging demand curve.

Change in supply vs. change in quantity supplied. This distinction is the same for supply as for demand, so see **change in demand vs. change in quantity demanded**.

Checking accounts (or **bank money**). A deposit in a commercial bank or other financial intermediary upon which checks can be written and which is therefore transactions money (or M_1), also called "checkable deposits." Checkable deposits are the largest component of M_1.

Chicago School of Economics. A group of economists (among whom Henry Simons, F. A. von Hayek, and Milton Friedman have been the most prominent) who believe that competitive markets free of government intervention will lead to the most efficient operation of the economy.

Classical approach. See **classical economics**.

Classical economics. The predominant school of economic thought prior to the appearance of Keynes' work; founded by Adam Smith in 1776. Other major figures who followed him include David Ricardo, Thomas Malthus, and John Stuart Mill. By and large, this school believed that economic laws (particularly individual self-interest and competition) determine prices and factor rewards and that the price system is the best possible device for resource allocation.

Classical theories (in macroeconomics). Theories emphasizing the self-correcting forces in the economy. In the classical approach, there is generally full employment and policies to stimulate aggregate demand have no impact upon output.

Clearing market. A market in which prices are sufficiently flexible to equilibrate supply and demand very quickly. In markets that clear, there is no rationing, unemployed resources, or excess demand or supply. In practice, this is thought to apply to many commodity and financial markets but not to labor or many product markets.

Closed economy. See **open economy**.

Coase theorem. A view (not actually a theorem) put forth by Ronald Coase that externalities or economic inefficiencies will under certain conditions be corrected by bargaining between the affected parties.

Collective bargaining. The process of negotiations between a group of workers (usually a union) and their employer. Such bargaining leads to an agreement about wages, fringe benefits, and working conditions.

Collusion. Agreement between different firms to cooperate by raising prices, dividing markets, or otherwise restraining competition.

Collusive oligopoly. A market structure in which a small number of firms (i.e., a few oligopolists) collude and jointly make their decisions. When they succeed in maximizing their joint profits, the price and quantity in the market closely approach those prevailing under monopoly.

Command economy. A mode of economic organization in which the key economic functions—*what, how,* and *for whom*—are principally determined by government directive. Sometimes called a "centrally planned economy."

Commodity money. Money with **intrinsic value**; also, the use of some commodity (cattle, beads, etc.) as money.

Common stock. The financial instrument representing ownership and, generally, voting rights in a corporation. A certain share of a company's stock gives the owner title to that fraction of the votes, net earnings, and assets of the corporation.

Communism. A communist economic system (also called Soviet-style central planning) is one in which the state owns and controls the means of production, particularly industrial capital. These economies are also characterized by extensive central planning, with the state setting many prices, output levels, and other important economic variables.

Comparative advantage (in international trade). The law of comparative advantage says that a nation should specialize in producing and exporting those commodities which it can produce at *relatively* lower cost, and that it should import those goods for which it is a *relatively* high-cost producer. Thus it is a comparative advantage, not an absolute advantage, that should dictate trade patterns.

Compensating differentials. Differences in wage rates among jobs that serve to offset or compensate for the nonmonetary differences of the jobs. For example, unpleasant jobs that require isolation for many months in Alaska pay wages much higher than those for similar jobs nearer to civilization.

Competition, imperfect. Refers to markets in which perfect competition does not hold because at least one seller (or buyer) is large enough to affect the market price and therefore faces a downward-sloping demand (or supply) curve. Imperfect competition refers to any kind of imperfection—pure **monopoly, oligopoly,** or **monopolistic competition**.

Competition, perfect. Refers to markets in which no firm or consumer is large enough to affect the market price. This situation arises where (1) the number of sellers and buyers is very large and (2) the products offered by sellers are homogeneous (or indistinguishable). Under such conditions, each firm faces a horizontal (or perfectly elastic) demand curve.

Competitive equilibrium. The balancing of supply and demand in a market or economy characterized by **perfect competition**. Because perfectly competitive sellers and buyers individually have no power to influence the market, price will move to the point at which it equals both marginal cost and marginal utility.

Competitive market. See **competition, perfect**.

Complements. Two goods which "go together" in the eyes of consumers (e.g., left shoes and right shoes). Goods are **substitutes** when they compete with each other (as do gloves and mittens).

Compound interest. Interest computed on the sum of all past interest earned as well as on the principal. For example, suppose $100 (the principal) is deposited in an account earning 10 percent interest compounded annually. At the end of year 1, interest of $10 is earned. At the end of year 2, the interest payment is $11, $10 on the original principal and $1 on the interest—and so on in future years.

Concentration ratio. The percentage of an industry's total output accounted for by the largest firms. A typical measure is the **four-firm concentration ratio**, which is the fraction of output accounted for by the four largest firms.

Conglomerate. A large corporation producing and selling a variety of unrelated goods (e.g., some cigarette companies have expanded into such unrelated areas as liquor, car rental, and movie production).

Conglomerate merger. See **merger**.

Constant returns to scale. See **returns to scale**.

Consumer price index (CPI). A price index that measures the cost of a fixed basket of consumer goods in which the weight assigned to each commodity is the share of expenditures on that commodity by urban consumers in 1982–1984.

Consumer surplus. The difference between the amount that a consumer would be willing to pay for a commodity and the amount actually paid. This difference arises because the marginal utilities (in dollar terms) of all but the last unit exceed the price. Under certain conditions, the money value of consumer surplus can be measured (using a demand-curve diagram) as the area under the demand curve but above the price line.

Consumption. In macroeconomics, the total spending, by individuals or a nation, on consumer goods during a given period. Strictly speaking, consumption should apply only to those goods totally used, enjoyed, or "eaten up" within that period. In practice, consumption expenditures include all consumer goods bought, many of which last well beyond the period in question—e.g., furniture, clothing, and automobiles.

Consumption function. A schedule relating total consumption to personal disposable income (DI). Total wealth and other variables are also frequently assumed to influence consumption.

Consumption-possibility line. See **budget line**.

Cooperative equilibrium. In game theory, an outcome in which the parties act in unison to find strategies that will optimize their joint payoffs.

Corporate income tax. A tax levied on the annual net income of a corporation.

Corporation. The dominant form of business organization in modern capitalist economies. A corporation is a firm owned by individuals or other corporations. It has the same rights to buy, sell, and make contracts as a person would have. It is legally separate from those who own it and has "limited liability."

Correlation. The degree to which two variables are systematically associated with each other.

Cost, average. Total cost (refer to **cost, total**) divided by the number of units produced.

Cost, average fixed. Fixed cost divided by the number of units produced.

Cost, average variable. Variable cost (refer to **cost, variable**) divided by the number of units produced.

Cost, fixed. The cost a firm would incur even if its output for the period in question were zero. Total fixed cost is made up of such individual contractual costs as interest payments, mortgage payments, and directors' fees.

Cost, marginal. The extra cost (or the increase in total cost) required to produce 1 extra unit of output (or the reduction in total cost from producing 1 unit less).

Cost, minimum. The lowest attainable cost per unit (whether average, variable, or marginal). Every point on an average cost curve is a minimum in the sense that it is the best the firm can do with respect to cost for the output which that point represents. Minimum average cost is the lowest point, or points, on that curve.

Cost-push inflation. Inflation originating on the supply side of markets from a sharp increase in costs. In the aggregate supply-and-demand framework, cost-push is illustrated as an upward shift of the AS curve. Also called **supply-shock** inflation.

Cost, total. The minimum attainable total cost, given a particular level of technology and set of input prices. Short-run total cost takes existing plant and other fixed costs as given. Long-run total cost is the cost that would be incurred if the firm had complete flexibility with respect to all inputs and decisions.

Cost, variable. A cost that varies with the level of output, such as raw materials, labor, and fuel costs. Variable costs equal total cost minus fixed cost.

Crawling (or **sliding**) **peg.** A technique for managing a nation's exchange rate that allows the exchange rate (or the bands around the rate) to "crawl" up or down by a small amount each day or week (say, 0.25 percent per week).

Credit. (1) In monetary theory, the use of someone else's funds in exchange for a promise to pay (usually with interest) at a later date. The major examples are short-term loans from a bank, credit extended by suppliers, and commercial paper. (2) In balance-of-payments accounting, an item such as exports that earns a country foreign currency.

Cross elasticity of demand. A measure of the influence of a change in one good's price on the demand for another good. More precisely, the cross elasticity of demand equals the percentage change in demand for good A when the price of good B changes by 1 percent, assuming other variables are held constant.

Crowding-out hypothesis. The proposition that government spending or government deficits reduce the amount of business investment.

Currency. Coins and paper money.

Currency appreciation (or **depreciation**). See **depreciation** (of a currency).

Current account. See **balance of trade**.

Cyclical budget. See **actual, cyclical,** and **structural budget**.

Cyclical unemployment. See **frictional unemployment**.

D

Deadweight loss. The loss in real income or consumer and producer surplus that arises because of monopoly, tariffs and quotas, taxes, or other distortions. For example, when a monopolist raises its price, the loss in consumer satisfaction is more than the gain in the monopolist's revenue—the difference being the deadweight loss to society due to monopoly.

Debit. (1) An accounting term signifying an increase in assets or decrease in liabilities. (2) In balance-of-payments accounting, a debit is an item such as imports that reduces a country's stock of foreign currencies.

Decreasing returns to scale. See **returns to scale**.

Deficit spending. Government expenditures on goods and services and transfer payments in excess of its receipts from taxation and other revenue sources. The difference must be financed by borrowing from the public.

Deflating (of economic data). The process of converting "nominal" or current-dollar variables into "real" terms. This is accomplished by dividing current-dollar variables by a **price index**.

Deflation. A fall in the general level of prices.

Demand curve (or **demand schedule**). A schedule or curve showing the quantity of a good that buyers would purchase at each price, other things equal. Normally a demand curve has price on the vertical or Y axis and quantity demanded on the horizontal or X axis. Also see **change in demand vs. change in quantity demanded**.

Demand for money. A summary term used by economists to ex-

plain why individuals and businesses hold money balances. The major motivations for holding money are (1) **transactions demand**, signifying that people need money to purchase things, and (2) **asset demand**, relating to the desire to hold a very liquid, risk-free asset.

Demand-pull inflation. Price inflation caused by an excess demand for goods in general, caused, for example, by a major increase in aggregate demand. Often contrasted with **cost-push inflation**.

Demography. The study of the behavior of a population.

Depreciation (of an asset). A decline in the value of an asset. In both business and national accounts, depreciation is the dollar estimate of the extent to which capital has been "used up" or worn out over the period in question. Also termed **capital consumption allowance** in national-income accounting.

Depreciation (of a currency). A nation's currency is said to depreciate when it declines relative to other currencies. For example, if the foreign exchange rate of the dollar falls from 6 to 4 French francs per U.S. dollar, the dollar's value has fallen, and the dollar has undergone a depreciation. The opposite of a depreciation is an **appreciation**, which occurs when the foreign exchange rate of a currency rises.

Depression. A prolonged period characterized by high unemployment, low output and investment, depressed business confidence, falling prices, and widespread business failures. A milder form of business downturn is a **recession**, which has many of the features of a depression to a lesser extent; the precise definition of a recession today is a period in which real GNP declines for at least two consecutive calendar quarters.

Derived demand. The demand for a factor of production that results (is "derived") from the demand for the final good to which it contributes. Thus the demand for tires is derived from the demand for automobile transportation.

Devaluation. A decrease in the official price of a nation's currency, as expressed in the currencies of other nations or in terms of gold. Thus, when the official price of the dollar was lowered with respect to gold in 1971, the dollar was devalued. The opposite of devaluation is **revaluation**, which occurs when a nation raises its official foreign exchange rate relative to gold or other currencies.

Developing country. Same as **less-developed country**.

Differentiated products. Products which compete with each other and are close substitutes but are not identical. Differences may be manifest in the product's function, appearance, location, quality, or other attributes.

Diminishing marginal utility, law of. The law which says that, as more and more of any one commodity is consumed, its marginal utility declines.

Diminishing returns, law of. A law stating that the additional output from successive increases of one input will eventually diminish when other inputs are held constant. Technically, the law is equivalent to saying that the marginal product of the varying input declines after a point.

Direct taxes. Those levied directly on individuals or firms, including taxes on income, labor earnings, and profits. Direct taxes contrast with **indirect taxes**, which are those levied on goods and services and thus only indirectly on people, and which include sales taxes and taxes on property, alcohol, imports, and gasoline.

Discount rate. (1) The interest rate charged by a Federal Reserve Bank (the central bank) on a loan that it makes to a commercial bank. (2) The rate used to calculate the present value of some asset.

Discounting (of future income). The process of converting future income into an equivalent present value. This process takes a future dollar amount and reduces it by a discount factor that reflects the appropriate interest rate. For example, if someone promises you $121 in 2 years, and the appropriate interest rate or discount rate is 10 percent per year, then we can calculate the present value by discounting the $121 by a discount factor of $(1.10)^2$. The rate at which future incomes are discounted is called the **discount rate**.

Discrimination. Differences in earnings that arise because of personal characteristics that are unrelated to job performance, especially those related to gender, race, ethnicity, sexual orientation, or religion.

Disequilibrium. The state in which an economy is not in **equilibrium**. This may arise when shocks (to income or prices) have shifted demand or supply schedules but the market price (or quantity) has not yet adjusted fully. In macroeconomics, unemployment is often thought to stem from market disequilibria.

Disinflation. The process of reducing a high inflation rate. For example, the deep recession of 1980–1983 led to a sharp disinflation over that period.

Disposable income (*DI*). Roughly, take-home pay, or that part of the total national income that is available to households for consumption or saving. More precisely, it is equal to GNP less all taxes, business saving, and depreciation plus government and other transfer payments and government interest payments.

Disposable personal income. Same as **disposable income**.

Dissaving. Negative saving; spending more on consumption goods during a period than the disposable income available for that period (the difference being financed by borrowing or drawing on past saving).

Distribution. In economics, the manner in which total output and income is distributed among individuals or factors (e.g., the distribution of income between labor and capital).

Division of labor. A method of organizing production whereby each worker specializes in part of the productive process. Specialization of labor yields higher total output because labor can become more skilled at a particular task and because specialized machinery can be introduced to perform more carefully defined subtasks.

Dominant equilibrium. See **dominant strategy**.

Dominant strategy. In game theory, a situation where one player has a best strategy no matter what strategy the other player follows. When all players have a dominant strategy, we say that the outcome is a **dominant equilibrium**.

Downward-sloping demand, law of. The rule that says that when the price of some commodity falls, consumers will purchase more of that good when other things are held equal.

Duopoly. A market structure in which there are only two sellers. (Compare with **oligopoly**.)

Duopoly price war. A situation where the market is supplied by two firms which are engaged in an economic warfare of continual undercutting of each other's price.

E

Easy-money policy. The central-bank policy of increasing the money supply to reduce interest rates. The purpose of such a policy is to increase investment, thereby raising GDP. (Contrast with **tight-money policy**.)

Econometrics. The branch of economics that uses the methods of statistics to measure and estimate quantitative economic relationships.

Economic good. A good that is scarce relative to the total amount of it that is desired. It must therefore be rationed, usually by charging a positive price.

Economic growth. An increase in the total output of a nation over time. Economic growth is usually measured as the annual rate of increase in a nation's real GDP (or real potential GDP).

Economic regulation. See **regulation**.

Economic rent. Refer to **rent, economic**.

Economic surplus. A term denoting the excess in total satisfaction or utility over the costs of production. Equals the sum of consumer surplus (the excess of consumer satisfaction over total value of purchases) and producer surplus (the excess of producer revenues over costs).

Economics of information. Analysis of economic situations that involve information as a commodity. Because information is costly to produce but cheap to reproduce, market failures are common in markets for informational goods and services such as invention, publishing, and software.

Economies of scale. Increases in productivity, or decreases in average cost of production, that arise from increasing all the factors of production in the same proportion.

Economies of scope. Economies of producing multiple goods or services. Thus economies of scope exist if it is cheaper to produce good X and good Y together rather than separately.

Effective tax rate. Total taxes paid as a percentage of the total income or other tax base.

Efficiency. Absence of waste, or the use of economic resources that produces the maximum level of satisfaction possible with the given inputs and technology. A shorthand expression for **allocative efficiency**.

Efficiency-wage theory. According to this theory, higher wages lead to higher productivity. This occurs because with higher wages workers are healthier, have higher morale, or have lower turnover.

Efficient market. A market where all new information is quickly understood by market participants and becomes immediately incorporated into market prices. In economics, efficient-market theory holds that all currently available information is already incorporated into the price of common stocks (or other assets).

Elasticity. A term widely used in economics to denote the responsiveness of one variable to changes in another. Thus the elasticity of X with respect to Y means the percentage change in X for every 1 percent change in Y. For especially important examples, see **price elasticity of demand** and **price elasticity of supply**.

Employed. According to official U.S. definitions, persons are employed if they perform any paid work, or if they hold jobs but are absent because of illness, strike, or vacations. Also see **unemployment**.

Equal-cost line. A line in a graph showing the various possible combinations of factor inputs that can be purchased with a given quantity of money.

Equal-product curve (or **isoquant**). A line in a graph showing the various possible combinations of factor inputs which will yield a given quantity of output.

Equilibrium. The state in which an economic entity is at rest or in which the forces operating on the entity are in balance so that there is no tendency for change.

Equilibrium (for a business firm). That position or level of output in which the firm is maximizing its profit, subject to any constraints it may face, and therefore has no incentive to change its output or price level. In the standard theory of the firm, this means that the firm has chosen an output at which marginal revenue is just equal to marginal cost.

Equilibrium (for the individual consumer). That position in which the consumer is maximizing utility, i.e., has chosen the bundle of goods which, given income and prices, best satisfies the consumer's wants.

Equilibrium, competitive. Refer to **competitive equilibrium**.

Equilibrium, general. Refer to **general-equilibrium analysis**.

Equilibrium, macroeconomic. A GDP level at which intended aggregate demand equals intended aggregate supply. At the equilibrium, desired consumption (C), government expenditures (G), investment (I), and net exports (X) just equal the quantity that businesses wish to sell at the going price level.

Equimarginal principle. Principle for deciding the allocation of income among different consumption goods. Under this principle, a consumer's utility is maximized by choosing the consumption bundle such that the marginal utility per dollar spent is equal for all goods.

Exchange rate. See **foreign exchange rate**.

Exchange-rate system. The set of rules, arrangements, and institutions under which payments are made among nations. Historically, the most important exchange-rate systems have been the gold exchange standard, the Bretton Woods system, and today's flexible-exchange-rate system.

Excise tax vs. sales tax. An **excise tax** is one levied on the purchase of a specific commodity or group of commodities (e.g., alcohol or tobacco). A **sales tax** is one levied on all commodities with only a few specific exclusions (e.g., all purchases except food).

Exclusion principle. A criterion by which public goods are distinguished from private goods. When a producer sells a commodity to person A and can easily exclude B, C, D, etc., from enjoying the benefits of the commodity, the exclusion principle holds and the good is a private good. If, as in public health or national defense, people cannot easily be excluded from enjoying the benefits of the good's production, then the good has public-good characteristics.

Exogenous vs. induced variables. Exogenous variables are those determined by conditions outside the economy. They are contrasted with **induced variables**, which are determined by the internal workings of the economic system. Changes in the weather are exogenous; changes in consumption are often induced by changes in income.

Expectations. Views or beliefs about uncertain variables (such as future interest rates, prices, or tax rates). Expectations are said to be **rational** if they are not systematically wrong (or "biased") and use all available information. Expectations are said to be **adaptive** if people form their expectations on the basis of past behavior.

Expenditure multiplier. See **multiplier**.

Exports. Goods or services that are produced in the home country and sold to another country. These include merchandise trade (like cars), services (like transportation), and interest on loans and investments. **Imports** are simply flows in the opposite direction—into the home country from another country.

External diseconomies. Situations in which production or consumption imposes uncompensated costs on other parties. Steel factories that emit smoke and sulfurous fumes harm local property and public health, yet the injured parties are not paid for the damage. The pollution is an external diseconomy.

External economies. Situations in which production or consumption yields positive benefits to others without those others paying. A firm that hires a security guard scares thieves from the neighborhood, thus providing external security services. Together with external diseconomies, these are often referred to as **externalities**.

External variables. Same as **exogenous variables**.

Externalities. Activities that affect others for better or worse, without those others paying or being compensated for the activity. Externalities exist when private costs or benefits do not equal social costs or benefits. The two major species are **external economies** and **external diseconomies**.

F

Factors of production. Productive inputs, such as labor, land, and capital; the resources needed to produce goods and services. Also called **inputs**.

Fallacy of composition. The fallacy of assuming that what holds for individuals also holds for the group or the entire system.

Federal Reserve System. The **central bank** of the United States.

Fiat money. Money, like today's paper currency, without **intrinsic value** but decreed (by fiat) to be legal tender by the government. Fiat money is accepted only as long as people have confidence that it will be accepted.

Final good. A good that is produced for final use and not for resale or further manufacture. (Compare with **intermediate goods**.)

Financial economics. That branch of economics which analyzes how rational investors should invest their funds to attain their objectives in the best possible manner.

Financial intermediary. An institution that receives funds from savers and lends them to borrowers. These include depository institutions (such as commercial or savings banks) and nondepository institutions (such as money market mutual funds, brokerage houses, insurance companies, or pension funds).

Firm (business firm). The basic, private producing unit in an economy. It hires labor and buys other inputs in order to make and sell commodities.

Fiscal-monetary mix. Refers to the combination of fiscal and monetary policies used to influence macroeconomic activity. A tight-monetary–loose-fiscal policy will tend to encourage consumption and retard investment, while an easy-monetary–tight-fiscal policy will have the opposite effect.

Fiscal policy. A government's program with respect to (1) the purchase of goods and services and spending on transfer payments, and (2) the amount and type of taxes.

Fixed cost. Refer to **cost, fixed**.

Fixed exchange rate. See **foreign exchange rate**.

Flexible exchange rates. A system of foreign exchange rates among countries wherein the exchange rates are predominantly determined by private market forces (i.e., by supply and demand) without governments' setting and maintaining a particular pattern of exchange rates. Also sometimes called **floating exchange rates**. When the government refrains from any intervention in exchange markets, the system is called a pure flexible-exchange-rate system.

Floating exchange rates. See **flexible exchange rates**.

Flow vs. stock. A flow variable is one that has a time dimension or flows over time (like the flow through a stream). A stock variable is one that measures a quantity at a point of time (like the water in a lake). Income represents dollars per year and is thus a flow. Wealth as of December 1998 is a stock.

Foreign exchange. Currency (or other financial instruments) of different countries that allow one country to settle amounts owed to other countries.

Foreign exchange market. The market in which currencies of different countries are traded.

Foreign exchange rate. The rate, or price, at which one country's currency is exchanged for the currency of another country. For example, if you can buy 1.9 German marks for one U.S. dollar, then the exchange rate for the mark is 1.9. A country has a **fixed exchange rate** if it pegs its currency at a given exchange rate and stands ready to defend that rate. Exchange rates which are determined by market supply and demand are called **flexible exchange rates**.

Four-firm concentration ratio. See **concentration ratio**.

Fractional-reserve banking. A regulation in modern banking systems whereby financial institutions are legally required to keep a specified fraction of their deposits in the form of deposits with the central bank (or in vault cash).

Free goods. Those goods that are not **economic goods**. Like air or seawater, they exist in such large quantities that they need not be rationed out among those wishing to use them. Thus, their market price is zero.

Free trade. A policy whereby the government does not intervene in trading between nations by tariffs, quotas, or other means.

Frictional unemployment. Temporary unemployment caused by changes in individual markets. It takes time, for example, for new workers to search among different job possibilities; even experienced workers often spend a minimum period of unemployed time moving from one job to another. Frictional is thus distinct from **cyclical unemployment**, which results from a low level of aggregate demand in the context of sticky wages and prices.

Full employment. A term that is used in many senses. Historically, it was taken to be that level of employment at which no (or minimal) involuntary unemployment exists. Today, economists rely upon the concept of the **lowest sustainable rate of unemployment** (*LSUR*) to indicate the highest sustainable level of employment over the long run.

G

Gains from trade. Refers to the aggregate increase in welfare accruing from voluntary exchange. Equal to the sum of consumer surplus and gains in producer profits.

Galloping inflation. See **inflation**.

Game theory. An analysis of situations involving two or more decision makers with at least partially conflicting interests. It can be applied to the interaction of oligopolistic markets as well as to bargaining situations such as strikes or to conflicts such as games and war.

General-equilibrium analysis. Analysis of the equilibrium state for the economy as a whole in which the markets for all goods and services are simultaneously in equilibrium. By contrast, **partial-equilibrium analysis** concerns the equilibrium in a single market.

GDP deflator. The "price" of GDP, that is, the price index that measures the average price of the components in GDP relative to a base year.

GDP gap. The difference or gap between potential GDP and actual GDP.

GNP. See **gross national product**.

Gold standard. A system under which a nation (1) declares its currency unit to be equivalent to some fixed weight of gold, (2) holds gold reserves and will buy or sell gold freely at the price so proclaimed, and (3) puts no restriction on the export or import of gold.

Government debt. The total of government obligations in the form of bonds and shorter-term borrowings. Government debt held by the public excludes bonds held by quasi-governmental agencies such as the central bank.

Government expenditure multiplier. The increase in GDP resulting from an increase of $1 in government purchases.

Graduated income tax. See **income tax, personal**.

Gresham's Law. A law first attributed to Sir Thomas Gresham, adviser to Queen Elizabeth I of England, who stated in 1558 that "bad money drives out good"—i.e., if the public is suspicious of one component of the money supply, it will hoard the "good money" and try to pass off the "bad money" to someone else.

Gross domestic product, nominal (or **nominal GDP**). The value, at current market prices, of the total final output produced inside a country during a given year.

Gross domestic product, real (or **real GDP**). Nominal GDP corrected for inflation, i.e., real GDP = nominal GDP divided by the GDP deflator.

Gross national product, nominal (or nominal GNP). The value, at current market prices, of all final goods and services produced during a year by the factors owned by a nation.

Gross national product, real (or real GNP). Nominal GNP corrected for inflation, i.e., real GNP = nominal GNP divided by the GNP deflator.

Growth accounting. A technique for estimating the contribution of different factors to economic growth. Using marginal productivity theory, growth accounting decomposes the growth of output into the growth in labor, land, capital, education, technical knowledge, and other miscellaneous sources.

H

Hedging. A technique for avoiding a risk by making a counteracting transaction. For example, if a farmer produces wheat that will be harvested in the fall, the risk of price fluctuations can be offset, or hedged, by selling in the spring or summer the quantity of wheat that will be produced.

High-powered money. Same as **monetary base**.

Horizontal equity vs. vertical equity. **Horizontal equity** refers to the fairness or equity in treatment of persons in similar situations; the principle of horizontal equity states that those who are essentially equal should receive equal treatment. **Vertical equity** refers to the equitable treatment of those who are in different circumstances.

Horizontal integration. See **integration, vertical vs. horizontal**.

Horizontal merger. See **merger**.

Human capital. The stock of technical knowledge and skill embodied in a nation's work force, resulting from investments in formal education and on-the-job training.

Hyperinflation. See **inflation**.

I

Imperfect competition. Refer to **competition, imperfect**.

Imperfect competitor. Any firm that buys or sells a good in large enough quantities to be able to affect the price of that good.

Implicit-cost elements. Costs that do not show up as explicit money costs but nevertheless should be counted as such (such as the labor cost of the owner of a small store). Sometimes called **opportunity cost**, although "opportunity cost" has a broader meaning.

Imports. See **exports**.

Inappropriability. See **inappropriable**.

Inappropriable. Describes resources for which the individual cost of use is free, or less than the full social costs. These resources are characterized by the presence of externalities, and thus markets will allocate their use inefficiently from a social point of view.

Incidence (or tax incidence). The ultimate economic burden of a tax (as opposed to the legal requirement for payment). Thus a sales tax may be paid by a retailer, but it is likely that the incidence falls upon the consumer. The exact incidence of a tax depends on the price elasticities of supply and demand.

Income. The flow of wages, interest payments, dividends, and other receipts accruing to an individual or nation during a period of time (usually a year).

Income effect (of a price change). Change in the quantity demanded of a commodity because the change in its price has the effect of changing a consumer's real income. Thus it supplements the **substitution effect** of a price change.

Income elasticity of demand. The demand for any given good is influenced not only by the good's price but by buyers' incomes. Income elasticity measures this responsiveness. Its precise definition is percentage change in quantity demanded divided by percentage change in income. (Compare with **price elasticity of demand**.)

Income statement. A company's statement, covering a specified time period (usually a year), showing sales or revenue earned during that period, all costs properly charged against the goods sold, and the profit (net income) remaining after deduction of such costs. Also called a **profit-and-loss statement**.

Income tax, negative. Refer to **negative income tax**.

Income tax, personal. Tax levied on the income received by individuals in the form either of wages and salaries or income from property, such as rents, dividends, or interest. In the United States, personal income tax is **graduated,** meaning that people with higher incomes pay taxes at a higher average rate than people with lower incomes.

Income velocity of money. See **velocity of money**.

Incomes policy. A government policy that attempts directly to restrict wage and price changes in an effort to slow inflation. Such policies range from voluntary wage-price guidelines to outright legal control over wages, salaries, and prices.

Increasing returns to scale. See **returns to scale**.

Independent goods. Goods whose demands are relatively separate from each other. More precisely, goods A and B are independent when a change in the price of good A has no effect on the quantity demanded of good B, other things equal.

Indexing (or indexation). A mechanism by which wages, prices, and contracts are partially or wholly adjusted to compensate for changes in the general price level.

Indifference curve. A curve drawn on a graph whose two axes measure amounts of different goods consumed. Each point on one curve (indicating different combinations of the two goods) yields exactly thc samc level of satisfaction for a given consumer.

Indifference map. A graph showing a family of indifference curves for a consumer. In general, curves that lie farther northeast from the graph's origin represent higher levels of satisfaction.

Indirect taxes. See **direct taxes**.

Induced variables. See exogenous vs. induced variables.

Industry. A group of firms producing similar or identical products.

Inertial rate of inflation. A process of steady inflation that occurs when inflation is expected to persist and the ongoing rate of inflation is built into contracts and people's expectations.

Infant industry. In foreign-trade theory, an industry that has not had sufficient time to develop the experience or expertise to exploit the economies of scale needed to compete successfully with more mature industries producing the same commodity in other countries. Infant industries are often thought to need tariffs or quotas to protect them while they develop.

Inferior good. A good whose consumption goes down as income rises.

Inflation (or **inflation rate**). The inflation rate is the percentage of annual increase in a general price level. **Hyperinflation** is inflation at extremely high rates (say, 1000, 1 million, or even 1 billion percent a year). **Galloping inflation** is a rate of 50 or 100 or 200 percent annually. **Moderate inflation** is a price-level rise that does not dis-

tort relative prices or incomes severely.

Inflation targeting. The announcement of official target ranges for the inflation rate along with an explicit statement that low and stable inflation is the overriding goal of monetary policy. Inflation targeting in hard or soft varieties has been adopted in recent years by many industrial countries.

Innovation. A term particularly associated with Joseph Schumpeter, who meant by it (1) the bringing to market of a new and significantly different product, (2) the introduction of a new production technique, or (3) the opening up of a new market. (Contrast with **invention**.)

Inputs. Inputs (or **factors of production**) are commodities or services used by firms in their production processes.

Insurance. A system by which individuals can reduce their exposure to risk of large losses by spreading the risks among a large number of persons.

Integration, vertical vs. horizontal. The production process is one of stages—e.g., iron ore into steel ingots, steel ingots into rolled steel sheets, rolled steel sheets into an automobile body. **Vertical integration** is the combination in a single firm of two or more different stages of this process (e.g., iron ore with steel ingots). **Horizontal integration** is the combination in a single firm of different units that operate at the same stage of production.

Intellectual property rights. Laws governing patents, copyrights, trade secrets, electronic media, and other commodities comprised primarily of information. These laws generally provide the original creator the right to control and be compensated for reproduction of the work.

Interest. The return paid to those who lend money.

Interest rate. The price paid for borrowing money for a period of time, usually expressed as a percentage of the principal per year. Thus, if the interest rate is 10 percent per year, then $100 would be paid for a loan of $1000 for 1 year.

Intermediate goods. Goods that have undergone some manufacturing or processing but have not yet reached the stage of becoming final products. For example, steel and cotton yarn are intermediate goods.

International monetary system (also **international financial system**). The institutions under which payments are made for transactions that reach across national boundaries. A central policy issue concerns the arrangement for determining how foreign exchange rates are set and how governments can affect exchange rates.

Intervention. An activity in which a government buys or sells its currency in the foreign exchange market in order to affect its currency's exchange rate.

Intrinsic value (of money). The commodity value of a piece of money (e.g., the market value of the weight of copper in a copper coin).

Invention. The creation of a new product or discovery of a new production technique. (Distinguish from **innovation**.)

Investment. (1) Economic activity that forgoes consumption today with an eye to increasing output in the future. It includes tangible capital such as houses and intangible investments such as education. Net investment is the value of total investment after an allowance has been made for depreciation. Gross investment is investment without allowance for depreciation. (2) In finance terms, investment has an altogether different meaning and denotes the purchase of a security, such as a stock or a bond.

Investment demand (or **investment demand curve**). The schedule showing the relationship between the level of investment and the cost of capital (or, more specifically, the real interest rate); also, the graph of that relationship.

Invisible hand. A concept introduced by Adam Smith in 1776 to describe the paradox of a laissez-faire market economy. The invisible-hand doctrine holds that, with each participant pursuing his or her own private interest, a market system nevertheless works to the benefit of all as though a benevolent invisible hand were directing the whole process.

Involuntarily unemployed. See **unemployment**.

Iron law of wages. In the economic theories of Malthus and Marx, the theory that there is an inevitable tendency in capitalism for wages to be driven down to a subsistence level.

Isoquant. See **equal product curve**.

K

Keynesian economics. The body of thought developed by John Maynard Keynes holding that a capitalist system does not automatically tend toward a full-employment equilibrium. According to Keynes, the resulting underemployment equilibrium could be cured by fiscal or monetary policies to raise aggregate demand.

Keynesian school. See **Keynesian economics**.

L

Labor force. In official U.S. statistics, that group of people 16 years of age and older who are either employed or unemployed.

Labor-force participation rate. Ratio of those in the labor force to the entire population 16 years of age or older.

Labor productivity. See **productivity**.

Labor supply. The number of workers (or, more generally, the number of labor-hours) available to an economy. The principal determinants of labor supply are population, real wages, and social traditions.

Labor theory of value. The view, often associated with Karl Marx, that every commodity should be valued solely according to the quantity of labor required for its production.

Laissez-faire ("Leave us alone"). The view that government should interfere as little as possible in economic activity and leave decisions to the marketplace. As expressed by classical economists like Adam Smith, this view held that the role of government should be limited to maintenance of law and order, national defense, and provision of certain public goods that private business would not undertake (e.g., public health and sanitation).

Land. In classical and neoclassical economics, one of the three basic factors of production (along with labor and capital). More generally, land is taken to include land used for agricultural or industrial purposes as well as natural resources taken from above or below the soil.

Least-cost rule (of production). The rule that the cost of producing a specific level of output is minimized when the ratio of the marginal revenue product of each input to the price of that input is the same for all inputs.

Legal tender. Money that by law must be accepted as payment for debts. All U.S. coins and currency are legal tender, but checks are not.

Less-developed country (LDC). A country with a per capita income far below that of "developed" nations (the latter usually includes most nations of North America and Western Europe).

Liabilities. In accounting, debts or financial obligations owed to other firms or persons.

Libertarianism. An economic philosophy that emphasizes the importance of personal freedom in economic and political affairs; also sometimes called "liberalism." Libertarian writers, including Adam Smith in an earlier age and Milton Friedman and James Buchanan today, hold that people should be able to follow their own interests and desires and that government activities should be limited to guaranteeing contracts and to providing police and national defense, thereby allowing maximum personal freedom.

Limited liability. The restriction of an owner's loss in a business to the amount of capital that the owner has contributed to the company. Limited liability was an important factor in the rise of large corporations. By contrast, owners in partnerships and individual proprietorships generally have **unlimited liability** for the debts of those firms.

Long run. A term used to denote a period over which full adjustment to changes can take place. In microeconomics, it denotes the time over which firms can enter or leave an industry and the capital stock can be replaced. In macroeconomics, it is often used to mean the period over which all prices, wage contracts, tax rates, and expectations can fully adjust.

Long-run aggregate supply schedule. A schedule showing the relationship between output and the price level after all price and wage adjustments have taken place, and the *AS* curve is therefore vertical.

Lorenz curve. A graph used to show the extent of inequality of income or wealth.

Lowest sustainable rate of unemployment (or *LSUR*). The lowest sustainable unemployment rate (*LSUR*) is that rate at which upward and downward forces on price and wage inflation are in balance. At the *LSUR*, inflation is stable, with no tendency to show either accelerating or declining inflation. The *LSUR* is the lowest level of unemployment that can be attained for long without upward pressure on inflation. Equivalently, it is the unemployment rate at which the long-run **Phillips curve** is vertical.

Lump-of-labor fallacy. The mistaken idea that the total amount of work to be done in a society is fixed. It is false because labor markets can adjust through wage changes or migration to accommodate changes in the supply and demand for labor.

M

M_1, M_2. See **money supply**.

Macroeconomics. Analysis dealing with the behavior of the economy as a whole with respect to output, income, the price level, foreign trade, unemployment, and other aggregate economic variables. (Contrast with **microeconomics**.)

Malthusian theory of population growth. The hypothesis, first expressed by Thomas Malthus, that the "natural" tendency of population is to grow more rapidly than the food supply. Per capita food production would thus decline over time, thereby putting a check on population. In general, a view that population tends to grow more rapidly as incomes or living standards of the population rise.

Managed exchange rate. The most prevalent exchange-rate system today. In this system, a country occasionally intervenes to stabilize its currency but there is no fixed or announced parity.

Marginal cost. Refer to **cost, marginal**.

Marginal principle. The fundamental notion that people will maximize their income or profits when the marginal costs and marginal benefits of their actions are equal.

Marginal product (*MP*). The extra output resulting from 1 extra unit of a specified input when all other inputs are held constant. Sometimes called marginal physical product.

Marginal product theory of distribution. A theory of the distribution of income proposed by John B. Clark, according to which each productive input is paid according to its **marginal product**.

Marginal propensity to consume (*MPC*). The extra amount that people consume when they receive an extra dollar of disposable income. To be distinguished from the **average propensity to consume**, which is the ratio of total consumption to total disposable income.

Marginal propensity to import (*MPm*). In macroeconomics, the increase in the dollar value of imports resulting from each dollar increase in the value of GDP.

Marginal propensity to save (*MPS*). That fraction of an additional dollar of disposable income that is saved. Note that, by definition, $MPC + MPS = 1$.

Marginal revenue (*MR*). The additional revenue a firm would earn if it sold 1 extra unit of output. In perfect competition, *MR* equals price. Under imperfect competition, *MR* is less than price because, in order to sell the extra unit, the price must be reduced on all prior units sold.

Marginal revenue product (*MRP*) (of an input). Marginal revenue multiplied by marginal product. It is the extra revenue that would be brought in if a firm were to buy 1 extra unit of an input, put it to work, and sell the extra product it produced.

Marginal tax rate. For an income tax, the percentage of the last dollar of income paid in taxes. If a tax system is progressive, the marginal tax rate is higher than the average tax rate.

Marginal utility (*MU*). The additional or extra satisfaction yielded from consuming 1 additional unit of a commodity, with amounts of all other goods consumed held constant.

Market. An arrangement whereby buyers and sellers interact to determine the prices and quantities of a commodity. Some markets (such as the stock market or a flea market) take place in physical locations; other markets are conducted over the telephone or are organized by computers, and some markets now are organized on the Internet.

Market economy. An economy in which the *what, how,* and *for whom* questions concerning resource allocation are primarily determined by supply and demand in markets. In this form of economic organization, firms, motivated by the desire to maximize profits, buy inputs and produce and sell outputs. Households, armed with their factor incomes, go to markets and determine the demand for commodities. The interaction of firms' supply and households' demand then determines the prices and quantities of goods.

Market equilibrium. Same as **competitive equilibrium**.

Market failure. An imperfection in a price system that prevents an efficient allocation of resources. Important examples are **externalities** and **imperfect competition**.

Market power. The degree of control that a firm or group of firms has over the price and production decisions in an industry. In a monopoly, the firm has a high degree of market power; firms in perfectly competitive industries have no market power. **Concentration ratios** are the most widely used measures of market power.

Market share. That fraction of an industry's output accounted for by an individual firm or group of firms.

Markup pricing. The pricing method used by many firms in situations of imperfect competition; under this method they estimate average cost and then add some fixed percentage to that cost in order to reach the price they charge.

Marxism. The set of social, political, and economic doctrines developed by Karl Marx in the nineteenth century. As an economic theory, Marxism predicted that capitalism would collapse as a result of its own internal contradictions, especially its tendency to exploit the working classes. The conviction that workers would inevitably be oppressed under capitalism was based on the **iron law of wages**, which holds that wages would decline to subsistence levels.

Mean. In statistics, the same thing as "average." Thus for the numbers 1, 3, 6, 10, 20, the mean is 8.

Median. In statistics, the figure exactly in the middle of a series of numbers ordered or ranked from lowest to highest (e.g., incomes or examination grades). Thus for the numbers 1, 3, 6, 10, 20, the median is 6.

Mercantilism. A political doctrine emphasizing the importance of balance-of-payments surpluses as a device to accumulate gold. Proponents therefore advocated tight government control of economic policies, believing that laissez-faire policies might lead to a loss of gold.

Merchandise trade balance. See **trade balance**.

Merger. The acquisition of one corporation by another, which usually occurs when one firm buys the stock of another. Important examples are (1) **vertical mergers**, which occur when the two firms are at different stages of a production process (e.g., iron ore and steel), (2) **horizontal mergers**, which occur when the two firms produce in the same market (e.g., two automobile manufacturers), and (3) **conglomerate mergers**, which occur when the two firms operate in unrelated markets (e.g., shoelaces and oil refining).

Microeconomics. Analysis dealing with the behavior of individual elements in an economy—such as the determination of the price of a single product or the behavior of a single consumer or business firm. (Contrast with **macroeconomics**.)

Minimum cost. Refer to **cost, minimum**.

Mixed economy. The dominant form of economic organization in noncommunist countries. Mixed economies rely primarily on the price system for their economic organization but use a variety of government interventions (such as taxes, spending, and regulation) to handle macroeconomic instability and market failures.

Model. A formal framework for representing the basic features of a complex system by a few central relationships. Models take the form of graphs, mathematical equations, and computer programs.

Moderate inflation. See **inflation**.

Momentary run. A period of time that is so short that production is fixed.

Monetarism. A school of thought holding that changes in the money supply are the major cause of macroeconomic fluctuations. For the short run, this view holds that changes in the money supply are the primary determinant of changes in both real output and the price level. For the longer run, this holds that prices tend to move proportionally with the money supply. Monetarists often conclude that the best macroeconomic policy is one with a stable growth in the money supply.

Monetary base. The net monetary liabilities of the government that are held by the public. In the United States, the monetary base is equal to currency and bank reserves. Sometimes called **high-powered money**.

Monetary economy. An economy in which the trade takes place through a commonly accepted medium of exchange.

Monetary policy. The objectives of the central bank in exercising its control over money, interest rates, and credit conditions. The instruments of monetary policy are primarily open-market operations, reserve requirements, and the discount rate.

Monetary rule. The cardinal tenet of monetarist economic philosophy is the monetary rule which asserts that optimal monetary policy sets the growth of money supply at a fixed rate and holds to that rate through thick and thin.

Monetary transmission mechanism. In macroeconomics, the route by which changes in the supply of money are translated into changes in output, employment, prices, and inflation.

Monetary union. An arrangement by which several nations adopt a common currency as a unit of account and medium of exchange. The European Monetary Union is scheduled to adopt the "Euro" as the common currency in 1999.

Money. The means of payment or medium of exchange. For the items constituting money, see **money supply**.

Money demand schedule. The relationship between holdings of money and interest rates. As interest rates rise, bonds and other securities become more attractive, lowering the quantity of money demanded. See also **demand for money**.

Money funds. Shorthand expression for very liquid short-term financial instruments whose interest rates are not regulated. The major examples are money market mutual funds and commercial bank money market deposit accounts.

Money market. A term denoting the set of institutions that handle the purchase or sale of short-term credit instruments like Treasury bills and commercial paper.

Money supply. The narrowly defined money supply (M_1) consists of coins, paper currency, plus all demand or checking deposits; this is narrow, or transactions, money. The broadly defined supply (M_2) includes all items in M_1 plus certain liquid assets or near-monies— savings deposits, money market funds, and the like.

Money-supply effect. The relationship whereby a price rise operating on a fixed nominal money supply produces tight money and lowers aggregate spending.

Money-supply multiplier. The ratio of the increase in the money supply (or in deposits) to the increase in bank reserves. Generally, the money-supply multiplier is equal to the inverse of the required reserve ratio. For example, if the required reserve ratio is 0.125, then the money-supply multiplier is 8.

Money, velocity of. Refer to **velocity of money**.

Monopolistic competition. A market structure in which there are many sellers who are supplying goods that are close, but not perfect, substitutes. In such a market, each firm can exercise some effect on its product's price.

Monopoly. A market structure in which a commodity is supplied by a single firm. Also see **natural monopoly**.

Monopsony. The mirror image of monopoly: a market in which there is a single buyer; a "buyer's monopoly."

Moral hazard. A type of market failure in which the presence of in-surance against an insured risk increases the likelihood of the risky event occurring. For example, a car owner insured against auto theft may be careless about locking the car because the presence of insurance reduces the incentive to prevent the theft.

MPC. See **marginal propensity to consume**.

MPS. See **marginal propensity to save**.

Multiplier. A term in macroeconomics denoting the change in an induced variable (such as GDP or money supply) per unit of change in an external variable (such as government spending or bank reserves). The **expenditure multiplier** refers to the increase in GDP that would result from a $1 increase in expenditure (say, on investment).

Multiplier model. In macroeconomics, a theory developed by J. M. Keynes that emphasizes the importance of changes in autonomous expenditures (especially investment, government spending, and net exports) in determining changes in output and employment. Also see **multiplier**.

N

Nash equilibrium. In game theory, a set of strategies for the players where no player can improve his or her payoff given the other player's strategy. That is, given player A's strategy, player B can do no better, and given B's strategy, A can do no better. The Nash equilibrium is also sometimes called the **noncooperative equilibrium**.

National debt. Same as **government debt**.

National income and product accounts (NIPA). A set of accounts that measures the spending, income, and output of the entire nation for a quarter or a year.

National savings rate. Total saving, private and public, divided by net domestic product.

Natural monopoly. A firm or industry whose average cost per unit of production falls sharply over the entire range of its output, as for example in local electricity distribution. Thus a single firm, a monopoly, can supply the industry output more efficiently than can multiple firms.

"Near-money." Financial assets that are risk-free and so readily convertible into money that they are close to actually being money. Examples are money funds and Treasury bills.

Negative income tax. A plan for replacing current income-support programs (welfare, food stamps, etc.) with a unified program. Under such a plan, poor families would receive an income supplement and would have benefits reduced as their earnings increase.

Neoclassical model of growth. A theory or model used to explain long-term trends in economic growth of industrial economies. This model emphasizes the importance of capital deepening (i.e., a growing capital-labor ratio) and technological change in explaining the growth of potential real GDP.

Net domestic product (NDP). GDP less an allowance for depreciation of capital goods.

Net economic welfare (NEW). A measure of national output that corrects several limitations of the GDP measure.

Net exports. In the national product accounts, the value of exports of goods and services minus the value of imports of goods and services.

Net foreign investment. Net savings by a country abroad, also approximately equal to net exports.

Net investment. Gross investment minus depreciation of capital goods.

Net national product (NNP). GNP less an allowance for depreciation of capital goods.

Net worth. In accounting, total assets minus total liabilities.

New classical macroeconomics. This theory holds that (1) prices and wages are flexible and (2) people make forecasts in accordance with the rational expectations hypothesis. The main implication of this theory is the policy ineffectiveness theorem. See **rational expectations hypothesis** and **policy ineffectiveness theorem**.

NNP. See **net national product**.

Nominal GDP. See **gross domestic product, nominal**.

Nominal GNP. See **gross national product, nominal**.

Nominal (or money) interest rate. The **interest rate** paid on different assets. This represents a dollar return per year per dollar invested. Compare with the **real interest rate**, which represents the return per year in goods per unit of goods invested.

Noncooperative equilibrium. See **Nash equilibrium**.

Nonrenewable resources. Those natural resources, like oil and gas, that are essentially fixed in supply and whose regeneration is not quick enough to be economically relevant.

Normative vs. positive economics. Normative economics considers "what ought to be"—value judgments, or goals, of public policy. Positive economics, by contrast, is the analysis of facts and behavior in an economy, or "the way things are."

Not in the labor force. That part of the adult population that is neither working nor looking for work.

NOW (negotiable order of withdrawal) account. An interest-bearing checking account. See also **checking accounts**.

O

Okun's Law. The empirical relationship, discovered by Arthur Okun, between cyclical movements in GDP and unemployment. The law states that when actual GDP declines 2 percent relative to potential GDP, the unemployment rate increases by about 1 percentage point. (Earlier estimates placed the ratio at 3 to 1.)

Oligopoly. A situation of imperfect competition in which an industry is dominated by a small number of suppliers.

Open economy. An economy that engages in international trade (i.e., imports and exports) of goods and capital with other countries. A **closed economy** is one that has no imports or exports.

Open-economy multiplier. In an open economy, income leaks into imports as well as into savings. Therefore, the open-economy multiplier for investment or government expenditure is given by

$$\frac{\text{Open-economy}}{\text{multiplier}} = \frac{1}{MPS + MPm}$$

where MPS = marginal propensity to save and MPm = marginal propensity to import.

Open-market operations. The activity of a central bank in buying or selling government bonds to influence bank reserves, the money supply, and interest rates. If securities are bought, the money paid out by the central bank increases commercial-bank reserves, and the money supply increases. If securities are sold, the money supply contracts.

Opportunity cost. The value of the next best use (or opportunity) for an economic good, or the value of the sacrificed alternative. Thus, say that the best alternative use of the inputs employed to mine a ton of coal was to grow 10 bushels of wheat. The opportunity cost of a ton of coal is thus the 10 bushels of wheat that *could* have been produced but were not. Opportunity cost is particularly useful for valuing nonmarketed goods such as environmental health or safety.

Ordinal utility. A dimensionless utility measure used in demand theory. Ordinal utility enables one to state that A is preferred to B, but we cannot say by how much. That is, any two bundles of goods can be ranked relative to each other, but the absolute difference between bundles cannot be measured. This contrasts with **cardinal utility,** or dimensional utility, which is sometimes used in the analysis of behavior toward risk. An example of a cardinal measure comes when we say that a substance at 100 K (kelvin) is twice as hot as one at 50 K.

Other things constant. A phrase (sometimes stated "ceteris paribus") that signifies that a factor under consideration is changed while all other factors are held constant or unchanged. For example, a downward-sloping demand curve shows that the quantity demanded will decline as the price rises, as long as other things (such as incomes) are held constant.

Outputs. These are the various useful goods or services that are either consumed or used in further production.

P

Paradox of thrift. The principle, first proposed by John Maynard Keynes, that an attempt by a society to increase its saving may result in a reduction in the amount which it actually saves.

Paradox of value. The paradox that many necessities of life (e.g., water) have a low "market" value, while many luxuries (e.g., diamonds) with little "use" value have a high market price. It is explained by the fact that a price reflects not the total utility of a commodity but its marginal utility.

Pareto efficiency (or **Pareto optimality**).   See **allocative efficiency**.

Partial-equilibrium analysis.   Analysis concentrating on the effect of changes in an individual market, holding other things equal (e.g., disregarding changes in income).

Partnership.   An association of two or more persons to conduct a business which is not in corporate form and does not enjoy limited liability.

Patent.   An exclusive right granted to an inventor to control the use of an invention for, in the United States, a period of 20 years. Patents create temporary monopolies as a way of rewarding inventive activity and, like other intellectual property rights, are a tool for promoting invention among individuals or small firms.

Payoff table.   In game theory, a table used to describe the strategies and payoffs of a game with two or more players. The profits or utilities of the different players are the **payoffs**.

Payoffs.   See **payoff table**.

Perfect competition.   Refer to **competition, perfect**.

Personal income.   A measure of income before taxes have been deducted. More precisely, it equals disposable personal income plus net taxes.

Personal saving.   That part of income which is not consumed; in other words, the difference between disposable income and consumption.

Personal savings rate.   The ratio of personal saving to personal disposable income, in percent.

Phillips curve.   A graph first devised by A. W. Phillips, showing the tradeoff between unemployment and inflation. In modern mainstream macroeconomics, the downward-sloping "tradeoff" Phillips curve is generally held to be valid only in the short run; in the long run, the Phillips curve is usually thought to be vertical at the lowest sustainable rate of unemployment.

Policy ineffectiveness theorem.   A theorem which asserts that, with rational expectations and flexible prices and wages, anticipated government monetary or fiscal policy cannot affect real output or unemployment.

Portfolio theory.   An economic theory that describes how rational investors allocate their wealth among different financial asset—that is, how they put their wealth into a "portfolio."

Positive economics.   See **normative vs. positive economics**.

Post hoc **fallacy.**   From the Latin, *post hoc, ergo propter hoc*, which translates as "after this, therefore because of this." This fallacy arises when it is assumed that because event A precedes event B, it follows that A *causes* B.

Potential GDP.   High-employment GDP; more precisely, the maximum level of GDP that can be sustained with a given state of technology and population size without accelerating inflation. Today, it is generally taken to be equivalent to the level of output corresponding to the **lowest sustainable rate of unemployment**.

Potential output.   Same as **potential GDP**.

Poverty.   Today, the U.S. government defines the "poverty line" to be the minimum adequate standard of living.

PPF.   See **production-possibility frontier**.

Present value (of an asset).   Today's value for an asset that yields a stream of income over time. Valuation of such time streams of returns requires calculating the present worth of each component of the income, which is done by applying a discount rate (or interest rate) to future incomes.

Price-elastic demand (or elastic demand).   The situation in which price elasticity of demand exceeds 1 in absolute value. This signifies that the percentage change in quantity demanded is greater than the percentage change in price. In addition, elastic demand implies that total revenue (price times quantity) rises when price falls because the increase in quantity demanded is so large. (Contrast with **price-inelastic demand**.)

Price elasticity of demand.   A measure of the extent to which quantity demanded responds to a price change. The elasticity coefficient (price elasticity of demand E_p) is percentage change in quantity demanded divided by percentage change in price. In figuring percentages, use the averages of old and new quantities in the numerator and of old and new prices in the denominator; disregard the minus sign. Refer also to **price-elastic demand, price-inelastic demand, unit-elastic demand**.

Price elasticity of supply.   Conceptually similar to **price elasticity of demand**, except that it measures the supply responsiveness to a price change. More precisely, the price elasticity of supply measures the percentage change in quantity supplied divided by the percentage change in price. Supply elasticities are most useful in perfect competition.

Price flexibility.   Price behavior in "auction" markets (e.g., for many raw commodities or the stock market), in which prices immediately respond to changes in demand or in supply. (In contrast, refer to **administered prices**.)

Price index.   An index number that shows how the average price of a bundle of goods has changed over a period of time. In computing the average, the prices of the different goods are generally weighted by their economic importance (e.g., by each commodity's share of total consumer expenditures in the **consumer price index**).

Price-inelastic demand (or **inelastic demand**). The situation in which price elasticity of demand is below 1 in absolute value. In this case, when price declines, total revenue declines, and when price is increased, total revenue goes up. Perfectly inelastic demand means that there is no change at all in quantity demanded when price goes up or down. (Contrast with **price-elastic demand** and **unit-elastic demand**.)

Private good. **See public good.**

Producer price index. The **price index** of goods sold at the wholesale level (such as steel, wheat, oil).

Product, average. Refer to **average product**.

Product differentiation. The existence of characteristics that make similar goods less-than-perfect substitutes. Thus locational differences make similar types of gasoline sold at separate points imperfect substitutes. Firms enjoying product differentiation face a downward-sloping demand curve instead of the horizontal demand curve of the perfect competitor.

Product, marginal. Refer to **marginal product**.

Production function. A relation (or mathematical function) specifying the maximum output that can be produced with given inputs for a given level of technology. Applies to a firm or, as an aggregate production function, to the economy as a whole.

Production-possibility frontier (PPF). A graph showing the menu of goods that can be produced by an economy. In a frequently cited case, the choice is reduced to two goods, guns and butter. Points outside the *PPF* (to the northeast of it) are unattainable. Points inside it are inefficient since resources are not being fully employed, resources are not being used properly, or outdated production techniques are being utilized.

Productivity. A term referring to the ratio of output to inputs (total output divided by labor inputs is **labor productivity**). Productivity increases if the same quantity of inputs produces more output. Labor productivity increases because of improved technology, improvements in labor skills, or capital deepening.

Productivity growth. The rate of increase in **productivity** from one period to another. For example, if an index of labor productivity is 100 in 1990 and 101.7 in 1991, the rate of productivity growth is 1.7 percent per year for 1991 over 1990.

Productivity of capital, net. See **rate of return**.

Productivity slowdown. The sharp decline in U.S. productivity growth that occurred around 1973.

Profit. (1) In accounting terms, total revenue minus costs properly chargeable against the goods sold (see **income statement**). (2) In economic theory, the difference between sales revenue and the full opportunity cost of resources involved in producing the goods.

Profit-and-loss statement. See **income statement**.

Progressive, proportional, and regressive taxes. A progressive tax weighs more heavily upon the rich; a regressive tax does the opposite. More precisely, a tax is progressive if the average tax rate (i.e., taxes divided by income) is higher for those with higher incomes; it is a regressive tax if the average tax rate declines with higher incomes; it is a proportional tax if the average tax rate is equal at all income levels.

Property rights. Property rights define the ability of individuals or firms to own, buy, sell, and use the capital goods and other property in a market economy.

Proportional tax. See **progressive, proportional**, and **regressive taxes**.

Proprietorship, individual. A business firm owned and operated by one person.

Protectionism. Any policy adopted by a country to protect domestic industries against competition from imports (most commonly, a tariff or quota imposed on such imports).

Public choice (also **public-choice theory**). Branch of economics and political science dealing with the way that governments make choices and direct the economy. This theory differs from the theory of markets in emphasizing the influence of vote maximizing for politicians, which contrasts to profit maximizing by firms.

Public debt. See **government debt**.

Public good. A commodity whose benefits are indivisibly spread among the entire community, whether or not particular individuals desire to consume the public good. For example, a public-health measure that eradicates smallpox protects all, not just those paying for the vaccinations. To be contrasted with **private goods**, such as bread, which, if consumed by one person, cannot be consumed by another person.

Pure economic rent. See **rent, economic**.

Q

Quantity demanded. See **change in demand vs. change in quantity demanded**.

Quantity equation of exchange. A tautology, $MV \equiv PQ$, where M is the money supply, V is the income velocity of money, and PQ (price times quantity) is the money value of total output (nominal GDP). The equation must always hold exactly since V is defined as PQ/M.

Quantity supplied. See **change in supply vs. change in quantity supplied**.

Quantity theory of money. A theory of the determination of output and the overall price level holding that prices move proportionately with the money supply. A more cautious approach put forth by monetarists holds that the money supply is the most important determinant of changes in nominal GDP (see **monetarism**).

Quota. A form of import protectionism in which the total quantity of imports of a particular commodity (e.g., sugar or cars) during a given period is limited.

R

Random-walk theory (of stock market prices). See the **efficient-market theory**.

Rate of inflation. See **inflation**.

Rate of return (or **return**) **on capital.** The yield on an investment or on a capital good. Thus, an investment costing $100 and yielding $12 annually has a rate of return of 12 percent per year.

Rational-expectations hypothesis. This hypothesis holds that people make unbiased forecasts and further that people use all available information and economic theory to make these forecasts.

Rational-expectations macroeconomics. A school, led by Robert Lucas, Robert Barro, and Thomas Sargent, holding that markets clear quickly and that expectations are rational. Under these and other conditions it can be shown that predictable macroeconomic policies have no effect on real output or unemployment. Sometimes called **new classical macroeconomics**.

Real-business-cycle theory. A theory that explains business cycles purely as shifts in aggregate supply, primarily due to technological disturbances, without any reference to monetary or other demand-side forces.

Real GDP. See **gross domestic product, real**.

Real interest rate. The interest rate measured in terms of goods rather than money. It is thus equal to the money (or nominal) interest rate less the rate of inflation.

Real wages. The purchasing power of a worker's wages in terms of goods and services. It is measured by the ratio of the money wage rate to the consumer price index.

Recession. A downturn in real GDP for two or more successive quarters. See also **depression**.

Regressive tax. See **progressive, proportional**, and **regressive taxes**.

Regulation. Government laws or rules designed to control the behavior of firms. The major kinds are **economic regulation** (which affects the prices, entry, or service of a single industry, such as telephone service) and **social regulation** (which attempts to correct externalities that prevail across a number of industries, such as air or water pollution).

Renewable resources. Natural resources (like agricultural land) whose services replenish regularly and which, if properly managed, can yield useful services indefinitely.

Rent, economic (or **pure economic rent**). This term was applied to income earned from land. The total supply of land available is (with minor qualifications) fixed, and the return paid to the landowner is rent. The term is often extended to the return paid to any factor in fixed supply—i.e., to any input having a perfectly inelastic or vertical supply curve.

Required reserves. See **reserves, bank**.

Reserves, bank. That portion of deposits that a bank sets aside in the form of vault cash or non-interest-earning deposits with Federal Reserve Banks. In the United States, banks are required to hold 12 percent of checking deposits (or transactions accounts) in the form of reserves.

Reserves, international. Every nation holds at least some reserves, in such forms as gold, currencies of other nations, and special drawing rights. International reserves serve as "international money," to be used when a country encounters balance-of-payments difficulties. If a nation were prepared to allow its exchange rate to float freely, it would need minimal reserves.

Resource allocation. The manner in which an economy distributes its resources (its factors of production) among the potential uses so as to produce a particular set of final goods.

Returns to scale. The rate at which output increases when all inputs are increased proportionately. For example, if all the inputs double and output is exactly doubled, that process is said to exhibit **constant returns to scale**. If, however, output grows by less than 100 percent when all inputs are doubled, the process shows **decreasing returns to scale**; if output more than doubles, the process demonstrates **increasing returns to scale**.

Revaluation. An increase in the official foreign exchange rate of a currency. See also **devaluation**.

Risk. In financial economics, refers to the variability of the returns on an investment.

Risk averse. A person is risk averse when, faced with an uncertain situation, the displeasure from losing a given amount of income is greater than the pleasure from gaining the same amount of income.

Risk spreading. The process of taking large risks and spreading them around so that they are but small risks for a large number of people. The major form of risk spreading is **insurance**, which is a kind of gambling in reverse.

Rule of 70. A useful shortcut for approximating compound interest. A quantity that grows at r percent per year will double in about $70/r$ years.

S

Sales tax. See **excise tax vs. sales tax**.

Savings function. The schedule showing the amount of saving that households or a nation will undertake at each level of income.

Say's Law of Markets. The theory that "supply creates its own demand." J. B. Say argued in 1803 that, because total purchasing power is exactly equal to total incomes and outputs, excess demand or supply is impossible. Keynes attacked Say's Law, pointing out that an extra dollar of income need not be spent entirely (i.e., the marginal propensity to spend is not necessarily unity).

Scarcity. Scarcity is the distinguishing characteristic of an economic good. That an economic good is scarce does not mean that it is rare, but only that it is not freely available for the taking. To obtain such a good, one must either produce it or offer other economic goods in exchange.

Scarcity, law of. The principle that most things that people want are available only in limited supply (the exception being **free goods**). Thus goods are generally scarce and must somehow be rationed, whether by price or some other means.

Securities. A term used to designate a wide variety of financial assets, such as stocks, bonds, options, and notes; more precisely, the documents used to establish ownership of these assets.

Short run. A period in which not all factors can adjust fully. In microeconomics, the capital stock and other "fixed" inputs cannot be adjusted and entry is not free in the short run. In macroeconomics, prices, wage contracts, tax rates, and expectations may not fully adjust in the short run.

Short-run aggregate supply schedule. The schedule showing the relationship between output and prices in the short run wherein changes in aggregate demand can affect output. Also represented by an upward-sloping or horizontal *AS* curve.

Shutdown price (or **point**, or **rule**). In the theory of the firm, the shutdown point comes at that point where the market price is just sufficient to cover average variable cost and no more. Hence, the firm's losses per period just equal its fixed costs; it might as well shut down.

Single-tax movement. A nineteenth-century movement, originated by Henry George, holding that continued poverty in the midst of steady economic progress was attributable to the scarcity of land and the large rents flowing to landowners. The "single tax" was to be a tax on economic rent earned from landownership.

Slope. In a graph, the change in the variable on the vertical axis per unit of change in the variable on the horizontal axis. Upward-sloping lines have positive slopes, downward-sloping curves (like demand curves) have negative slopes, and horizontal lines have slopes of zero.

Social insurance. Mandatory insurance provided by government to improve social welfare by preventing the losses created by market failures such as moral hazard or adverse selection.

Social overhead capital. The essential investments on which economic development depends, particularly for sanitation and drinking water, transportation, and communications. Sometimes called "infrastructure."

Social regulation. See **regulation**.

Socialism. A political theory that holds that all (or almost all) the means of production, other than labor, should be owned by the community. This allows the return on capital to be shared more equally than under capitalism.

Speculator. Someone engaged in speculation, i.e., someone who buys (or sells) a commodity or financial asset with the aim of profiting from later selling (or buying) the item at a higher (or lower) price.

Spillovers. Same as **externalities**.

Stagflation. A term, coined in the early 1970s, describing the coexistence of high unemployment, or *stag*nation, with persistent in*flation*. Its explanation lies primarily in the inertial nature of the inflationary process.

Statistical discrimination. Treatment of individuals on the basis of the average behavior or characteristics of members of the group to which they belong. Statistical discrimination can be self-fulfilling by reducing incentives for individuals to overcome the stereotype.

Stock, common. Refer to **common stock**.

Stock market. An organized marketplace in which common stocks are traded. In the United States, the largest stock market is the New York Stock Exchange, on which are traded the stocks of the largest U.S. companies.

Stock vs. flow. See **flow vs. stock**.

Strategic interaction. A situation in oligopolistic markets in which each firm's business strategies depend upon its rivals' plans. A formal analysis of strategic interaction is given in **game theory**.

Structural budget. See **actual, cyclical**, and **structural budget**.

Structural unemployment. Unemployment resulting because the regional or occupational pattern of job vacancies does not match the pattern of worker availability. There may be jobs available, but unemployed workers may not have the required skill; or the jobs may be in different regions from where the unemployed workers live.

Subsidy. A payment by a government to a firm or household that provides or consumes a commodity. For example, governments often subsidize food by paying for part of the food expenditures of low-income households.

Substitutes. Goods that compete with each other (as with gloves and mittens). By contrast, goods that go together in the eyes of consumers (such as left shoes and right shoes) are **complements**.

Substitution effect (of a price change). The tendency of consumers is to consume more of a good when its relative price falls (to "substitute" in favor of that good) and to consume less of the good when its relative price increases (to "substitute" away from that good). This substitution effect of a price change leads to a downward-sloping demand curve. (Compare with **income effect**.)

Substitution rule. This asserts that if the price of one factor falls while all other factor prices remain the same, firms will profit by substituting the now-cheaper factor for all the other factors. The rule is a corollary of the **least-cost rule**.

Supply curve (or **supply schedule**). A schedule showing the quantity of a good that suppliers in a given market desire to sell at each price, holding other things equal.

Supply shock. In macroeconomics, a sudden change in production costs or productivity that has a large and unexpected impact upon aggregate supply. As a result of a supply shock, real GNP and the price level change unexpectedly.

Supply-side economics. A view emphasizing policy measures to affect aggregate supply or potential output. This approach holds that high marginal tax rates on labor and capital incomes reduce work effort and saving.

T

Tariff. A levy or tax imposed upon each unit of a commodity imported into a country.

Tax incidence. See **incidence**.

Technological change. A change in the process of production or introduction of new products such that more or improved output can be obtained from the same bundle of inputs. It results in an outward shift in the production-possibility curve.

Technological progress. See **technological change**.

Terms of trade (in international trade). The "real" terms at which a nation sells its export products and buys its import products. It equals the ratio of an index of export prices to an index of import prices.

Theory of income distribution. A theory explaining the manner in which personal income and wealth are distributed in a society.

Tight-money policy. A central-bank policy of restraining or reducing the money supply and of raising interest rates. This policy has the effect of slowing the growth of real GDP, reducing the rate of inflation, or raising the nation's foreign exchange rate. (Contrast with **easy-money policy**.)

Time deposit. Funds, held in a bank, that have a minimum "time of withdrawal." Included in broad money (M_2) but not in M_1 because they are not accepted as a means of payment.

Token money. Money with little or no intrinsic value.

Total cost. Refer to **cost, total**.

Total factor productivity. An index of productivity that measures total output per unit of total input. The numerator of the index is total output (say, GDP), while the denominator is a weighted average of inputs of capital, labor, and resources. The growth of total factor productivity is often taken as an index of the rate of technological progress.

Total product (or **output**). The total amount of a commodity pro-

duced, measured in physical units such as bushels of wheat, tons of steel, or number of haircuts.

Total revenue. Price times quantity, or total sales.

Trade balance or **merchandise trade balance.** See **balance of trade**.

Trade barrier. Any of a number of protectionist devices by which nations discourage imports. Tariffs and quotas are the most visible barriers, but in recent years nontariff barriers (or NTBs), such as burdensome regulatory proceedings, have replaced more traditional measures.

Transactions demand for money. See **demand for money**.

Transactions money. A measure of money supply (also known as M_1) which consists of items that are actually for transactions, namely, currency and checking accounts.

Transfer payments, government. Payments made by a government to individuals, for which the individual performs no current service in return. Examples are social security payments and unemployment insurance.

Treasury bills (T-bills). Short-term bonds or securities issued by the federal government.

U

Underground economy. Unreported economic activity. The underground economy includes otherwise legal activities not reported to the taxing authorities (such as garage sales or services "bartered" among friends) and illegal activities (such as the drug trade, gambling, and prostitution).

Unemployed. People who are not employed but are actively looking for work or waiting to return to work.

Unemployment. (1) In economic terms, **involuntary unemployment** occurs if there are qualified workers who would be willing to work at prevailing wages but cannot find jobs. (2) In the official (U.S. Bureau of Labor Statistics) definition, a worker is unemployed if he or she (*a*) is not working and (*b*) either is waiting for recall from layoff or has actively looked for work in the last 4 weeks.

Unemployment, frictional. Refer to **frictional unemployment**.

Unemployment rate. The percentage of the labor force that is unemployed.

Unit-elastic demand. The situation, between **price-elastic demand** and **price-inelastic demand**, in which price elasticity is just equal to 1 in absolute value. See also **price elasticity of demand**.

Unlimited liability. See **limited liability**.

Usury. The charging of an interest rate above a legal maximum on borrowed money.

Utility (also **total utility**). The total satisfaction derived from the consumption of goods or services. To be contrasted with **marginal utility**, which is the additional utility arising from consumption of an additional unit of the commodity.

Utility-possibility frontier. Analogous to the **production-possibility frontier**; a graph showing the utility or satisfaction of two consumers (or groups), one on each axis. It is downward-sloping to indicate that redistributing income from A to B will lower the utility of A and raise that of B. Points on the utility-possibility frontier display **allocative** (or **Pareto**) **efficiency**. For Pareto- efficient allocations, it is impossible to find feasible outcomes that would make one person better off without making someone else worse off.

V

Value added. The difference between the value of goods produced and the cost of materials and supplies used in producing them. In a $1 loaf of bread embodying $0.60 worth of wheat and other materials, the value added is $0.40. Value added consists of the wages, interest, and profit components added to the output by a firm or industry.

Value-added tax (or **VAT**). A tax levied upon a firm as a percentage of its value added.

Value, paradox of. Refer to **paradox of value**.

Variable. A magnitude of interest that can be defined and measured. Important variables in economics include prices, quantities, interest rates, exchange rates, dollars of wealth, and so forth.

Variable cost. Refer to **cost, variable**.

Velocity of money. In serving its function as a medium of exchange, money moves from buyer to seller to new buyer and so on. Its "velocity" refers to the "speed" of this movement. The **income velocity of money** is defined as nominal GNP divided by the total money supply $V \equiv P \times Q/M \equiv GNP/M$.

Vertical equity. See **horizontal equity vs. vertical equity**.

Vertical integration. See **integration, vertical vs. horizontal**.

Vertical merger. See **merger**.

Voluntarily unemployed. Describes an individual who is unemployed because she perceives the value of wages to be less than the opportunity use of time, say in leisure.

W

Wealth. The net value of tangible and financial items owned by a nation or person at a point of time. It equals all assets less all liabilities.

Welfare economics. The normative analysis of economic systems, i.e., the study of what is "wrong" or "right" about the economy's functioning.

Welfare state. A concept of the mixed economy arising in Europe in the late nineteenth century and introduced in the United States in the 1930s. In the modern conception of the welfare state, markets direct the detailed activities of day to day economic life while governments regulate social conditions and provide pensions, health care, and other aspects of the social safety net.

***What, how,* and *for whom*.** The three fundamental problems of economic organization. *What* is the problem of how much of each possible good and service will be produced with the society's limited stock of resources or inputs. *How* is the choice of the particular technique by which each good of the what shall be produced. *For whom* refers to the distribution of consumption goods among the members of that society.

Winner-take-all games. Situations in which payoffs are determined by merit relative to other competitors/players rather than by absolute merit. These contests generally are characterized by rewards heavily or entirely concentrated among the very best competitors.

Y

Yield. Same as the **interest rate** or **rate of return** on an asset.

Z

Zero-profit point. For a business firm, that level of price at which the firm breaks even, covering all costs but earning zero profit.

INDEX